elicit

elicit

elicit

Chronicles of Awakening

Your Guide to Liberation!

Her Holiness **The Common Snook**

STONYBROOK
PUBLISHING

elicit

 Published by Stonybrook Publishing, Gainesville, Florida
www.elicitthebook.com

To protect the privacy of the individuals involved, some identifying information, such as names, locations, and certain characteristics, have been altered in this book. While the essence of the events and experiences described remains true, these minor changes have been made to ensure anonymity.

Any name or artist mentioned in this book is solely for entertainment purposes and does not constitute an endorsement of this book.

Book cover artwork and design by my son, *Li'l Snook van Gogh*

Printed in the United States of America

ISBN 979-8-9989379-0-3
Library of Congress Catalog Card Number 2025913999

First Edition

To everyone who identifies as human, especially those who feel the world has robbed them of freedom, and to my sons, who survived eating Maggi (ramen noodles) for a year while I was writing.

TABLE OF CONTENTS

elicit

Pseudo-Chapter One
(Start here!)

Welcome to liberation! You must be here because you're ready for something new, or someone told you this book is filled with funny stories. Forgive me; I have an early confession about my mental state. For me, joking and giggling are like an *uncontrollable tic*. Honestly, I can't help it. Even when I was a quiet child, I was constantly chuckling inside. Anyhow, regardless of what brought you here, I'm excited and look forward to embarking on this mental transformation with you and, of course, laughing and rolling along the way. (Additionally, it is worth noting that I wrote a significant portion of this book in a finely attuned Southern accent.)

In the summer of 2023, I founded ***Betwixt,*** a spiritual community in the college town of Gainesville, Florida—*Betwixt* website, double-u, double-u, double-u, dot…, lol. (You can look it up! I don't want to date the book prematurely with a website that always needs updating. Ugh!) The vision behind *Betwixt* is to build community between our differences. It functions as both a physical community and a movement. Being local to Gainesville isn't necessary to participate because *Betwixt* represents a mindset and way of life. There's no religion, preaching, teaching, or politics; however, as a spiritual teacher, I write on topics that divide people and separate us from the Divine. I also offer practical solutions to life's challenges and share simple wisdom to encourage a different perspective. These writings, which I refer to as my sermons, are meant to be read in the comfort of your home to bring people together and awaken your higher selves. But don't be mistaken; this doesn't mean I shy away from referencing your scriptures or current events. Nothing is off-limits.

While my teachings inspire people to see things from new perspectives, I would best be described as a "seer," a term we seldom encounter. Being a seer is not an identity but rather a way the Divine works through me…today. I use Consciousness to perceive things clearly or for what they truly are, and at times, I may seem to contradict myself because I don't naturally take a side on any given issue. Taking sides isn't necessary. Additionally, I don't believe anyone needs a spiritual teacher in the traditional sense, since everything we need to know is already within us. Some of us simply need a little guidance to help us look in the right direction.

To increase human Consciousness, I observe the world around us, drawing deeply from my life experiences to uncover a more profound truth or perspective beyond what is seen as the norm. Writing about my personal experiences is an effective way for me to present these topics, but please don't think it's all about me. It never is and never will be. (As noted on the copyright page, some minor identifying details in a few sermons have been omitted or changed to protect privacy. [wink])

I've had an extraordinary life in such a short time. I hope my multidimensional perspective will benefit others and help dismantle some of the walls that separate us, often tied to our personal mental veils. I will also discuss race and racism extensively, as they are two of the most significant divisions among Americans and are also evident in many other countries. I guarantee it will be unlike anything you've ever heard. (You know, race needs racism to survive, and racism needs race.)

In this book, we will explore how the mind creates and adopts identities and beliefs that serve as veils in our lives, becoming something for us to argue about and defend. Some of the collective veils we will discuss include sexism, racism, nationalism, "feminism," racism, religion, and culture. Yes, I intentionally mentioned racism twice. Now, White folks, don't get nervous; it will be fun, like an ice cream sundae with plenty of toppings. First, we'll start with fruits and nuts…a dash of cardamom and green tea…topped with a heap of vanilla flakes. Then, we'll finish off with a heavy drizzle of artificially flavored chocolate syrup.

Having lived with one foot (and often two feet) in a White world has intriguingly exposed me to greater doses of what I call "the mental disease of racism." I once asked a family member if she experienced racism as often as I did, and she replied, "No, I don't live with them." (Hmm…that was eye-opening! And I wasn't sure if I should be offended.) I consider my living situation a blessing, as my experience has given me valuable insight into how programming and ideologies shape our lives, becoming the veils through which we perceive the world. (We must understand how programming works or risk being programmed.)

When discussing race, you may notice that I capitalize Black, Brown, and White, a practice adopted by many organizations and writers to promote equality and respect. The MacArthur Foundation explains that when "Black" and "Brown" are written in lowercase as adjectives rather than as proper nouns, some feel it fails to recognize those who identify with these terms as part of their own identity. However, when "White" is left lowercase or not mentioned at all, it allows White people to remain the standard. This approach overlooks that "White" is also a racial category, exempting them from engaging in conversations about race. For example, when terms like "people," "men," and "women" are used without a leading racial or ethnic label, they are typically designated for White people as the default. Capitalizing Black, Brown, and White, and using proper nouns consistently, encourages and welcomes all perspectives to the discussion. Yet, humanity will truly thrive when free from these labels and mental identities. (Additionally, I sometimes use "White" instead of "Whiteness" to emphasize my point.)

Elicit was inspired by my encounters over the past twenty years. My wonderful husband, my greatest inspiration, also happens to be White and has navigated many veils. He has experienced and expressed nearly all the social constructs—the ideas humans and society create and agree upon—such as "gender," "race," "disability," "money," "value," "sexuality," "religion," and so forth. Some of these constructs are helpful, while many, like sexism and racism, are damaging. I refer to these social constructs as collective veils and will discuss them in greater detail in the pages to come. However, he has overcome them all and is left with the most daunting challenge: the self. Most will dance with this one throughout their lives, but it can also be tamed and conquered. (By the way, if you ever hear me say, "Babe," "Honey," or "that man," I'm speaking to or talkin' 'bout my beloved husband.)

Many of us dislike reading the preface or introduction in a book that isn't labeled as a chapter because it feels like we haven't officially started and are wasting precious time before getting to the core content. (That's why self-help books tend to be brief. *We humans* are naturally impatient.) This book aims to help you overcome your mind, so it's structured differently from a traditional book. Instead of requiring you to read the preface or introduction without any satisfaction, I've made those sections the book's first chapter, allowing you to receive the credit your mind believes it deserves. That's your first lesson on how the mind rules your life. But doesn't it feel satisfying to know that you're already well into "Pseudo-Chapter One," even though it is the only chapter in the book?

Hopefully, you won't read the rest of the book with the same urgency, as doing so may lead you to miss its main points. So, slow down. Inhale and exhale. Some readers will finish this book quickly, while others may prefer to absorb the stories over several weeks or months. You'll discover what works best for you. That said, let me walk you through the layout of this book and show you how to use it to free yourself from the mental veils that rule your life.

Learning to Help Yourself Through Humility

Among mental health professionals and spiritual teachers, there are strong beliefs regarding allowing individuals to act independently. To be considered a reputable professional or enlightened figure in these communities, one must agree and adopt this perspective to avoid being labeled as someone who infringes on personal boundaries. "Oh yeah, they absolutely must take charge. It's their choice." No one wants to be labeled a "boundary violator," especially considering how often the term "boundaries" appears in today's self-empowerment circles. These days, everybody is focused on boundaries and protecting their space. (What is going on?)

When you agree with the notion that "they must help themselves," this, in a sense, elevates you above those who are struggling with challenges they can't identify. You and your authority reached this conclusion. However, it's possible that *someone* may have had their feelings hurt. Instead, the professional rarely pauses to consider whether they might be the one unable to assist this individual. And why would they do this when all their colleagues have reached the same conclusion? It's simply that those who champion the idea of "independence" don't realize they themselves support this widely accepted conclusion, because they have also encountered obstacles. (How arrogant of them!)

They point fingers at the victim. Instead of saying, "I can't help this person," they assert, "They can't be helped or must help themselves." Sadly, mental health and spiritual circles often unknowingly arrive at these irrational conclusions. This is a passive-aggressive way of shifting blame onto those they cannot assist.

It takes humility to say, "I can't help you, but that doesn't mean you're hopeless." Instead of concluding, I like to believe that everyone can find liberation. Not making such a firm conclusion allows for new understanding. After all, when you've decided you're right, that's the end of the discussion. (Hmm...what a waste of time!)

Even though most situations in life require us to step up to the plate and make decisions, we were never meant to handle many of these things alone. Furthermore, there are some challenges from which we can only find freedom with the assistance of others, since we did not become bound by ourselves. (The keyword here is "bound.") If your hands are tied behind your back, you may need help getting untethered. Deep down, we know that most people require a little assistance, but the issue is that many are also bound. Who can lend a hand? We can't guide someone through a situation we haven't overcome ourselves. Simply put, I can't help you untie your hands if mine are also tied.

The knack for helping someone "free themselves" from mental veils involves assisting them in recognizing the invisible veils they face, which might seem contradictory because how can we know what is invisible? It's undoubtedly a challenging task since attaining freedom necessitates the ability to perceive a mental behavior that, once again, is invisible. (Hmm…that twisted my brain.) Adding to this seemingly impossible challenge, many professionals struggle to assist these individuals because they cannot see these mental patterns in themselves. You know, the blind can't lead the blind.

Here's the trick! If you can see one veil in yourself or another, it can provide you with enough insight and willpower to recognize other veils that your mind conceals from you if you let it. As you will read and learn in this book, my husband and I spent our early years in a cult that also operated as a Christian church. ("But isn't religion a cult?" some may ask. [giggles]) We learned a great deal from this experience, which will be a recurring theme in this book. I will elaborate later on how the mind tends to conceal things from us when we are conditioned to think in a certain way, which can occur in any ideology, from specific relationships to simply being part of society.

For my husband and me, recognizing and accepting our reality after leaving the church was humbling. If you can remain humble, you can allow your experiences to reveal the possibility of other veils. We all have them, but we can't perceive them because they have become part of our beliefs, which shape our identity. I will help you step outside yourself and observe by first showing you the hidden veils in others. I will be the first subject for you to examine. I wish you the best as you awaken to your own madness. I'm joking—*kinda*—but let's say "their madness" because noticing flaws in others is something we excel at; however, this can also serve as a gateway to our own liberation.

Pointing Fingers

Let us point fingers freely without judging ourselves, as this can become our superpower, setting us free. We will also point fingers, speculate about a few public figures, and assign lay diagnoses, even though professionals remind us that it's crucial to remember that only they can make a proper diagnosis. Disclaimer: Nothing we point fingers at or use our mental label maker (a.k.a. the mind) to describe a set of behaviors should be considered significant. Any such labeling should not be taken to heart; it should only serve to make a point.

You may notice that the mind feels uneasy with this freedom because it prefers to be seen as good, and finger-pointing is generally frowned upon. It also wants to avoid being on anyone's list or facing finger-pointing, so it promotes neutrality and respect for all individuals and religions to evade criticism. (Not today, sucka!) I encourage you to point fingers in every direction, and hopefully, if you let it, that finger will return to you. And if you can humble yourself in secret, can we agree that most people have at least five to ten veils they can't see? No worries, "It is true!" I've already fact-checked it. (And those numbers were conservative. [giggles])

Furthermore, we will discuss and observe everyone under the sun, if possible. And if I don't touch on "your specific mental group," please know this is for you, too, if you identify as human, of course. (Just so you know, in this book, race and religion become irrelevant.) I have also included Jewish people equally in this call to liberation. Hopefully, that was not a mistake. (Can I say that?)

Still, let me apologize in advance for all the attention I will give White and Black folks. If you're American or live in America, you know these two groups have *issues and issues* with each other that impact all the rest of us. (Hold on a *sec*! Step out of yourself. That last sentence was a test. It would have been more offensive if I had only said White or Black, but I threw both groups under the spotlight equally. If you identify with one of the two groups, let me know if you could see the mental wall that went up. [Yeah, that veil can be so thick it would qualify as a wall.] If you could see it, you might have discovered your first veil. Seeing is half the battle! That means you're ready for the good *stuff.* Take notes.)

As you engage in this observation process, you'll notice that I teach by making visual or mental comparisons and highlighting similar or identical

Our cat Zen is checking to see if anyone is home. (My apologies if the photos are grainy. Amazon offers a "retro" addition. It's still good! Save a tree!)

behaviors. By the time we identify all the parallels and patterns, you'll gain a clear understanding of how the mind works for and against you.

Speaking of pointing fingers! I had a White, Jewish, gay, transgender, gender-fluid, queer, non-conforming, non-binary acquaintance who wanted to be seen as inclusive and progressive. However, during one of my discussions on awakening, they became excited when I addressed some of the struggles I noticed around religion in many African American communities. This person had been holding back and had a thing or two to say about Black people and their Jesus. (Yes, Jewish people like to talk to me about Jesus. We all must start somewhere, right?)

Still, I could see how *he/they* and their behaviors were rooted in something *he/they* couldn't see in *himself/themself,* yet *he/they* felt comfortable pointing out what some Black people might not see. And, of course, he/they used his insight to elevate *himself/themself.* "Oh my god, you can't talk to them without them

6

praising Jesus." (If you listen closely, egos will always tell you what they think.) *He/they* missed an opportunity to point the finger at *himself/themself.* (Please don't let the exaggerated pronoun usage weed you out before we get the party started. It's a test! Only the strong will survive to the end.)

Your Scriptures, Spiritual Gurus, and Learning from All

As I mentioned in the opening, I will sometimes reference your scriptures, primarily from the Bible. This is not intended to promote religion or Christianity over any other faith. It's just that I am surprisingly still well-versed and fluent in "Christianese," even though I don't read the Bible. Please don't confuse this with suggesting that I align with a particular faith. If you choose to count the number of scriptures I use, you may notice a pattern: I only really use two to convey my teachings because they align with my focus areas. Everything else is just for your entertainment.

Whether we care for scriptures or not, these spiritual books, from the Bhagavad Gita to the Quran, were created to help us navigate major human concerns and debates. They can still be valuable. Ultimately, they were intended to guide humanity toward the common goal of awakening to human Consciousness, which we will explore. My writing aims to show you the path without the need for fancy scriptures because the path is already within you.

As you read, I will occasionally reference a well-known world leader or spiritual guru, which simply means teacher; however, this is not intended to promote or endorse their teachings or agendas, nor am I implying any *specialness*. I also refrain from listing their titles to maintain a neutral position. "Those who mind don't matter, and those who matter don't mind" (some attribute this quote to Dr. Seuss). At the same time, understand that we can learn from almost anyone or any spiritual teaching if we allow it; as my cult leader used to ironically say, "God can speak to you through a jackass." (That'll preach!) I am incredibly grateful to those who have taught me valuable lessons; their inspirations remain a part of me and have influenced many of my teachings.

Still, many of these folks are entrepreneurs who have repackaged jewels (spiritual truths) and decided to sell them back to us or use them to advance a political agenda. Essentially, there's nothing new under the sun. It's just that some people (some gifted and some crooked) have discovered clever ways to present the same material, giving it a facelift or simplifying it for better understanding. This is similar to how Christianity has many denominations and approaches to rejuvenate the faith; "Church like you've never seen before!" is one of my favorite church slogans.

I've also noticed this phenomenon coming out of India: you might have someone revered (highly respected) as a guru. However, the ancient teachings shared outlive these modern sources and are far older than the gurus we see on social media today. These teachings are effective not because of the guru but because they come from the same Source. Yet, my reluctance to promote any leaders arises from the fact that, through veils, we all perceive them differently. I don't want my use of a specific name to distract you from the purpose of this book.

With that said, I listen and learn from every walk of life. For instance, I have a secret: I'm on an email list for a group that urged its subscribers to rally at the Capitol on January 6, 2021. I've been on their list for the past twelve years. I was suspicious of the couple providing the information because they reminded me of charismatic church leaders and were rather flamboyant in their style. I watched them evolve from an organization that promoted natural healthcare into a political group with one-sided views resembling *White Christian Nationalism*, appealing only to a select few. No, I am not a supporter of their movement.

On the other hand, I decided to stick around instead of removing my name from their list because their content was enlightening. I learned a lot from their messages and guest speakers. Many of these folks were my neighbors and members of my community. I wanted to understand their desires and viewpoints, so I listened closely. How can we understand our nation and its many perspectives if we isolate ourselves from others? (Some of you have just been schooled.)

Let's Talk About Structure

In this collection of sermons, I share lessons through the power of storytelling. And sometimes, I use these stories to grab your attention, similar to how prescription drug commercials distract you with visuals of intergenerational birthday parties while selling you drugs...I mean, their products.

Each sermon is structured in a letter format to enhance the personal experience. A few include the date, but this is simply because they are either older writings, or I chose to include the date. Some people appreciate details and enjoy following patterns, while others may find them unimportant. Either way, it doesn't matter.

Anyhow, this ancient method of storytelling also helps increase engagement and stimulate critical thinking skills. (wink) Each will begin with the disclosure below. Instead of including it in every sermon, it will be listed at the beginning of each section for your convenience. Still, in its place, you will see **Disclosure Reminder...,** followed by three dots (an ellipsis) and a comma. It will read:

Before diving in, I will say this: I'm simple. I love to laugh. Please don't confuse my humor with sarcasm; I always mean what I say. I test the limits. My words are plain. I often use "own" redundantly. I don't claim to know all the answers; my only intention is to be a vessel. Also, to connect with different experiences, I interchangeably use the terms "Consciousness," "Presence," "God," "Universe," "Source," "Divine," "Energy," "Christ/Krst," and "Light." Above all, reading my humor with a Southern accent is best. Enjoy!

Moving forward, I hope to remember to capitalize those big spiritual words, but you might "catch me slipping." Also, if my teachings ever become an audiobook, I would love a voiceover that combines the tones and personalities of Carol Burnett, Maya Angelou, and Wanda Sykes—funny, wise, and sassy. However, it's best to read my book with both your eyes and hands so you don't miss the humor expressed through my unique use of grammar. For starters, you'll notice a comma following **Disclosure Reminder...,** an art form to create the illusion of a letter, "Dear Such and Such," because you missed the service, of course. When you see the comma, please know I am directly addressing my sermon to you. (wink)

You can skip the mental reminder once you fully accept my communication style. Some people prefer to browse around, read subtitles, bypass the introduction, etc. Therefore, they may need a reminder to keep their thoughts in check and avoid becoming overly arrogant, as the mind often elevates itself by discrediting others. "You can't use 'own' redundantly and publish a book." Whatever! I'm *absolutely certain* I can, and this book will be full of *unexpected surprises*. Since we're pointing out mind behaviors, let's call that veil or attitude "academic arrogance" as a nod to a few of my good friends. You can check that one off your list. On the other hand, if the page doesn't have a **Disclosure Reminder** noted, then the sermon isn't something to take lightly. Some sermons tackle sensitive issues, and I do lay aside my humor.

(Here's an afterthought!) As I was editing the book, I decided to quit. (Good Lord, I was tired of editing!) I thought perhaps leaving some unknown grammatical errors might be beneficial because a segment of America takes pride in well-placed grammatical symbols, much like decorating a Christmas tree. Sure, I understand that grammar and editing help make communication clearer (*more better!*), but this is for those who have made their writing ability their god. (They know who they are.) These tree decorators can sometimes be the most arrogant and fail to see that they have created a "superior" sense of self based on where they hang the mistletoe, so to speak (a.k.a. control issues or mom or dad issues). They cling to this validation like a parasite hanging from a tree.

That said, I left a few errors unknown to me just for you. (wink) Notice how your ego reacts when you find the elf on the shelf. Please send it to me! I'll have a *"special"* prize for you. But there are no prizes for calling out my exclamation points in the middle of sentences or my passive sentences that only English majors care about. (You know, the more exclamation points the better.) And umm…homophones sound the same, so you'll know what I'm talkin' 'bout. Still, sometimes I flat-out choose the wrong word or forget that not everyone speaks my language. (giggles) Hopefully, I've corrected my creativity. If not, it's because I was schooled in Alachua County, Florida. I also use quotations instead of italics when necessary or vice versa. (It depends on how I'm feeling.) And sometimes, I don't intend the word's meaning, like how I used *"special"* above. However, at other times, I use quotations or italics to convey my slang or to emphasize my intentions. Even so, some slang or Southern African American Vernacular English (SAAVE), such as "<u>*ch'rn*</u>," should be standard American English and used without quotations or italics. (No worries…I'll explain *ch'rn* later. Also, if I use "whassup," it's not a question; it's a greeting.)

I also *really* enjoy using words like "really," "just," "even," "actually," "absolutely," and a few other unnecessary ones, of course, you know. You'll see! And if you notice me using a word twice in one sentence, it's because it's powerful that way. More to come.

Furthermore, I had to find myself a somewhat independent thinkin' Jewish "editor" who might have had a Black nanny and raised him bilingual to give the book a proofread. I wasn't sure whether I could rely on the feelings or motivations of the typical politically correct liberal or conservative editor. You know, Jews can help with this kind of *stuff*! I just hope he can handle the goods when I start talkin' 'bout Jewish people. *(Shalom!)*

Anyhow, did y'all notice I *completely eliminated* the need for an editor and permitted myself to write however I want? Let's just call it "poetry"! It's also cheaper that way. You know, I couldn't even afford an editor with a book this size. I had to ask myself if our message was more important than following the rules. I'm tryin' to give y'all a gift, not go broke! I'd much rather spend ten grand on printing and give my book away for free with a few—hundred errors…like long-ass sentences and paragraphs; omitted, misused and abused commas; dangling modifiers; and strange punctuation, you know. But who's countin'? With that said, you have been introduced to The Common Snook (TCS) version of *The Successful Writing Guide* and ~~APA~~ TCS writing style.

In Section I, "Encountering My Own Veils—Awakening and New Vision," I will begin by sharing the story of how I started to see veils in my own life and the lives of others. I have always had the gift of a multidimensional perspective, but I can still see the people or situations that helped to enlighten me. (Yep, I'm enlightened, lol.) I did not achieve this awakening without assistance. Even so, my greatest superpower was sitting in stillness *with myself.*

Next, we will move on to Section II, "Massaging and Expanding Your Perspectives." These stories may seem unrelated, but they are "the caressing" to get you comfortable before I drop some of the heavier bombs…I mean, topics. These sermons are to challenge your perspectives, which are smaller veils that don't fit neatly under the broader categories we will discuss. Hopefully, these stories will make you laugh and, of course, prompt you to think. I will intentionally refrain from sharing too much of my opinion and avoid drawing firm conclusions, if any, to leave room for you to think for yourself. *We humans* like feeling independent and making our own decisions, even though most of who we are is never something we choose.

That said, it is essential not to skip around until you have read the book once to fully appreciate its effect. My sermons build on each other and expose layers of the mind's behaviors. (I love it when I almost rhyme.) There are also a few recurring themes and characters I don't want you to miss. Individually, my writings would make excellent church sermons or daily devotions because they'll enhance your life by liberating and expanding your mind. I can promise you that. I also promise that there will be one (more likely two, three, or four) sermons you won't like because they challenge a belief that has likely become part of your identity. That will be just the sermon to observe your reactions and how your mind behaves. Take notes. (Also, take notes because I don't have an index yet, which I plan to post online someday when I have time.)

Unfortunately, some will close the book to protect themselves and their feelings, never to open it again, as if there's a scary monster inside. It is fascinating to watch the mind practice information control without any external direction, like a momma telling it what to do. If you can inhale, exhale, and keep going, I promise there's a pot of gold at the end. (Who doesn't want gold?) Yet for some, the mind isn't always ready to let go and must create another veil to justify why the book is not for them. It might even go so far as to call the book "crap" to permit itself to create a veil to dodge the book. (Good Lord, that's complicated!) This is also my preemptive defense, a behavior we'll discuss much later. Hopefully, it will be effective in keeping you engaged. (Warning! Critiquing this book will be difficult without facing your own veils.)

Please don't play dodgeball with these jewels. I aim to *elicit*—draw forth and bring out—your higher self. This is called awakening! I hope that you will leave with fewer veils and without acquiring another. (I said this while shaking my head.) Since we are pointing out behaviors again, you can call this "the dodgeball veil." And, of course, you can check it off your list.

As you can see, I will have many comments to share with you as I present my sermons. I want you to feel at home and experience what I might say if we were in the same room. My goal is to be as distracting as possible to keep your attention. (wink) You'll also get a taste of Southern humor, as I'll speak to you as if you lived in my hometown of Gainesville, Florida, which I heard described as a microcosm of the world during a school tour at the University of Florida (UF) with my son. (Big things happen here!) My communications will sometimes have a Southern flavor and, at other times, follow a more traditional academic approach. As you know, this is a college town, right? (Go Gators!) Count it a blessin' to experience culture in the great state of Florida.

I will also try to use fewer than 304 different words to make my points. (I'm joking; I won't be counting.) In the Quaker faith, the principle of plain speech has always resonated with me. Who cares if you use fancy words like "hubris" to enhance your pride while attempting to share the world's secrets when nobody can understand you? Sure, right (eye-roll)…the Divine is speaking through you while you stroke your own ego. (Hmm…what a waste of time!) I will show you that brilliant *stuff* can be simple, and that you are more intelligent than the "smart" hubris folks have fooled themselves into believing.

Strangely, one of my "editors" suggested removing some of my commentary. I quickly replied, "No, I desire to communicate with real people." I believe my humor will help you continue reading without feeling offended, as you will soon realize I'm not a threat to anyone. In fact, I'm someone you would enjoy hanging out with, regardless of your background or hidden biases. Also, please don't worry about understanding all of my humor. You will probably not understand everything unless you have lived among as many different cultures as I have. For instance, Indian folks, except for the Patels, likely won't understand SAAVE or its jokes unless you are the one Indian girl who played high school basketball at Buchholz in Gainesville. Still, Americans may not fully grasp my humor about the Indian mother-in-law phenomenon. However, the challenges women face concerning mothers-in-law uniquely unite us…oops, I mean, them…and break down cultural boundaries, all while men across the globe are unsure if it's safe to laugh at this moment. (Wow, did I just hear a Hungarian-Chinese woman giggle? Awesome!)

And umm…sometimes, I'm a bit freer than most spiritual teachers with my language. However, I do follow some basic rules; I tell my sons that if you're going to curse, you must watch what you say. "MF" should never be used. Never call women "bitches," and never cuss/curse/swear *at* somebody. (Hmm?) Let's say I'm here to confirm the Divine has a sense of humor and isn't judgmental, as most cultures have personified their "male deity" to be. (If *it* were, I'd be the first to be condemned.)

My freedom of expression is also my insurance policy. First, it prevents anyone from putting me on a pedestal and making me *special* because I'm just like you. For example, when I say "bonehead," it doesn't mean "stupid" to me. Nobody is *stupid*. Still, bonehead is a word that I really like. (giggles) I use it to refer to people who don't listen, ignore what's right in front of their faces, or do *really ridiculous* things. That's all. Also, "beeyotch" should not be confused with the "b" word. It's just an expression of exuberance! Secondly, those who are offended and unable to handle my humor (solid food) are likely not ready for new understanding and are not exactly the population closest to waking up. Although the world is spiritually malnourished, you might not be hungry yet.

Some of these folks are best suited to glean from ancient personalities and posturing, as observed in religious leaders who serve milk or Kool-Aid. However, this book is for "the fruit ripe for picking," which Jesus mentioned. If you are ready for solid food, I promise to serve it to you gradually, sprinkled with a bit of "humor enzymes" to ensure the best digestion.

Lastly, a spoiler alert: each sermon will conclude with the following statement: "Sit in stillness with your eyes closed for 15 minutes a day; I promise it will transform your life!" Alternatively, you might see this little chair ♟. I'll use this visual reminder if I run out of space. "Why the 'subliminal' message?" No worries…I'll explain more later in the book. But hopefully, you will read it consciously. (giggles)

Some of you may think this is a long-ass book, and I say that's because it will take some of you a long-ass time to wake up. Some folks are hardheaded. Also, writing a comprehensive book of sacred scriptures to guide your life in under 500 pages is nearly impossible. Essentially, it's two books in one, with a few mini coffee table books scattered in there for your enjoyment. No worries

(*Hakuna matata*)…the sermons are brief. Don't rush through the book. Self-awakening requires time and doesn't occur overnight, so take your time with the stories and let your perspective expand and evolve. And don't worry about agreeing or believing in every perspective presented. It isn't necessary; this isn't a cult. Even so, the mind will not allow you to believe many of the stories. With that said, you only need to approach each sermon with an open mind, ready to consider new and uncomfortable perspectives. (Also, before I forget, feel free to drop the "-ass" as needed throughout the book. I'm being inclusive. Some folks speak a form of Pig Latin where many adjectives end in "-ass.")

Awakening to mental veils is a process that unfolds beautifully, much like a flower. First, a bud emerges, slowly expanding in all directions. You'll notice things you hadn't seen before, which were always right before you, hidden by your mental veils. You may find that everything physical remains unchanged; only your perspective has grown. Once this unfolding process begins, it continues without pause, and the expansion becomes exponential. Seeing and accepting things just as they are, without the need to draw conclusions, marks the beginning of a new chapter that I hope will lead to liberation in your life, where everything and everyone you encounter will be like a beautiful flower.

Let's conclude with a poem I titled "Projected Success":

> In Florida, this masterpiece will be scanned
> And then likely banned
> But if read as a whole,
> I promise it will liberate your soul.
> (Oh, that reminds me, it must be translated into Español!)
> Either way, if banned or canned,
> That would be stellar
> Because that means it is sure to be a best-_ _ _ _ _ _.

See, it was a short pseudo-chapter. Now you feel successful!

1 CHRONICLES

Section I: Encountering My Own Veils—Awakening and New Vision

In case you decided to skip the introduction and browse around, here's the **Disclosure Reminder**: Before diving in, I will say this: I'm simple. I love to laugh. Please don't confuse my humor with sarcasm; I always mean what I say. I test the limits. My words are plain. I often use "own" redundantly. I don't claim to know all the answers; my only intention is to be a vessel. Also, to connect with different experiences, I interchangeably use the terms "Consciousness," "Presence," "God," "Universe," "Source," "Divine," "Energy," "Christ/Krst," and "Light." Above all, reading my humor with a Southern accent is best. Enjoy!

Most of these sermons offer a different perspective on life. As noted, this book does not provide definitive conclusions, allowing for introspection and self-reflection. You are encouraged to journal and explore the reasons behind your feelings. While you read, you may notice a wall going up or that you are forming a new perspective, which may be more flexible than the previous one. However, if you encounter a wall of defense, I encourage you to express your feelings in writing. This often leads you to confront a mental veil or programming you were unaware of, and you may wish to spend some time with these emotions. You aren't required to abandon the belief; regardless, it takes time either way. This is simply an exercise to reveal hidden veils in our lives that we didn't create and that we might want to overcome.

Spend enough time in rural New Hampshire, and you, too, will stick your face in the snow one day. The 3D effect is an optical illusion. (TCS)

1. Waking Up

WARNING!!! If you haven't read the introduction "Pseudo-Chapter One," you likely will not understand the collection of sermons in this book.

Disclosure Reminder…,   July 2023

Hello! My name is Sher (pronounced like "Cher" or "share"). Some people refer to me as The Common Snook, which is appropriate since I am a Pisces.

I was going to jump in and start my story with my marriage, but then I realized that some locals might want to know I'm from Gainesville, Florida, and a graduate of Eastside High School. Nope, not from the International Baccalaureate (IB) program, as I'm often asked. This question stems from a perspective that perhaps someone like me could have only attended Eastside because of the IB program. Nope, I'm the product of their general education population, known as East Gainesville, a community that can only be understood by those who attended Eastside. (Go Rams!)

My parents are both from New Jersey, sharing varying degrees of the same multiracial background: Native American, Black, and White. My father was culturally raised as an African American, while my mother grew up as a Cherokee with a lot of Irish pride, as reflected in our family surname. (These were the Cherokees who declared, "The hell with *The Dawes Final Rolls*" and resisted leaving the Carolinas, Georgia, Alabama, Tennessee, and Kentucky when White men forced many local Native communities to migrate west to Oklahoma. As a result, these families were denied tribal citizenship and federal benefits. Many integrated within African American communities.)

My family relocated to Gainesville in the summer of 1978, when the city was still largely segregated. My father, a businessman, boldly decided to pay cash for a beautiful home on over an acre of land across from Glen Springs Elementary School in the Edgewood Hills community on N.W. 29th Street, which connects to Brywood on N.W. 16th Avenue—two neighborhoods where "People of Color" did *not* mix or mingle with "People of Pallor" at the time. (Hmm…let's continue to capitalize the phrase "People of Color" and its various forms moving forward. "Why?" No worries…you'll figure it out?)

I began attending school in the early 1980s when there were still very few "Children of Color" west of Main Street. However, the county was starting a new busing program, which meant new friends were coming.

*

Awakening to Race

Somewhat oblivious to race, I sensed something was off when my predominantly White classroom underwent a complete transformation. My neighborhood was in an uproar over the new zoning program that, for instance, relocated Black families from Lincoln Estates and bused them across town to Buchholz High School, which was predominantly White at the time. The White kids were also in for a bumpy ride. My White classmates clung tightly to their backpacks and matching lunch boxes because Duval Heights, a well-known African American neighborhood in town, was "in the house."

My new friends looked at me like a foreign creature and asked me almost non-stop, "What *is you*, mixed?" as if I weren't purebred. "Why *you* talk like a White girl?" Some would even pull my hair, perhaps to collect a specimen. I was in the dark about what that meant and became fascinated by their fascination with me. I noticed they seemed to have a sense of community that I didn't share with any one group of people, and they all attended this thing they called "church" on Sundays. With that reality, I needed to figure out who I was.

In middle school, I experienced what I call "The Great Racial Divide," reminiscent of the parting of the Red Sea. It all revolved around finding a group to survive this terrible experiment. Hanging out with my White friends from Girl Scouts, whom I had grown up with, and my soccer "homegirls" wouldn't help because the world remained predominantly Black and White. I needed to pick a side quickly, and given the teasing was b-r-u-t-a-l toward biracial and multiracial children at the time by African American children from disadvantaged communities, it was wiser to join them than to be the target of their jokes and covert aggression. (giggles) Oh my goodness, what a culture shock.

In the summer of 1989, as I prepared for middle school, I asked my mother to drop me off in Duval Heights for the day so I could hang out with my new friends. As we roamed the neighborhood, all my classmates were surprised to see me come to visit them, and I was astonished to find *everyone* at home. They treated me like an honored guest. Someone even bought me a *squeeze cup* (frozen Kool-Aid) from the *squeeze cup lady* as a warm welcome to the neighborhood. After my strategic visit, my peers from Duval never teased me again. (Wisdom is to love your enemies and turn them into friends. Many became my best friends.) Love is how I survived.

After two years of middle school, I became somewhat fluent in Southern African American Vernacular English (SAAVE), *King James style* (yep, I *be* code-switchin'), despite not speaking it at home. Nobody would have guessed I was born in Princeton, New Jersey, to parents from the Northeast. However, thanks to my older sister, who was also fluent after middle school, I knew there was hope for me.

Embraced by a Vibrant Culture

By the end of 7th grade, I had made a new best friend from an African American community that I so desperately wanted to be a part of. She had flawless, deep brown skin and was breathtakingly beautiful. In high school, nobody could match her style and flair. Surprisingly, even the White girls competed for her attention. If she were grown today, I'd imagine she'd resemble the well-known celebrity ghostwriter and screenwriter Ardre Orie, who just happens to be from Gainesville and graduated from Eastside High School the same year as me. (She's beautiful; look her up! [giggles])

Anyways, my good friend and my homegirls introduced me to a whole new world: those *painfully delicious,* lip-puckering salt and vinegar potato chips, secret societies like the Black Pre-Collegiate Club, Historically Black Colleges and Universities (HBCUs), Alpha Kappa Alpha Sorority (AKA), and nifty tricks like how to wrap my hair at night so it would behave the following day. *(Whassup, Carlarta! I bow to you.)* Anyhow, those were the kinds of tricks my Cherokee bohemian momma hadn't quite figured out yet. Lord knows I was a little rough around the edges and sweaty from playing soccer with the boys, but I learned to be a lady just by experiencing their graceful presence. And I like to think they were drawn to my boldness and that I didn't exactly conform to cultural or gender expectations.

I loved my new secondary culture, although I maintained a foot in many other worlds. My friends welcomed me even when I knew nothing about Southern African American cultures, and I introduced them to my unique multiracial experience. It might have seemed bizarre to them, but they loved coming to our house to experience my mother's carefree spirit and, of course, to enjoy yogurt, pasta, waffles, and bagels. Even though I was often teased for eating these things, they appreciated the fruits of my mother being raised in a racially ambiguous household situated between a Jewish and Italian community in New Jersey. (Pardon me; saying carefree might be an understatement; my lovely mother did not coexist with rules.)

Ms. Juliette

When I was ten or eleven, I met the most extraordinary woman, Ms. Juliette Watts McCoy, who was in her late sixties at the time. She was unlike anyone I had ever met because she could see into the illusion of the past, present, and future. She could see your entire life and its many paths. Although she used to frighten me, I eventually understood there was nothing to fear, as she mainly tried to warn people that they needed to change their lives, since she could also see their end. And it was **not** a prediction. Sometimes she would let you know your time was up and might even tell you that your youngest child, who has Down syndrome, "…will grow up to become a poet, but you won't be around to know him." That's pretty specific. (You know, not even Buddha had this ability, and Jesus would have been like, "Wow!" confirming his words, "You will do greater things than me.") *Anyways*, with nothing to hide, I decided we would be friends.

I could spend hours sharing stories about Ms. Juliette, and I will tell you more about her later. Still, two moments that stood out for me in my early twenties were these: She saw my husband through her vision and asked in a sweet, soft Southern accent, "He hasn't courted you yet?" Then she said, "He is so handsome, he's so handsome." I didn't know what she meant. The use of "yet" made me feel like this person was already a part of my life. (Some might argue that the future does not exist because we can only experience it in the present. Technically, that's true. But are they right about that? I watched Ms. Juliette experience my future. "He is so handsome" sounds like an *in-the-present* experience to me, but of course, the courtship would only ever occur in my present. Yet, it could be said that I also experienced a glimpse of my future that day, as well—in the present moment, of course. Is it possible that the present and the future coexist?)

Still, the only guy I knew back then was this funny White dude with a strong New England accent from the backwoods of *Yankalachia*…I mean, New Hampshire. (It's okay if I lost you. I know, I know, most Southerners still don't even know where the geographic region of New England is located.) *Certainly, she couldn't have been talking about him*, I thought. Never in a million years did I imagine that White men were an option for marriage :0). So, if that were the case, I would probably overlook him. Indeed, it would have been easier and saved me a lot of time and heartache if she had just hinted that he was White.

Interestingly, Ms. Juliette also told me, along with another young lady named *Detra*, who stopped by during one of my visits (whom I have yet to see again), that the Divine had instructed her to teach us to carry on her work and that we should be friends. *(Whassup, Detra! It's been a while.)* One lesson was to recognize the good in all people beyond their self-created identities and personal struggles. For instance, I remember sharing that my first job after college was working for a well-known local politician, whom she also knew, which lasted three loooong months. Before I could share my experience, she responded, "Isn't she a wonderful person?" She left me speechless. Ms. Juliette was teaching me to see through the eyes of Love and not to condemn people because of their faults.

Union in the Ministry

My husband and I met and married at a well-known church in town, where we served in the ministry for many years. We once led one of Alachua County's most extensive faith-based after-school programs. With over thirty volunteers from Santa Fe College and the University of Florida, we reached more than 300 children each week with faith-based lessons on practical life skills. Our ministry impacted the church and community so much that, during praise and worship, the church leader once told us, with a warm hug and a back rub, "Keep up the good work; you might find yourself in the [paid] ministry one day." (eye-roll)

Kicked Out of a Cult that Rocked Our Little World

As a naturally curious person, I'm not surprised that I didn't last long in a conservative, predominantly White, patriarchal Christian church that didn't handle questions too well. The church's covert controlling tendencies were becoming more visible to us, and their immense power to control information and silence individuals, often for years, was frightening. One thing led to another, resulting in a narrative that could serve as the basis of a self-help book, titled *The Exodus: How to Free Your Mind or Your Loved Ones from a Cult*. We found ourselves disturbed that we had spent our early years in a cult that was a well-known whisper in town. (Remember, rumors often hold a nugget of truth. [wink])

We wanted to get further and further away from that place because the pain of deception and being shunned by the congregation was more than we could bear. It was much like being one of the prisoners in Plato's *Allegory of the Cave* who finally left the cave to see the light and a new reality. We learned that our minds had kept us from seeing what they were programmed to defend, contributing to our trap and pain. (We must understand how programming works or risk being programmed. No worries...*common and country folks*, you can grasp Plato's *Allegory of the Cave*. Plato always used plain speech. There are numerous good sources for his work. One of my favorites is Ebenstein's Great Political Thinkers: Plato to the Present, sixth edition. Sorry, it's an old textbook from the University of Florida.)

Anyways, if you left the church without "the covering" or "the blessing," which meant—you left without permission—you weren't blessed, which was just as bad, if not worse, than being "unsaved," not Christian, in their eyes. And they ensured you felt their disapproval: either they avoided you or were too scared to talk to you. Sadly, no one dared to say goodbye when we left. It was *absolutely devastating* to lose every friend we had—overnight, especially since we considered them family or, worse, treated them better than our natural family. We loved those people, which made leaving even more heartbreaking. (Later, I will share the full story.)

We learned that conflict and pain are vital to usher in awakening. (Ouch!) Questioning and conflict are our doors to freedom, but not without crawling through the thorns first. As I tell my children today, "On the other side of conflict, there's always gold! Never be afraid to face it head-on." We had no clue this would kickstart a twenty-year transformation, awakening us to life. *Boy*, were we in for a surprise!

Goodbye to Gainesville

After leaving Gainesville, our first stop was Charlotte, North Carolina, known as the Bible Belt (the land of vinyl siding and urban sprawl) and home to the late American evangelist Billy Graham. We departed Gainesville with a small group from our church exodus to help launch a new church in Charlotte. However, my husband and I grappled with the fact that we had just escaped a cult and questioned what right we had to start a church. Still, it was our opportunity to leave Gainesville. (giggles)

Every Sunday, as we drove from the University Area to South Charlotte to set up at the local high school for the morning service, I often wondered how the parents would feel about us teaching their children in the children's church if they knew our recent history. No one ever inquired about our former ministry experience. Nevertheless, as we struggled to make sense of life, we didn't feel right about what we were doing. Even so, not everyone agreed with our perspective, though.

Those who share our views are seen as detrimental to "church business." We were likened to Lot's wife in the Bible, who turned into a pillar of salt for looking back at the ruins of Sodom and Gomorrah as she fled. Scriptures can be beautiful tools to justify any position. Some people are willing to look back a thousand years to reference biblical stories in hopes of gaining wisdom, but they won't look back five months, let alone five years, to truly grasp what they have escaped. The truth can sometimes be too painful for the ego to bear.

The idea of moving forward sounds excellent and can be practical at the right time; however, when you have participated in something inappropriate, you may need a time-out. A criminal inclined to arson can't tell a judge, "Hey, that was the past. We need to focus on the here and now." This individual needs time to reflect on their life and behavior before reintegrating into society.

Instead of being a dead weight or a block of salt to this ministry, we decided to take our chances because we felt it was necessary to look back at "Sodom and Gomorrah" to understand what we had been a part of and avoid repeating the same behaviors. We didn't need a judge to decide for us; we sentenced ourselves to a time of solitary confinement and finally started our young lives. It was scary as we walked out the doors again, but this time, we were utterly alone in a new town, which we later renamed "Little India" due to the significant South Asian population. (Can you hear the sitar, an Indian instrument, and the wonderful smell of incense and spices?)

Embraced by Little India

I was big and pregnant with our first son when I met my first friend in the real world, who was from Mumbai, India. She was my massage therapist and was also pregnant, having trained as an Ayurvedic practitioner, a traditional Indian doctor. I could barely pronounce "Ayurveda," so I didn't understand the significance of the field and how it would impact my life. (She basically has a Ph.D. in Soul Food.) During one of our sessions, I told her we should be friends. She couldn't have entered my life at a better time and had no idea that I was recovering from being in a charismatic cult and needed space from Christianity to determine what was a keeper in my life versus what was merely a product of destructive religious programming.

Many people would extend their apologies upon hearing our story, assuming it couldn't or wasn't happening to them. This was the condescending kind of "I'm so sorry" that made you never want to bring it up again. However, we came to accept that experiencing and breaking free from religious abuse or…abusive religion was the greatest blessing bestowed upon us, even though we didn't realize it at the time.

Inspired by my new friend, I quickly mastered the art of South Asian cooking, almost as if I had prepared these dishes in a past life. (*Shout out* to my homegirls, Hetal and Anuja!) I fell in love with the endless possibilities. *This food truly embodied the essence of soul food!*

The only thing that could have made life better would have been my own curry tree, a popular tempering spice in South Asian cuisine. I started eyeing a baby tree that sprouted from my friend's plant. As I watched the new shoot grow, I asked if I could have the sapling. She responded, "Shetty," *with attitude,* which often sounded like "Shitty" to me, as she shook her head from side to side. (I always needed clarification on her pronunciation of my name and the direction of her head wobble.) "Do you know how many Indian women are waiting for that tree to mature?" she said. With that, I knew I had to act quickly if I were to have any chance of beating the other women who shared my hopes. I almost didn't feel worthy of having the tree because I was so new to South Asian cooking. Nonetheless, I selfishly pulled up the poor sapling, which was no more than an inch tall. Unbeknownst to me, this little tree would become a part of my family, blessing us through the years, and would be the door to many more marvelous friendships.

Healing from Religion

I cherished the safety I found in healing among my Hindu friends. They never tried to impose their religion on me or label me with names like "sinner," "heathen," or "unsaved." The environment was perfect for my curious nature, as observing their rhythm and culture sparked my interest and fueled my studies.

As I researched Hinduism and why they all had little altars in their homes, I noticed how strikingly similar some Christian stories were to Hindu stories that were thousands of years older than Christianity. *How could that be?* Of course, with my limited perspective at the time, I justified the similarities to defend my Christian rightness by saying something like, "These Hindu stories foreshadowed the coming of Christ." (giggles) Without first ensuring I was "right," I might have felt compelled to conclude that I had witnessed a case of plagiarism or that we might be talking about the same God. (I couldn't have that! And is it plagiarism if I write your story before you do?) But as you probably know, it's always safer to construct a belief that reinforces your viewpoint instead of considering other uncomfortable possibilities. Well…that's at least what I did.

Homogeneous New Hampshire

After seven loooong years in Charlotte and much time spent alone, our next stop was the bitter cold of New Hampshire, where my wonderful husband was born and raised. There's nothing like good old-fashioned unemployment to propel you to the other side of the globe. I highly recommend that everyone experience living as a "minority" in a homogeneous culture at least once. It will change you—forever. (Migration changes you.)

Oddly enough, I started to miss home right away. Something was unsettling about how some locals interacted with me. I noticed and began to express that many who appeared friendly were treating me as if I were Black, which may sound like something I'm not supposed to say, depending on your perspective. But it might be helpful to ask what it means to treat someone as if they are Black. This was a foreign feeling, but it brought me closer to realizing that I benefited from certain privileges in the South connected to "white or light skin seen as better." (I believe this quote is mine, but I'm concerned I might have read it somewhere in 2014.)

However, in New Hampshire, where diversity was less than 2%, my previous identity as a multiracial or light-skinned person faced a rude awakening. I had become the very definition of Black. Without knowing who I truly was, they molded Black into my ethnicity. *Boy*, did I hate what that meant to them and how it felt! "You're 'black,' and this is who you are as I see it," was the message. (If that isn't abusive, I don't know what is.) They acted as if they owned my identity and that of every "Person of Color." You only notice this when you refuse to accept what they force-feed you, and some of them will make sure you swallow the programming if you resist. Unfortunately, I was a character recruited to play a role in their imaginary world. Shucks! For the first time in my life, there was no one darker to take my place at the table.

New Hampshire stripped me of my privileged multiracial heritage and slapped me. People acted as if they had never encountered someone like me, treating me according to their stereotypical views. I wanted to tell them *with attitude*, "You must not know who I am." Yet, I felt conflicted because I longed to return south to a world where my light skin placed me a little higher in the ranks. I was baffled. *How could that ever be something to desire?* This notion was intertwined with a system that required someone else to be less than me. (Yikes!)

One day, filled with emotions, I reflected on all my elementary school girlfriends who had to endure me being chosen for every *special* event and photo opportunity. I experienced an awakening that revealed a variation of White privilege in my life. Living as a second-class citizen in New Hampshire was good for my soul. Don't get me wrong; I wasn't oblivious to racism or colorism. It's just that I had never faced it as harshly as many of my friends with darker skin do daily.

*

The Husband's Awakening

New Hampshire had something for us all! My husband, who had experienced zero diversity in his life before meeting me, wanted to believe that the world was peaceful and that racism wasn't as severe as some described. He thought it didn't affect White people in the Northeast as much as it did in the South. He also believed that maybe he was exempt from being racist (which I consider a disease of the mind) or from examining his beliefs simply because he was married to a "Woman of Color." Nope, I told him from the start, "You're not exempt, and you don't earn any points or a pass by marrying me." While he was trying to collect points, he also didn't realize that Black people didn't exactly recognize me as Black. *(Sorry, no points for you, "brotha.")* Many of us who are biracial or multiracial are often only claimed when convenient ☹. *(Right, Obama? Harris, did I hear you say, "Amen!"?)*

Similar to the way I used creative mind tricks to avoid examining my Christianity, my husband faced his own struggles, as well. However, this situation revolved around him calling out the behaviors of "his people" who looked like him when we encountered racism. He was unknowingly defending the notion of being White and would deny, justify, or downplay the behaviors he observed to escape feelings of personal conviction or responsibility. I often asked him, "***Who*** or ***what*** are you defending?" This question helped him realize that racism is often hardwired in the mind like a religion, and that the notion of *White* wasn't the essence of who he was.

We both learned that the mind has a remarkable ability to create alternative perspectives to support our beliefs, even when the truth is right in front of us, allowing us to avoid confronting a deeper reality. "Don't challenge my beliefs," the mind insists, "because all I am is good, perfect, and right." When you question the ideologies that the mind holds dear, the ego begins to think, "Something is wrong with me!" We can't have our little feelings getting hurt because we are conditioned to believe that our identities, shaped by the mind, define who we are and are worth defending, and even dying for.

But he, too, was in for a rude awakening. His beloved New Hampshire would start treating his children as if they were "Black," particularly our youngest, who has a darker complexion, sweet potato brown. He walked up into our son's Christian preschool as a proud father, and man, did they give him a good smack in the face. A boy loudly questioned him for everyone to hear, "How are you even his father when you're White and he's Black?" The boy's mother, who was also the preschool director and the pastor's wife, didn't know how to respond. (Ouch!) Someone wasn't teaching these children; we all come in many colors.

New Hampshire snatched my multiracial heritage and was now taking his parental rights. He was *38-hot.* I remember smiling at him and asking how it felt. It took him some time before he was willing to drop the...R-bomb...toward "his people," but it was coming and loooong overdue. Maybe it was the funeral we attended, with all the giant red, white, and blue flags with the stars and bars draped from pickup trucks. (Those Yankees surprised me. You would have thought this was the South.) I don't know, but this man's transformation has shown me that anything is possible! When we can move beyond our mind, culture, or religious programming, we begin to see things for what they truly are. It's called awakening!

*These friends remind me of the heartwarming film, **Ernest and Celestine**, I saw at the Hippodrome Theatre in Gainesville.*

Friendship Without Walls

Surprisingly, in a state with less than 2% diversity, I was again blessed with a friend from India, this time from Punjab! She was thrilled to have fresh tropical curry leaves from my tree in New Hampshire year-round, even when it was below zero outside. Neither of us had much going for ourselves. In fact, we were rather pitiful. (giggles) We were both living in a foreign land, just trying to survive day by day. It's incredible how quickly the notions of nationality, religion, and race fade away when you're desperate for human companionship.

Destined to be friends, we discovered much in common: husbands we didn't date (more on that in a later sermon, lol), mothers-in-law, raising boys, and a shared love for South Asian cuisine. I happily took a break from mustard seeds and the South Indian rice staple to say hello to North Indian chapatis and parathas! *Extra ghee, please!* We began cooking and sharing our passion for food, transforming our modest abodes, barely 800 sq ft, into what felt like luxury housing. Yet, if this were the South, it would have been a step up from public housing. Man, it was such a chore to put on snow boots, a jacket, a hat, and gloves to carry that damn laundry down a flight of stairs, passing through three locked doors, through the snow, across the street, "to Grandma's house we go"...oops, I mean, to the laundromat.

Our boys would race up and down the stairs in the winter when it was below zero outside. From our frosty windows, we would watch the sunset each day around 3:45 p.m. And it was gone by 4:13 p.m., sometimes with us never leaving the building. Life felt like one…long…dark…day. But our friendship made what could have been a dreary winter feel like the middle of summer. We didn't have much, but we had each other. (tears)

I encouraged her to return to dental school so she could transfer her credentials and work as a dentist in the U.S., and naturally, surpass her husband's earnings. And she gifted me a giant book on mysticism as a spiritual path, a gift from her brother that she had no intention of ever reading. In truth, she observed that spirituality radiated from my very essence. Unbeknownst to me, this hefty book served as the introductory manual for the life I was living. It became my Bible! The book revealed that others were grappling with the same questions I had and perceiving the world through a similarly inquisitive lens.

Welcomed by the Quakers

During our time in New Hampshire, my family and I joined the Religious Society of Friends, commonly referred to as the Quakers. *(Whassup, New England Yearly Meeting!)* They refer to themselves as *Friends* with a capital "F." Worshiping with them was peaceful, though sometimes it felt like pulling teeth. They certainly tested our patience at times.

Most Quaker Meetings don't have pastors or leaders, but they sit silently—closing your eyes is optional—for an hour on Sundays. This gathering is called "silent worship" or an "unprogrammed meeting," which is the Quakers' preferred way of connecting with the Divine or inner Christ. Beautiful!

There's a children's film called *Zootopia* where the sloth character inputs the numbers of a tag at the DMV at a painfully slow pace, just enough to drive you crazy or "quazy." This is Quakerism! If you haven't seen the movie, take a moment to look it up.

Some people took living in the moment to an extent that could make the *now* vanish. "Oops, did we lose Ed?" said in a slow, sleepy voice. "Let's call a business meeting to decide what shape hole would be best for his burial. *(Whassup, Ed!)* Does anyone know where the shovel labeled '*shovel for burial*' was left?" Good Lord, it took us forever to reach a decision. Respectfully, the process or involvement in life was more important than the product. This can be described as Love.

Quakerism can also be a challenging faith because it naturally attracts individuals, like the wolf in sheep's clothing, who secretly want to lead and control the group. One of my favorite *Friends* once said, "This [big bad wolf] is the age-old problem with Quakerism!" Most meetings, as congregations are called, have a "leader" or "leaders," whether they realize it or not. This wolf character exists in most churches, but you don't have to worry as much about where it's hiding because it's usually already in the pulpit. Still, these Quakers will welcome the naughty sheep, who is passively-aggressively tormenting the herd while hoping to crush...I mean, awaken this individual with their silence. Sometimes, it worked; sometimes, it was painful, like watching paint peel. (Unfortunately, some swapped out Presence for the silent treatment instead. [wink])

In principle, Quakerism appeared to be a great faith, but its structure and lack of accountability proved abusive in practice. My husband and I used to refer to the Second Hour discussion as the *Meeting for Beating.* (giggles) The misuse of power may explain why Quakerism, like many other churches, is dying or experiencing decline, with its numbers diminishing.

Although Quakerism was too tolerant, sleepy, and slow for me, its founder, George Fox, like many earlier teachers of Consciousness, experienced what Eckhart Tolle describes in *The Power of Now* as an awakening to life. In truth, most major world religions began with a clear and pure path to the Divine. However, they gradually transformed into religious rituals focused on strict adherence to "rules" or worshiping a person, losing sight of the essence of the original teaching.

Fox believed that God resided within the faithful and that each person could follow their inner spirit to guide themselves instead of relying on scriptures or clergy. Fox also aimed to prevent people from transforming his movement into merely something to believe in. His only objective was to guide these folks "to be" and connect with the Light within. He also believed that traditional church

leadership held no value and did not want to risk inflating his ego by positioning himself as the holy leader. Fox was clearly aware of how easy it was to lose touch with the Divine with the slightest shift in one's heart. "*I* did that," as the ego likes to say.

Awake and Letting Go of Identity

Meanwhile, what I now refer to as Consciousness and Presence flourished within me. I could see things before my face that I hadn't seen before. I could draw parallels between social constructs like racism and religion, or how

When you are bold enough to shave your head, it's a good indicator that you are letting go. However, it is not recommended—more on this in a later sermon.

one abusive system was merely a microcosm of another. They all exhibited similar thought and defense patterns.

I could no longer align myself with one perspective, religion, or political ideology. I perceived things for what they were—temporary and merely existing in time and space—which pushed me further away from identifying with anything. I was becoming free. I wasn't White, Brown, or Black...Democrat or Republican...rich or poor...gay or straight...a heart or a liver...saved or unsaved...smart or dumb...you get the idea. There was nothing left for me to argue about or defend. I was nothing, yet so much more.

These Russian nesting dolls were a beautiful visual of the endless microcosms of abuse and control I had to overcome in life. They were never-ending! The last one was me, and I beat her to death!

At times, this revelation became more than I could bear. I would occasionally experience burnout from witnessing the absurdity of our society, and my mind would shut down completely. Nothing was running through my mind. Not a single thought! My therapist at the time thought for sure something was wrong with me. (She didn't realize "that man" was driving me sane.)

The more time I spend in this state of Presence—what some might call meditating—the more substantial the force within me becomes, and my sense of knowing, peace, and faith strengthens. At times, I feel as high as a kite...without any substance abuse. I am free to live in this world while not being of it at the same time. Indeed, I recognize the labels the world imposes on us and the boxes I must navigate in this physical realm due to my "demographics," which exist solely in people's minds. Occasionally, I find it necessary to participate to make a point. Still, these labels no longer define me, nor do they hinder my connection to the Divine source.

*

Reimagining Life

I spent the last ten years reimagining a spiritual community focused on awakening to life. I even joined my Reform Jewish brothers and sisters for a while. I had a rabbi for a minute there, where I learned about their beautiful faith and God, who is intentionally nameless—"YHWH" (which isn't a name)—made accessible and universal to everyone. How amazing is that?

There was nothing I wanted more than to share that the Cosmos, or the Kingdom of God (which *is* God), is always within us (*you*). (It's like having *free power* from the electric company—more to come!) It isn't just a scripture to quote, an idea to discuss, or a mystical place many believe exists outside ourselves. We are a microcosm of God, a reflection of the Universe. I found the door, and it was open! It didn't require a key or a unique religious path. You just have to quiet your mind, turn off a few distractions, let go of a lot of mental clutter, and allow the Source within you to begin to flourish. It's like a plant that grows only when the conditions are right. (You, too, can birth this Krst.)

The fourteenth-century mystic Meister Eckhart was a controversial Catholic theologian who believed that ordinary people could find God without relying on religion, simply by looking inward to connect with the power some call Christ/Krst. His message was not well received by the church because it bypassed their teachings and threatened their control and influence over the people, who were essentially led to believe they needed the church for their "salvation." As a result, he was tried as a heretic, and his teachings were condemned. We can't have simple people thinking for themselves, right? The Catholic Church nearly silenced the poor guy, similar to Fox's experience, for suggesting the same. Perhaps they were onto something!

In the sixth sermon from The Complete Mystical Works of Meister Eckhart, "Truth is Not Merchandise" (referencing Matthew 21:12 from the Bible), Meister Eckhart explains that the merchants Jesus sought to expel from the temple are essentially the voices living in your head, constantly engaging in transactions. They consistently negotiate, aiming to strike a sweet deal that satisfies their superficial desires and bolsters their sense of self. Some of these characters would exchange the experience of knowing God for a luxury car. Quiet the temple, clear out the merchants, and you will meet God there.

He also wrote in Sermon Sixty-Nine, "The Kingdom of God is Near to You" (referencing Luke 21:31 from the Bible), not as something coming in the future, but more like in your face, close up and personal, **closer to you than you are to yourself**. Well, that's *pretty damn* close and intimate! Just as Jacob realized this

31

in the Old Testament and said, "[Well, I'll be damned!] God is in this place (his vessel), and I didn't even know it" (Genesis 28:16 from the Bible). (You know, it's like discovering you have *free power* from the electric company—more to come!)

I Had "Company" and Friends

Fast-forward to the present, with our two sons, my husband and I moved back to Gainesville after nearly twenty years away. After settling in, I quickly began making new friends. One day, during a conversation with a friend from South America who has a strong presence, I caught a glimpse of how others perceive me. We discussed parenting and our worldviews when she reached out, touched my hand like a passionate Italian or a *Brazillionaire*, close-up and personal, and said lovingly while rolling the "R's" in my name, "Sherry, you're Catholic!" I suspected she was looking at the Divine in me or the "Christ within." Later, when I shared this heartwarming story with another friend, she turned to me and said, "And to us, Sherry, you are Hindu." I had never felt more touched in my life. We don't have to live divided; we must reflect Love.

I realized both connected to the God within me—the Light and the Source of all creation. The Catholics saw Christ/Krst within, while the Hindus saw peace, love, and understanding (along with a whole bunch of gods). I remember telling my husband, "It's okay with me; I'm Catholic." I winked and added, "To the Catholic, I'm a Catholic, and to the Hindu, I'm a Hindu."

The phrase sounded so familiar that I asked my husband if it was something Jesus had said. I grabbed my dusty Bible, finally looked it up, and realized it was a scripture attributed to Paul in 1 Corinthians 9:19-22:

For though I *be* free from all *men*, yet [I have] made myself [a] servant unto all, that I might gain the more. And unto the Jews I became as a Jew, that I might gain the Jews; to them that are under the law, [I became] as under the law, that I might gain them that are under the law; to them that are without law, [I became] as without law, (being not without law to God, but under the law to Christ,) that I might gain them that are without law. To the weak *became I* as weak (giggles), that I might gain the weak: I am made all things to all *men*, that I might by all means save some. (King James Version of the Bible, the good stuff, as it's free to use, no permission needed. Feel free to open your devices for a more up-to-date version of the Bible. However, those who speak SAAVE likely understood this version just fine.)

Not only did I see myself in my friends, but I was the same as them. I could relate to them, and they seemed to see their God in me. Well, I'll be damned with a slap on the knee! It was the most beautiful revelation. It was enough to unite the nations!

There's Something Up with That Curry Tree

A month after we settled into our home, my youngest approached me, giggling, and asked, "Mom, how come you always have an Indian friend as a neighbor and a bunch of Indian ladies as friends?" (Because Indian friendship is exponential; make one Indian friend, and by the end of the year, you'll have twenty new friends. [giggles]) Still, I smiled, realizing I didn't have an answer for him. This time, however, I was to learn about the Islamic side of India, as my new neighbor and friend wore a hijab.

I found it peculiar that my son was also starting to notice the pattern. Then it dawned on me that it had something to do with my now thirteen-year-old, ten-foot curry tree. I remember thinking, *Could this tree have been helping me make friends over the years?* Unaware of the outcome, I often sought out my Indian neighbors after pruning my tree to avoid throwing away the precious leaves. Ask any Indian woman: curry leaves are like gold! Until then, I never realized that sharing my leaves always led to a new, delightful friendship. (Wow, leaves!)

Freed by Love

Overall, I was living a quiet life, distancing myself from my past in Gainesville. Oddly enough, it was my Indian friends, guided by the Divine, who cornered me with questions that led me to share the story of why my husband and I had fled Gainesville in the first place. These ladies were helping to set me free! I felt safe sharing with them, perhaps because they didn't fully grasp the significance of what we had escaped. I told them they might not have liked me if I had never left Gainesville because I was ignorant of the spirituality and diversity of people that existed beyond my limited experience.

Reflecting on my years, I find comfort in how a young mom from India embraced and welcomed me to Charlotte when I ran away from Gainesville. Then, folks of the same vibrant culture, which had been sparse when I left, played a key role in welcoming me home. I still don't quite understand it. I told my dear friends—one Sunni Muslim, another Jain, one *Mormon*, another Catholic, and two Hindus—that **I wouldn't be the woman I am today** if I hadn't been pushed out of Gainesville. This experience forced me to grow and awaken to the limitless, unifying power of Consciousness, which transcends all religions! (Migration changes you.)

Today, I present to you ***Betwixt***, a community focused on building bridges between our differences. I don't hold a fancy title. I'm simply a vessel, a teacher of Consciousness and stillness accessible to all, regardless of faith.

Namaste,

—Sher! (The Common Snook)

Pause. Inhale. Exhale. Reflect.

P.S. My struggles and displacement were the best things that ever happened to me—food for my soul. CeeLo's verse (1:09) in the Goodie Mob song "Soul Food" expresses this idea well. However, I do not condone F-bombing O.J. Simpson's prosecutor, Marcia Clark. She demonstrated the resilience of women in a society that seeks to devalue us and crush our spirits. I'm sure she can also relate to CeeLo's verse, but instead, she would be rapping, **"I wouldn't be the woman I am today."** *(Whassup, Marcia!)*

P.P.S. Speaking of "The Great Racial Divide" in middle school! How 'bout we get the Gator fans excited? One of my classmates from the west side of the tracks in Gainesville, Doug Johnson, who later became a Florida Gators football quarterback in 1996 under coach Steve Spurrier and then moved on to the NFL, would likely remember me as the girl who straddled two worlds. I spent my weekends with my country White friends, from birthday parties on the Suwannee to watching baseball games at Westside Park. Then, on Monday, it was back to the segregated cafeteria, of course. *(Doug, don't pretend you don't know me. Quarterbacks are supposed to have good brain function, you know.)*

P.P.P.S. My homegirl from Punjab, whom I met when our boys were babies, became "Doctor!" by Western standards in the spring of 2023—graduating first and *eldest* in her class from a top-ten dental school—beeyotch!

(Sit in stillness with your eyes closed for 15 minutes a day; I promise it will transform your life!)

2. No Labels

Disclosure Reminder…,

The only power available to overcome sexism, racism, and a slew of other *isms* in the form of social constructs is to raise human Consciousness. We can change policies to create a more inclusive future, but the heart must change to make the world a more loving place. Most specifically, overcoming the mind identifications that define and separate us is essential.

Let's look at the Quaker faith again. And no, I'm not talkin' 'bout the Amish or the man from the Quaker Oats box…well, *kinda.* As mentioned, Quakerism was inspired by George Fox, who experienced God (or the Divine) by looking within, as the Bible suggests, *for the Kingdom of God is within—you.* (It's like having *free power*….) Fox found God without any fancy preaching from a pulpit. Who would have guessed that was possible? He just sat in silence as a form of worship, which I call meditation or stillness. (Y'all remember William Penn, who established Pennsylvania, a.k.a. the pure and honest "fictional character" on the Quaker Oats box? He, too, was a Quaker.)

Forgive me for giving an abbreviated history of this once-powerful group. Today, small groups of Quakers remain, with many, unfortunately, missing the profoundness of Fox's original teachings. Any great movement can become diluted over time and lose its original ethos. Even so, to this day, Quakers remain strong voices for social justice.

One of the most recognized Quakers was John Woolman, who was recognized as a leader in freeing enslaved people before the Civil War. Many Quakers recognize him as more successful than the battle itself because he was able to free enslaved people and enslavers from the evil practice of slavery without any loss of life. He achieved this by invoking the conscience of the enslavers through his talks and writings, as conveyed (in a manuscript by Gray Fitzgerald, set to be published in 2025).

Many Quakers take pride in this idea, but sometimes, provoking strong feelings is necessary since not everyone responds to peaceful requests. At times, creating tension is essential. However, this "peaceful" approach often serves as the oppressor's favored method for fighting for your freedom. "First, say please!" Still, nonviolence remained the only practical way to confront the White hatred and violence directed at fellow Americans. Anything less would have provoked and justified their desire to use deadly force, as Martin Luther King Jr. often expressed.

In mid-June 2023, I dropped my son off at a well-known summer camp that has been in operation for many years. As much as the camp is about the children, it is also about the parents making the investment and needing to feel reassured that they are sending their children to a safe and welcoming place. I should have been able to peacefully drop off my son and leave camp like the other families. Instead, I had to gently address a three-by-five-foot Blue Lives Matter flag that was allowed to hang on the wall in my son's cabin without considering how families of different backgrounds might perceive it. Some argue that the Blue Lives Matter flag is designed to show support for law enforcement, and others feel it is used as a counter-protest to the Black Lives Matter movement and is divisive.

I didn't have any issues with anyone's connection to or expression around the flag…outside of the camp; however, it would not be a flag I would have my son sleep under in our home. When I spoke to the appropriate staff member about the flag and its meaning to different people, I asked whether camp could be a place where everyone felt welcome, as this symbol had become divisive and a source of conflict. When he suggested that the flag was displayed because one of the counselors had law enforcement in their family, I could respect the notion, as I, too, had a family member who served as an officer for over thirty years with the Gainesville Police Department. (Hmm…but what did that have to do with camp?)

Though we disagreed on the meaning behind the flag, we both agreed that the camp should be a neutral place and that many symbols have been politicized. Then, the staff member mentioned the pride flag as another example. Oddly enough, I don't think he noticed I agreed with him, perhaps because I look like the type who might cover my car in bumper stickers. I thanked him for his willingness (pluralism) to hear and respect my views, regardless of whether he agreed. He was a gentleman, and I'm thankful for how he handled the situation. The bottom line is that camp should be where everyone feels welcome.

That brings me to our label-free position with *Betwixt*. A spiritual community that is open to *all* should also be a place where *all* feel welcome. We are not a spiritual community trying to rebrand from a history of past discrimination and hate, where we must try to convince newcomers that *all* are welcome— genuinely means *all*. We don't want anyone to be deterred from experiencing life beyond the labels because we mistakenly choose to align with a political or social movement, as I did in the cabin that day.

We are not interested in mixing our mission with the often violent wars invoked to change policies. We are interested in helping people find the door to change their own hearts. We want to attract both sides: those who counter-protest efforts for fundamental human rights and those who intentionally wear a pin or symbol into a church to make a statement to the congregation that has rejected them. I can't say I haven't thought of using similar warfare tactics to express my views. However, when we realize that it is about accessing Consciousness, connecting to the Divine, and waking up from our state of sleep, a similar perspective emerges, akin to the Quakers' awakening to their sin or separation from God due to slavery. One begins to see all human life as oneself, worthy of dignity and respect.

Woolman realized his non-violent approach helped his fellow Quakers free themselves and their enslaved people. They began to see slavery as an evil they didn't want to be a part of, and by freeing enslaved people, they released themselves to learn to love. *(Whassup, Gray!)*

Having said that, this changing of hearts didn't happen as widely, some would say, in the South, but racism was just more subtle in the North. Unfortunately, the freeing of enslaved people resulted from policy changes due to the war and not love. The Civil War freed enslaved people but didn't change the mindsets or hearts of the enslavers, segregationists, or their descendants, as evidenced by the many racial struggles we still face today, which again is also still evident in the North.

With *Betwixt*, our vision is to grow consciously, allowing our hearts, attitudes, and minds to be transformed. Staying neutral will enable us to welcome all and avoid getting involved in polarized arguments. It will also open the door for more people to be genuinely transformed (the ones we need to be transformed) by the power open to all of us, regardless of faith.

Peace,

—Sher! (The Common Snook)

Pause. Inhale. Exhale. Reflect.

P.S. *And don'tcha be calling to see if this is your camp. I ain't disclosin'. Yet, you know this is your camp because you hired mostly "Rednecks" down to the woman in the chair with the stare who gave me attitude for addressing the flag. Just make sure it doesn't happen again. You might need a policy that upsets everyone.* Even so, I bow to those "Rednecks" for putting up with my son during his musky years, so they can rest assured I won't give any names. I owe them my life! They gave me two weeks off to catch my breath. Priceless! You know, everyone needs a "Redneck" as a friend, right? More to come! 🍸

3. Sent by God, Thank You!

Disclosure Reminder…,   August 1, 2023

The Divine has placed me in a neighborhood where every house and yard must look the same. We pay people low wages for services so we can maintain our picture-perfect lifestyles with minimal stress. Rather than keeping these individuals in quarters behind our homes and feeding them our dinner scraps, they are offered pennies for the work we refuse to do, allowing them to find their own *Porter's Quarters* and their own scraps to eat. It's easier this way, preventing us from confronting how we enslave our fellow man. We arrogantly proclaim, "We are providing them work!" (Well, not me…saying "we" helps people buy-in and own their sins. Unfortunately, I still cut my own grass—ugh! [giggles])

I'm so grateful to the numerous landscaping companies, DoorDash, and Amazon for making our neighborhood more culturally diverse. Who doesn't enjoy the bass blaring in the middle of the day from an Amazon truck with its side door flung wide open as the driver tosses packages up and down the street? Whoever said, "Santa isn't Black," hasn't visited my neighborhood.

Because I think I know everyone, or maybe it's because I've taught many kids in Gainesville through my previous children's ministry, JAM on the Streets (where JAM stands for Jesus and Me), and in the public schools. I recognize faces that might be related to one of the children I taught. In any case, I became friendly with the "bros" who kept my neighbors' picture-perfect lives nice and tidy. I asked one young man if I knew him, and he suggested I might know his father, who was in his fifties. He *tried me* with that age reminder! Talkin' 'bout,

"Yes, ma'am." I often perceive myself as younger than I actually appear. For all he knew, I could've been his age; some of us go gray early.

Anyhow, because I'm curious, we got to talking about life. I asked him where he attended high school. Knowing I was an educator, he seemed embarrassed to admit that he dropped out of high school. He offered some excuses to ease his discomfort because society often shames or cancels people for not meeting certain standards. I said, "No worries...school isn't for everyone." But as I watched him holding the edger, I added, "But learning is," because I could tell he was more intelligent than many people with a college degree, as he slipped me his business card for the landscaping company he was starting with his brother. (Man, I wish I could have bought that young man a piece of lawn equipment to help jump-start his business.)

He also mentioned that he didn't enjoy high school and hated being there. The *Betwixt* alternative middle and high school, a vision I have, would have been an excellent option for him. I would have guided him toward the trade programs at Santa Fe College so he could earn enough to support his family. That young man would have made an excellent plumber or electrician since he was hardworking and skilled with his hands.

Furthermore, I recall thinking about a friend from middle school who is now a successful plumber in town. This friend mentioned that he would never have stuck with the program if it hadn't been for his instructor at Santa Fe, who encouraged him to persevere despite the challenges, as the trade programs primarily catered to White men. His White instructor noted that "*They* are trying to keep the trade industry White" by not recruiting Black men or failing to support them emotionally in a predominantly White program. (Hmm...maybe because landscaping fees would skyrocket if Alachua County Public Schools ensured these young men learned a trade before graduating high school.)

As our conversation continued, he shared that life had been tough for him as a kid and that he's still dealing with anger today because of how he grew up. I'll give him credit; he did look a bit hot and angry taking care of White folks' lawns for pennies. But thank God he wore a bright yellow shirt to show my neighbors which team he was on. His pain ran so deep that I could feel it. Despite that, I admired his spirit and vulnerability because even though life was hard, he had the heart of a real man. He wasn't all that broken after all.

I mostly just listened. Still, I told him to acknowledge the past but not let it hold him back because it no longer exists. Then he looked me in the eye. He was tall, dark, ripped, and handsome, with the heart of a boy who, unfortunately, had a rough start in life. He said to me boldly, as if he were an angel sent to me by

God, "You know, you could help young Black people like me. They'd listen to you." The angel of the Lord left me speechless. (I still have tears in my eyes.)

He surprised me because I hadn't really said anything other than offering him my undivided attention and Presence. I knew then that my role was changing, and my time served in the prison of uniformity was coming to an end as I returned to my picture-perfect grass and my picture-perfect house, where the sheets *smell* like *Downy*.

Big *Li'l Bro'* Hugs,

—Sher! (The Common Snook)

Pause. Inhale. Exhale. Reflect.

P.S. *Shout out* to my beloved students from Mebane and Lincoln Middle Schools in the greater Gainesville area. *Give it up for* the good times in the "behavioral self-contained class"! "What you talkin' 'bout, Ms. S?" as my country-ass students from "Alachu-ay" used to say. (Alachua is a city and county in Florida, named by the Timucuan Native Americans, which means "land of the sinks or sinkholes." Yikes!)

And to those who are "behaviorally self-contained" behind bars today, I haven't forgotten about you. Y'all used to have me refereeing professional wrestling for Alachua County Public Schools. *(Hey, li'l bro with the million-dollar smile! Well, you know, I read your story in the paper some years ago. Wow! That was a big deal, banana peel. I'm glad you missed, or perhaps* he ducked.*)*

Anyhow, **I wouldn't be the woman I am today** without you. You were among the brightest boys who, unfortunately, had a rough start in life. But remember, it isn't over.

P.P.S. What if a student threatens to kill their teacher? *("Child please.")* Often, these students are arrested and expelled for being scary, and then the school system must offer them an alternative learning arrangement with a home-based teacher. But what happens if nobody takes the job? Oddly enough, I once received a job offer for a home-based teacher assignment with an hourly rate that I couldn't refuse. (giggles) Sometimes we say things we don't mean, right? 🪑

40

Section II: Massaging and Expanding Your Perspectives

In case you decided to skip the introduction and browse around, here's the **Disclosure Reminder**: Before diving in, I will say this: I'm simple. I love to laugh. Please don't confuse my humor with sarcasm; I always mean what I say. I test the limits. My words are plain. I often use "own" redundantly. I don't claim to know all the answers; my only intention is to be a vessel. Also, to connect with different experiences, I interchangeably use the terms "Consciousness," "Presence," "God," "Universe," "Source," "Divine," "Energy," "Christ/Krst," and "Light." Above all, reading my humor with a Southern accent is best. Enjoy!

My son, Li'l Snook van Gogh (LSVG), age 9, was inspired by an unknown artist from Athens, Georgia.

1. Speaking of Angry Men in My Neighborhood

Disclosure Reminder...,

Once upon a time, my happy self ran into the wrong *brotha* on the wrong day. He wasn't in the mood for my *"bougie-ness."* (No, I ain't bougie.) He was preparing to unload some supplies to take care of a few items at my neighbor's house, which had just been vacated, and I was serving as their point person since they were out of state. I said with a smile, "Hello, are you here for the next project?" I asked because I was the one who left the house unlocked—that he was about to enter.

"Is *dis yo* house?" he asked with a nasty attitude. I replied, "No," and explained that I was the primary contact for the property and was helping my friend coordinate the maintenance services. (That was the wrong answer.)

When I asked which company he was from, he refused to tell me the name and became aggressive. "I'm just here to do a job!" he said. Man, he was testing me; I was about to bend his young-ass over my knee. I couldn't figure out what had gone wrong. So, I stepped into his personal space, close up, as if I were his momma and was going to tickle him (not recommended), and said through my tight teeth, "I'm not a threat, and you know that." I must have really upset him because he became even more aggressive with me while simultaneously apologizing. (What a strange combination.) Sadly, I could tell he was accustomed to being questioned and spoken to in a condescending manner.

Then he said, with all that testosterone that forced his chin up in the air, "You shouldn't have walked up on me like *dat* without *introducin' yoself*!" (*Oh no he didn't.* [That's SAAVE; no commas.]) He was being slick, trying to make himself right when he knew he was dead wrong for being mean, especially since I only approached him with kindness. (Perhaps he thought I was armed.) I said, "You're right. I'm sorry," which caught him off guard. *Li'l bro'* was ready for a fight. Yet he continued apologizing and growled at me simultaneously, and his stubborn-ass still wouldn't tell me what company he was with. *What happened was*...we had problems with the first company that needed to be resolved before he began his work. (It's complicated.) Nonetheless, his ego had to hold on to a little bit of "I'm right" because, with a little bit of "I'm wrong," he would have had to face his weakness and admit that he was being mean.

The White woman in me, the Schmeirer (y'all, I'm 65% European, and 35% of that is German, my primary ethnicity), thought about blocking the door with my arms wide open until he answered me. However, I decided that helping my friend was not all that important, and *I didn't give a flip* about who walked into her house that day. I told that young man, "You have a nice day," and texted my friend, saying, "There's an angry man in your house. Good luck!" That sweet young man with the early receding hairline broke my heart. He was raised to watch his back and has lived feeling unwelcome. I had never seen someone apologize and growl the way he did.

He was split in two; that's called cognitive dissonance. One side of him said, "She's okay; she won't hurt me," and the other side said, "I WILL NOT BE WRONG BECAUSE THIS WORLD HAS HURT ME!" Unfortunately, the world was not a safe or welcoming place for him, which likely required him to qualify his right to exist in certain spaces. A part of me can respect why he didn't answer me, even though I wasn't his problem. But thank God he wore a bright-ass yellow shirt so my neighbors would know which team he was on.

At the same time, this was a valuable observation, and many of us find ourselves in these defensive, reactive patterns. First, good news! This is not you, but instead, the false self, pretending to be you, that feels threatened. Defensiveness is a crucial sign that the mind is in attack and defense mode. That means you are no longer home; you have checked out. Engaging people in that state of mind is often fruitless and dangerous.

I encountered the essence of this sweet young man, which is why he kept apologizing and growling. He was torn because he struggled with conflicting beliefs in his mind. After all, there were two entities in there. Still, his mind was the dominant beast running his life, working hard to protect his younger self, which he hid inside.

When we connect to the Source (some call it "Christ/Krst"), we no longer have to protect our multiple selves. If we observe this behavior, we can begin to deactivate and defuse the monster who pretends to be us. It can *actually* be a lot of fun because *you*, the real *you* (connected to the Source of all creation), are watching the madness through the lens of awareness. Also, don't judge the madness with your words or thoughts because that's just the mind showing you who the boss is and running this temple. Keep an eye on that sucker, and it will surrender to the Divine. As the Bible says, as in most spiritual books, *darkness cannot dwell in the light*. Either way, that precious lamp is already inside of you.

Big Black *Bro'* Hugs,
   —Sher! (The Common Snook)
                    Pause. Inhale. Exhale. Reflect. 🧘

2. If Jewish People Never Joined the Notion of *White*—I Probably Can't Say That

The following sermon is a conversation, so read it as if we were sitting in a circle eating cheese puffs.

Disclosure Reminder…,

Some of you may be too young to realize that Jewish people haven't always been viewed as White. This concept is incredible, coming from the perspective that *White* is an ideology. It clearly illustrates that being White isn't just about skin color; rather, it encompasses a specific set of beliefs.

However, if Jewish people had rejected *White* instead of joining *Club White* after the Holocaust, I imagine the world would be further along in the fight against racism. It might have ended sixty years ago if every Jew in America had shown up wearing either black hats with candy curls or wigs, for the 1963 March on Washington for Jobs and Freedom. Even so, many did. Still, for most Jews, eighteen and a half years after the Holocaust wasn't long enough. Shoot, I don't blame them. Over six million Jewish lives were lost in the name of "White Supremacy." Damn. That's choking. I can't believe *we humans* allowed something so horrific to happen. (I'm sorry; I need to pause for a moment. It's challenging to tap into my humor after writing something so sobering. I'll return shortly.)

Jewish people have historically been among the most influential social advocates in the Western world. For instance, Reform Jews, formerly known as the Union of American Hebrew Congregations, played a significant role in establishing and funding many important civil rights organizations, including the National Association for the Advancement of Colored People (NAACP) and various Black colleges and schools. Unfortunately, for many, the experience of the Holocaust, which was of biblical proportions, transformed a once-powerful group into literal believers of their text, similar to the followers of Christianity or Hinduism, for that matter.

Judaism evolved from being just a lifestyle into a full-fledged *belief system*. Douglas Rushkoff's *Nothing Sacred: The Truth About Judaism* is an exceptional read for those wanting to explore Abrahamic faiths through a fresh perspective. Interestingly, I discovered this book shortly after leaving "the cult." This book played a crucial role in helping me rise above religion.

Even so, if Jewish people denied *White* as they were rejected, we'd have a powerful visual of an ethnic group with fair skin proclaiming, "We are not

White," which would allow the rest of the world to see what *White* truly denotes...or perhaps just White people. (No worries...there's still time to represent.)

Similarly, as I tell my husband, "You don't have to be White if you don't want to," because it's an ideology that tries to hide behind skin color. It's sneaky. Even so, the privileges of ~~Whiteness~~...I mean, *White* were sometimes too hard to resist, and Jewish people joined the force. Still, you shouldn't accept the cookie after your brother spits on it. In all fairness, if you knew that brother had homicidal tendencies, I would eat the cookie too and maybe drop "the N-word" or "schvartzer" a few times so they would know you were committed to the cause.

Sadly, many Jews lost their way when tempted by the allure of *White* despite already possessing "the jewels" (diamonds and rubies), a connection to the Cosmos. No worries...some fruits of their faith and ancestry are still reflected in their lives, similar to what we observe in many Indian communities and others whose ancestors also lived in connection with the Source. Nevertheless, the blessing of Divine intelligence tends to diminish over time when neglected, leading them to act like heathens.

These babies singing "Oh Hanukkah" and reciting Jewish prayers, "Baruch atah Adonai Eloheinu Melech ha-olam..." would have gladly checked Jewish on demographic forms.

If I were Jewish, I would never trade my faith for an illusion and some extra cookies. Imagine if there were a separate category for Jewish people on demographic forms. Please stop. (eye-roll) I'm not talkin' 'bout a yellow star to force Jews to identify themselves, just a separate checkbox. Some people would call it "racist" today to separate them from White. Hmm…maybe that's what they want you to think.

It's also important to recognize that not every culture views Jewish people through a White, Western lens. This perspective is complicated because the White Western world, in a sense, expects everyone to adopt its perspectives. For instance, not seeing a Jewish person as White can have different meanings for different people. It truly depends on how you interpret what it means to be *White*. Some of my family worked for Jewish families their entire lives, who were considered better employers than White folks. These Jewish families treated their "help" well, as outlined in the Torah, specifically in Deuteronomy. (Multiracial Cherokees, similar to the ancestry of many Lumbee Native Americans, with tan or fair skin, had better access to these good jobs…but still no federal benefits.)

Unfortunately, the perspective of the dominant class regarding the notion of *White* overrides individual thought and seeks to stifle freedom of speech through collective claims of "antisemitism." For many Jews, not being seen as White is viewed as a compliment, you know. Let's take a moment to discuss the concept of antisemitism, a.k.a. "You can't say that." Y'all okay with that?

Jews have stronger protections than any other "minority" group. Honestly, you can't say anything about a Jewish person without it being labeled antisemitic. Later in this book, we'll discuss how we create demonizing language to silence, discredit, and dismiss opposing perspectives.

The protections surrounding Jewish people sometimes don't even make it worth discussing them because of the backlash from their supporters enforcing these measures. (Hmm…I wonder who programmed these puppets.) A good visual representation of this dynamic is the missile defense system known as the Iron Dome, which Israel created. Americans seem conditioned to react to any mention of Jews, regardless of their understanding of what antisemitism entails. It must be advantageous to have a human-powered missile defense system doing this work, and there's a certain level of honor in knowing that some feel it's their religious duty. To me, that describes a form of mind control. We will explore this topic in greater depth later in the book, examining how individuals respond to feelings of being controlled. However, discussing any other group remains *completely acceptable*, which surprisingly makes me sympathetic to White people for a moment—only for a moment.

Yes, I'm completely serious. Examine the frameworks that define antisemitism while holding opposing views, and you may briefly experience the muzzling effect that can fuel White anger and antisemitism. This is similar to how "minorities" are conditioned never to speak about the rude and hurtful things that White people say, which may hurt their feelings if we were to share. Oh my god, I've got the perfect *jacked-up* example of why the muzzle might be necessary, contradicting my whole argument. (I told you, I only felt sympathetic for a moment.)

Okay, I'm already laughing. Many years ago, we had some good Christian friends over for dinner. They were frustrated with all their Jewish neighbors. They should have checked the neighborhood demographics before moving in. (Shhh! Real estate agents can't help you with that.) This neighborhood was packed with Jews because these were the folks who only walked to the synagogue on Saturdays. It was a Jewish neighborhood!

Well, my White friend, a PW (pastor's wife), was tired of seeing big-ass wooden menorahs strapped to the tops of their neighbors' cars during Hanukkah. She said at my table, in my home, while we were fellowshipping and enjoying dinner together, "The menorahs looked ***nigger-rigged*** with duct tape and rope." (White folks are always so comfortable around me; I love it!)

She reached deep into her heart and inner strength to passionately express her disgust. Overflowing with scorn, she pulled out her Uzi, taking out Black and Jewish people in one sweeping statement. Her husband, the pastor, almost *pissed* on himself. (No, I didn't hurt their little White feelings then.) She never realized what she had said, and I allowed the husband to leave our house peacefully with his dignity intact, convincing himself (delusional as it was) that I hadn't noticed. Yessum, I'm guilty of protecting White folks' feelings. I felt embarrassed for her, and I'm embarrassed for myself. Still, I don't identify with "the N-word" *anyways*.

Hmm…was that antisemitic? Was it? Or was it too closely tied to racism to matter? Is that why the protections are so extreme? Dammit! What about me and my feelings? There should be laws against such language! She should have been stoned for dropping "the N-word"…at my table. This is all so confusing to me. Even Whoopi, with the last name "Goldberg," was confused about Jewish people's multi-layered identity and was shot down by the Iron Dome for not knowing.

The Iron Dome says, "Remember your place, and stay in your lane!" Shoot, maybe the menorahs were "rigged." We have the right to our opinions, right? This isn't to say that some of the protections that Jewish people receive aren't necessary, but it crosses a fine line regarding freedom of speech and is likely anti-Judaism. (I probably can't say that.)

Even so, some may argue this is due to how they have been treated...by White people, of course. Yes, Jewish history in White Christian Europe is atrocious. Christians had (or have?) been killing Jews since the inception of Christianity. Still, perhaps the concept of antisemitism needs reevaluation as Christians have grown and matured, much like what occurred with laws protecting "minority" access to higher education. Were these protections meant to last a lifetime? The idea of progressiveness is to continue to evolve and align with current times, right? And my Reform Jewish friends said, "Amen!" (Still, my friend Patel said, "Black people and Jewish people need to...." I'm sorry, I had to cut Patel short. He has a lot of opinions, and I'm not sure if y'all can handle Patel at this point in the book. No worries...we'll hear more from Patel later.)

We can't grow as a society with the current setup and extensive (broad!) definition of antisemitism. It's also complicated because Christian beliefs are tied to the idea of supporting Jews. This clouds their understanding and compassion for others who are impacted by Jews, as if Jews can do no wrong. (I probably can't say that either.) It's so bad that there's very little room for publicly objecting to anything related to Jews or Israel, which, in turn, makes people distance themselves further from Jews. (It's like being terrified to use pronouns, so you avoid them altogether.) The exclusive pro-Jewish belief in America is counterproductive. Jewish people need to object to this *special* treatment, yet, at the same time, the Iron Dome missile defense system makes it just about antisemitic for suggesting that.

Looking out from inside this dome is like peering through a veil from the 1970s, a time when antisemitism began to fade. It's a harvest green fabric adorned with gold specks that was once fashionable but now feels outdated. Do you know anyone who still has these curtains? They're so thick that light struggles to enter the homes, which could be an issue. Don't let anyone drape a veil over you or trap you under a dome. Nowadays, we have young Jewish people wearing polyester like it's stylish. (Can I say that?)

White folks, with their disturbing jokes in the past, have made it nearly impossible to joke about Jewish people today. (Damn!) They made cruel jokes, like naming segregation laws after the racist Jim Crow character created to ridicule Black people. (Who on earth does that?) Furthermore, I must be cautious with my observations...I mean, my jokes because they could fuel White people's suspicions. More on that later.

America, wouldn't it be easier to teach history, given that many Americans have such a vague understanding of what racism is, let alone the detailed list of what antisemitism entails? Or is remaining ignorant how they want us to be? Even so, those of us from marginalized communities bear the responsibility of moving forward. If we don't, we, in a sense, dishonor those who came before us. I can only imagine that our ancestors who lost their lives while dreaming of civil rights and equality would be disappointed if we turned their stories into our identities.

Years ago, I shifted my focus from fighting racism to what I could change: myself. I realized that getting Americans on the same page is what the war on racism required, which is an impossible feat, especially with the definition of the word changing every few years. The world may take or redefine the language you once used to describe your battle. They don't know your history, and they don't care to learn it, even if you write them a little book. What do you do with that? (Hmm…how is it that the term "antisemitism" is shielded from being redefined, while White people can now use the term "racism" against those they still oppress and whose ancestors were enslaved, terrorized, and controlled—by their ancestors? Who are they kidding?)

Continuing from where I left off, speaking about history, you must almost embody the past and transform it into your identity to capture their attention. Who wants to live so far in the past? Maybe it'll work, and you'll prove something or change a few minds. But is it worth your time when the world is leaving you behind? What will you do when the protections are no longer in place? Will you evolve, or will you simply sit there and make demands from an entitled mindset that has disadvantaged many "minorities"? Is that the Judaism you know? (Can I ask that?)

I could probably write a book just on how the belief system created to protect Jewish people further perpetuates their struggle and experiences of antisemitic attacks. (That, too, I probably can't say.) When someone feels muzzled or their words are restricted, it can lead them to respond violently. (Even my husband understands how that works. *Honey, can I say that?*)

Most people feel uncomfortable receiving privileges or benefits they don't need. For instance, I used to shop at a predominantly White *healthy store* and would buy lunch for my boys on BBQ Tuesdays. A gentleman of African American descent always gave them the largest piece of chicken and extra holy mac 'n' cheese, so much so that I didn't need to buy two lunches unless I wanted to. And I always had leftovers! Walking to the counter with what felt like two meals in one box never felt right. I didn't like what he was doing, which seemed more about him and his frustration with the White customers he served than about me. Receiving more than others only sits right in the mind with mental justifications, a veil you must wear to avoid personal conviction. "I deserve this because...."

For many Jews, their place in society breeds discontent when they confront their privileges. This is particularly true considering the many others who suffer in this country and share an ancestral narrative that is comparable, if not worse, than the tragic loss of Jewish lives during the Holocaust. Yet, their loss has not received the same visibility or been acknowledged with equal remorse. (And Patel said, "Amen!")

The privileged protections for Jews are intertwined with White guilt and shame, as many Jews today share similar physical features and beliefs. This loyalty also stems from the mindset of "us against them," which refers to perceived threats in the Middle East. Meanwhile, others try to avoid confronting the veil, which only distances them from their true selves. This mental struggle has led many to leave Judaism entirely. In doing so, they beautifully assimilate into the diverse family of God. (Speaking of "us against them"! Do you know who has been the greatest threat to Jews? You might be thinking it's Muslims, but you are dead wrong. Guess again!)

However, as a well-known guru once said, something to the effect of: you won't meet God in the temple if you create mental justifications. More to come. Additionally, "It's harder for a rich 'man' (one who is rich in protective privileges) to enter the Kingdom of God," which could very well imply.... (We'll finish that sentence in a later sermon. *Don't get worked up, Chuck!*)

It's a harsh reality to face or acknowledge because letting go of the best of both worlds is a difficult sacrifice, and many will create a veil of entitlement to avoid confronting it. Who would address something that offers them protective or even *special* privileges? (And White people said, "Amen!")

Do you mean to tell me that you are a racial "minority" and White, too? That doesn't seem like a logical combination. Would that qualify as an oxymoron...or is that a paradox? (giggles) Benefiting from two perspectives like this resembles narcissism—you know, where one is both the victim and the victor. (I probably can't make that comparison either.) Even so, it's a powerful position to be in.

What are the risks with the current setup?

For one, many "minorities" can see loopholes and *gremlins* that White people might overlook. Yet, White privilege can nicely position some individuals to exploit those loopholes. (Hey, I'm talkin' 'bout myself. Again, I'm 65% European, and my primary ethnicity is German. But some may think I'm only Black, thanks to the influence of "White Supremacy" and foolishness. Anyhow, I can see loopholes!) The gift arises from learning to observe and navigate life as an outsider, and one must be cautious never to wield this superpower for self-serving means.

Overall, Jews have low blue-collar crime rates because very few live in poverty, and they can take advantage of White privilege. However, this cannot be said for white-collar crimes, which often involve the ability to see loopholes, right? (I might not be able to say this either since some White people are suspicious of Jews, but it's acceptable to say that.) Many Mexicans, or even more so Guatemalans (I have family in Belize), also possess this ability but are too clever to get caught. I can say this, but not that.

Let's make this fair! Can we agree that Black folks have some of the lowest white-collar crime rates? Still, that can't be said for blue-collar crimes. Does that make it better? I would imagine that Mexicans and Guatemalans, "...Julio Down by the Schoolyard," would be some of the finest white-collar criminals because they're brilliant. Don't be fooled by their height! They can see things from completely different angles. However, I'm almost 100% certain that Christians have the highest white-collar and blue-collar crime rates of any religious group. (Disproportionately high!)

Also, the protections in place to prevent antisemitism make it nearly impossible to examine how religion (including Judaism) and ideas of *specialness* or chosenness create trouble and can give birth to concepts like "White Supremacy." (Society's *gremlin*!) Unfortunately, this leads some people to feel that one is implying Jews can be blamed for the cruelty they suffered, which would be a brutal form of blame-shifting. However, because the crimes against Jews were so severe, we are all denied the right to genuinely examine how religion and exclusiveness can separate people in the worst ways. Furthermore, this silencing of others to protect Jews is, in a sense, anti-Judaism since Judaism, like Quakerism, is a faith that encourages and values uncensored queries, even if it involves questioning the very religion itself. (Can I say that?)

The broad concept of antisemitism is counterproductive. Its multidimensional system of controls limits freedom of speech, hampers the spiritual growth of Jewish people, and forces them to navigate their lives while defending an identity. This kind of mental prison is, once again, self-defeating and isolating. This complex struggle, along with the mental concepts involved, is an enormous burden for anyone to bear, which unfortunately leads to mental health issues for many of my Jewish friends.

Returning to my original point, Jews opting out of being classified as White could have been, or might still be, a powerful force against racism. In reality, the notion of *White* might feel somewhat threatened by this. Honestly, I'd check Jewish as well on demographic forms if it weren't an exclusive club, and so would African American Jews, Ethiopian Jews, and, of course, the Black Israelites. (It's fascinating how the separation of Jews from *White* may offend some, but what about non-White Jews? Are they unimportant, or is being labeled as "other" sufficient for them?) I thought for sure Jews weren't a race. (Oh shoot, can I express that?)

That could be a great place to stop, but I believe I have Part II brewing, "If Jewish People...." Grab another bowl of cheese puffs, and I'll meet you here in a minute.

Shalom Hugs,
—Sher! (The Common Snook)
Pause. Inhale. Exhale. Reflect.

P.S. I know, I know, not all Jewish people wear black hats with candy curls/curly sideburns or wigs, but it still would have been a sight to see.

P.P.S. Yes, yes, I know—you can be one goofy label and another similar to the ridiculous notion of being biracial or multiracial. If race is a joke, then multiracial is an even bigger joke. Shouldn't "multiracial" cancel out the concept of race entirely? But folks won't let it go.

P.P.P.S. Speaking of the muzzling effect! Biracial and multiracial people with African American ancestry are conditioned never to speak about the cruel things that Black people say to them. *Youse* in trouble if you do. *Youse* supposed to take it. (giggles) It's supposed to be fun and games. Can you see a familiar pattern here? (And all the biracial and multiracial folks who share this experience very very quietly said, "Amen.")

(Sit in stillness with your eyes closed for 15 minutes a day; I promise it will transform your life!)

3. If Jewish People Had Shared Their Faith—I Probably Can't Say That

Reminder: This is Part II of "If Jewish People…." We took a short break to replenish the cheese puffs before continuing this conversation.

Disclosure Reminder…,

What if Jewish communities had *shared* their faith, like Christianity and Islam, and welcomed converts as if Judaism weren't an exclusive club? Perhaps Westerners might be more enlightened today. Imagine that! (Don't get worked up. It was just a thought.)

But thank God India has our back. They have enough software engineers to "evangelize" the world with the ancient wisdom of yoga, and I'm not talking about stretching. I'm talkin' 'bout yoga, which means to unite—the union of your body, mind, and spirit. You know, if we don't make something sacred, there's no one to leave out, no supremacy, which isn't fun because *we humans* like feeling *special*…superior…chosen…or called.

Still, as Rushkoff explained, you must be careful when choosing *specialness* because it often doesn't resonate well with the rest of humanity. (Shhh! I had similar thoughts, but passing the buck to Rushkoff felt safer.) He mentioned that we all know what happened to "*special* Joseph," right? (No worries…he's Jewish. Can he say that?) This position of *specialness* is only as strong as its ability to defend itself. Someone with a bigger ego will always seek to prove you wrong because you've hurt their little feelings. The notion of supremacy or chosenness is what taints an excellent path to the Divine. As soon as the ego and his *bros* enter through the back door, it's over for that religion. It happens every time! *(Specialness stirs up trouble!)*

Nobody likes being written into a script as a second-class citizen, just as White Christians portrayed Africans as "infidels" to justify their enslavement. (Hmm…I wonder where they got that idea. "Infidel" sure sounds a lot like "heathen" to me.) Whites in Europe had been using religion to their advantage as a mental token of "superiority," just as some did with Judaism. No matter how it's framed, supremacy, *specialness*, and chosenness are all the same—mere figments of our imagination.

Regardless of the faith's purity, egos tend to craft insurance policies to serve their interests. Judaism had a policy aimed at inspiring and elevating Jews, which has never settled right with many Christians, who either choose to believe or feel compelled to think that Jews are God's chosen people. (Someone needs to inform Christians that these stories were allegories.)

No matter how much Europeans embraced Christianity, I'm sure the notion of not being God's "chosen" people (in Jewish storytelling) still lingered in the back of their minds. It's really frustrating when someone suggests they are "superior" to you or, worse, *chosen by God*, and they have scriptures written by man to support their *specialness,* and you believe it. That's about as difficult to swallow as *man* writing *woman* into the scriptures of the Bible to submit to him because he's the big ol' head of the wife, claiming God inspired it. (giggles)

Unfortunately, what we don't correct continues to grow. As Christianity gained strength, justifying its wrongs in the name of religion, so too, a plan began to unfold that would update and override the scriptures by merging religion with the ideology of "White Supremacy" (hence the capitalization of this unique religion and *gremlin*). Establishing a conglomerate is a surefire way to dominate and confront any opposing religious supremacy. It's not hard to get people to join the movement because they, too, want to feel chosen. Do we see a pattern here of those who feel inferior needing to make themselves "superior"? Gathering the wounded for their day to shine, we will witness this happening again—sooner rather than later.

That being said, the Jews did help the heathens. Jesus, the mystic, and his *bros* gave the Western world a book, but they had no idea that people would turn his profound yet straightforward teachings into a franchise. Oddly enough, Jews might appreciate the Bible, too…if they read it…at home…since it is relatively easy to understand, possibly clearer and more direct than the Old Testament. *Anyways*, Jesus knew that his people loved stories, so he and his *bros* wrote some for us, too. (That was so thoughtful.)

He said, "The way ain't no secret." Good Lord, somebody should've warned Jesus about telling secrets and sharing the idea of *specialness* with the rest of us. Then he said, "If mysticism (the practice of connecting with the Divine by "looking" within) is too difficult for you boneheads, I'll hide mysticism in the scriptures for the deep folks and establish a path of devotion, like *CliffsNotes,* that's equally effective for the simpler man. Follow me—dammit! Do what I do, say what I say, and the bouncer will let you through the door." However, *Elicit* will help you connect with the Divine, with or without religion, in the way Jesus intended before men turned his scriptures into a franchise. (Shhh! There truly is nothing to seek; you just need to learn "to be.")

You can also thank the Hebrews for restoring your credit after seven years of bad luck. (Hush! I'm not being derogatory; I'm connecting with simple folks who still read Leviticus, Numbers, and Deuteronomy for fun.) The Hebrews are also responsible for why many of *you* still circumcise your boys, as they tricked heathens into believing that the foreskin of the penis was sufficient to please your fierce God, convincing your barbaric ancestors to stop sacrificing their firstborns...for no good reason. They put an end to that nonsense! "Just give *Him* some skin," they said. They even brought in angels to speak to Abraham! You can read about this drama in Genesis from the Bible for yourself. *Those* Hebrews were clever...screenwriters, in fact! I love the theater! Nothing beats angels and fire to deliver a good message. Read this scripture from Genesis 22:10-12 in a dark, scary voice:

And Abraham stretched forth his hand, and took the knife to slay his son. (Yikes!) And the angel of the LORD called unto him out of heaven, and said, Abraham, Abraham: and he said, Here *am* I. And he said, Lay not thine hand upon the lad, neither do thou any thing unto him: for now I know that thou fearest God, seeing thou hast not withheld thy son, thine only *son* from me (King James Version of the Bible).

Problem solved! The Hebrews were hilarious, like Seinfeld. Please stop. (eye-roll) This isn't antisemitic! And umm...I have Jewish friends and my own rabbi, so. You didn't know I was Jewish? I've been called a Jew most of my life. (Can I say that?) Perhaps these people see me as a middleman, which I take as an honor. Anyhow, *Jewish people*, just like *Black people*, are not lifetime victims who need to be coddled to reinforce a sense of inferiority or superiority for some, depending on the kind of attention they prefer. If anything, *we humans* are all responsible for this madness inflicted upon humanity. (See, I'm teaching Jews to think like Jews and not like a race.)

They don't need you, the Iron Dome, getting upset or racking up brownie points whenever someone says something that doesn't sound in their favor. And they certainly didn't need an invitation to *Club Assimilation.* Or maybe they're just fooling everyone. (Can I say that?) But thankfully, Jesus and his *bros* did welcome non-Jews, heathens, to join the *family of God.* Perhaps being invited into the *family of White* was just a way of returning the favor. Before I wrap this up, why weren't *Black people* invited to the club? Careful, "White" Cubans; some of you are next!

As I mentioned, we're just sitting in a circle, enjoying cheese puffs. Please wash your hands and avoid touching anything if possible.

Shalom,

—Sher! (The Common Snook)
Pause. Inhale. Exhale. Reflect.

P.S. Not allowing the inclusion and prosperity of all people creates opportunities for isolated communities to establish their own governments, often led by a tyrant. This situation does not function as a political democracy. These tyrants can maintain power for a loooong time, wreaking havoc on our youth and communities—more, much later.

However, migration and adaptation foster spiritual growth. This also explains why some cultures have remained unchanged or stagnant: they lacked opportunities to migrate. For example, Blacks and Whites who left the South often had a different mindset compared to those who stayed behind, and the same goes for Blacks and Whites in the North. Once again, migration and adaptation change us. As I mentioned in my first sermon, if I had never left Gainesville, I would have remained ignorant of the world and told my friends they might not have liked me. Interestingly, many spiritual teachers share a common experience of being banished or abandoned. (Hmm…I sure hope the "s" at the end of Black doesn't ruffle any feathers. Okay, Black people, I'll drop the "s" moving forward or use "x" if I can't avoid the plural noun, but I think Whites can handle the "s" since they're familiar with its usage. [giggles]).

(Sit in stillness with your eyes closed for 15 minutes a day; I promise it will transform your life!)

4. Fashionista or Lesbian

Disclosure Reminder...,

I have a secret: I wouldn't say I like shopping, window shopping, or sightseeing. I can't think of anything worse to do.

My husband and our young men were returning from a road trip to New Hampshire and decided to visit Pennsylvania Amish Country. I couldn't understand why. For a moment, my husband said he wished I were there to experience this with them, but then he considered how I might behave and how unbearable it would have been for me to tour an Amish house museum. If I want to visit a hot Amish house, I don't have to go far since Florida author Marjorie K. Rawlings' humble abode is just down the street. I couldn't imagine it would look any different. (Y'all remember *The Yearling*, right?)

The next day, my "*sistas*" from the neighborhood called and said we were going to T.J. Maxx to browse around, and they told me to be ready in fifteen minutes. I got up and was ready to roll. It's been years since I've hung out with the ladies like this, and I forgot how much...I wouldn't say I like shopping.

The ride to the store was a blast. I love hanging out like I'm twenty. One of my homegirls is almost fifty, beautiful and sassy with that gorgeous hair; another is thirty-five and cute. Since they are Indian, you know Grandma, the mother-in-law (MIL), was rolling with us, too. We were four ladies deep, just like in high school. We arrived at 12:30 sharp, and the parking lot was packed like the State Fair. Women were everywhere! The two in the backseat even had the nerve to hop out before I found a parking space. *This wasn't Black Friday,* I thought.

I walked into the store. My 'fro was tight. I had my Birkenstocks on and thought I was ready to take on the challenge. My homegirls, who said they weren't shopping, grabbed carts and vanished, much like the Supermarket Sweep television game show. Looking around, it felt almost like an illegal swap meet. These women seemed to be up to something suspicious and didn't want their husbands to know where they were. The store managers must have sprayed something because all the customers behaved similarly. This must have been what Jesus was talkin' 'bout when he said, "Get these merchants out of my temple."

I strapped my purse across my chest (which had been hanging open because its zipper had broken off after five years of carrying it) and began observing the chaos. You'd think a hurricane was on the way, and the ladies were stockpiling bottled water, milk, eggs, and beer. The shelves were well-stocked with the finest *stuff*. I was certain a fight was about to erupt. I was ready to announce over the loudspeaker, like Wyclef Jean in Shakira's song "Hips Don't Lie," "Ladies, I don't want to see any fighting…absolutely no elbow blows!"

The customers, including my friends, browsed through purses, sandals, jewelry, bowls, pots, towels, chips, candles, thongs, clothing, and couches. The loot was endless. To me, it felt like a house of horrors. To anyone else, it might have sounded like I said, "house of whores," and I still wouldn't be wrong. I got no pleasure in the experience, but these women were like the men you see in old Western movies as they pile into the brothel with a sign that says, "Today only, ½ off." Now, please don't get confused; ain't nobody calling these sweet women "whores." I'm just sayin', as men are to brothels, women are to T.J. Maxx. Okay…*some* women.

I started to feel like I was about to lose Consciousness and completely disconnect from the Source. I grabbed my chest and frantically ran from aisle to aisle, searching for a safe space to avoid getting sucked in. I couldn't let my friends see me suffering like this. I dashed down the candle aisle for relief and began smelling as many as possible before the dust started collecting in my nose. While rubbing my nose, I glanced at my watch and realized we would be there for an hour. *What the heck was I thinking?*

I have never spent that much time in a home décor store. Maybe Home Depot, but in most cases, I'm in and out in five minutes if I need something. Some people say I'm wired like a lesbian (giggles), and I take that as a compliment. That's something lesbians and I have in common; I would much rather be building a house on Habitat's Alachua Women Build team if they would have me and welcome my feminine advice. Those tough gals aren't hanging out at T.J. Maxx. But that day, I didn't know what to do to survive this zombie apocalypse. I started texting my son, "Hey, sweetie, I miss you!"

Luckily, I found a spot to hide among all the bored husbands in the furniture section. Since I didn't want to spoil their time with the piss-poor look on my face, I started making phone calls. And I would have balanced my checkbook if I still had written checks and had a check ledger.

I was getting antsy, so I called my son and pleaded, "What should I do? Please help me, please." He replied, "Mom, sneak out the door and walk to Earth Origins Market, the health food store." He's so brilliant!

Ducking with my 'fro, I ran for the door. At last, I was free! It was hot as hell, walking uphill, but nothing compared to the zombie apocalypse I had just escaped.

Walking around the health food store, I could smell and see life. The vegetables greeted me. I caught a delightful whiff of patchouli. The store was quiet and peaceful. Nobody seemed interested in healthy food. All the ladies were down the hill, buying *stuff* they didn't need and talkin' 'bout organic food being expensive. I got myself some cashews and asked the young ladies at the counter what treat they would choose if given the chance. One sweet girl with beautiful, long braids and smooth, glossy baby-hair edges lit up and said, "A cookie!" She tickled me pink. (Strangely, I do blush pink.) Her lovely smile was the highlight of my day, better than any wooden bowl or thong from down the hill. She was full of life!

I returned to Maxx J.T. (Maximum Jail Time) with my nuts, not the ladies, silly. I'm talkin' 'bout my cashews. And nobody even noticed I was missing. I couldn't believe that so many women had free time in the middle of the day and knew that the Habitat Women Built Team needed some feminine energy. I was surprised that anyone would choose to spend it that way, wasting hard-earned money on *stuff* that brought them no inner joy and only temporary pleasures that required returning in a couple of days…for more *stuff*. (*Kinda* like sex outside of marriage. [giggles] I'm sorry, I couldn't resist. I'm just joking. Y'all can do what you want.) Still, there must be more fulfilling things to do. We could all have been painting, building a house for Habitat, doing yoga, enjoying each other's company, chopping some real food, helping at our kids' school, or engaging in *anything* more enriching than wandering around the cemetery with all those zombies.

It makes me wonder whether lesbians know something that the rest of you ladies haven't figured out yet. I sometimes think lesbianism is less about attraction and more about common sense. They recognize that *we women* are more capable than the world lets on and might have experienced some awakening because when your perspective doesn't align with the norm, the insane "normals" push you out and call you names like "lesbian" or "man-wired," which I hear often. (giggles) In my case, I'm blessed with these names just for having common sense or for not conforming to the male's perverted standard of femininity. Yep, I said it! I don't play roles. I'm as real as it gets.

I would choose to hang out with a group of lesbians any day over a bunch of women who mindlessly buy shit they don't need. (giggles) We label this madness "feminine," but it just doesn't make sense. It feels like someone hijacked femininity and redefined what it means to be feminine. I thought for sure that being feminine meant being smarter than men.

By the way, I can build a house and cook, too—beeyotch! But I do appreciate my husband's muscles and testosterone, which I act like are an extension of my own…and I do call him for roaches. (I'm ashamed.)

I designed and built that kitchen myself—beeyotch! I hate cabinet doors.

Anyhow, it was a sight that could take your breath away—a living nightmare! After I got home, I told my husband, "Never again."

Friendly Lesbo Hugs,
—Sher! (The Common Snook)
Pause. Inhale. Exhale. Reflect.

P.S. I do know some materialistic and wasteful lesbians. Unfortunately, times are changing.

P.P.S. By the way, I was on the first Alachua Habitat for Humanity Women Build team in 1996, representing Eastside High School. We built a home for our beloved janitor. I learned to wrap a house, install windows, and shingle a roof without a nail gun—beeyotch!

P.P.P.S. Did I ever tell y'all I installed a second full-size dishwasher, so I *never, ever, not ever* have to unload the dishes—*ever again?* Pretty great, right? See, better than any thong!

(Sit in stillness with your eyes closed for 15 minutes a day; I promise it will transform your life!)

5. It's the Black Kids Who Start All the Fights at School

"Who me?" Photo by my son, Li'l Snook van Gogh.

Disclosure Reminder...,

I had a friend whose husband works at the University of Florida (UF) ask me one day how to respond to her son, who said, "It's the Black kids who start all the fights at school." She wasn't sure how to react to his statement, perhaps because progressive folks feel uneasy when their children sound a bit racist. (They know what they *be seeing*!) No worries...this boy wasn't being racist.

First, I told her it was okay to acknowledge his observations. (He knows what he *be seeing.* ☺) This was also a teaching moment, as I often used similar situations with my children. I said, "Children who fight at school are unhappy at home." It's really that simple. I explained that Gainesville rests on the backs of its marginalized African American communities, with nearly half of the African American children in Gainesville living in poverty, which does not account for those living just above the poverty line.

I suggested that my dear friend encourage her son to take a moment each day to reflect on his life. He's got a sweet housewife for a momma (well, *kinda*) who is home managing their lives, doing his laundry, picking him up from school, greeting him with a snack, and having dinner ready by 5:00 p.m., allowing time for an evening family stroll to socialize with neighbors who lead similarly sweet little lives. He cuddles up for the night in his neatly made twin-size bed, lying down with his matching quilt and sheets from Target that *smell* like *Downy.* *When life is sweet to you, it makes school that much sweeter.*

61

However, for many *Black and Brown kids* with those hard-working, underpaid parents, nobody is home when they come back from school, or worse, too many people are. They often share a room with multiple siblings. *Mom-dad* doesn't have time to prepare a wholesome meal because they work two jobs and run DoorDash on the side, yet they still can't make ends meet.

Sometimes, when these kids get home and go to rummage for a snack in the fridge, they finally realize it's hot in the house because the power is off—again. Some must even deal with or avoid an unemployed neighbor or relative who always looks at them strangely. If you had to deal with that bullshit every day, you'd be showing up to school *pissed off*, too. (Alachua County school teachers and administrators, stop damning these students—calling them hopeless!)

Poverty is unfortunate, yet it can also be a pathway to awakening.

Gainesville has a constant turnover of professors and college students who never take a moment to recognize the individuals who keep this town running. One day, I was waiting in traffic on S.W. 13th, near Museum Rd. on campus, when I saw a sign that read, "Come work for UF!" I remember thinking, *Wow, UF is really trying to recruit!* Then I noticed it was one of those tacky yard signs positioned facing the bench next to the city bus stop. The job advertised was for kitchen services. They understood that the demographics of the employees they needed to work in the kitchen to feed their students likely didn't even have transportation. The sign stated something like: Great benefits…*please come work for low wages and feed these kids.* (Ugh, I know the city bus counts as transportation (eye-roll), and it should be our primary form of transportation!)

When these kids graduate, secure good jobs, and start families of their own, their children will one day ask, "Why is it always the Black kids who start all the fights at school?" Hopefully, they'll recount a similar story to the one I shared with my friend, rooted in compassion without judgment.

Alright, I'm *gonna* seal the deal!

Poverty is a complex beast to overcome. Many families in Gainesville have lived in the same public housing community for generations. Thankfully, Gainesville demolished the Kennedy Homes apartment complex in East Gainesville, helping to break that vicious cycle for many families. (Migration changes you.) No worries: Lake Road projects, Cedar Ridge, and several others are still accessible for viewing if you want to take your kids on a tour of "Why is it the Black kids who start all the fights in school?"

If you really want to teach a valuable lesson, you can follow my example. We had just moved back to Gainesville, and on my son's first day of school, I put him on the Cedar Ridge bus to take him home from Buchholz High School. (RTS Bus seventy-five will work, too.) He mentioned that before leaving the schoolyard, the resource officer threatened the kids if they didn't behave, saying he was coming after them. Naturally, they laughed the officer off the bus and then gave my son the ride of his life while he hugged his violin and lunch box—vigorously. It was better than a trip to Orlando. I told him, "Welcome to Gainesville!" I was so glad he had that experience because life has always been good for my little angel.

To make matters worse, the bus driver quit, and for more than six months, "those kids" sometimes stood on the corner for hours, hoping Alachua County Public Schools would send them a ride. It just didn't seem fair; they were indeed headed for summer school.

Well, we didn't have time for that mess! When nobody from the school or the county transportation department followed up with me after I demanded a safe ride to school for my son, I quietly moved him to the Haile Plantation bus, where the bus driver handed out treats for the sweet kids whose sheets...*smell* like *Downy*.

Wink,
　—Sher! (The Common Snook)
Pause. Inhale. Exhale. Reflect.

P.S. I'm confident that the county transportation department and the school sent me a subliminal message to move my son to the other bus as they couldn't move all those babies to the happy bus, which *smells* like *Downy*, without turning sweet Haile Plantation into Hell. (Hmm...they don't want these *ch'rn* anywhere near the plantation today. However, it's easier for "a creamy" to sneak onto the plantation bus than for "a brownie" who might not...*smell* like *Downy*. *Shout out* to the White woman from *Haile* who used to give me the middle finger at the bus stop and then ride my bumper every day. Ugh, motherhood!)

P.P.S. Speaking of Orlando! Did I ever tell y'all I met the real "Tipsy Mouse" right here in Gainesville at her parents' house? She was short and cute with a curvy figure, and they loved some wine and cheese, of course.

(Sit in stillness with your eyes closed for 15 minutes a day; I promise it will transform your life!)

6. I'm Takin' Sexy Back

Disclosure Reminder…,   9/15/2023 – World Afro Day!

When I was born, my father remarked, "Wow, look at her hair; at least she's

light-skinned." He came from a generation that understood life could be a little sweeter for "People of Color" simply because of skin tone. He was right; I benefited from "white or light skin seen as better," a.k.a. that sweet White privilege that White folks hate to admit is real. It was real in my life—real good!

If my father were here today, he'd be surprised to see me rockin' my 'fro, which is my best feature, if you ask me. Now I understand why White folks back in the day didn't like afros. This *thang* is powerful, intimidating, and demands respect. I had no clue this soft hair, like wool, was Divine.

My 'fro will stop you in your tracks!

I must be careful with my 'fro because it's also sexy, a.k.a. "Oops!" ("Oops" is what you call a flattering outfit that wasn't intended to be sexy or a person who is sexy and can't help it.) Unfortunately, many women around the world have been conditioned to believe that "yellow" or "blonde" hair is what makes you sexy. *Wrrrrr!* (That's the sound of a car from the 70s backing up, to make a screeching U-turn.) *Skrrrrrrt!*

Y'all didn't know that some of us call it "yellow," "white," or "brown" instead of giving White women "pet names," helping to idolize, sexualize, and dehumanize them? Treating these women as objects or toys of pleasure strips all women of dignity and forces many to compete among themselves for the attention and validation of men—like fools. That is how porn stars are created, who are most often "blondes." (No, I don't watch porn; I learned this from a well-known American politician.)

Many of these women are perfectly fine with the dehumanizing labels. *(Taylor, what do you think? Should they "Shake It Off"?)* Being called "a blonde" instills a sense of pride and reinforces feelings of "superiority" through idolization. Yet, this phrase devalues and sexualizes them, again, reducing them to objects for men's pleasure. "Who am I without the label?" This leaves many White women feeling worthless unless they possess the most "valued" hair color. (That's ridiculous!) Some even psychologically assert they are "blonde," as if it were an identity, when their hair appears "brown" or "light brown" to the rest of us. It's the name they so crave.

I once mistakenly told a little White girl, a family friend, "How cool! You and my son have the same complexion, hair color, and curls." This eight-year-old appeared to panic and freak out. She replied, "No, my hair isn't the same color as his," which was light brown then. She added, "My mom said I have 'blonde' hair," while her expression seemed to question whether she believed her mother. Unfortunately, my innocent remarks caused her considerable discomfort. (Strangely, many Jews also cling to the "blonde" identity. Hmm...I wonder what that's about.)

Suddenly, I could see the shackles of mind manipulation that have many White women competing for the prize. Interestingly, she recognized that my son's hair was light brown, but not her own; instead, she clung to a word her mother had given her. We often believe what we are told, regardless of its truth. As I frequently say, how others perceive us can influence how we see ourselves, reflecting on the "looking-glass self" theory by Charles Horton Cooley. As we will discuss in a later sermon, words can profoundly affect our minds, whether "White," "Black," "blonde," or "brunette." This innocent little girl understood that there was something significant about the "blonde" label. She was in denial while positioning herself for the prize. *(Hey, Taylor, you know, you have enough influence to swiftly heal and save an entire generation of White girls from playing this game if you, too, can see it.)*

I have also noticed this struggle with White people, both women and men, who have dark hair. You may compliment their hair or notice the melanin in their skin. They respond, "You wouldn't believe I have a sibling or relatives with 'blonde' hair and blue eyes," as if it's a badge of honor that affirms their "superiority," never considering whether the rest of us also value this hair color as much as they do. ("Nope, I don't believe it," I reply.)

Did you know that on the U.S. passport application, "blonde" is listed as a hair color, rather than "yellow" or "white," but not "brunette"? See, "brunette" is complicated because some of y'all who the sweet name isn't intended might check that box, and most White men don't particularly like to be called "a brunette." However, "blonde" still stands as a badge of honor! Sorry, "brunettes," you didn't make the cut. (Shake it off!)

Still, if you have brown hair, which is second best, you will at least be elevated above other "minorities" with the mental token of "brunette." It must be somewhat psychologically abusive to be so close to first place in society, yet never quite enough, much like the terrible mind game of being called "White trash." For some, it's better than nothing, while men manipulate their minds, and they fight for their recognition and sexualization when they are beautiful, without needing men to turn them into sex toys.

Many White women fail to recognize this idolization and favoritism, as it serves as a veil that maintains their position—directly beneath men. Do you think I might be mistaken? Leave it to a Black woman; she will pinpoint and expose what this labeling is truly about. Many will put on a yellow wig, but she doesn't necessarily desire yellow hair; she seeks full recognition, some of the same attention, affirmation, and action associated with being "a blonde." She will say, "Shoot, I'll throw on a yellow wig if that's what it boils down to." Unfortunately, while she seeks equal affirmation, she also seeks the same dehumanization. (Hmm…unknowingly?)

Pop culture promotes the notion that "blondes have more fun." I wonder what that's all about since they depict White women squealing and giggling. (That's bullshit!) Unfortunately, many men, White, Black, and Brown (right, India?), are guilty of supporting this harmful stereotype rooted in physical appearance. They want some of that action as well and have chosen to participate in the idolization, sexualization, and dehumanization of White women. For many, acquiring a trophy—a phony treasure—boosts their desired self-image.

Watching all this foolishness sometimes makes me want to cover my head or slip into my hijab in protest against this kind of manipulation. Yes, I have an emergency hijab; you never know when you might get invited to a halal Indian party. They make the most excellent halal biryani! Still, the Afghans have them beat with "Kabuli pulao," which reminds me of biryani. (*Shout out* to my Afghan peeps of Gainesville!)

Anyhow, I'm surprised that the #MeToo movement didn't end that mess. "Don't define me by my hair color like I'm a piece of chocolate or a trophy! Don't refer to me as 'a blonde' or 'a brunette' like I'm a sex toy; say my name— dammit!" It's interesting what we'll tolerate when it makes us feel good, *special*, or "superior," even though "blonde" and "brunette" are traditionally pet names (gender-exclusive names) used to describe White women and girls.

I found it interesting that the 2023 movie *Barbie* didn't address or let go of the idolization of White women either. (Oops, let me say first, it was still a thought-provoking film before I ruffle any feathers.) Sure, the character Barbie, or "stereotypical Barbie," reflects a White woman with "yellow" or "white" hair. Still, I question how many "Women of Color" struggled with the film, with some not being able to pinpoint the disconnect. Yes, it's important to challenge unrealistic body standards and gender roles imposed on women…*but*…many might not have allowed themselves to articulate that it was a twisted experience watching the movie from a White woman's perspective on "feminism," one that overlooks the idolatry of White women. (giggles) This idolatry, embraced by many White women, helps to perpetuate the objectification and sexualization of all women and reinforces a system of racial stratification.

Within this hierarchy, White women occupy the highest position in society. It's challenging for White women to confront this issue, as doing so would require them to step down from their "privileged" positions, which allow them to benefit from *special* treatment (like more opportunities, better jobs, and higher salaries), unfortunately, at their own expense. "You mean to tell me you got this job because you did what!?" Here we have sexualization and dehumanization infused with privileges. (Hmm…twisted.)

White women, even talented writers like Greta Gerwig, one of the co-writers of the movie *Barbie*, want to rise above male dominance. Yet many wear massive chains they can't see. Still, if they look closer in the mirror, they might catch a glimpse of what also holds them back from true liberation just seconds before bleaching their roots, which could leave them coming in second place, but at least still above the rest, right? That highlights (no pun intended) one example of why many argue that White "feminism" is a separate movement that prioritizes itself, failing to acknowledge the needs of all women and how its "superiority" casts a shadow over others just as severely as the sexism they believe they are trying to dismantle.

Hmm…can you embrace the sexualization of women and be a feminist at the same time? (giggles) This should not be confused with being naturally attractive (sexy or *oops*). Don't get me wrong; I'm not a "feminist" in the label sense. It was just a question.

A more inclusive portrayal of liberation at the film's end could have been to dye the main character's bleached-white hair jet black, resembling either Israeli or Palestinian traits. However, the film concludes with a bang as Barbie decides to join the human race as a woman and visits the gynecologist for the first time. Perhaps unintentionally confirming that women have vaginas. (*Give it up for* Barbie for protesting in the end, making both lesbians and conservatives proud!)

Well, I shouldn't forget to mention that Black men use a degrading and divisive label for light-skinned women, much like "blonde." I hated the terms "redbone" and especially "red." Many of my *sistas* felt the same way because of the attention these labels attract, which creates competition among women. (Ken said, "Let's make these women fight amongst themselves." We'll call some of them "blondes" and a few others "red.") Men need to stop that nonsense and show us some respect. (We must understand how programming works or risk being programmed.)

When my husband and I were just friends, he quickly learned that whenever I was called "Red" (as if that was my first name), it meant I was about to be sexually harassed in the communities where we volunteered. (Don't tell me to shake it off! Today, sometimes my husband jokingly says to me when he wants his ass kicked, "Whassup, Red!")

Back to White women, where I left off: These women and girls are idolized for their features first, not as people. It would be more appropriate to say, "She has brown or yellow hair," rather than using a pet name or a noun to replace her human-first identity. Saying she is "a blonde" or "a brunette" is similar to saying autistic children instead of children with autism. Believe me, I make mistakes too, but this sexualizing and dehumanizing of women needs our attention—and must stop. However, in this book, proper nouns related to racial identity and other labels will continue to be used first to promote equality and awareness between those labeled and those who are not. Ultimately, freedom is when we have moved beyond the labels.

Returning to Takin' Sexy Back

But when it comes to the 'fro and femininity, there's one significant difference! I am a woman with an afro and not "an afro." (giggles) I am first, which brings me back to my point. It is the 'fro that is sexy, not a sex toy, *Foxy Brown*. The 'fro says, "Excuse me, did you not notice me?" In fact, I passed some *brothas* from Fiji while visiting New Zealand, who informed my husband that the 'fro was like gold and demanded respect. These men had not been completely "whitewashed" by the Western world. Those Fijian eyes spoke louder than words. You should have seen my husband's ego after that. I reminded him, "I am not an afro; I am a beautiful woman *with* an afro."

To tell you the truth, the 'fro is for everyone! In the 1960s, some women recognized that the 'fro was like gold and demanded respect. They attempted to call it a "beehive" and worked hard to make their hair stand tall, which is nothing more than a sexy 'fro. It's also inclusive because 'fros come in many shapes, colors, sizes, and ethnic backgrounds. (My first BFF [best friend forever] was an incredibly flexible five-year-old Jewish girl with the most fantastic afro! She could put her feet behind her big ol' light brownish 'fro and walk upright on her hands. *Whassup, Erin!*)

Today, as I walk past my husband, *stylin' and profilin'* my 'fro, he oddly falls silent and keeps his eyes on me. Again, it demands respect. I have surprisingly noticed this with children, but White *ch'rn/chil'ren/children* seem to love it the most. They will stare into my soul, and I hear them saying, "Whassup!" from within. It's quite a phenomenon to witness.

Recently, a sweet White baby nearly broke his neck trying to catch a glimpse of me when I entered T-Bones restaurant in Concord, New Hampshire, stylin' my 'fro. He *completely rotated* his head backward like in *The Exorcist,* staring me down along with everyone else. (Ain't nothing changed since I left?) His thought bubble seemed to say, "Mom and Dad, who or what the heck is this!? You didn't tell me about her! I love it!"

The 'fro is both breathtaking and can take your breath away if needed. However, I'm tired of "that man" always asking me if I've cut my hair. "No, I haven't cut my hair," I tell him, which is past my shoulders when pulled straight. He still doesn't get it. My hair retracts almost 90% like a spring. It's that beautiful hair that defies gravity and, once again, demands respect. I would have been rockin' this 'fro since kindergarten if I had known...and if my momma hadn't put that box relaxer on my head and had me thinking my hair was straight.

What do you want, dehumanization or respect? No worries, I'm takin' sexy back—with dignity for all women!

Power to the people,
—Sher! (The Common Snook)
Pause. Inhale. Exhale. Reflect.

P.S. Today, this 'fro, my crown of glory, is helping to "regulate" my energies. More to come!

P.P.S. Once, one of my many little friends, Vishnu, a young boy from my neighborhood in Little India, asked to pull a piece of my hair straight. He responded, "Wow, it's long!" I was so touched because he didn't compare me to anyone else. He only saw me, even with his mother's hair extending past her waist. We'll hear more about Vishnu much later.

P.P.P.S. Speaking of "redbones" from Gainesville! One day, I was big and pregnant with my second child, and I returned to Gainesville temporarily to deliver him with the support of The Birth Center of Gainesville, the oldest birthing center on the East Coast. (You'll hear about that delivery later.) Anyhow, while at the old retro Publix at Westgate Shopping Center near campus, located at N.W. 34th Street and University Avenue, a man (who looked Jewish) stopped me with a nervous, giddy smile and said, "You're Maya

69

Rudolph! You were in the movie *Away We Go*!" I just gave him a confused look because I didn't know who he was talking about and couldn't recall the movie. Then he glanced at my husband, with our son riding on his shoulders. I could tell he was doing some mental calculations. Before I could convince him otherwise, he walked away, looking so excited, as if he was helping me not to blow my cover.

When I got home, I had to look up who this Maya was. Surprisingly, she looked like me: big and pregnant with her second child, and she had a White husband. Then I recalled her from the movie *Away We Go,* which at the time strangely made me feel like I was watching a film of my own unusual life. You'll read more about this in my sermon, "Perception is Reality" or "Away We Go."And then…I was confused because her life and the movie seemed to resemble mine. To complicate things further, she was from Gainesville!!! Now, I completely understood why the guy knew without a doubt that he had met Maya Rudolph that day in Publix. He's probably still tellin' people his story. (Hmm…Maya would also be a fantastic audio narrator for this book. *Whassup from Gainesville, Maya!*)

(Sit in stillness with your eyes closed for 15 minutes a day; I promise it will transform your life!)

7. When Saudi Ladies Gained the Right to Drive

Disclosure Reminder...,

A few years back, I spent a season in another part of Florida. (Yep, I was still avoiding Gainesville.) Each morning, I would hang out with my homegirls from Saudi Arabia while we waited for our children to catch the school bus. These ladies were covered from head to toe, even when it was sometimes hot, humid, and nearly a hundred degrees outside. We were similar in that we were all hot...in hot-ass Florida.

I'm sure they thought I was rather strange because I spoke to them like we were BFFs. One day, as a conversation starter, I asked some friendly questions about their culture and asked them to explain the mutawa. (I'll clarify that in a

minute.) I also quickly learned that "qaf," pronounced like "cuff," means *to stop* in Arabic because we moms speak the same language: "Stop—dammit!"

Anyways, one gal wasn't so fond of me asking about the mutawa and responded defensively, "You get your perspective from the American media," she said *with attitude*. (*Child please.* [That's SAAVE; no commas.]) If I were influenced by "the American media," I probably wouldn't have been hanging out with them and would have kept a *safe* distance. I learned about the mutawa through my own research. I grew curious about their culture after spending time with them every morning.

I had no clue that those handsome men with the five o'clock shadows and red checkered head coverings, held on by black headbands, shemaghs, were the equivalent of religious police. My, my, the mutawa! I thought that would be the perfect conversation starter because we "People of Color" in the U.S. always talk about "the po-po." She must not have done her research, talking to me *with attitude*.

Back then, I was bald, so we'll let Sara #1 off the hook since all women tended to look at me suspiciously. (By the way, # does not mean hashtag.) My Muslim sisters faced discrimination for covering their heads, and I received the same treatment for shaving mine. We were like two peas in a pod.

Anywho, I was just trying to connect with a culture that had been so closed off from the rest of the world—like forever. Some of these women have a chip

71

on their shoulder or seem guarded because none of y'all stop to give them the time of day, and it's not just Americans. It's as if they are given a universal cold shoulder; even in India, life can be challenging for Muslim women.

I am amazed at how many American women accuse others of dressing for men while failing to see that they do the same. Some cover-up, while others reveal more, all in the name of whatever makes men happy. (Just my opinion, ladies.) I promise, once we get over ourselves and our Western sense of "superiority," which we confuse with women's liberation—like walking around with our 'cheeks hanging out—we'll discover we are more alike than different. (Still, tribal or primitive styles can be cute, too.)

You know, most of us also have a friend who misinterprets things and talks to *who they think we are*. (*Youse* talkin' to the wrong person—dammit!) Besides Sara #1, who was being defensive, the rest of my homegirls seemed cool and enjoyed my company each day.

September 26, 2017: While walking my young fellows to the bus stop, I read in the news that Saudi ladies had finally earned the right to drive. I approached my homegirls *with attitude*, twisting with my hand on my hip, as if I were sixteen and had just received my license. I exclaimed excitedly, as if it were the latest gossip, "I know y'all heard the news!" I then declared, "Saudi ladies can now drive!" I extended my arm stiffly, almost like I was saying, "Give it to me!" At that moment, "my girl" in the niqab, Sara #2, whose eyes were the only feature visible, jumped up from the bench and gave me *a Michael Jordan high-five slam dunk*, while the rest of the gals looked to Sara #1 to see if she was offended. (Shoot, I was scared, too.)

Sara #2 was letting me know that we were the same and had the same desires—beeyotch! Nonetheless, she saw herself in me even when I was bald and a bit rebellious. Sara #2 was "my girrrl." That day, she showed me there were no limits to friendship.

Wa'l-salaam,
    —Sher! (The Common Snook)
                    Pause. Inhale. Exhale. Reflect.

P.S. Hmm…can you drive safely while wearing a niqab? It might be safer just to tint the windows.

(Sit in stillness with your eyes closed for 15 minutes a day; I promise it will transform your life!)

8. Pro-Choice and Pro-Life—Dammit!

Disclosure Reminder…,

Nobody would believe my body has always been pro-choice…and pro-life! In my early years, I had a shitload of miscarriages. My body would sometimes say, "I choose my life—dammit!" and had the nerve to kick the baby out.

After my third, fourth, or fifth miscarriage, my doctor asked if anyone had tested my progesterone levels. Sometimes, we "Women of Color" just don't receive the necessary testing unless our organs are hanging out. (They must not have realized I had a White husband.)

Bless her heart, she ordered some labs and found that I indeed had low progesterone. This hormone is necessary to carry a baby to at least twenty weeks, after which the baby no longer requires the mother's hormonal support, meaning that the baby is a full-fledged being after twenty weeks of gestation. Imagine that! (We have two handsome young men in the family who were kicked out at around twenty-seven weeks.)

Anyhow, progesterone is also the hormone that is blocked by the early abortion pill. She essentially told me, "Your body is both pro-choice and pro-life." And if someone had paid attention to how often I was in the office, they could have easily helped me avoid all those miscarriages (spontaneous abortions).

Don't be jealous because I could only carry a pregnancy if I wanted to, if I **chose** to, and **chose** to apply the cream (progesterone cream). I thought, *Well, I'll be damned; the rest of those poor women who use early progesterone blockers must live with so much shame because of their choice* when I had a built-in blocker. Sometimes, I was like, "Not today, Baby!"

One time, I visited one of those free pregnancy centers for an ultrasound, you know, the ones that *smell* like a cross between *Downy* and vanilla potpourri (or candles if you don't remember the 1990s), with all the pictures of happy moms and lovely scriptures to support their happiness. I explained that I needed to know if I was pregnant so I could get a prescription for progesterone from my doctor since I was traveling out of state at the time. They didn't want me taking crazy progesterone without an ultrasound.

Those women thought I was up to something. They were ready to scare me straight like a Halloween haunted house and weren't expecting me to share their perspective. We were both concerned about saving babies. They just stared at me like ants that had lost their path. Even so, something about my story didn't sit right with them. They were suspicious, and rightfully so.

Sure enough, I was pregnant, and they were rejoicing. Man, it was tough for me to crack a smile, but I had to do so in order to avoid their life-affirming "Creepshow." (I'm just being funny. *Creepshow* is just a simple horror comedy from the 1980s.) I expressed my gratitude for their services and even sent them a donation. Their free services were indeed a blessing. *Still, something distracted me when I got home.*

When I fell pregnant again (that's what the Brits say) with my last child, I was done with babies. I asked the baby, "Are you finished *trying me*?" because I knew it was the same soul knocking three times. Folks used to dramatize my pregnancies, encouraging me to name the miscarriages so I could feel horrible for the rest of my life. Good Lord, I'd have a bunch of kids if I did that. Who would do that to themselves? I said, "Nope, it's always been the same baby knocking. He only needs one name. But we'll give him a long-ass name since it took him a long-ass time to get his act together."

But did you know that I threatened Baby and made a deal? I told Baby, "I will give your butt some progesterone cream for twenty loooong weeks, twice a day, having me acting crazy, but don't you pull any fast ones, putting your foot in my back, trying to give me morning sickness. *Try me!*"

Wouldn't you know, he agreed to be kind to my body, ensuring no sickness or new stretch marks? He even gifted me a delivery that was contraction-free and pain-free because he understood how terrible those four-hour miscarriages were. Sometimes, they wouldn't even prescribe me a prescription painkiller, the good *stuff*. I guess they thought I would share it with my husband or sell it. Of course, I would. My name is *Sher*, right?

Anyways, I got out of the tub one day, and he just popped out without even telling me he was coming. (*Those are those* good hips…aligned by my chiropractor a few weeks before my delivery. *Whassup, Dr. Schargel!)* My husband said I locked hold of the bathroom sink and looked like I was concentrating like mad. I said, "He's coming!" He quickly got on his knees to take a look. Then, to get a better view, he peeked behind me, only to be greeted by our son's face, looking at him upside down. He grabbed an unsanitized towel and positioned it just in time to catch his slippery butt. He moved the umbilical cord and the mucus from his face. The baby spit and then cried like he knew the routine. After an instant of complete shock at what had just happened, the three of us (they were behind me) slowly shuffled off to the bed because the cord was still connected to me, and the baby was in his arms, talkin' 'bout, "Hey, Momma." I told him, "Don't you *be* stoppin' by our house (Anglewood a.k.a. Sugarfoot today, SW 2nd Avenue) without calling first" (Snook, "The Unassisted Birth"). Thankfully, he didn't hit his head on the bathroom floor. I told Baby, "That wasn't funny. Do you wanna have to come knocking on that door again?"

You may be wondering why I was delivering in Florida from home. Well, here's the short version: I was uninsured. I couldn't find a single practice in Mecklenburg County, North Carolina, that would see me without insurance. They wouldn't even let me in the door. The rejection was awful! I had never felt so poor, despite my husband having a good job. I drove thirty minutes to *backwoods* China Grove just to be seen at a local clinic. (Folks in Charlotte used to say, "Don't get caught in China Grove after dark," lol. Hmm…that's not funny.)

I was told that American women are guaranteed, at minimum, pregnancy Medicaid. Don't believe the lie! The lowest quote I received for a hospital delivery was $20,000, which didn't include an epidural or any extras like a stitch.

I told my husband, "I'm going home to deliver our baby at the Birthing Center of Gainesville." They said I had to arrive before I reached my 20th week, or they couldn't take me. I packed up with our four-year-old, leaving my husband behind to work in Charlotte, and arrived at nineteen weeks. (tears) Even though the midwives didn't make it to assist with my delivery, despite being

My son, Sweet Potato Brown.

warned an hour earlier that I knew he was coming, I'm still thankful for the invaluable services they provided me. (Regardless, they still should have trusted my insight because the body speaks!) The total cost for their services, including prenatal care, classes, companionship, delivery, and post-delivery follow-up, was less than $2000, which I gladly paid upfront in cash. I let them keep the change because I would have been *pissed* if I had delivered this five-minute transaction in the hospital and left with a $30,000 bill.

By the way, I didn't even need to call my doctor for a prescription for that "wild thing." I used Wild Yam Cream, derived from African yams, which acts like natural progesterone. Those sweet Christian midwives recommended the cream before any doctor ever tested my levels.

Today, I refer to my son as my wild yam baby. Yep, he's wild, and he has the complexion of a sweet potato.

Unconditional Hugs,

—Sher! (The Common Snook)

Pause. Inhale. Exhale. Reflect.

P.S. Are pro-lifers also vegetarians?

P.P.S. Hmm…do you think I could get arrested for not applying the cream? "Nope, I ain't puttin' it on!"

P.P.P.S. Most people who don't have a third baby are pro-choice because it's the third pregnancy that triggers an awakening. "We need to do somethin' about this mess," they say.

(Sit in stillness with your eyes closed for 15 minutes a day; I promise it will transform your life!)

9. Everyone Needs a Redneck as a Friend

This is one of those sermons where the minister rambles for an hour before delivering a one-liner message at the end. At least you can read my sermons while still in your PJs. Also, be warned, I will use the term "Redneck," but only to mean middle-class, hard-working White folks, as it was originally intended and not as a slur against my friends and family. And for those of you who think I can't or shouldn't use the term, remember, I'm 65% European or "North Carolina Redneck," according to my DNA, so I'm more "White" than anything. Race is *stupid*, and it's racist of you to think I can be Black but not White. Hopefully, one day, someone will begin addressing that nonsense instead of the *"sexual buffet"* we have today. (More on "the buffet" in a later sermon.) Also, feel free to read the entire sermon in a Southern accent; this one is *special*. Sometimes, reading my sermons aloud provides a more effective way to fully grasp the message.

The house was a mess, but a jewel! All the windows were nailed shut, and someone stole the air conditioning unit in hot-ass Georgia.

Disclosure Reminder...,

Anyways, way back when my well-educated, undercover "Redneck" husband decided he wanted a farm, we bought a hundred-year-old farmhouse that we were going to fix up in Athens-Clarke County, right on the border of Oglethorpe and Oconee Counties in northern Georgia. Had it been in Florida, this area would have been culturally similar to Levy or Dixie County.

Let me share a fun fact about our house before I tell you my story of life in the country. We purchased this Central Hall Colonial-style home as a foreclosure. The central passageway was magnificent and could have easily been mistaken for a bowling alley. It measured over five feet wide and over fifty feet long, give or take, featuring some of the most gorgeous heart pine boards, with many extending more than twelve feet in length. (Strangely, we all had a favorite board.)

Additionally, we learned that it was initially the farm manager's house at the University of Georgia (UGA) in the early 1900s before being converted into the UGA Visitor Center. Still, the historic home was given away for free to any "Redneck" bold enough to cut it in half, move it, and put it back together again. The university wanted to make room for a fitness center, of course. If you ever visit UGA, the silo that once stood near our home still stands on campus in remembrance of the original farm.

Today, on "This Old House," as we used to say.

As you can see, some bold "Redneck" moved the house to the country and abandoned it during the 2007 recession, and it became our beloved fixer-upper! But of course, my New England lad would always be out of the country, leaving me at home fixing that old-ass house and holding down the farm by myself.

I never feared being out in the country alone with my young fellows because I had a big-ass maroon-colored Chevy pickup truck that conveyed, "Don't mess with me; I have a gun." But I didn't, of course. I realized the pickup truck was enough for most people to back off. I should have installed a gun rack in the back window for extra security. It would have been interesting to show up to the local Quaker Meeting I attended in town, where there were anti-violence, gun-hating pacifists…like me, or as I strive to be. (War is unjustifiable, and choosing not to engage in war is a daily decision for me.)

Living in the country was great, and there were many great odors! Surprisingly, we lived not far from one of those awful chicken houses that can grow a ten-pound chicken in just forty-five days. I still don't understand how that was possible or how we lived so close to one of those houses without smelling the shit. I heard it can be brutal if you live close to one, but the locals were right: "It all depends on which way the wind blows," whether you smelled the shit or not. We were lucky since we only smelled the chicken house during cleaning time when they harvested the manure. The neighbors used to say, "What smells like shit to you...smells like money to us."

As a matter of fact, there was shit everywhere in the country. *Horse shit. Cow shit. Pig shit. You name it!* (We can count that as a poem, too.) Some of that shit used to seep into our well, a.k.a. coliform, which politely indicated that we had fecal matter, somethin' like E. coli, in our water: "not recommended for drinking." Our young boys learned a wide range of valuable agricultural science lessons while being homeschooled in the country.

Did y'all know you can earn a Ph.D. in poultry nutrition? My good friend's husband was a poultry nutritionist, and their last name, wait for it—was "Byrd." I shit you not. (Y'all better be laughing.)

You know, chicken is an essential commodity in Georgia, especially since Chick-fil-A is the state's capital. Pardon me...I mean, the first Chick-fil-A is *in* the state's capital—*kinda*. You know that questionable-looking "Dwarf House" (the original name of the Chick-fil-A restaurant) that has a separate entrance for short people.

You can feel the history of the White South in that place, "from cotton fields to skyscrapers," as they say. Visit for yourself! There's an eerie ambiance in that crowded little building with all those Black and White folks eating chicken *sammiches* together. I would guess it's also one of America's Blackest-staffed Chick-fil-A restaurants. Instead of Christian White teens serving you your food, you get to experience the old South, like a Paula Deen dream wedding. (Hmm...I bet she's been there! Deen's from Georgia, you know.) Oh Lord, as the Baptist pastor might say, "Someone must have needed some poultry preaching. Can I get an 'Amen!' for Chick-fil-A?" (Now for my story!)

It never failed. Whenever my bougie, undercover "Redneck" husband left town, the most horrific things would occur. These included the tornado that flipped our shed and ripped all the shingles off our roof...and the pack of dogs from *A Christmas Story* that ate Bunny one night and had the nerve to spread cotton tail all over our yard for my poor babies to see the following morning. (And I know where those dogs came from because White folks' dogs live in the house and sleep with them in their beds at night.)

On another horrific day, I nearly cried the morning I saw that our herd of deer had devoured and plowed down our sixty-by-thirty-foot garden—even the tomato plants, which they were supposedly allergic to. I refer to them as "our herd of deer" because about fifteen of them came to our house every night like family. (They used to be playin' in our front yard all night, smokin' and drinkin'.)

One day, I noticed a buck going buck-wild on our property in the middle of the day. I didn't know what was happening, but it was scary to watch. I jumped in my Chevy with my boys and followed the deer around, where it fell to the ground and appeared to be having a seizure. I could see the deer was in pain. Perhaps it had been hit by a car and somehow wandered onto our farm because someone left the damn gate open.

I needed to find someone—a sportsman—to help me. This was no job for the Black folks living in the woods behind me off "Ella Mae." (They must have named the street after grandma, and I always felt safe knowing Ella Mae's *ch'rn* were in the woods behind me with all those loud-ass dogs barking.) However, I knew that my neighbors across the street in Oglethorpe County would know what to do. Honestly, I thought one of those guys might want the meat.

As I crossed over to Oglethorpe, I knew I was getting closer to help when I saw a "Redneck-dog" come from under the trailer and catch a squirrel for lunch. Then, I drove through the rural development. Each house sat on a few acres. Everyone had big-ass flags, four-wheelers, motorcycles, tractors, above-ground pools, chickens, pickup trucks, and guns. I was looking for someone outside so I could look silly, asking if they had a gun and would be willing to help me. Sure enough, finding someone with a gun didn't take long. Imagine that! I met the sweetest young man and tried to entice him with the meat. He agreed to help but mentioned that roadkill is never good to eat since the adrenaline released in the animal's body after being hit makes the meat tough. (He must have tried some before. [giggles])

I found myself an "Ass-Kicking White Boy," which I saw written across a Confederate flag as far north as the backwoods of *Yankalachia*…oops again, I mean, New Hampshire. (Hmm…I think "kick-ass" better describes him.) He went inside, grabbed his rifle, and followed me back to my house, which he said he passed every day on his way home, noting that he'd been watching me restore that old-ass house. He confirmed the deer was injured and agreed to put it down for me. (It reminded me of the movie *Sounder*.) Before shooting the deer, he turned to my sons, ages four and eight at the time, and shared that his father taught him to always pause before taking a life because it was never something to take lightly. Then, he turned to shoot the deer as my young boys watched.

This is an example of how children cope with pain. My sweet boy even pointed out that it was female. You can see his li'l handwriting in the bottom left corner. (LSVG)

It was terrible—absolutely terrible! My oldest was nearly in tears, and my youngest pushed me away as I tried to block his view. They were in shock. They'd never witnessed anything like that in their young lives. The young man apologized for what we had to endure and took the deer away to dispose of it in the woods down the road. He was such a gentleman. Listen up! A real man never leaves a woman with a mess to clean up. (Mm-hmm…that, too.)

I will always cherish this labor of love.

I don't know what I would have done without this young man. Without his kindness, I would have been stuck with a decomposing carcass and a yard full of vultures circling and *praying* over their meal ("Father, we thank you….") since my husband wasn't due home for another week. (Yes, ladies, we need men to move *stuff* when rigor mortis sets in. I am so thankful for men.)

Thankfully, I chose not to view the neighboring Oglethorpe and Oconee counties through the lens of the past. This area of Georgia, bordering Athens-Clarke County, has some of the most recent lynching dates, which is one reason Oconee County remains predominantly White to this day. (That's where many White families move to escape the lovely children in Athens-Clarke County Schools. I kept "move" in the present tense since this White flight is still ongoing.)

I could coexist with "these people" because I lived in the present. Any story I allowed to live in my head about "these people" felt too heavy to carry when the past no longer existed. Sure, I knew that the last name "Lumpkin," also a street name in town, was connected to the descendants of enslavers and the descendants of the enslaved in my area; many of them were my neighbors. Still, change only happens when you allow the present moment to replace the past.

However, some of us cling to the past instead of growing and moving forward because we wouldn't know who we are without the story. (And my Reform Jewish friends said, "Amen!") The story becomes an identity—on both sides. Nonetheless, when you hold onto the past too tightly, you will always receive more of it in some shape or form, and your perspective may cause you to miss an opportunity to make a friend...or be left to clean up a dead deer by yourself.

This young man who blessed me was no different from my husband's people in New Hampshire, who enjoyed the same leisure activities as my "Redneck" brother or neighbors in Levy or Dixie County, Florida. They had big-ass flags, four-wheelers, motorcycles, tractors, above-ground pools, chickens, pickup trucks, and guns; one of them I could have sworn was a taxidermist. (No worries...they ate everything they killed, no different than y'all who buy meat from Publix.)

Til' we meet again,
—Sher! (The Common Snook)
Pause. Inhale. Exhale. Reflect.

(Sit in stillness with your eyes closed for 15 minutes a day; I promise it will transform your life!)

10. Tales from Little India

Well, for starters, Little India was great for my hair but not so good for my complexion.

Disclosure Reminder...,

As you may have noticed by now, I reference many different ethnicities in my sermons, and the people of India hold a *special* place in my heart. This is because Indian cultures are incredible, and we lived in a predominantly Indian community in Charlotte, North Carolina—you know, Little India. The culture was so rich that it touched my life without my realizing it, and it will forever remain with me: dhal, dhokla, and chapatis.

Let's rewind to one of my favorite experiences. (Hmm...some of y'all don't even know what "rewind" or "fast-forward" means. [giggles]) Y'all remember the pandemic, right? Well, interestingly, I became the neighborhood art teacher during that time—this was unplanned, of course. Let me walk you through the events that led to our delightful afternoons of art, peace, healing, and personal growth. And then we'll end with a story of shared empowerment. How does that sound to you? (Enjoy some milk and cookies while you listen to the story.)

Each day, in the magical place of Little India, my youngest and the neighborhood boys played cricket to help pass the long days while the schools were closed, a game I never imagined my son would learn. I still don't understand how they say, "It's like baseball." Nonetheless, with nearly twenty boys aged eight to ten within a few blocks, it wasn't uncommon for a blood fight to break out. These boys used to brawl, which had me googling because, you know, children only mimic their parents' behavior, right? (They always had me googling.) I had never witnessed so many *ass-whoopings* in my life. Relax, no worries...we all have our issues, which I could see in the smacks my son frequently received upside the head. (Now, now, let's keep going. There should be no defensiveness. We are—one world, one people, especially if you ask Europeans. You know, we're all Indians, right?)

I recall thinking that Little India was the ideal place for my son to learn some self-defense. After all, he wouldn't have to worry about being shot as he rolled with all his Brown brothers, unlike the neighboring community where those White boys used to rev their engines and race through our neighborhood in their big-ass pickup trucks. (They were just giving my Indian neighbors a taste of the South.) And speaking of Brown! Interestingly, most of my son's friends, except for the *North Indian Nepali* boy, were darker in complexion than he was. More on complexion later.

Anyhow, I introduced a day of art to keep the boys from fighting. Too much masculine energy can be overwhelming and rarely ends well without some balance from feminine energy—and some food, of course. (More on energy in a later sermon.)

They were so Zen after our afternoon of art that I overheard one boy, a nine-year-old whom I called the CEO, coordinating their next class. (They were hooked!) I was amazed by his leadership skills. He checked the availability of the ten or so boys present that day. "Does anyone have Kumon on Monday?" he asked. (Now, if you're Indian, you know that's funny.) And so, it was decided: Every Monday at 5:00 p.m., they would come for art in the garage. I loved that they just assumed I was available and willing to teach them. (You know, *we women* are always available, right?) Who would turn down that kind of collaboration?

Each week, they would come running to class, eager to learn, and some would arrive early to help set up the materials. This class truly became the highlight of my year. Some parents even offered to pay me, but I said, "Thank you, but no," because that would lead to expectations of me. This class was a blessing that no amount of money could provide. These boys brought me more joy than I could have asked for that year. (Share your talents freely, and you will be blessed!)

Meanwhile, a few of the younger sisters wanted to join in, too. They gradually began to work their way into the class. One day, I noticed one of them had her hair oiled…I mean, oiled down, baby! This moment took me back to my childhood and seemed to clear a pain I didn't know I had.

I remember the White kids teasing us, Brown and Black kids, for having "greasy" hair, which needed to be oiled to prevent breakage. Many of us stopped using oil on our hair to fit in better with our White peers, who produced oil daily, unlike us, leading to severe damage to our hair.

Yet, this little girl had enough oil on her head to condition the hair of about ten African American children, and it was completely safe to walk around the neighborhood without facing teasing. This was a place where Brown people ruled while the five White families raged, trying to take HOA voting rights from non-compliant Indians with their big ol' viny gardens and unkept lawns. This seemed like the promised land! (Yes, a select few planned to take voting rights [disenfranchisement!]. Hmm…I wonder where they got that idea from.)

I was so moved that I texted one of my sisters in South Florida to share my experience, which nearly brought tears to my eyes. Although I was technically a "minority" in Little India, it was the first time I had lived in an entirely Brown and "black" community and did not have to tolerate White dominance. (Yes, black! Some were significantly darker than *me* and often referred to as black or dusky.) From that moment on, I learned to care for my scalp and hair in a new way. I used pure coconut oil and applied as much as I wanted—dammit! Those little girls and some boys had set me free and healed little Sherry's tender heart.

That being said, one day, my youngest said abruptly to one of his friends during art class, "Ew, what is that smell, and why is your hair so greasy!?" Oh my, I couldn't believe what I was hearing. My half-White son, with his limited exposure to African American cultures, was making my eye twitch. I was about to grab his ass, but thankfully, the future CEO who coordinated our art classes wasn't havin' it either. He turned to my son, thankfully without a smack upside the head (giggles), and corrected his nonsense because, in this neighborhood, it was India—beeyotch! They didn't have to give in to White Americans or American ignorance. They would light up the whole damn neighborhood of about 400 residents during Diwali with TNT and fireworks, which, of course, left the five White families enraged.

Later that evening, I pulled my son aside, with his wild hair tangled from root to tip. I shared my story of being rejected as a child for having my hair oiled and how our Indian neighbors had brought me healing. For once, he was silent. I slapped some coconut oil into his dry scalp and hair as he melted under my hands from the massage.

Now, back to black! I noticed that many of my Indian friends would compliment my complexion, which struck me as strange because I had always believed that darker-skinned Indians were among the most captivating people— in the world. However, that was not how they viewed themselves. Colonialism and colorism had gotten to them, too, and perhaps even more so than in African American circles.

Black women have counteracted the attack of anti-blackness by reminding the world that "black is beautiful." *(Whassup, Beautiful!)* Yet, my Indian *sistas* regularly talked about their imperfect skin and seemed to idolize fair skin thanks to Bollywood, and I found myself at a loss for words to explain how misguided that was. It felt like they couldn't hear me, or perhaps I spoke a foreign language. They didn't want to acknowledge their colorism while they lusted for lighter skin. As I've mentioned before, "white or light skin is seen as better," and this was regarded as a fact in my Indian circles. There was no alternative narrative.

My experience living in Little India healed a childhood wound, yet it also left me saddened by the fact that many Indian women believe they aren't beautiful because of their dark skin. If you've ever met someone from the South Indian regions of Andhra Pradesh and Telangana, they're stunning—all of them! *(Whassup, Sowmya!)* And don't even get me started on the people from Tamil Nadu or Karnataka. Their beauty will truly take your breath away. I used to be sittin' on the porch, *rubbernecking* at some of the most beautiful people. I even had a neighbor I named "George Michael." He was gorgeous—tall, dark, and handsome. Oh my, what a "Careless Whisper." (Those neighbors would be surprised to see my youngest, who is now as tall and attractive as the neighborhood George Michael. Hmm…Old Navy should try to recruit him as a model.)

One neighbor, who had her eye on my oldest son because he's a good catch, asked if I would permit him to marry an "Indian girl" (woman). I replied, "Sure, one of those beautiful young ladies whose hair matches her skin tone." She looked at me as if I were crazy. I said, "The blacker the berry, the sweeter the juice." I was channeling empowerment through African American Vernacular. (However, I have a strange suspicion this saying was something White men created. But what a great metaphor, even if its origin may have been racist, raunchy, or true. Black folks said, "We can work with that, too." Pardon me, *Wallace Thurman, is this your work? Was I mistaken?*)

Still, that's not how Indians see it (well…*most* of them). One of my girlfriends even joked, calling me North Indian because of my complexion, which would be similar to calling a light-skinned or biracial person a "redbone" in the South. They were so funny. I even watched a few of my Indian *sistas* dodge the sun as if it would kill them. One said something like, "Girrrl, get me out of this sun. I'm not 'bout to get blacker," ending with a profound "sonic pop." I could've sworn I was hanging out with a bunch of Black women—no pun intended! (More on the "sonic pop" later.)

I wish more "People of Color" could experience the liberation I felt while living in that vibrant community. (In Gainesville, it would be called Lincoln Estates or Hollywood.) However, we still have work to do worldwide to combat colorism and reprogram society to value all forms of beauty. In *fact*, I will be takin' sexy *back*. (Once again, I love it when I almost rhyme.)

Let us be a gift to one another as we rise in Consciousness!

Cheers to sweeter juice,

—Sher! (The Common Snook)

Pause. Inhale. Exhale. Reflect.

P.S. Alright, Indian mommas, please send your daughter's inquiry to the attached email. My son will likely study architecture and urban design and needs an intelligent and strong-willed gal—the type who says, "No, it's your turn to cook—dammit!" (*Black mommas, I hear you, but unfortunately, many Black girls prefer a cool guy; however, cool isn't sustainable. If your daughter is interested, I encourage her to apply for a date, too.* Hmm…maybe a Haitian girl (woman) would be suitable for him.)

P.P.S. Thanks to my homegirls, I've had the privilege of wearing a saree/sari. Y'all, the saree is so sexy! (*Oops!*) You should have seen my husband watching me. How did the world miss this brilliant fashion statement? *Nothing* compares to the feeling of royalty while wearing a saree!

Thank you to my team of fashion advisors and saree drapists. Celebrity drapist, The Mahaan of Gainesville, draped the traditional red cotton saree with a li'l skin showin'.

P.P.P.S. Did I ever tell y'all nineteen of my favorite Indian names are "Sugasuranya," coming in first place with that sweet name, then "Meerambika," "Sailaja," "Shanvika," "Sraavani," "Swetha," "Sumita," "Toshitha," "Adrika," "Abhay," "Sai," "Sanjay," "Sivadha," "Shriyan," "Suresh," "Deepu," "Dilesh," "Yuvan," and "Parthiv"? "Parthiv" is awesome! (wink) Come on, Black women! Pick one! ♟

87

11. Gentrification: The End of Segregation

I won't say anything funny until the end because this one isn't funny. Also, I want to thank Bushel and Peck Pop-up Bakery for the amazing pretzels and for inspiring me to share this story. *Give it up for* **Eastside High School's Institute of Culinary Arts!**

Disclosure Reminder...,   10/13/2023

I lived outside of Gainesville for almost twenty years, and upon my return, I was astounded by the redevelopment of the Fifth Avenue and Pleasant Street Community. From bass-blaring boxed Chevies to Tesla-driving composting millennials, White people were everywhere! I learned of friends and friends of friends whose families had been pushed out, so to speak. And I wasn't sure how I felt about this. The general sentiment was one of sadness because the historical community where I attended preschool and where my friend, Ms. Juliette McCoy, lived was all there was for "People of Color." I guess it hurts to see White people take it for themselves. At least, that's how it appeared when I chose to view the situation from my perspective as a "Person of Color."

To add insult to injury, I tried to purchase property in the area and was nearly bulldozed by investors. It was comical to think I could compete with these beasts. I wanted to help...somehow...or, at the very least, support the residents in getting their money's worth for their property and hopefully avoiding being robbed. But then I realized I could do nothing to save the community, even if I bought a few pieces of property and built a house. Some properties may remain Black-owned, but most would eventually be sold because who wouldn't want to profit off their real estate? Certainly, I would prefer that the property go to the highest bidder. Moreover, we can't expect Black owners to hold out for history's sake.

Finally, some families are receiving fair market value for their property, even though African American communities have historically been undervalued. My only wish is that Realtors would give these communities a break since the National Association of Realtors is largely responsible for the undervaluation of Black real estate in the first place. This is acknowledged today, but no one is taking action to rectify the situation by lowering real estate fees.

Six percent is an outrageous amount to charge anyone, let alone members of communities that have been deprived of generational wealth. Call me! I'm still happy to offer free advice so marginalized families get their money's worth. And yes, I used to be a Realtor, so I know enough to be creative or to point you in the right direction to get free legal advice (hint, hint—in Gainesville, Florida, you can contact the UF Law School or Three Rivers Legal Service), especially if you have "heirs property," meaning properties without wills left to the heirs, which is common in historically African American communities. (Those with generational wealth love targeting these valuable historic properties. "I'll pay the taxes!" they say.)

Twenty twenty-four update! Did you know a local Realtor threatened me, saying agents would throw my listing in the trash because I offered a generous 1% and used flat-rate listing services like Beycome.com? Hmm…her threat definitely sounded like a confession that agents engage in steering practices that help keep commission rates high and choke out sellers like me. I guess they still believe they're the ones who determine the commission rate. Shoot, she must not have been keeping up with the news. She's old-school and old, too…nobody prints listings anymore.

Back to my point! Unfortunately, money ultimately prevails, and it is often held by White hands. When I accepted the hard-to-swallow reality, I realized that this unique community, which was the heart of the African American community in Gainesville, was never something that Black people created. White people started these segregated communities, and it is clear they still hold the power to dismantle and level them, as we see today. They said, "You people, 'the help,' can live here for 150 years in proximity to service the University of Florida, the Duckpond area, and Florida Park. But when we say it's over, it's over—just like affirmative action."

C'mon, y'all, folks should have seen this coming! Nobody greedy wants a Black neighborhood in the middle of town, occupying valuable land. What I initially viewed as White people taking the land because they now wanted it (still partly true) also indicated that segregation was coming to an end. The Fifth Ave Community has been predominantly Black for over 150 years, and that period is now over. This trend will continue in Gainesville. You know, you can't keep building west forever, especially with all those sinkholes in the local areas of Tioga and Oakmont. (giggles)

Indeed, there will always be economic segregation if we don't intentionally design our communities to welcome diverse income levels and strive to prevent economic displacement. However, gentrification is a sign that segregation is a thing of the past, not only because of a law signed in 1964 but also because the landscape is changing. In another two hundred years, many of those unattractive,

89

greed-driven high-rise buildings will be torn down for whatever humanity has in store next, where terms like "segregation" and "gentrification" won't be relevant or even understood.

When we see ourselves defined solely by skin color (and what is *Black* if the concept of *White* never existed?)—a concept unjustly imposed on "People of Color" as our identity—we may find ourselves resisting the change for which our ancestors prayed and fought. Let me put it this way (please don't take offense), but it's like choosing to eat chitterlings when you can now enjoy steak willingly. (giggles) It seems somewhat contradictory and counterproductive to fight for the freedom to live where we want while simultaneously cherishing the confinement as a prize. (Migration changes you.) Please don't get me wrong; I recognize the significance of history and the need to create space for "People of Color," as there is still much work to be done. Nevertheless, we must grow and embrace change. (And the White people snatching up land with their dependable real estate appreciation and generational wealth—exhaled.)

Speaking of preserving space! *Betwixt* hopes to acquire Ms. Juliette McCoy's house on 2nd Street (also known as Pleasant Street) and set it aside as a sacred space for people to visit and connect with the Divine. Better yet, a donation would be lovely.

Peace and blessings,
   —Sher! (The Common Snook)
        Pause. Inhale. Exhale. Reflect.

P.S. If holding on to the Fifth Ave Community was necessary, I'm confident Ms. Juliette would have had something to say about it. I sometimes imagine asking her, "Why didn't you tell me the White people were coming?" Without a doubt, she saw the coming change and never mentioned it—at least not to me. She also didn't look at the world through the lens of race.

P.P.S. You know, having your *shit jacked* (phony wealth) by White people again and again can be a door to awakening. I'm serious, though! I'm surprised more Black communities haven't used this pain to access the true wealth within. It's time, Black people…White people, too! These perpetual slaps are a blessing in disguise.

(Sit in stillness with your eyes closed for 15 minutes a day; I promise it will transform your life!)

12. You're a Victim—and a Survivor?

Let's kick off this service with a song: "The Message" by Grandmaster Flash and the Furious Five. Bow your heads, please.

Disclosure Reminder…,

I love survivors! We can share our sad stories until the cows come home. If you think your story is terrible, I bet mine can top yours.

Did you know that I nearly died once? But not really; the angels were just trying to get my non-emotional husband to shed a tear. Someone must have told him when he was young that "boys don't cry" and robbed him of a lifetime of emotions. (More on my amazing husband later.)

Nevertheless, some years ago, I found myself in the hospital with a brain aneurysm that was about to pop. (Yikes!) However, the correct term would be "rupture." I had never been hospitalized or taken any medication before this event because I was rebellious and "anti-Western-medicine-establishment." (Isn't that how country folks or those who feel inferior use that phrase?)

Still, I was lucky, and I'm thankful for Western medicine, which provides the world's best emergency services…as they say. That juicy baby (the aneurysm bulge in my brain) landed on my optic nerve…and so graciously turned off the lights.

My left eye was closed entirely, and it felt like someone was stabbing me in the head with an icepick. Indeed, the pain was unimaginable! I remember sitting in the middle of the bathroom floor and peeing…just because. I…did…not…care about anything anymore in this world. I kept telling my husband to take me to the urgent care center because I wouldn't exactly say I liked hospitals.

I just assumed it was a cluster headache since I had experienced headaches for years and had received a shot in the butt at another urgent care center just two days earlier. However, something about me hanging my head in a cooler full of ice cubes while in the car made him believe he should take me to the hospital instead. I'm so glad his emotional intelligence and invaluable emergency medical technician (EMT) training from Santa Fe Community College (SFCC) kicked in.

They did their doctor *stuff*. "Look left; look right." I thought I looked left while smiling at the doctor with my disfigured face. Even so, the doctor said again, "Follow my finger to the left side of the room," and I complied. Well, at least I thought I did. This time, Blondie…I mean, the doctor got testy with me for a moment because, I guess, she assumed that we "Women of Color" enjoy coming to the emergency room to play games, or maybe she had forgotten the rules of her doctor game. "Please call for emergency backup when the patient's eyeball doesn't move." (Here's a fun fact: Studies have found that Black patients live longer when more Black doctors are in a hospital. Hmm…I wonder what the correlation is. *What do you think, Dr. Tyndall?*)

When she finally accepted that I wasn't playing games and had no peripheral vision, she almost shitted on herself. Her face looked like I was about to die right then and there. *That wasn't appropriate bedside manner*, I thought. Sure enough, the hospital staff scanned my head, and Dr. Testy said, "We're surprised you're still walking on this earth, talking and laughing." Then, they began aggressively pumping me with steroids.

I blame "that man" and those *ch'rn*…and that woman on my mom's side, who I won't name. Okay, okay, I blame myself, too, for allowing this to happen to me. Men might be physically stronger than women, but we carry ten times more emotional weight in the name of family. They used to be driving me crazy, and ladies, don't fuck around and shave your head as I did without knowing how powerful we are. (For the record, I came into the hospital with a bald head.) I had enough supernatural power to flip the kitchen table when "that man" would *piss me off*! (No, I did not flip the kitchen table. I flipped something else. Shhh!)

I once learned from an Indian guru, Jaggi Vasudev, that shaving your head without a plan to balance yourself spiritually could lead to trouble because it creates an upsurge of energy. He said your head is like any plant. When you trim the stems or branches, it concentrates all its energy in that area to promote new growth. The same thing occurs when you shave your head.

He explained that this was why many spiritual seekers, monks, and others who desire a union of mind, body, and spirit shave their heads at a specific time of the month, enhancing spiritual awareness and growth when done correctly and consciously. (Baloney?) This explanation prompted me to reflect on my own situation. Try it for yourself! Mistakenly shave your head on a full or new moon and get angry. You'll see! And if you're feeling adventurous, consider rubbing some all-natural progesterone cream on it, too.

Women are indeed different from men. (Who would have guessed?) Apparently, we have a bit more energy, particularly around that time of the month. You should really be careful when tapping into those energetic forces. Without a surge protector or a plan to balance yourself, it could be dangerous (she could be dangerous), or you might go insane, especially if you're spiritually inclined, Vasudev said. (Do you know any intense or wild bald women who shaved their heads, aside from those undergoing chemotherapy?)

Vasudev added that once certain energy pathways are activated in the body, it's advisable to grow the hair long and tie it up in a bun to protect the individual and help regulate the energy leaving the body. He explained that this lack of understanding was why many young teachers, sages, and others never reached the age of forty. (Hmm...that's interesting. See references.)

I paid close attention to this explanation due to my own near-death experience. Interestingly, my mentor, Ms. Juliette, gave specific attention to me, covering myself. She noticed that I was losing excess energy from my body. She also had a similar practice to many yogis, wearing her long hair styled in a bun on top of her head. (Yes, on top of her head, not the back.) This is a significant observation for me because many Western spiritual seekers often only recognize Eastern spiritual practices, gurus, and yogis, even though this wisdom is readily available in the West. Moreover, it was as local as the Fifth Avenue and Pleasant Street Community—*right here* in Gainesville!

As I chuckle, this might explain why my doctor kept asking if I had been snorting something. Deep down inside, he was suspicious; he knew I had done something since young people rarely come in with brain aneurysms. I was high, but it wasn't from snorting coke. (Speaking of high! With that fentanyl they gave me, I could see home movies of families from the 1970s playing on the wall in my hospital room. [giggles])

Be warned, rebellious ladies and queer ladies! Again, you can explore Eastern spiritual practices to gain a deeper understanding of this knowledge and how our life energy, referred to as Spirit, Prana, or Chi, functions. I only mention this because those of you who knew Ms. Juliette didn't write down your stories. No worries...there's still time.

For the record, to y'all holier-than-thou folks, yes, I drop the F-bomb sometimes. I don't relate to words as most people do, but I'll try not to do it in front of your *ch'rn*. (Oh my, I see a bunny trail coming!)

Speaking of F-bombing! One day, I dropped the F-bomb before my husband and kids, a habit I had picked up after moving to New Hampshire. I blame "his people." This man corrected me because he feared our youngest might pick it up, too. Of course, he would! Children only repeat what their parents say, right? He acted all high and mighty like he didn't drop F-bombs, too. "Not in front of the kids," he would say while asserting his "superiority." I had too many cognitive issues and didn't have time for his *bougie-ness* (that which is bougie).

During that time, I couldn't form a word or sentence to save my life. I even wore earplugs for about three years straight because everything sounded razor-sharp in my left ear, like someone was stabbing me in the head with an icepick. I looked at him with my angry-wife face and said, "You need to be more concerned about what's happening in my head than what's coming out of my mouth—*brotha*!"

Anyways, when I was transferred to the neuro and dementia floor for emergency brain surgery, my roommate, a hundred-year-old White woman, had a foul-ass mouth. Her daughter was so embarrassed—just like my husband. I said, "No worries, I can be a little foul, too." Then our good-looking neurosurgeon, Dr. Wow, walked into the room to wash my mouth out with soap. (Shoot, I could still see him with my one eye.)

He was so handsome with that charming Kennedy smile that would make any woman want to hold his hand and hear him say, "I can't guarantee that you will live to see tomorrow, and if you do, I can't promise a full recovery." It was like being in Heaven or Rishikesh! According to Dr. Wow, cussin' can be a sign of brain trauma. I knew I was right! My only wish was that my husband was in the room to hear the good news so I could be right one last time.

Scientists once believed that the primal or reptilian part of the brain (the downstairs brain you didn't know you had) lacked language. However, science has discovered that some of us can express a prehistoric F-bomb that makes everyone in the house or village know to leave you the fuck alone. It's like a caveman grunt that communicates a great deal with just one word, merely a sound. Who gives a shit what people think? We all drop F-bombs from time to time, yet we strive to meet some false standard that even the fundamentalists don't adhere to. Our egos enjoy the thought of being approved and accepted by others while despising the idea of being rejected. (No worries…I have self-control. I must act somewhat normal if I hope any of you will listen to me. I understand how the *B.S.* game operates.)

Anywho, back to my head and being a victim—and a survivor—beeyotch! You know, after my brain surgery, my husband was *38-hot* because not one of "his people" called to see if I lived…ever, lol. (Not even an email to wish me well.) Maybe they were saying *special* prayers for me. Honestly, I think he was mad at them because it was finally his turn to take the stage or for someone to acknowledge his existence. That's what being a survivor is about, right? (Oh my god, I almost died, everyone! Me!)

He was going to steal my story because it was a good one. Anyhow, I don't blame "his people." I wouldn't have called me either if they had known I would write about them one day. That aneurysm was supposed to be the jackpot, but it turned out to be worthless and a waste of time when you couldn't milk it for anything. "That poor man" had to take care of me for six months while I stared back at him with one eye, saying, "You almost killed me, *bro*! It's time for you to deal with those issues!" (It's time, husbands!)

Some of us seem happy that we almost died—like all of us aren't going to die one day. It creates a new identity, a new label. You can even get a bumper sticker that says, "I'm a survivor!" If anything, we are all survivors just by continuing to live each day despite our difficulties. However, when we're all survivors, it doesn't make identifying as one feel all that *special*. Even so, the ego loves to express itself through your stories of victimhood and survivorship. It makes you feel *special*—for a moment. I'm here to tell you that you are much more than a survivor story. Since you're still here with us, what are you doing? Who are you today? (Here's a song to encourage you to keep pushing forward: "I'm Still Standing" by Elton John.)

Today, I'm like a $190,000 Mercedes-Benz you can't insure. No life insurance will cover me, and most health insurance companies would drop me if it weren't for Obamacare. I'll survive, though!

Survivor Hugs,
—Sher! (The Common Snook)
Pause. Inhale. Exhale. Reflect.

P.S. When the doctors took me back to put me under, my son reported seeing something resembling a teardrop in my husband's eye. Probably just one eye and one tear, but we'll take it. I love and thank "that man" for putting up with me. We've been laughing together for over twenty years.

P.P.S. Some of y'all might think God saved me, but "Ain't no God coming down to do this work for us." Many people helped me that day. I thanked Dr. Wow for all those years of school to fix *my* head. Christ said, "You will do greater things than me." Christ was right! Dr. Wow outdid Jesus. Now, don't y'all *be trippin'*. Read the Bible and start doing great things. I hope Dr. Wow has BFFs and cool peeps in his life.

(Stop F-bombin' for 15 minutes a day; I promise it will transform your life!)

13. Love Who You Want

Love is a complex and often misunderstood word. (Ugh!) But we'll simplify it today.

Portland, Maine.

Disclosure Reminder…,

Spiritually speaking, if love is Consciousness (living connected to the Source of creation), and very few people behave as if they know Love, do "straight" or "gay" people love who they *want*, or do they love devouring, consuming, and controlling who they *want* to meet their needs? Not you, of course. Still, most of those "wonderful" relationships end up sounding something like this: "Blow Me (One Last Kiss)."

May we all connect with the Source of creation to genuinely love everyone without conditions. Presence can help us access this true Love so we can share it with our partners. Still, there's nothing quite like a dysfunctional relationship to trigger an awakening to the madness we mistakenly call love. *(Right, Babe?)* You know, the ones that you can't quite control, and that bring you varying levels of pain and disappointment. Or better yet, the ones you bestowed the badge of hatred were probably your most profound teachers and, ironically, the ones you learned to love. Not everyone earns that badge, you know. Some *suckers* you couldn't care less about, but for those who evoke the emotion of "hate," there's somethin' *special* about them…where songs like "Hell At Night," bring you joy with deep satisfaction. (How's that for a perspective on love?)

Learning from the phenomenon of love goes beyond physical relationships. Parents and siblings can also contribute to our understanding of this. The bond of true Love in physical relationships mirrors that in any other connection. You know, that's how powerful and universal Love is. Remember, Love has no opposites, and its joy doesn't rely on anything external, sexual, or physical. When we understand this, we can stop searching for this Love in others and access it ourselves. Love is to live connected to the Source within...not who you *want*.

In the meantime, sure, everyone should be with whom they *want* to be with or emotionally "love." It's only fair, right? Sometimes, I used to *want* a housewife, too, but I was blessed with a husband instead. Having someone to do your laundry and cook your meals must be lovely. (giggles)

Gotta-wink Hugs,
 —Sher! (The Common Snook)
Pause. Inhale. Exhale. Reflect.

P.S. Speaking of complicated love! I stopped routinely and emotionally telling my husband and sons, "I love you." I didn't want them to confuse love with empty words of habit. I've noticed that some of the *most unhealthiest* families use this phrase frequently, often as a psychological means to maintain their control. They used words to substitute for what didn't actually exist. Instead, I express my love by giving them my undivided attention. Those who can't grasp this truth will arrogantly defend themselves by saying, "I will *neva'* stop telling my family how much I love them," as if it earns them brownie points. Meanwhile, the little one looks confused and says, "But Mommy says she loves me," while holding conflicting beliefs.

P.P.S. I dedicate "All My Life" by K-Ci & JoJo to my dear husband.

(Sit in stillness with your eyes closed for 15 minutes a day; I promise it will transform your life!)

14. I Wouldn't Exactly Say I Like Them

I *hate* it when people complicate simple *stuff* unnecessarily.

Disclosure Reminder...,

To dislike or hate is an emotion. It's interesting that people act as if they don't experience these feelings. Instead, they manipulate language to deceive themselves. Phrases like "I dislike you passionately" are used to avoid the word "hate" and the judgment it carries. "Hate is a strong word," some say. *(Right, Yolanda?)* Certainly, there are different levels of dislike, but the reality is that it's merely an emotion—a reaction to an experience.

However, there is a difference between evil and hate. Racism, a mental construct, is often a manifestation of evil, right? The Holocaust was evil, right? Of course, there are many other examples of this kind of mental illness throughout humanity, particularly in American history, such as Mary Turner's story from Brooks County, Georgia, right? Unfortunately, evil becomes intertwined with the term "hate," preventing people from effectively processing these emotions within themselves. Some individuals "dislike" or "hate" how they've been treated by *Evil*, and they are made to feel that their emotions or reactions should not be processed or are equivalent to the evil they have faced. (It's wild how that works.)

I don't want to dig too deeply into this to avoid overcomplicating something that should be simple. I just want to say that this book invites you to explore your emotions without judgment. Unfortunately, when we shame or cancel people for disliking or hating someone—often for good reasons—we force them to suppress their feelings instead of confronting them. We make them play tricks on themselves. Again, saying, "I don't exactly hate them; I just don't really like them that much," is the same. They're grappling with religious condemnation.

The battle is tied to a religious belief about hate. Let's replace the word "hate" with something like "lima beans." Please don't try to swallow what you dislike; instead, observe and understand the pain or frustration it causes you. "On the other side of conflict, there's always gold! Never be afraid to face it head-on." Playing mind games to evade religious shame (control) is child's play.

In our society, language and religion compel us to suppress our feelings. Only after years of ~~oppression~~ (oops...wrong word, but it *kinda* works) are you permitted or justified to release and let them out. Your therapist might even urge you to scream and shout. *(Whassup, will.i.am and Britney—beeyotch!)* This results from a buildup, likely caused by societal or religious pressures that encourage you to swallow it. Clench your teeth and tell us how you really feel. (Oh my, butterfly!) But we can work with that. Inhale and exhale that toxicity. Repeat this a few times if necessary.

I hope I got you thinking because learning "to be," connecting with the Divine, can alleviate your pain or frustration without shame. However, hiding from it, denying it, dodging it, or rephrasing it is what separates you from ever experiencing Consciousness. Please come as you are. Your experience is valid! You are truly a wonderful person, and I'm sorry this world has caused you so much pain.

I love you,
—Sher! (The Common Snook)
Pause. Inhale. Exhale. Reflect.

P.S. I had a friend who almost killed her mother-in-law (MIL). (giggles) Like a good Christian, she swallowed the "lima beans," which can be dangerous. But after wrapping her hands around her MIL's neck, she realized she should have never swallowed those terrible beans for all those years, because she hadn't been digesting them properly. They were giving her violent gas.

P.P.S. Spoken in a dark, eerie voice that resembles a demon, "But what if my feelings are not rooted in pain?" Oh, okay...I suppose we can work with that, too. (See, some of these folks are dealing with *Evil* and not an emotional response that some call "hate.")

(Sit in stillness with your eyes closed for 15 minutes a day; I promise it will transform your life!)

15. I Was Indian, Specifically Gujarati

This sermon is a lovely short story about friendship.

Disclosure Reminder...,

When you become true friends, the notion of race should fade away as you begin to see your friends as yourself. However, if you continue to focus solely on "race," it's a clear sign that you're not truly connecting with your friends; instead, you're engaging with them from a mental perspective. You're not home, and this person is interacting with a robotic version of you.

One of my BFFs is, of course, from India, whom I met in Little India, NC. *(Whassup, Spicy Cinnamon!)* While driving to visit another friend I had met in the neighborhood—who is also Indian yet considered fair-skinned—she asked me if the other gal was North Indian. Her question was posed much like how an African American woman might express some reservations about attending a "country chic" barnyard party with hay bales, cowboy hats, and "Daisy Dukes" in the backwoods of Levy or Dixie County, Florida. (It's all in the face.) I laughed and said, "No, she's Telugu, from the Telangana region," which means she's South Indian. Then she challenged me because her fair complexion suggested a different story, and I replied, "I promise she's South Indian!" She never stopped to consider who she was asking. She spoke to me like I was one of her homegirls from India, as if to say, "Where is this 'redbone' from?"

On a different day, the same gal talked about a friend who wanted to borrow money to buy gifts for her family to take back to India. She said, "You know how it's good to bring presents back home." I looked at her and replied, "Yes," while giggling. Apparently, I was born in India.

Lastly, when I hang out with my *sistas,* the conversation is always a mix of Hindi and English or any other shared mother tongue, since each Indian state has its own language. The country has more than 120 languages and over 1,900 different mother tongues. (Holy cow!)

That day, my friends spoke a mix of English and Gujarati, which I could follow because there was plenty of English. I also understood enough Gujarati thanks to their body language, facial expressions, and intensity, especially when talkin' 'bout husbands and mothers-in-law. I also spoke the language of love and food, so I kept up with the conversation just fine. However, my friend wanted to know if I understood what was being said because the gossip was important. I assured her I was following along, and she responded sternly, "But did you understand in Gujarati?" She was dead serious. All I could do was laugh and say, "Yes," because I knew what they were discussing.

For the record, I don't speak Gujarati—except for the language of food: dhokla, thepla, khandvi, kadhi, and so on.

"Aww...that's sweet," I hear you say. I was feeling the same.

Dher saara pyaar (Lots of love),
—Sher! (The Common Snook)

Pause. Inhale. Exhale. Reflect.

P.S. Nothing makes me happier than when my friends stop by for curry leaves...with dhokla, of course.

P.P.S. Patel wants me to let America know he is fed up with ignorant-ass White and Black Americans telling him to go home. Patel said, "Indians were here first. Why don't *y'all* go home?"

P.P.P.S. Speaking of friendship! I have two grandma friends. One grew up in the Philippines, and the other is from India. They share no common language apart from love, yet they can be seen walking together almost daily and chatting in the garden. It's one of the most heartwarming sights to behold.

(Sit in stillness with your eyes closed for 15 minutes a day *[Roz 15 minutes apni aankh band kar ke bina hile baitho]*; I promise it will transform your life *[Ye karne se tumhari life badal jayegi]*!)

Section III: Lowering Your Defenses

In case you decided to skip the introduction and browse around, here's the **Disclosure Reminder**: Before diving in, I will say this: I'm simple. I love to laugh. Please don't confuse my humor with sarcasm; I always mean what I say. I test the limits. My words are plain. I often use "own" redundantly. I don't claim to know all the answers; my only intention is to be a vessel. Also, to connect with different experiences, I interchangeably use the terms "Consciousness," "Presence," "God," "Universe," "Source," "Divine," "Energy," "Christ/Krst," and "Light." Above all, reading my humor with a Southern accent is best. Enjoy!

Lake Winnisquam, Laconia, New Hampshire. Perhaps swimming with alligators in Lake Wauburg, Micanopy, Florida, as a child wasn't so bad after all. (TCS)

1. Everyone is Defining "Boundaries" Nowadays

*This may be my backyard, but it's one boundary I do not cross. Everybody thinks this is where my visiting alligators come from. But they're mistaken! They crawl out of the city's storm drain. I **be** watchin' 'em!*

Disclosure Reminder...,

If you've been to therapy lately or spent time with someone who has, you've likely heard something about boundaries. *Boundaries* have become a buzzword, much like *empowerment*. It sounds appealing, but what is all this talk about boundaries?

In a nutshell, boundaries are the rules that govern our lives. They represent what we will and won't tolerate and encompass how we respond when someone decides to cross the limits. Depending on your background or personal experiences, boundaries can be loose, moderate, or rigid.

There was a time when boundaries didn't need to be described or listed. They were simply part of being raised in a healthy family. However, many people find themselves in therapy or support groups where a therapist or leader suggests they have weak or nonexistent boundaries. This is often true for those who struggle to say "no" and those who have unfortunately endured experiences that should never have occurred. Such experiences can desensitize us to the risks or dangers of specific behaviors. For instance, I'm completely comfortable talking with people who are a bit eccentric or even *crazy* because they remind me of my family, and I often see them as reflections of myself. And it's okay to laugh. I will elaborate on the latter later.

103

I have seen and experienced a lot in my young years without anyone to confirm or deny the appropriateness of what I went through, even though I could clearly recognize the unhealthiness in others. I remember telling my husband that I wished he would investigate my life as thoroughly as I do his. I wanted someone to analyze my childhood and highlight some of the unusual aspects (craziness!) of my life. My husband looked up and said, "What, like being kidnapped by your father and living in Hawaii?" He was being a smartass. Yet, he ultimately shed light on a period of insanity in my family that I couldn't fully see because of a blind spot.

Some of you might be thinking, "Duh-uh!" But living in Hawaii and exploring while eating roadside kuawa (Hawaiian for guava) with my father was an incredible experience, or at least that's what I like to believe. (wink) However, my older siblings, who were school-age at the time, don't seem to share the same nostalgic memories as I do. I wonder what that's about. (giggles)

Now, with my husband's judgment of my family weighing on me, just as I "judge" his, I can finally view that situation through a different lens. Oh my, what my father did—taking my siblings and me across the Pacific for two years without my mother knowing where we were—was fucked up! (Forgive me; I can't think of a more fitting word.)

But here's what I think happened before my siblings and I abruptly left Gainesville for Hawaii, tossing our belongings into black trash bags. In an ego war, my mother likely challenged my father with something like, "Take 'em!" (giggles) And he, with a slightly bigger ego, called her bluff (or maybe she wasn't bluffing, lol). They were toying with our lives. She never imagined how far and how long he would take us or how it would impact us emotionally—for years! I'm sure it affected her, too, because she didn't know us for two years. I was no longer a baby when I returned home, even though my crib was still set up. This experience will always be a part of me. Unfortunately, it also means there's not much anyone can say to surprise me. Coming from such a unique family, I became desensitized to what was appropriate in life as early as three. That should never have happened. More to come.

Today, boundary building is becoming a standard practice because many of us come from *dysfunctional families* and encounter others from *dysfunctional families*. I'm not talkin' 'bout your average annoying friend or neighbor who helps build your character. I'm talkin' 'bout people who outright step on your toes and show no respect for your personal space. These are the contrary and passive-aggressive folks who "jab" you when you're not paying attention.

I had a relative visiting after my first son was born who had the nerve to open our bedroom door without knocking and ask if she could take the baby. I remember quickly covering myself with the blanket. My hair was a mess, and there was a good chance my engorged boobs were leaking all over the bed that morning—*a need for privacy* was putting it mildly. Still, she just stood there, asking if she could take the baby. I felt so violated that I almost threw a shoe at her (non-violently, of course). And this was just the beginning of this individual's strange, boundary-violating behaviors that would last for years.

She had me laying down the law with her and even accused me of having too many rules. *Was I bossy?* I thought certain boundaries were understood, such as knocking and waiting for a response before entering a private room or not opening my refrigerator without permission. (Oops, bunny trail!)

However, I realized I had made a good friend when a relatively new acquaintance checked my refrigerator for some sauce—probably pickled mango—before returning to the pot for seconds. This was fine with me because we had a sister-like bond from the start. Indian people often don't have the unhealthy formalities or rigid boundaries that can make forming friendships a slow and overly cautious process for Americans...and the Chinese, too. See, Americans and the Chinese share something in common.

Anyhow, that unbalanced relative would teach me a valuable lesson about boundary violators and reveal areas where I lacked the rules that should govern my life. Man, I was lacking because she walked all over me. I hated having to correct a grown-ass woman. I did not think it was my job, but she had no plans to stop violating me until I learned to put my foot down. She required the kind of stomp powerful enough to crack the earth and make the heavens tremble. It was boot camp for me!

She taught me never to expect boundaries to be understood and that no one will treat you the way you want to be treated unless you communicate your needs. After encountering her, I thought, *The hell with the Golden Rule! Please, don't treat me the way you want to be treated.* Even so, it's your responsibility to tell others what you like and don't like, even if some may be offended, while others seem to grasp this naturally without words.

After surviving boot camp, I realized that this seven-year *ass-whoopin'* came from someone with a personality disorder. Why didn't anyone tell me she wasn't just a normal, difficult person? Nonetheless, she trained me well. She helped me become alert and present, stepping on my toes to keep me on my toes. We only get what we need in life, right?

Looking around, I can see that many of you have encountered similar personalities or lack alertness. I recommend living and learning so you don't require a repeat lesson.

On the flip side, these same personalities are now using the lessons that your therapists might have taught you or those you picked up from a self-help empowerment book to manipulate you. This is why boundary-setting isn't as great as it's cracked up to be. Boundaries have turned into tools for controlling others. If we all establish rigid boundaries, what is left of the idea of community?

A "good friend" once surprised me with this new pop psychology point of view on setting boundaries, which seemed to have a one-size-fits-all approach when I asked for a favor that I would have gladly done for her. For a moment, I thought she might decline my request (perceptiveness), but I decided to ask *anyways* because friendship is supposed to be a two-way street. I had already given so much; it was time to see where I stood and to test the strength of the relationship.

As expected, she immediately started to backpedal. (We know our friends' true nature without asking.) When I suggested she could come through for me, she hit me hard with a boundary. She was calling the shots, and it was a take-it-or-leave-it kind of boundary, letting me know where I stood.

Certainly, I accepted her position. *But did I not have rights in this friendship, too?* This type of boundary setting felt controlling and one-sided. I realized she created rigid boundaries with everyone by not having healthy boundaries for so long, allowing herself to be violated. Unfortunately, this also led to her denying her ethical responsibility to friendship.

However, I have some good news! I have tips for individuals with weak or rigid boundaries that stem from their upbringing. Sure, spend 15 minutes a day in stillness, but this process involves slowing down and connecting with your body. When you do this, you will no longer need to build unnecessary walls to protect yourself or your ego. You must learn to make decisions confidently within your own skin without compromising your comfort.

Chances are, you're building boundaries because you tend to let people violate you. After all, you're not home in a sense. You won't have to leave situations feeling violated when you actively connect to your body. You can process everything right then and there and ask how you feel. Pause, respond, and move on.

Most people are okay with the outcome if they can express themselves or advocate for their needs. The frustration driving the need for "Jersey walls" and concrete boundaries arises from not being home and missing out on life as it unfolds before you. Most boundary-building stems from the fact that you are not home (present) to create space for yourself.

Building the fortress is only necessary when dealing with personality disorders or those who are missing a few screws. You know, the ones who will dominate the conversation without hearing a word you say. Walls may seem appealing, but that's the opposite of liberation. Instead of setting boundaries, I suggest being present and focusing on giving space.

Here's the final story: an unhoused young man asking for money—whom most would have avoided (so-called healthy boundaries)—came alive when I told him I didn't have any money but asked how he was doing and where he was from. I saw myself in him.

The articulate young man mentioned that he was from Miami and had relocated to Gainesville a decade ago. I could tell he was reflecting on the passage of time. Strangely, he remarked, "I don't know what happened," as if justifying himself to his mother. "I just got stuck. I can't believe I've been living on the streets for that long."

I told him that being stuck can feel like forever, and then one day, you wake up. The boy in him then said to the mother in me, "Some people are so mean out here." He thanked me for the conversation, and the light turned green as I drove off to Whole Foods, filled with empathy. His vulnerability and humanity touched me.

While constructing your fortress, be cautious not to entirely close yourself off from real people (giggles), as this can become a type of control masquerading as healthy boundaries. You don't require more boundaries when you possess Presence and awareness. For some individuals, their being will suggest continuing to move forward; for others, it will say to give them room "to be." If you permit this, those are all the boundaries you need.

Boundless Hugs,
—Sher! (The Common Snook)
Pause. Inhale. Exhale. Reflect.

(Sit in stillness with your eyes closed for 15 minutes a day; I promise it will transform your life!)

107

2. Choked by the Bra

Imagine eating a big meal and then wrapping a belt around your rib cage. It would be terrible! However, many women are accustomed to being constricted in this way.

Disclosure Reminder...,

A friend looked at me a few years ago and said, "Wow, you really are free!" I could tell what she was implying, and yes, I was—dammit!

We live in a world where women still dress for men. We'll know women have been liberated when we stop dressing for them, and they stop dressing us. You ain't fooling anyone when you say, "I wear these back-breaking pole-dancing high heels for myself." Who wants to deal with back pain? Well, if you're selling real estate, then I understand. Anyhow, I was unaware of how much men ruled my life and wardrobe.

As you may know from a previous sermon, I underwent a significant surgery that, had I skipped it, I wouldn't be talking to you today. Well, if you know anything about surgery, the body goes buck-wild afterward. My body said, "Nope, no more bras," and every time I put one on, it choked the shit out of me. Going bra-free wasn't about making a statement; it was about avoiding severe pain and discomfort.

Similar to going natural with my hair back in the day, I didn't know what to do with these boobs. I couldn't wear a bra anymore, but how was I supposed to leave the house? It was hard enough to find clothes, let alone get past women who wouldn't frown at me. You know, *we women* can be worse than men with the "shame factor." At least men smile when they see boobs.

Interestingly, I came across a group of researchers who studied bra-free women. They offered suggestions on clothing styles and patterns that helped women feel more comfortable in this judgmental, male-dominated world. I decided to participate in their study. According to their research, they found that women who were bra-free had no greater chance of breast cancer than men. (Well, I'll be damned!) They believe that bras restrict the flow of the lymphatic system, which helps rid the body of toxins and germs, including cancer cells and infections, and that bras trap these cells in the breasts. (I love *me* some simple science.)

Did you know that breasts are meant to move? Movement helps ensure proper circulation. And you know what happens when water doesn't move, right? Need I say more?

Anyhow, the research team checked in with me over the years with some of the strangest questions. One was, "Do you like your new breasts?" I told the person interviewing me, "I've never had a relationship with my boobs; I'm sorry, I can't relate to that question." That evening, I looked in the mirror and noticed they were standing up just a little higher than they had previously drooped. I said, "Sure, I do like my new boobs."

I emailed the team back and apologized for the difficulty and for not noticing my progress. I started to notice that my breasts were becoming lighter, and I could now do things I once couldn't do without a bra. In fact, I caught myself running across the yard one day like a five-year-old. The muscles in my back and chest that had never developed were beginning to carry their weight. I even noticed that my digestion improved, and I experienced no more reflux. Once that happened, there was no turning back.

First, it was medically necessary, but today I say, "Screw you if you can't handle seeing nipples." *My life* is not about you. (Hmm…I have a feeling the future is bright for boobs that move. We also need fashion designers like you to create comfortable clothing that respects and honors our natural bodies, emphasizing color, fabric, and style rather than figure.)

Cheers to no-shoulder grooves,
—Sher! (The Common Snook)
Pause. Inhale. Exhale. Reflect.

P.S. Tissues or breast pads work great to catch the unexpected under-bust sweat in the summer. I *actually* use nursing pads. Just cut or fold them in half and gently place them under your breasts. Lift and stick. (No, not the sticky ones.) If your boobs are at least a size C, your "girls" should be big enough to hold the pads in place. Additionally, applying a little lotion or moisture can also help. I know this because I live in humid Florida.

P.P.S. Hmm…have any of y'all ever heard of breast cancer prevention? Oh…nobody?

(Sit in stillness with your eyes closed for 15 minutes a day; I promise it will transform your life!)

3. As-salamu Alaykum—a COVID Experience

Disclosure Reminder…,

In January 2022, my neighbors across the street, both doctors with unpredictable schedules, completely disappeared without a trace. No one was coming or going from their house. However, I would see DoorDash or a grocery service drop off items at the door every few days, so I knew someone was home. I realized it must be the coronavirus because there was no activity.

I texted my friend to check-in. I remember thinking that if I were sick with three children and a husband, all I would want was a home-cooked meal. She confirmed it was COVID, Omicron, which was an ass-kicker. I told her I would send dinner, and of course, she said I didn't have to, perhaps because we had only been friends for a few months. But the truth was, I did have to…because we were responsible for each other, whether we accepted that responsibility or not. We should love our neighbors as ourselves.

It was time for me to overcome my insecurity about cooking South Asian food for Indian folks. My neighbor, as I mentioned, is a physician with a bunch of kids and was raised in the U.S. She didn't have time to "throw down" (a Southern phrase meaning to make excellent food) like a traditional Indian woman. So, I thought perhaps I could fool her palate and that she and the kids wouldn't find my food bland. I made them chana masala from scratch, served with basmati rice, a delightful ginger broccoli and carrot side dish, and samosas from the Indian store. I set the dinner by the door and ran for my life.

Later that evening, I received a text from my neighbor that was the best compliment ever. She said it was so good and "tasted legit," like it was from India. She even sent a picture to her mother-in-law, who was concerned about all five of them being sick at the same time. I felt fantastic! I didn't have a medical degree, but I could whip up a concoction better than any pharmacy or recommendation from Dr. Fauci. Food is medicine!

Fast-forward to July 2022. I registered my youngest for the Santa Fe College for Kids program and instructed him to wear a mask since COVID-19 had spiked again. The situation was so bad that an article in the newspaper reported that a local program, Camp Crystal, had to shut down for the rest of the summer that same week.

To my dismay, I picked him up from camp each day, only to find his mask dangling from one ear. I'm sure you can imagine where this story is headed, and within a week, he was out sick. I didn't think the virus could affect a youngster so severely, but he displayed every symptom on the list. I felt terrible for him, but he had been warned. However, I must admit, I was feeling my German roots as schadenfreude welled up in my eyes. (Oh my, I can hear the bitching now. They say, "What kind of mother says that!?"). *Perhaps next time, he'll listen to me.* Yet, this pleasure I found in his suffering didn't last long, for soon I was next, as schadenfreude filled his eyes. (They get their humor from their father.) The coronavirus viciously ripped through our house like the plague, taking us out one by one in just a few days.

My husband had us all quarantined in different parts of the house. I was confined to the room I called "The Room Where Nothing Moved." I would have been thrilled to see a fly. It was awful because my condition remained the same for about four days straight. Thankfully, my husband finally succumbed to the virus so he could stop avoiding me, as I was beginning to go insane in "The Room Where Nothing Moved." Luckily, he experienced a mild case (yep, he was the only one who got the booster) and, unfortunately, had to play "nurse" for all his naughty patients.

At the end of the week, I received a text from my neighbor across the street saying, "Where are you? We haven't seen you in a while," whose mother-in-law was visiting from India. I explained that we were all sick with COVID, and within a few hours, authentic Indian food appeared on the front porch. My husband, who had been holding it down for over a week, was nearly brought to tears (probably just one tear) because he, too, was sick but couldn't catch a break.

We devoured the dahl, made with fresh vegetables, herbs, and spices, served with flawless, perfectly round chapatis and rice with a Muslim flair. I could feel my body rising from the grave, expressing gratitude. The food was medicine for my soul, even though I still couldn't get out of bed. The next day, dinner showed up—once again! I was blown away! Allah, which means God in Arabic, was watching over me. *Shukriyaa, thank you, Auntie!*

Not in a million years did I imagine that cooking a simple meal for my neighbors would become my lifeline, coming all the way from Hyderabad, India, to help nurture my family back to health. The story almost felt unreal; it was as if I were making it up. It was so beautiful and showed me how far Love can travel. The Quran says to love your brother as yourself (*an yuhibba li-akhî-hi*). (Hmm...does that mean sister, too?)

As-salamu Alaykum (Peace be with you),
— Sher! (The Common Snook)

Pause. Inhale. Exhale. Reflect. 🕉

4. What are Your Pronouns—Man?

This sermon here is dedicated to those on the far right and left who hold the "I'm right" belief. As you read, you may begin to feel assured that I'm on your side, but I assure you—I'm not.

Disclosure Reminder...,

In 2020, I was accepted into a well-regarded Master of Social Work (MSW) program. My goal was to focus on spirituality in social work and empower individuals to help themselves through non-religious spiritual education (like this book, my dissertation).

At first, I struggled to determine whether the school was a good fit for me and whether social work was the right path to develop and deliver my program. Additionally, I was unaware of the culture I was entering. I believed this was a safe environment dedicated to training a diverse group of social workers.

My first class was an introductory course on the history of social work and the programs developed to "promote the social well-being of all Americans." The idea was great, but I second-guessed the program after the first few chapters. Unfortunately, I felt as though I was being trained to embrace government social services, as we covered a wide range of topics, from poverty to Temporary Assistance for Needy Families (TANF) and even Social Security. Even though these services are necessary, and I support the idea of a universal basic income (UBI), this wasn't exactly my area of interest.

I also found the standards by which most Americans assess poverty in comparison to wealth and poverty in other countries to be conflicting. It was disturbing to think that our nation's greed for more possessions would set a baseline for what the average person felt entitled to or needed to live a simple and comfortable life. For instance, my husband and I often debate whether air conditioning is a necessity (giggles); I remind him that I attended school in Alachua County, Florida, when the classrooms only had ceiling fans. Many of these ideas that bring us comfort left me conflicted. Clearly, my heart did not align with a career in social work.

My experience as a case manager at Meridian Behavioral Healthcare in Gainesville left me scarred; I felt that social work provided only temporary solutions to chronic problems. I was saddened and discouraged as I turned the pages in my textbook, unsure if I could stomach much more. I quickly emailed my professor, worried that the program might not be right for me. Nevertheless, she believed my vision of helping people help themselves still aligned with the program and encouraged me to keep going because *they had more surprises in store for me.*

Well, things became real, *really fast,* when I was assigned an "Introduce Yourself" Flipgrid project as a type of online communication. (I felt like an eighty-year-old who had just learned how to use a smartphone.) I had to cover five main points in my introduction, and one caught me off guard, perhaps because of my age: "What are your pronouns?" they asked. This made me think about this new concept, and I wasn't sure how I felt about it. I remember reflecting on the issues that matter to me and my experiences with "transgender" children and *Friends* who had transitioned. With that in mind, I couldn't find common ground with any of the perspectives being presented, and I was surprised that they didn't give me an option. (We must understand how programming works or risk being programmed.)

The school's approach reminded me a lot of how religion, or even White dominance, imposes its views without considering that others might think differently. *I had seen this shit before,* I thought. I also realized that by not conforming, I would be singled out from the program's start, which seemed to suggest that "This is how we social workers perceive the world." There was no room for another perspective.

I didn't come this far to drink the Kool-Aid just because someone passed me the cup, so I chose not to take a position. With over thirty people in this online class, no one dared to stand by their views. Or maybe I was the only oddball, which is also quite possible.

It felt like they were all being initiated into the club of "I'm welcoming and on the right side of history." They seemed proud to display their allegiance, which appeared more about constructing their own sense of self-worth—a message saying, "If I am this, then I am definitely not one of the ignorant haters." Who wouldn't want to join the club when not taking a stand or agreeing with their stance faced so much more judgment? "Americans tend to lean toward political correctness and likability and seldom their true feelings" (unknown source, maybe NPR).

While introducing myself, I explained that I hadn't jumped on the pronoun bandwagon. I mentioned that I was still here, addressing this notion called "race," and I couldn't take on every new movement. I then added that perhaps in the future, I might feel differently. That...did...not...go...well, and I was marked before I ever got my feet wet in the program.

The situation was extremely awkward because I was isolated from everyone. This was a strategic maneuver, like military encirclement. They got me! "You're either for us or against us," but that wasn't true. I wasn't a religious conservative, hater, or bigot. I just had a different perspective (dammit!) based on my experiences. If anything, I am for the people, from those who wave colorful Confederate flags as a form of inexpensive home security to the man who believes he's a woman and insists you embrace and affirm him as such. (Ladies, forgive me for focusing on these men today.) In fact, I love them both equally.

Interestingly, the experience with my class made me curious about the types of people who pursue an MSW, as there appears to be an underlying core belief. I hope the world remembers that our diversity of thought helps us grow and thrive. *(Whassup, Colonel Jim!)* To my surprise, the test of the pronouns would continue to follow me personally.

Once, I encouraged a *Friend* with a transgender teenager to welcome a *Friend* like me who doesn't share the same views. When we all think alike, we risk becoming a stagnant collective and, at times, even collectively insane. Sadly, because my thoughts didn't align with hers, she boldly accused me of violence, encountering once again the mentality of "You're either for us or against us," which I believe is violence—dammit! I remember just wanting to hang my head like a sad puppy and say, "Please let me be. I don't mean any harm and don't plan to take a position anytime soon." (Hmm...I'm starting to see a pattern of certain types of parents accusing me of violence.)

To make matters worse, have you noticed that "People of Color" are often made to feel they can't express their own opinions? This stems from the fact that the entire conversation about equality seems to rest on the shoulders of those still fighting for fundamental human rights—such as the right to walk down the street.

I'm sure many "People of Color" hold diverse perspectives because, of course, we are not a monolithic group. Unfortunately, many remain silent due to the severe backlash and tight muzzle. This muzzle, in a sense, has also been placed over the mouths of numerous women's rights advocates who have worked tirelessly to create safe spaces for women and are now being silenced if they express differing views. You can't be a "Person of Color" or a women's rights advocate and hold your own opinions without the risk of being labeled a "hater." The table is now being turned against the very individuals the Civil Rights Movement once represented.

114

What's the real issue?

One way to dismantle the systems or social constructs that support inequality is to first address the notion of race and eliminate the antichrist forever. After that, we should tackle false or toxic masculinity. No worries…I'm not a "feminist." (You can call me "conscious and reasonable.") I am equally interested in the liberation of both men and women. In fact, men today need liberation just as much, if not more, than women. (Uh-oh, the progressive White women are now looking at me crazy as they often do whenever I speak on male liberation.)

I value freedom of speech and welcome diverse perspectives. Unfortunately, many people live confidently, believing their perspective is the only correct one, leaving no room for growth. Throughout history, many groups have thought they were collectively right, yet still so wrong, as demonstrated by the Jim Crow laws in this country.

When it comes to the *sexual buffet* we see today, my feelings run deep. They are deeply rooted in how male dominance and other forms of "superiority" and control have gone unchecked for centuries, dictating who we are and how we should behave. Many fail to see that humanity is simply self-correcting to end this nonsense. It's just that the movie isn't playing out the way most would have imagined. I accept everything we witness today because our species is creative and powerful, and those who struggle for acceptance are, interestingly, the ones who are closest to awakening.

Two Scenarios for You to Consider

In one scenario, there's a shortage of about two million African American men, primarily due to racism linked to poverty due to racism. These numbers are staggering! Do "Women of Color," who've had to navigate multiple gender roles in life, who are psychologically branded and told that they are not beautiful or feminine, not have the right to a family, a dual income, and companionship?

China experienced a similar hiccup with an imbalanced male-to-female ratio after thirty years of aborting or sending their baby girls to be raised abroad, all due to an ideology valuing sons over daughters. Humanity will self-correct this kind of injustice. The outcomes are remarkable, as they will upset many people who fail to consider how the past influences the present and how trauma can persist for generations, often referred to as karma. Humanity will capture our attention in one way or another. (Stay tuned for my upcoming sermon on why "the N-word" persists today.)

The Once Beautiful World Created by Men

Please take a moment to consider the pressure this world places on men to suppress their feminine nature. Coupled with testosterone and feminine energy, men are some of the most remarkable artists and creators that *we women* will never be able to reach, regardless of how some may wish to believe we are the same. (Please, don't flip out. Is it not okay to say something nice about men?)

Who do you think built all the glorious cathedrals in the Middle Ages? Strong-ass men with enough testosterone who had the balls to "hang upside down" to create paintings like Michelangelo's in the Sistine Chapel. These men also carved intricate stonework, creating beautiful spaces where everyone could connect with the Divine. Moreover, these artists possessed a good balance of masculine and feminine energy flowing through their bodies, blessing us with such a breathtakingly beautiful world. These were true homemakers. No worries, ladies; childbirth will always have us coming in first place.

Today, visit any new development in Gainesville, Florida, from the sterile Celebration Point complex, featuring retail stores and housing in a live-work-play environment, to the typical speculative home community, where developers have recklessly removed all the trees to maximize profits. You'll witness the consequences of suppressing feminine qualities in men in favor of ultra-masculinity and its cousin, Greed. Life gets ugly!

Please don't draw conclusions or form beliefs based on anything I've said. It's just a teaser meant to encourage some to stand in the middle and be okay with not choosing a side or claiming to be right. This flexibility is known as Love.

Regardless, it doesn't matter if someone agrees with you about whether picking your nose is acceptable. What truly matters is respecting each other's views without resorting to name-calling or imposing our own agenda on others. America has already employed that tactic. The world needs individuals who are unwilling to conform and can view this world through a lens of historical understanding and acceptance. It's called Love.

I hear some of you shouting into this book, "Policies matter!" And I commend your hard work. Still, only awareness can transform human behavior. That said, I can't deny my experiences or observations, regardless of what the far right or left may believe. *(No worries, King; I, too, subscribe to the "social gospel.")*

Hugs from the middle,

—Sher! (The Common Snook)
Pause. Inhale. Exhale. Reflect.

P.S. Since *we talkin' 'bout* pronouns, femininity, and gender rebellion, have y'all noticed that the White woman's obsession with thinness resembles gender dysphoria? (giggles) For instance, discomfort or distress with female curves and cellulite could be seen as gender dysphoria, right? This obsession favors masculine features or a thin, boyish look, setting them apart from the average woman as a symbol of "supremacy," which is exhausting for these women and psychologically harmful to those who don't measure up. *(Uh-oh, skinny liberals, you didn't know? Hush, I don't want to hear your health nut argument.)* I know I'm not the only one who has observed this; study the history of American fashion or look at the average runway model ("sexy" dudes, causing Matisse to snap his pencils). *Anyways,* I studied fashion and art at SFCC in the late 1990s, so I can speak on this.

P.P.S. Speaking of those who struggle for acceptance! An HIV diagnosis has left many feeling ashamed, as if HIV defines who they are. However, HIV can catalyze awakening because it compels you to rethink or reconsider the concept of identity, shifting your perspective.

If someone can avoid making HIV their identity and overcome the mental anguish of shame—while consistently taking their medication—they will likely naturally separate themselves from identifying with their body, recognizing that it does not define them. "This is not who I am." (Those who struggle with obesity or any other health condition may also have a similar awakening.) This realization is powerful because it helps them see life for what it truly is, fostering a connection with the Divine—Consciousness. (Hey, *anybody* strugglin' with being labeled a felon for life? This is for you, too.)

Many may have experienced this reality, but the mind can interfere and pull you back into identifying with the virus or disease. (*You've seen the door! Even if just for a moment.* Some of you know what I'm talking about.) For many, what felt like the end of the world could be the beginning of an awakened life. (Here's a song for those rising above HIV and AIDS: I wish you "Good Times" with this freedom.)

(Sit in stillness with your eyes closed for 15 minutes a day; I promise it will transform your life!)

5. Florida's Abortion Laws are "Tight"

Disclosure Reminder...,

Now, don't be confused, "tight" does not mean cool. As the laws continue to change around abortion rights, I gladly welcome something new until we can vote for something different. I believe it's time for a new conversation. These days, you can't even discuss abstinence because sex is for everyone.

Have you been to the mall lately? You should see all the sex toys they have for children...I mean, adults in the mall retail store, Spencer's. I felt like an old woman on the verge of a heart attack while walking through that store with my son. There were penises everywhere! The right to sex is now on par with the right to fresh water and air. You need to get some; otherwise, you might not survive.

What the hell happened to humanity? (Hmm...never mind, the ancient Greeks remind me that it has always been this way.) As I tell my son, folks must be bored because there are far more incredible experiences than sex. You need to wake up, "woke generation." I'd choose a pint of Häagen-Dazs *Rum Raisin* ice cream any day. "I'm sorry, Honey; I'm busy."

I don't understand why teenagers would want to mess around with that five-minute fire that could have them serving a twenty-year sentence. Someone isn't teaching these kids ratios because five minutes to twenty years doesn't make a damn bit of sense. Most high school students are smart enough to recognize that ratio and say, "Hell no!" But nobody can teach that kind of practical math because this state's economy relies on some of you living in poverty. After all, if you received a good education and put sex on hold, you might change this world.

Children need to know they are more than a penis or a vagina. It's just an organ, like the tongue, to which pleasure has been attached because nobody in their right mind would have sex. The key phrase is "right mind." It's *actually* quite gross if you think about it. Nobody would do it. Nobody! (giggles) And humanity would cease to exist. So, we are being used to keep society alive. It's time to smarten up—y'all.

We also face population and resource issues. You can't even buy an affordable house these days because people have been having too much sex. You ain't sick of high rental rates? This is simple economics—supply and demand. And those who are concerned about global warming should be the first advocates to stop having sex. In any case, it's a quick solution to a terrible problem. You really don't need to have sex unless you are trying to create a monster race or religion that dominates the world, and your focus is on recruits born into the fold or faith to keep the numbers high. (India, did I hear you say something…I mean, the Bharatiya Janata Party [BJP]? Hmm…if smart folks stop reproducing, what will we be left with?)

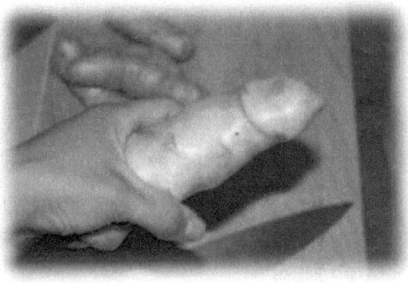

I needed a picture to keep you engaged. This "fingerling" arrived in my CSA box from my cherished Brookford Farm in Canterbury, New Hampshire. What a peculiar name for a dictator…I mean, a potato. I bet I could have sold it for at least twenty bucks.

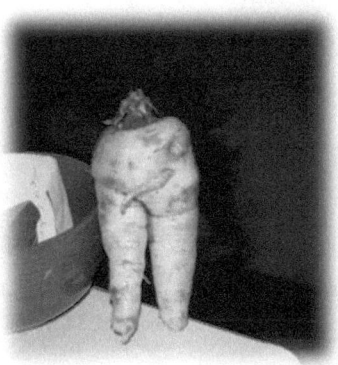

Uh-oh, Principal Parsnip (or replace with your favorite principal's name) forgot her pants and has a li'l head like some of y'all. (As you can see, I used to teach middle school.)

Anyhow, some may ask, what am I if I'm not a penis or a vagina? I'm glad you asked. You're also not a heart or a liver, either. Unfortunately, body obsession can sometimes deceive us and become a central part of our lives.

However, we can learn from cultures that don't let sex dominate them. They focus on developing themselves instead. You know, we are all mini-biological machines that can be trained and programmed to accomplish amazing things. That's why many Indian children excel academically in school. Their parents view them as an investment and understand that a good education will yield the

119

greatest return. They say, "Don't worry about sex; I'll find you someone to marry and have fun with just as soon as you're finished developing yourself." I admire Indian parents; they don't mess around with their 401(k).

I hope to assist young people in moving beyond "sexuality" as an identity, or at least in establishing that it is not their primary identity. Certainly, there are more extraordinary accomplishments than a five-minute sexual encounter. (Can I get an "Amen!"? said with a hint of hesitation.) Or is that the extent of your abilities? (Aww...boner-shrinker.)

When "sexuality" latches on like a parasite, we begin to generate all sorts of ideas, which is okay because embracing the absurd helps us recognize other unchecked forms of insanity. Sometimes, you must flow with it. All things work together for the glory of God, right?

Until then, keep having unnecessary sex in the Sunshine State. But I already sense that some young people will start considering a different perspective. You're smarter than they think. You just needed to hear something that made sense. Don't worry; sex won't go stale if you wait a couple of years. Ask your parents! By the way, young ladies, you might find it more enjoyable with a committed partner rather than in the bushes or the janitor's closet at school. Again, ask your parents.

Smart Hugs,
 —Sher! (The Common Snook)
Pause. Inhale. Exhale. Reflect.

P.S. If you weren't feeling this sermon, turn the page, and I'll take another stab at it.

(Sit in stillness with your eyes closed for 15 minutes a day; I promise it will transform your life!)

6. The Sex Secrets of Virgins

To all the gods in the world, "Why have you forsaken me?" I don't want to be the one to share this sermon…but I will…if I must.

Disclosure Reminder…,

First, I apologize to young people, full of stimulating hormones, who want to connect physically to express this hormonal surge of life we mistakenly call love. It's tough being on sex steroids with half a brain, and I don't mean that to be rude. The brain is still developing during puberty.

I'm sorry that we live in a world that contradicts your natural development. In high school, many students had to wake up before sunrise, having just fallen asleep shortly after midnight. Florida has finally passed a bill allowing these wonderful teens to sleep in a little longer, but it's still not enough.

You fall in love at the sight of a young man or woman, regardless of their material possessions or status. (That's romantic!) You should be getting ready to marry the love of your life and indulge in as much sex as your young heart desires. Instead, some fools structured the Western world in opposition to life.

We don't have trades in high school, so you graduate with no skills, which forces you to put life on hold until you acquire enough post-secondary skills or education to get a job. By then, you might need Viagra, or your eggs could be too old to conceive. If I had time to explore this thought, I'm sure it would lead to capitalism and man's greed for more, which fueled slavery in America. So, why wouldn't it also fuel your enslavement to the system? Our society needs you to join "the rat race," requiring you to put your natural desires on hold. However, if you can't resist the force of nature without your parents beating or shaming you, I may have some valuable advice. Grab the popcorn and hold onto your seats.

I was reading an article in a well-known health journal that examined sexual preferences among various races and ethnic groups of sexually active teens. The findings were eye-opening. The average age of first sexual encounter was still around sixteen, regardless of religious or racial background. However, certain groups still had higher rates of pregnancy and sexually transmitted diseases (STDs). Some might assume this was due to access to healthcare, such as birth control, but surprisingly, it wasn't.

First of all, Asian and Muslim American teens weren't messing around with five-minute sex because they did the math or feared their parents; therefore, the sample size wasn't large enough to yield meaningful contributions to the research project. Kudos to Asian and Muslim teens, and great job, Asian and Muslim parents, for their effective use of fear! Let's hope that didn't involve a childhood of beatings.

Regardless, the Asian and Muslim teens who are sexually active yet feel "invisible" due to the survey results should view their "invisibility" as a blessing. Isn't the goal to avoid getting caught? If the statistics were higher, Asian and Muslim parents might uncover your sex secrets.

But the rest were getting it on equally with no shame; however, the rates of pregnancy and STD transmission were higher among Black and Latino teens. Again, it wasn't due to a lack of resources or access to healthcare. *So there*, you sex-for-all advocates.

"So, what was the secret?" you ask. Well, it all came down to penetration—no pun intended! (Hmm…perhaps I'm the only one who can make out that pun.) Basically, how do you like it? Of the hundred or so teens surveyed, Latino and Black adolescents were less likely to engage in oral or alternative forms of sex.

Listen up, Black and Brown teens! White kids have found a way to technically be virgins when they get married and fool their parents. Yep, it's brilliant! "Minorities," let's say it together: "Penetration equals causation!" Yep, sometimes it causes pregnancy and STDs. (I know "STD" is outdated. *What do y'all call it these days?* Oh, okay, sexually transmitted infections (STIs). That does sound a little less complicated.)

Young ladies, don't allow that old man or young man to penetrate you. Tell the old nasty man to go home to his momma and tell that good-looking, youthful young man with all those muscles that you can't resist, "It's time to go downtown" because "Penetration equals causation!"

Young men, I apologize. My mind has overtaken me, and the Divine's channeling has been interrupted. I can't stop laughing and doubt I can write another description just for you. Please forgive me. However, I'm sure you don't need my help with creativity. Just remember, "Penetration equals causation!" Let me say it to you directly: Your penetration is causing problems.

The survey also said that "minority" women had a stigma around oral sex but were perfectly okay gambling with an STI-infected penis. (Well, that was my translation. Sorry about that.) However, that doesn't make any sense to me. With unprotected oral sex, there is a significantly lower risk of STI transmission and no chance of pregnancy, of course. Now, don't get me wrong; I'm not advocating for either (oral or unprotected sex). Still, it seems to me that the teens engaging in oral sex were not using protection (similar to lesbians), hence the need to report low levels of STI transmission. Who knows? Use protection either way because, you know, they say human papillomavirus (HPV) can lead to throat cancer. See, that's your answer! And I imagine stores like Spencer's might sell the hundred-pack mint and vanilla-flavored dental dams. (Oh God, help me with this sermon.)

The moral of the story is that White kids have figured it out. Don't be confused. I'm not talkin' 'bout the Mormon kids who have concluded that penetration without movement doesn't technically count as an act of sex. Still, last I checked, that method without movement can still lead to STIs and pregnancy because "Penetration equals causation!" You got it!

I can only imagine it must be *pretty explosive*. You might even have to hose the couple down like you do when two dogs of varying genitalia sizes get stuck together. If you have never witnessed this, it's truly a sight to behold, particularly as I did at the age of twelve. "Penetration equals causation!" And I was responsible for doing the "hosing."

Returning to my point, White kids are having just as much sex and just as much youthful fun without all the *causation* and religious *condemnation*. Good job, White kids!

In my last sermon, I encouraged some of you to do the math around sex. A five-minute pleasure can be expensive, which many "minorities" and underserved communities cannot afford to mess around with if they wish to provide themselves and their children with a better chance at a slightly more comfortable life. Essentially, that's all it boils down to—comfort.

You might say, "To hell with future comfort; I'm choosing pleasure today!" And you're not wrong for doing that. Just remember, "Penetration equals causation!" Most Americans collectively consume enough food to feed a starving nation. Pursuing pleasure today is no different than going back for an extra piece of cheesecake. It's all good! (Phew, I'm done!)

Secret Hugs,
  —Sher! (The Common Snook)
            Pause. Inhale. Exhale. Reflect.

P.S. Many of the rappers that these teens admire make it clear they prefer to "stick it" rather than "lick it." However, perhaps one of the more talented ones could come up with a chant to help these *ch'rn* "skip it"…because I'm sure they know by now that "penetration equals causation," along with baby-mommas, back child support, and so on.

Hey, maybe that old dude who was jammin' on NPR Music Tiny Desk last year could come up with a chant for "penetration equals causation," similar to the famous beat of "Back That Azz Up" by Juvenile. And umm…maybe the other old dude who resembled Mannie Fresh could give the *ch'rn* some ideas on where to put the dipstick instead. They'll listen to these old dudes because they were on NPR. Let me see *whatcha* got!

P.P.S. My friend Ms. Juliette used to warn young people not to share clothing because it retains the owner's energy for a loooong time and could become *mixed up* with their own energy. Hmm…I wonder if lots of unnecessary sex poses the same risk. (giggles)

P.P.P.S. Speaking of sex secrets! Did you know that Consciousness is a divine conception, no sex required to embody and birth this Krst (Christ) or Krsna (Krishna)?

(Sit in stillness with your eyes closed for 15 minutes a day; I promise it will transform your life!)

7. You Can't Always Rely on the Past

Are you letting your past experiences shape how you view the present?

In mid-December 2012, my family and I were headed up the highway, moving from North Carolina to New Hampshire, where my husband grew up. (Yes, we had stock in the truck rental company, Penske.) I was driving our car with my mother-in-law and our one-year-old in the back while my husband and our almost six-year-old were lagging behind in the big yellow Penske truck, pulling our wagon on a trailer with an engine governor that wouldn't let him drive over sixty-five miles per hour.

At some point, I lost track of him and became distracted by an endless procession of police cars. They kept coming one after another. It got to the point where I could feel the wind displacement whooshing against my vehicle, moving in the opposite direction. I had never seen so many police cars speeding down the highway. The energy felt breathtaking as I listened to Rihanna's song "Diamonds."

In the meantime, my youngest was getting restless from being in his car seat for so long and needed a diaper change. I couldn't find my husband, so I pulled over at the next rest stop. My mother-in-law rushed off to tend to her needs, leaving me in the car with my son. I changed him on the front seat instead of taking him inside to use the changing station. He was tired of being in the car and was arching his back, doing everything he could to escape me. I remember firmly instructing him to be still when an older White woman who was watching approached me as I was pulling his pants up. With a disappointed look, she said, "I hope you cherish your children."

I was thinking, *How rude!* I was tired and had been on the road for two days, and man, that really irritated me. I felt judged. *Did she think I was someone who needed her intervention? Was she suggesting I didn't care for my children?* My mother-in-law, with whom I had never found any common ground, was just as surprised by the woman's remarks.

When I got back in the car, my fear of moving to the Northeast—a region surprisingly marked by segregation that isn't as obvious since entire towns are divided by race—started to fester in my mind. I recalled how, in college, a friend and I were wrongly pulled over by a police officer in Morristown, New Jersey. The officer asked us what we were doing in *their* town, assuming we were from the lower urban county where more "minorities" lived. From that moment on, I unknowingly held a belief (that undoubtedly held some truth) that some

125

communities of New Jersey and the tri-state area were racist. I began to feel that the woman at the rest stop was "one of those people" who stereotyped me because I was a "Person of Color" passing through "one of those towns."

I finally met up with my husband and son, who were getting gas at the next exit. I told him about my experience. By then, I was convinced it was a personal attack.

I settled back in to continue our long ride and decided to flip through the radio stations, which were playing Christmas songs. A local news anchor said, "We mourn together the loss of our youngest at Sandy Hook Elementary School," and went on to state that the number of casualties was still unknown. My heart sank. As I paused for a minute, trying to gauge my location, I realized I was in the vicinity of Newtown, Connecticut. It was December 14, 2012, just a day before my oldest turned six. These children were his age. (I'm still overwhelmed by emotions every time I read this.)

Then, suddenly, I could see again the face of the woman who had approached me at the rest stop. This time, I noticed tears in her eyes, which I hadn't seen before. She was distraught. Instantly, I recognized that she was talking about the school shooting. She said, "I hope you cherish your children," because twenty families that day wouldn't see their children return home from school that evening, along with the families of six educators who had also lost their lives that day. (Why are assault weapons still legal?)

People seem to come together when tragedy strikes. We seek comfort from those around us, breaking down superficial boundaries like "race" and "religion" that typically divide us. She was reaching out to me. Unfortunately, I missed the opportunity to receive her interaction because I wasn't present and was lost in my own thoughts and fears about moving back to the segregated Northeast and White New Hampshire.

I allowed my *jacked-up* inner experience of crossing through a predominantly White town in New Jersey as a college student to influence how I perceived the present moment fifteen years later. It would have been nice if I had taken a moment to notice her.

A few clear points here are that pain and racism can affect individuals for many years to come. The scars don't fade quickly when our communities are slow to change, and we cling to them so tightly that our memories replay as if they happened just yesterday. We shouldn't let the past shape our present understanding. While our experiences can be valuable, they should merely serve as resources to help us respond with awareness. If we continue to view the present through the lens of the past, there will be no room for anything new.

Perhaps I was entitled to my perspective, which I can defend until the cows come home. But do we really want to be held captive by the past to the extent that it obscures our ability to experience what's happening today? Absolutely not. May we be transformed into diamonds.

Sobering lessons,
—Sher! (The Common Snook)
Pause. Inhale. Exhale. Reflect.

P.S. Yes, my timing and experiences are strange. Sometimes, there's a lesson like the one in the story above, or I can use the story to draw your attention to something greater. When people lose their lives, the Universe leaves us with valuable lessons to raise our awareness and improve ourselves. You must pay attention because they're there.

I started noticing that the Divine was trying to get my attention through these unsettling experiences after I met one of the five college students in 1990, when I was twelve, who lost her life here in Gainesville after a monster had haunted our town for weeks. Her name was Christa Hoyt. As a clerk for the Alachua County Sheriff's Office, she helped my mother and me file a police report after my purse was stolen from my sister's car at the old Lyons Apartments on S.W. 20th Avenue. This was when the old Sheriff's Office was located on Depot Road.

About a week later, I saw her beautiful face on the news. I remember gasping and calling for my mother in complete terror, and from that moment on, she became a permanent part of my memory. I recall admiring her lovely figure as she styled her uniform with sheriff green pants that perfectly hugged her hips. She was graceful, with neatly trimmed dark brown hair and the most beautiful, angelic eyes that I can still see smiling back at me. (Wow, I had no idea Consciousness was observing her closely through me.) Meeting Christa, possibly an angel, transformed my young life that year by shifting my attention inward.

(Sit in stillness with your eyes closed for 15 minutes a day; I promise it will transform your life!)

8. "Can You Teach Me to Roll My Neck?"

Backwoods of New Zealand. Photo by Li'l Snook van Gogh.

A Southern accent *with attitude* is required from the start.

Disclosure Reminder...,

One day in Little India, while chilling with my *sistas*, a little girl asked if I could show her how to snap her fingers and roll her neck. (That's who I am to some people, lol.) I remember thinking she *tried me,* but then I saw her sweet little face smiling back at me, eager to learn. I said to the ladies in the room with a gentle glare, "You know, you Indian people *got* more head movements and tongue clickin' and poppin' than Black folks." It's all good; all roads lead to Africa—one world, one people!

Suddenly, I realized that the sweet child wasn't mocking me; she saw the gesture as valuable and believed I was her door to "Black Girl Magic." She would take the Indian head wobble to a whole new level! Wobble. Swivel. "Sonic pop." Snap. (That'll make you dizzy! *Shout out* to content creator "Meen Fried Chicken Curry" for naming the "sonic pop." Listen carefully as I "sonic pop" my tongue for you, Alachua County style. I learned from the best.)

Unfortunately, she was talking to the wrong *sista.* (Shoot, I ain't got no magic.) She was speaking to whom she believed I was. Many of us mistakenly

128

do this, interacting with people based on our stereotypical views instead of recognizing the essence of who that individual truly is. Sometimes, we're accurate, but most of the time, we're dead wrong.

This sweet child needed someone with deep roots in the African American communities to teach her how to master the head swivel paired with a coordinated finger snap, and she didn't have to look far for the magic. I turned to my friend, who was both graceful and commanding, and had owned liquor and convenience stores across the Southeast that served this demographic. I said, "Shoot, why don't you teach her?"

It's all good! Everyone could use a little Brass Monkey or gin and juice therapy now and then. (Let's dance to "A Bar Song Tipsy" by Shaboozey.)

Cool Hugs,
—Sher! (The Common Snook)
Pause. Inhale. Exhale. Reflect.

P.S. Speaking of dead wrong but spot on! One day, I took some good friends to see the alligators at La Chua Trail on Paynes Prairie in Gainesville, Florida. During the winter, you can see hundreds, like thousands, of alligators sprawled out on the banks. Like a true paparazzi (paparazzo sounds better plural), one of my friends started filming to post videos on the "Little Red Book" or "RedNote," a Chinese social media platform. (They're always filming me on the sly, posting me and my 'fro all over China.)

I was thinkin', *Chinese people would probably stir-fry and eat these gators.* Then, as if they could hear my thoughts, one said, "You know that picture you sent of the gator at your front door? Everyone on my thread asked what they tasted like and if Americans eat them." They were all imagining a new dish! I told my friends, "That's exactly what I was just thinking." One laughed and replied, "Chinese, we eat everything!"

(Sit in stillness with your eyes closed for 15 minutes a day and add some ice; I promise it will transform your life!)

9. This Is Who You Are

With this type of imprint, you won't get too far in life. (TCS)

Disclosure Reminder...,

Not being Black enough is unacceptable for those who need Black folks to be Black. When my youngest joined the Alachua County Public Schools, White kids harassed and trash-talked him because he was *tall* and couldn't *ball*. Then, Chinese kids teased him about his hiking shoes. (Give him a break! My boy has a White daddy! Geez!) He wasn't Black enough for them. And if he ever complained about how he was being treated, the White teachers seemed oblivious to his feelings. (Hold off on rolling your eyes at these devoted White teachers. There's more to this situation, and it becomes increasingly complex.)

Their reaction to my son stemmed mainly from their mental concepts regarding how they viewed "Boys of Color." However, their mindset was partly shaped by the local population they were accustomed to observing. It created a vicious cycle. Ultimately, my son needed a teacher and friends who could see beyond the mental conditioning and refrain from unfairly classifying him based on his skin color. He was expected to embody the stereotype of being "Black tough" rather than being seen as an individual or a boy deserving of empathy. He had no knowledge of or family ties to the local culture, but he was force-fed the culture as if it were his own. They treated him as if he were "Black," specifically reflecting their view of a Black person in Gainesville. (Poor Sweet Potato Brown, who can play cricket, does not enjoy the same privileges as the rest of his lighter-complexioned family.)

What if Black and Brown children were stereotyped like Asian students are treated? Who would they become? Promoting positive images of "Boys of Color" while challenging and dismantling negative stereotypes is essential for their social development.

Gainesville told my son, who wants to study astrophysics, "This is who you are. You're Black, you're a baller, and you're meant to wear stylish *kicks*." They needed him to be "cool." If he had been left to the Alachua County school system, with that kind of encouragement, my future astrophysicist would likely have ended up cutting grass. (No worries...I was schooled in Alachua County.) After four months of indoctrination, I pulled him out and signed my violinist up for basketball, of course. (Thankfully, he's still privileged enough to come home.)

I was surprised to find that the collective understanding of "Black" among non-Black people in Alachua County was still relatively shallow compared to larger cities. (It felt like I had stepped back in time.) Unfortunately, how others perceive us can influence how we see ourselves. (We didn't have time for that.)

Interestingly enough, the well-known actor Bill Cosby produced a film in the 1960s that advocated for Black and Brown children to have teachers who looked like them. (Hey, don't get worked up. We'll talk more about Cosby later.) My son's experience shifted my husband's and my perspective on whom we wanted to teach him during his formative years. As you can see, I'm advocating for more diversity among classroom teachers. We need educators who can see children through the eyes of Love because anything less is detrimental. "If there were no other reason for wanting to keep [Black and Brown] kids out of school, the social life would be reason enough" (John Holt, 1981). (Relax, I'm talking about homeschooling.)

Cool Hugs,
—Sher! (The Common Snook)
Pause. Inhale. Exhale. Reflect.

P.S. Strangely, I've had a few "progressive" White women give me *attitude* and challenge me for having pulled my boys out of public schools. Their liberal, privileged perspectives fail to see that public education doesn't serve all children equally. However, I do award them brownie points because we need White families to continue supporting public education, whose children will never face the challenges "Children of Color" face.

For many White families, private school tuition and vouchers are a waste of resources (shhh!), especially when the teaching methods are primarily the same and racial diversity is arguably the most valuable experience of all. However, there are further reasons why these families choose to segregate their students.

10. Heroes Don't Get Vacations

Deputy Nickolas Tilliman (02/12/1983-02/15/2023) of Gainesville served in the Navy and the U.S. Army. After five years with the Alachua County Sheriff's Office, he was deployed to Afghanistan before returning to serve our community. He even chased an alligator in our neighborhood and had everyone rolling with laughter as the crowd of children cheered him on. We will forever remember his warm smile and wonderful sense of humor.

On average, twenty veterans take their own lives each day, totaling about 7,000 women and men per year, with those who have served in Afghanistan seeming to be the most at risk.

Careful when someone bestows upon you the title or label of a hero. You might lose control over your own life as you feel pressured to live up to and align your behavior with the expectations others place on you. Those are big boots to fill when you should be free to be nothing more than who you are.

Have you noticed how the term "hero" can become a form of bondage that intertwines with our human need for validation? Many individuals who enter service fields often unknowingly seek affirmation and validation of their existence. The validation they seek is called Love—unfortunately, many search for it externally, even though Love does not come from anything outside ourselves. When the world makes you a hero, it can sometimes cause you to lose focus on your own life. I assure you that this is not how Love functions.

Someone once called me a hero because I worked in the public schools, and I replied, "Heck no, not me. I'm not your hero." I'm just like everyone else. And I will walk out of this door and not let myself be manipulated by those who hope I will continue serving underpaid for my work or commit to multiple tours in the military, as some do.

Speaking of underpaid! As a mom hero, I learned that no one wins or benefits when someone sacrifices themselves. I always tell moms that they must prioritize their own needs, which contradicts our traditional belief system. I often ask, "Who will care for the kids if you don't survive?" Your children want and need you to prioritize yourself. I learned that lesson the hard way. No one looks after the needs of heroes.

I met an officer a few years ago who shared his struggle with stepping down from the force. He recalled feeling trapped, as if he couldn't make a decision without letting down his fellow officers. The mentality was, "Once a cop, always a cop." I wonder who instilled in these women and men the belief that they had to give their lives for this job. However, he discovered his own strength—Love—and chose himself along with the family he hoped to have. He mentioned that he had to choose because the only people in his life who could genuinely rely on him were his fellow officers. After all, law enforcement was a 24/7 commitment.

Even after leaving the force, the mindset and conditioning remain with many of them, and these former officers approach life with a sense of obligation and responsibility. Unfortunately, this admirable character can make these women and men easy targets for someone to take advantage of because "no" was not part of their vocabulary. No one should have to live like that, carrying the world's weight on their shoulders. Being a hero can really suck. I'm sorry about that.

At *Betwixt*, we don't have any heroes—just ordinary, good people. We aim to be a community where parents, nurses, law enforcement personnel, military service members, teachers, and others feel loved and can release the burdens placed upon them, because our job does not define our identity. We want to know who you are, not whose mother this is.

Certainly, we need women and men to serve our community. Still, I hope they can serve without the mental token of "hero." Heck, I would say, don't give me a "hero"; give me a pay raise and a vacation instead! "Hero" sounds like a six-figure income, or is "hero" just a bone?

I have watched many "heroes" in my life. My grandfather was a World War II veteran; my father dodged the Vietnam draft; we have a bunch of nurses in the family; my "TV-dad" was a police officer in Gainesville; my husband was an emergency medical technician (EMT) who worked at Shands UF Alachua General Hospital (AGH); one in-law was a secret Marine; and I was a former teacher and mental health case manager. We could all use some love instead of being sandwiched with "hero." (Just so you know, my "TV-dad" was a gentleman present for the early episodes of my life, known as Gainesville's beloved Officer Friendly in the 1980s. You'll have to guess which one.)

Heartfelt Hugs,
—Sher! (The Common Snook)
Pause. Inhale. Exhale. Reflect.

P.S. Did I ever tell y'all my husband is a real-life superhero? This man has been the first on the scene of an accident well over a dozen times, and not as an

EMT. It doesn't make sense for this to be possible. In fact, he once held the neck of a drunk driver one night off Hwy 27, west of Gainesville, who was pinned in his car while waiting with him for a rescue unit to arrive, all while the person in the other vehicle had lost their life.

P.P.S. Speaking of another hero, me! In the late 1990s, while attending college, I worked at a new suite hotel in Morris County, New Jersey, just off Route 10. The guests who conducted business in the area became like family because of their extended stays. I always worked the holidays to keep them company since my family was in Florida.

One weekend, around 9:43 PM, the fire alarm went off. I raced upstairs and smelled smoke. It was a real fire! That evening, only two of us were working. Unfortunately, with no manager on duty, we were responsible for knocking on the door of every occupied room in case someone ignored the alarm, and many did, including the Orthodox Jewish couple with all those kids. (giggles)

As Christmas music played in the background, my buddy and I raced up and down the halls and stairs of the three-story hotel, with over 135 rooms, in under three minutes, yelling "Fire!" When I finally made it outside safely, exhausted and nursing my sore knuckles, bent over with my hands on my knees, I looked up at the handsome young man who smelled of smoke. "What happened?" I asked. He explained that he was frying something that caught on fire, and he doused it with water. I was too tired to laugh, but his friend had enough laughter for all of us as we waited for the fire department to arrive. *(Whassup, Smooth Jazz! Thank God you have a chef today.)*

Anyways, some of you may remember this young man from the 1994 Coca-Cola commercial where he beautifully sang the jingle "Always Coca-Cola" as he walked to the back of the city bus. He was "the Coca-Cola guy" to us, better known today as the singer and actor _____ (you get to fill in the blank). (You know, I pay close attention to the interesting folks who cross my path for whatever reason and seem to stand out like this experience. Most of them I find are rather spiritual and are close to awakening. [wink])

(Sit in stillness with your eyes closed for 15 minutes a day; I promise it will transform your life!)

11. A Double Standard Enforced by Capitalism

Disclosure Reminder…,

Should we ever rely on the media of a capitalistic society to raise our children? Talk about brainwashing! I learned that in early 2024, thousands of Christians signed a petition to boycott the Pandora jewelry company for a Valentine's Day ad that briefly showed two women kissing. They argued that the commercial was in danger of "corrupting" their children.

When I heard their argument, I didn't form an opinion or draw a conclusion; instead, I investigated further and began to digest their response. I wanted to gain an understanding beyond my personal views. Y'all know I have serious concerns about the *sexual buffet* we lay before our children today, but grown folks' business is not my business. Whether someone identifies as "gay" or "straight" isn't a debate for me.

I struggled to understand how someone could hold such strong views or perspectives that they believe their position should be universal. I couldn't grasp how one could expect another to conform to their religious beliefs. I could only imagine that these views originated from individuals who had never had to live in submission to the dominant viewpoint or culture…or consider that others might see things differently than they did.

When you live as a "minority," you always live in submission to the dominant culture, from Christmas celebrations in school to Fido pooping on your front lawn. (More on Fido another time.) It's an excellent opportunity to build character and understand the concept of give-and-take, learning that you can't always have everything your way. The fact that some people still behave with these expectations is concerning. (Okay, I'm sick of the term "minority." These "equalizers" are a valuable asset to any community and help bring clarity and balance due to their unique perspective.)

Two questions may emerge: Who defines the ideal vision for society, and who decides what information should be kept hidden from specific faith communities? We proudly showcase a variety of things that people might feel positively or negatively about. Here are a few:

- The Muslim or Christian lifestyle, diversity, cigarettes (I was born in the 1970s), minivans and SUVs, interracial marriage, rap music and country music, Walmart, "Grab her by the pussy," fast-food, credit cards, domestic violence, bread and butter, assault rifles, Playmate of the Year and pageants, white-washed history, bras, candy, social media, ice cream, racism, economic segregation, big-ass houses, lawn irrigation, front yard gardens, coffee, alcohol, Mary Jane, air conditioning, defund the police, cream, cake, and cookies. (One big ol' bulleted list helped to save a tree.)

People have attempted to suppress humanity and stigmatize various expressions that differ from their own, seeking to dictate what everyone else should see. What is bad for one is heaven for another.

We can hold our beliefs and make personal decisions without trying to control everything. For instance, I teach my son to do what makes sense. He decided he didn't want a credit card, even after I mentioned he might need one to rent a car or a hotel room someday. I believe it should be illegal to market credit cards to college students. (Oops, I meant not to share any opinions.)

Most of humanity's problems stem from control issues, which lead to the complete opposite of harmony. Focusing on our neighbors' choices distracts us from confronting our own issues. Unfortunately, forcing our perspectives on one another is a significant challenge for both sides.

However, to find common ground, we must consider opposing perspectives. One might argue, "Could you please not play that minivan commercial before my daughter? I can't believe anyone would show a minivan commercial featuring loads of children hopping out with a mom smiling as if she adores the chauffeur soccer-mom lifestyle while I'm trying to raise a woman with free will."

Are seeing Muslims in traditional dress a threat to the Christian faith or the other way around? (Muslims are like, "No, 'Daisy Dukes' with boots do not interest us.") Is it possible that grabbing a woman "by the pussy" or grabbing a fast-food milkshake is more concerning than two women in a Valentine's ad? Isn't faith supposed to be stronger than shielding our children from the world? If they're too young not to be influenced, maybe it's time to turn off the TV or get rid of it. My boys managed without one. (Speaking of milkshakes! I wish Chick-fil-A would stop listing the calories for each item on their menu. I haven't bought a strawberry milkshake since 2013. They are to die for! The hell with calories; I'm going to Chick-fil-A today!)

The bottom line is that religion, sexism, racism, and "White Supremacy" have failed us for hundreds of years. Humanity has lost patience with these controlling constructs, so power is shifting. As a society, we are entirely responsible for this shift, regardless of whether it is in the "right" direction or not. Hopefully, as power changes hands, we will be cognizant of what didn't work in the past. If this new direction fails to address our problems, humanity will shift again.

I wouldn't be surprised to see people begin promoting various economic systems that have never been heard of before. Currently, anything outside of capitalism is frowned upon, much like how some view "right religion." But perhaps it's time for a change!

For one, you can see how this group, which signed the petition to boycott the jewelry company, was leveraging economic power to make its voice heard and push its agenda. Sadly, many attempt to use this effective form of communication as a means of control rather than for liberation. That kind of behavior provokes innovative ideas from the opposing side because it shows how money is wielded to punish what we disagree with. And some will say, "Maybe it's time we did away with an economic system that supports foolishness and bribery." *(Whassup, Kapil!)*

Yet, those who feel supported by the commercial have also become symbols of capitalism. Is equal exploitation truly a measure of equality? (giggles?) What a dreadful way to gauge progress. Some proudly say, "They recognize our buying power."

No worries…don't get worked up. I was just making a point. Please understand that I can see it from both perspectives. While capitalism exploits us, it also reflects what we choose to support, as evidenced by the disparity in salaries between the NBA and the WNBA. Brittney Griner likely would not have found herself in Russia if the WNBA earned even a fraction of what the average NBA player makes.

I wholeheartedly embrace change, hoping it will lead us to new levels of Consciousness. There are signs that the future is promising for new minds, as there is often a struggle before power shifts hands.

Hugs for sale,
  —Sher! (The Common Snook)
Pause. Inhale. Exhale. Reflect.

P.S. Speaking of buying power! (No, I'm not talkin' 'bout the house I had that had *free power*, lol. Shoot, I didn't buy any power; it was "off the grid" for sure. *[Anybody else have a house that's off the grid in the city limits!?]* I told the electric company *three times* that they were providing me services for free, but you can't locate what's not on the grid, right? [giggles] It was hopeless. Ms.

Loophole can't tell anyone the truth these days, even when they have a *gremlin* in their system.) *Anyways*, sorry for being distracting. Back to buying power!

Did you know that some American home builders intentionally design neighborhoods to create more north and east-facing homes, aiming to attract Indian buyers who may prefer this Vastu architectural style? (Look it up!) These builders charge a premium for north or east-facing homes without fully understanding how the sun's energy and natural light impact the residents. Either way, it shows they are flexible and eager to attract these buyers.

If Indian people recognized their buying power, they might also be able to persuade builders to move away from creating tacky McMansions and instead promote more thoughtful home designs and sustainable building practices that enhance health and community. Indians understand the risks of land scarcity better than most, so they should also recognize that McMansions alongside the suburban landscape and design are neither healthy nor sustainable, especially given global housing shortages, the rapid deterioration of agricultural land, and the agrarian crisis (farmers are struggling). "Amen!"

Anywho, thank goodness nobody wanted the small, sunbaked, west-facing house we bought; without it, we would never have landed a home in Little India. See, west-facing can be auspicious, too!

(Sit in stillness with your eyes closed for 15 minutes a day; I promise it will transform your life!)

12. Train 'Em Young

Disclosure Reminder…,

Upon entering school
A new friend
I didn't know she was White
Or I, other
We spent endless hours playing
Oh,
How I love the smell of Barbies
We were best friends

~

I loved vacationing with her family
White momma turned on the radio
She said,
You probably don't want to listen to
Cracka music
How thoughtful
Having never called anyone a *Cracka*
I couldn't relate
I loved the same music
I didn't know what to say

~

We met some kids at the beach
From Alabama
Apprehensive I was
Yet,
She was comfortable
We hung out at the pool
Gathered in the warmth of summer
Straight out of a poem
Or a Fourth of July photograph

~

Big brother whispered
In the baby girl's ear
The wind blew
The ocean roared

elicit

Sweet White baby
Shifted like the current
Called me a *nigger*
Wasn't she a cutie
Getting her feet wet
A first time for everything
Eleven years old
I didn't know what to say

~

As we grew older,
I kept her close,
My *special* friend
Maturing to express
Full cognitive dissonance
She said,
You're not like the rest of them
The rest of whom?
I thought
By then,
I was fully aware
Still,
I didn't know what to say

~

Why was she raised to see me as different?
Why was I assigned an identity?
Why couldn't she see me as I saw her?
Only as a *special* friend

Poetic Hugs,
—Sher! (The Common Snook)
Pause. Inhale. Exhale. Reflect.

P.S. Hmm…I wonder if anyone else has been called a "nigger" by a one-year-old. I may need to submit that to the Guinness World Records. (giggles)

(Sit in stillness with your eyes closed for 15 minutes a day; I promise it will transform your life!)

140

13. Old-Fashioned Courtship Still Works

Today, this sermon is dedicated to all the young ladies with an eye on a *special* young man. (No worries, Gen Z-ers; I'm not telling anyone what to do.) This is just one perspective among many ways to find a life partner.

Disclosure Reminder...,

Many have asked me, "What do you teach your children about dating and relationships?" This is a good question, but I can only respond from my perspective as a mother of two boys and from my personal experience of having religion, righteousness, and purity shoved down my throat.

First, let me take a moment to boast about my son, who is now at an age where he attracts the interest of the *opposite sex* (uh-oh, bad word). Young ladies, he must be one of the finest catches in the county. (Yes, I'm proud of him.) He's kind, caring, and a true gentleman. He isn't perfect by any means but is growing into his own man. Any young lady who captures his attention should be thrilled because he doesn't offer much time to anyone.

Hopefully, a young lady will be patient with him since he's *never* in a rush—*ever*. At home, we call him "Snook the Sloth" from the old PBS children's program, *It's a Big Big World*. The show seemed to suggest, "Though Snook is slow, he is smart." (This is funny because "Snook" is our last name.)

Thank goodness, being slow is coupled with being meticulous. (The slower the processing, the more you see.) My son can clean a bathroom thoroughly from top to bottom, knows how to have my back when I'm in the kitchen, and will take the mower from me when he catches me cutting the lawn. My masterpiece is nearly finished.

I am often very grateful that he consults me about *everything* and trusts me enough to seek advice on women, particularly regarding their emotions and nonverbal communication. The smart ones are like that because few relationships thrive if Mom disapproves of the gal. You can roll your eyes if you wish, but it can be hell! And the only reason for your eye-rolls is that you've never had a mother-in-hell. Every woman should be aware of that nugget of truth. More to come. (Strangely, many of my Indian friends admire my relationship with my son because of our closeness, but their admiration doesn't sit well with me, as I observe them with a hint of suspicion. My goal is to raise an independent and interdependent young man, not a codependent man-boy or *baby-husband*. What some fail to realize is that he enjoys spending time with me because I treat him like a man, without handicapping him.)

141

With that said, let's talk about dating. As you can gather from the title, my husband and I are a bit old-fashioned and only encourage dating or close companionship with the intent of finding a life partner. We are not interested in our son having a *lover*, lol. I tell him there are far better things to do than to indulge in physical pleasures outside of marriage. (Ugh…I mean, outside of a committed relationship, y'all. I don't care about legal paperwork.) Go to a theme park! Study astrophysics! It's far cheaper than the risk associated with youthful physical pleasures. (Don't get offended, Gen Z-ers or the latest generation. *You!* This doesn't mean I have anything against those who focus on the body. As the saying goes, "there are different strokes for different folks"—no pun intended!)

Still, my son understands that he doesn't have much to offer in a dating relationship at this age because he wants to build a future for himself and provide for his family if he chooses that path. Interestingly, young women want to capture a guy's attention, but any guy chasing girls at that age is likely not focused on his future but rather on boobs. It's okay…but balancing both is challenging.

Understanding that my husband and I didn't date might help you grasp my "strange" perspective. You know I mentioned we met in an ultra-controlling church, right? Dating was prohibited! That's where my Hindu ladies and I can *relate*. We both married a man we didn't *date*.

I loved not having to worry about sex and unwanted pregnancies in my twenties. What a relief! I hope more young women can experience the same freedom. Additionally, after twenty years of marriage, I can attest that there is nothing in dating that can truly prepare you for marriage. On average, based on my statistics, it takes about *thirteen years* to understand the creature you said, "I do," and "to death do us part." So scary!

As a matter of fact, my abusive church might have been onto something! There is a strong possibility they were right: dating is a waste of time. They must have been observing Hindus or Muslims, who don't mess around with dating or only date to find a life partner, and noticed they have some of the lowest divorce rates. (Now, I know there's more to the story, but we aren't talkin' 'bout the oppression of women right now.) Many Hindus understand what marriage is truly about. That gift called a spouse is meant to refine you and will have you on your knees, connecting with the Divine for grace and increasing human Consciousness. It's beautiful!

Oddly enough, my husband and I were friends for many years, and then, one day, our relationship blossomed. I don't know what the heck he was thinking when he decided to court me, especially since you had to ask the controlling church leader for permission to pursue a young lady. That said, my husband was a rule breaker (a bad-ass, as White folks like to say). He decided to *holla*, which is Southern African American Vernacular English used to express interest in a woman. He said, "I have loved you for years and always believed you were meant to be my wife." Oh my, I almost fainted. He must have rehearsed that line because I haven't heard anything so romantic since. (Shhh!) And guess what? We married in exactly three months after the date of the proposal. Any idea why? Yep, good guess! We weren't fuckin' around—pun intended!

Anyhow, I tell my son that he should look for someone he enjoys spending time with and who also appreciates his company. And, of course, does Mom like this person? Marriage is never just about two people; rather, it is about two families coming together. (Once again, the Hindus and Muslims were right.) If more people viewed it that way, they might make better choices from the beginning, avoiding unnecessary conflicts that could last a lifetime.

You want hell? Marry who you *want* or a guy whose momma hasn't agreed to let him go. For many women, if they had known then what they know now, they might have gone to a theme park instead. As a result of my teachings, my son is wise. He has seen…and has learned…and hopes to avoid unnecessary conflict. (It may be worth mentioning that momma's psychological control is cultural and accepted in many Indian families.)

Besides that, nothing else matters because marriage is about growing up, waking up, and becoming a better version of yourself. "Love Is A Loooong Road," so stop with your list. Or, as I tell my son, steer clear of the woman who has a list and insists on dating only men of a specific height. In any case, her elaborate list may help her find the man she needs. She doesn't understand that friendship is what will help you through the tough times when there are no warm fuzzies or romance to lean on. Just ask "Jack & Diane."

Ball and Chain Hugs,
　—Sher! (The Common Snook)
　　　　Pause. Inhale. Exhale. Reflect.

P.S. Once, my son asked, "Mom, why are all the pretty girls gay?" Now, you can't tell anyone what I told him; this was between momma and son. But I said, "She just hasn't met the right guy." I told him to *holla*, tell her she's beautiful ("Chanda Re Chanda Re"), and watch the magic…or duck. (You can see how a boy's upbringing shapes his view. He appreciates natural beauty, those who are like "*Oops*…I really didn't mean to be sexy," just like his momma's.) 🐟

143

14. Asian Americans: A Force to Be Reckoned With

Disclosure Reminder...,

To all my Asian friends, I challenge you to listen with an open heart, just in case you're concerned about the direction I'm about to take. No worries, I see humanity as—one world, one people! Also, it may be comforting to know I had two Asian stepmoms (technically three) at one time, not to be confused with "at some point in time." (It's called polygamy. Don't knock it until you try it. It does have its benefits. [giggles]) I have four half-Asian (Blasian) siblings (my dad's second litter), which means absolutely nothing, of course. That's like someone saying, "I have 'Black' grandchildren," to avoid being called racist. Nonetheless, I will share this story at another point in my life. Maybe in a future book, *It's Time to End the Exploitation of Asian Women.*

Pardon me for a moment. If you're Blasian, born in the early 1990s in Charlottesville, VA, and don't know your daddy but resemble me, give me a call, li'l bro! You were the first of two babies born that year, so you have a "twin." Your mother was brilliant; she never returned home from the hospital after your birth. Women must be strong enough to raise a child, with or without a man.

My family jokes that I invent these stories because I can genuinely connect with anyone in the world. Unfortunately, they're all true. We are more connected than you could ever imagine.

Anyways, I hope you aren't too closely identified with the geographic identity assigned to the "Far East." (If that isn't Eurocentric, I don't know what is.) And far from what? I must ask.

Additionally, we won't be talkin' 'bout Asian "invisibility," as I hear that term being used more frequently these days. Half of my neighborhood is Asian, and I can see them—clearly. And I'm sure many of you are expecting this sermon to endorse the stereotype of Asians as model citizens; don't worry, we aren't headed in that direction either. My family has effectively debunked that myth. But nursing runs in the family, if you want to guess which country their ancestry is from.

Due to overpopulation in Asia, particularly in China and India, there aren't enough seats for all children to receive a traditional education. It's mathematically impossible. Because of limited resources, Asian cultures have become increasingly competitive. Only the best will secure those seats, and, as the saying goes in China, they will have the opportunity to change their destiny.

Many Asians pride themselves on being people who perhaps value education more than others, while many Westerners feed the stereotype and hold similar beliefs about these cultures. However, for most, this identity isn't rooted in passion or a love for sleepless nights but rather in desperation, which has become ingrained in the culture. (You know, fifteen to twenty hours of school and studying each day will make you crazy...and weird. Careful now!)

For many Chinese, excelling in school can mean the difference between a life of poverty and one filled with opportunities. Additionally, let's not overlook the fact that being the top student can help one avoid physical punishment at home. Unfortunately, this also rings true for many Indians. A gifted child can be a ticket to a better life, a ticket out of communism for some, or even a ticket to America. This is a heavy burden for a child to bear.

Most Americans don't realize we benefit from Asia's top talent (the crème de la crème). What a gift to our spoiled little nation. And keep in mind, I live in a college town, not Chinatown, where you'll find everyday Asians who are just like the average American.

Many people might argue that Americans need to work harder to measure up, but I can't say I agree with that perspective unless I think life is not worth enjoying. (I love to chill, which I learned from my Indian friends.) However, the drive that some Asians possess isn't something that can be taught to Americans, no matter how much we try to improve our *outdated* educational system. At the same time, that doesn't mean there isn't more work to be done. Also, if Americans approached education the way many Asians do abroad and in the U.S., it would be considered child abuse.

Still, this conversation could very well be viewed from the shallow perspective of "us against them." If we did "for a moment," White America might regret "for a moment" not fighting to preserve affirmative action, as that would have guaranteed seats for "Americans." (Hang tight, Asian Americans, I hear you. I'll address you in a moment. It's a set-up. Right now, I'm focusing on White Americans.) Nonetheless, change is good because it enables us to evolve and grow. I believe Black Americans, Latinos, and Native Americans are ready for that change. But are White folks?

Will White folks be able to compete with the machines Asia is sending us, even with their access to better schools, private tutoring, and the ability to bridge the gap between state vouchers (second-generation "segregation academy" tricks) and private school tuition inconveniently or conveniently set just high enough to keep the riffraff out? (Yes, I love long-ass sentences!) Is it fair to race against a biological machine? Don't get offended; a well-trained mind is indeed a machine.

Did you know that the average Indian (or Patel) running your local convenience store knows their multiplication tables (pause while you're still counting on your fingers) up to "twenty times twelve"? Yet, most Americans still struggle with "six times eight." (Good Lord, I hate "six times eight" passionately. Yes, I know…there are far better things to memorize in life.) Still, they are walking calculators. The force coming out of Asia is a force to be reckoned with—beeyotch! Academically, they stand out above the rest. (Let's not forget my peeps from Nigeria! *Báwo ni!*)

Pardon me for a minute; I might be a bit biased because if I had not met my husband, I would have totally married an Asian man. I'm serious! Ask my husband. And don't miss the opportunity, Black *sistas*!

You know there's a "man shortage" or "shortage of men" in African American communities, and the mindset behind White American masculinity has worked to emasculate Asian men, making them less likely to marry in America, similar to what African American women face. Still, running a university sure the heck looks masculine to me and sexy, too. (But not exactly the "*oops*" kind of sexy.) Given the sex-ratio imbalance in both groups in America, who knows, Blasian might be the face of the future. Can I get an "Amen!"?

Returning to the issue of White Americans feeling threatened by walking calculators. Denying visas and complicating life for Asian immigrants is one approach, as American as apple pie. Still, it will only be effective temporarily or perhaps only in the "country of Florida."

The "country of Florida" must realize that the circumstances these individuals have endured or witnessed firsthand foster a desperation that can take generations to overcome. It's like an *invisible mental veil* that governs their lives. (Hmm…that sounds like an excellent title for a spiritual self-help book.) Finding liberation from such an experience is challenging because it serves as a constant reminder upon returning home to visit. This drive or curse is passed down from one generation to the next.

Once again, from the shallow perspective of "us against them," when we neglect the needs of those who have been oppressed in this country and instead hold the belief that hard work alone opens doors of opportunity (that has proven to be a myth), we may be in for a direct lesson about why we have specific policies in place to help level the playing field. America will need a lot of dirt to level that field, and White Americans are struggling to keep pace with our Asian counterparts.

Okay, Asian Americans, now I will get on some of you! Asians are in this country and rising to the top 100% because of the efforts of the Civil Rights Movement. When the third Monday in January comes around, many people believe that Martin Luther King Jr. Day is primarily about Black Americans. Still, I remind my Asian friends that King fought for them too, and they wouldn't be living as well today without those who paved the way for them. If I were Asian, I would march alongside Black folks yearly on MLK Day. (You cannot conquer what is united.)

Despite this, many Asian Americans fell victim to the same mindset that blocks visas. The White conservative movement used Asian Americans to advance their agenda by claiming affirmative action was discrimination against Asian students because "White Supremacy" (society's *gremlin*) cannot stand alone and claim unfairness. They were now supposedly looking out for Asians. Elon Musk, a well-known businessman, used a similar approach in 2023 when he accused the media of discriminating against White and Asian people. Again, this *gremlin* cannot stand alone and claim discrimination.

Jewish history in America was also used as a "supporting pawn" where "Kenneth L. Marcus, who served as assistant secretary for civil rights at the Education Department in the [early] Trump administration, said Harvard's treatment of Asian students was reminiscent of its efforts to limit Jewish enrollment" (*The New York Times*, 2023). It was so kind of these *White folks* to use ~~their~~…I mean, *White folks'* historical acts of discrimination against Jewish people as a heartfelt example of why affirmative action should be eliminated to protect Asian Americans. (That was beautiful, right? And if I had stuck with "their," many would have said they weren't "there." "I didn't do it," they say.)

Nonetheless, these cunning individuals with old tricks used Asian Americans as leverage. Sadly, some took the bait and allied with the very force that perpetuates the myth of the model Asian, depicting emasculated men and then women as *exotic sex toys* for White men (and, of course, my late father, who also joined the movement).

America needs Asians to view meekness as both honorable and cultural. This behavior reminds me of a time when a religious leader referred to me as a "sweet girl," which led me to never speak up, because I liked the idea of being sweet. After all, humility and meekness were highly valued. Still, it's a form of mind manipulation, regardless of whether its origins are Asian or not.

Unfortunately, many Asians continue to buy into this mentality, which, again, works well for America. Some will defend their silence as if it earns them brownie points. (Hmm…is that what they told you to think?) And then they get frustrated when they don't feel seen. Hey, lean in so I can whisper this to you: *Perhaps it's your programming causing your frustration.* However, instead of taking responsibility, we often resort to blame-shifting, especially when we fail to recognize our own programming.

As I'm sure you know, there is discrimination against Asians in the West. However, Asians must also recognize that what you put in is what you receive in return, which complicates things for cultures conditioned to value meekness and humility at the expense of their own emotions. Collectivism and authoritarian regimes favor compliance, and this obedience, "…undue influence, as it's termed today, is that once you're wired, you don't require regular tune-ups because your friends and family typically share the same beliefs and speak the same language. You will pass these teachings down to your children, keeping the tradition alive. This mental programming ensures that oppression becomes cyclical and continues to thrive for generations" (*Elicit* sermon, "Guard Your Heart—from Whom?"). Deprogramming takes time, and the process doesn't start until you can recognize the programming.

However, more Asians, especially the Chinese, are finding their voice. Still, thank goodness Asians, in a sense, support and protect their lack of visibility (not being seen or heard) as cultural, because when you do speak and are ignored, Martin Luther King Jr. said it produces something a bit more violent. Remember that the civil rights we all enjoy in America were achieved because people spoke up and demanded change—more in a later sermon.

Many Asians with higher incomes than most White Americans, whose children populate tutoring centers and who were having no problem getting into excellent universities, came out of nowhere and were just shy of chanting that affirmative action was discrimination against them. They mindlessly supported the Harvard and University of North Carolina cases, which made it more difficult for universities to support voluntary race-based admissions. Some Asians willingly decided to be used by "White Supremacy" as puppets. Standing equal to the notion of *White* sometimes feels good, especially when you can't see that you're being used. "Now I feel seen," some may say. Careful; this same ideology will block your cousin's visa without hesitation.

If that were me, and a lot of other Asians would agree (because they are not a monolithic group), I would have thought twice about that move, especially if I still needed allies in this country. Even so, the Silicon Valley Chinese Association Foundation supported the Harvard case. That's how a one-sided perspective sees the world. It looks out for itself and can be manipulated by "White Supremacy." What's done is done, and we must rise to the occasion.

White people, back to you again, of course! This is what happens when we ignore our history. White America has failed to teach comprehensive American history; subsequently, we will all learn the significance of history together. Without it, folks forget where they came from and what paved their way from a broader perspective. This is akin to how many Americans overlook that this "second nation" was founded on the principles of religious freedom and that we reject the cross-contamination of government and religion. Sadly, we can be so forgetful.

Desperation also squashes compassion for anyone in your way—Black folks, Latinos, Native Americans; you have been trampled once more from a one-sided perspective, collaborating with another one-sided perspective. It may not appear fair; however, life has never been fair. Economic systems, such as communism and capitalism, illustrate this to us every day.

Suppose Asians didn't need the seats set aside for students from marginalized communities because they have no trouble gaining admission to excellent universities. Then, who suddenly needed those seats? When you examine the racial demographics of Harvard before the end of affirmative action, Whites made up about 30% of the population. That means roughly 70% of Harvard students identified as non-White. (You know we can't have that in America!) Is it possible that, instead of embracing the future, in 2040, some in America viewed the 70% result as a threat? Perhaps this better illustrates the mentality of "us against them." In that case, targeting affirmative action was a waste of time.

Anyhow, I can't leave without my Chinese friends knowing that I hear and see them. I was blown away by their boldness at the 2024 protest on the University of Florida (UF) campus. These were not quiet Chinese folks. They demonstrated American bravery because, as a patriot, I, too, am skeptical of the "country of Florida." Applause to you, Chinese people, for speaking up during these challenging times. But…I was a bit concerned by some of the protest slogans. Hear me out.

In *The Independent Florida Alligator*, the local University of Florida newspaper, I read, "We make UF!" Say what!? That sounds like an *only child* to me. Still, I completely understood the purpose behind the protest against Florida "Senate Bill 846, which [banned] 'partnerships,' including recruitment programs, between state universities and any non-U.S. citizen living in one of seven countries of 'concern'" (*The Independent Florida Alligator*). Regardless of the counterarguments supporting the ban, many Chinese individuals feel they are being discriminated against due to their ethnicity, especially since this has happened before in the U.S. Does anyone remember learning about the Chinese Exclusion Act signed in 1882 in their American History class? Oh…nobody?

At the same time, someone on campus needed to advise them—perhaps one of my *sistas* from the Marston Science Library, preferably the one with the "Raspberry Beret," needed to pull these *only children* aside and say, "We make UF?" with a local African American accent, complete with a head swivel and snap. "You might not want to say that, even if your department is all Chinese, because it wasn't always that way. That won't go over too well with the rest of us or the general faculty, who also 'make UF' and see you as a valuable school partner—shoot."

One protester even went so far as to say, "The law will also lower the quality of graduate students at UF." (*Oh no he didn't!* [That's SAAVE; no commas.] That must have been another *only child*.) And the quality, well-qualified local population, including American-born Chinese (ABCs), who struggle to get a seat at UF these days, say, "We'll gladly take those seats back." (Y'all know I'm a Gainesville, Florida, patriot; I graduated from Eastside High School!)

We will discuss further at another time how collective *trauma*—such as that experienced under communism—can lead to *drama*. We must show compassion for those who have suffered. Sometimes, "they know not what they do" when their minds rule their lives. (Hmm…wasn't that somethin' Jesus said?) We can all fall into this pattern. Chinese Americans and ABCs should read the *Tao Te Ching* and honor their ancestry and rich cultural heritage. I understand that "it's old," but it's still relevant, especially since the "old ideas" have endured destruction and continue to live with us—*now*. It would be beneficial for you to read it, too. (We'll talk more about that mind of ours later.)

Either way, change is happening. Overpopulation is contributing to global diversification as people migrate in search of resources and opportunities. I embrace humanity, my brothers and sisters, whom some call Asian. Certainly, rising to the top in education above Whites, who selfishly brought opium and Christianity to China against their will, can't be such a bad thing. (Do you see how opium and Christianity were both used as weapons to disrupt the Chinese way of life? I sincerely hope they don't retaliate by sending opioids to the West. See, teaching world history is essential!) My only hope is that Asians will remember their history and origins. Chinese humility is what America needs.

And, of course, we welcome the wisdom and spirituality of India. (My Indian friends are like, "Phew, she didn't get on us too much," because you know, Indians aren't really considered Asians, right? [giggles])

We are—one world, one people! Let's end this one with a song that unites us all: "Kung Fu Fighting" by Carl Douglas.

Cool Hugs,
—Sher! (The Common Snook)
Pause. Inhale. Exhale. Reflect.

P.S. "But 'those people' are buying up all the real estate!" Let's put that into perspective. Canada owns 30% of the foreign-owned land in the U.S. Those Canadians are clever because they know we aren't watching them. The Netherlands owns about 10%, but they're also predominantly White and can easily blend in, even though they're giants. And the Chinese, who are *buying up everything*, own less than 1%—last I checked.

Why is everyone getting upset with the Chinese? Have you ever tried renting out a unit in a college town? Only the Chinese have the expertise to deal with American college students who will trash your property.

Did I ever tell y'all my first home purchase was in Shell Rock, which I mistakenly rented out to a college student? Do you know that country gal trashed our house and let her cat boo-boo on top of my kitchen cabinets, which I didn't discover for over a year after she left? My second tenant, who moved out, didn't have a cat. Those old turds were petrified! Gainesville should thank the Chinese for tolerating all these kids.

P.P.S. Every time I hear the mental justification, "We're Indian, so," I recognize that the following statement typically condones cruel and unusual amounts of schoolwork. However, I have one Indian friend who managed to break free from the programming and fears that contribute to the competitiveness among Asians. I did not believe she was free until she declared, "I don't have time for Kumon and competing with Indians." She was a liberated woman; she even packed up and returned to school so her husband could learn to cook.

P.P.P.S. Speaking of success and rising to the top! Careful, Indians, as you allow your values to shift because the American lifestyle (success-driven) and community design (car-dependent) may one day leave you feeling just as lonely as Americans—and the Chinese too—questioning why you traded the chaos of India for this lonely existence. (Come on, Indians! *Raise the roof!* Let's get this *chapati* started right!) ☙

151

15. Perception Is Reality

"Mom and Dad, let's go for a ride. This life is boring here."

Disclosure Reminder…,

In the early years of our marriage, my husband and I were among the many unemployed during the recession and real estate crisis from 2007 to 2010. Our oldest son was just a youngster then, and my husband was completing his Master of Business Administration (MBA) degree.

At the beginning of his program, he was told that the MBA would guarantee a nice income and mark the start of a promising future. Instead, his graduating class was the first to receive the message, "best of luck," as over half of the class of banking and finance executives were unemployed, including my husband, who was pursuing work in non-profit management in Charlotte, North Carolina.

Snook Art, Charlotte, North Carolina.

See, now my studio is famous! I was an apprentice under the most notorious arts and crafts teacher in Gainesville, Florida—the Purple Lady—and by the time I graduated from middle school, I had earned a Ph.D. in arts and crafts.

Our little house, which we called "The Attic" above my art studio, Snook Art, began to feel smaller and more suffocating by the minute. When we realized we were bringing in less money than it cost us to live each day, we needed to make a change quickly. Every evening after teaching art class, I outlined the worst-case scenarios to see if we could survive until the recession passed, but the end never seemed to come.

After nine months of unemployment and hustling with no end in sight, we decided to stop paying our mortgage and use our remaining money more wisely. We discovered that you could only receive government assistance after exhausting every penny of your savings. We were appalled by our *bassackwards* country—the equation to qualify for assistance equaled starvation. America wasn't interested in helping people while they could still help themselves.

These policies were indeed created by selfish folks who were not interested in sharing food, not even a crumb. The approval process for assistance was maliciously designed to ensure you didn't receive anything unless you had absolutely nothing. As a result, an individual or family could only qualify when they could no longer afford to keep a roof over their heads. However, if you lost your roof, you couldn't apply without an address, meaning one would essentially be forced to hustle on the side to pay their rent in hopes of getting a slice of cheese from the government. If they caught you paying your rent or mortgage, you'd be in trouble. Basically, if you weren't starving, you didn't qualify for assistance. The application might as well have said, "You can't apply for help until your stomach starts to growl." With that said, I continued working in my art

153

studio, where my students began to look like steaks and probably felt that a butcher was teaching them.

My husband must have applied for over a hundred jobs, and that's when reality set in. Our house was no longer a home; it quickly became a burden. I wanted to be free of the impending doom, so I began to joke, dancing and singing to the B-52's song "Roam." I said, "Do you hear the wind calling us? Is it whispering sweet nothings in your ear?" Oddly enough, my husband could hear the wind, too, and felt a similar itch. We were going to roam because we wanted to, fueled by the love we shared. We started questioning, "Why sit here and lose everything when we could see our country [literally] on our last dime?" I love his spirit; *Sagittariuses* (or Sagittarii) are adventure junkies!

We packed up our house and put everything in storage, just in case the bank decided to take it before things improved. I closed my art studio, and we hit the road with our little one in our classic 1992 Volvo station wagon, which we still have. When my sister invited us for an extended visit, we headed for Arizona, which had some of the worst unemployment rates in the country.

I remember my mother being disappointed when I closed my business. I was letting down many people who dreamed of being self-employed. However, self-employment wasn't as liberating as folks imagined. I was responsible for bringing in every dollar I earned. There was no salary, no vacations, and no paid time off. But this was supposed to be the American dream that was sucking the life out of me. I decided I would rather be poor than lose my passion for the arts and take my chances to see what the world had to offer, rather than follow the rules and sell my soul to keep the suburban nightmare alive. (Yes, I hated hot-ass suburbia with its no trees!!!)

The cross-country trip was loooong overdue. We drove through the Blue Ridge Mountains, the farthest either of us had been west and crossed the Mississippi together for the first time. Her sheer vastness was impressive as we drove into the night. We fell asleep at a rest stop in New Mexico because pulling over for a nap there wasn't against the law. That was because you weren't guaranteed to find a hotel in rural America.

The following day, which was too early to be morning, we woke up to the most magnificent sunrise around 4:00 AM. (I'm starting to think I forgot to change my clock because the time doesn't add up.) The view was breathtaking. I had never seen anything so beautiful; flat-topped mountains called mesas caught my eye as we listened to Billy Idol's "White Wedding." At that moment, I realized how little I knew about the world and how much I had yet to explore. I felt free and excited by the potential of the unknown. (Migration changes you.)

154

We climbed through beautiful northern Arizona and rolled into dusty Tempe, where my beloved sister lived while attending Naturopathic medical school. It felt terrific to leave everything behind and discover what a fresh start could offer. While applying for jobs, we explored the surrounding areas daily and even fried an egg on the back patio under the scorching sun.

We learned a lot by observing the local Latino culture. For some reason, the locals wore cowboy hats and sombreros, carried gallons of water as they walked, and only took their children out to play at night. It was quite a sight to see.

The parks were deserted during the day, and you occasionally saw a tumbleweed rolling by. But these parks came alive at sunset, infused with a taste of Mexico. You could hear Spanish guitar music coming from car radios, and kids ran around joyfully munching on corn on the cob that smelled like a cross between funky, cheesy feet and your favorite pizzeria. The snack smelled awful to me, but the kids seemed to love it. I remember my husband and son, with their now Arizona-tanned skin, were starting to blend in with the locals. They said the cheesy Mexican street corn on a stick was starting to look appetizing.

There was somethin' *special* about hanging out with the Mexican community every day, allowing our son to enjoy some playtime. Although we all had very little, they possessed a joy and connection to life that many of us can't fully grasp. They might have thought, "Did those poor Americans lose their big house? They look so miserable when they could be dancing, playing soccer, chilling in the grass, and eating cheesy street corn." After all, perception is reality!

Eventually, we explored every corner of Arizona while continuing our job search. At some point, we considered camping and hiking up the West Coast because that's what hippies do—or at least what my White husband wanted to do.

We contacted my family in Belize for advice, as they had RVed each year from Central America to Washington State. They quickly informed us that camping with a baby would get old after a week and suggested we consider purchasing a used RV. They likely did not realize we were unemployed and living off our last dime, which we feared would run out by the end of summer.

They advised us to check Craigslist for an old RV with low mileage. Arizona was the ideal place to find one, as many retirees dreamed of RVing but hadn't ventured beyond the local lake. In Tucson, we discovered a 1989 Minnie-Winnie for sale for $6,000. It had only 30,000 miles, which was impressive given its age. We decided to make the purchase. *(Thank you for believing in us, Mr. Newnan!)*

The camper featured a mauve interior from the 1980s and required a bit of TLC since the current owner was using it as a "toy hauler," as my "Redneck" friends would say. With plenty of free time on our hands, we gutted and replaced the interior. I found a brand-new sewing machine on Craigslist for $20 and purchased some beautiful upholstery fabric from Walmart to give it a facelift. I was getting excited and convinced my husband that we could change the flooring. We found vibrant red tiger hardwood flooring scraps at a yard sale for $5, along with some carpet scraps from Lowe's. Our little humble abode was the first tiny house, long before tiny houses became a thing.

I remember my husband and I jokingly saying that this camper could easily become our home since we didn't know which direction life would take us. My family in Belize explained that the gamble with the RV was to relist it on Craigslist for sale by the end of the summer so that we wouldn't lose any money we didn't have. (Bunny trail!)

We needed a place to work on our RV, so I convinced my husband, my spokesperson and interpreter, to ask a church near the self-storage lot where we parked our RV in Mesa if we could use their back parking lot. They weren't very open to hosting us, so we had to give them a story to *invoke* the spirit of Christ within them. (No worries…it was a true story, depending on our perspective that day.)

We would get up before sunrise each morning to avoid embarrassing the church folks but mostly to beat the heat. The temperature was close to a hundred degrees and became unbearable by sunrise. Unfortunately, the old RV made us appear worse off than we really were. No one would have guessed that my husband had just graduated with honors, alongside classmates who were making six figures, before the recession struck. Each day, we watched church staff and members keep their distance from us, perhaps because we looked like *homeless people* who might ask for something.

Never once did they ask if we were thirsty, hungry, or needed help during the entire week we spent on their property. However, I'm grateful for the water hose they allowed us to use. Without that water, the heat exhaustion with fever that one of us experienced might have been worse. Damn, it was hot out there!

Forget about needing access to a restroom; it was so hot that urine never reached the toilet. The sun would suck you dry the moment you stepped outside. I bet those church folks praised God for not having to let us in. Little did they know they were helping to set us free from religion, which would happen a year later.

156

*

We left our Volvo wagon with my sister in Arizona and decided to continue our adventure before we lost everything. Buying the RV was terrifying because we had almost nothing left to our name, which meant we were getting closer to facing hunger. However, we weren't hungry enough for the government to assist us willingly. They required our pockets to be squeezed to less than $1,200 before they would show us any mercy. That's why smart folks bury their money in a big pickle jar in the woods. Still, we must have felt okay about the RV purchase, which was a gamble, yet we could live in it if things took a turn for the worse.

At some point, our "bank in America" realized we were having too much fun and turned off our credit cards, even though we had never defaulted on them because we needed them. Unfortunately, there was a red flag in their system because our house in Charlotte, along with about 3 million other homes across the country, was in foreclosure. Everything we had relied on—excellent credit, kissing the ass of the system—was now working against us. They didn't care about our good credit or that we were trying to survive.

Still, that didn't stop us from living it up. We hit the road again, but this time in style. We visited the Grand Canyon, Vegas, Hoover Dam, the Mojave Desert, Sequoia National Forest, and Yosemite. We parked for two weeks in Vacaville, just outside San Francisco, searching for work because we *loved* the area. After spending an afternoon sipping some of the finest wine and enjoying cheese in Napa Valley with our son, who trusted his parents to provide him with food each day, we had to consider our next steps because winter was just around the corner.

We sought free parking to reduce our expenses and extend our luxury stays at national parks and the pristine campgrounds managed by the U.S. Army Corps of Engineers. This included boondocking, free camping in national forests (which is likely now illegal due to the 2024 Supreme Court decision), and Walmart parking lots that graciously welcomed RVers.

Some of these places were downright scary. I can now recognize the smell of crack cocaine and many other street drugs that require heating. However, the trick to saving money and waking up alive was to stay at Walmart while commuting from place to place, a thought I initially found intimidating. But I ended up *loving* Walmart! Who doesn't enjoy having a 24-hour grocery store in their backyard? *(Right, Kellers?)* Sometimes, I would take laps around the store with other unhoused individuals to get my daily exercise. I always felt safe at *Wally World*, as other RVers would nestle around us at night. I would sleep like a baby, except for that one night outside Lincoln, Nebraska, when a cattle truck pulled right up next to us, smeared with feces from top to bottom. The smell of shit is still in my nose. (*Cousin Sherry will be stopping in Lincoln, Nebraska, "coincidentally" on the 28th of August to wish you a happy birthday. [wink] If you pay attention and listen, the Universe is always speaking.*)

Here's a quick story about how we landed a fantastic *site* in Yose-*Mite,* which we later discovered required reservations months in advance. The night before, we stayed at a campground that looked like you might not wake up alive the following day, only to be found floating in the river. And there was a river! There were only two families of campers in the entire park, and a pickup truck with a strip of lights across the hood, which I thought was security, drove through every couple of hours at full speed, scaring the daylights out of us. I told my husband I didn't feel good about the place and wanted to leave. I hated putting this pressure on him because he was responsible for unhooking the sewage hose and electric cable and driving Princess, a.k.a. "A Horse with No Name," which sounded like a 1950s Ford pickup without a muffler.

He agreed to go, so we decided to head to Yosemite early. To our surprise, we arrived just as the ranger handed out the last available sites for the day, which we got because "the early bird gets the worm."

I remember hearing a disappointed couple around our age talking to the ranger. They wanted to pitch their tent but would have to drive back to San Francisco to find accommodations since they weren't as lucky as we were. Naturally, we stopped them and asked if they wanted to share our campsite. They were thrilled, and we were happy to have their company. They even offered to chip in $20 for half of the site, which felt like a double blessing to us then. We felt prosperous and blessed in Yose-*Mite.*

We learned that the couple sharing our site was on their honeymoon from England. Both worked in the film industry, and one was relatively well-known. We slept soundly in our RV, and a curious bear paid them a visit. It was fun to share a laugh with the startled couple over breakfast the following day—our treat served up fresh from our RV kitchen.

Sheep Creek Overlook in Utah.

Back to drinking *wine*…on our last *dime*…in Napa Valley. While reorienting, we discovered that Northern California was on fire, as one might expect, so our only option was to head back east. From Lake Tahoe to Salt Lake City, Utah, to dinosaur country in

Wyoming, we ended up at a Walmart just outside of Steamboat Springs, Colorado, at the end of summer. It was a lovely Walmart that looked like a cozy log cabin, with red cedar logs adorning the entrance against the mountain backdrop—a sign we should have never ignored. Nobody warned us that the temperature in the Rockies could drop below freezing and that snow could unexpectedly fall in August. It was so cold that night that I cuddled with my baby boy just to keep him warm, all while dreaming of being inside, sitting by the crackling fireplace.

At one point, I remember asking my husband in the middle of the night if he was awake, and he responded as if he'd never fallen asleep. I said, "Babe, are you freezing to death?" He replied, "Yes, do you want to leave and turn on the heat?" At 3:00 a.m., we packed up and left the most charming Walmart ever...just to be warm.

But of course, we needed to follow our charismatic Christian roots south to Colorado Springs, Colorado, the home of megachurches and the Focus on the Family Christian ministry, led by Dr. James Dobson. These are the folks from the far right who lobby against the folks from the far left in the name of Jesus.

But first, we stopped in Denver and discovered the original Udi's gluten-free bakery. They were just beginning to expand, with their products appearing on the shelves of small health food stores on the East Coast. They can now be found in most major grocery stores—even Publix!

The bakery café was closed when we arrived, but some cool dude unlocked the door and welcomed us in. We told them we were visiting local gluten-free bakeries on our cross-country trip, hoping to find the best gluten-free bread for the café we planned to open, which was all true. It was so kind of them to give us free samples—loaves of bread, their specialty granola, and a tour of their industrial bakery. Udi's treated us better than the church folks in Mesa, Arizona. And those Colorado hippies even saw our old-ass RV and didn't discriminate against us; they thought we were cool. Perception is reality!

During our tour of Focus on the Family, which left us with a warm, fuzzy feeling, I attempted their three-story "thriller slide" and nearly had a heart attack. I do not recommend it for anyone over thirty.

Then, my curious side persuaded my husband that we should also attend a service at New Life Church, the 10,000-member megachurch previously led by Ted Haggard, who was once the head of the National Church of Evangelicals. This was the well-known pastor who was plastered across the news media in 2006 due to his long-term relationship with a male prostitute. As expected, my husband seemed annoyed with me, but I couldn't pass up the opportunity.

We pulled up like it was a Florida Gators football game and parked our Minnie-Winnie in the tailgate section right in front of the *massive* church. It was intoxicating singin' and praisin' Jesus like we did in our old church days back in Gainesville, Florida. We felt completely at home, swaying back and forth into a trance. Seriously, it was amazing!

One of my favorite experiences and lessons learned while on the road came from the retirees; they pursued the American dream and adhered to the rules. They all had pensions and excellent retirement savings, yet they expressed to us, "Enjoy life while you can still get out and enjoy it." They were cheering us on. Many had finally realized that possessions were pointless to live for when life was short. They were now living freely and unburdened by material things. However, many weren't physically able to enjoy the freedom they had worked so hard to attain.

I can't share the entire story because we saw and experienced so much on the road. However, we ended our trip with a stop at Niagara Falls before heading to our final destination, New Hampshire, to visit my husband's family. Niagara was a delightful layover, and we were surprised to find more Indians there than in Charlotte, North Carolina. It felt like home was just around the corner.

When we arrived in New Hampshire, the leaves were turning bright red, orange, and yellow, signaling that winter was on its way. Thankfully, Grammy lent us a heater and a power cord for our stay. Life in our self-contained unit was wonderful. We had minimal possessions and woke each morning in some of the most beautiful places in the world. However, we knew our life on the road was coming to an end because we couldn't endure the winter in our RV.

We returned to Charlotte, where we feared we had lost our home, only to find that sucker patiently waiting for us—dammit! We moved back in, still owing the bank about a year's worth of payments. We qualified for a loan adjustment, and they urged us to sign the paperwork to keep paying the bill of the American dream.

My husband's start-up company, for which he had been raising capital while on the road, was finally funded, with the team having secured $1.2 million. He began *paid work* again after sixteen months of unemployment, as if nothing had ever happened. I remember thinking, "Is that it?" After all that drama, with the bank harassing us with phone calls, they

Back to the prison of uniformity and three meals a day.

160

didn't take the house because they had too many homes to take. (See, there's power in numbers!)

I recall sharing our story with a more affluent friend who seemed envious that we had the time to live it up and break free from the grind, even though her income should have allowed for such an adventure. Perhaps I should have told her we were broke, but she knew we were unemployed. Still, nobody wanted to envision the worst, so instead, we were seen as spoiled brats and even accused of "gallivanting" around the country. Maybe they were right. Perception is reality!

That's when I realized both stories were true. One was that our home was in foreclosure, a fact we hadn't disclosed to everyone at the time. We believed we were leaving our house behind and could have easily made the RV our permanent residence. We knew what it felt like to be "homeless" and live in an RV at various Walmarts across the U.S. for over fourteen days between campgrounds, experiencing extreme heat and cold. (Hmm...heat and cold?)

The other story was that, stirred by our unemployment, we craved adventure and decided to hit the road to see what the world had to offer. Nobody ever crunched the numbers or questioned whether we had any money due to our "status." We were just lucky because of the force called faith, which allowed us to escape one of our many mind-made realities.

Our friends were jealous when we had nothing to envy. The only thing we possessed was a willingness to let go of everything rather than fight to maintain our standard of living. While others played by the rules and waited for the

Classy, Class-C!

recession to end, we had an absolute blast. Both were valid options. Sure, there were days we were scared as shit, especially when we looked into our son's eyes. After all, he trusted us to provide him shelter and three meals a day.

Unfortunately, we never lost anything—not a penny—even when we believed we had. We listed the RV on Craigslist, flipped it, and sold it for $8,000 because it had been completely gutted and updated. It was classy! "Clarke, that there's an RV" (*National Lampoon's Christmas Vacation*). To my surprise, we made enough profit to cover our gas bill and returned to "the rat race" and the perfectly linear, subdivided life in suburbia.

Ultimately, both stories were true, but it depended on our perspective of the life story we chose to live on any given day. Most days, we roamed because we wanted to. "Our beliefs...cause us to focus our awareness according to their content, thereby creating our reality" (Dr. Hanoch Talmor, M.D.). Perception is reality!

Shout out to my Mexican brothers and sisters who refuse to let life take away their joy. And to my unhoused friends, I feel you.

Roam Hugs,
   —Sher! (The Common Snook)
   Pause. Inhale. Exhale. Reflect.

P.S. A food stamp card is like a Euro; it can be used anywhere in the U.S., including the *Farmers'* Market and Whole Foods! (wink) The nonsense that some liberals promote—that "poor people" on food stamps can't afford to eat healthy or buy organic—is a complete lie! It's just that these folks *love* Walmart! Give the same budget to a Haitian; you'll see. (Hush…I know it's called SNAP, the Supplemental Nutrition Assistance Program. It's just that referring to them as "food stamps" is nostalgic for many people.) Also, never ask someone if they were able to get help after they're back on their feet. Wow!

P.P.S. Rest in peace to my uncle, who passed away in January 2025 at the age of sixty-nine, living on the streets of New Jersey. (The harshness of winter and the blaze of summer can be the hardest on the homeless population.) He held a bachelor's degree in political science, followed a vegetarian lifestyle, and was a self-taught herbalist. He considered his big brother to be his best friend and hero. *(Well, I'll be damned, Kevin, you made the book!)*

(Sit in stillness with your eyes closed for 15 minutes a day; I promise it will transform your life!)

16. Don't Correct My Dog or Me

Disclosure Reminder...,

On the first day of 2023, I sent a friendly New Year's greeting to my neighbors and their hundreds of dogs. I politely asked them to refrain from letting their dogs poop on my front lawn. Many assumed it was just their dog using a specific spot. However, I asked if they had considered how many other dog owners were permitting their dogs to do the same and pointed out that they should observe the number of dogs pooping and peeing on our front lawn—in that same spot—sometimes up to five times a day. (No joke!)

I explained that this excess in "fertilizer treatment" had also burned and killed the grass in that area. Honestly, I couldn't care less about that grass. *(Please forgive me, Horticulture Tom, Ph.D.)* I conveyed that my top concern was my children and that it wasn't hard to imagine how Fido's grass-skids and urine would inevitably find their way onto them and into the house. We needed to find a middle ground where everyone could live here safely, happily, healthily, and skid-free.

I even made this cute, all-organic sign with little ants and butterflies attached. One sign says, "Curb your dog means over there...not here!" And the other one says, "Please...won't you be my neighbor?" (Even my mailman loves my signs. He's tired of dogs, too.)

But my letter didn't go over too well. I can't imagine why. I even included a cute little insert of Mr. Rogers' song, "Won't You Be My Neighbor," on a pastel piece of paper. Who doesn't like Mr. Rogers? In fact, the best part of my letter was borrowed from my husband, who said, "Could we have a hidden defecation epidemic at the 'tail end' of this pandemic?" ("That man" is so funny!) Yet none of them had enough life to muster a good laugh. Holy cow, who holds in a good

163

laugh? If that were me, I would've been laughing and rolling all over my front lawn.

In our neighborhood, we've got a big ol' dog park but no space for kids. And I can't believe folks were offended that I didn't want poo-poo on my front lawn. There was a collective belief that it was acceptable as long as it was picked up, but does Fido really need to come that close to my front door with his 20-foot leash? I asked one neighbor if she would mind if I *took a dump* in her front yard to relieve myself, but I promised to clean it up afterward. She looked at me as if I were crazy. I can't imagine why.

I was astonished by how many people believed this practice was perfectly acceptable. I told my husband I would prefer to live on N.E. 13th Drive, with no grass and chain-link fences, rather than pay high-ass HOA fees to partake in the collective mindset of "Don't correct my dog or me." These *"right" folks* did not like being corrected or redirected. I thought for sure everyone held a soft spot for Mr. Rogers' Neighborhood.

It's time we start thinking outside our little boxes and pay attention to how we impact the folks around us. There's no "right" or "wrong" here. Please continue picking up your poop. However, you're wrong when you only think you're right. (That's some shit—no pun intended!)

Hakuna matata…I like dogs. I even allow them to sit on my couch when they're visiting. You know, I dog-sit sometimes. (*Shout out* to crazy Lolo and the Rottweiler with the bad hips who tried to bite my ankle. *RIP, homegirl.*)

Stank Hugs,
　　—Sher! (The Common Snook)
Pause. Inhale. Exhale. Reflect.

(Sit in stillness with your eyes closed for 15 minutes a day; I promise it will transform your life!)

2 CHRONICLES

Awakening is a process that unfolds beautifully, much like a flower.

Section IV: Destructive Veils

In case you decided to skip the introduction and browse around, here's the **Disclosure Reminder**: Before diving in, I will say this: I'm simple. I love to laugh. Please don't confuse my humor with sarcasm; I always mean what I say. I test the limits. My words are plain. I often use "own" redundantly. I don't claim to know all the answers; my only intention is to be a vessel. Also, to connect with different experiences, I interchangeably use the terms "Consciousness," "Presence," "God," "Universe," "Source," "Divine," "Energy," "Christ/Krst," and "Light." Above all, reading my humor with a Southern accent is best. Enjoy!

Destructive veils…are like waking up to a gator at your front door. (LSVG)

1. Guard Your Heart—from Whom?

While nothing I share in this sermon will be humorous, I'll do my best to make you chuckle. Sound good?

The sermon we have here is intended for all my friends, the residents of Gainesville, and those who have lost a family member to a controlling personality or group, seeking a deeper understanding of how some individuals or institutions wield such significant power over their loved ones. It's particularly aimed at church folks (mainly Christians, due to the "Christianese") who may have missed the opportunity for their own liberation because they ignored, silenced, or failed to investigate someone's pain and withheld the love of Christ. Church folks, if you're guilty, say, "Amen!"

WARNING: NO PHOTOS BEYOND THIS POINT!

Many claim to know God yet fear listening to someone's story about how the church or religion negatively impacted them, as if this same God will somehow vanish. Interestingly, former church folks are often the most feared by the congregation, even scarier than the idea of reaching "the lost." I wonder why and where this fear originated. Strangely, the notion of "guard your heart" echoes in my mind.

167

Do we really believe that something as powerful as our connection to the Divine can be revoked or that something terrible might happen to us simply by showing compassion and listening to someone's story? I did, with my head held low and my hand raised high. The church subtly taught us not to listen to "complainers" or to "take up another man's offense" because the enemy comes to "kill, steal, and destroy." This nonsense has no basis in scripture or common sense but is used to "silence the lamb" and cover sin.

In my twenties, I turned an *ignorant ear* to a good friend, a sweet grandma, who was trying to warn me. She was "complaining" about the toxic, charismatic church we were involved with in Southwest Gainesville. She said, "They are not who you think they are." What kind of foolish person would ignore Grandma's warning? Was she the Devil? *(Whassup, Ms. Sylvia!)*

The church had a profound influence over us, affecting everything from our voting choices to our marital decisions—and *when* we got married. The leadership once stated from the pulpit that they couldn't understand how one could be both Christian and a Democrat. (No worries...I've always been a registered independent, but they did influence my vote.) They even encouraged us to live with church families, as I did with my beloved Jamaican momma, who gave me my first warning after she left the church.

We even had our own commune...I mean, villas, "Shell Rock Villas." (What a perfect name!) Within two years, the members collectively owned more than twenty units. As the pack's leader in the neighborhood, I was the fourth member and played a key role in successfully building the commune. (It was so much fun! It reminded me of the TV show *Melrose Place*. Hmm...I bet the neighbors hated us because we dominated the neighborhood. [giggles])

My friends and I were responsible for the unprecedented property value increase of over 125% in Shell Rock. Our community was once deadlocked behind Linton Oaks, also known as the old Sugarfoot neighborhood, located off SW 61st Street, which intersects with SW 20th Avenue and connects to SW 8th Avenue. (Somebody from the county had a bad idea in the 1990s to block the road, significantly impacting property values in Shell Rock. That should have been illegal!) Today, the road reconnects with what was once called Cedar Ridge (lesser-known today [giggles] as Gordon Manor and Holly Heights) because, you know, White folks from Tioga needed a second route into town, right? (Shhh!) And, of course, we bought up the neighborhood and kept the commission only to Realtors who paid a 10% tithe to the church.

Speaking of tithing! Those who didn't tithe at the church weren't technically Christians. (giggles) You were also barred from participating or "serving" in the church if you didn't tithe. And just in case you didn't take tithing seriously (like tithing on your gross income instead of net), lessons about being a giver in the community, such as not being a cheap tipper, helped ensure you were generous when giving to the church. The leadership would say, "Don't tell people you attend this church and then leave a sorry tip." (The mind would think, "Wow, their love and care extended down to the waitress." We were trained well!)

Sure enough, my foolishness led me to serve another year because I had plugged my ears like a child after being warned. (But it was still seed!) However, when I faced my own struggles with the same leadership, I understood what my friend was trying to warn me about. I also realized the church would ignore and silence me, too, just as I had been conditioned to do the same. In fact, I was muzzled before I ever opened my mouth. The church's internal security system (in your head) was remarkable and almost impermeable, as it prevented any informative content from ever reaching its members. We were programmed to expect opposition and were always preparing for war and "the attack of the enemy," but we didn't know the enemy was "truth."

Has anyone ever ignored or filtered out someone who left their church or religion out of fear of the boogeyman…I mean, that the Devil might take you down with them? Interestingly, there's a way to ignore people while avoiding responsibility for your actions. Here's how it works! You lean into your fear and *never, ever, not ever* look under the bed…I mean, ask what happened to them because it might be a frightening story involving a real-life boogeyman (and your chance at freedom!). And you will *never, ever, not ever* know what happened to them, like in my situation with the charismatic preacher who was trying to break me. I'll share a bit of that traumatic story now.

What ever happened to the Snooks?

As mentioned in my sermon, "Waking Up," my husband and I led an outreach children's ministry called JAM on the Streets. He oversaw the bus aspect of the ministry, while I managed the popular after-school program JOTS, which stands for JAM on the Streets. On average, we reached about 300 children each week through our one-hour program, supported by over thirty volunteers. When we arrived with our food truck-style pop-out trailer that resembled something from Nickelodeon, the children would come running and cheering.

Today, our trailer probably looks somethin' like this.

As the ministry grew larger, the responsibilities became more significant. We relied heavily on the church staff for much of our support, as we volunteered while holding full-time jobs. Communication issues and differing opinions emerged, which significantly impacted the ministry's efficiency. Individuals who had never set foot on a JOTS site suddenly found themselves responsible for deciding what we did or didn't need. In short, if we needed "A," we were given "E," and if we required "seven," we received "three." Their disorganized process was incredibly frustrating.

We could no longer navigate the inadequate administrative support that hindered this ministry's effective operation. We were nearing the end of our tenure, as the challenges with the administrative team were taking their toll on me. We were confident that 2004 would be JOTS's final year if things did not change. We communicated with all the supporting pastors and team members to address some of the issues, but the situation never improved.

With that, we decided to give it one last try. During our five years of serving the greater Gainesville community on behalf of the church, we had never spoken to the church leader about the details of our ministry, even though they enjoyed the public recognition the church received thanks to our presence in the community. The general feeling was that the leader was too busy for the minor details of ministry work, despite my husband and me leading the church's two most significant outreach ministries.

The leader often preached from the pulpit that if you ever need help and have done everything you can, don't give up before allowing him to assist. We were confident that he had no understanding of the logistical demands placed on his administrative staff, which often exceeded their scope of knowledge. JOTS was not given the administrative respect it required because effective leadership originates from the head of a healthy organization.

After several weeks of being removed from the church leader's "busy" calendar, we finally secured a date to discuss our frustrations and need for support. It was the strangest meeting ever. We were invited into a peculiar, heavily decorated room, where he lay on his side on a low-profile cushion, surrounded by a bed of pillows, like a Greek god, while we spoke to him. It felt as though we were there to stroke—his ego. (wink) I still don't understand what that room was about.

After the two-hour love fest, which felt like a significant amount of time for a man who was usually too "busy" to meet with his congregation, he asked us to write down all our needs and frustrations. He mentioned that we would meet again to discuss and resolve each one. We felt excited, as we believed our issues would finally be acknowledged and the ministry could move forward successfully.

In response to our letter that he requested, my husband and I were invited back for a business meeting with the church leader, which was supposed to be just the three of us, a one-to-two ratio. His responsiveness surprised me. (For the record, my husband's corporate-style bulleted "situation and recommendation" letters can be intimidating for some, even though they are always written with good intentions.)

We were led to believe the meeting was about supporting the logistics of our growing outreach children's ministry, JOTS. However, four additional leaders were invited to the meeting without our knowledge, and we were informed of this only an hour beforehand. The ratio became five-to-two. (Uh-oh!)

As we entered the room, they were all seated around the large conference table, perfectly positioned to encircle us. He explained that he had provided each participating pastor with a copy of our letter, and they would all speak first. Then, we would have the opportunity to respond.

I couldn't understand why four additional people to whom the letter wasn't addressed would have the opportunity to comment without hearing us first. However, we justified the order of the meeting, noting that they held higher positions, and we needed to "submit" to them, as was the order of the church. Still optimistic, we believed the meeting would be successful, especially with so many participants. In the counsel of many, there is wisdom, right?

The pack leader arrogantly laughed as he opened the meeting, claiming they felt bad. He said, "We love you all very much, but..." and described our letter as a "red flag." He also mentioned that our complaints were petty and that he wouldn't be having this discussion with us again.

It became clear they were highly offended by our letter and wanted to put me in my place, of course. "Submit, woman!" was a significant theme of the meeting. I can only guess the church must have feared me because they knew I had God's favor while in the church, along with the respect and ear of many members—enough to cause an exodus. More to come. (giggles)

He casually criticized us, tearing us apart word by word, speaking without allowing us to comment, clarify, or question. He claimed our letter suggested we were not "cut out" for the ministry. "This is the ministry!" he declared. "If you can't handle this, then maybe you're not called to this work. If you think you've got it bad, you should walk a day in my shoes. If you think you've got it bad, try...[managing] what my wife does with the choir." I couldn't understand where the meeting was going, and I didn't realize he was deliberately attacking and undermining my self-esteem.

For *forty-five minutes*, we listened to him talk about what we didn't have. (giggles) We came for assistance to succeed in our ministry, but they were unwilling to provide it. After all that lecturing, we weren't allowed to speak, and the next two "leaders" of "the united front" had their way with us for another hour, behaving like bullies in an elementary school. (The second one, the leader's main puppet, was the most pathetic of all. Without this church, he, his wife, and their children would have been living in a trailer park, where he might have become a "real man.")

I was unaware this person was targeting me before I ever walked in the door. The assaults on my character were well planned, as three of them took turns trying to break my spirit. They gave us no opportunity to speak because it was never part of their plan for us to have the floor. Still, one of the five pastors refused to participate in the abuse because he cared about us. He mistakenly said, "I don't know what's happening; I want to hear from you first." That was not part of the plan. But by the time my husband opened his mouth and tried to bring them back to the point of the letter, the leader had regained control of the meeting. Surprisingly, they turned on this pastor as well, belittling him in front of us. (Here's a *special* note for abuser #5, who sat to the right of us. *You dishonored yourself because you condemned the abuse and never spoke up. Your silence was morally unacceptable, and you live knowing you are a fraud, along with the rest.*)

I didn't understand what was going on. They were indeed a united front with a clear mission. It wasn't necessary to respond so aggressively. Even if we asked what seemed like threatening questions or highlighted their operational issues, we were still mentally subordinate to the church. In a sense, they overreacted (that's what egos do), pulling out their guns, so to speak, instead of just smacking our hands. (Thank you, Jesus! Asking questions could be your door to freedom!)

More than *three hours* into the meeting, the interrogation became increasingly specific. The head pastor questioned me with full authority, "Who else knows what you know? Who else knows your connections in the city? You need to write down everything you do. What if you decide to get pregnant within a year? What will happen to this ministry? Maybe your grace to lead this ministry has run out." (See, he could see my Divine favor, too.) Once again, all this came from a man who had never set foot on a JAM on the Streets site and had not formally spoken to us in five years.

That's when I realized the meeting wasn't entirely about us but my ministry, which they wanted to keep because it enhanced the church's reputation in the community. They wanted my ministry and intended to take it away from me when all we needed was their support.

Our top two requests were for administrative assistance and help in preventing church members from showing up at our community sites without prior notice. I had an agreement with the city's Parks and Recreation Department that all our volunteers would be uniformed and have photo ID badges along with background checks. (Being Christian was not an exemption.) Today, I have come to accept that men with big egos feel threatened by strong women.

When we finally gained the floor to speak, I picked up my copy of the letter and addressed an issue while tears streamed down my face. I just knew they would understand where we were coming from if given the chance to speak. I emphasized that the issues needed to be considered as a whole, as one aggravated the other when they were ongoing and repeated.

When I refused to bow down after sitting through *four hours* of verbal assaults and having spoken for less than *five minutes*, with the (5:2) unified front (also known as a "breaking session") where they intentionally excluded the Black pastors and leaders who might have felt compelled to come to our rescue, the coward, the head pastor, sucker-punched me in front of his all-White male "entourage" (The Pussy Posse) and his sister with a few select words that could crush any woman's heart. He was enraged that I wasn't broken after *four hours* of abuse and had no plans to yield to his arrogance and self-proclaimed "superiority."

When the *tyrant* concluded our session of interrogation and psychological abuse, he remarked, "We're finished?" as if everything had been resolved. He glanced at my husband for confirmation. My husband nodded because he had nothing more to say, and as I wiped away my tears, I replied, "No." He hadn't fulfilled his promise to address our ministry concerns, so I wasn't about to nod in submission. (He must not have heard about me. [giggles])

I later realized that the problem with addressing our concerns was that this man would have had to admit there was something flawed about the operations of his church. Therefore, crushing my spirit was a better use of their time and, of course, a way to protect their egos. *Oh boy*, was I in trouble then! I had no idea what awaited me, but I was about to awaken to reality with a mountaintop view of what I couldn't see before due to a powerful two-letter word, "No."

Spitefully, he stood up angrily while I remained seated beside him, perhaps attempting to intimidate me. He declared, intending to hurt me one last time,

173

"Sherry, there are some things that I can't do for my wife, and there are some things [your husband] will never be able to do for you." He instructed me to schedule an appointment with the female minister, his sister, and then, looking at me with contempt, said, "Maybe your miscarriage is causing you to magnify this whole situation." (Ouch!)

He suggested that I was being irrational because I had just lost my first pregnancy and perhaps needed some feminine counsel due to my refusal to submit to his *specialness*. (What a pitiful man.) He was trying to shatter my already disappointed heart and attributed all the issues presented in our letter that day to my miscarriage. He ended with a smug little smile, full of disgust, saying *with attitude,* "Sherry, there's nothing I can do for you." (Hmm…he was right about that.) Then he walked out arrogantly as if something was profoundly wrong with me. Of course, I was crushed and bewildered because I had bought into his "teachings." (I was going to use another word, but I don't want to distract you with my mouth.)

Thank you. We saw what we needed to see up close and personal, and later that night, we would learn that some of those *Black ears* were listening outside the door, which still makes me giggle to this day. They knew something was up when they were excluded from the meeting. Thank God one of them would come to our rescue later that evening to soothe my uncontrollable wailing and validate what we experienced before our minds sucked us back in.

A Pastor Called to Check on Us

Late in the evening, the phone rang. A pastor who wasn't at the meeting (nor a part of the posse) called to check on how we were doing. He wanted to know how things went. My husband said, "It didn't quite go as we had hoped, but we did get some answers." (No answers can be just as powerful.) What my husband didn't share was that I had been wailing for hours and that we were living in mental torment since we couldn't figure out what we had done wrong to deserve such mistreatment.

At this point, we were finished with this church. Yet we couldn't figure out how to leave, knowing we wouldn't have the leader's blessing, which we were programmed to believe we needed—and couldn't leave—without it. The pack leader used to say, "It's better to be 100% blessed than 10% cursed." Leaving without "the blessing" meant leaving cursed. (It was a brain-twister!) Being blessed (prayed over) and sent out (released by the leader) as the leader used to teach sounded terrific—until it was your time to leave, lol. (More specific details later.)

The pastor, sounding genuinely concerned about the situation, asked if we could stop by his house to drop off a project my husband had completed for him. He then told my husband, "Bring your wife."

I remember thinking, *Screw you*! I told my husband I wasn't going. I'd been crying for hours and looked like a mess. Still, he encouraged me to come along. Eventually, I gave in because I was losing my mind—almost to the point of vomiting. I set all shame aside as I washed my face and pulled myself together. I couldn't hide what had happened.

We got in the car and drove back down the street, this time to the Abbey Glen community off SW 24th Avenue. The pastor and his wife warmly hugged us as we entered their home. They could see from my red, swollen face that our meeting with the five pastors had much more depth. They excused their children and invited us to sit in a private living room. Then, they encouraged us to share about our meeting. However, we were extremely hesitant. Although we had a close relationship with them, we weren't sure if we could trust them, given that they were part of the pastoral team.

At that point in our lives, nothing really mattered anymore. What we had with the church would never be the same again, and it wouldn't make much difference if one more pastor rejected us. Once more, the pastor and his wife opened the floor, which seemed to be a sincere invitation, so we decided to share our experience.

We sat there, waiting for the husband-and-wife pair to turn on us, just as the others had. I shared our experience and even remarked, "The general feeling I took away from the meeting was pure evil," not expecting them to believe us and unaware that he had been listening outside the door. Instead, while not realizing that the church he worked for was historically toxic, they looked at us, and the wife, with tears in her eyes, said, **"You are not crazy."** We did not expect to hear that from them.

They both repeated, **"You are not crazy."** Between them, they said it three or four times. Amid my emotions, a light came on. *Was this pastor on staff saying that we were not crazy? And if we were not crazy, then what was happening?* He was warning us. He confidently stated, **"You have been close enough to see. Now you see...now you know."**

The light grew brighter and brighter. My vision was getting more precise. I could hear my friend's warning again: **"They are not who you think they are."** I could now see that the breaking session interrogation was planned. And yet, this pastor and his wife said nothing more than a few words. They validated us. I knew I had encountered something, and that something was evil. Their simple, cryptic responses gave us something to hold on to and changed our lives forever. To them, I am *forever* grateful.

Given our emotional state, he couldn't tell us much more than that he was distancing himself from them due to a similar experience. He was also still in a position where he wouldn't dishonor those in "authority," as we were all conditioned never to do; "Don't speak against the man of God. It's a dangerous place," as the church leader used to say. With that, nothing more was said between the four of us. Who were we fooling by abiding by the church's rules?

Back to the sucker punch!

I'll give it to him; the lead pastor got me good. That sucker $@#*** rocked my world, twisted my brain, and laid me out to dry in front of all those White men. Nobody knew I had just lost my first baby, but during that meeting, they all found out. (You must laugh with me…laughter can help overcome pain.) That sucker punch still takes the cake to this day!!! But as you can see, what couldn't break me only made me stronger—beeyotch! (Kanye was right! However, this "beeyotch" could rightfully be used in a more traditional sense. [giggles])

Ministers need to wake up because psychological abuse and control are now recognized as crimes in many European countries. Thankfully, the U.S. is also beginning to acknowledge these behaviors as criminal. Times are changing, and psychological abuse is rampant.

Former church members are often afraid to share their stories because they're unsure of their rights to *their stories* and fear being sued by a brat with unlimited resources from tithes and offerings. Thankfully, I've already been sued before! (cartwheel) It was a small price to pay for freedom of speech, and it set me free.

It's tough to sell the model home when your neighbor also puts their house on the market. The builder sued me to intimidate me. They issued a "cease and desist" order, but they didn't get very far since only the size of my sign was an issue. By that point, it was all over social media. I like big-ass signs!

Today, we have GoFundMe to help level the playing field against these kinds of attacks. Also, similar to the stories you hear about those who attempted to speak out or leave gangs, some church members fear for their lives because the leaders can influence their followers to take their lives. *(Y'all remember Charles Manson, right?)*

176

Churches are *actually* the ones who should be concerned about being sued because these stories are now receiving the attention they deserve in the courts. Furthermore, regardless of the verdict, a lawsuit in either direction would have been monumental, as the attention alone might have helped prevent the abuse from continuing. Perhaps more individuals, especially vulnerable college students, would have found their freedom or avoided such a place altogether.

Today, if someone treated me the way that *impostor* did (listen closely; this can only be expressed in the present tense and can also be referred to as a "word of the Lord" sermon where the individual uses their medium or the pulpit to speak directly to you), *I will protest your ass. You will regret ever messing with me. Try to silence me! I'm the type to stand on the corner with a sign in front of your school—for weeks.* "Let my people go!" Moses said.

Without a doubt, I'm sure he created his own karma because you can't live a peaceful life while hurting and deceiving others without making amends for your wrongs. "Woe be to the shepherds who only care for themselves" (Ezekiel 34:2 from the Bible). God is not pleased. In fact, life is miserable when people despise you. You find yourself afraid to shop alone and living like a prisoner. However, I will say this: one of those men did break away from the unified front. They didn't realize their weakest link still had a heart. Before we left the building, we spoke privately with this pastor, and he showed us compassion. He apologized for what my husband and I went through and took the blame, but sadly, he is still there *to this day.* (Can I get a witness!?) He knew we were done after that, and the good days of preaching the love of Jesus were over. Instead, the dark days, like the plagues of Egypt, were approaching, along with *the EXODUS.*

Although our instinct was to flee, we delayed our official departure for as long as we could endure to handle some business. (Those were some loooong weeks.) A close friend was getting married that summer in 2005, and a few other dear friends were scheduled to go on a mission trip to China in June, just weeks after our breaking session. I couldn't leave without them.

It was both stressful and intriguing to walk around in there with fresh eyes, fully aware, while one person was constantly harassing me because I hadn't returned her calls. (I never scheduled the appointment with his sister as instructed. Her job was to convince me further that I was the problem.) This person was annoyed with me. She couldn't stand not knowing what I was thinking and would whisper commands in my ear during praise and worship while gripping my arm. "I need you to call me, sweet girl. You just don't

177

understand." (Nope, I was no longer a *sweet girl*; I was a *grown-ass woman*, done being manipulated. Oh my, here comes a bunny trail!)

*

By the way, this is the same woman I met for premarital counseling, who advised me never to deny my husband sex because "he needs a physical release to relieve stress," as she spiritualized and explained ejaculation in detail. ([giggles] Aww…bless her heart, she probably didn't know that women release, too.) She said it was my role as a wife "to minister" to him in this way, even daily, if necessary. She seemed to enjoy discussing sex, but the underlying lesson was about making him sexually dependent to control him. However, this was not for my benefit, but so *they* could control him with sex by making me a sex slave.

Men would be taught that they were the priests of the home and how to lead, rather than skipping church, as many men tend to do (because it's boring). The woman's job was to reward his good behavior, unaware that the church was manipulating her to control him. They, too, recognized the influence *woman* has over *man*. (Many men would love to be gorged with sex, but the motive is wrong. *RIP, homegirl.*)

*

As we became more aware of the leader's preaching style, we could now hear how former messages were crafted to influence and control the congregation, and we began to hear subtle messages directed at us and other key members. Again, this is referred to as "word of the Lord" preaching. However, they were unaware that we were awake and observing their paranoia. How strange it was that they were willing to abuse us yet concerned that we might retaliate. (Hmm…what a waste of time!) It was hard not to lose control, but we had to maintain our composure if we hoped to save any of our friends. Our silence was our most powerful weapon. We held the upper hand.

Spiders move quickly when they notice a hole in their web. Our friend, the pastor on staff, warned us that if we stopped paying our tithes, they would suspect we were up to something (a hole in the web). So we continued paying the bill and attending church until we got our closest friends out. Damn, it was tough to write those tithe checks while awake, but it was worth every penny. Then, the official announcement and warning came from the pulpit (the hole in the web) because this pastor was ready to abandon ship and get the hell out of there.

When we decided to officially leave because we had already been forced out and so graciously awakened, we lost everything we knew overnight, akin to the pain of losing your entire family in a house fire. We later discovered that we would not be allowed to return to take part in our friends' weddings. The shunning would be severe. After seven years of serving that church, only one person (a Puerto Rican gal) out of a few hundred was brave enough to say goodbye when we walked out the door that night, where the congregation had been warned to stay away from us ("guard your heart") and not to take our calls.

The church couldn't exactly call us out by name since we were sitting not far from the front on the right. By this point, word had spread that we were leaving, and we had informed many of our friends and ministry volunteers by letter. We attended the service because we knew we would be conveniently tied to this pastor by name if we weren't there. He also encouraged us to go. Attending that service as an enemy or a perceived threat was one of the hardest things I had ever done in my young life.

However, I'm not sure why more people didn't wake up or leave after that night when the head pastor became irate and started yelling multiple times, "I ORDAINED HIM!" referring to our friend, the pastor, who had just stepped down. (It was terrifying!) His anger probably stemmed from the fact that this pastor and *successful businessman* was incredibly valuable to him, as he was the direct link to a significant portion of the racial diversity. He also brought considerable funds into the church and attracted professional Black families. That year, he also served as the official chaplain for the *Florida Gators* football team, and many of the teammates attended the church. (Can you hear my Tim "The Tool Man" Taylor grunt? Uuhhahaha! Go Gators!)

The church meeting that day and the sense of urgency reminded me of the night in 2002 when we, the congregation, were briefed before a sex scandal involving the church's school hit the front page of the local newspaper, *The Gainesville Sun*. It isn't easy to awaken or reach people when one individual holds so much power over them and controls the narrative. Unfortunately, in our case, nobody was aware of what was happening behind the scenes, and it was made to seem as though we were leaving due to the pastor who had just stepped down. The timing was convenient for covering our story.

At the end of the service, the congregation was invited to come to the front if they needed a fatherly hug, and the leadership team would stand there all night if necessary. As they lined up like obedient sheep, they were unaware that this "kind gesture" conveniently painted a clear picture of who was still on their side. I skipped to the front of each line, again wailing in tears, and said goodbye because we were taught that people who leave only sneak out the back door and don't have the decency to say farewell. (My poor husband, who wanted out of there, so lovingly escorted me to the front of each line. I love "that man"!) I could see the fear of God in their eyes as I looked each of them in the face. There was no hug for me.

Finally, on the Outside but Not Entirely Free

Surprisingly, or maybe not, my White friends gave me the strongest stiff arm, except for two who were closely connected to "People of Color." Nevertheless, Black folks were ringing our doorbell in the night as if it were the Underground Railroad. They were fearful yet still asked questions afterward because they knew my character and were uncomfortable with the leader's rant, where he was just shy of saying, "I MADE HIM!" That night, his behavior helped validate our story about the breaking session that rocked our world—no pun intended!

I asked a friend who escaped with us why she believed so many Black people could access *the first level* of freedom. (I refer to it as *the first level* because leaving an abusive church doesn't guarantee mental freedom unless you genuinely understand *and* are willing to accept the truth about succumbing to manipulation and losing your free will. [Wow! Can you see where else this could be applied?]) *Anyways*, she said, "Grandma taught all of us to be 'suspicious' of the White man," which can be interpreted as being alert, steadfast, and guarding your heart. What was perceived as a character flaw in Black folks— *suspiciousness*, a.k.a. *alertness*—proved valuable in accessing *the first level* of freedom. Unknowingly, many didn't fully trust him in their subconscious.

I must also note, which I will explain more in my future sermon, "The Parables of Controlling Personalities," that being in a controlling and abusive church is like wearing a veil. You can't see what the mind has been programmed to hide from you. Furthermore, it was more difficult during that time for a White person to find their freedom because they had multiple mental veils to overcome. Even though it was clear to many Black members that further investigation was needed, most White members could not empathize with or heed the warning from a "Person of Color." They still wore a veil of "White Supremacy" (disguised as loyalty to God) that prevailed and prevented them from listening to "racial outsiders." Unfortunately, their deeply ingrained cultural beliefs secured their allegiance to the leader, *their God*, beyond the traditional programming that we all experienced. When your mind aligns with an ideology of supremacy, which reflects the mindset of a fool, you will live life as a prisoner separated from the truth and—"Truth." (Truth with a capital "T" is Christianese. In this case, Jesus is "the truth.")

My husband jokes to this day that his White butt would still be there jumping up and down for Jesus if it wasn't for the "People of Color" he welcomed into his life. Despite this, my husband (our bless-*id* White savior) and his research (who was thinking like a Black man, harboring reservations) educated all those Black and Brown folks and leaders about what we were a part of. (I bow to "that man.") People who follow a charismatic leader who exerts undue influence and manipulation to control their followers easily fit into the broad definition of a religious cult. Steven Hassan, in his book *Releasing the Bonds,* outlines the distinction by noting that cults exhibit a destructive nature by employing deception and mind control techniques to "undermine a person's free will and make him (or her) dependent on the group's leader."

We noticed peculiar behaviors after deciding to leave but before announcing it to our friends. Those moving boxes we had concealed in our upstairs bedroom made my husband *suspicious*, and we started asking who, exactly, we were hiding from. (What the hell!?) We thought the same thing but were too afraid to voice our concerns. Then my husband asked *the question*, "Are we part of a cult?" Strangely, we sensed the Amish shunning approaching like a tidal wave. (Pardon me, I had to read this paragraph twice. The drama is priceless!)

We needed to be strategic if we wanted to save any of our friends, as they all had the same "thought-stopper" programming that would shut you down if you triggered their threat response. This response could lead to a situation where nothing gets through. We worked day and night for nearly two weeks straight, hoping to deprogram as many people as possible before *the spider* could repair the portal we had torn into its web. And we were relatively successful! (It would make a great Lifetime movie today!)

In addition, *the second level* requires individuals to study and humbly accept what they have been part of and the ugly role they may have played. This is where things become complicated for the mind and might cost you your marriage if you and your spouse aren't on the same page or don't tackle this process together. The mind (the ego), which is primarily responsible for keeping you bound by your programmed belief system, doesn't like to feel humiliated and will do whatever is possible to save face. Nobody wants to admit they've been fooled, another reason these organizations continue to operate unchecked. We protect our egos. Moreover, it doesn't reflect well on a resume, especially for those who feel "called" to teach, pastor, or lead the church. Sometimes, it's better for business to keep your mouth shut and safeguard your own interests. Thankfully, teaching stillness and alertness isn't a business for me.

The mind will say, "It may have been a little toxic, but I wouldn't go so far as to call it a cult," even when the definition of a cult suggests otherwise. To label it a cult requires one to face and own how they behaved and treated others. Accepting that one has been deceived can be crushing to the ego. Others may argue, "No church is perfect." This mindset enables you, your ego, to walk away with your dignity intact, often at the expense of those who join after you. Many UF college students lost their careers and futures because this organization did not prioritize higher learning, as much of the leadership team was uneducated. Also, denying your friend's experience or the truth is a mental game that fosters a sense of "superiority," sometimes just enough to keep you confidently on the same path. The Bible teaches that the last or the least among us will be first. Salvation at every level, including escaping a cult, requires humility.

The mind also struggles to accept and believe the abusive experience because it is conditioned to view the abuser as *special* and incapable of wrongdoing. Sometimes, it cannot reconcile its own knowledge or accept reality due to these programmed "thought-stoppers." It must navigate its own belief that the spiritual leader is *special* or has a unique connection to God before it can progress. This mental process is draining.

The tragedy of leaving a cult or abusive church is that the mind seeks something familiar if it was never deprogrammed—similar to the patterns seen in abusive relationships. Some women are known to gravitate toward the same type of abusive men repeatedly. Spiritual abuse is no different and perhaps the hardest to overcome because it affects your psyche, leaving you unsure of what to keep and what to throw out.

Unfortunately, it can sometimes feel easier to discard everything and start anew. As mentioned, overcoming the ingrained belief that we needed a blessing from the "man of God" to leave his church was one of the most challenging tasks. He often passionately expressed sentiments like: *Today, the church acts much like the world, and the divorce rate within the church reflects that reality. This is the family of God! God takes the solitary and places them into family! Don't imitate the world; don't abandon your spiritual family and just walk out one day! If you believe God is leading you in a different direction or if a "girl" has captured your heart for marriage, let us pray with you about these significant life decisions and rejoice with you as a father should with his children! (Yikes!) Allow the family of God to celebrate with you and "bless you in your going"!*

Do you see how subtly one can make oneself privy to another's personal information? Having someone "cover you" in prayer, as they used to say, sounds terrific. Can you see how leaving the church is compared to divorce in a marriage? Departing from the church was also equated with leaving God. Certainly, nobody wants to resemble the world, which is viewed negatively. And who wouldn't want to be blessed as they go?

Many held this belief for years, never realizing when it was their time to move on; those "praying" with them would conveniently hear a different message from God. They would say, "I can't stand with you today or bless you to go because I believe God has more work for you here—perhaps even leadership."

I witnessed many people who could barely feed their families turn down job offers in other cities or states because of this man and his games. His followers easily bought into the notion of being "sent out" since he occasionally publicly prayed over and sent people out. (The theatrical performance is somethin' *special*. Some ministers will even anoint you with olive oil. [giggles]) In my view, many of these individuals were ones he never valued in the first place or lacked the power to fully control, as evidenced by the young Black man he used to publicly describe as a "wild stallion." Lucky for them!

Another strong "thought-stopper" was the fear and danger of holding the tithe check for too long because "it was holy." (Again, in a gang that also operates like a cult, this fear of leaving may be a legitimate concern about losing one's life, though the conditioning is the same.) Essentially, these two "thought-stoppers" boiled down to the reality that nobody could leave our church, and we had to keep giving them our money.

In the end, out of the hundred or so adults and children who left as part of our exodus, I only know one (maybe two), besides my husband and me, who overcame the programming and completed *the second level* of mental freedom. However, I'm hopeful there are more. Yet most remain stuck in the same mind patterns. (Sadly, expressing this can be very offensive to the minds that are still trapped. Those who are free have nothing to defend.)

Others may believe they're free because their leader has supposedly "changed" or is less active. The great thing about mind manipulation or undue influence, as it's termed today, is that once you're wired, you don't require regular tune-ups because your friends and family typically share the same beliefs and speak the same language. You will pass these teachings down to your children, keeping the tradition alive. This mental programming ensures that oppression becomes cyclical and continues to thrive for generations. In fact, it's tough to find freedom without conflict or the power of empathy to see through your friends' eyes. The mind needs something to awaken it to a higher level of thinking, questioning, and awareness. That said, I always prayed for a good slap in the face for my friends who weren't privileged enough to experience the inner circle. Still, *the third level* involves figuring out what got you there in the first place, but that's a conversation for another day.

You might be thinking, "Not me!" If you believe this can't happen to you, you've already been deceived. Today, I correct myself if I think I'm above getting caught up in foolishness again, though it's unlikely because of Presence; it doesn't take me long to smell the breath or sense the signs of manipulation. I've been trained well to listen and stay alert. Once I'm inside, I can see all the mind games.

Interestingly, I noticed that most individuals who were attracted to or recruited by religious cults often came from broken families, experienced traumatic childhoods, had controlling parents, or were raised in a restrictive church or religion. That's just about all of us, so be warned—it could happen to you. We were all looking for what we lacked (a.k.a. deficiencies) in our upbringing or a familiar authoritarian personality.

Furthermore, college towns are breeding grounds for these types of leaders. If you want to know which churches to steer clear of, ask around. While most people might not recognize what qualifies a church as a cult, I've learned that rumors often originate from a valid source and typically contain a nugget of truth. Also, suppose someone refers to your group or the personality you follow as a cult. In that case, I strongly advise humbling yourself, resisting your ego, and investigating because the people know the truth. Gainesville certainly knows this truth! Ask ten people and average your results. The group I was involved with was the largest and most well-known at that time. Nonetheless, every party must come to an end.

Of course, it would be easier if I listed the church's name to satisfy some of you, but not doing so encourages you, the reader, to do your own research and stimulates critical thinking. Have fun investigating and asking good questions! Again, rumors often contain a nugget of truth.

Let's wrap up this sermon!

Unfortunately, this spider, intoxicated by power, had no qualms about destroying your life. I describe this experience as having my mind raped, sucked dry, or like waking up to discover that the love of your life for the past ten years has been unfaithful. The pain runs so deep that you don't know if you can love or trust again. You're unsure if anything you believe is the truth. It was awful. There's no other way to express it, and I had no idea it would take us three solid years to fully deprogram and reprogram ourselves for a life of independent thinking. Given that I was recruited at eighteen (by my classmate at SFCC), joined at twenty, and served a seven-year sentence, three years of deprogramming (plus two additional years of weirdness) wasn't all that bad.

Why seven years? Cults are fun! Everyone thinks the same, and to keep you hooked, the parties are endless. (And earning a Ph.D. takes time.) Also, very few therapists understand cults, and you can't reach the individual and their programming unless you know their language. Additionally, I had to learn how to make friends again because, in a cult, you are love-bombed and given instant friends, which is another reason why these churches can be so appealing. (Sorry if I love-bomb you; it's still in me because it has always been real Love.)

We packed up our ministry like a traveling circus. We closed out everything with our six after-school sites across Gainesville by sending letters to the Boys and Girls Clubs and the City of Gainesville's Parks and Recreation department. We informed them that our ministry, JAM on the Streets (JOTS), had relocated out of state. If anyone showed up at any of their after-school programs claiming to be associated with our ministry, we didn't support any such action. We informed them that we had severed ties with the church and made our reasons very clear. Believe me, they picked up the phone without hesitation. I assured them that everything was safe on our end and thanked them for the opportunity to serve our community. (*Shout out* to Clarence R. Kelly, a Gainesville legend.)

It was bad enough knowing I left behind so many of my beloved friends. Still, I didn't want any of the children from our ministry to grow up thinking, "If Ms. Sherry went there, then it must be a safe place." Kudos to the "Hebrew meek" mom in the former Village Green Apartments, who angrily shouted at me to leave their neighborhood because the church I was connected to was harming people. No worries...parents had to sign permission for their children to participate in our program. (wink) This policy was initiated by the director at the Boys and Girls Club then, which we carried over to our city programs.

In Proverbs 4:23, the Bible instructs us to "guard your heart," emphasizing the importance of being aware and mindful of what resides in our hearts, and more specifically, our minds. We must protect ourselves against the temptations of wealth, power, attention, "superiority," *specialness*, luxury cars, sprawling houses, and other similar enticements, as well as the risk of falling prey to manipulation. This is what Jesus was talkin' 'bout when he came to cast out the bullshit...I mean, the merchants from the temple. If you do, you'll meet God there!

"Guard your heart!" Don't let deception and the longing for phony treasures take root in your heart or invade your mind. Unfortunately, while this was one of the most significant lessons of my life, I didn't realize I needed to guard mine from the church, having been conditioned to believe it was "the complainers" I should be wary of.

Unfortunately, many pastors, preachers, priests, and ministers have used this scripture to instill fear of losing something that has always been a part of you. As you should know by now, the Kingdom of God is within—*you*. (It's like having *free power* from the electric company, you know.) You can't harbor crap in your heart when you are the temple of God. (If you didn't understand, reread it.) These individuals fear their members will discover the truth about their behavior—possibly how they have harmed people and destroyed lives and marriages. They exploit this scripture for their own benefit and to cover their tracks—their sin. I wonder what the consequences might be for manipulating hundreds or thousands of people for personal gain? Indeed, there was a price to pay spiritually, mentally, and physically for those of us who had the burden of carrying and processing this pain. (Samskara, look it up!)

Guarding your heart (staying alert) is about being present. Moreover, if you fear connecting with your brothers and sisters in Christ with compassion, "fear" is the keyword, revealing your relationship with God and your level of spiritual awareness. Don't ignore your friends or those your church has hurt because God isn't coming to do this work for us or rescue you. We are responsible for caring for and advocating for one another, regardless of whether anyone chooses to listen. The Bible calls us to do this in Proverbs 31:9. We must open our mouths and speak out against injustice! For instance, "Taking up an offense" against injustice might have helped save six million Jewish lives lost in the Holocaust and "crush the oppressor," as the Bible instructs us to do in Psalms 72:4.

May the church awaken to Love—Consciousness! May we forgive those who have wronged us, as Jesus said, "for they do not know what they do." (Pardon me, did you know that the challenging task of "letting go or forgiveness" isn't necessary with Presence? The past and psychological pain only exist in your mind. They don't have to exist today, and they do not exist with Presence. Presence is the peace that surpasses all understanding.)

Alert, steadfast, *respectfully* unfiltered with love bombs,
   —Sher! (The Common Snook)
Pause. Inhale. Exhale. Reflect.

186

P.S. No worries…I'll accept a check for $30,000 plus interest in tithes and *special* offerings that were shaken from our poor pockets at such a young age as an apology. And to my dear friends and those who came after me, whether through the church or its school, I apologize for taking so long to put this manna into words. After all, I had to raise myself while also raising my children. I hope this summary nourishes those ready for solid food.

P.P.S. Also, what I've shared isn't limited to religious groups. (I know of a few "cultish" private schools, religious and "hippie-ish," in Gainesville that worship their leaders, too, and pit their teachers against each other or students against students. [wink]) About ten years ago, my husband and I had the privilege of helping a dear friend rescue her father, who had been in a martial arts cult for over thirty years. He was able to receive help from my husband and be deprogrammed because the language we spoke in our church was very similar to the language and mindset of his group.

The Flock of Gainesville worship service, Santa Fe College, Gainesville, Florida. "Church like you've never seen before!" (TCS)

P.P.P.S. When my husband and I searched for a new church in Charlotte, North Carolina, a friend who had attended church with us in Gainesville appeared at the same church 500 miles away. Upon seeing each other after the service, we were both terrified! We were like, *"Oh hell no!"* I said, "I don't care if the music is good. I ain't coming back!" We both agreed we would never return to that church because it was clear we were drawn to something familiar, and there was a recognizable odor. We ran for our lives!

Here's a personal P.S. to my cult leader: *You may be surprised to hear, but I have only prayed you would live to see this day.*

(Sit in stillness with your eyes closed for 15 minutes a day; I promise it will transform your life!)

2. Spiritual Assholes, *Specialness*, and You

In this *special* sermon, I hope to use the words *"special"* or *"specialness"* at least twenty times to emphasize my point. What I will discuss is not limited to any religious or spiritual group. All are at risk!

Disclosure Reminder…,

I'm glad this title caught your attention. First, no one is more important or *special* than you (pause for dramatic effect). Unfortunately, since this applies to everyone, it also means that no one is important or *special*. I'm so sorry to share this news with you.

As you have read in my sermon, "Guard Your Heart—from Whom?," you learned I spent my early years in a charismatic cult in Gainesville. My husband and I joke that those were some of the most fun days of our lives. Because cults notoriously control every minute of your day with activities and events to keep you hooked, the fun is endless! For us, it was all in the name of *Jesus*. For you, it might be whatever belief system the cult subscribes to.

Yes, it was fun, but please don't take joining a cult as a recommendation. Who would willingly sacrifice their free will for endless parties? Some of you might be thinking, "It doesn't sound all that bad," except that the consequence might be that it could take you years to learn to think for yourself again. Like with weed, there is such a thing as *too much*. Yes, I'm talkin' 'bout being *stoned on Jesus* (just kidding…sort of). You could spend your whole life in a cult, and many do, since most cannot identify what a cult even is, let alone realize that they might be in one. This is why many go unchecked for years.

After studying religious cults and controlling groups for the past twenty years, I've noticed a few factors that lead to the development of *spiritual assholes*. These spiritual assholes, commonly referred to as cult leaders, also include the parasitic individuals who worship them. This brings me to the notion of *specialness,* which often appears in three forms, and we'll explore each one in detail.

The first form is the cult leader with an inflated ego. They believe they are *special* and make sure everyone around them knows it, too. They're the ones at the center of the circle (or at the top of the pyramid) who knowingly manipulate the congregation to nourish their sense of *specialness* and derive an emotional high from the power that comes with it.

Spiritual teachers and leaders are at the highest risk of ego inflation and losing their connection to the Divine simply by embracing the identity of specialness. Once they accept the phony crown, their teachings no longer originate from the Source; they become mere words without substance or a theatrical performance that only stirs emotions. Many mistakenly refer to this emotional experience as the word of God.

The second form consists of the parasites who feed off the *specialness,* sometimes referred to as *the inner circle* or, for us, "the remnant." This could include the entire congregation or just "the groupies" surrounding the leader. These parasites draw from the leader's *specialness* to maintain their own *specialness* while simultaneously reaffirming the leader's *specialness.* That's a lot of *specialnesses*! (giggles)

If you're part of a church, don't worship the leader because they're no more *special* than you. The moment you elevate someone in your mind, you lay the groundwork for a cult or a cult leader. By doing this, you become a part of the problem and become just as alluring as a woman swinging from a pole in one of those "gentlemen's" clubs. Cut it out; you might get what you secretly desire, a spiritual asshole. *(Specialness stirs up trouble!)*

Then, there is a third form of *specialness:* spiritual parasites that spontaneously form around any "*special* movement" or influential person. This doesn't necessarily imply that the influential person, who may be a leader, regards themselves as *special.* They might be completely detached from any sense of *specialness*, while the parasitic group has made them *special* in their minds and acts accordingly.

These spiritual parasites are the least threatening because they will always be present in any organization or movement, regardless of whether the organization is doing good or not. They might be the ones who answer the phone when you call your favorite ministry or community organization and leave you thinking, "What an asshole!"

*While visiting this local "church," I noticed that some spiritual asshole installed barbed wire to prevent the children from playing in what resembled a magical place from the children's book **Bridge to Terabithia**. As you can see, the cat also couldn't resist. The purpose of the barbed wire was to stab and cut them. "That'll teach 'em!"*

Once, I contacted two organizations representing these big-time (prominent) spiritual leaders (you'd recognize the names if I mentioned them). Interestingly, I stumbled upon this outer parasitic ring, which was beneficial because you can't learn unless you're willing to get close enough to these inner circles to see how these individuals truly behave. Apparently, the person I spoke with didn't appreciate my familiarity with their *special* leader and became quite resistant to me moving forward. If I failed to view their leader as *special*, my interaction became a personal attack on their *specialness*, which was, in effect, an attack on their own *specialness* by association. (Ugh, exhausting!)

Thankfully, a healthy, knowledgeable spiritual leader recognizes they aren't *special* and understands that many people who choose to connect with them are unknowingly drawn to the Light or God within them. They also realize that others may want to connect to the *specialness* they have constructed in their minds about them. As mentioned earlier, these individuals believe that if the teacher is *special*, then they become *special* by association. Take a moment to observe the politicians, spiritual teachers, and church leaders you know; you might notice they often have a shitload of spiritual parasites *circling around* them. Careful now!

What is interesting about all this *special spiritual stuff* is that we are all just humans who have lost the way that came naturally to our ancient ancestors. Thankfully, we have people attuned enough to help humanity return to the path. These universal truths are not new revelations. All these truths are within you; however, having a teacher or guide can sometimes help you reconnect with what is innate or already a part of who you are.

Unfortunately, many of these "*special*" folks merely repackage *free gifts*, selling them back to you and making millions. For example, when I read a popular spiritual book from a book club years ago, I told my husband that the author just repackaged the essence of Hinduism and Buddhism for the Western world. There weren't many new or original ideas in the book. The author simply made the teachings appealing to a Christian or Western audience, which was great. Still, I was suspicious of this individual's intentions as Westerners often have a terrible habit of repackaging age-old concepts as business opportunities. For instance, hot wings, "an age-old concept," once considered scraps that wealthier people discarded, are now marketed as delicacies. (Thank you. I, too, appreciate my excellent analogies.)

I'm here to tell you that there's nothing *special* happening, and you can grow spiritually closer to the Divine with or without help. Careful now! If you mistakenly believe you're *special*, you've joined The Club of Spiritual Assholes and have returned to the back of the line, so to speak. Warning: The ego is the ruler of the human condition, and to assume you're above becoming like these individuals is simply a sign that you are already one of them.

However, if you don't get caught up in *specialness*, keep in mind that you will encounter endless spiritual assholes and parasites because these folks are human, and their poo, my poo, stinks just like yours. If you understand that they are always around, you won't be caught off guard and risk throwing the baby out with the bathwater when you encounter them, especially within your spiritual community. Observing spiritual parasites can also be beneficial, much like noticing grubs versus earthworms in a garden: one signals the need to explore deeper due to possible problems, while the other indicates that the soil is healthy. Still, I strongly advise distancing yourself (running) from the spiritual asshole leader since their well is dry and cannot nourish your soul. Alternatively, you might stick around just long enough to have your world rocked—no pun intended! That should set you on the right path—at least, that's how it worked for me.

Keep pressing forward,
—Sher! (The Common Snook)
Pause. Inhale. Exhale. Reflect.

(Sit in stillness with your eyes closed for 15 minutes a day; I promise it will transform your life!)

3. Don't Throw the Baby Out with the Bathwater

Beware, this sermon is not for the black-and-white thinkers!

Disclosure Reminder...,

Many of us have been harmed by religion and its leaders. However, we must be careful not to let these individuals or experiences extinguish our yearning to connect with the Divine or limit us in life. If you allow your experiences to teach you something, I promise nothing will ever be lost.

As I mentioned in "Pseudo-Chapter One," I'm on the email list of a group that encouraged its subscribers to ~~storm~~...I mean, rally at the capital. I'm sure that surprised some folks. Still, I will reiterate joyfully, "There is something to learn from every walk of life."

For instance, as part of our boys' education, my husband and I are open to them choosing to attend any religious or *special* ideological school of any sort, even if it may be controlling or slightly abusive. (giggles) Hands-on practical learning is the best way to understand how programming works or risk being programmed, right? However, we didn't realize this until we took a closer look at the reality of the options, the dirty bathwater.

Students can consciously participate as observers in one of these organizations or unwittingly fall victim to manipulation and control elsewhere in life. Unfortunately, the experience *will* come either way since an individual or a collective always looks to program or influence them. *(Hey son, I hope I've taught you well. Good luck!)*

Indeed, most institutions have their share of the dirty bathwater: a culture, hierarchy, and various forms of stratification that quickly reveal students' places within the community. Sometimes, the leadership of these schools will toss out books on gender studies or purge their libraries of Black scholars to provoke liberals or to subtly indicate where they stand. *(Hmm...was that enough to run you off?)* However, larger state institutions are perceived to be free from this undue influence, as if they are better or safer than the alternatives. Still, "minority" students (the equalizers), more so than White students, often become aware of the culture and the expectations for them to self-segregate on the first day they step on campus. (giggles) Thankfully, many choose to take on the role of observers rather than conforming to the one assigned to them. This profound awareness resembles that of the unique individuals who attend, say, a Catholic school, yet surprisingly manage to graduate as agnostics or atheists. That's impressive!

I asked my husband, "Can you imagine what it's like going to a predominantly White university and how the experience might impact the spirit of 'minority' students?" However, without that consideration, he believed that the dogma of religious or ideological schools was worse than anything one might encounter at a "diverse" state school. I challenged him to re-evaluate his notion of "worse": the obvious or the not-so-obvious brainwashing of a religious school, or the "ideological brainwashing" rooted in the culture of the organization. I could see he was experiencing an awakening. He realized he had the privilege (similar to many White liberals) to judge a school as "good" or "bad" because he didn't have to deal with the "cultural brainwashing" or White dominance that "minorities" face, regardless of whether a school is religious or not. One institution was only better or worse due to a blind spot. Perhaps the small religious, conservative, or ultra-liberal school with its manageable environment was less threatening than the massive secular state school with lingering racial tension and oppression expressed through a feeling of insignificance.

Then, I asked him, "Cult or 'White Supremacy'? Honey, certainly you can see they are the same, right?" He responds, "But that one has a shady history." And then I asked, "Does your alma mater not have a shady history?" I left him to chew on his cud.

Another excellent example of not throwing the baby out with the bathwater is the dilemma many people face with actor and comedian Bill Cosby. Cosby, unfortunately, became (or was) a disappointing figure—*a celebrity asshole*. No one is immune to facing a similar fate. Yet, sadly, people began to *cancel* his legacy, even though his contributions were crucial in paving the way for African American actors to gain respect in the film industry. Cosby *is* largely responsible for the existence of Black sitcoms today. We often find it difficult to separate an individual's flaws from the good they may have contributed to the world. Please don't get me wrong. What Cosby did was terrible. Having faced sexual violence for much of my life, the stories of these women hit close to home. In the Quaker faith, it is believed that everyone has something good to offer; however, some people unfortunately stray from their path.

Separating an individual from their actions allows you to recognize God in everyone. (And Trump supporters said, "Amen!" [giggles] Reread it! It depends on your perspective on how you interpreted that.) When we condemn a man like Cosby by dismissing his legacy, we are, in a sense, committing a crime, as well. If we can hold that possibility for a moment, this may raise questions about how to best address similar historical situations, such as our Confederate history, *cancel culture.* White people will confront this history appropriately when they are ready and willing, and I believe their final stance will one day resemble the message preached in Christianity: "Hate the sin but love the sinner."

Unfortunately, humanity remains relatively immature. We tend to judge others, categorizing them as completely "good" or "bad." Nelson Mandela took a vastly different approach to addressing apartheid and White South African cultures. It's evident that he recognized the Divine in all people and refused to participate in erasing them.

Some people dismiss the idea of relationships with men, labeling them all as toxic, while others reject women and harbor animosity toward them due to unresolved issues with their mothers. (Shhh!)

Humbly,
—Sher! (The Common Snook)
Pause. Inhale. Exhale. Reflect.

P.S. How will the world ever watch me "dip and hay-day" if we wash the baby out with the bathwater? What a waste of a *perfectly good* line dance...and chant! (May my book reach every corner of DeKalb County, Georgia. *Whassup, Cuz!*)

P.P.S. If you ever see me yelling (in righteous anger) at a former "church member," perhaps in Trader Joe's as I have before (giggles) or getting dragged away or tased for speaking *truth*, don't dismiss my teachings. They still hold value because they come from the Source, not me. But no worries...I'm on my best behavior these days. (wink)

(Sit in stillness with your eyes closed for 15 minutes a day; I promise it will transform your life!)

Section V: Insightful Perspectives on the Trauma of Abuse and Control

In case you decided to skip the introduction and browse around, here's the **Disclosure Reminder**: Before diving in, I will say this: I'm simple. I love to laugh. Please don't confuse my humor with sarcasm; I always mean what I say. I test the limits. My words are plain. I often use "own" redundantly. I don't claim to know all the answers; my only intention is to be a vessel. Also, to connect with different experiences, I interchangeably use the terms "Consciousness," "Presence," "God," "Universe," "Source," "Divine," "Energy," "Christ/Krst," and "Light." Above all, reading my humor with a Southern accent is best. Enjoy!

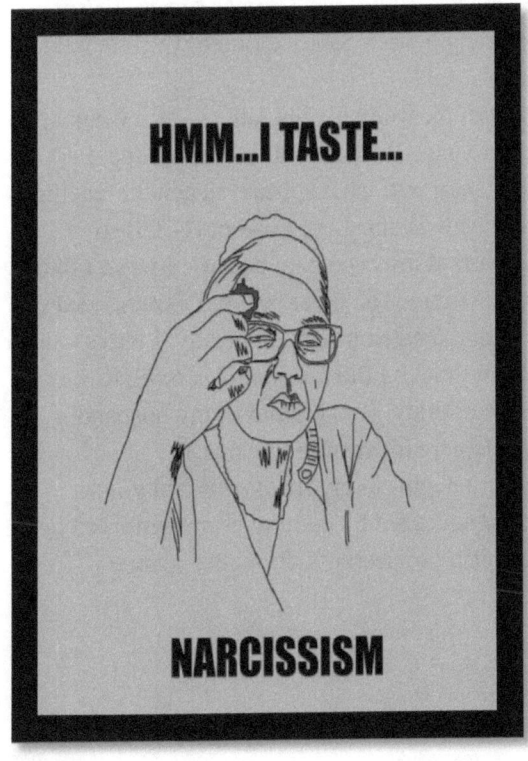

1. Go Queer, but We Need Some of Y'all to Come Back

Disclosure Reminder...,

Observing my own expression and style for most of my life, I could reasonably be described or labeled as queer when defined as non-gender conforming if I allowed it. But who wants another label? Not me. I enjoy the freedom just "to be." However, my husband calls me a non-compliant non-conformist. (Whatever! I follow the rules. That's why I spent seven years in a cult.) But he's just jealous of my freedom to live in this world without being defined or controlled by it. It's tough being a White man.

I played soccer with the boys before girls realized they could also play. Five of us girls in Alachua County played for Sandy's Blueprints with Youth Soccer Inc., creating a safe space for girls like me. *(Whassup, Christi, Karah, Kristy, and Nita!)* The experience was liberating. Coach Sandy ensured we were treated as equals to our male peers.

And today, I'm still holding it down for women's liberation—as a woman, even though I rolled with the boys for years. With that bit of knowledge, I believe I'm qualified to offer some insight into what appears as gender rebellion.

Fast-forward to my adult years in New Hampshire; I had never felt so beautiful until the day I completely shaved my head bald because I wasn't living up to anyone's definition of beauty anymore. The inner beauty I experienced was freedom that radiated from my heart and created true outer beauty. I was shocked to receive so many compliments, even though I did *absolutely nothing* to conform to the absurd definition of femininity. But, of course, my husband's ego *loved* the attention I received. (Men are interesting like that.)

Queerness (non-gender conformity) begins to unfold as girls and young women find themselves restricted and squeezed by cultural norms enforced by the gender police. Let's express the birth of queerness through a poem:

Don't tell me how to behave
Don't tell me how to dress
To cross my legs
To close my legs
To shave my legs
To cover my legs
To open my legs
To shave betwixt my legs
To hide my armpit hair
Fuck you!

Living in New Hampshire taught me a lot about seeking freedom. When I wanted a haircut, the locals would suggest an *African* salon run by *African refugees* in the rough part of Manchester, a.k.a. Manch-Vegas. In the diverse South where I grew up, I was used to walking into any "classy" American hair salon. They couldn't seem to understand; as the saying goes, "We may be *skinfolk,* but we ain't all *kinfolk.*" (*Hakuna matata,* American Africans; y'all are my peeps, too. I was just making a point.) I wasn't any more African (refugee) than they were. I was American—dammit! (And umm…some Africans twist and braid hair super tight, leaving you with a facelift and alopecia. [giggles])

Thank God for the cosmetology student I cornered in Sally's Beauty, a beauty supply store, who I convinced to cut my hair in my kitchen while she was still working to get her license. (Shhh!) She was apprehensive, all while defending White fear of curly hair. To ease her mental discomfort, I reluctantly straightened my hair, hoping to get a haircut and style after years of wearing my hair naturally. She did a great job and, hopefully, learned that hair is just hair, regardless of texture. I remember her sounding surprised, "Wow, it's soft!" What the heck was she thinking?

To my surprise, I took the clippers and shaved my hair off completely the very next week—bald! Those relaxer chemicals just weren't for me.

It took a lot of balls to walk down the street without hair to define me. My bald head was a big big "fuck you" to New Hampshire, who wouldn't cut my gorgeous hair in the 21st century. My bald head was also a "fuck you" to the White standard of beauty, which declared I wasn't beautiful in a state where the local Walmart in the state capital, Concord, didn't carry a single hair product for "People of Color" like yesterday. What the heck was I supposed to do with my hair? And the last "fuck you" was to my husband, who should have boycotted all those cheap strip-mall walk-in hair salons and barbers that claimed to be welcoming, especially when I didn't have the same privilege as him. (No worries…I *passionately* love "that man" with all my heart. Marriage is about growing up and rising together. **I wouldn't be the woman I am today** without "that man"—sent from Heaven.)

Strangely enough, I was often given a pass for my "rebellion," in part because I am a "Woman of Color," indicating that this privilege wasn't extended to or acceptable for all women. Additionally, being an artist also afforded me a pass for a lot of shit. I loved it! However, I realized this ticket to freedom carried more weight for other women, particularly White women, who face the pressure of serving as the standard of beauty and femininity.

You wouldn't notice if I didn't shave my legs, but a fair-skinned White woman with bushy dark brown or black hair can't hide it. She's bold! You wouldn't notice if I didn't shave my armpits unless I raised my arms, but you can spot the hair of a White woman from a mile away, waving back at you. For some, queerness is the easiest way to say, "Fuck you! Fuck all your rules! And back the fuck off! 'You Don't Own Me.'"

To prevent any confusion, please note that I am addressing *women*. If you were born female, with a uterus, I'm talking to you. I apologize for any awkwardness and sincerely regret if I misrepresent anyone—be it *they, them, she, her, he, him, her*, etc.—as I work to clarify my position and viewpoint. What other terms do y'all queer folks with ovaries go by?

Some brilliant young women are tired of being told how they should behave and dress. They start to test the limits by rejecting the standards that society imposes on them. When they taste this freedom, it's a liberation from a psychological prison.

Did y'all know that nearly half of gay and queer women are neurodiverse? (Do your research!) The term "neurodiverse" describes the broad range of differences in how human brains function, indicating that there is no "correct" way for an individual to think or behave. For y'all technical folks, I will say there are significantly higher numbers (high-ass numbers!) of neurodiversity within queer communities of women. They often go undetected because women, unlike their male counterparts, excel at mimicking bullshit socially acceptable behaviors. (I wonder why that is, lol.)

These girls and women are like, "We are tired of toxic masculinity dominating our lives; I'm going queer!" They have no trouble recognizing the nonsense in this world. Today, "the normals," stereotypical folks, might say these women are odd, but perhaps they are just non-conforming ordinary women, and the problem lies with the rest of the ladies. It's all a numbers game that determines who gets to be right, right?

But tasting this freedom comes at a cost—judgment and condemnation. You no longer get to carry the bullshit label of "lady." Your gender and femininity may be questioned simply by choosing to pursue freedom. I say go for it, but don't go too far. Don't let queerness get into your mind and turn into an identity, something for you to argue about and defend. Then we might start acting like men. (Shhh!)

It may also be beneficial to distinguish psychological and physical freedom from mere sexual pleasures that we mistakenly make into identities. You'll need to consider that on your own without too much opinion from me. That said, we need some of you to come back and reclaim your seat and insist on being respected as a *woman* without any alternative label. Don't let those fools run you off.

The label of queer sure the heck makes it much easier to be yourself, supposedly. But often, when you aren't psychologically free, this is merely a crutch. Instead, you have only swapped one label for another. "This is who I am," you say, but it's just a label. When it's no more who you are than not shaving your legs makes you less feminine. *Anyways*, what you want is to be free. This idea may be challenging for some of you to grasp, especially those in the middle of the "fuck-you" stage. Regardless, understand that you can experience freedom without taking on any labels. It isn't you who needs to adopt "a tag or a logo" or change gender identity or sex; rather, it is the system that dictates who we're supposed to be that needs to change…or die.

Y'all must reclaim what is beautiful, sexy, and rightfully yours. (We must understand how programming works or risk being programmed.) And you don't have to be sexy either. You can just be. *We women* have armpit hair, pubic hair, hairy legs, "soft cushions," *and* nipples. You know that pheromones (love chemicals that get trapped in hair) can be sexually arousing. If men were wise, they'd say, "Grow me some of that weed." (However, some folks should continue shaving, as removing body hair can be an effective form of pest control.)

I also heard that some women are sporting the appearance of a young girl's vagina…without hair. I wonder what kind of confusion that might create for men who are supposed to be attracted to *adult women*. Anyhow, that's too much for me. That's for the other gals who have gone too far the other way. *Hakuna matata*…I'll be sure to address the issue of false femininity soon enough. We need some of them to come back, too. (Don't get worked up, I understand that trimming the bushes is important *stuff*. Hmm…I won't tell y'all what my youngest said to me last time we went to the beach.)

Anywho, please understand that if you go too far or fail to return, they win; toxic masculinity wins, and false femininity wins. Please know you are lovely just as you are. It's not easy to believe that when so many have been misled into engaging in false femininity.

As for you queer girls, you are my heroes! Oh my, I just said "girls." Please don't yell at me, ladies. (You know, some of these "girls" are girls.) I often struggle with what to call y'all: *they, them, she, her, he, him, her, or all the above*. Please have mercy on me. Have mercy on us. Careful, you might find yourself in this seat one day when the world changes around you and flips out because you don't relate to—*them*. Love me.

With Love and Peace,
   —Sher! (The Common Snook)
   Pause. Inhale. Exhale. Reflect.

P.S. Did you know that research shows half of obese women experienced sexual abuse during their youth and that obesity is notably higher among women who identify as gay? What might this tell us? For one, food can serve as a source of comfort. Trauma might have affected them hormonally, or weight and "sexuality" could create a sense of safety from unwanted advances.

P.P.S. Women who experience menstrual cramps often unknowingly use stillness and specific breathing techniques to alleviate the pain. *Ladies, pay close attention to yourselves next time; it could teach you a valuable skill.*

P.P.P.S. This public announcement might seem random, but it's important. Is *anybody* interested in joining my *Betwixt* anti-high cholesterol, blood sugar-regulating kickball league? No worries…you don't have to be queer to join, but women without body hair will initially be frowned upon. You must be at least forty-five and a minimum of five pounds overweight for women and thirty-five pounds overweight for men to create *equity*, and that applies to *you, trans women,* as well. This league, where bunt kicks and run-walking are *completely acceptable*, is specifically designed for middle-aged folks who are tired of the aimless circles…I mean, walks around the neighborhood that become your destiny after forty-five. (*Shout out* to Nancy!) *Hit me back* if you're interested! (*Hmm…Patel, you and your wife would qualify for this league.*)

P.P.P.P.S. Speaking of refugees…I mean, *fugees*! Did I ever tell y'all that the only reason I passed physics with calculus was because of my good friend in college? She was a Haitian young lady who came to the U.S. "by way of the sea" as a child without any family (awe) and tutored me once a week in calculus for free. (*I bow to the Divinity in DACA!*) She showed me I was capable of so much more and that I just needed a good teacher who believed in me. (Check this! *My dear friend* is now a board-certified physician—beeyotch! You know, Haitians have good genes, right? *I bow to you, sister.*)

(Sit in stillness with your eyes closed for 15 minutes a day; I promise it will transform your life!)

200

2. Queerness Provides Safety for Some in African American Communities

Disclosure Reminder…,

When I entered the public schools in Alachua County, Florida, in the early 1980s, I was groped from kindergarten until I left the halls of the public school to participate in the Santa Fe Community College (SFCC) High School Dual Enrollment program. A few months into kindergarten, a boy I will call "*Li'l Pervert*" put his nasty hand under my dress and dragged it between my legs. Thank God I wore saggy tights because I would have felt even more violated if his hand had made direct contact with my body. **(Young children are watching you closely, so be mindful of what you teach them!)**

When I told my mother what happened to me, she said that the next time someone touched me, I should "beat him over the head with a chair." I remember thinking, *Has she lost her mind?* (Hmm…maybe it was wisdom, after all.)

However, by the time we reached high school, "*Li'l* Pervert" had broken both of his legs, so again, schadenfreude filled my eyes even though I was still being sexually abused. Seeing him at the mall with that walker helped me find my Divine healing, my inner strength, my *uzi*. I don't think he remembered me since I hadn't seen him since kindergarten. Still, what goes around comes around, right? (By the way, uzi is a Hebrew word that means inner strength. I know, it's so "ghetto" to take such a beautiful word and use it to name a submachine gun. It's like the well-known "Doggie Be Good Stick.")

To my surprise, the same boy and another (who later ended up in prison) threatened my mother, who was chaperoning a field trip. They told her that if she didn't sit with them on the bus, they would grab her boobs. Little me was so offended, but "the wildflower" didn't pay them any attention. She also didn't tell me this would be the beginning of the sexual harassment that would trouble me throughout my high school years. (You know, she didn't grow up in the South.) I was unaware that "redbone," which I learned was a nickname for light-skinned women, meant "free meat for grabbing" in some African American communities.

By the time I reached middle school, I had had every body part grabbed, caressed, and violated. I hated living that way and began to believe this was just how things were.

During my preteen years, I lived not far from Howard Bishop Middle School, and that year, the county had a great idea to provide my neighborhood with a bus ride home. Back then, it felt like someone cared that we kids were walking almost two miles to school, but my adult eyes can now see somebody wanted to get "those *ch'rn*" off the campus—quickly, especially "those kids" from Village Green Apartments, which housed low-income families. (I don't blame them.) Those of us from Highland Court Manor were just lucky to catch a ride.

I loved the idea of a ride home, but it turned into a nightmare if I arrived late on the bus. Sometimes, there were three kids per bench, forcing me to squeeze through to find an open seat. I was surprised I managed to maintain my virginity, just getting to an available bench. I quickly learned that I needed to pack my backpack before the bell rang and then run for my life to be the first on the bus. I could tell the bus driver, an older White woman, understood how difficult it was for me because she always seemed thrilled to see me make it to the bus early and secure the seat next to her. She realized I was just as terrified as she was but for slightly different reasons. (Bus 8911 should have read 666.)

Sometimes, I considered just walking the two miles home, but the five-minute ride from hell was often preferable to the thirty-minute sexual abuse I might have faced by walking alone with two or three boys. At that time, I really didn't know how to defend myself against those guys like my friends did. Some of the tough girls from the neighborhood were impressive; they were skilled and would come out swinging fists first. Sadly, others had the nerve to say they were rough or acted like men. *(Thank you to my bros from N.E. 28th Ave for always walking my homegirl and me safely to the neighborhood when we missed the bus. Except for that time…one of youse…shot my homegirl in the leg with a BB gun.)*

Thankfully, by the time I reached high school, segregation was disguised as honors, Advanced Placement (AP), or International Baccalaureate (IB) classes. The "Men of Color" I encountered from that point forward were mostly gentlemen. There is something about poverty, stemming from oppression, that also breeds toxic masculinity. (I'll explain more below.) I felt sorry for the girls who couldn't escape the abuse by taking these segregated classes.

No worries…here's a life jacket to keep you from sinking with this heavy sermon. There's another door to escape the abuse! When I think of all my queer "Sisters of Color" who have biological children from a man (a penis and not a turkey baster [giggles]), I see a woman who was fed up with that shit. If being groped and treated like a piece of meat doesn't make you queer, I don't know what will.

Have you ever befriended or hung out with a queer "Woman of Color" or any background, for that matter? You might have noticed they are some of the brightest, most caring individuals. Queerness can provide an alternative, safe space for girls and women while this world tries to figure out what the hell is going on with men.

Unfortunately, when my husband was courting me for marriage, I didn't realize he had feelings for me. I was so accustomed to having my ass grabbed first that I overlooked his genuine, gentlemanly signals of affection.

Tears,

—Sher! (The Common Snook)

Pause. Inhale. Exhale. Reflect.

P.S. Let's pause for our first lesson on **Consciousness for *Common and Country Folks***. The ego, the mind-made self, which is not who we are (since we are neither the mind nor the body), tends to project itself through the mental labels and possessions that give us a sense of self-worth. They shape our identities and influence how we perceive ourselves. This false sense of self is more diversified among middle-class or wealthier populations.

Those without additional mental labels leave the ego with very few options for self-expression. Many often identify with their bodies and sex since that's something we all share, regardless of education or material possessions. Cheap pleasures can sometimes be the best, and we all said, "Amen!" to the Big Sixty from Winn-Dixie. This is why I said poverty, stemming from oppression, can be a breeding ground for toxic masculinity in the Western world. Projecting that kind of "superiority" doesn't require intelligence or skill. However, it's essential to recognize that poverty is relative and varies globally, as its definition differs across cultures. Not all poverty stems from oppression or impacts a person's self-worth.

At the same time, those who are in poverty are closest to awakening or the Kingdom of God because it is the mental and physical possessions that can separate us from the Divine, depending on how we use them in our lives. The Bible states that wealth can hinder our entry into the Kingdom of God. I'm sure you've heard the scripture from Matthew 19:24, which states, "It's harder for a rich 'man' to enter the Kingdom" because they have so much to let go of.

Poverty sucks, but it can be a door to awakening if you allow it to teach you a lesson about what is valuable in life. Unfortunately, many will live their whole life just one step away from the door.

P.P.S. Hmm…there are many full-figured women in our Black communities. What might this tell us? 昙

3. Autism: A Gift to Humanity

Disclosure Reminder…,

Not only is autism a gift of mastery for many, but it's also a gift to humanity because these individuals are not wired like the rest to engage in the social games that can erode the "fabric of our society." (I pulled that *artificial* phrase from a book written by *artificial intelligence*.) Having one less person involved in the collective madness we call normal is a blessing and a step toward universal Consciousness.

Heck, if you ask me, autism is humanity saving itself from itself. I have always been fascinated by the autistic mind because "aspies" (a word for people on the spectrum) have somewhat of a social immunity to bullshit. I notice this specifically when it comes to racism.

For instance, White children with autism are difficult to influence or program, and they can often see through the veil of racism a little easier. Of course, some never develop the veil at all. They will ask bold questions, like during a school tour at a historically White "segregation academy" that I once visited here in town. "Do you teach a 'whitewashed' version of American history?" she asked kindly. (giggles) This lovely girl touched my heart and had me shoutin' like I was at a Gator Women's soccer game. Her passion for social justice gave me hope! She was truly a gift to humanity.

Still, I can't understand why no one was willing to answer her question. I admired the parent who went wild like a Chihuahua chasing its tail. He wanted to talk to this girl and wasn't leaving the halls that day until he understood what "whitewashed" meant. (Don't believe the lie; White people are hungry for truth.) *Li'l Greta* had touched the lives of all the tour participants that day.

Hugs to those who are improving our world,
　　—Sher! (The Common Snook)
Pause. Inhale. Exhale. Reflect.

P.S. Hmm…have any of y'all ever noticed the neurodiversity among the Indian population? (Disproportionately high!) Is it possible that some of them are further along in the evolution of human Consciousness? Neurodiversity is the norm! *(Hey, Indians, just so you know, this is a compliment, by the way.)*

(Sit in stillness with your eyes closed for 15 minutes a day; I promise it will transform your life.)

204

4. The Fruit of the Same Tree

In this sermon, I aim to reach both the head and the heart.

Disclosure Reminder...,

A few topics are dear to me beyond spirituality and Consciousness—with a capital *C*. These include autism spectrum disorder (ASD), "homosexuality," *Cluster B* personality disorders, veils/false personas, cults/controlling groups, and the mind. I recognize this is quite an intriguing selection, but essentially, it represents humanity in a nutshell...oops, I mean, in a nuthouse. *(We're talkin' 'bout all of humanity here. Not you. Ugh!)*

Today, I will touch on all of the above to some extent. I will also keep it straightforward because I want you to think and observe for yourself. That's my only objective.

I'm also confident this sermon may offend some; however, that's not the intention. If you can go along with me, I encourage you to notice your reactions and ask why you feel a certain way. Being aware of our feelings can lead to a deeper understanding.

To begin with, I've observed that narcissistic parents—those exhibiting traits or having a full-blown personality disorder—often have a child on the autism spectrum, one with attention deficit hyperactivity disorder (ADHD), or one who identifies as lesbian, gay, bisexual, transgender, or queer (LGBTQ), and the list goes on. I won't focus on ADHD, but please understand that when I discuss ASD, ADHD is implied. (Shhh! For many undercover aspies, ADHD sometimes serves as a stand-in for ASD since it's more socially acceptable.) From a spiritual perspective, I view ADHD as a close relative to autism, like first cousins, so I don't spend time distinguishing between them.

I am acutely aware of the emotions that may arise when discussing "sexuality" in America, particularly as many continue to fight for their fundamental human right to exist. Before I lose anyone who might not be ready for alternative perspectives that differ from the most prominent viewpoints or ideologies, I encourage you to keep reading. What I will discuss isn't focused on adult "homosexuality"; rather, it is meant for our youth, who may need to hear another narrative that resonates with their experiences and diverges from the current mainstream direction.

For one, "homosexuality" was removed from the *Diagnostic and Statistical Manual of Mental Disorders* (DSM) in the mid-1970s. I'm grateful for books like the DSM that enable us to track and categorize certain behaviors and abnormalities observed in humanity. However, if you take the book too seriously, you might create a belief system for or against specific behaviors. As I've mentioned before, normal and abnormal are merely a numbers game that determines who gets to be right, right?

Today, reflecting from an American psychiatric perspective, "homosexuality" is regarded as a normal expression by a large portion of Americans, and conditions like autism, which are currently viewed as disordered, may one day be considered normal, as well. Still, both autism and "homosexuality" can be seen as equally disordered by some people and not by others.

Here, the good book, the DSM, is not the final authority, as any book can reflect biases based on the perspectives and prejudices of its authors and those who vote for or against specific behaviors. Ultimately, today's behaviors and expressions reflect humanity, whether we like it or not, as we evolve in response to ourselves and our circumstances.

Since "homosexuality" is largely off-limits for discussion, it's difficult to address issues of "gender" and "sexuality" in our youth that may arise from mental disturbances. Unfortunately, many families that have negatively impacted their child's development are escaping accountability because modern psychiatry no longer welcomes objective conversation on this topic. Those who dare to express viewpoints that differ from mainstream opinions are silenced and labeled with ugly names. It's almost as if one can only belong to the far right or left: there's no room for independent thinking in the middle.

With that said, for those of you who understand I'm not a threat to anyone's identity and that your "sexuality" or situation isn't a debate for me, is it okay that we take a look at ourselves from a spiritual and psychosocial perspective?

At one point, I thought I was the only one noticing this pattern, which I call "the fruit of the same tree." Surprisingly, I discovered two psychologists who also observed the high frequency of autism in children of narcissistic parents, suggesting a possible genetic connection. Furthermore, I am not interested in determining whether a condition or behavior arises from nature versus nurture or before or after birth; it doesn't matter to me either way.

The only takeaway I gained from my observation is that events from several generations ago still affect us today. I'm sure you've heard the intriguing stories about how lab rats that received an electric shock while eating a specific food or listening to a sound, oddly enough, caused their descendants to avoid that food for generations or react in fear to the sound. In either case, trauma became embedded in their DNA.

206

Children with autism often have a narcissistic parent, and narcissism is frequently associated with early childhood trauma, which is also known to run in families, just like autism. There are a few narcissistic politicians with very public families that would serve as good examples to observe and analyze for these patterns. (Observe their *ch'rn!*) When I notice these patterns, again, it leads me to believe there may be a connection between ASD and generational trauma, which might also explain why the numbers are so high today, as we are all dealing with something. (This is the simple science we learned in junior high.) Observe and hypothesize!

Okay, we will take a break here and set autism aside. Still, I promise to write a whole sermon on observing how narcissism and ASD are likely two sides of the same coin, rooted in generational trauma. And that autism may be humanity's response to dealing with an unchecked, mind-dominant society. Notice that people with autism aren't as quick, if ever, to buy into the nonsense of this world. Please don't take offense; my feedback will enlighten you and offer practical solutions.

Moving forward from where I left off, I want to focus on the parenting styles of parents whose children later identify as LGBTQ, excluding the intersex population and children with various chromosomal abnormalities. Nevertheless, I consider these developments when examining the influences of DNA and generational trauma, as well as how they manifest in coping with society. This discussion primarily explores how parents' experiences and influences affect their children. This is merely one perspective.

Interestingly, as I continued to observe the offspring of narcissistic parents, I noticed that narcissistic fathers often have daughters who are gay, autistic, or both. In contrast, narcissistic mothers tend to have sons who are gay, broken, or narcissistic...or some combination of the three. However, they typically do not have gay and autistic sons, as is often seen in daughters. (No worries, *bro*; I know you exist and likely have a difficult mother. [wink]) Additionally, personality disorders—demons—aren't usually diagnosed until adulthood. Instead, one might see behaviors indicative of a lack of empathy and a disconnection from their emotions, or behaviors like oppositional defiant disorder (ODD) and conduct disorder (CD). All of these children will likely report episodes of depression and may secretly suffer from feelings and thoughts of suicidal ideation. Both parents, of course, create these situations with children who have the same gender as themselves and foster narcissism equally, which we call normal. *(So why not just say narcissistic parents? Because I really want you to catch this pattern that I think is important.)* Again, I'm not trying to take away anyone's identity or label from them. Your "sexuality" or situation isn't a debate for me.

Furthermore, I use the terms "narcissism" or "narcissistic" to encompass all *Cluster B personality disorders* and "mind-dominant behaviors," which I also describe as complete absenteeism from the body. For your reference, *Cluster B disorders* include antisocial personality disorder, borderline personality disorder, histrionic personality disorder, and narcissistic personality disorder. This approach of sticking with "narcissism" simplifies matters since very few people understand *Cluster B disorders* or even the clinical concept behind narcissism as someone who lives behind protective mental veils. While behaviors can differ among these conditions, they often share overlapping narcissistic traits. The average person experiences this to varying degrees, with the condition being more pronounced in those labeled as disordered. (Just as a heads up! Some of you may start to see patterns because you want to see patterns. [giggles] Careful now! That's another one of those mind games *we humans* enjoy playing. Take a breath, stay present, and simply observe.)

Freeing the "Innocent"

Before we get this party started and dig deeper into the behaviors of toxic parents, I would like to briefly take a detour to discuss "the fruit of the family tree," which needs to be included in this conversation. This tree encompasses parents and communities who have suffered narcissistic abuse or oppression (traumatized folks). Some of these parents may not have done anything wrong to their children; however, due to experiencing narcissistic abuse—either firsthand or inherited through their DNA (yes, generational)—they may sometimes produce the autistic or narcissistic children we just discussed, or worse, a little demon, regardless of whether they exhibit narcissistic traits. Once again, this happens because the damage from the abuse remains in their DNA. (This may become confusing for those who subscribe to the "nature versus nurture" perspective when trying to determine or justify *particular abnormalities*. Even so, being born with a demon doesn't mean one should remain with that demon for life. [giggles])

These expressive li'l demons can paint, too. (Elementary student)

*

Trauma and Drama

Since we will focus significantly on "sexuality" in this sermon, let's examine a unique demon with which many of us are familiar and whose manifestation may have very little, if anything, to do with upbringing. Can we all agree that the "gay" guy (the one who was not violated as a child) with the vindictive attitude and the twitch in his left eye has a demon, and there's more to his story? (And all the gay men who have unfortunately crossed his path said, "Amen!") He has a strong need to be hated. After all, he can't love himself because he was never loved. There is a block in his life energy, called Chi, that prevents him from receiving Love (it's like being cut off from God), and his deceitful behavior ensures that no one shows him affection. Still, your hatred ensures that he feels something—anything is better than nothing. Again, these young men typically have *fairly decent* parents (the innocent). However, these parents may have also dealt with severe depression, feelings of hopelessness, or even codependency (hmm…the not-so-innocent, toxic, covert abuser). (More on codependency much later.)

Women often lack patience with this guy and tend to argue with him. Heterosexual men fear him because he will physically *whoop* their asses like a man or psychologically like a woman. (giggles) This person is often labeled as "gay." After all, he frequently seeks out gay men for attention and behaves…or acts like a woman due to his enjoyment of being annoying. (Hmm…does that mean some of these women are *acting*, too?) Still, it's merely a strange manifestation of what some may call oppositional defiant disorder (ODD). (Uh-oh, I can hear some of those men "sonic poppin'" and "sucking their teeth" into this book.)

Many parents begin to notice this demon around preschool age because, for many of these kids, it has been present since birth. If it has been there from the start, can we agree it's a DNA demon? Even so, a few demons linger in the house with the family that can reach the baby within its first year. (Gotcha!) That's where things get confusing. (Some of y'all are like "Oh my god, she is so right!" Don't let just anyone hold your baby. Look at the baby's face. The baby knows!)

Anyhow, notice the twitch in Mr. Vindictive's left eye that says, "I'll cut you if I must," because he's a *survivor* in a world that has failed to understand the unique pain he carries. At the same time, he is almost completely cut off from Love. He can't find the door to escape and doesn't know what he is running from. (Do you?)

Prolonged narcissistic abuse, often generational, creates conditions such as ODD and CD, which can become genetic in individuals and cultures that have endured this abuse. These individuals struggle to connect to Love due to an energy block that arises from their gene expression, which is essentially a reaction to trauma. This response helps ensure the survival of the physical body while, unfortunately, neglecting the spiritual self. They don't know how to occupy space without this disruptive behavior (their crutch) because someone in their family was never given the opportunity "to be." Still, this pain can be healed. The pain of their ancestors can be healed. Remove the block, heal the body, and retrain the mind, and this person will be free. (More on Chi in a later sermon. I appreciate your patience.)

Interesting Patterns in Toxic Families

Once again, we return to our discussion of toxic or narcissistic parents while the innocent parents exhale. Below is a list of harmful, controlling parenting behaviors rooted in generational trauma that can influence a child's development, including, but not limited to, self-esteem, independence, "sexuality," and "gender identity," affecting their Chi or life energy. A common reaction or response among these youth is also noted. While some may view these behaviors as cultural, being "cultural" doesn't mean it's okay. Here are some examples:

- The parent gets their emotional needs fulfilled by their child. For some, this resembles covert emotional incest. (He's not your man, or she's not your woman.)
- The parent and child are too close for comfort. Children raised in such proximity often reflect their parent's gender behaviors and "sexuality."
- Overprotective and coddling parents fail to provide their children with the opportunity to develop independence, individuality, and self-esteem.
- Verbal and physical abuse, which includes corporal punishment. This psychological and physical pain can impact a child's life energy.
- The child is overwhelmed and choked by toxic masculinity and false femininity. Children exposed to this crap will resist indoctrination at all costs, and sometimes, the complete opposite provides the greatest sense of autonomy. (Queer girls don't have time for this nonsense.) As you already read in my sermon, "Go Queer, but We Need Some of Y'all to Come Back," which examines one of the driving forces behind queerness in women.

- Demonizing femininity in boys and men.
- Mocking masculinity in girls and women.
- The parent hinders or handicaps their child by fostering an unhealthy dependency to guarantee they always occupy a place in their lives. These parents, mainly the mother, say authoritatively, "This is your mother speaking," to reinforce her position and power over the child, keeping them subordinate. Or even worse, they'll say, "He will be my baby forever." (Eww, that's sure to cause mental health issues. Pardon me; it may be worth noting that creating dependency is cultural and accepted in many Asian families, and they would likely not use the word "hinder." More on this later.)
- Mom intentionally raises a transgender or gay son to ensure they wouldn't raise a self-absorbed *White man* like their racist father or have to compete for the son's attention from another woman.
- The child attempts to escape or resist their controlling parents by identifying as transgender or gay. Furthermore, the child may also display narcissistic traits and will use their "sexuality" to distinguish themselves from their parents, cultivating a sense of *specialness* and uniqueness that their parents never permitted. This also grants them the opportunity to narcissistically correct their parents, compelling them to conform and submit to their chosen pronouns. In response, the narcissistic parent spitefully and conveniently decides to support and pamper them during this *monumental* time when all the child truly seeks is freedom from that "bitch," as they put it. Instead, the parent— typically the mother, who believes they are "worthy" of admiration— exploits their child's quest for freedom to fulfill their own emotional needs for attention. "My child identifies as transgender," they insist, demanding that you now use the correct pronouns. It's all a power struggle, where they now control both you and their child. (Hmm…that was a loooong bullet point.)
- (We must understand how programming works or risk being programmed.)

There are a few celebrity families with interesting children, particularly non-gender-conforming boys, who would make excellent mother-son pairs to observe. One day, I was watching an online show, and something about the hostess's behavior felt very familiar to me from my observations of many other narcissistic women. Without any knowledge of her past actions, I told my husband, "I smell narcissism" (or we could call it an "energy block" in her Chi), and this was before many reached a similar conclusion due to the couple's odd behaviors. I'm not sure how these children were raised. However, the list above may provide some insight since narcissistic and controlling parenting follow a unique pattern. (Please stop trying to make this a perfect science; just observe.)

*

Our Childhood Impacts Our Parenting

As noted above, I observed that many who experienced difficult childhoods and needed safe boundaries in their homes (many who are now codependents) are now purposefully raising their boys without any boundaries or acknowledgment of their masculinity. This seemed to be the latest trend, seen as better than following in the footsteps of their controlling, bigoted parents. It felt as if they were making sure they wouldn't raise a racist, self-centered, privileged White man. When we ignore issues like sexism or racism, a force within humanity will ultimately address these challenges and respond as needed. While it's clear that I'm referring to White parents in this example, this doesn't imply that certain conditions are more prevalent in one group than in another. Sexism is universal, you know.

With that, there was a sense of pride among these parents for doing something different. I agree that change is necessary to help boys because having them deny their femininity contributes significantly to the problems we see in our *bassackwards* world today. However, I wasn't confident that my generation—the most unsupervised in history, growing up in the 1980s and 1990s—was equipped to make the best decisions for the next generation of boys, and those that have followed are just as concerning. Most of us were still working to overcome old wounds from our childhoods. We were raising our children while also trying to raise ourselves. Many choose to do the opposite of what their parents did, which is one option. But as we know, unchecked abuse leads to more abuse.

Strangely, this pattern, "the fruit of the same tree," has followed me throughout my life. As I continued to watch my friends and community struggle with pain, I couldn't help but conclude that there was more to what I was witnessing. Refusing to take sides and participate in the gender and "sexuality" wars was dangerous; egos do not favor pacifists like me—or at least as I strive to be. (I consciously try to avoid engaging in these conflicts.)

*

Is *anybody* listening?

You might be curious about how well my observations have been received. Once, I shared my thoughts with a mother who stopped by for support a few years ago. Her husband was highly controlling, a mix of narcissism and high-functioning autism. Like many others who sought my help, her family confirmed my observations. They were inundated with "the fruit of the same tree." Both of their parents were emotionally unstable and controlling, the type who didn't allow their boys to develop their manhood. That day, sitting across from this woman, I learned that sharing my observations could be risky because everyone fears being blamed, leading us to support anything that doesn't require self-reflection or draw attention to ourselves.

As you are aware, we play a significant role in shaping how our children develop and become who they are. Most people who have raised children would agree that their personalities are set from the moment they enter this world. However, identities formed by the mind are different and can be influenced by parenting and social conditioning.

My feedback caused such an uproar because this mother, too, had adopted a fluid and flexible parenting style with no clear boundaries. She kept her son very close, giving him plenty of attention to his feminine nature because it was better than the pain of being White and bigoted. She was angry with me because my observation may have indirectly implied that she was responsible for her son's growing femininity, which she indulged in and seemed drawn to. He paid more attention to her than her controlling, militant husband did. Unfortunately, he was fulfilling an emotional need for her. I see it all the time.

Side note: The male awareness of *woman* is impressive. It must be instinctual since they can anticipate a vicious roar from the slightest shift in her eyes. *We women* need to stop underestimating men just because they seem like they aren't listening or stop taking advantage of boys who can sense danger and will handle it right then and there. I often hear women say, "Why are men always trying to offer solutions?" Because they can sense death, the predator approaching, whether it's a lion or their mother. They know how to meet needs, pounce, or put out fires. Men are skilled like that. "Here, *woman,* you happy now?"

Children need space from their parents to grow; however, we all respond differently to parental influence. Let's explore how *Mother* has been perceived throughout her tenure.

*

213

Boys are Chained to Their Mothers

With so many families that have psychologically or physically absent fathers, women rely heavily on their sons for emotional support. Women hold significant power and sometimes use it to benefit themselves. Some women intentionally do not allow their sons the space to develop independently because, when children feel dependent, it ensures they will always need their mother. These types of women can make their sons despise women and long for the companionship of men because they took that away from them in their youth. I told my oldest that if I ever tried to pull that shit on him, I would permit him to cut ties with me. But of course, he won't because boys often have a stronger bond with their mothers than girls.

Please don't confuse this bond with Freud's peculiar idea of the *Oedipus Complex*, in which the boy has a sexual desire for his mother. (Gross!) I'm simply referring to the spiritual bond boys share with their mothers, which arises from the emotional support and physical comfort they provide. Freud must have also recognized this connection; many cultures would agree that the two often share an inseparable bond.

Girls Require Space from Their Mothers

On the other hand, when it comes to mothers, many of us girls say, "Please get this woman out of my life." (And we all said, "Amen!") We are wired that way because we must be strong enough to raise a child with or without a man, "the head of the *woman*." (Ha!) It's a part of our responsibility to keep humanity alive. We don't have time for Momma's games and will squash her like a bug if necessary. It starts in high school. Observe for yourself, and you will see this is mainly true.

Crushed Doesn't Mean Wrong

As I'm sure you can imagine, I've been attacked and overwhelmed for sharing my observations. Like an attorney would argue, most of those I've encountered often tried to dominate me with their words. They would assert defensively that the general population produced these conditions at the same rate, rather than considering what I was saying. Or they ask a twisted question like a journalist attempting to discredit and deflate my perspective, as if not being able to respond as aggressively and defensively proves anything. Sadly, they will do anything to avoid hearing an alternative viewpoint. So, I listened quietly as they crushed, minimized, and dismissed me with their passion and progressive jargon. This is America! The loudest and most dominant voice prevails without having to use common sense and confront their emotions. For me, it has never been about starting an argument. I'm simply curious why the same fruit keeps falling from the same tree, and I believe it deserves attention. ("Whoomp! There It Is," again!)

I can hear my sociology major classmates like a voice from a dusty textbook, shouting into this book, "CORRELATION DOESN'T EQUAL CAUSATION," blah blah. This was often a way to quickly dismiss anything they wanted to silence while appearing intelligent. One might also say, "This is a spurious correlation," meaning that even though the events seem related, they don't necessarily lead to a particular outcome. Still, research and questioning are our duties, even on topics that make us uncomfortable.

Even though many have tried to dismiss me, their defensiveness only strengthened my argument, as the truth often lies behind what people fiercely defend. I welcomed their feedback, and in a way, my experiences were validated; the general narcissistic population was producing this fruit at a similar rate. Narcissism, a condition of those who have been emotionally hurt and who hide behind veils or false personas, is rampant in our society. I could recognize the patterns because I had no interest or belief that needed defending.

Some of you understand me because I'm only discussing observations that we can all see. This isn't rocket science. Even so, many are frustrated because I may have struck a nerve. Others are upset because this conversation is unwelcome and has been deemed over. (And the guilty parents from both sides of the aisle said, "Amen!") People like me are silenced and labeled with ugly names like "hater" or "violent" just for refusing to agree with what's being presented today.

Young men and women are exhausted and worn out trying to decipher life and identity without realizing they have been raised by wolves, so to speak. Yes, when parents live ruled by their minds, they can behave like wolves. These children now say, "This is who I am," or "Please allow this to be who I am." Meanwhile, without making eye contact, these parents say, "This is who they are. They were born this way. Don't point any fingers at me." Both sides agree on something for the first time, reinforcing the narrative—one driven by exhaustion and rejection, the other by avoidance and self-preservation.

Your personality and energy are what make you unique. Everything else is a product of the mind coping with society, which isn't truly you and is instead shaped by our experiences and conditioning.

Many prominent spiritual teachers seem aware that "sexuality," whether one identifies as "gay" or "straight," has become a central issue influencing people's lives. However, they often opt to steer clear of discussing it. One reason could be that the topic is frequently weaponized and used to categorize individuals based on their perceived alignment in the ongoing cultural war between the far left and right. Some may inquire about your stance, suggesting that agreeing or disagreeing with their agenda determines your value as either "good" or "bad" or whether you are "for us" or "against us." In truth, none of these considerations holds any significance concerning spiritual awakening. When a person awakens, everything we once identified with ceases to matter. Sometimes, it's safer to remain silent to avoid vicious attacks, as the outcomes of awakening are ultimately the same in the end.

Discussing "sexuality," you may notice it triggers reactions that lead to the same defensive patterns we encounter when discussing racism, religion, or other aspects of identity. We often feel compelled to defend our need to be right and avoid anything that makes us uncomfortable. I've decided to share my observations because we all need clarity and insight. My generation and those that have followed are raising these children while struggling to understand themselves. I'm on their side and their children's side. I want to express compassion and present another scenario that doesn't require conflict or alignment with the far right or left cultural wars.

Academia Doesn't Get to Draw All the Conclusions

Some years ago, I wanted to study my observations through a doctoral program and see where it would take me. However, I knew that no institution would support my research because, as they say, "These mainstream schools are run by liberals." (giggles) My only option would have been a religious institution, which I could never align with because my perspective isn't rooted in an ideology that claims to be right. Nobody has the right to condemn human lives that differ from their own.

The autistic communities I mentioned briefly might have welcomed some of my observations, but unfortunately, my focus is on the family or family history. I also don't view individuals with autism as disordered or handicapped. Many parents with children on the autism spectrum prefer that they be seen as *special*. "He has autism," they say in a tone to garner sympathy. This perspective provides them with a sense of *specialness* and purpose in life. Who would want to give that up? Once again, the ego will close off any path that might hold parents or generational trauma responsible. Sadly, most people dodge responsibility instead of seeing it as a duty to enhance life and improve our world.

216

*

Do you know this parent, or are you this parent?

For parents, humility and healing begin with a willingness to understand ourselves and acknowledge how our behaviors may have impacted our children. There's no avoiding this process, although the mind will attempt to shield us from it. In our quest for healing, we discover that overcoming the mind was half the battle. It may feel frightening to let go of the beliefs built to avoid pain, but fortunately, there's no one to punish you on the other side. You'll only be met with love.

For the children who may very well be adults and have experienced this kind of parenting, this doesn't imply anything is wrong with you. That's where the world is mistaken. However, there is something wrong with all of us if we are human and ruled by the mind. Not everyone is willing to do the work to rise above the identities constructed by our minds or to acknowledge that our parents may not have been perfect. This realization is painful for most. But it's okay. They weren't ideal, and neither are we. Fortunately, we don't have to pass down trauma that is repackaged and labeled as normal. As I mentioned to the parents above, which also applies to children and adults, healing begins with a willingness to understand ourselves and confront what we defend or avoid.

I write to increase human Consciousness, which some refer to as awakening. What's interesting about those who had difficult childhoods or feel different from the world is that they are surprisingly the closest to awakening or discovering their true selves as they strive for freedom. (Yes, I refuse to say, "authentic self.") As the 16th-century German theologian Meister Eckhart stated, "Those who are in darkness are closest to the light." This is hard for "the normals" to understand, as their minds judge what appears "right" or "wrong." With that in mind, you can consider your childhood a blessing if you use it to uncover the essence of who you are.

Thanks for welcoming the conversation today. If anything, humanity has only taken baby steps toward understanding life, our purpose, and the paths we choose to take. We could do ourselves a favor by agreeing that it's okay not to draw conclusions. "CORRELATION DOESN'T EQUAL CAUSATION," these frustrated folks continue to shout into this book as if we have everything figured out. (eye-roll) We've been ruled by religion and other controlling constructs for ages. Indeed, we don't suddenly have it figured out, especially those of us from my generation or the fruit we produced.

Furthermore, humanity remains largely unaware (asleep), living behind veils and false personas designed to shield ourselves from pain and reality. This is a trick the mind plays to protect us from suffering. I've observed that our world, which primarily participates in this self-preservation practice, produces the same fruit as if we were victims of the same condition. Observe, and let's continue to grow together.

Sincerely,
    —Sher! (The Common Snook)
                Pause. Inhale. Exhale. Reflect.

P.S. Speaking of the most unsupervised generation! I can understand why many progressive White parents desire a different outcome for their boys, especially after an entitled sixteen-year-old "redneck" White boy pointed a loaded shotgun in my twelve-year-old face while laughing with his friends. It was an awful feeling; I didn't know what to say. (He, too, eventually ended up in jail. I sure hope they taught his ass a lesson.)

(Sit in stillness with your eyes closed for 15 minutes a day; I promise it will transform your life!)

5. Narcissism and Autism: Two Sides of the Same Coin— Awakening Through Consciousness, Part I

I hope you've read my introductory sermon, "The Fruit of the Same Tree." If you haven't, I recommend starting there first.

Disclosure Reminder…,

From my observation, both narcissism and autism spectrum disorder (ASD) stem from "environmental toxins" called fear and generational trauma, and the two reproduce these conditions equally. Although both are rooted in fear, they interact with the world quite differently. These children were told in the womb by their parents that the world was not a safe place, a belief that was reinforced during their first year of life, leading many to retreat completely by age two.

Children are born brilliant and are more intelligent than you might think. These children quickly make decisions about how to protect themselves. One decides to remain inside the body where it's safe, perhaps because there's a temple in there, only coming out when necessary. Another chooses to engage with the outside world yet emerges hostile and may sometimes try to demolish the connection to the temple in the process. But it's still there.

As you likely guessed, it is the child with autism who finds safety within, while the narcissistic child eventually emerges armed and dangerous. If we place that kind of mind or trapped soul in need of security in a leadership position, we'll be headed for war.

The narcissistic mind observes how the world operates and utilizes this knowledge to its advantage. Everything they express is a façade…not much different from the roles most people play, but just a bit over the top. They're like the woman who wears too much makeup and doesn't realize she's scaring everyone—with her larger-than-life personality. Or better yet, in Keenan Ivory Wayans' *I'm Gonna Git You Sucka*, where Isaac Hayes, who played Hammer, loaded up with one too many guns and accidentally shot himself in the foot.

The autistic mind is hiding inside. In fact, most of my family is still locked away inside their minds and bodies, and I have a few you may want to hide from because narcissism or body absenteeism, if left unchecked, can become a monster.

Sometimes, autism may initially surface but can later manifest as narcissism to navigate the world safely and confidently. I can think of a few well-known individuals and some infamous people who display traits of both—such as the young perpetrator who was responsible for the Sandy Hook shooting in 2014, which claimed twenty-six lives. I only mention him because he was diagnosed with autism, yet many observed anti-social or narcissistic characteristics in him. This did not sit well with the autistic community, which became upset, as they prefer to acknowledge only one aspect of autism, not the part that might skillfully army crawl on top of a building like a trained soldier and attempt to take you out. You know, the individuals whom we coddle and bully, treating them as if they are emotionally handicapped. Again, "He has autism," they say with sad puppy eyes and pouty lips to gain sympathy or attention. (Autism with a demon can be a beast!)

I held on to this story for a while because it was the first time I saw in the news that ASD appeared to intersect with another condition, supporting my theories. There was a blur between the two that most of us would prefer to keep separate. (Shhh!)

You will find many individuals with autism in academia. They discovered their escape from the inner world by becoming completely mind-identified, similar to a narcissist, but with less clutter than the rest of you folks. Once again, they were told in the womb and early in life that the world was not a safe place. There's nothing better than to hide behind a book. Give it a try! No one will notice you.

They remain inside where it's safe, allowing their minds to operate like a computer while they hide. For instance, when some of these folks speak, they sound like a computer or a book. "I am career. I am biology. I am science." They become one with their interests. This isn't all that troublesome because they often hide behind only one or two veils, unlike those who struggle with narcissism and the rest of you humans we call normal.

I know that anyone who has attended a university has encountered one of these human robots who are incredibly smart yet can be rude as shit, leaving you to wonder how they got the job. You've just encountered the ASD and narcissism combo. (Spiritually speaking, yes, both behaviors can manifest because trauma and drama are in their DNA.) They often exhibit extreme arrogance because you're merely engaging with a brain. Brains don't have hearts, you know. Nobody is home inside the body. However, if you spend enough time with these individuals and manage to get them to stop talking nonstop, some will smile back and wink at you because the child is still there. He enjoys li'l LEGO bricks, video games, and comic books; she typically likes cats, horses, and exotic plants. Place a LEGO brick or a picture of a horse in front of them, and you will witness this child emerge.

I'm confident both can be awakened, although it might be a bit more challenging to grab the attention of those who struggle with narcissism due to the many mental veils they wear. Nevertheless, mental health professionals frequently claim that narcissism is hopeless, while autism can only be treated with therapies, and some cognitive symptoms may improve with diet. Perhaps it would be helpful to describe this generational trauma as "cyclical karma" that repeats itself until one can rise above the repetitive cycles. (Hmm...that sentence had me twirling.) Alternatively, if you're Christian, you might resonate with the notion of generational curses, which sounds scary to me. At the same time, there appears to be a consensus that traits or conditions are passed down through our genetic code, specifically our DNA. Okay, are some of you following what I'm saying? I can introduce more new-age or Christian terminology if necessary. (You know, some of our leaders believe this. They've likely been reflecting on our country's European ancestry and how this immigrant gene pool continues to impact our nation. Some of these folks start to realize, "This shit is in my DNA, Sherguru!" Yes, it is!)

Overcoming fear and learning to inhabit both the body and the world can improve and even alleviate the challenging aspects of ASD and narcissism. Still, I don't see autism as something that needs a cure; rather, it's a gift that offers the world a unique perspective, and you truly can't earn a Ph.D. without a narrow interest, right? Without autism, we wouldn't have many of the technological advancements we see today.

If they had been diagnosing autism in the 1980s, my family (both maternal and paternal) would have been a hotbed of "aspie-ness" (and I quietly whisper) and narcissism, complete body absenteeism. Being of Cherokee, Catawba, Nigerian, German, Palatine, Italian, and Irish descent can have a significant impact on your DNA. (giggles)

Some people don't realize...but "aspies" are survivors! How do you think I managed to survive living in the South Pacific as a three-year-old without my mother? This was before it was illegal for boneheads to kidnap their own children. I like to think I helped change policies in this country. If your ass tries to cross the county line today with your children without permission, you're in trouble! Still, I survived emotionally by staying inside where it was safe, relying mainly on my sense perception to understand the world. It was a gift in disguise. Some of y'all are now lowering your defenses. Your mind is making room for me. "Okay, she's not a threat…that's why she's weird." Nope, I'm not weird; I'm just free.

For the record, don't let the traditional medical and psychiatric mental health communities convince you that you can't recognize these behaviors or conditions yourself just because you don't have a Ph.D. Parents diagnose their children every day when they bring them into the clinic and say, "I would like to have my son or daughter evaluated for autism." That's a very specific request; it sounds like a diagnosis…to me. Of course, some come into these clinics oblivious to their child's specific diagnosis. However, most parents are acutely aware of their child's behaviors and don't require a practitioner without children to inform them of what's going on. An official diagnosis is something we purchase on a piece of paper, similar to an MBA (Master of Business Administration).

Here's a bit of information about my father for those who are sizing me up against the *Diagnostic and Statistical Manual of Mental Disorders (DSM-5)* to determine if I know what I'm talking about. In 1968, the same year Martin Luther King Jr. was assassinated, my sixteen-year-old father was one of the youngest self-made millionaires in New Jersey (representing Newark) who was not a pimp, preacher, or performer. And he never finished high school. Careers were limited for "Men of Color," so thinking creatively and recognizing loopholes was crucial. My father embodied the determination of many "Men of Color." (For more insight, read James Baldwin's 1962 essay *A Letter from a Region in My Mind*.)

Let me prove it to you! There is an article from *The New York Times* in 1974 about my father, who was indicted by a federal grand jury in New Jersey for $1.3 million in mail fraud. (giggles) At just sixteen, my father conducted business under his father's name while running a mail-order business and would foolishly neglect to issue refunds, a close family member once said. However, from my adult perspective, the case seemed a bit more complex and resembled a network marketing "business." This concept was difficult for people to grasp back then. That same family member would always say, "He was the original developer of network marketing"—beeyotch! But she didn't realize that Amway and Mary Kay had him beaten by a few years. Regardless, this is worthy of Black history! He employed his whole family and saved his children from growing up in Newark. If you ask *me*, those who sued my father should have been held liable for doing business with a minor. (See, that's the ego being defensive.)

He never finished high school and never worked for anyone in his short life. The only explanation for my father's brilliance and uniqueness, besides being a Pisces, is ASD (accompanied by traits of narcissism, of course), as he needed to find a way to navigate and survive in this world. The man never learned to ride a bike, couldn't swim, lived in his head, and all his older Jewish friends were twice his age. (They advised him to move his business to New York, a.k.a. to a P.O. Box, since he was banned from the post office in New Jersey. Interestingly enough, Jews were among his biggest supporters and some of his most loyal employees.)

Luckily, *The New York Times* was printed in New Jersey at the time, which might explain why New York was unaware of his arrival. (wink) I'm grateful his buddies could see that loophole, allowing three-year-old me to cross the George Washington Bridge or the Holland Tunnel with my father each day, depending on which post office we visited. Young people found it difficult to relate to him. You get the picture: my father had Asperger's syndrome with narcissistic traits, similar to a well-known billionaire. (Dedda always said, "Make sure you have a P.O. Box.")

Indeed, something was up with me when I returned home from Hawaii. My favorite songs were "Down Under" by Men at Work, "Africa" by Toto, and "Sexual Healing" by Marvin Gaye. (The music selection in Hawaii was limited back then.) I didn't say much. I observed *you strange people*, unaware that I lived in a safe bubble. At five years old, Michael Jackson's "Thriller" was making its debut, and I had already experienced more of life and seen more of the world than the average twenty-eight-year-old in 1983. That's how old my mother was when I returned home. I also noticed that she seemed to be having a great time, partying and living it up as a college student in Gainesville, while we were living in the Pacific Rim of Fire with our hippie, "fresh fruit" eatin', vegetarian father. (It's hard not to party in Gainesville, even when your *ch'rn* are missing. [giggles])

As a young mom of three who had her first child during her senior year of high school, I'm sure she felt a bit disappointed not knowing where her crazy, covert, emotionally abusive ex-husband *(my daddy!)* had taken her children for two years. At least she managed her free time well and earned a nursing degree from the former Santa Fe Community College (SFCC). Women rarely get free time or opportunities to better themselves, so please don't let your *drama*...pity my *momma*. (She knew my father would bring us back because the man had never changed a diaper, let alone taken care of three children. He was just being a blessing.)

Anyhow, in 1983, if they were diagnosing autism, I would have qualified to join the club. If I didn't have autism before I left for Hawaii, I sure the heck had it when I got back. Given that I have vivid early childhood memories, as early as six months, and wasn't too keen on being held, I think strangeness and trauma were already in my DNA. For instance, as a toddler, when I heard the theme song of the daytime soap opera *General Hospital* playing in the background, I knew I needed to get my mother out of the house to pick up my siblings from school. I would say, "Let's go pick up the kids; you're late again!"

As I mentioned, I was quiet and observant. I also struggled with language, speech, and processing sound, which contributed to my rapid speech. Nonetheless, I was a math whiz and, of course, all-around quirky. (Those from my generation are now thinking "retarded." *Shame on you!* It's referred to as "neurodiversity" today.)

However, today I'm fully awake. (But I won't tell you about the rest of my family, though.) *Anywho,* it takes some time to burn off those extra neurons, you know, but it's possible. Plus, free extra channels are always a bonus, right?

Unfortunately, I no longer qualify for any diagnosis because ASD can be awakened. The gift of autism/Asperger's syndrome allowed me to access the temple, the inner world, freely, because I spent a lot of time in my body. It helped me avoid putting on any unnecessary veils, you know, the things that you "normal" people believe define who you are. (giggles)

Thank goodness, Asperger's is considered outdated since it was essentially a unique diagnosis reserved for White men and boys. Diagnoses like oppositional defiant disorder (ODD) and conduct disorder (CD) seemed more appropriate for Black and Brown men and boys. Additionally, Black and Brown boys on the spectrum who would align more closely with the former Asperger's syndrome— often charming and well-behaved—are frequently overlooked and never diagnosed because many White and Asian professionals hold implicit biases against "Children of Color." "Wow, what a sweetheart," they say, having expected worse behavior. Some of these delightful children (with their backpacks full of rocks and sticks) will never be diagnosed until they encounter a psychologist who is also a "Person of Color." (By the way, Tallahassee has a strong pool of Black professionals who can recognize the difference. Go Rattlers! Additionally, I plan to allocate $100,000 from the proceeds of my book to establish a foundation fund, which I invite you to match, to support diversity in research. Yep, my book is going to be big!) *Anyways,* I'm sure there are other reasons for the removal of Asperger's that White people would mention to shift the focus from this perspective. (giggles)

I imagine that Eckhart Tolle, Bill Gates, and many other unusual people...I mean, unique individuals would fall into the same boat. No worries...it's always a compliment. Unfortunately, many people hold a stereotypical view of autism, such as hand-flapping, which is why they (most of my friends, lol) can't recognize it in themselves, even though "birds of a feather flock together," right?

You know, most of the world's great discoveries have come from individuals who seemed to be locked away as children or who took nontraditional paths in life. At one point, I dropped out of high school to homeschool myself. Then I shifted gears. I enrolled in the Santa Fe Community College dual enrollment program and graduated high school with an A.A. degree—one of three in the county that year—beeyotch! It was unheard of back then. You can often recognize these individuals by their unique speech patterns, *sense of humor*, interests, communication style, or physical appearance. Whether awakened or not, most don't feel the need to adjust their uniqueness to fit in and blend in like clones...with the rest of you. (wink)

Let's pause for a moment. I need to split this into two sermons, with a "To be continued..." just like they did in the 1980s. Please don't fret; I've got you covered!

In the following sermon, I will share how you can awaken yourself, your spouse, and your children—whether they are autistic or narcissistic—from the sleeping state of fear, anxiety, and defensiveness typical of narcissistic folks. I might even venture to say this applies to those with antisocial personality disorder, but that might frighten some of you.

However, before you get too excited, some individuals on the autism spectrum may not awaken to the definition of normal you might desire in this physical world. Yet, they are deeply connected to the spiritual realm. Please don't get offended. But the fact is, there's a possibility they are already awakened, and you can't tell because you are asleep. (Ouch! I'm really sorry about that.) Some of y'all are praying for someone to save you while overlooking the gift of *Christ/Krst Consciousness* staring back at you.

You know, this awakened state is often overlooked in children with Down syndrome. Want to see God? Look into their eyes. Instead, we seem eager to eliminate this "condition" because what we perceive as a good life isn't the simplicity of living in connection with the Source. Thus, *Christ/Krst*

Consciousness is sacrificed once more. (Strangely, these angels are known to visit White families for some reason.)

When individuals lack language or a traditional social life, they often possess a well-developed sense of perception and a deeper connection to the Divine and nature than most. This is more real than the illusion we create that we believe would be best for them. This might explain why some people with autism don't mess around with storms; it's almost as if they can sense them approaching and gauge their magnitude. That's a gift!

As I conclude today, a few questions should arise if you have been following me. "If what you're saying holds any truth, are we mistaken about autism? Is it autism, or have we mistakenly labeled individuals?" First, a person is no more autistic than they are a lemon. Autism is simply a word or label used to describe similar behaviors. Personally, I wouldn't choose to adopt the label of autism, especially since it carries significant judgment from the general population, which is rooted in ignorance. Moreover, ignorance can be even worse when dealing with those who are "professionally" trained to assist individuals with the condition. Ignorance is rampant!

For instance, I've seen many who are unknowingly on the spectrum belittle and talk down to a person with autism as if they couldn't understand basic instructions and weren't the same as they are. The only difference between the two lies in when a person was born or whether they had been evaluated. One had the privilege of growing up without the label; however, due to the lack of a diagnosis, one shamefully creates a sense of "superiority" over people just like them.

You will find many undiagnosed "aspies" or individuals with autism within the Quaker faith, as it attracts an *older White autistic population* who have discovered a safe space to be their quirky selves in this world. Yep, I just said Quakerism is a hotbed of "aspie-ness." Ordinary people don't fight for social justice as a pastime. Once again, it's meant as a compliment.

Anyways, the answer to both questions, "Is it autism, or have we mistakenly labeled people?" is twofold. Indeed, we are noticing changes in human behavior more rapidly than would be considered a normal rate of human evolution. Observing and labeling patterns is part of our nature, but our conclusions are limited to the mind's understanding of the world. That's always been our issue, from Karl Marx to Sigmund Freud. What the world calls autism is both a challenge and a blessing, both a condition and not a condition, both a defense mechanism and humanity self-correcting itself. It addresses societal issues from multiple angles. Without autism, the gift of mastery, and (let's not forget, narcissism and ADHD, the gift of risk-taking), we would still be living in the Stone Age.

Perplexing Hugs,
—Sher! (The Common Snook)
Pause. Inhale. Exhale. Reflect.

P.S. Let's find some narcissistic folks and observe their children and grandchildren together. You'll see!

P.P.S. Speaking of retarded! I was schooled in "retarded" Alachua County Public Schools shortly after they were integrated. (Shhh!) I should have been in *special* education, but nobody noticed I struggled with language and processing because I was cute, light-skinned, quiet, well-behaved, and didn't speak SAAVE then.

Instead, they segregated our school by placing almost *all* the Black kids from Duval Heights into *special* classes. But Raheem's momma wasn't havin' it! She hopped off the city bus, bypassed the front office, walked up into our 4th-grade classroom at Stephen Foster Elementary, and *went off*! It was amazing! She was the first Black momma to impact my life. I had never seen anything like it, while the kids from Duval, who were just lucky to be in class that day, cheered like they were at a Pepsi Florida Relays Track and Field event. Her love for her son was beautiful, and I took notes, of course. (*Hey Inyo! Were you there that year? That was the year Governor Bob Graham's daughter was our student teacher. I hope she told her daddy that segregation was still alive and well in Alachua County, and that all the Black kids, except for you and Stephanie and a few others, were detained in special ed.*)

The very next day, Raheem was in regular ed, sitting right next to me. (She didn't even have to call a meeting.) He was thrilled to be a part of the class and was a real gentleman. You could tell his momma threatened him, though. He turned out to be one of the best students that year. Even so, I wish they'd given me Raheem's seat in *special* education and an individual education plan (IEP). Being light-skinned had failed me. (*Shout out* to Raheem's momma, a.k.a. Ms. Jackson! *Ms. Graham, do you remember Ms. Jackson?*)

P.P.P.S. Speaking of needing *special* education! As a result, I was entirely self-taught because I couldn't process anything in the chaotic classroom. In a sense, I was hearing-impaired, or as some describe this condition, the "hearing

227

deaf." I didn't learn much of anything in Alachua County schools, but I was always on the honor roll. (Hmm…maybe traditional school is a waste of time.)

The only reason I can write today—or at least know where to place a few commas—is that my professor, Robert Connelly, while I was in the high school dual enrollment program at Santa Fe Community College (SFCC), could teach—beeyotch! He awakened my mind and was the only English teacher I ever heard speak. He had an *attitude* when it came to English.

Surprisingly, I still have a copy of the textbook he wrote, *Writer's Resources: From Paragraph to Essay*, which he co-authored with Julie Robitaille. Once, I ran into him at the old Cuban restaurant down the street from Ward's Grocery Store in Gainesville. I said, "You wrote the book!" He looked at me like I was crazy. I always loved his *attitude. (Robert, I sure hope you're proud of me.)*

P.P.P.P.S. Speaking of talkin' too much! Did I ever tell y'all I was Florida's youngest public school teacher in 1998? The kids in the school used to say…well, I mean, the White kids, "You're not even old enough to get wasted!" It was a blast! *(Right, guys?)* They needed someone to supervise those *awesomesauce* students in the "behavioral self-contained class," and I needed a job. I adored those boys! (But let me not forget the sweet girls I taught. *Y'all were the best.*)

(Sit in stillness with your eyes closed for 15 minutes a day; I promise it will transform your life!)

6. Narcissism and Autism: Two Sides of the Same Coin—Awakening Through Consciousness, Part II

Disclosure Reminder...,

Okay, I'm back, and I promise to keep this short and simple. For the record, you don't have to believe anything I say for this to benefit you and your family. It doesn't require belief to yield transformative results. I'll begin with parents of *challenging* children or those with autism. I use the term "challenging" because personality disorders (demons) are rarely diagnosed until adulthood.

Children reflect your inner turmoil. (Hmm...my demons?) They reflect who you are, whether you accept it or not. If you're looking for a good reflection of the fears and struggles you try to hide or mask from the world, your children won't let you off the hook. Every time you feel frustrated with them, remember that they mirror something within yourself that you may not recognize. It's such a beautiful relationship! (I might need to give Lawrence Williams from Oak Meadow homeschool curriculum some credit here. I read his book/course, *The Heart of Learning,* about fifteen years ago, so I can't always remember who to thank for inspiring me. We'll talk more about Lawrence later.)

If you elevate your state of Consciousness, your children's behavior will improve, regardless of whether they have autism. As you continue to read, you might find yourself asking, "What exactly is Consciousness?" Simply put, it's your level of awareness. Essentially, are you home or not? Are you occupying your body, or has something else taken up residence? Do you get the point, elbow joint? Even so, children who are difficult or have autism cannot perceive the world as a safe place unless that becomes your reality first.

You will tackle this at various stages of your child's development. Certainly, it's easier to connect with a younger child than with a teenager, but it remains possible even during the teenage years. You just have to coach them with patience. Still, they will ultimately have to choose this path themselves. We can't force this awakening on anyone, but maintaining a state of Presence (being present in your body) can be transformative for them. The difficulty lies in that it will require time to achieve and sustain a state of body awareness, which ultimately enables both you and your child to awaken.

The cool part is that you don't have to solve one problem in any specific order. Just practice stillness (occupying your body), and you will transform your child's life while simultaneously transforming your own. It's beautiful and works every time...guaranteed!

Still, some rascals may benefit from deep prayer or even acupuncture to help release blocked energy that *you* might lack the will to move. Yes, some of these *ch'rn*/children may require an exorcist. It's all good! We all need a little cleansing from time to time. (This includes behavioral conditions like ODD and CD as already discussed.)

Now for the other side of the coin!

Some years ago, while exploring the idea of stillness and how to overcome and quiet the mind, I almost reluctantly recognized that there was hope for a narcissistic family member—the boundary violator I mentioned earlier—who had been putting me through hell. It's powerful when you can see a path forward for someone you didn't care for. I exclaimed, "Dammit, there's hope for her, too!"

Just because mental health professionals have little hope for these individuals, due to their inability to treat them, doesn't mean *jack*. As I've likely mentioned before, many of those drawn to the mental health field require treatment, as well. You know, only *crazy people* are willing to work with *crazy people*. (giggles) We sometimes fail to recognize that we are drawn to *ourselves* in hopes of gaining a better understanding of *ourselves*. Still, as I've previously stated, you can't treat what you don't understand or haven't overcome.

Now, please don't send me your crazy relatives. "They need to decide if they want help." Whatever! That's what the "professionals" say.

Individuals with personality disorders or facades often avoid seeking help because they perceive their false persona as their true identity. This belief is the most challenging aspect of reaching those with partial or full-blown personality disorders. The emotional layers they adopted as children to endure some of the harshest circumstances are thick and burdensome. It's as if their minds have entirely taken control, fiercely protecting them from confronting a reality they consider too painful to face.

Hmm…that has to be what is portrayed in vampire movies, where one must fight to get a mirror in their face before sunrise. In a later sermon, I will explain how veils impact all of us and how to shine a mirror in the corresponding vampire's face without getting bitten. Fingers crossed!

In the meantime, please don't do anything drastic until you've read my sermon, "The Parables of Controlling Personalities," and the grand finale, which isn't exactly the last sermon, but you'll figure it out. Yes, I'm intentionally providing just enough for you to continue learning with me. Warning: They may retaliate if you hold the mirror directly in front of their face, so please refrain from doing so. To keep you engaged, I'll give you a lesson to occupy you until then.

Interestingly, they respond to a gentle redirection from a loving person, yet like vipers, they can sense your intentions from afar. The most effective way to reach them is through practicing stillness. Strangely, they may perceive Presence, the result of stillness, perhaps more acutely than the average person due to its unfamiliarity. They (or it) will still be assessing whether they like the calming feeling. They'll ask *with attitude,* "What are you doing to me?" which indicates that it's working! I love how "nothing" can be so powerful. This concept is difficult for many to grasp, but once it sinks in, call me. We'll celebrate! (I love observing the analogies that come out of me. I know nothing about vipers, but I was right when I fact-checked myself.)

Practicing Presence or stillness with people with heavy veils can increase your own Consciousness because it's the only way to interact with them without getting drawn into an altercation. If you can remain present without being swayed by their gaslighting, blame-shifting, redefining, magic tricks, backstabbing, undercuts, dodging, lying, and minimizing, you will be like a spiritual Rocky! These are merely defense mechanisms they learned as children, making them difficult to deal with as adults. Just say under your breath, "It's time to put away childish things." It's worth your time because sometimes you can't escape these individuals, and they do need your help in a sense...but not too much.

With human transformation, everything physical remains the same; the only thing that changes is your perspective. We can all experience transformation through the practice of stillness.

Good Luck Hugs,
　　—Sher! (The Common Snook)
Pause. Inhale. Exhale. Reflect.

P.S. The answer will always be the same. It's sort of like eating at Taco Bell, or is Chipotle a better comparison? There's hardly any difference in flavor between a burrito, taco, quesadilla, or bowl; it's just wrapped and presented differently.

P.P.S. Speaking of coaching teenagers! Did I ever tell y'all I used to coach high school JV Boys Soccer for The Rock School in Gainesville over twenty years ago? Mm-hmm, that's right! The Rock School only selects the finest coaches! (wink)

When we traveled to away games, the referees and other coaches would overlook me and address the White bus driver, who wore a school polo, as if only a White man could coach those boys. I guess they assumed I was a "water boy" and not the *awesomesauce* coach handling all those White boys. And we only lost one game that year—beeyotch! They would *try me* like UF *tried* coach Clarence McCoy. More about him later. (Hmm…actually, he's coming up next!)

(Sit in stillness with your eyes closed for 15 minutes a day; I promise it will transform your life!)

Section VI: A Fresh View on Spirituality and Consciousness

In case you decided to skip the introduction and browse around, here's the **Disclosure Reminder**: Before diving in, I will say this: I'm simple. I love to laugh. Please don't confuse my humor with sarcasm; I always mean what I say. I test the limits. My words are plain. I often use "own" redundantly. I don't claim to know all the answers; my only intention is to be a vessel. Also, to connect with different experiences, I interchangeably use the terms "Consciousness," "Presence," "God," "Universe," "Source," "Divine," "Energy," "Christ/Krst," and "Light." Above all, reading my humor with a Southern accent is best. Enjoy!

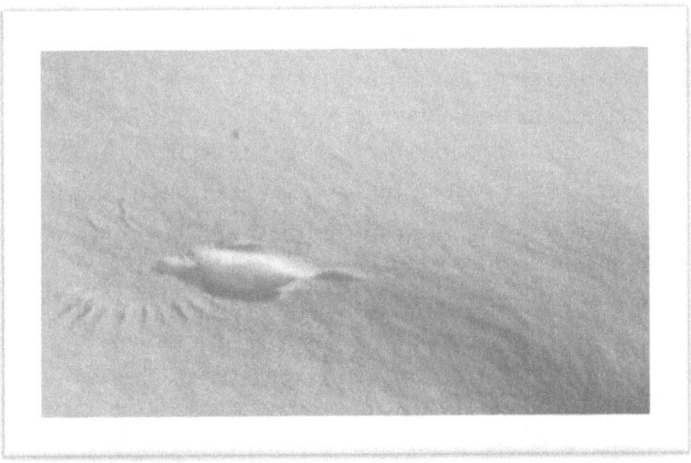

Nature says hello. (TCS)

1. Ms. Juliette of Gainesville

The vision behind my program, *Betwixt,* was partly inspired by and dedicated to the late Juliette Watts McCoy (10/11/1918–11/14/2003) of Gainesville, Florida. She was a resident of the Historic Fifth Avenue and Pleasant Street Community and a member of Mount Pleasant United Methodist Church, the oldest Black congregation in Gainesville. Additionally, she had deep roots in the neighboring historical Arredondo community, with enslaved family members who worked on the Historic Haile Homestead at Kanapaha Plantation alongside the Chestnuts, whose descendants are well-known in Gainesville for their civic involvement.

Ms. Juliette married Clarence McCoy (6/15/1889–6/5/1967). He served as a Corporal in the U.S. Army during World War I. Additionally, he was among the first African American assistant football coaches at the University of Florida (UF), which remained predominantly segregated even after the school was officially "integrated" in 1958. While unrolling a large black-and-white panoramic photo of her husband with the all-White team, Ms. Juliette mentioned that he was never honored with the title of *Coach McCoy* and was less recognized by a title closer to a "water boy." It was clear he was a remarkable man, as she beamed with pride when speaking about him. (If anyone has a copy of the University of Florida football team photo featuring *Coach McCoy*, we would *love* for you to share it. Perhaps it's time for UF to step up and officially acknowledge their African American "water boys" as coaches with a capital "C" after waiting all these years, and a spot in the University of Florida Athletic Hall of Fame would be sufficient. *Right, Ms. Juliette?*)

Ms. Juliette graduated from Bethune-Cookman College in Daytona Beach, Florida. She worked as a music teacher and was a first-class pianist. She dedicated her life to serving the community and the greater Gainesville area as a spiritual teacher. It wouldn't be fair to describe her with just one word, as she lived fully connected to the Source; therefore, she embraced multiple roles as the love and light of God radiated through her being. She was a mystic, seer, prophet, meditator, sage, visionary, guru, missionary, saint, intercessor, friend, teacher, psalmist, chanter, musician, naturalist, herbalist, and so much more. At the same time, she made it very clear she was "no fortune-teller." She often advised people to *pay attention to nature while walking, to enjoy pineapple for its healing properties, and to eat apples to calm the system.*

Furthermore, her Presence was so strong that sometimes the church would ask her to stay home. I would ask my mom, "Did Ms. Juliette get suspended from church again?" People felt uncomfortable when she showed up to church in the same black dress every Sunday, which she didn't like wearing but said she wore in obedience to God. (Shoot, I would have been scared and suspended her, too.)

Moreover, the descriptions above are merely limiting words as we attempt to express the indescribable—above all, Ms. Juliette embodied Love so much so that she didn't die but lived a full life, transitioning seamlessly from her body when her time was up. (Peace out!) Having said that, this phenomenon is subject to your perspective, as some may say God came for her, while others might argue she left her vessel, which was found standing in a walking position in front of the bathroom sink, reaching for the door to exit the room. (That was quite an exit, for sure!) It was no surprise to those who knew her that she would depart this physical world with such an astonishing gesture of the Divine or a glimpse into the Cosmos. There was no denying that she was both in and not of this world.

Ms. Juliette lived a modest life in a one-bedroom, wood-framed house that still stands next to Mount Pleasant Methodist Church on N.W. 2nd Avenue. Her life was filled with true wealth, unlike the phony wealth many people accumulate, which holds only material and temporal value. She set aside all labels and used only limited descriptions to make a point or appeal to the mind's limitations. What an average person might perceive as a cruel or undeserving individual, she viewed as someone of good character and sensed the Light within each person. Unlike those who see the world through the lens of "race," "gender," or "sexuality," she recognized them simply as humans deserving of respect and love. (Hmm…she must have also thought, *age is just a number*, as dear Clarence was twenty-nine years older than her. [giggles])

In 2001, Ms. Juliette asked me while I was sitting in her living room, "Sherry, what are you doing in Palatka?" I decided to dodge the question because I didn't know which direction she was going. She then exclaimed in a high-pitched, surprised tone, "You're at a ballgame! What are you doing at a ballgame!?" I had no idea what she was talking about. *I didn't follow any sports*, I thought. (Apparently, this event already existed. Again, she was experiencing my future or my "Now and Later.")

A year later, I was shouting, "Down the line!" during our final soccer game of the season for the team I coached. I glanced to my right at the spotlights illuminating the dark field. Everything paused momentarily, and I felt I was observing myself from another dimension. I said to myself, "Wow, you're at a ballgame in Palatka." The experience was surreal! (To my quantum physics friends, how was my friend, Ms. Juliette, able to identify the city from her vision of me at the game? Let's think about this together! Understanding where I was on the planet required knowing the time, which is the fourth dimension (spacetime). Did she see a street sign or somethin'? Please send me your thoughts!)

There are many incredible spiritual books out there, but nothing compares to sitting in the Presence of Ms. Juliette. Her inspirations run through the core of *Betwixt* as we strive to access the door that fundamentally connects us with all life on this planet. Gainesville was fortunate to receive her love and guidance, and we are grateful that her spirit and encouragement continue to thrive among us.

Betwixt plans to author a book featuring the stories of those who knew or experienced Ms. Juliette's Love. Pardon me; I know it's tacky to promote a barbecue in the middle of a book, but I'm giving away free barbecue for anyone who wants to come and share their "Ms. Juliette" story. I don't have time to track y'all down on social media. (Call me!) And maybe my homegirl, the celebrity ghostwriter, could help with this book. Whatever, y'all...you can be tacky, too. Still, *Elicit* wouldn't be possible without G'ville—dammit! When you aim small, you hit big! (That'll preach!) And Black folks love free barbecue in these parts! Just be grateful that someone recommended my book to you. Hmm...you must be *special*.

I believe these stories are invaluable and will provide insight into Albert Einstein's theory of relativity and the concept of the block universe. ("Say what!?") You heard me right! This phenomenon can be heard in Ms. Juliette's questions, which seemed to suggest there was a blur between past, present, and future. It was almost as if there was no concept of time to distinguish the difference. Some scientists believe that only a small percentage of people can see this dimension and beyond. Ms. Juliette was one of them.

It's hard to believe the University of Florida had such an incredible woman right under its nose, just one mile from campus, and missed the opportunity to glean from her Divine intelligence. (That damn segregation!) Nobody would have imagined that these jewels might be preserved through stories buried in the local African American communities and the greater Gainesville area. Well, it's time to dig them up!

To my local folks, if anyone has a photograph of Ms. Juliette, please share it with us. I'm starting to think she may not have been captured in photos, which could explain why nobody has a picture of her beautiful face, long hair, vibrant hazel-green eyes, fair skin, and keen Native American features. And White folks, if you lived in the Duckpond neighborhood before 2003, she was the distinctive older woman often seen walking to Publix on Main Street, wearing an A-line dress.

No worries…there are more Ms. Juliette stories on the way. She's limitless!

Inspiring Hugs,
   —Sher! (The Common Snook)
   Pause. Inhale. Exhale. Reflect.

P.S. I love sharing her life story boldly because many people can validate this account. I aimed to capture the late Charles S. Chestnut's story of knowing Ms. Juliette, as she held a deep fondness for him and his work as a civil rights leader. I hope a family member will ensure that his story is included in the book. *(No worries, I'll send another letter by snail mail.)*

P.P.S. Speaking of paying attention to nature! *Alice Walker, you might be surprised to hear that I have never seen "The Color Purple" (and now, some condescending Black folks are snickering into this book), which probably further disqualifies me from being Black. It's all good; I don't identify with "race" anyways.*

If it weren't for my brother watching "I'm Gonna Git You Sucka" and then the movie "Friday" almost daily, I wouldn't be able to quote any Black films like my classmates did. They quoted "The Color Purple" so often that I could rightfully say I'd seen the bootlegged version performed by middle schoolers. That said, I never had much interest in television or movies because I was always looking out the window or had something better to do.

Each day after school, I would stretch across my bed and gaze out the window. Sometimes, I spent hours watching the bees buzzing around "the purple flowers," wisteria, or the palm tree outside my bedroom. More was happening in that tree than in any movie; it felt so peaceful.

Still, I'm embarrassed to admit that I've seen the movie "Barbie" but not "The Color Purple." To make matters worse, I didn't even know there was a remake of the original film until yesterday, almost a year later. I spend most of my days writing-dancing or walking in nature. I blame the two Black women in my neighborhood and the one I walk with for not keeping me informed. How else am I supposed to get the news?

However, some years ago, I visited the MacDowell Colony for artists in rural Peterborough, New Hampshire, where you created some of your work in the late 1960s and early 1970s. (Wow!) James Baldwin was there, too; they even named the new library in his honor.

Anywho, while sneaking around the campus one weekend, I thought of you because I sometimes felt like I was the only "Person of Color" who had ever lived in the state. As I experienced the stillness and tranquility of that magical place, I saw a single tulip amidst the woods, surrounded by snow. I never thought winter would end. Still, that flower gave me hope that my alienation from the world wouldn't last forever. Alice, did you see this flower, too, or the yellow forsythias that always arrived a week later, even when snow was still on the ground?

(Sit in stillness with your eyes closed for 15 minutes a day; I promise it will transform your life!)

2. Angel's Wednesday

At first, I was hesitant to share this story from such a pure perspective of the Divine because many people live disconnected from the Source of life and might find a story like this difficult to relate to, making it seem somewhat fictional. Nevertheless, I chose to share it from my original perspective, of course.

On February 8th, 2023, while waiting to be seen in the dentist's office in the Park Avenue complex off Newberry Road in Gainesville, I noticed a text message from a woman I was supposed to meet at the end of the week. I was thinking, *I really hope she isn't canceling.* The text said she couldn't make it on Friday and asked if I could meet in the next hour. I just stared for a minute. I so wanted to meet with her, but I wasn't sure how long my appointment would take.

The staff called me back and discovered that the records from my previous dentist had not yet arrived. To avoid over-billing my insurance company, the sweet gal suggested, as if it were no problem at all, "Just reschedule for next week and make sure we get your records." (She was also an Eastside High School graduate fluent in Southern African American Vernacular English.) It felt like she was an angel, helping to work out the plan, and said, "Gone 'head, go take care of your business now." You should have seen her face. I could have sworn she winked at me. What a pleasant surprise. I texted the woman, letting her know we could meet in the next fifteen minutes.

The woman and I had never met before; however, we shared a mutual friend, the late Ms. Juliette Watts McCoy, again of the Fifth Avenue and Pleasant Street community in Gainesville and who had roots in the historic town of Arredondo. We enjoyed a lovely conversation and exchanged stories about our experiences with our friend. I expressed my hopes of starting a school and a spiritual community in Ms. Juliette's honor, as well as writing a book of stories from those who knew her.

Oddly, while conversing with her, I also felt Ms. Juliette's presence. I won't share any specifics since it might seem creepy to some of you. Unsure of what was happening, it was difficult to determine whether the woman before me was speaking or something was speaking through her. (Yikes!)

I returned home just as my husband was finishing lunch. On his way back to the office, he mentioned, almost reluctantly, that a close friend from his childhood, with whom he had originally moved to Gainesville from New Hampshire, had passed away. He was considering attending the funeral to support the family. I said, "Great, let's go together," since the funeral was at the church we had fled almost twenty years prior. However, this would be their new church location. I don't think he welcomed my enthusiasm, as he wasn't sure if he wanted to attend either. This was a significant event, and I needed to prepare myself mentally and spiritually. I asked when the funeral was, and he replied, "Tomorrow." I almost choked. I realized this visit would require some intense sitting in stillness. There was no time to waste.

My husband returned to the office, leaving me with only a few hours to quiet myself before my son came home from school. Once he arrived, I decided it would be best to send my sons by city bus to their dad's office (the man cave), so I could have some time to myself. We checked the clock and realized the bus was on its way. I told them to hop in the car and planned to drop them off at the corner of S.W. Tower Road.

Just as we were about to leave the house around 3:45 pm, my neighbor's boys frantically rang the doorbell. They said, "Ms. Sherry, our sister is missing; we need your help to look for her." Remaining present, I agreed to help while ushering my sons out the door. My oldest responded, "Shouldn't we stay to help search?" Thinking it would be a quick search around the neighborhood, I told my son, "No, you need to take your brother downtown." Sitting in stillness was serious business for me to prepare for this funeral.

I crossed back into the neighborhood and began calling for the missing child, whom I will refer to as Angel, and noticed that the community had started to fill up with deputies. I figured we would likely find her soon with all the help. As the hours passed, neighbors I had never met were out searching for Angel, including some I found questionable. The entire community was coming together, and I purposefully avoided my friend, Angel's mother, because I knew my emotions would get the best of me. She didn't need me for emotional support. It was best that I continued searching for her daughter.

In the neighborhood, there were more sheriff cruisers than there was space to park along the roadside. The heaviness began to weigh on me. That's when I decided we had enough help in the neighborhood. I would head to Wiles Elementary School and then to nearby Kanapaha Park (also known as Veterans Memorial Park) to look for Angel.

As the sun set, my heart sank, and I didn't know what else to do. I remembered thinking I wouldn't go home if this were my child, so I stayed in the backfield behind the park. It was pitch black, and all I could see were the flickering lights of the officers' flashlights in the woods and the distant lights of the soccer game. As I passed one officer, I asked, "At what point do you issue an Amber Alert?" He replied, "We're getting close to that." I remained out there, staying present, chanting. I had their back and wouldn't go home until she was found.

A little while later, the same officer emerged from the darkness and recognized me. He was so joyful, just shy of skipping and dancing, that he said something like, "They got her!" as if she were a little criminal. I said, "How? Where?" He said, "The helicopter spotted her in the woods behind the school."

The good news erupted from my body as I shouted like a maniac across the park and texted our neighborhood chat group to celebrate. Then I caught myself; I needed to call my friend first. I just assumed she had gotten the news, of course. But I called *anyways*. "Did you hear? They got her!" A wail of relief came from her that I will never forget. Then, of course, the phone got disconnected.

As I continued to rejoice in the park, I could hear others celebrating with me at the soccer game. It was remarkable to see everyone so excited. The news spread so quickly, like a game of telephone, that it popped up on Facebook before it was officially announced. I hurried back to the neighborhood and called my friend again. Then, the lead investigator asked her—to ask me—to confirm where she had been found, as he hadn't received the news yet. (Say what!?) Thankfully, within a matter of minutes, she was home!

As I hugged my friend, a feeling of peace washed over me. Something more significant than both of us was crafting the whole evening. I had initially planned to be home, sitting in stillness, but Angel had me out in the woods in the middle of the night for a more profound meditation and connection with the Divine. The news of her recovery landed in my hands like catching a feather falling from the sky—truly the best catch I have ever received. However, how was it possible that a close friend of this family just so happened to be the one to bring them the good news when hundreds of people across Gainesville were searching for Angel? It was a tremendous honor to join the inner circle and team of the Alachua County Sheriff's Office. (giggles) The Divine was speaking to both of us, and we couldn't deny it. I boldly told my friend, "You know this is Arredondo, right?" She was probably thinking, *Sher is strange.*

I simply followed the Divine energy, and it was just the heightened awareness I needed to prepare for the funeral the following day. Nothing compares to it.

Angel changed the lives of the Sheriff's Office on February 8th. These officers work so hard and rarely come home with a win. They used their training and technology to meticulously comb across Gainesville, inch by inch. Can you imagine how that one officer in the air unit felt, a man who usually chases suspects, when he spotted a precious little girl, barefoot, navigating the woods in complete darkness? When I watched the rescue video on Facebook, it almost didn't seem real. Angel seemed to instinctively know what she was doing. Most of us would have stumbled all over the place, but she appeared to navigate the woods with ease. Angel, who has Down syndrome and is nonverbal, was talking to the officer in the car. **"Am I going home?"** she asked. We witnessed a miracle! Or at least that's what we believe. (I get choked up every time I read this.)

My friend saw her baby girl, but I saw a remarkable human being who seemed to transcend this world. She activated her mind to communicate with the officer, understanding that his language was composed of words, while the rest of humanity struggles to suppress their inner beast. She never accepted the labels and baggage that, unfortunately, often separate us from the Divine. Her temple is pure! Angel single-handedly changed the course of Gainesville for four hours. She demonstrated that we could unite and rise together for a greater purpose. She reminded us that every human life is of great significance. No one is superior or inferior; we all have something to offer. (And Alabama said, "Amen!")

When I saw this angelic child "Reunited" with her family, I felt as though she looked at me and said, "Ms. Sherry, I've got this, and I've got your back."

I couldn't sleep that night, and many others in the neighborhood shared the same experience. I was filled with joy and the urge to dance, as if I had found my own child. I felt liberated and realized that my passion for dance was actually a type of meditation that had connected me to the Divine for years. It didn't require being physically still but rather an intense Presence that allowed my life energy, or Chi, to flow through my body. A strong sense of knowing reassured me that my friend Ms. Juliette understood I was attending a critical funeral the following day and needed her support. My dentist appointment was canceled. I met with her friend. Then, she passed me something; she tossed me the baton. I have been dancing nearly every day since Angel's Wednesday. (It all started with "Start Me Up" by The Rolling Stones.)

Peace,

—Sher! (The Common Snook)
Pause. Inhale. Exhale. Reflect.

P.S. How 'bout anotha' lesson on **Consciousness for *Common and Country Folks***? If you've been paying attention while reading, you might have noticed I'm a strong visual, logical, and pattern thinker. These skills contribute to my multidimensional perspective, allowing me to see what others often overlook. It's almost as if I have an extra set of eyes and antennas. Many Indian people, unknowingly, also have these antennas. I've seen them! (giggles)

Strangely, I could see parallels in human behavior before I found the language to express my understanding, which made me realize there was knowledge beyond words and human intelligence. For a while, all I could say was, "This *shit* is the same *shit*!" Or I would try to warn people, "There's a *gremlin* on the wing!" Or even worse, "He killed her!" But nobody could see what I saw, perhaps due to a mutation in the human mind. (giggles) The *simple-minded* needed me to translate my visual understanding into words, and most hold the belief that if you can't express it verbally, you don't know it.

However, as you can see now, I have found my voice to convey my observations by quieting my mind and employing storytelling. Either way, that's when I realized that the mute population could be some of the most intelligent people on the planet, even though we call them dumb—no pun intended. Nonetheless, it's *dumb* that our schools and educators lack insight into how to extract this wisdom from these brilliant thinkers. Again, Angel asked, **"Am I going home?"** She probably hasn't said anything since, yet apparently, she speaks just fine. But who cares whether a person speaks when their touch feels like a touch from God?

(Sit in stillness with your eyes closed for 15 minutes a day; I promise it will transform your life!)

3. Tell Me More About Stillness

Say what!? You ain't never read the Bible!? Times are changing, that's for sure, although it's perfectly fine. Quiet time fosters stillness, a practice that aids individuals in awakening from the sleeping state of insanity or the zombie apocalypse, the walking dead. (Some of you need to be born again.) I bet you didn't know that most people today are asleep and disconnected from themselves and humanity. Ain't nobody home.

When we embrace silence or stillness, we tap into a universal energy, a source of life that connects us all. Some may refer to it as "God," while others, who prefer to distance themselves from religion, may use terms like "Divine" or "Source." But let's keep it a secret; it's all the same; it's all part of the same intelligence that permeates our existence.

At first, some people can't handle the peace of stillness when they close their eyes because they're addicted to activities and live entertainment (sense gratification). They start to wiggle and fidget, but that's alright. We all must start somewhere. Begin small and be patient with yourself; that's all it takes. When you aim small, you hit big!

I'm not even talkin' 'bout meditation at this stage of spiritual development or awakening. Just try sitting with your eyes closed for 15 minutes. You will be blown away at how much your mind is running its mouth. You'll catch a glimpse of why you might be driving yourself crazy. If you've never meditated before, I encourage you to do this first and observe your mind. You can't start meditation until you realize how this device controls you. Imagine living your entire life with the TV blaring in the background. Well, that's how most people live; no wonder there is so much madness today. Nobody has peace.

Interestingly, spending time alone can be a lot like therapy. You can express all your thoughts and opinions without interruptions, yet without any therapy bill. After that, you'll be ready to take baby steps toward meditation, a state of no mental activity. Nope, you're not dead. I promise the mind is a tool, like a computer, and when you understand that, you can turn that thing off for some much-needed rest.

Oftentimes, meditation happens without you actively trying to practice it. As you discover peace within yourself, you will notice your thoughts fade away with your undivided attention. You might even find yourself observing your breathing patterns, or perhaps the length of your stillness session will increase because you enjoy the calm. You may also decide to quiet yourself twice a day or whenever you find yourself getting stressed. Please don't share my secret with the big-time gurus who have folks positioned with both legs behind their necks, eyes closed while pinching their noses, or who suggest their method is "the only way" or "the best way" to experience Consciousness.

Once, I was talking to a student at Santa Fe College here in Gainesville about sitting in stillness. He said, "Why the fuck would I want to do that!? There's some crazy shit going on in my head! I turn the music on just to escape my thoughts!" I replied, "So you're aware of your madness?" He looked at me and said, "Huh, you're right." He nearly finished my sentence and acknowledged, "Awareness is half the battle." I responded, "Yes, you got it! You're further along than most people." He and his demons walked away a little prouder that day. If you can't handle sitting with your own chaos, consider taking a daily 15-minute walk in nature. It can be just as profound. Keep your eyes open so you can see where you're going.

However, stillness is not enough for most people. It can serve as a sufficient spiritual practice for those without significant mental baggage, such as mind identifications. So, what prevents most of us from growing or having a transformative experience? You guessed it—baggage! This lack of transformation is evident among many individuals who regularly engage in stillness or meditation practices. If it worked, why aren't more people from these groups awakened to life or liberated? I've specifically noticed this in Quakerism. Many leave meditation groups yet continue to display the same mental patterns, suggesting it isn't quite working.

For instance, one group may be racially exclusive and not open to outsiders. This clearly shows that their practices offer no benefits beyond lower blood pressure and other health improvements. You can't pretend that meditation is transforming your life while you're still dealing with issues like racism or even sexism. They don't go together like oil and water. This doesn't imply that the Divine has abandoned you; instead, it suggests that you are living disconnected from your full potential.

While observing my *Friends*, I contemplated why sitting in silence worked for me and only for some of them. Of course, I couldn't see their "inner transformation," but the outer reflects the inner, right? Again, their baggage, mental rewards, and spiritual identity as Quakers prevented them from this awakening. We used *the same method* and *the same wooden chairs*, yet we had strikingly different results. You will find the door to Consciousness when you are nothing, so the opposite is also true. (I'm sure my observations will be unsettling for some Quakers, yet the insight is too valuable to conceal for the sake of feelings. And George Fox said, "Amen!" from the grave.)

Left Without Identity

Let me share where I was in life when I joined the Religious Society of Friends, a.k.a. the Quakers: By the time I embraced Quakerism, very little of the person I believed myself to be remained. I had no religion, no town to call home, an 800-square-foot apartment, no washer and dryer, joint pains, a headache that would not go away, no solid racial identity, no close family ties beyond my husband and children, no help in raising our children, no breaks, no job title, and no culture…but the food was good. Additionally, I had experienced poverty and near homelessness, and I never identified with the labels of mommy or wife. Yes, I have children and a husband, but those labels were never me, or at least not a mental concept or a role I acted out in my head. I lived life to the fullest and always gave my best while preserving my mental independence from labels.

Here's a little detour for moms who feel challenged by the label or mental concept of "mommy." Women who believe that an identity can save them or provide the mental significance and purpose they seek often transform the idea of being a "mom" into an abstract concept. This is why many people unwittingly ridicule the actions of suburban housewives. It's a role they play along the path of insanity. If you take a moment to observe, you'll see this is largely true.

I abandoned the idea of the "mommy" identity early on when I saw my young "mom friends" in the church setting clinging to the title and brainwashing as if it made them into somethin' *special*. I was no breeding machine and wouldn't fall for that nonsense. I wanted nothing to do with that exclusive club or title. In fact, "mommy" felt like a replacement identity, akin to joining a cult. I hated mom's groups, strollers, spandex, runny noses, "Clownfish" Cheddar Cheese Crackers, "Cereal O's," and the word "hubby." (giggles)

However, my nonconforming nature led me to homeschool, making me look like a "*special* mommy." At least, that's how I was treated. "Wow, you homeschool?" as if I were *special* for doing so. Cringing inside, I reluctantly replied, "Yes," while they tucked me into a mental box. (Now you understand why folks call me man-wired. However, I prefer Yang-wired, and pink is one of my favorite colors. And umm…I like unnecessary exclamation points alongside my pink, so. Also, if you stop feeding it "Clownfish" crackers, the nose will stop running. Hmm…I can hear one of my *jams* from back in the day. Hey, moms, let's sing it together, "I Love the Mountains.")

*

With that said, I was absolutely nobody, yet I had no idea I had discovered the jewels and the door to the Kingdom of God. (It's like discovering you have *free power*....) Stillness sucked me in and began to transform my life. "I was nothing, yet so much more" (*Elicit* sermon, "Waking Up").

As you can see, sitting in stillness is merely a ritual for many, making them feel *special* while seated in a circle of chairs or on a mat on the floor. They become religious followers—meditators—instead of individuals who meditate and live in union with the Source. They neglect to realize there is work (homework) to be done on this side of life. Awakening is not a passive process; it requires your active participation. You can't even find the door to the inner world with all those veils obstructing your view. Learning to see can help you overcome veils; simultaneously, stillness enhances your awareness to see them. They work together beautifully!

Many are unaware that they can learn to see...and hear! (*Listen* will be the title of my next book.) Others can *see clearly* yet lack awareness, so they, in a way, miss what they observe. However, as soon as you validate them or bring something to their attention, they say, "That's what I was thinking!" or "I knew it!" But it wasn't really them because they weren't home. Their innate connection to the Source allowed them to observe life while they were away.

I often explain that my guidance is similar to my work as an art teacher. I never hold anyone's hand to teach them to draw; instead, I teach them to see what is already there or to perceive things as they are. (Wow, art teachers, photographers, and computer programmers may have an advantage if they're willing to do their homework.)

You will be unstoppable if you practice stillness and focus on decluttering your mind, removing the veils. Interestingly, you don't have to do any sweeping; you simply need to recognize the mess and observe it. As Jesus firmly stated, and I will continue to quote, "It's harder for a rich 'man' to enter the Kingdom of God," regardless of how long they sit in stillness. They won't make it through the door with all that mental clutter—identifications and concepts of "superiority." You must learn to see first. Practicing stillness and clearing your mind is essential; being among diversity can speed up the process.

Lastly, the peace that surpasses all understanding is a state of complete mental stillness. No one is in the temple constantly reminding you of past hurts, unpaid debts, offenses, your MIL (mother-in-law), lost love, and deadlines. And here's the icing on the cake: this is where the Divine begins to strengthen you to keep those crazy merchants out of the temple for good. Y'all remember when Jesus came into the temple (Matthew 21:12-17 from the Bible) and was *38-hot* because people were running a swap shop? Yep, he was talkin' 'bout your head. It's a transformation you cannot measure because it changes you by leaps and bounds, with nothing required other than being still and quiet. You got this! This book can help!

Don't worry if you fall asleep; it happens. There's always someone snoring during silent worship in a Quaker Meeting. (Meeting is often capitalized, too.)

Stillness Hugs,

—Sher! (The Common Snook)
Pause. Inhale. Exhale. Reflect.

P.S. Both theists and non-theists have reported benefits from spiritual practices like stillness and meditation. Being a believer isn't necessary to experience transformation in your life. (Frankly, it often holds many people back.) Nevertheless, I'm a believer in you!

P.P.S. Speaking of stillness, with your eyes closed for 15 minutes! Have any of y'all ever played possum? In 9th grade at Gainesville High School, this goofy Hispanic boy pulled the desk from under me. I fell back, smacking my head on the desk before hitting the floor. I thought for sure I was dead, but then consciousness kicked back in.

The bell rang, and I could feel a crowd forming around me. "Is she dead?" I heard from the concerned onlookers. However, getting off the floor felt like too great a social risk. I remember thinking, *Ain't no way in hell I'm getting up,* so I decided to practice stillness that day. They were going to have to take me out on a stretcher. *Boy,* did I teach that kid a lesson! (Whatever! I did have a headache and might have broken my neck, and of course, my ego was hurt.)

Still, high school was tough; I had to make the best decision for my social well-being: being the laughingstock of the school or a victim were my only choices. And I chose wisely. (Oh my, I just confessed my biggest secret! Only my husband knew I once "played dead." Please send me your best confessions.)

When I returned to school on Monday, the poor troublemaker was hated and shunned, and I was a victim—and a survivor! "Damn, you almost killed her," I heard echoed through the halls in my support. (For the record, he never meant to hurt me. Acclimating to Gainesville through the English as a Second Language (ESL) program was challenging for students since Gainesville wasn't particularly diverse back then. That boy was just trying to be *cool* but lost all his *coolness* in one day. More on *cool* much later.)

4. Mysticism as a Spiritual Path

Mmm...frankincense. It smells like the Catholic Church up in here!

Youse* ready for anotha' lesson on Consciousness for *Common and Country Folks?

Well, depending on who you ask, mysticism (with a lowercase "m") can have a broad and complex definition. However, I prefer to keep things simple and define it as nothing more than connecting with the Divine (universal intelligence) by "looking within" and not allowing religion to limit one's experience. (To my literal thinkers, please understand that I primarily use "looking within" in a figurative sense, even though it is possible for some. [giggles])

I use the word "Divine" because it helps the average person grasp this idea. However, I also prefer to use "intelligence," which doesn't always create a mental image. Mysticism differs from religion because there is nothing to believe in or a prescribed path to follow. It's not a belief, but a commitment to life, a dedication to seeking and being open to innovative ideas and new understandings. It represents a lifestyle of inquiry and introspection. One may call it "Judaism," and another may call it "Quakerism" or nothing at all. The names are irrelevant. (More below.) Nevertheless, mystics can rightfully be described as seekers of spiritual knowledge.

Some individuals might conflate the concepts of a seeker and a believer. Even so, believers often accept what they are told without personal experience and typically dismiss any perspectives that do not align with their limited views. On the other hand, a seeker is unlikely to dismiss new ideas unless they have

249

experienced them firsthand. This leaves them in a state of curiosity and a willingness to explore uncharted territory. Seeking embodies a desire to know and an acceptance of the unknown. This may be uncomfortable for some, but it opens the mind in fresh ways and enhances your awareness because you haven't surrendered to the convenient explanations you've been told to believe since childhood. You will never discover new possibilities once you declare this is "the only way."

However, when you live in a state of acceptance, completely at ease with not knowing everything, you won't miss experiencing life as it truly is. There's no rose-colored lens distorting the view.

Modern scientists, whom I greatly respect, or those who align strictly with science, sometimes act like "believers" when they resist exploring human spirituality or mysticism due to its unfamiliarity. However, Albert Einstein was an exception and exceptional as a result.

Unfortunately, very few people in religious communities realize that mystics exist in every major religion. They often view themselves as united, regardless of the faith with which they are most closely affiliated or how they choose to express themselves. Almost every major religion has a path of mysticism.

Another remarkable aspect of mysticism, or mystics, which is not an identity, is that we may appear to contradict ourselves because we do not instinctively take sides. Instead, we aim to see things for what they truly are.

Mystics often disagree with their friends, which can be challenging for friendships. They do not endorse all facets of nationalism or any political party and seldom identify with either. Family members are not given *special* privileges; everyone, including friends, is generally treated equally, with no attachments to familial status. (In religious terms, this embrace and honor of all can be seen as a beautiful example of the family of God [Love] or the essence of humanity, which is understood as equal and one.)

Living without mental labels or a conventional, mind-made identity is difficult for many people to understand. *We humans* have a frustrating tendency to categorize everything and everyone into neat boxes tied with pretty ribbons. "This is who you are!" we proclaim. Others might ask, "Do you believe in the death and resurrection of Jesus or a higher power?" which may reflect a little man in their mind. Who knows? What does it matter if one's mind believes in something nearly indescribable and unseen, given that we are not our minds, and they are so unreliable? Most of these people (Westerners) are trying to figure out whether the individual they're conversing with is a Christian or an atheist. It's disheartening to reduce the world's vastness and human experience to just two categories.

Some people find it challenging to grasp the magnitude of the human experience when a set of beliefs rules their minds. This limitation leads them to assume that others perceive the world in the same way. Such an attitude can understandably be regarded as immaturity and narrow-mindedness. I recognize their intent to satisfy the mind; however, mysticism doesn't function that way. (I often yield to these folks because their mental barrier hasn't yet made room for this knowledge.) It's all good! Humanity is still blooming.

Moreover, mysticism is not about adhering to or restricting the human experience to a specific set of beliefs. It is about experiencing limitlessness, which can be viewed as the antithesis of religion, which is often seen as quite confining. Some eventually realize that holding and embracing diverse beliefs that don't conform to traditional categories is liberating. By avoiding taking sides and learning to see things clearly, you can foster friendships with everyone since there is no identity to protect.

Here are a few brain teasers and contradictory views that people often struggle to process: Black and Republican, Jewish and not White, Indian and not clever, White and not right, Black and not Christian, Christian and not pro-life, Republican and supporting teaching diversified American history, Arab and not a terrorist, Black and not a Democrat, Filipino and not fabulous, Lesbian and not trans-supportive, Woman in Hijab and friend, Black and not monolithic, autistic and more intelligent than you, hard-working "Redneck" and not racist, Hindu and not vegetarian, White and not ignorant, alternative LGBTQ views and not a hater, Mexican and American, Republican and not pro-life, Patel and not a Democrat, Puerto Rican and American, Republican and not a hater, Indian and not Hindu, mute and intelligent, autistic and not socially challenged, Hispanic and White, Chinese and American, Black and Latino, introvert and social. (That was fun!)

Let's keep the fun going with a list of alternative spiritual paths for your studies that remain unconfined when not practiced as a religion. Choose one; they're all the same:

- Sufism or Christ/Krst Consciousness in Islam
- Jainism, with its meditative and self-introspective approach
- Advaita Vedanta in Hinduism
- Gnosticism and the essence of Quakerism in Christianity

- Kabbalah, Hasidism, Christ/Krst Consciousness in Judaism
- Zen in Buddhism
- Pure mysticism without an umbrella religion that considers all faiths equally (That's me, looking at you.)

Now You Know Hugs,
  —Sher! (The Common Snook)
  Pause. Inhale. Exhale. Reflect.

P.S. Jews, humanists, and atheists, please don't let your minds get hung up on religious terms. The intelligence we all possess remains the same, whether you refer to it as a god or not—to the Jew, I'm a Jew; to the atheist, I'm an Atheist. (Atheists, particularly angry Atheists, can be very sensitive about capital letters when some attempt to make atheism a one-size-fits-all—identity (doctrine or ideology) for some. It's also a handy word to help ensure religious people back off. It's scary!)

However, I have met many "Atheists" who are just fed up with religion or angry at their parents or culture for valid reasons, yet they are secretly somewhat spiritual. (Shhh! I get it; humanity expresses many ideas and words that are rather primitive [cavemanish]. A few of my favorites are god, fire, man, foot, mouth, and bone.)

P.P.S. Speaking of Patel! Black folks, White folks, and folks on meth, Patel is tired of having his 7-Elevens robbed. (That jewelry store armed robbery in New Jersey was terrible!) Just so you know, Patel has a gun, but he chooses not to *pop a cap in your ass*. He respects your life and asks that you respect him in return. Law enforcement could learn a thing or two from Patel.

Patel, I bow to the Divinity in you for sparing lives. Even so, you work in the heart of African American communities. (It's like being in India, right?) They put food on your table. You know, you have more to offer than alcohol. Indians in America, more so South Indians than my friend Patel, could help lift African American communities out of poverty by simply sharing their love of mathematics and science through free tutoring programs. Remember, share your talents freely, and you will be blessed! Also, don't forget where you came from and, for some, how it feels to be trapped at the bottom of the caste system, with some never able to escape the oppression. Namaste!

(Sit in stillness with your eyes closed for 15 minutes a day; I promise it will transform your life!)

5. Is It ADHD or Your Parenting?

Disclosure Reminder...,

In my early years, I read *The Heart of Learning* by Lawrence Williams, Ed.D., a homeschooling guide specifically designed to educate parents on how to parent and teach, rather than entrusting them with a homeschool curriculum. It was an incredible mini-course and one of my most memorable experiences of mental transformation. I am referring to the original, meaty version of *The Heart of Learning*, likely written in the 1970s or 1980s, where Williams mentioned that women should stay home and give up their careers if they want to have children. He also suggested that if they wished to have a career, they might need to reconsider having a family. (Ouch!) I'm sure that didn't sit well with this modern generation of women. However, if I may be so bold as to agree just a tiny bit, there was some truth to his statement. (Oh shoot, I'm in trouble now.)

Unfortunately, the illusion of staying home with the *ch'rn* is often a privilege reserved for the more affluent, making it challenging for many who desire a family. Although he opened the opportunity for either parent to stay home, I sensed Williams was eyeing *Mom* because she is the primary teacher during the early years. (More about this in a later sermon.) Nonetheless, he offered advice on living simply, which may have still fallen short for this generation to fully grasp his message. For instance, I know a couple of physicians whose spouses are also physicians, for whom it doesn't make sense for both parents to work while their children need them; as a result, they end up being absent more often than most parents. Given this example, can you see where he was coming from? Childhood is short, and our children need us more than ever.

Williams was being insightful and striving to help families achieve success. Even so, I'm sure he irritated some folks in ways similar to my book. Unfortunately, Oak Meadow updated their course to be more inclusive, tending to the needs of this generation. (I almost said, "disgruntled generation," but I didn't.) In my view, the new version has lost its soul. But you know, I'm old school.

Pardon me for a second: *Lawrence...Lawrence! I understand you're in Vermont, but there are brown folks in the South using your curriculum. We need our faces reflected in the artwork, book covers, character descriptions in the stories, brown hands teaching knitting—anything!, especially with this Oak Meadow Curriculum shout-out. Otherwise, I will send folks to eBay.*

*

Anyhow, one section of this comprehensive course discussed and attributed children's behavior problems, such as hyperactivity and argumentativeness, to an imbalanced flow of energy within the household. It classified certain behaviors or expressions as either feminine or masculine energy, which had nothing to do with the parents' sex or "sexuality." (Please note, this is not the masculine and feminine energy nonsense you may have heard about on social media that claims to help women attract a man and that excuses toxic masculinity. This is entirely different. Don't be confused.) As I was saying before I interrupted myself, we all possess masculine and feminine energy, for lack of a better description. (You can call them orange and blue if that helps.) As I followed his train of thought, having very little knowledge about feminine versus masculine energy at the time, I was open to testing the theory. Because the behaviors they described, I was dealing with in my children.

Without going into depth, they essentially stated that if your children are bouncing off the walls, there is too much masculine energy; if your children are flighty and detached, there is too much feminine energy. A well-balanced family exists somewhere between these two extremes. By adjusting the two, adding or reducing certain behaviors and activities, you will notice that your children start to behave more positively or return to planet Earth. I didn't need to believe in this teaching to give it a try.

Our household was perceived as hyperactive and argumentative, which meant there was an excess of masculine energy and a corresponding lack of feminine energy, characterized by a deficiency in intimacy, creativity, and fun. All those alpha males couldn't handle the force coming from this "alpha female," as our house cat likes to call me. My husband and I both lean toward organizing, planning, building, and achieving; these activities are associated with masculine energy. (But he does like to chill and have fun!) Additionally, those who could relax in a messy house and paint a picture in the middle of the living room floor without establishing any structure were viewed as *feminine energy dominant*.

I had always envied the woman who could chill in a messy house (like my BFF from Chhattisgarh, India). That was not me. I ran a schedule (pronounced with an English accent) from the moment you woke up until I kissed you goodnight…right on time. (Crazy!) Our house functioned like a well-oiled machine, clean and sterile…just as I preferred it. It was so bad that my husband and I joked by singing a few lines we heard from the father in that famous movie with the "British" nanny: "Order is the blood we bleed!" (Be creative; you'll figure it out.) That said, I realized that perhaps I had more masculine energy; yet thank God, I was also an artist, which always helped to balance me. Likely, this stemmed from growing up without structure during my childhood and without a father at home to balance my mother's energy. (Or maybe I was born that way!!!) Strangely, this also aligned with all the asshole comments I heard throughout my life. "Sher, you think like a man; you're man-wired." Oh, how I wished to be like sweet Mother Mary, who caressed and cuddled with her babies, even when they had sticky hands touching the couch. But I wasn't havin' that; I grew up in a sticky house.

Once I understood where my husband and I fell on the energy spectrum, I aimed to incorporate more feminine energy activities into our family life. These were activities I had to schedule, of course. One in particular comes to mind! I started playing and free-building structures with my youngest. I wouldn't say I like li'l LEGO bricks, especially when I accidentally step on them or have to clean them up. Sometimes, I would suck them up in the vacuum—just because. Still, I gave in because I knew my youngest would enjoy my company.

One afternoon, I set aside my agenda and spent hours building meaningless LEGO brick towers with my son. I even constructed a mega-church from the plastic pieces and placed some crows on the roof. I could see the joy in his eyes as he received my undivided attention.

The very next day, I noticed that he seemed relatively peaceful. He approached me and asked, "Mom, is there anything I can help you with?" My jaw dropped. I gave to him, and he gave back to me. He noticed me because I noticed him. I saw this miracle occur repeatedly in our household, which began to transform my state of Presence. Moving forward, I let go of my schedule. Nothing was more important than spending quality time with my sons.

Lastly, I want to share a story that still touches my heart. This balancing act was something I had to do consciously, so indeed, I would occasionally fall back into old habits, running our house like the crazy principal from the movie *Matilda*. "Don't put your sticky hands on the couch, and clean up those crumbs!" My love for order is what enables me to flip a house or commit to a thirty-day diet of just vegetable juice. I have no problem with dedication and discipline, which means that sometimes...I'm no fun.

As part of the thirty-day program that included juicing and journaling, I was supposed to take time for a daily walk to experience nature. Well, I attempted this flush in the middle of winter in cold-ass New Hampshire. I wouldn't say I like cold weather, so I skipped that part of the program. Yet, by the end of the month, I realized I hadn't spent much time with my son outdoors, so we bundled up in our jackets, snow pants, hats, gloves, and boots, then set out for a hike in the heart of winter. He was unaware that I was practicing Presence during our walk. My goal was to be completely present with him.

As we walked through our community, I pointed out things I noticed. Some hedges resembled cupcakes dusted in snow. There was a tree that resembled a man with his head plunged into the snow, performing a handstand. One intriguing bush was covered and appeared like a full-size sofa. We even saw where a bird had landed, leaving an imprint with its wings spread wide in the snow. As we continued our walk, some of those cupcakes transformed into gumdrops. At that time, my son couldn't have been more than three, and to this day, he still says, "Mom, do you remember that day we went for a walk and saw those cupcakes and the sofa?"

I'm so glad I didn't roll my eyes at this teaching and assume that medication was the only solution for my children's hyperactivity. I learned that I was primarily responsible for what my children expressed—they were my barometer. Today, I'm proud to say that both are relatively balanced and fall in the middle of this energy spectrum. I no longer play with LEGO bricks; instead, I give them my undivided attention—Presence. *(Thank you, Lawrence!)*

Please don't be mistaken; even though I focused on hyperactivity, children who are disconnected and flighty are just as much of a concern. In families without structure or order, these children yearn for the stability that helps them build confidence and feel secure. (I felt unsafe growing up without rules, even though everyone loved my mother's carefreeness. *"Mother brought home strays…many of them with two legs some days…whole families with four or more…oh dear, not a baby!…when most would have closed the door."* I don't think my wonderful mother has ever appreciated the beauty in this poem. Still, you can see she's a lovely person.)

Again, sex and "sexuality" are irrelevant when trying to balance this energy. For instance, you can still have a household dominated by feminine energy with a masculine husband who enjoys relaxing, cuddling with the children, and socializing. (Stop calling him gay…because he may believe your lie…someday.) By the way, these homes usually *smell*…sticky. The kitchen is a mess. The cat is sleeping on the counter. There's pee still in the toilet. Nobody makes their beds. Children are not well-groomed. Their hair resembles a hornet's nest. They do as they please, whenever they please. They can eat a box of cookies if they like. Unfortunately, these children often feel lost in the world. Introduce a schedule with a spoonful of structure; you will see them come alive and their fears diminish in such a pleasant way.

256

Single parents don't get *hot* with me because of my initial focus; this is also for you! It was a test of your patience and character. I hope you passed.

Many single parents lean toward *masculine energy dominance* primarily because they are responsible for providing structure, which is the primary need. This pattern can also be observed in many African American single-parent households. One might assume that this is due to the absence of fathers. While that is a contributing factor, the necessity to be the primary provider or the experience of living in poverty has an even more significant influence. In this situation, there is often little opportunity for feminine expression and leisure time. Again, this applies regardless of whether the parent is male or female. However, when single parents collaborate with grandparents to raise children, it tends to reduce the masculine energy. Simply having support from elders can be immensely beneficial for single-parent households.

My mother received substantial financial assistance from my grandmother, who worked the night shift as an RN supervisor in New Jersey to earn enough to support us. (She put her masculine energy into overdrive.) Thanks to Grandma, we never lacked anything. Mother, "the wildflower," never lost her fragrance, even as a single parent. She never had to worry about having a roof over her head, so she was chill...*all the time.* (The front of the house could have been falling off, yet she knew I'd fix it.)

Here are some patterns I've noticed across the energy spectrum:

- Children raised in households with strong masculine energy may be energetic and argumentative, and they often require more intimacy with their parents.
- Children raised in households where feminine energy predominates may cultivate masculine energy as an internal effort to establish balance, structure, and safety in their lives.
- Children often find this balance outside their homes through school, neighbors, or extracurricular activities. For example, dancing and reciting poetry in the streets can benefit families dealing with an overload of masculine energy due to various circumstances. This therapeutic, feminine artistic expression, known as rap, is prevalent in African American communities. (wink) I love seeing these men and boys connect with their femininity. (Go Shakespeare...it's your birthday!)
- The dominance of masculine or feminine energy has nothing to do with "sexuality," as many people mistakenly believe. Cut it out!

- Most people tend to lean strongly in one direction, as this imbalance was also evident in our parents and grandparents. We often find ourselves drawn to what we perceive as missing in our lives.
- Sadly, many individuals seeking structure or intimacy may fall prey to predators offering these qualities. Severely challenged youth often gravitate toward military careers, while others turn to religion or controlling institutions. These institutions provide both structure and intimacy, supplementing any deficiencies—if you don't. Young people from economically disadvantaged communities sometimes join lesser-respected controlling institutions known as gangs. Nevertheless, their needs remain the same, and gangs function similarly to the two mentioned above. This serves as a warning: some of these children may be lost to you—*forever*. (They say, "Give me some guidance—dammit!")

Enjoy experimenting with your children or finding balance for yourself if you don't have kids. Remember that you shouldn't try to make this a perfect science by strictly assigning behaviors of feminine or masculine energy to either sex, as it just doesn't work that way. You'll see excellent results simply by tweaking your routine, habits, or approach to life based on the behaviors you observe in your children to suit your family's needs.

Sticky Hugs,
—Sher! (The Common Snook)
Pause. Inhale. Exhale. Reflect.

P.S. Please don't confuse controlling behavior with masculine energy, as many people do. Controlling behavior is self-serving and seeks specific outcomes; it often stems from an individual's experiences of being controlled or violated. As you know, both women and men can be controlling, and we have already discussed the children they produce in my sermon, "The Fruit of the Same Tree."

P.P.S. Speaking of balanced energy! Before my husband and I married, he used to coordinate the volunteer chaplain and healing arts program at the old Shands UF Alachua General Hospital (AGH). As part of his job, he attended *special* conferences around the state in the field of healing arts. (You know, those whom Western medicine refers to as quacks—them!)

Once, he went to a conference in Orlando. He was still young and somewhat narrow-minded then. He approached a table with several Reiki practitioners to pick up some materials. Apparently, the head guru (the Reiki Master!) got a good whiff of his powerful energy. She was so excited that she asked if her posse could gather around him to experience his energy. (I'm not joking!) She said, "You're so balanced. Your energy is amazing!" *("Hey ladies! There's a brain in this one!")* They worshipped him almost as if he were Jesus. And I'm sure his supervisor, who was also there, was rolling her eyes. Unfortunately, my husband didn't take them too seriously because he was still deeply involved in religion at the time. Honestly, he thought they were crazy and needed Jesus.

About five years later, we were married and lived in Charlotte, North Carolina. A group of Reiki practitioners, high on something, stopped by my art studio, looking for space to rent in the area. As the posse left, one gentleman, an African American Reiki practitioner and minister from Virginia Beach, Virginia *(whom you can see, I'm trying to locate)*, stayed behind for a few minutes to chat with me. He asked for my permission to share a few things with me. I said, "Sure." He mentioned that I needed to nourish my reproductive system and made some recommendations. I thought that was good news, as if I might have been expecting a baby. Unfortunately, I suffered another miscarriage that same year and many more in the future.

My husband, unemployed and growing increasingly stressed each day, came downstairs to the studio with our son on his back to tell me that lunch was ready. He was at the back of the room, about twenty feet away, and only popped his head in the door for a second. This gentleman abruptly stopped our conversation and said, "Wow, who was that!? He has amazing energy!" I said, "Who, Mr. Wonderful? That's my husband." And he began to tell me all about him. Everything he said about his character was accurate. (Yes, he's "Some Kind Of Wonderful.") And his remarks about his energy were almost verbatim to what the crazy Reiki practitioners (the quacks!) had said back in Orlando. I became a believer that day!

I went upstairs and told my husband the story that he was radiant! I asked, "If you're such an angel, why aren't you in Heaven with the others?" Either way, I knew "that man's" *sammiches* were Divine! From then on, I made room for my grandmother and mother, who also practiced Reiki.

(Sit in stillness with your eyes closed for 15 minutes a day; I promise it will transform your life!)

6. How to Make Life Work for You: Faith and the Power of Your Words

Disclosure Reminder...,

Did you know that you can use your mind to create what you want? I'm sure you've seen those unusual ads on social media that attempt to capture your attention with Law of Attraction videos, or perhaps that's just what the algorithms suggest to me. However, what I will share with you has nothing to do with the Law of Attraction, although the philosophy of improving and replacing your thoughts can be an excellent tool for enhancing mental health. Today, we will discuss simple, old-fashioned faith like a mustard seed! And if you're not Indian, you may have never seen one. (Those tiny seeds are bursting with flavor!)

I'm sure you've heard ministers preach and teach about this idea of faith. However, I would guess that very few people, including ministers, genuinely or consciously experience this power. (I promise; it's nothing *special*.) Christianity encourages its followers to have faith like a child. Thankfully, the practice and results of faith are not tied to religion but rather depend on our ability to tap into the power of creation and focus our energies. Many don't understand what it means to have faith like a child or how other forms of faith operate. Let's take a closer look!

Alright, when the Bible says to have faith like a child, it means believing without doubt. Most people are so full of themselves and full of nonsense that they will never experience this kind of faith in their lives. However, very few children carry the same level of baggage and mental clutter as the average adult. You tell them Santa Claus is real, and they believe it. It's that simple. They don't need much convincing.

Most people don't realize that faith is straightforward. Every person possesses the power of creation, the Source, or the God within. (And the Hindus shouted, Brahma!) Once our minds are set, we naturally begin working toward our goal. Everything made by humans first originated as a seed in the human mind; good soil for planting is essential.

Faith requires work, yet results can occur with minimal effort if your energies are strong enough. Once the seed is planted, the state of *believing* becomes a thought, and energy is generated. Next, *speaking* the idea into existence represents a form of energy transfer from the mind to words. This is powerful, so we must be careful what we say.

For some seeds, you must actively tend to them with persistence. Other seeds require only the focused energy of a clear mind, free from mental clutter. This is where stillness and meditation can help those seeking to achieve or obtain something. Unfortunately, many people are lazy and expect results without active participation and persistence, which the Bible calls *works*. "Faith without works is dead" (James 2:14-26 from the Bible), and others struggle to use their faith to generate focused energy because their minds are cluttered.

Let's explore three different forms of faith. Remember, faith knows no limits. And, of course, I have stories for you!

Seeing, Believing, Acting, and Not Wavering

Once, I had a vivid "dream" about the house my husband and I would buy. In the "dream," we were fixing it up. I felt confident I had caught a glimpse of the future (peeking through a portal, not just dreaming) and began searching for this house (works). It was a farmhouse, well over a hundred years old, a foreclosure that we bought for around $125,000. The house was painted the same color both inside and out, had a dirt-floored basement, and featured bushy pink flowers out front. The details of this "dream home" were remarkable!

Upon returning to New Hampshire from a snowbird vacation in Florida, I browsed Zillow for entertainment and spotted a well-priced foreclosure that piqued my interest. We took a detour to Athens, Georgia, to check out the property. As I stepped inside, I observed that everything was painted a light creamy peach color. I felt this was the house from my dream or the portal I had peeked through.

We offered $125,000 in mid-February because I was confident that no one would pay more for the house. After all, it needed a lot of work. Coincidentally (or not), the numbers matched those in my "dream."

Unfortunately, the bank denied our offer. I told my husband I wouldn't increase our offer because no one would pay more for the house due to the work needed. A week later, it went under contract. I wasn't too worried because I felt confident the person would back out after the inspection due to all the issues.

The scenario was exactly as expected, so I submitted another offer for the same amount. I explained why the house wouldn't sell for over $125,000 to justify my proposal. I'm sure that really *pissed off* the banker because egos don't appreciate logic, and of course, our offer was rejected. The attitude is, "You might be right, but I'd rather sell it to someone else." I did everything I could, and my son was so disappointed.

We moved on from the house, but I didn't realize that my eight-year-old son was drawing pictures of the house he thought was ours. The images were so precise that I was amazed by his eye for perspective, which takes adults years to develop.

I discovered I was living with little Frank Lloyd Wright—his visual-spatial intelligence falls in the 90th percentile. The University of Florida School of Architecture or the College of the Arts should consider recruiting him. My boy can probably see beyond 3D. (Come on, UGA! That's your old visitor center!)

That summer, we returned to the area where we hoped to relocate, searching for more properties. To our surprise, the foreclosure house was still on the market. I'm sure you can guess what happened next.

I decided to forgo another property and made the same offer again on the house. My agent was growing increasingly annoyed with me and thought I was being cheap (similar to my husband). She wanted me to raise my offer to avoid disappointment. But money was tight; I needed them to pay our closing costs. (Who cares about disappointment? She had little faith but is still one of the best Realtors I have ever met because a straight one [and I don't mean the opposite of gay] is like finding a needle in a haystack.)

Of course, I refused to budge because I knew it was the house from my "dream" and already knew how much we paid for it. Despite her recommendation, I made the offer again, and as we packed up to head back north, we stopped by the house one last time. Surprisingly (like a wink from God), pink Knock Out roses were growing out of control in front of the house, which had been dormant during the winter.

While sitting on the porch, I was slightly disappointed to think it would be a "Cruel Summer" and that we would head home without a contract. (Sorry, Swifties, but nobody can replace Bananarama's "Cruel Summer," Kindergarten 1983, my theme song that year. [giggles]) Meanwhile, my husband checked his phone and noticed an old voicemail from our agent. She said, "I don't know what kind of faith you have, but the bank accepted your offer!" My son jumped up and danced, witnessing the power of his own faith for the first time. Priceless!

Even though I saw the house in my "dream," I still struggled with disbelief (the mind getting in my way) because this was a new experience for me. Honestly, I don't think anything would have been possible without my son. His faith never wavered. Poor kid, stuck in the *freezing cold* of New Hampshire, felt depressed being confined to his seat in the classroom. He wrote in his school journal to his teacher that his parents would soon buy a farm and homeschool him again. I'm sure she thought my sweet boy had a wild imagination since she knew we lived in the modest apartments down the street from the school. She didn't realize my boy had the kind of faith that could move mountains.

Believing, Speaking, Acting, and Aligning Energy

The story I'm about to share qualifies as a miracle, and I promise to share more details at another time, perhaps on my website. However, I will briefly describe how, through faith, I was able to find my long-lost half-siblings, with whom I had lost contact for over twelve years after my father passed away when I was thirteen.

In 2003, I realized they might be in Central America, where my father once lived. This insight came from a photo my older brother found online of our nine-year-old "baby sister" swimming in the Macal River in Belize's Cayo District. The picture was taken randomly (or divinely!) by Carlton Ward Jr., an ecology graduate student and now-famous National Geographic conservation photographer, who was interning with a group from the College of Journalism at the University of Florida—**in my hometown**!!! (Do you understand the odds of this happening? This person could have been from anywhere in the world. All I had to do was open the "phonebook" [giggles] and call the college. The "secretary" was surprisingly familiar with Carlton, mentioning that he was in Africa at the time, so she referred me to one of Carlton's peers who, of course, **lived up the street in High Springs**…and came to the house in *Shell Rock. Whassup, bro!*)

The second miracle (the fruit of faith) was that I found them in a foreign country with no phone number or address in less than twenty-one minutes, by following clues provided by this student (the dude from High Springs), who was also on the trip and had met my younger sister. He said they took thousands of photos, and the only reason he remembered her and her approximate location was that she was on one of the first "rolls of film." After speaking to her mother,

263

they found it strange that this woman, living along the river in the rainforest, claimed to have a connection to Gainesville. Small world! *(You can run, but you can't hide! Yep, I'm talkin' 'bout you.)*

Anyways, our journey was likely closer to fifteen minutes, but we had to briefly hike down a mountain in the jungle before reaching their home (an old Mennonite plantation with no electricity, purchased by my "naturalist" father just outside Christo Rey *Mestizo* village near San Ignacio). So, I added six minutes for accuracy. (Sometimes, my quirkiness helps drive my point. No, I don't round my numbers. I prefer to be precise.)

Anywho, before we embarked on our adventure, folks were trying to quench my faith when I told them I would get a passport and search for my half-siblings in the jungles of Belize without a phone number or an address. I still remember one gal addressing me as if I were a fool. "You're going to do what?" I didn't let her disbelief hold me back. Thankfully, five friends, including one I would later marry, aligned with my faith and witnessed this miracle. (Gloria Dios!)

Seeing, Believing, and Speaking

Lastly, you sports fans might find it interesting that I once "spoke over" (which is Christianese terminology meaning to declare something) the world-famous professional track and field athlete, bronze medalist at the 2020 Olympic Games (held in 2021 due to COVID) and three-time gold medalist at the 2023 World Athletics Championships, who also became known as "one of the fastest men in the world" that year. He also broke Usain Bolt's record that summer for the most "sub-20s" in the 200-meter. (I sure hope the stats are correct.)

When "Little Man" was around four, suffering from asthma, I observed him and his brother (my favorite of the two) play "Jump like Tigger," as they used to say. (I'm just joking about favorites. [wink]) Still, I should've had both boys in my wedding, but the little one, "The Boss," stole my heart. I love that boy so much! "Don't go, Ms. Sherry!" he used to say in that sweet, frustrated little voice. (He loved me, too.) Unfortunately, "Big Brother," although always a delight, was *a lot* for me to handle. I couldn't risk him bouncing down the aisle in my wedding. *Anywho,* I had never seen what looked like normal, joyful children jump so damn high. I'm surprised they didn't punch holes in the ceiling.

One time, when they were older, in the middle of July, I escorted their bouncing butts to the backyard and gave them some cardboard boxes and ice water. (I have pictures.) I told those *ch'rn*, "I know it's hot, but you ain't coming inside until you build something!" I was just trying to escape the constant bouncing off the walls. (Hmm…that sounds like too much masculine energy.) I remember peeking out the window as they fumbled with the boxes. But thank goodness, there was a little lady there who could offer them advice. I love those *ch'rn*. (Can you hear me singing "We Are Family"?).

Back to when "Little Man" was four! I confidently told his mother *(Whassup, Mami!)*, who was homeschooling the boys at the time, that asthma would not hold him back and boldly said, "He will be a world champion" (unlike the NBA, of course, lol). I added something to the effect that the world would know his name…in the name of Jeesuuus! (That was pretty damn accurate! Sometimes, I *be* peeking through portals [seeing in 4D and beyond] and don't even realize it, but we'll stick with the simplicity of faith for this sermon.) It came from deep within me and aligned with my energies, which is called "faith." If you don't know his name, maybe I was mistaken. And *don'tcha* bring me your *ch'rn*/children to bless; you can do this, too.

Pardon me for a *sec. Hey, little bouncing bros, remember when we stopped by the house on Christmas Day a few years back? That was my boys' first Black Christmas with collard greens, holy mac 'n' cheese, yams, sweet potato pie, turkey, and ham…damn! I had never seen my ch'rn so excited…sneaking ham. I bow to you. Tell your peeps I said hello! (Whassup, Kevin!)*

Church folks, whom some associate with faith, often wonder how I do it. Over twenty years ago, the leadership at The Rock of Gainesville church invited me to share the remarkable story of finding my half-siblings in Belize with their congregation. They even published my story in their monthly news magazine and remain in awe of how faith has worked in my life, both within and *outside* of religion. I recently ran into one of their delightful *brethren*, and the first thing he mentioned was the Belize reunion story: "I've never forgotten that incredible story you shared!" Faith isn't just for church folks; it's a power we all possess, a skill that anyone can learn to apply in their life. The faith I've experienced at this level is limitless!

Careful What You Speak Hugs,
   —Sher! (The Common Snook)
Pause. Inhale. Exhale. Reflect.

P.S. I can't close this sermon without acknowledging that Mr. Carlton Ward is also behind the new "Protect the Panther" Florida license plate, featuring a picture of a female panther with her cub. (Initially, I had said "kitten" instead of "cub" because that's what I read in an article, but a veterinarian who chases big kitty cats…oops, I mean, tigers for fun—whom I met this year in India near Jim Corbett National Park—said these big kittens were called cubs. I stand corrected, even though it sounds goofy—*Saket. Whassup, Doc!*) This marks the first sighting of a panther north of the Caloosahatchee River in over four decades. *(Hey bros! Y'all should be friends since you share the same hobby—#HelloKitty.)*

Photojournalism is a remarkable art form that connects the everyday person with the world, allowing us to see through the eyes of modern-day explorers.

Hey Carlton! I hope we cross "paths" and meet face-to-face one day…before we both go completely gray. I bet you didn't realize you were taking photos for The Common Snook. We're "partners in crime," you know, and more connected than most would imagine.

Well, I'll be damned! It turns out you were in town, buddy. That was a powerful commencement speech you delivered for the 2024 graduating class of your alma mater. (Go Gators!) However, you missed an excellent opportunity to mention our story, "our shared path," as you called it, to your audience of 10,000. Still, as you originally suggested, our Belize story deserves a bigger audience, like the former Oprah Winfrey Show—more another time.

Lastly, a bicyclist I met at Kanapaha Botanical Gardens (my hangout…whassup, Chris!), who cycles from state to state, gave me the song "Seminole Wind" by John Anderson after I mentioned the beauty of the swamp, particularly in Micanopy, which he had just passed through. Now I give the song to you. Have you heard it? It made me think of you, Swampman. Thank you for your efforts to preserve our state.

Hold up, wait a minute! Carlton, you didn't tell me your great-grandpappy was a Florida Governor! Well, how about that!

P.P.S. Pardon me; I almost forgot to mention that my sons will one day wow the world like Frank Lloyd Wright. I have two amazing artists!

(Sit in stillness with your eyes closed for 15 minutes a day; I promise it will transform your life!)

7. Chanting for Relaxation and Mental Clarity

Disclosure Reminder...,

As you may know by now, I spent my early years in a controlling, charismatic church that I later recognized as fitting the definition of a cult. (Yikes!) While every person has the potential to fall from grace, especially in an intoxicating, power-hungry environment like the church I was part of, there were practices within the church community that I found still worked to access the inner dimensions. Although this inner world has many names, some might refer to it as "the Kingdom of God."

The church believed that everyone "who was saved," those who accepted Christ as their savior, should *pray in tongues*, a.k.a. *praying in the Spirit or glossolalia*. This is a type of spiritual babbling that can scare the crap out of the average person if they are unfamiliar with charismatic and Pentecostal Christian practices.

Still, "scary tongues" was something I learned from my mentor, Ms. Juliette. She often prayed in tongues. Of course, this scared the crap out of me at first. But to my surprise, I picked up the habit from her before fully understanding the details of organized religion or how this behavior or skill might overlap with charismatic churches. She used this chanting to gain clarity and connect with the Source within.

After fleeing the charismatic church for dear life, I became repulsed by many of their ways and wanted to distance myself from them completely. Yet, I recalled that I had learned to pray in the Spirit from my friend. *Was this praying in tongues a keeper?* I needed clarification.

Oddly enough, I sometimes found myself slipping back into old habits of babbling when I felt stressed, and I noticed how quickly I began to relax. My mind would clear, and whatever was causing me concern or that I wanted to resolve would improve. In the back of my mind, while giving myself the side-eye, I wondered what this tongue-praying was all about. As someone not affiliated with any religion or church, I realized that something beyond myself was at work in my life, and I began to draw wisdom from within. George Fox, the founder of the Quaker movement, was correct in stating that we do not need the church or religion to connect with the Divine.

I eventually came to accept that praying in tongues was beneficial, and it was merely a type of Christian chanting or a way to enter a meditative state. Come on, two points for Christianity! (And the Catholic monks, who have been chanting for centuries, said, "Duh-uh!")

At the same time, this chanting can also be risky because one can easily be manipulated in this state of "no mind." (wink) This is why so many charismatic churches will have you praying in tongues…all day, jamming to a rhythmic beat, and they might slip in a second offering request above your regular tithe. The timing couldn't be more perfect. But careful! It's like asking someone to open their wallet while they're high. They'll have you "willingly" tossing out your hard-earned money like rose petals. (I've participated in one of those jam sessions before.)

Once I understood that it was a type of chanting that connected me to the Source, I realized how calling it the Holy Spirit made sense. It could also be described as your Spirit praying on your behalf to bring you great wisdom, peace, and understanding. With that, curiosity began to inspire me to investigate further. Would chanting mantras like Hare Krishna/Krsna yield similar results?

Guess what I did? I threw on my kurti/long shirt, leggings, dupatta/scarf, and bindi/the third eye (or the dot, as some ignorant folks like to say) and headed for the Hare Krishna Temple in Alachua, Florida, the largest Hare Krishna community outside of India, right here in my backyard! (College towns are breeding grounds. [giggles])

> *Hare Krishna Hare Krishna*
> *Krishna Krishna Hare Hare*
> *Hare Rama Hare Rama*
> *Rama Rama Hare Hare*

I quickly learned the mantra because it's simple and catchy, and I "rocked out" with my new friends. It felt like a dose of serotonin straight into my veins: "High with Krishna!" Strangely, it reminded me of my days at the charismatic church in Gainesville.

Warning: if you ever try chanting Hare Krishna as a newbie, it will likely stay in your head for nearly twenty-four hours, similar to a hangover, although I've never experienced one. It will follow you even when you close your eyes to sleep. But I promise, it will fade with patience.

With this mantra, they say, "Chant and be happy," which is both powerful and addictive. To my surprise, I witnessed new levels of Consciousness unfolding right before my eyes. My creativity began to expand, and my anticipation grew. (Uh-oh, Sher was as high as a kite!) I was unaware that this energizing would aid me in selling my neighbor's house. After chanting Hare Krishna for about a week—no less than 108 times a day—I unknowingly focused my energy, called faith, quite powerfully. (Why 108? Because it's auspicious! [wink and giggles])

One night, something shifted in me after chanting the Hare Krishna mantra and swaying in my hammock. I "dreamed" (slipped through a portal as I woke up), "You and Tiffany will 'evoke' a buyer today; 'evoke,' not 'invoke,'" I was told. Interestingly, the Source knew I might need clarity between the two words. In our case, "evoke" meant to call forth or draw out emotions, such as "I want this house." It sounded a bit creepy for a minute, but I was game either way!

That morning, I told my homegirl about my "dream" and mentioned that her buyer was coming to our open house that day. Surprisingly, she didn't react to my remarks, which might have sounded bizarre to some. Since her husband had already started a new job in another state, my homegirl, a mother of many with a baby in a bouncer plus Fido, was responsible for selling her house and coordinating movers within a tight timeframe. She was the ideal candidate for a Realtor to convince her she couldn't sell the house herself, and many tried to work their magic…I mean, deception. (wink) I don't know what she was thinking when she chose to partner with me, but I was honored by her faith.

I have sold houses in under twenty-four hours, but it usually takes at least a week or two, at the minimum. And the interest rates that spring were not in her favor. Still, I didn't let my real estate knowledge overshadow the faith I sensed in this momma who had never sold a house. I told her, "We'll have the house wrapped up in thirty days." She replied, "No, I'm moving in two weeks." I almost choked. I figured she'd need a cash offer to make that happen.

We were a flawless match, and I have yet to meet another who has complemented my faith as she did. Don't mess with a momma, the head of the household, who has business to take care of. (By the way, I did this as a friend without any hidden expectations because it's fun and a significant gift of financial savings I could never have provided anyone from my pocket.)

I met many people as "the hostess of the *mostest*" at the open house, but I had a memorable conversation with a sweet young couple, specifically with the "missus." As I began to share some of the house's features, I could see her interest spark. I wasn't trying to sell her; I was just being honest. (That'll preach!) In the meantime, I gave them some space so I could greet other buyers.

As the young couple wrapped up their tour, the young lady turned around and firmly shook my hand. Oh my, it was invigorating! I could feel the power; I had scored big! I knew she was the buyer—evoked, called forth, and didn't even write down her name. The following day, my dear friend received a cash offer she couldn't refuse—for sale by owner, baby, barely fifteen days on the market with rising interest rates! Hare Krishna! (This story still has me shouting to this day!)

That said, I officially welcomed praying in tongues back into my life. I promise I won't do it around you because it can be creepy for some folks…like head-spinning and snake-tossing creepy. I get it! (You know, I sound Jamaican when I pray in tongues.)

Naturally, each religious group I honored today would view it as a testament to their God and faith. I certainly would, as well! However, would anyone pause to reflect on how the power of chanting appears to be universal? I don't want anyone to take my word for it; instead, I encourage you to test it yourself. I refuse to let beliefs or fear keep me from exploring unfamiliar territory. I will investigate, even if it makes me uncomfortable or someone advises me against it. (wink)

Additionally, I bet you didn't know that there's an element of old-school hip-hop, Southern-style African American dance music (both within and outside the church), and some modern forms that reflect chanting mantras and create the same heightened awareness I experienced through chanting the Hare Krishna

mantra. Once again, chanting—regardless of the words—can alter your state of Consciousness, especially dancing and chanting, so be careful about what you decide to do. (Try these songs: "Bhool Bhulaiyaa-3!" for techno folks, "Hare Krishna" by Krishna Das for White charismatic church folks and beatnik folks, and "Hare Krishna" by Alice Coltrane for Black church folks.)

Some of these chants are so addictive that they stay in your head for days.

Li'l Snook van Gogh, age fourteen.

Unfortunately, many of these guys don't recognize that the talent they possess could transform lives. They must not understand the origin of this desire to chant. Honestly, you can say just about anything, even something as ridiculous as "scrub the tub," and turn it into a chant. Try a little chant and dance for yourself! Hopefully, someone will create a chant one day that's as banging and powerful as John Lennon's "Give Peace A Chance." Let me see *whatcha* got!

Also, please keep in mind that this is not a recommendation to join the Hare Krishnas (who are listed on many cult registries and have a history of child sexual abuse in the U.S., similar to the Catholic Church). However, let me know if you'd like to visit one Sunday afternoon. We can ride together! Their food is excellent, and the kirtan is delightful. Interestingly, after attending one of their services (though they aren't called "services"), their message of Krishna felt remarkably similar to the devotional path of Christianity. Either way, it was lovely…and familiar. (wink) And, of course, I'm not advocating for religion, but rather humbly acknowledging that chanting is powerful, regardless of one's religious or spiritual background. The words don't matter (most of the time), especially when we have power over them instead of them over us, because it's all about clearing the mind to make room for greatness. (Hmm…I wonder if Tiffany knows Krishna helped sell her house.)

Hare Krishna Hugs,
—Sher! (The Common Snook)
Pause. Inhale. Exhale. Reflect.

P.S. "Hold on a *sec*, lady, you Common Snook! You went from talkin' 'bout faith to chanting. Now you've got me curious. Are you suggesting that people can see the future? If so, does that mean life is already predetermined?" *(Hmm…you sound like my son.)*

No, life isn't predetermined, except for boneheads. Some might argue that the block universe remains static. However, I'm not speaking scientifically but from experience. For instance, in the story I shared about buying the foreclosure, there was a key person in that "dream," and she chose not to be part of our lives at that time. The story continued to unfold and was rewritten around her. At that time, I couldn't comprehend how altering what had already happened was possible.

"Lady, did you say 'happened'?" Yes, there's a chance that what we perceive today is merely a projection of reality, kind of like a hologram that's influenced by our perspective. Consider how long it takes for starlight to reach Earth. By the time that light arrives, the star may have been dead for years. The fundamental reality isn't necessarily what we see or believe. (Hmm?)

One day, I will tell you why Ms. Juliette, to my knowledge, never got back into a car—even after her death. I bet they just carried her across the street to

271

Dorsey's Funeral Home on Pleasant Street. She had classified information and changed the outcome as a result.

P.P.S. Do y'all know Krishna means black, blue-black, or the all-attractive one? Yep, Krishna, like Jesus, was black. Just kidding! We all know that Jesus *has* yellow hair and blue eyes from his photographs. *Anyways*, I know some Haitians and Africans who are blue-black…so dark they appear navy blue. *(Whassup, Berm!)* That has to be the most stunning skin tone on earth! Hare Krishna! Praise to the black God!

P.P.P.S. Speaking of slipping through portals before waking up! Unaware of the results, the morning after the 2024 election, I heard, "Trump won by a landslide." Holy cow, I thought it was a nightmare! Some of y'all may believe it was a fake news portal, but I still heard it. *(Trump, did I hear you say, "Amen!"?)*

Regardless, I see good things in our future. You know humanity doesn't progress backwards, as "*Misery*" would like to imagine. Sure, history tends to repeat itself, but it's just that humanity hasn't progressed as much as we like to fool ourselves. America is getting closer to becoming—one nation, one people! (wink) Unconventional leadership is an awakening for some of y'all who have become complacent. It allows the blind to finally see "there's a *gremlin* on the wing!" (giggles) Agitation ignites a fire under your feet. Injustice raises human Consciousness.

Soon enough, you'll find me at the White House as the honorable spiritual teacher, Sherguru. "Sit in stillness—dammit, and stop peeking." I'm sorry to disappoint some of you; sitting in stillness, connected to the Source, can be transformative for anyone. "Let's make America great!" together. (Hmm…that sure sounds familiar. *Right, King?*)

(Sit in stillness with your eyes closed for 15 minutes a day; I promise it will transform your life!)

8. From the Bottom Rung to Purpose and Potential

PARENTAL ADVISORY: EXPLICIT CONTENT AHEAD!

Disclosure Reminder...,

The following question may seem strange for starting a sermon, but when did rap become porn? I remember the uproar surrounding the Miami bass group 2 Live Crew in the late 1980s and their groundbreaking album "As Nasty as They Wanna Be," which featured their hit song "Me So Horny." (giggles) However, I wasn't aware that this rap style had become the norm. What happened to fun rap like "Whoomp! There It Is"? Thank goodness I was in a cult in my twenties, so I missed out on a lot of "Southern bass and bounce music."

I had no clue that body part obsession had gotten so out of control in African American communities. I understand that sex sells albums, but what about the youth who try out these tricks while these musicians profit from being as explicit as possible? With so much anatomy and loooong cock talk, you'd think these guys were majoring in medicine and would soon discover a cure for prostate cancer and erectile dysfunction, which, of course, they don't have. Still, when I listen to audio porn, which I've explored quite a bit lately to get myself caught up, I hear young men who still have hope—and who need and want job opportunities. This is the bottom rung of Maslow's hierarchy of needs at its finest.

Some of these guys possess remarkable visual-spatial intelligence. They could achieve so much more. How can I tell? I can sense it in their words, much like my son, who is contemplating a career in architecture and urban design and is also an outstanding descriptive writer because he can visualize.

Those who take on the challenge of becoming a rapper don't all reach the top—still, those who do have genuine talent. We should ask who this young man is and what gift he brings. Once again, I want to highlight the rapper Juvenile, who likely possesses the mind of an engineer. (Yes, I've listened to a lot of "Back That Azz Up" to gain this perspective; however, I won't mention the other song where I became convinced he was an engineer or should have been a writer because I could visualize what he was portraying in a strange, slow like...locomotion. *RIP, Soulja Slim.*)

Let's examine the African American version of Maslow's hierarchy of needs. *(Honey, could you create a pyramid for my book?)* Or maybe my readers can picture one, with self-actualization at the top and physiological needs at the bottom, since we can't even afford to make a real pyramid here.

Here's the homemade pyramid (read it from the bottom rung up since those needs need to be fulfilled first before reaching self-actualization):

- Self-Actualization (beeyotch!)—one becomes the best they can be, reaching their full potential and soaring above audio porn.
- Esteem—confidence, respect for others, inner strength (uzi), recognition, freedom, self-esteem ("Pan Alpha" will address this issue. More details to come.)
- Love and belonging—family, family members who aren't incarcerated, friendship, intimacy, vulnerability, and a sense of connection. (Why don't people understand me?)
- Needs—walking safely while Black, access to healthcare without fear of death due to biases, progesterone and progesterone blockers, employment opportunities beyond landscaping White folks' and Busta Rhymes' lawns ("Dangerous"), property that hasn't been *jacked* through gentrification, family connections, and overall safety.
- Physiological Needs—air, food, water, shelter, clothing, sleep (Supreme Court!!!), and reproduction. (Hmm…I guess sex is as essential as air and water. I stand corrected. Y'all need to fact-check me.) Additionally, some rather distasteful sociologists include excretion on the list. Must we? (This reminds me of the Key and Peele episode where a passenger said to "Mark with a K," the passive-aggressive flight attendant who wouldn't let him use the restroom, "I have to piss, and I have to shit." "Amen, amen!") Still, it's a fundamental human need. You shouldn't have to hold it in.

Audio porn, similar to basketball and football, doesn't require much equipment…or actors, making it a potentially excellent start-up business. Yet, it indicates that there are pockets of Black communities struggling and suffering, potentially having lost hope in the idea that religion can heal and save them. (Hey, this could be my opportunity! Hmm…I might need to launch a spiritually focused middle school for boys sooner rather than later so they can grow from the inside out and tap that uzi, which once again means inner strength in Hebrew.) This is the consequence of allowing poverty to fester. Poverty creates desperation and innovation…like audio porn. *(Oh my, Spotify! I had no idea audio porn was a thing. I was just being goofy.)*

Regardless, these get-rich-quick schemes, bottom rung survival mentality, are distractions for boys who need real career opportunities. We have all these boys positioning themselves to become ballers or rappers. But what will they do when that doesn't work out for them? What!? Work for the University of Florida (UF), feeding those kids while their *ch'rn* are starting fights and scaring the shit out of my son on his first day of school? (Don't get me wrong. UF does offer good benefits, and its service staff has a legend in its lineage.)

As I mentioned, the renowned writer and civil rights activist James Baldwin discussed how careers were limited for "Men of Color." (Bottomless bottom rung.) Unfortunately, a pattern has emerged of striving to "catch the comet," so to speak, to survive, a.k.a. get-rich-quick schemes that range from pimpin'...to preachin'...to performin'...to the financial boom of the crack epidemic in the 1980s...to football, basketball, and rap. My father caught this comet, but he was one in a million. We must stop promoting these careers, especially considering the high risk of death by homicide, particularly in the rap industry. (Wikipedia's list of murdered hip hop musicians reports over seventy-seven rappers killed since 1987, with ten deaths in 2022 alone [Damn!]. These deaths are linked to impoverished communities and lesser-respected controlling institutions, a.k.a. gangs.) These youth seek to satisfy a deficiency in their lives, as discussed in my sermon, "Is It ADHD or Your Parenting?"

For one, I always ask my Indian friends who have to hustle to catch a similar comet, "I know you're in the IT field, but what did you want to be when you were a kid?" One friend responded with enthusiasm and said, "A botanist!" He loved studying plants and nurturing them. Could he have been a scientist or even a farmer? (Hmm...that reminds me, I'm going to give that sweet man a sapling from my curry tree.) Still, desperation often paves a different path for so many of us.

One of my favorite philanthropists, (Bucky) R. Buckminster Fuller, once said:

> We should do away with the absolutely specious notion that everybody has to earn a living. It is a fact today that one in ten thousand of us can make a technological breakthrough capable of supporting all the rest. The youth of today are absolutely right in recognizing this nonsense of earning a living. We keep inventing jobs because of this false idea that everybody has to be employed at some kind of drudgery because, according to Malthusian Darwinian theory, he must justify his right to exist. So we have inspectors of inspectors and people making instruments for inspectors to inspect inspectors. The true business of people should be to go back to school and think about whatever it was they were thinking about before somebody came

along and told them they had to earn a living (R. Buckminster Fuller, *New York magazine*, 1970).

Today, Amazon and a few other companies have demonstrated what Fuller believed: that we possess enough resources to meet everyone's basic needs and advance society toward self-actualization. This concept is challenging for many to grasp, which is why I included Fuller's quote. Still, I enjoy planting seeds for creative and unconventional thinkers. (Hmm…have you noticed that Western countries with low diversity, or at least fewer Black individuals, tend to have better retirement benefits and universal healthcare that is often free? Could racism be complicating life for all Americans because we're less inclined to share? The attitude of "I'm not paying for those lazy…" creates hell for all of us. [That's *stupid*, White people.] Lean in close so you can hear the critics shouting into this book, "Socialist!" *Whassup, Bernie!*)

Back to audio porn! With so much emphasis on male genitalia, size, power, and the sexualization of women (bottom rung mentality), this "egoic disorder" should be included in the *Diagnostic and Statistical Manual of Mental Disorders* (DSM). Someone should have recognized this cry for help long ago. Instead, we have therapists twerking on the weekends.

Yes, I said the words don't matter…most of the time. But there is always an exception to the rule. I'm not labeling audio porn, like prostitution, as "good" or "bad" because it reflects the collective mental health and the need for opportunities in some pocket-communities. Even so, I advise being cautious about what you do while chanting and dancing. We can all picture how a porn chant and dance might conclude. Remember, I had my pockets picked while chanting and dancing in the church, and I even sold a house with a more focused chant. What do you prefer?

With that said, I can't believe I'm guilty of listening to porn! Condemned again, I said, with my head held low. But it might be inspiring to know that I wrote this entire sermon while moving my Chi and chanting to "Back That Azz Up" by Juvenile…before I stumbled upon the censored version of "Back That Thang Up." (Holy cow, was that a violin or a cello I heard!? Please don't fret; I promise we'll discuss Chi in more detail in the following sermon. Again, thank you for your patience.)

I bet you didn't know that the Divine doesn't judge hip-hop…like some of y'all do. If you do judge, it was likely divinely written—just for you. Also, it may be worth noting that pornographic music grabs your attention like a fire alarm. Some people want to silence the alarm or pass judgment on those sounding it. Please don't turn off the fire alarm until someone has effectively put out the fire.

We don't change people by shaming or canceling them. Shame is a type of manipulation rooted in abuse and control. Remember, the tendency to shame others is often connected to a need to avoid feeling inferior or embarrassed—for some reason.

Many people weaponize shame to relieve their inner distress, which is the mental grip that another person, group, or belief has over them. This behavior indicates they are too closely identified with a label (their ego), and what another mental or social construct might think, or mostly what *they* think...*they* think...*they* think. (lmao!) Embarrassment is a self-destructive mind game and effectively serves to control and shame them. They become slaves to their programming and attack others when it's all in their heads. Literally! The question is, who is their programmer?

In any case, may the world cease sacrificing potential and purpose when survival should never be a concern. Our goal should be to elevate all of society from the bottom rung to self-actualization.

Superstar Hugs,
—Sher! (The Common Snook)
Pause. Inhale. Exhale. Reflect.

P.S. Speaking of prostitution! Did I ever tell y'all about my BFF from 2nd grade, Mennette Colón? She grew up to become an actress and played Gabrielle, a prostitute, on the series *Dexter*, which is now available on Netflix. Yep, we attended Stephen Foster Elementary in Gainesville and became friends the same year the "Conga" song was released. I only remember this because those Ricans *(Hola, Mami!)* could break it down better than the band, Miami Sound Machine. *(Ricans and Cubans, you can thank Gabrielle and me, of course, for being her friend and an honorary Puerto Rican that year, for paving the way for your ch'rn in Alachua County schools. There weren't many of y'all around in these parts back then. Alright, Ricans, "Despacito" it is!)*

(Sit in stillness with your eyes closed for 15 minutes a day; I promise it will transform your life!)

9. Listen to Yourself Even When No One Else Will

Disclosure Reminder…,   12/31/2023

As a seer and feeler who perceives and interprets things plainly and uses perceptiveness to understand the world, I am seldom taken seriously. People ignore my warnings and insights. Others resort to the "discredit the messenger" method by attacking me angrily in an attempt to evade facing the truth. Please understand that I am not here to alter anyone's reality. Only you can do that.

Many years ago, I became increasingly interested in our ability to sense and perceive energy because I consistently gained insight into people without them revealing much about themselves. (This should not be confused with the codependent, paranoid behavior of trying to gauge a person's emotions: "What are they thinking?") Even though I possessed this unique ability, I never had the words to describe it, and honestly, I didn't really understand what I was doing.

One day, a neighbor walked by our house, and as she did, I looked out the window and said to my husband, "Oh, she's a screamer." At that moment, I laughed. After all, my husband always got a kick out of these remarks because I didn't know where or how I came up with these ideas. I suspected that this ability was simply reading energy since I commented as she passed by, and this often happens when I'm around people. These kinds of comments always spilled from my mouth. I confidently declared, "Oh, he looks at porn!" (giggles)

People sometimes called me psychic, and churchgoers said I was a prophet. Although I utilize the profound power of faith to speak the unseen into existence, neither label suits me. I don't have any superpowers beyond my sense perception.

I later realized that people emit intense energy related to their struggles or secrets, and that we can all perceive this energy if we enhance our perceptiveness. This isn't about being nosy; it's a part of our animal instinct that helps us avoid danger. Sometimes, the feeling alone is enough to make us step back and pause, keeping us safe without needing to translate the energy into words. ("Oh Lord, what the hell was that!?")

As I became more aware of my experiences, I began to pay attention to how I described people moving forward. (*Hakuna matata*…I'll try to keep my mouth shut around you.) There was one person whom I strangely described as "negative," like *a void*. I told a friend I felt uncomfortable about this one. I rarely encountered individuals who seemed to produce what felt like a baseline, flat reading—no heart or soul. *What was this all about?*

Earlier in my life, I knew another seer and feeler—Ms. Juliette, of course. One day, she casually mentioned that I would witness a specific type of *crime*, which didn't sit well with me at the *time*.

I spent most of my life believing I would witness something dreadful. To my relief, I came to understand the broader definition of being a witness.
In courtroom cases, the judge often calls a character or expert witness who may provide information about a person or topic. Many witnesses are merely there to provide information.

That day came and went as Ms. Juliette described. I felt the energy of something terrible and noticed a troubling phrase escaping my lips. I thought, *What the heck was I supposed to do with that?* Nobody listens to seers or those who say they "felt" something. I even went so far as to share this experience with a few friends; most didn't take me seriously. (They must not have perceived me correctly.) I was left to carry this feeling alone—for many years.

As I've aged and matured, my understanding of life has evolved, and I no longer seek validation from others to trust myself. Once again, I chose to rely on my intuition, feeling more confident in my insights. I was in for a surprise and would discover firsthand why some crimes remain unsolved. This is primarily due to the egos of the law enforcement personnel answering the phone. (They don't seem to be very perceptive.) *I'll share more about that another time.*

I also learned that you can't tell people the truth without adding a bit of drama, even if it's to save their lives (or to confess you have *free power*). You must project inflated confidence and respond defensively to be heard since most people are accustomed to this communication style. "You won't believe what happened! Let me tell you, it was surreal. You don't believe me!? God help anyone who doesn't hear me!" You know the kind of dramatic story you enjoy hearing. ("I have every light on in the house—dammit!")

Ultimately, I decided to take matters into my own hands. I gathered my notes and transformed what started as a simple energy reading into the most compelling story I have ever written. I didn't realize how much I understood and carried all these years. Not only can we see and feel, but the story that expresses and organizes our feelings comes from a place deep within, far beyond the mind. Finally, I got someone's attention!

I know I'm leaving you with a cliffhanger, but this is the kind of drama you enjoy, right? Eat it up! Let's grow and listen together. To be continued...

Namaste, I bow to the Divinity in you,
—Sher Rishi! (The Common Snook)

Pause. Inhale. Exhale. Reflect.

P.S. This story will likely become a movie if published.

P.P.S. I once had a Muslim doctor who could read your energy and didn't even know he was doing it. He seemed to understand what people were thinking before they completed their sentences. Praying five times a day can have a profoundly positive impact.

P.P.P.S. Speaking of reading energy! I was at the mall in town, which might not be open when you read this, and some good-looking young men entered the trendy establishment (which looked like an old Banana Republic store to me), filling the room with a powerful, positive energy that caused all the young ladies and *me* to smile. I remember thinkin', *These must be Haitians. (Whassup, Chicken Sandwich U to the D!)*

P.P.P.P.S. Speaking of listening to yourself! Please pay attention, too! You know, if you find yourself tired of cookin', your knives are probably dull (I'm completely serious)…or your kitchen is too big and was designed by the same goofy men who design McMansions. (giggles)

(Sit in stillness with your eyes closed for 15 minutes a day and sharpen your knives; I promise it will transform your life!)

10. You Can Move Your Own Chi

Disclosure Reminder...,

Meditation or stillness can be whatever you make it: processing and bringing closure to your week, reflecting on your thoughts, calming and quieting your mind, or simply sitting in silence while connected to the Divine energy or Presence. Stillness is a practice that grows and evolves. However, I have something else to share with you!

Holi celebration! I had never seen a White man so free.

Dancing as a form of meditation to connect with the Divine can transform your life, allowing the life force within to flow and circulate freely. Some refer to this life energy as Spirit, Prana, Chi, or the universal life force. What you call it doesn't matter; it is available to us all and isn't limited to practices such as yoga or qigong. The key is to listen and learn how to move your body in a way that integrates breathing and meditation to access this energy. Quieting the mind is a process that takes time to develop; yet dance and movement are forms of expression that we can all achieve with little effort. Once again, dance can be a transformative experience!

I dedicate this part of my teachings to the Spirit-filled woman known as the "Dancing Lady" of Mount Pleasant United Methodist, Gainesville's oldest African American church. Many people may have found humor in her expression, but they failed to realize she had discovered a door to becoming one with God. (Ms. Juliette often said she was one of the few who truly knew God in that place. [*Hmm...ouch!*] We might need to ask her to stay home with that.) Watching dance is witnessing the heart speak; participating in dance is the ultimate expression of unity with life. Let us celebrate the universal language of dance together!

There has been some blending of worship styles involving dance in African American and Native American cultures. And no, I'm not talkin' 'bout "Apache (Jump On It)" by The Sugarhill Gang. I'm serious! If you are part of these communities or familiar with these cultures, you may have noticed a distinctive dance pattern often described as "catching the Spirit." These two cultures tapped into the Source, allowing the life energy to flow without being aware of qigong or yoga.

Interestingly, Martin Luther King Jr. once expressed frustration in his autobiography with the rhythmic and physical abilities often displayed by Black folks (King, p. 15). However, he likely didn't realize that Black people enjoy dancing (stompin' and stampin') because it's powerful and, like yoga, can create a direct connection to the Divine. The rhythm of the Spirit, Prana, or Chi ignites this desire to dance.

Some of you who have witnessed the "catching of the Spirit" may think it's just a theatrical performance, and for some, of course, it is. Who doesn't love to dance? However, that doesn't lessen the impact this power has had on so many people. There's also a strong chance of experiencing this energy in the traditional Black church, as one of the key components for connecting with the Source is to come without all your baggage, mental labels, material possessions, and property. "I ain't got a title, and I don't have much."

Poverty, whether defined by a lack of resources, limited material possessions, or a diminished sense of self-worth, often disguises true inner wealth and serves as a direct link to the Divine. However, folks must be careful, as body obsession can ensnare them when it is the only thing they possess. It's intriguing how this works. As scripture states, "It's harder for a rich 'man' (rich in ego and possessions) to enter the Kingdom of God." "It is true!"

Do you know anything about Sufism? Sufis have also discovered a direct link to the Divine through dance. Nothing uplifts the Spirit quite like a sweet Melody, such as "Kulli," an old Sufi song remix by Tech Panda and Kenzani. If you enjoy bass, check out their song "Dillagi."

Speaking of dancing like a Sufi! I'm one of "those people" who dance freely in public and whom everyone films. One day, I was jammin' at the beach when a White woman around my age from Jacksonville (originally from *Joisy*) suddenly appeared out of nowhere and did a cartwheel past me. It was amazing! *(Whassup, Mami!)* That's when I realized moving the Chi was contagious.

The movement to music that we call dance is virtually limitless. The world often categorizes a great deal of music as either "good" or "bad." But did you know that the Divine doesn't give a shit about what you listen to? Certainly, some rhythms can have a negative impact on the body, but for the most part, music is generally safe. The lyrics are irrelevant since we are the only ones who assign meaning to the sounds we label as words. However, instrumental music may be an excellent starting point if you find yourself easily distracted by lyrics.

Additionally, many unknowingly hyper-focus or meditate on the rhythm of a song. Have you ever gotten a really great idea after jammin' to one of your favorite beats? You must have inadvertently tapped into the Source. You see, you didn't even realize you could meditate and move your life energy to music through dance. Give it a try!

Here are a few all-time favorites: "Give Peace A Chance" by John Lennon (chants are powerful!), "Lovely Day" by Bill Withers, "Miss You" by The Rolling Stones, "Niwel Goes to Town" and "Following the North Star" by Rhiannon Giddens, "I Love Rock 'N Roll" by Joan Jett, "Scream & Shout" by will.i.am and Britney Spears, "In the Air Tonight" by Phil Collins, "Sweet Dreams" by Beyoncé, "I'm Blessed" by Charlie Wilson, "Midnight Sky" by Miley Cyrus, "Eye of the Tiger" by Survivor, "Party Mashup" by DJ Nyk, Badshah, Sachin-Jigar, AKASA, Rashmeet Kaur, Asees Kaur, Shamur (Oh my, that's a house party!), "Play at Your Own Risk" by Planet Patrol, and "Hypnotize" by The Notorious B.I.G. (*Yes I did!* [That's SAAVE; no commas.] By the way, "Hypnotize" is a clause on my insurance policy. [giggles] And I promise not to play it for your kids, but it's nothing more than the great Herb Alpert's 1979 instrumental piece, "Rise.")

However, moving to classical music, particularly Indian classical music, can liberate our life energies. (Consider listening to "Talking Fingers" by Dr. L. Subramaniam & Roby Lakatos.) May we dance together!

Enjoy,
　—Sher! (The Common Snook)
Pause. Inhale. Exhale. Reflect.

P.S. I dedicate "In the Air Tonight" by Phil Collins to my "birthday twin." (*Whassup, Nessa!*)

P.P.S. Hmm…I'm wondering whether Ms. Juliette put the dancing hex on me.

P.P.P.S. Speaking of yoga! With or without yoga, Indians tend to be more flexible than most. (I've observed this for years! [giggles]) That's why they invented yoga. They were putting their feet behind their necks long before yoga was yoga. If you drop something under the car seat, ask an Indian; they can get it for you while driving. (White folks, I'm not being cruel or "racist." It's called being observant—just like Black people can run faster than most. *[Whassup, Josephus and Noah!]* Or like my *hubby,* who is fatigue-resistant and stocky, which is why he can hike for days or choke you with his legs—like the Chinese.)

(Crank the bass for 15 minutes a day; I promise it will transform your life!)

11. The Door to Consciousness Found in Jainism, Too

Disclosure Reminder...,

Have you ever heard of Jainism? I didn't think so. Jainism is one of the oldest spiritual practices known to humanity, and of course, it originated in India. Some might categorize it as a religion, but its teachings extend beyond mere belief and are more widely embraced as a way of life. However, it has undoubtedly become a religion for some, something to believe in rather than a practice, which is how most good intentions in any religion end up.

I won't go deeply into Jainism to avoid coming across as too ignorant. However, I will discuss one of the most profound principles that resonates with me, along with one of their daily rituals. And, of course, I have a story for you!

When people learn about Jainism, I notice a pattern of mockery aimed at the practice of "ahimsa," non-violence, which emphasizes the non-injury of all living beings. Jains are strict vegetarians and even avoid consuming root vegetables because they value every life that could be harmed, including those of insects and other organisms that may be killed during tilling. So yes, that means no French fries or onion rings dipped in garlic sauce for Jains. This is when the typical American lets loose. "Oh my god, that's crazy," they exclaim and mock the Jains as if they are foolish, acting as if eating everything under the sun is essential.

I once spoke to a neighbor who was frustrated with our Indian neighbor for not maintaining his yard. This neighbor was also overly cautious when planting or pruning, preferring not to disturb the soil. Please don't ask me how he managed that.

From a distance, his property looked like a jungle in neatly edged suburbia. Still, after he moved and listed his house for sale, I wandered into his yard (yes, I'm nosy), and the bounty of his love for gardening was overflowing. It was like the Garden of *Eatin'*! Trees were free to be trees. Fruit was even dangling in front of me, seriously! The labor of his love left on his property would be worth a fortune.

I'm sorry, Jains. I frantically dug up plants everywhere because the new owner was bulldozing everything. I even saved the root system of a curry tree that had been completely chopped down, but I could still smell it was there. The root system was so extensive that it filled a fifty-gallon flowerpot.

Anyways, this neighbor mocked him for not conforming to the suburban American standard of using cancer-causing pesticides, Florida springs-destroying fertilizers, and water-wasting practices. (wink) He just knew he was right and described him as if he were crazy. "Look at this mess!" Immersed in nature's bounty, I said lovingly, "He was probably Jain," and explained some of their practices, which, of course, sounded ridiculous to him. I remarked, "Isn't it beautiful to think we have an ancient culture that taught early humanity to value all life down to the smallest organism? If we valued the tiniest life forms, how much more would we value the lives of our fellow humans?" I couldn't think of anything more delightful at that moment.

Instead of inspiring awe and wonder in him, he reacted like most Americans I've shared this idea with: "Have they ever eaten peanut butter?" We all know it can be loaded with many interesting, crunchy creatures that are accidentally roasted along with the peanuts. (Meanwhile, my Chinese neighbors exclaimed, "Yummy!") We Americans have a talent for transforming something beautiful into something downright ugly.

At the same time, I have been perplexed by my Jain friends, who adhere to strict vegetarianism yet overlook one of Jainism's most essential practices: daily stillness or meditation. Jains were a group deeply connected to the Cosmos through their dedicated practices, but many have lost the original ethos of the teachings and now focus more on idol worship.

Don't they realize that Jainism is effective and that many Jains have attained a level of knowledge and awareness that surpasses traditional intellect? Some even look down on the Jain monks who reject all possessions, including clothing. (giggles) If you are bold enough to walk down the street butt-naked, you have either lost your mind, like the woman who flashed my son and me on Main Street one day, or you've lost your mind's control over you.

Do you want to know how I know that Jains don't meditate? (Okay, some don't. Even so, my generalization wouldn't offend Jains who do.) I understand this because the fruit of stillness is powerful. It dismantles the root of violence that first originates from the tongue. It cuts the attachment to the self or the need to defend oneself. I can sense the fruit of stillness from a mile away. Still, I haven't detected the sweet fragrance of Jainism, except for the occasional irresistible *dal dhokli* simmering in the kitchen.

Hey, Jains, can I invite you to sit in stillness for 15 minutes a day? I know this is thirty-three minutes shorter than your traditional recommendation for meditation and introspective self-study, which I refer to as stillness. Even so, I have a secret: 15 minutes is a great place to start. It still works! I promise it will transform your life and the lives of those lucky enough to know you. And Lord Mahavira said, "Amen!" or "Aummmmm!"

America doesn't need more religion but could greatly benefit from the Consciousness of Jainism. (Yep, I just called out the Jains. Y'all thought I only spoke "Southern" and "Christianese.")

Hindus, you're next! Y'all have one of the best diets in the world, rooted in wisdom and science, yet unfortunately, now face diabetes and heart disease like everyone else. This wasn't supposed to happen. (And Vd. said, "Amen!" Pardon me, "Vd." does not stand for "venereal disease." It's an abbreviation for the Sanskrit word "vaidya," meaning doctor or ayurvedic practitioner.) *Anywho,* you're supposed to shop the outer aisles of American grocery stores and avoid the bakery, as the inner aisles are designed to kill you. Plus, you can't work in information technology (IT), sit at a computer all day, and safely eat rice and chapatis with extra ghee. *(Whassup, Satya! Whatever, Satya! I'm sayin' whassup to a different Satya. "The truth is," you're not the only Satya, of course.)* More to come!

Also, Indian folks! You know, the British could never conquer the minds of your ancestors because of Hinduism, but they're now slowly killing you with their diet. They've finally figured out how to defeat the Indian. They said, "The hell with guns and Christianity. Indians love good food; let's get 'em with cream, cake, and cookies…and, of course, tikka masala!" *(Whassup, Leon!)*

Pardon me, back to Jainism and Consciousness! *Jains, The Common Snook has called you out…to the Jain, I'm a Jain. It's time for you to represent!* And Lord Mahavira said, "Aummmmm!"

Namaste Hugs,
   —Sher! (The Common Snook)
                Pause. Inhale. Exhale. Reflect.

P.S. My friendians…I mean, my Indian friends *be asking* how I manage to maintain my weight, and I explain that it's because I eat a lot of traditional Indian food, low-starchy carbohydrates with double the veggies, avoid the inner aisles of American grocery stores, and *never, ever, not ever* bring home a tub of ice cream. And I love ice cream…*Rum Raisin*! (Thanks to *my daddy*!)

(Sit in stillness with your eyes closed for 15 minutes a day; I promise it will transform your life!)

12. Ph.D. in Soul Food

Disclosure Reminder...,

As you read in an earlier sermon, my first Indian friend was a doctor from India, an Ayurvedic practitioner. Yes, the gal with the Ph.D. in soul food!

Ayurveda, which means "science of life" in Sanskrit, determines that each person possesses a unique body energy pattern (Prana), known as Prakriti (a constitution), which encompasses physical and psychological characteristics. This pattern aims to balance the energies that connect the mind, body, and spirit, acknowledging that an imbalance can impact our physical or mental well-being. This concept parallels Classical Five-Element Acupuncture, which identifies each individual's primary meridian channel of energy (Chi), which is categorized into groups called elements, all aimed at achieving regulation and balance within the body.

Ayurveda categorizes all individuals into three main groups called "doshas": "vata," "pitta," and "kapha," which represent the essential characteristics of each constitution. Each dosha outlines a specific diet for individuals to follow. It also categorizes foods into three groups: sattvic (foods that are pure and nourishing), rajasic (foods that are stimulating), and tamasic (foods that are heavy and dulling). Additionally, foods are classified into simple categories, such as positive or negative pranic foods. Essentially, foods are organized into groups based on how they affect our energy; some can be nurturing, neutral, or stimulating, while others may lead to sluggishness.

Focusing on your body's specific needs sounds great, but what if a family of four has different doshas? How can you cook to accommodate so many specifications without a personal chef? No worries...there's a solution! Preparing positive, nurturing meals with whole-food ingredients for everyone was manageable for me, and catering to the needs of the most sensitive family member was another solution.

Most Ayurvedic practitioners allow for flexibility regarding food, much like my friend who loved soul food. I'm sure she would agree that balance is essential to life. (Shhh! Many of my vegetarian or Ayurveda adherent friends are often surprised when I share what a *white, sweet, and fluffy* "Western delicacy" consists of while touring their well-stocked "vegetarian" pantries. One friend exclaimed, "No, Shetty!" I thought, *"No shit" is right.* You know, American grocery stores are the Devil!)

Some may wonder if there is anything to this natural science that the White world does not recognize. Oh my, pardon me, I forgot I'm in mixed company.

Umm…I meant to say the right world. Oops again…I mean, the Western world. (giggles)

Interestingly, once I figured out my husband's and my dosha, the dietary restrictions surprisingly aligned closely with some of the recommendations he was now receiving from Western healthcare professionals, a.k.a. functional medicine. (As if the West is the ultimate authority on all truth, lol. Forgive me for sounding narrow-minded.)

For example, my husband has eczema or psoriasis (nobody is ever sure). Many Western doctors are now aware that nightshades, such as tomatoes, peppers, eggplants, and potatoes (not sweet potatoes), can trigger flare-ups in individuals with skin sensitivities or those with autoimmune and inflammatory issues. They now recommend avoiding these foods, of course, without recognizing the valuable contributions of Ayurveda medicine, which also inspired Naturopathic and other holistic treatments. You may also be surprised to learn that some researchers, including one local to Gainesville, believe that nightshades *cause* arthritis and other inflammatory disorders. But nobody wants to listen to that mess, right? According to Ayurveda science, most nightshade vegetables are either stimulating or dulling and are considered negative pranic foods. Either way, *give it up for* Western medicine for finally learning something about nutrition!

Several years ago, I removed nightshades from my husband's diet. Since I prepared many South Asian dishes, I needed to create my own spice mixes/masalas, such as garam and sambar masala, to eliminate the chili powder and find alternatives for tomatoes and white potatoes. Surprisingly, his dosha had suggested avoiding nightshades 5,000 years ago, as "pittas" tend to have skin sensitivities. This remarkable science of preparing food for the soul is older than Jesus, which many Western doctors believe in, but not in the brown people's science. (How can we give doctors, some of whom believe in Santa Claus, so much authority? Slow down. Don't get your feathers ruffled. Ain't nobody comparing sweet Jesus to Santa; I'm just making a point and trying to nudge some of you to think and not be so Western-narrow-minded. However, they do share the same birthday, right?)

Maybe if Ayurveda were included in the Bible, folks wouldn't be saying nonsense like, "There is no evidence to support Ayurvedic pseudo-science." (That is so rude. I'm embarrassed to be a Westerner.) Still, the creators of this practice must have known the Creator, as its profoundness is evident yet challenging for the commoner to understand.

Even so, the Western world claims there is no evidence that Ayurveda is effective, as it considers itself the self-appointed source of all truth. Most people in the West are just beginning to learn about nightshades, which may also be your first. I don't care if the West labels Ayurveda as pseudoscientific. I have discovered many parallels in modern health science that align with this ancient classical medical system, which was primarily designed to prevent illness, although it also provides treatments. Praise the Lord!

A Science of Life class taught by my good friend could have set many of us on the right path. It would be similar to a home economics class that incorporates spirituality. Unfortunately, most students graduate from high school knowing little about their spiritual selves or self-care.

At the same time, I found it strange that Indian cooking is now loaded with toxic nightshades, even though this science of life recommends avoiding them. (*We humans* just don't seem to listen.) The truth is that many of these foods were brought to India. For example, tomatoes and chilies originated in Mexico and South America. (Shhh!) Indians never consumed many of these nightshade vegetables, which clearly contradicts their ancient science of life, grounded in Divine wisdom. (It's sad how tempted we can be by flavor. I told you, there are far better things to enjoy than sex. Y'all ever had chicken biryani, a dish of chicken and rice layered and slow-cooked with aromatic spices, including cloves, cardamom, mint, and topped with fresh cilantro? I would abandon vegetarianism for a plate of biryani any day. Mmm…so delicious!)

I won't even discuss all the other negative pranic foods or central nervous system stimulants that Ayurveda advises avoiding. Instead, I will focus on onion and garlic, which belong to the Allium family, including their relatives: green onions/scallions, chives, leeks, and shallots. (Keep in mind that many cultures classify stimulants differently.) To learn about others, you must conduct your own research. Many believe these stimulants also hinder our ability to connect with the Divine, which, if you think about it, makes sense because it's the state of calmness and lack of mental activity that helps us stay connected. You can see caffeine likely makes it challenging to focus and be present enough to inhabit the body. But I will leave caffeine alone because some of y'all need your preferred substance to behave…I mean, to function. (Oops, did I mistakenly mention another stimulant? I apologize for that.)

That said, since my rebellious body had already put me on the "No-Food Diet," limited to grass and protein, testing the removal of onion and garlic from my life wasn't difficult. I ate the simplest foods for about a year, and when I tried onion for the first time, I nearly passed out. I became grouchy-tired, almost to the point of tears, and felt like I needed to be slapped just to keep my head up. I knew I felt amazing that year, being free of onion and garlic, yet I never imagined the change would be so significant.

The red onions I used in South Asian cooking were the most potent, even with their mild flavor compared to other onions. Once, an Indian friend slipped me about a teaspoon of raw red onion in a snack mix around 9:00 PM, which kept me up wired until 3:00 AM. It was incredible to witness how they made my body experience both highs and lows. (My husband calls me "the canary" because I react to anything unnatural or toxic.)

And my reaction to garlic, a natural antibiotic, was even worse. This made me suspicious about why I sometimes felt like I was going crazy, almost having an anxiety attack, after eating fresh homemade guacamole with fresh raw garlic, fresh raw onion, fresh raw jalapeño, and fresh raw tomatoes. That negative pranic shit was like snorting coke. (Again, no, I have never snorted coke, but some of you know what I mean.) And *don'tcha* dare crunch on a corn chip next to me after I've eaten *guac*. You might lose your life! I don't mess around with garlic anymore unless I can't avoid it, you invite me to a party, or I need to "address" an infection. A tiny bit of crushed garlic applied to the tooth can be powerful. Still, it will burn the heck out of your mouth and make you smell for days—but it "twerks"! (Please note that the Food and Drug Administration (FDA) has not approved this home remedy and *trumps* "freedom of speech." Additionally, I must say to avoid a lawsuit that "This here garlic or message is not intended to diagnose, treat, cure, or prevent any disease." Ugh!)

I made these thingamajigs…I mean, "garpons," but I won't say where I stuck them. Just sew a string to the clove so it doesn't get lost. It would be awful to need a doctor to remove it; it would stink up the whole office. (By the way, the FDA has not approved "garpons" either.)

As I'm sure you know, this got me thinking! I recalled how one of my sisters hated onions as a kid and claimed they gave her headaches, and another friend said the same. Were their bodies trying to tell them something, as our bodies often speak or signal with tears while chopping onion and garlic, or even diarrhea from eating hot peppers?

Then, I began to consider two religions that strangely avoid onion and garlic for different reasons. Nevertheless, they likely experienced the same level of calm and heightened awareness that I felt. If you're following me, you may have guessed that one is Jainism, which I discussed earlier. The other is the International Society for Krishna Consciousness (ISKCON), a.k.a. the Hare Krishna movement. They say, "Krishna doesn't like the smell, so you can't worship Krishna if you eat these two vegetables." On a deeper level, it can be said that it weakens our ability to remain conscious. For Jains, it was again about not harming any life, even the tiniest organism in the soil.

Suppose you look closer at these religions with parallel restrictions, both of which "coincidentally" originated from India. In that case, I suspect that a truly bright person created a helpful fable or allegory that many interpreted literally or even expanded upon. This literal interpretation, with strict adherence to rules, helped ensure that these two groups followed the path and reaped the benefits. Again, one group prioritizes not harming any living being, while the other is grounded in the fear of rejection from God because they would smell bad. Beautiful!

If we dig a little deeper, again with this, some Hare Krishnas will assert, "You cannot offer onion and garlic to Krishna." If we step outside of religion for a moment and embrace the belief that we are the "temple of God," the "Source of creation," or "that of God is in every human being," then the act of refraining from offering something foul, stimulating, or toxic to the Divine is in essence— *you.* (That's deep! And the Taoists said, "Amen!") Nevertheless, we don't need religion today because we can make conscious decisions without being fooled or bound by extreme religious laws.

Ayurveda makes it easy to make the best decisions for our bodies! It explains that many of us cannot handle the overstimulation of the central nervous system, leaving us to navigate our choices without religion guiding our behavior or conformity.

The late Elizabeth Alexandra Mary Windsor, the queen of the British monarchy, may have also experienced heightened awareness because she, too, avoided onion and garlic. She didn't want her breath to smell and may have unknowingly created a space to maintain peace, even while living under immense pressure and in the spotlight her entire life. Many people commented on her calmness and her Presence during interactions. The Japanese don't mess around with garlic either; they tend to be relatively calm compared to the rest of you.

Today, I mostly eat to nourish my body, not just for pleasure. I try to choose foods that provide me with the most energy. (While I'm sitting here typing, I glance over at my bowl of holy mac 'n' cheese from Trader Joe's, which I heated in my Breville Smart Oven Pro. Nope, this hippie does not have a microwave.) However, I still enjoy the occasional Indian buffet or house party at my neighbors', even if it gives me anxiety, hot flashes, a runny nose, irritability, and knocks me out afterward. (I feel *stupid* just writing that.) Who cares if garlic is a natural "aphrodisiac" if it makes you smelly from head to toe and then puts you to sleep? (Hmm…what a waste of time!)

Fresh Breath Hugs,
—Sher! (The Common Snook)
Pause. Inhale. Exhale. Reflect.

P.S. Greedy folks…ain't nobody tryin' to take any food from your mouth. No worries…conscious eating is rooted in being conscious. The more aware you become, the more conscious your food choices will be, and this applies to any aspect of your life that may conflict with your highest self. Be mindful, and you will change your own life without needing to be told what is "right" or "wrong," or "good" or "bad."

P.P.S. Warning! Unfortunately, many Ayurvedic practitioners in the United States have not received sufficient training and are collecting certifications, which is common in the healing arts. Your practitioner's spiritual state (not perfect, but also not too flaky) is just as important as the therapies they offer. (Also, *careful* when they put a name in front of the science, "Sher Ayurvedic.")

P.P.P.S. Speaking of soul food! If you're looking to take a weekend trip and eat to your heart's content, skip the hustle and bustle of New Jersey and book a flight to New England. (***Common and country folks***, *that was a test! The geographic region of New England consists of the six states in the most northeastern corner of the U.S.: Maine, Vermont, New Hampshire, Massachusetts, Rhode Island, and Connecticut. No worries…**common and country New Englanders** can't name them either.*) But most importantly, if you're after a good meal, head to New Hampshire.

And umm…if the restaurant is a hole-in-the-wall kind of place, like a barn on the side of the road, I highly recommend *stoppin'* because the food will be *poppin'*! Just be sure to skip the cream, cake, and cookies, of course.

292

13. Conscious Eating

Speaking of cream, cake, and cookies! This barn on the side of the road in New Hampshire serves the best ice cream! Plus, the animals are well cared for. Can you see the happy goat on the rooftop? Country is right! (TCS)

Disclosure Reminder…,

Many spiritual teachers and seekers are often assumed to be vegetarians. Some choose this lifestyle due to a commitment to nonviolence towards animals, while others have different motivations. Yet, many of these *"special* folks" still consume commercial dairy products. Need I say more? Violence is merely a matter of perspective or choosing to look the other way.

When we lived in Charlotte, North Carolina, my husband, who hails from New Hampshire and enjoys milk straight from the cow or goat, used to cross the border weekly into South Carolina (*with their* no regulations for anything) to buy raw milk from a farmer who loved his cows. He washed and sanitized their teats before milking them instead of opting for the alternative practice of boiling to kill "anything extra" that might have made its way into the milk. He treated the cows humanely, and you'd think that with so many cow-worshippin' Indian vegetarians in Charlotte, some would have joined the line alongside my husband, other hippies, and the "Weston A. Price followers" to buy the farmer's milk. But who wants to pay ten bucks a gallon for milk from humanely treated cows when you could buy boiled milk from Walmart for less than three dollars a gallon? (No worries…you can still boil it when you get home. Ain't nobody promoting raw milk consumption, said *with attitude.* However, last I checked, driving while Black was still riskier than consuming raw milk. Yet not even raw milk can kill the White man, and he sure *loves himself some* cream and holy mac 'n' cheese.)

Anywho, I'm not here to endorse any specific diet, but rather to listen to your body. But would you like to know why I stopped eating cows specifically? I know that doesn't sound very appealing, but to me, they are cows first, not just a piece of meat, as men often see women. I don't refer to my friends as "beef," "blondes," or "brunettes." Call it what you will; it's still associated with inflammation.

In my early twenties, I worked as a caseworker and traveled to some of the most tranquil places in the countryside around Alachua County, Florida. I noticed the breathtaking beauty of the cows and sometimes stopped to photograph them. I felt like I had never seen such heavenly animals. I was so in love that I began decorating my house with my photographs. I even convinced my friends that they, too, should take a moment to appreciate the cows.

I took a few of them in the church van to see the beautiful red-brown cows once found in the field next to the Jonesville Publix on Newberry Road before that area was developed. I also used to take selfies with the cows, using my 35mm camera, long before selfies became a thing. The more time I spent with them, the more I noticed they had a level of awareness and were observing me closely. Could this be the reason India declared the cow sacred? And this was long before Indian culture became a part of my life. I was still somewhat narrow-minded back then, yet I worshipped cows. (Hmm…I wasn't so bad after all.)

As my young fellows came along, I also introduced them to my love for cows. We had a herd that lived across the street from our house in Athens-Clarke County, Georgia, on the Oglethorpe side of the road, of course. We would sing to them, and they would come to listen, waving their tails in delight. If you've never seen a cow enjoying music, it's truly somethin' *special.*

Sometimes, the mothers with their curious calves were a bit more cautious, as if to say, "Y'all are too young to go to the music festival." Even so, the calves would come running against their mothers' wishes as if to say, "Gee, Mom, it's fine; it's just the woman with the two boys from across the street." They'd push their way to the front of the crowd, where it often seemed like well over a hundred cows gathered to enjoy the music. (You want to feel like a celebrity?

Try singing for a herd of cows. They'll bless your heart with love and appreciation.)

Observing cows over the years and identifying with them provided me with a clear idea of what chattel slavery must have looked like. These were the same plantations but with different inhabitants. But hey, as long as it's not us, right?

Americans often mock South Asians by calling them cow worshippers in a sarcastic, "superior" tone, as if they are fools. However, many of my fellow Americans have never paused to consider that other conscious beings share similar feelings and emotions. When you realize this, it can make cuttin' up and eatin' your friends rather challenging. It would be akin to cooking the family labradoodle or poodle with noodles for dinner. Numerous people in India also understand that they or their children wouldn't be here if it weren't for the cow. As a mom who struggled with breastfeeding and had to rely on formula, I found this idea profoundly moving. (How could I support the killing of a creature that gave my children life?)

The final conviction was, of course, my cow-worshipping Indian neighbors. Many Indians follow tradition without understanding the significance of the Consciousness reflected in these beautiful creatures, just as many Christians may not grasp the teachings of Jesus and his call to awakening. Nevertheless, living among people who saw the cow as lovely as I did, I haven't eaten beef since…unless my Muslim Indian neighbors slipped me some, calling it mutton. Indians didn't need to "evangelize" me. I was already a cow worshipper, and they were my people!

Today, if my neighborhood allowed it, I would have a cow mowing my front lawn. And, of course, I would take it on daily walks on a 20-foot leash and let it poop in my neighbors' yards. I wouldn't pick up after it either because cow manure is technically fertilizer, unlike Fido's acidic, human-like pee.

And thank goodness, Americans don't eat crows. (Wow, that's "cow" with an "r." I never noticed!) *Anyways*, they're another one of my favorite creatures. One day, I watched a crow enjoying a box of Bojangles chicken left in the parking lot. The bird picked up the entire drumstick and seemed thrilled to find a whole piece of fried chicken in the box while his friends chased him, begging him to share. Strangely, they reminded me of people I know who are always "shooting the breeze," laughing, and having a good time, even when they have so little. (You can learn a thing or two about enjoying life by watching crows.)

As I mentioned, this isn't about telling people what to eat. You can eat crow if you wish. At the same time, I encourage you to notice the life in all creation.

Vegetarianism isn't something Americans can easily adopt overnight, even though it can be a healthier choice. Avoiding meat or following a low-meat diet requires a level of awareness, as you must consider what you eat to maintain a balanced diet. Meat can be consumed with little thought and can be sustaining. (It's lazy eatin' for many people.) And it's necessary for a lot of folks, so please ignore those Whole Foods eatin' single-perspective vegetarians.

In fact, for about fifteen years, I couldn't eat dairy or legumes, and tree nuts triggered severe migraines for me. It was clear to me that promoting vegetarianism for everyone was nonsense. Animal protein was my only option for a long time.

Restrictive diets like vegetarianism or even paleo (grain-free) are often diets of privileged folks. (Shhh!) Many will continue to require meat simply because our lifestyles don't allow the time for conscious living. For instance, some members of the privileged vegetarian class or caste in India believe they are "superior" for never having eaten meat or eggs. However, when they finally stepped aside and stopped imposing their religious beliefs on a state level, affecting others who couldn't maintain the privileged lifestyle, they permitted schools to serve eggs to children, many of whom were living in poverty. Subsequently, they observed an increase in school attendance. Hungry children were coming to school for a hard-boiled egg. (Can you see the tears in my eyes?)

Furthermore, I don't recommend vegetarianism to anyone who lacks awareness or time because junk food and cheese-based "vegetarianism"—the diet many Americans adopt that excludes fresh vegetables or legumes—serves as a poor substitute for meat consumption. Ever wonder why there are so many "round" vegetarians? Well, many of them consume a lot of cheese and heavily processed meat alternatives packed with sodium that used to come from vegetables, or they fill up on carbohydrates like rice and bread products. They may not realize that this excellent cheese comes from milk designed to fatten a calf. American vegetarians, I'd be careful if I were you! (Uh-oh, here comes a bunny trail!)

Speaking of round! One time, I became good friends with the gal in the cheese department of one of my favorite *healthy stores*. (Not recommended!) Every week, she would give me an assortment of mouthwatering samples and send me home with blocks of gourmet cheese I couldn't afford. By the end of this "Tour de France," I had gained about fifteen pounds, which I couldn't explain. I thought it was my hormones. Still, my husband said, "It's your friend, the cheese lady." He was right; I had to end our friendship. She was worse than a dealer.

Guess what? I also don't eat pork. Pigs are pretty smart, too. Still, I often catch my husband and sons acting clueless about what bacon is made of. (Yeah, right!) Once, we were on a cruise, and my "Marine son"—whom I'll tell you about later—returned to the table with a plate piled high with bacon, along with our new friends we met on board. Bhutabhavyabhavatprabha (with the long-ass name), who grew up in India, had a big ol' plate of bacon, too, that his son Pi was enjoying. (No, I promise…these Indian folks found me for some reason.) *Anywho,* I thought perhaps my son needed me to read him *Charlotte's Web* again to go with his bacon, of course.

My Chinese friends have always treated me well for as long as I can remember. That said, I'm socially willing to try any little creature except for those stir-fried pig ears that I didn't realize were ears at my neighbor's Chinese New Year party. (Chinese people seem to enjoy getting a good laugh out of feeding some of us strange body parts. They find that hilarious.)

Also, I welcome the world-renowned chicken so my friends can bless me with their culinary skills. I never reject or turn my nose up at anyone's expression of love unless it might kill me. Ain't no chicken ever offended me. (Hmm…that's a lie.)

Have you ever eaten a humanely raised chicken from one of those all-organic, hippie Community Supported Agriculture (CSA) programs with the laughing chickens? That free-range bird was so tough from running around the yard that you couldn't even use it for stew and dumplings—*Lumbees.* (Lumbees, my cousin tribe, still fightin' for federal benefits, enjoy eating old, tough hens with pastry squares, which are like a cross between a dumplin' and a noodle. *Whassup, Locklears!* Uh-oh, here comes a final story and then a secret!)

As a matter of fact, I love chickens! I once rescued a chicken (not recommended!) that was sitting in the middle of the highway between fast-moving and on-merging traffic. It had fallen from a chicken truck in Athens, Georgia, on its way to Chick-fil-A. I couldn't stop to rescue the chicken the first time because I was headed to "Waseca" (giggles), but when I returned thirty minutes later, I could still see "my girl" on the opposite side of the highway, balancing on the solid white line with all her might. I could almost have sworn that she turned and looked my way all the way across the highway (that's a lot of ways) as if she knew I was coming back. She wasn't going to die on my watch, at least not then, and have me passing her the following morning flat on the road on my way to "Waseca." (giggles) I would have felt horrible. (Hmm…I wonder how many vegetarians passed my chicken that morning.)

I exited the highway onto Lexington Road, then got back on the highway, parking on the white merge lines. I grabbed the terrified chicken and rushed back to my Chevy, with semi-trucks on either side of me. I placed her in the back of my pickup and took the sweet girl home. She was fat and round like a "butterball" and could barely walk, which is bad news for a chicken. Still, she was free and enjoying life back on the farm as if she had escaped death by the skin of her beak. I won't share what happened over the next seventy-two hours, but it's true; everyone, indeed, likes chicken. (Also, if you're from Athens, you know Lexington Road is littered with dead chickens, probably coming from my old area on the Oglethorpe side of the road, of course.)

Speaking of conscious eating! I have a secret to share before I finish up. The year after my husband and I faced an extended period of unemployment and near homelessness, I finally regained my health and dental insurance. Unfortunately, I discovered that my dental health was in terrible shape. I needed about $15,000 worth of work. Essentially, they planned to take "all my teeth." But thank goodness, I couldn't afford the work, which led me to seek alternatives. And *boy*, did I discover some!

Let me say this quietly because you know my homegirl is a dentist. In any case, I learned that oral health is an indicator of overall health and that cavities aren't necessarily linked to sugar on the teeth, but rather to the amount of sugar in the body and bloodstream. The short version is that your teeth can heal and remineralize if you maintain a healthy diet. (Most dentists won't tell you this. Shhh!)

After I realized my husband was slowly killing me, feeding me cream, cake, and cookies as a form of therapy during the recession, I completely changed my diet, only eating whole food ingredients. (*Shout out* to Brookford Farm!) Within thirty days, my dental exam revealed improvement from 5–7 millimeter pockets between my teeth and gums to just 1–2 millimeters, indicating that I had no more inflammation and my teeth were beginning to remineralize. I also oil-pulled (a.k.a. oil-pulling) daily with coconut oil to eliminate bacteria from my mouth. (*Give it up for* Ayurveda!)

When I moved back south to Georgia and shared my dental history with my new hygienist, she said, "If what you're saying is true, this will put us out of business." (No, it won't...only Consciousness and conscious eating will put the *dentist* out of *business.* If you read the last sentence with a Southern accent, "dentist" and "business" should've rhymed. Just drop the "t's" in "dentist.")

Ultimately, I only lost one tooth by choice when my first dentist intended to extract five—beeyotch! I didn't want a root canal to minimize the risk of bacterial growth and infection, so I let my holistic hippy dentist take it.

I haven't needed any dental work in over ten years, and my children have never had cavities or used fluoride because I learned my lesson. When one of them had a soft spot on his tooth, I told the dentist, "I can fix that!" The soft spot meant we needed to adjust our diets, reducing sugar and grain, and doubling down on the veggies. Of course, there's more to it. Do your research! You can remineralize your teeth with the right minerals in your body. It's just that simple. This is why consuming organic vegetables and grass-fed products is essential. There are minerals in that grass!

Anywho, don't worry about what other folks are eatin'. Listen to your body and make the best choices for your well-being. Either way, take a moment to give thanks *to* or *for* the food that has given its life to you. (*Thank you, chicken. I bow to the Divinity in you.* And the Germains said, "Amen!")

Crispy Bacon Hugs,
—Sher! (The Common Snook)
Pause. Inhale. Exhale. Reflect.

P.S. The Indian boy named Pi is no joke. Once again, I always mean what I say. Additionally, here's a chant/poem, "Bhaja Govindam" by M. S. Subbulakshmi, which was given to me by Pi's father with the long-ass name. It's banging!

(Sit in stillness with your eyes closed for 15 minutes a day; I promise it will transform your life!)

14. I Bow to the Divinity in You

Youse ready for a sequel to Consciousness for *Common and Country Folks?*

You've heard the trending phrase "namaste" used in spiritual circles or even at your local yoga studio, right? This beautiful Sanskrit word means "I bow to you" or "I bow to the Divinity in you." It's a way of acknowledging that everyone deserves respect because that of God is in every individual. When someone says "namaste" back, it's like two souls saying, "Whassup," as seen in the beauty of the head nod exchanged between African American men. I believe George Fox of Quakerism would have been a *namaste enthusiast*, and the church would have condemned him, of course.

Some people manage to exist in this world while not being a part of it, as I describe my friend, Ms. Juliette. Being around these folks can feel like you are sitting in the Presence of God, which is true in a sense. Not because they are gods, per se, but because they have become one with the Source, as was likely the case with Jesus. This oneness varies from person to person and is more pronounced in certain teachers or individuals. This may also help explain why some gurus are "worshiped" and will sometimes have you dropping to your knees. This behavior, which resembles what some might call "worshipping," is not uncommon. It's just that those observing the behavior sometimes mistakenly think this is about the person, and occasionally, the worshipper doesn't know the difference either.

For example, I often bow to the Divinity I see in my acupuncturist and want to throw flowers at his feet. This is my way of expressing gratitude for the Divine in his life. Other times, he may accidentally burn my leg with moxa, a dry herb, while providing acupuncture because he's daydreaming about a beautiful place or eating something delicious for dinner. In that case, I see him. Regardless, God might also burn me to get my attention.

But as you know, some egos perceive this worship and petal-tossing as being all about them. People who are not very close to the Light may take these gestures of affection straight to the head, and sadly, we might have inadvertently contributed to the birth of another spiritual asshole. Humility and awareness are crucial to maintaining balance.

Namaste, —Sher! (The Common Snook)
Pause. Inhale. Exhale. Reflect. 🧘

15. I Have Never Accidentally Grown Anything This Big

The prophecy!

Disclosure Reminder...,

In the summer of 2022, I saved some seeds I had harvested from a melon I bought at the Indian Bazaar on 34th Street in Gainesville. *(Whassup, Jay!)* I took my seeds outside so they could cure in the sun. However, one of my seeds had other plans and decided to catch a ride with the wind.

The following summer of 2023, a charming little squash plant appeared near our front door in nice and tidy suburbia, where humans are expected to leave no trace of their existence. You know, they don't allow us hippies to have front yard gardens in these parts. Regardless, I ignore the politics of Homeowners Associations (HOAs) when it comes to choosing life.

It was so decorative that I let it grow to see what it would bring. That invasive Indian plant started grabbing everything in sight. It grabbed my hedge by the neck and worked its way up toward the house. Next, I noticed it peering in the window, pushing its little spiral shoots through my screen. It had *locked hold* onto the face of our house, like an octopus I saw on social media that a woman attempted to eat alive.

Bright yellow flowers were everywhere, but the plant wasn't bearing any fruit. For the life of me, I couldn't figure out whether the plant was male or female, which some of y'all might say is none of my business. (giggles) For a moment, I recall thinking about what Jesus said to the fig tree, but that sweet

nonbinary plant blessed me with all those beautiful flowers. I couldn't just curse it or rip it out.

As I sympathized with the plant, it dared to grow across the front entrance of our house and propped itself up in one of my lounge chairs. I told that plant, "You need to bear some fruit because the HOA police will be after me soon. This can't go on forever."

Sure enough, that tough broad was female and had a baby to prove it. She must have gotten some pollination from the seed bank growing behind the house and was now proudly dangling

"Theyby" (pronounced like "they-bee," like baby) in the dining room window so we could see her fruit.

We were so proud of the new addition to our family. But then that little rascal started to get fat and ripped away from the front of the house, tearing a big hole in the screen. You would have thought Theyby could have carried *their* weight, but since *they was* an only child, Theyby was eating nonstop.

We put little Hercules on a plate to support Theyby's growth, and that joker blew up, growing about a quarter of an inch in circumference every two days. With all the rain and unnecessary watering of lawns in suburban America, instead of growing food, her water was soon to break, so I scheduled an emergency delivery before Theyby got too big. I could barely pick *them* up when I cut the cord and pulled Theyby out from behind the bush. Theyby came in, weighing twenty pounds.

I was thrilled to embrace my new prickly addition. That same week, while building the *Betwixt* website in the summer of 2023, I told my husband, who took my picture, "I have never accidentally grown anything this big." I could feel the Divine speaking through me as I held what is called an "ash gourd" or "winter melon." This vegetable is commonly used in South Asian cuisine for soups, dahls, desserts, and juicing. It's one of the most versatile vegetables. I like diversity!

This 20-pound melon assured me that what I was building had nothing to do with me; all I had to do was prepare the seeds. Aww-yeah, Jesus…that'll preach!

Juicy Melon Hugs,

—Sher! (The Common Snook)
Pause. Inhale. Exhale. Reflect.

P.S. "Theyby" is a charming term used to describe a baby without enforcing the social construct of gender, which some people conflate and confuse with sex. I was just testing out inclusive language to see how I fared. It was fun! I like using my own language, too; as y'all can see, I make English work for me.

Language is supposed to be fluid and ever-changing. It's about time we used the English language to rightfully and honorably acknowledge people called "Black." African American was a good attempt by Jesse Jackson. But no worries...I'll have a term sermon coming soon!

P.P.S. Speaking of delicious ash gourd, which sounds like "ass-goat" with a Hindi accent! The three chefs at Jim's Jungle Retreat in Uttarakhand, India, must be nationally recognized. I have *never, ever, not ever* tasted such delicious food. It was Divine! Y'all hear me? Divine! *(I bow to the Divinity in Suresh, Michael, and Nawab. Y'all need to publish a cookbook and send me a copy!)*

(Sit in stillness with your eyes closed for 15 minutes a day; I promise it will transform your life!)

That's a magic pumpkin, for sure; beautiful!

Section VII: White Man's Reflection Through the Eyes of Love

In case you decided to skip the introduction and browse around, here's the **Disclosure Reminder**: Before diving in, I will say this: I'm simple. I love to laugh. Please don't confuse my humor with sarcasm; I always mean what I say. I test the limits. My words are plain. I often use "own" redundantly. I don't claim to know all the answers; my only intention is to be a vessel. Also, to connect with different experiences, I interchangeably use the terms "Consciousness," "Presence," "God," "Universe," "Source," "Divine," "Energy," "Christ/Krst," and "Light." Above all, reading my humor with a Southern accent is best. Enjoy!

Yosemite National Park in California, 2009. (TCS)

1. Black People: The Overlooked Similarities Between Racism and Religion and the Path to Liberation

Warning: this sermon is not for the faint of heart and may be a challenging read because it questions the literal belief in religion and speaks directly to African American communities. It's sharp and could leave both White and Black folks offended or, for once, united. Many will not be able to see beyond the title. Nonetheless, it's intended for those ready for solid food, as Jesus said. Still, I would forgo this sermon if I were building a business and collecting tithes.

November 3, 2016…,

For the past year, I've wanted to write a piece about what I refer to as *literal Christianity*, particularly in African American communities. Admittedly, this topic isn't widely popular, but it needs to be addressed. Stimulating new thoughts among those deeply engaged in any religion can be a challenging task.

Last year, a video of a religious talk supporting traditional Christian views was sent to me by a close friend who practices this literal form of Christianity. I highly value my relationship with her, as she has maintained our friendship even when others have used the Bible as an excuse to turn their backs on me due to my willingness to think outside the box. At times, I've wondered if she continued our relationship in hopes that I would return to practicing the faith as she was raised and believes it should be. I think this is called "friendship evangelism," right?

I can't say I wouldn't do the same if I were in her position. Either way, I'll take it because she's a valuable person to me, with an extraordinary mind. I'm almost certain she was looking forward to my response. I'm one of those people who loves a good thought-provoking experience, so I know she was at least confident I would watch the video. Little did she know that her recommendation, perhaps even used as a tool to evangelize me, was just the provoking instrument I needed to finally sit down and write a letter to the brilliant "People of Color" whose grandmothers' literal Christianity still binds them.

I used to feel hopeless discussing this topic with my friends because it often seemed impossible to encourage people to think beyond religion or their belief systems. Being Black and loving Jesus seemed like two halves of a whole.

While watching this film, I noticed for the first time how strikingly similar the thought patterns behind religion are to those of racism. It was intriguing, to

305

say the least. Because of that, I finally felt I had an opportunity to stand up against literal Christianity.

Christianity, like racism, is a belief system that is only as strong as its ability to defend itself, reproduce, and influence others. It also has the privilege of disregarding outsiders' perspectives. Christians need not strive to understand how their religion might harm others or be flawed in certain instances. In this religion, its adherents assign you an identity from a contrasting perspective of themselves: "nonbeliever," "wicked," "heathen," "unrighteous," "lost," "Pagan," and so on. This concept of religion demands to be upheld as the truth, even when society acknowledges its flaws and divisive nature. It is a belief deemed "superior," often without consideration for the spiritual practices of others. It is considered "right," just as the ideology of "White Supremacy" has been deemed "right" in our society. (This recognition stings and evokes discomfort because a muzzle on humanity suggests I'm not permitted to express this. Who dictates that?)

Furthermore, similar to addressing racism, the mind often refuses to admit involvement in these behaviors, trying to alter perceptions or to detach or exempt itself from self-examination. This ensures that nothing changes, allowing us to hold on to our beliefs comfortably; meanwhile, we remain frustrated by others' lack of understanding of racism and its effects on our lives. If we cannot see the control religion exerts over our own minds, how can we expect others to see the racist system that controls theirs? (Oh my, I can hear Frederick Douglass, W. E. B. Du Bois, and James Baldwin shouting into this book!)

It gets even more twisted! Besides religion paralleling the same thought patterns as racism, "People of Color" are fighting for equality while still believing in a religion that was clearly used to favor one group over another. Our ancestors were written into the script as second-class citizens, "infidels." "The Good Book," which is still very powerful when interpreted consciously, was used to justify chattel slavery! (See Judaism's Exodus 21:2-7 or Deuteronomy 15:12-18 from the Torah or the Bible.)

Let's consider a hypothetical situation for a moment. Imagine you are playing a game where you are enslaved. Your culture and religious practices are stripped from you because your enslaver fears the freedom that still exists in your mind. When he learned of your evening worship of nature and the Universe under the stars, he whipped you and then restricted your worship to his idea of God. He felt more secure in his position, knowing you shared the same beliefs, hopes, and fears. The fear of his deity and archangel became *yours*, and "obey your master" became the foundation of your religion.

306

Understanding your ideology enabled him to better control you without shackles, which perhaps made him feel less inhumane. Your only hope for escape from the misery lay in an imaginary place called Heaven. It was the ultimate prize for your suffering.

But it was too late for you once you were finally granted physical freedom. Too much time had passed, and you didn't know whether the enslaver's rules were relevant or not. So, instead, you continued playing by the rules of his game, physically free but still a captive in your mind. (We must understand how programming works or risk being programmed.)

Of course, today, this scenario wouldn't make sense to anyone. But how is it that even well-educated Black folks find themselves caught in this very reality? The enslaver no longer needs to teach his dogma because many Black people willingly pass down the teachings to their children, generation after generation, all while fighting a war against racism. However, many display thought patterns that reflect the same exclusive behavior they seek to dismantle. Additionally, many unknowingly support a mindset that continues to control them socially and psychologically. Some never escape the cult, so to speak. (Please know that while writing this, I have been particularly sensitive to the fact that God, through religion, was the only hope many Black communities had. It was, and still is, a hope that keeps many moving forward and living day after day through some of the harshest conditions. This isn't something I take lightly.)

But how can I challenge the religion of the great Martin Luther King Jr., the face of freedom and Christianity in many Black communities, if he too was a believer? Indeed, a man as wise as King wouldn't fall for the religion of the enslaver. However, if you knew a bit more about King, you would discover that he regularly questioned the faith of his youth.

In *The Autobiography of Martin Luther King Jr.*, King discusses questioning the literalization of Christian scriptures as early as age thirteen during his Sunday school class by boldly denying "the resurrection." He realized that failing to question religion contradicted his spirit, and he could no longer accept what he was being taught without question. He also expressed remarkable frustration with the emotional side of the Black church—all that [unnecessary] shoutin' and stompin'. (Don't look at me. I'm just paraphrasing King.) He goes on to share that he could not see how religion could harmonize with science or forward-thinking ideas. However, it was through his biblical studies and formal training that he experienced freedom from fundamentalism, which he described as "shackles." (giggles) Still, as he peered beyond the shackles and the great stories, legends, and myths [with "angels and fire," of course], he could see that the

307

Bible contained many truths and decided to dedicate his life to promoting the "social gospel." He made it his mission to change hearts in order to change society, and to change society in order to change hearts (King, pp 6-19).

King joined the ministry because he viewed the message preached by Jesus as a tool to help liberate Black communities, not because he was a literal believer in Christianity. He also regarded this Love as an instrument to appeal to the moral conscience of those who oppressed his people. I couldn't think of a better way to reach an oppressive population than by inspiring a massive awakening and teaching them to love. He used their very own belief system, as anything less would have been futile and would have also left Black people divided. Yet this Love is not religion or Christianity, for that matter. This Love is universal, yet most who resisted the Civil Rights Movement lived disconnected from Love.

My respect for King grew beyond the obvious reasons and far beyond the songs taught in school and the freedom marches I watched on television as a child. I read the autobiography of a man who didn't allow religion to prevent him from establishing his own beliefs, nor did he blindly follow his grandmother's ideology or conditioning. He embodied the essence of Christ/Krst Consciousness. He brought Consciousness (salvation) not only to Black and Brown Americans but also to millions of Whites and their descendants, freeing them from the mental hell of racism and guilt. He was brilliant and used what he had, nearly the equivalent of rocks and sticks, to ignite a revolutionary fire for change. His faith was powerful! And if you have lived or studied his legacy, regardless of your background, you would likely agree that he is the greatest American leader to have ever lived and one of the most incredible reflections of the Divine to have touched America. (Uh-oh, I have stirred some egos. Great! Do your homework! I'm sure if "Honest Abe" were around today, he would tell you the truth. And my awakened *Friends* said, "Amen!")

I find it interesting how many White people today don't believe in religion or, more specifically, Christianity. However, when I share my struggles with Christianity's stronghold over Black communities, many adopt the "respect all religions" approach, or they take the high road by viewing the Christian church as central to Black communities, despite it having never been core to African communities. In Africa, where some nations were initially seen by Whites as a collection of heathen nations without organized religion, today this autonomy is now ironically one of the world's fastest-growing religions known as "None." Many Whites now consider what is not suitable for them as a good thing for Black people. What a double standard!

I assume this position is similar to how I perceive religion's role in the prison system. It can serve as a valuable tool to encourage positive behavior among the prison population or those who are unruly. I'm tired of the respect that religion demands as "a good" for society. *So what* if it advises against lying or stealing. We recognize that goodness exists in all major world religions, as humanity possesses a measure of morality and kindness. However, "a good" that holds you back is not "a good" worth having.

As expected, my friend's video concluded that the afterlife is a place of peace and paradise. I added that it is free from literal beliefs in religion and its distortions of the truth.

I said those remarks because very few Black folks know that the core principles of Christianity were taken or even stolen from African cultures and other earlier faiths. Yet, many White historians will only go so far as to claim it "borrowed" from Africa…and, of course, repackaged to control the people.

Did you know that the notion of "Christ/Krst," the Source within, existed long before the establishment and "the establishment" of Christianity? This transformative power within was believed to be available to all individuals to do good works. The problem with that simple approach is that it does not allow space for a dictator to control the people. It'd be like trying to sell you an old Box Chevy (for those from the South) when you already owned a Cadillac. No one could sell you a knockoff.

I'm sure the story sounds familiar, but most follow the personified version of an idea that belongs to humanity. Ancient Africa, the mother of all nations, believes that man possesses the power of good, unlike Christianity, which teaches that we are all born evil and need a savior. (Yes, believes! The Spirit never dies!)

I used to feel isolated in my understanding of Christian history. However, one day, while participating in a Quaker worship and meditation circle, I was surprised when a retired professional, speaking from the Christian faith—or, better yet, as a follower of Christ's ways—humbly thanked the people of Africa for their valuable contributions to Christianity. Where were the Black people to hear this? Unfortunately, most were still literally believing in a book of allegories. To be fair, it is a meaty book with precious teachings, as most world religions have. But if they did hear his words, would anyone examine his understanding more closely?

I must ask: was it the White man's "destiny" to save our ancestors from their primitive nature worship (again, the religious practice many Whites are now pursuing)? Were our ancestors' spiritual practices wrong? Christianity does help make those with brown skin less of a mystery and more acceptable in society, similar to what a hair relaxer did for many years.

Please understand: I'm not here to take anyone's religion. The devotional path of aligning one's life with the Christ of Christianity remains effective for some. Yet, there is more. At the same time, recognizing our own exclusive thought patterns helps us understand how others may struggle to overcome theirs, whether we are examining issues related to religion or racism. We know that we can only change the world by first changing ourselves.

I hope to have sparked a desire for truth beyond religion. Pick up a new book, ask the tough questions, and seek your own answers. (Consciousness!) Unlike our ancestors, we are not enslaved; instead, we are free women and men with unlimited access to knowledge, which is power. As Barbara Hillary, the first Black woman to reach the North Pole, sharply stated, "Christianity [or literal Christianity] is a greater shackle than slavery ever was." Let us fight for freedom and equality today by seeking freedom of the mind.

In Love and Peace Hugs,

—Sher! (The Common Snook)
Pause. Inhale. Exhale. Reflect.

P.S. An excellent book to get the believer thinking: *Nothing Sacred: The Truth About Judaism* by Douglas Rushkoff —written for a Jewish audience. "What does this have to do with Christianity?" Everything! Also, *shout out* to Bet Emet Ministries! Thank you, Craig Lyons, Ms.D, D.D., M.Div, for your educational material. (Caution! Ignorance is bliss.)

(Sit in stillness with your eyes closed for 15 minutes a day; I promise it will transform your life!)

2. *BETwixt* for "People of Color": Growing in Awareness and Free from Racism

Disclosure Reminder...,

After outgrowing religion, I never lost my passion for spirituality, as some might assume. I no longer followed anyone's teachings blindly but became a lifelong seeker. This journey has taken me to places and allowed me to meet people that religion often restricts. As you read in "Waking Up," I describe this unfolding in my life; however, I omitted the details of how the vision of *Betwixt* was born. So I'll continue from here.

With the shoe of *literal Christianity* and its exclusivity no longer a good fit for me, I began to explore some of the other more "welcoming" spiritual circles, like the Unitarian Universalist Church (UU), the Religious Society of Friends (the Quakers), and the United Church of Christ (not to be confused with the infamous Church of Christ). I will provide a simplified definition for those unfamiliar with these churches that will quickly resonate with some. They are the White folks (super liberals!) who show up on MLK Day to march; they chant, "Black Lives Matter," hang the Pride flag with pride, and recycle everything! They are like little fan clubs for the far left. (Well...some of them.)

These groups assert that everyone is welcome. They differ slightly in that Unitarians and the United Church of Christ have ministers and follow a traditional church service program, while Quakers generally do not have clergy and instead sit in silence or engage in meditation. I sounded as if I were joking when describing these groups earlier. However, Quakerism is a meaty faith. I sure hope those old folks will awaken and not let it die due to stubbornness. *Hakuna matata*...George Fox, I've got your back.

The people I grew to love and accept sometimes greeted me more than I wanted to be greeted. It felt as if they were saying, "You are welcome here, and we are not 'racist' like the rest of our people. Do you see our pins and buttons?"

Unfortunately, the pins were never enough. I could see that racism was ingrained in many of them. Some never escape the cult, so to speak. These people weren't necessarily "haters." Sadly, they were products of social programming. Every conversation with some of the members seemed to revolve around the skin color of the person standing before them. It was evident that this was a serious mental health issue.

They often assigned me a culture and history so they could tell me about everything from their parents, who helped fund a well-known historically Black

311

university, to having a "Black" grandchild who was technically biracial and not Black. It was shocking to witness that White people would have the audacity to redefine my ancestry and tell me who I am. (But hold on a *sec*, I spy a Jew! I can now see it in his eyes. [Can I say that?] Well, I'll be damned! That was years ago. Aw, it's so good to see Reform Jews with my *Friends*.)

You know, members of the Reform Jewish community helped fund many Black universities. Maybe *someone* was just trying to tell me in code that he wasn't like the rest of our *Friends*. Shoot, if that were me, I would be telling every Black person in America about my parents. That's something to be proud of. *(I'm sorry, bro; you just didn't know how many Black stories I could hear in one setting. You're exempt!)*

And heaven forbid if one of the "coloreds" or true allies attempted to introduce anything new or diverse in one of these "welcoming" circles. In response, an intriguing spirit that I shall call "the resistance" would *rise up* like clockwork, yet "all were welcome," of course.

Speaking of the spirit of resistance! Two summers ago, when I spoke at a Quaker Meeting on two separate occasions, the same member…I mean, a crustacean…got up and walked out in the middle of my sharing. This crab was silently protesting my voice in *their* all-White community, which was painfully loud and clear. (Hmm…there's always lots of traffic whenever I speak. [giggles]) I glanced at it sideways as it scurried out the door in a similar fashion. (*You gotta love 'em.*) They didn't know I was a Quaker. Perhaps they mistook me for a Black person who had just popped in off the street and had never read Quaker Faith & Practice, the Quaker rulebook. *(Whassup, Friends!)*

However, some years ago, at another "welcoming" church, I was quite entertained by an older White "gentleman" who, when I expressed my surprise at the high housing prices in the area, suggested I look for a place in the new affordable housing community in "Antiquity," which had income restrictions. (giggles) Curious, I asked my husband if he received the same kind of recommendations, but he always engaged in lighter conversations with our interesting group of *Friends*. These folks were proud of being different and often used my reflection to enhance the validation they craved, while others worked hard to ensure I didn't stay too long.

Sure, some were attempting to make connections…that were *always* wrong. Good for them!

Speaking of making connections! A sweet older White woman who I met on vacation once shared a story of her deplorable house guest that kept using the word "nigger*S*." (Oh my, she was so loud with "the N-word," with a firm capital "S" at the end.) I remember thinking, *Why do you need to share this story? What's its connection to me?*

As you can see, this kind of communication gets old when you fail to realize there is more to the person than your stereotypical views. This person is a unique individual—human. Let's stop making excuses. (Here's a heartwarming side story to calm you, just in case I have triggered some defensiveness.)

The generation of Whites who attended middle and high school during the Civil Rights Movement and resided in sheltered communities that were never impacted by integration are now ready to talk. They want to engage in conversations about the Civil Rights Movement with young "People of Color," possibly because that's where their interest paused before being told what to think or never fully embracing King's message of love. However, I can't fairly express their reasons since each experience is unique. Still, they consistently share their stories with me, so I listen.

I have learned to discern the difference between ignorant comments, like "I'm not racist," and those that are race-focused but are more about helping a person heal from pain for various reasons. I especially learned this while enjoying the company of a White bicyclist I met at Kanapaha Botanical Gardens, who cycled through my area and Micanopy. (He and his friends caught my attention because of their noisy cleats scraping against the concrete path.) As we walked and talked through the garden, he became excited and wanted to show me a picture of a bridge he had crossed on his bike in Alabama. (He may have even said the bridge's name, but it likely didn't ring a bell.) Even so, I could sense it had a heavy history as he searched for the picture on his phone. As I braced myself, I thought, *What is the bridge?*

He showed me a picture of the Edmund Pettus Bridge in Selma, Alabama, where the late John Lewis attempted to cross during the Civil Rights Movement on March 7, 1965, a day now known as "Bloody Sunday." Lewis was nearly beaten to death on the bridge by a vicious mob of Alabama state troopers. Martin Luther King Jr. tried to cross the bridge two days later but was stopped by the same "united front" of mentally ill White state troopers. My new friend, who still showed glimpses of his youth despite being retired, shared a piece of history—*his history*—during a period I couldn't fully relate to as he did. His enthusiasm brought the story to life as if it had happened yesterday, which was likely how it felt for him. Even so, I may have appeared safe and approachable, and perhaps I had the right skin color, which I was okay with. I embraced his excitement and healing as he gave me a pin, a token of friendship, to wear on my shirt and asked to hug me before we parted ways.

He really warmed my heart. In a sense, he was taking responsibility for what happened that day and made amends by sharing his story with me. Even though he was old enough to be my father, he was still growing and ready to make new friends regardless of skin color. Hopefully, he got what he needed and wouldn't have to show his picture to another "Person of Color." (giggles) Or perhaps he should share his image with the world, because his joy was contagious! I will forever remember his passion…for "grow or die"—beeyotch! That gentleman had crossed the bridge! (Yes, he is the same man who gave me the song "Seminole Wind" by John Anderson, which I then gave to Carlton Ward, the National Geographic Photographer.)

Back to my main point! Man, I was sick of being the token "Person of Color" in these spiritual communities and the fulfillment of their emotional orgasms. Finally, I had had enough of their stories. Was anyone genuinely interested in getting to know *me?*

While leaving Quaker Meeting one Sunday afternoon, I said to my husband, who has evolved significantly in his thinking, "I am sick of White people and their need to share their 'I'm not racist stories' or to always address me based on my skin color." Oh man, did that trigger the White defense reaction in him! I thought for sure this man was cured!

My husband had to rescue *them* and attempt to "alter my perception" instead of acknowledging my frustration. He defended her by saying, "She means well." (*Child please.* [That's SAAVE; no commas.]) I almost karate-chopped his ass! I didn't need to be taught how to handle her mental illness, nor did she need him to defend her ignorance. And, oh man, did I unleash on him. I said, "***Who*** or ***what*** are you defending? This is your wife speaking." I expressed that I was also sick and tired of always having to take a parental role and excuse White people's behavior, prioritizing their feelings above my own or the truth of the situation. "White people aren't children," I said. This person was a grown-ass woman, and it was time for her to start considering how she impacted me. She always spoke to the person she believed I was. I am human and deserve to be known as an individual.

African American Jews share similar struggles, including the absence of a welcoming space to connect. (Yes, there are about 40,000 African American Jews in the U.S.) Fortunately, I had a positive experience with the Reform Jews. Perhaps because they were a "troubled group," as the rabbi described them, lacking direction and feeling frustrated with Judaism. The group was more of a progressive social community than a religious group, if anything. Unfortunately, many couldn't figure out how to leave Judaism without "the blessing." Some never escape the cult, so to speak. (giggles)

I couldn't believe there were still White people who behaved worse than children, frowning upon others because of their skin color. I'm even more shocked when Jews do the same, considering they have experienced so much discrimination and racism.

White folks don't realize that Black and Brown folks are here to remind them that their religion isn't all that *special*. Diversity offers these religious folks a reflection on their current state of awakening or connection to the Divine. Here's a hint: the answer to where they stand can be found in the frown. If you believe you have reservations in "Heaven" and want to ensure it before you leave this world, ask God to send a few Black families to join your church, and then observe your behavior without deceiving yourself.

Anyways, do you see who is always responsible for extending the pass or ignoring the ignorant or hurtful comments? *It was time to start taking turns.*

That's when I realized the mental disease of racism was too deeply ingrained to dismantle before I could ever show up to church as a human and have the same experience my White husband was afforded. He had lovely conversations with these people, sometimes even about art and poetry. But not me; it felt as if I were in a different movie, and they could hear the humming of "Negro Spirituals" every time they looked my way. I'm sorry, White people, but I'm not playing that character for you.

I was primarily interacting with my parents' generation of Whites, who still didn't have many "People of Color" in their personal lives. Now, I was feeling the brunt of a generation that wasn't mine. I couldn't understand why any "Person of Color" would tolerate this kind of firsthand abuse. Talk to a Black Quaker; they are some of the most frustrated people who belong to a community that, once again, advocates for social justice as a hobby but never takes the time to address the racial issues within their own circle. This is because "they are not racist" or consider themselves exempt from being racist due to their qualifying good deeds, having "Black" grandchildren, or their ability to intellectualize racism.

Many White progressives fought for or supported civil rights for "People of Color" because it's a tough inner battle to accept oneself while witnessing such injustice against humanity. However, many never progressed far enough to see a Black person as they see themselves. Instead, they lived justified by their actions without fully transforming their hearts. For many, activism served as a stamp of approval and a means to escape the inner turmoil of conflicting beliefs. They never realized that they were not their minds; instead, they became prisoners of societal programming. You remain a prisoner when you attempt to conceal and protect this ugliness. Activism can become a veil that covers other veils. This is why racism persists in many "progressive communities": the veil was never lifted.

The mental game of hiding from oneself, which "People of Color" often observe White people playing, occurs while simultaneously experiencing their underlying racism. I encountered some of the strongest civil rights advocates and, ironically, "racially charged" (wink) individuals in Quaker circles who spoke boldly about Martin Luther King Jr. and John Lewis. However, they still assigned me an identity and spoke to me as if I were who they believed I was in their minds. It was evident; the veil remained—and was "fully charged." Yet, they thought they were free of racism because they possessed the ultimate "get out of jail free" card known as "activism." (So that you know, those who are free of racism are not disturbed by my observation. I hope you passed the test.)

On a lighter note, I also grew consciously while sitting in silence with my *Friends*. (It was good to have them quiet.) This stillness allowed me to understand them better, accepting their struggle (or pride) with having my brown face present in *their* community. Yet, I could see how many more people could benefit from this silence, which can lead to awakening if you allow Presence to grow within you.

As you can see, many are stuck in old mind patterns (merchants in the temple). Some of these folks use former political and ethical positions within their community as tokens of "superiority." "Quakers didn't support slavery," some like to say, which is far from the truth, but it makes them feel warm and fuzzy inside. Others allow their religious identity as Quakers to cause them to miss the original spirit of Quakerism, which is simply connecting with the Divine by looking within. This approach works whether you are a god-believing person or not. The fruit is the same, but many never taste its sweetness.

Realizing this was it for alternative spiritual communities and acknowledging that "People of Color" would have to endure the lingering effects of racism for the sake of community, I began to envision something new. What if there existed a spiritual community that didn't rely on any particular religion and one that didn't require ignoring racism or seeking unjustified validation from "People of Color"? Conversely, it would not be a place that made the collective pain of Brown and Black people central or permanent, but rather one that moved

316

towards liberation and alleviated this pain. As I mentioned in the *Betwixt* description, "We noticed many institutions working to rebrand from a history of exclusion, control, and discrimination. Instead of rebranding and attempting to repurpose old traditions, we built a loving community from the ground up." As R. Buckminster Fuller best articulated, "You never change things by fighting the existing reality. To change something, build a new model that makes the existing model obsolete." (Coincidentally, Fuller was a Unitarian—my favorite Unitarian.)

Living independently of religion, I unfortunately don't find many "People of Color" like me. Still, I know we exist and likely have a limited community to connect with due to the stronghold I described in my sermon, *"Black People: The Overlooked Similarities Between Racism and Religion and the Path to Liberation."* However, I want those who walk in similar shoes to know that *Betwixt* was created first with you in mind and welcomes everyone from all walks of life who wants to leave behind treating people based on *who they think they are.* "Hey, girlfriend!" which I don't mind because it's stinking hilarious to hear a White woman say this.

Yep, you got it! Frustration with old White folks so graciously helped birth *Betwixt's* magnificent vision. See! Racism stirs innovation; we're all in this together! (Now, old White folks are not the same as older White individuals.)

I appreciate you for growing with me,
—Sher! (The Common Snook)
Pause. Inhale. Exhale. Reflect.

P.S. Speaking of delusional! Well, you know Gainesville, Florida, is notorious for petty theft. One day, my ten-year-old son witnessed two boys breaking into our neighbor's car in broad daylight. He raced home and exclaimed, "Mom, call the police, and let's hop in the car so we can catch them!"

Within a few minutes, I contacted the neighbor and explained what my son had witnessed. I asked if he wanted to call the police. Thankfully, he was able to catch the boys on camera, which also showed my son watching them and racing home to report the crime. Instead of thanking my son for looking out for him, he asked if those were his friends. (I could see where this was going.) I wanted to ask him if those were *his* son's friends since they had lived in the neighborhood much longer than we had. Instead, I chose not to respond defensively, which can be even more powerful. (wink)

A few days later, fresh-picked fruit showed up at the house. (Busted!) My neighbor thought he was fooling us, but he was only fooling himself. He had the nerve to give my son the "good job" speech when he should have apologized. (Some of you may think I should have recognized his efforts in how a parent might make room for a child, but you're missing that he wasn't apologizing. His ego was trying to cover his tracks, completing its dirty work. There's a big difference.)

Instead of stomping the fruit, we enjoyed it while I explained to my son what had happened and why the fruit showed up. Sadly, I could see that his feelings were deeply hurt. I warned my son to keep a safe distance from this neighbor because of the lens through which he viewed the world. I reminded him of *Ahmaud Arbery*, a young Black man who was shot while jogging in Georgia in 2020.

(Sit in stillness with your eyes closed for 15 minutes a day; I promise it will transform your life!)

3. "What About 'the N-word?'"

Disclosure Reminder...,

My sheltered *ch'rn*/children had thankfully never heard "the N-word". Although they were aware that there was a naughty word called "the N-word," they didn't know what it was.

One summer, I sent my son to Cherry Lake 4-H Camp in the Florida panhandle. It was his first time hanging out with African American youth from the country. I didn't even know Black folks lived in the panhandle outside of Tallahassee or attended camp, for that matter, and *boy*, did they drop "the N-word" far and wide.

I remember my son wanting to smile and laugh as he shared his camp stories with me, but he wasn't sure if that was appropriate or not. These kind-hearted boys even gave my son the greeting, "What's up, my nigga?" He had lived in a predominantly White world until then and was unfamiliar with Southern African American cultural practices. Yet Black folks possess a keen eye for those who carry the genotype of the Motherland, even when others seem to miss it. Strangely, my boy felt as if he had been welcomed into a new community. (Hmm...the rite of passage seems a bit concerning. I think I prefer "my *brotha*" or a basket of fruit.)

I said to him, "Let me share my perspective on the spiritual significance of "the N-word" and why it has yet to die. We live in a self-deceiving society that seeks to bury the ugly past to avoid pain—without teaching these *ch'rn* true American history. But I bet no one would have guessed that Black folks, along with the help of White folks, would poetically transform "the N-word" and apply it to nearly every part of speech in the English language. It has served as a noun, a pronoun, an adjective, and a verb. If you ask me, it's as if the Divine said, "America, you ain't going to bury this one until you resolve this mess."

It's interesting how those who have been silenced find the most creative ways to express themselves. For instance, "woke" originally meant awareness of racism, yet it has been hijacked by both the far right and left. One side uses it to casually erase the legacy of Martin Luther King Jr. by sweeping his work under this new umbrella. In contrast, the other side uses it to support a political movement. Additionally, we have the term "Karen," a lovely expression used to highlight the abuse of White power in society by White women. However, it has been broadened to encompass others who behave in an entitled manner. The term became mainstream following an incident in which a White woman called the police on an African American birdwatcher in New York City's Central

Park. These words have echoed throughout society alongside "the N-word," giving history and struggle a voice that sometimes manifests in a haunting form because they do not fade quickly.

The haunting of "the N-word" is akin to a husband who had an affair with a woman named "Nigar," prompting the family to call everyone Nigar when all he desires is to bury the past (yesterday!) as if it never happened. "Stop with the Nigar," he pleads, yet he still won't fully acknowledge the affair and its impact on his family even to this day. Then, his wife decides to name their firstborn after his mistress.

It seems rather cruel, almost as if God said, "You're going to face this, and don't you try to be slick and bury this one. I'm going to haunt you like the book of Exodus." The haunting will be so intense that folks won't even know whether it's a bad word or not. Teachers will be terrified to address it. One kid says F-you in class and gets a referral; another says, "*Nigga please*," causing the teacher to check out for a minute and stare into the abyss. It's powerful! It's like a hot potato. Nobody knows what to do with it.

The words and expressions from Southern African American Vernacular English (SAAVE) are remarkable forms of artistic expression. Today, with a slightly arrogant tone of "superiority," you'll hear White folks ask, "Why do they call themselves that?" Seriously!? (Hmm…that's an interesting question. It sounds like the beginning of a history lesson.)

Wink Hugs,
   —Sher! (The Common Snook)
   Pause. Inhale. Exhale. Reflect.

P.S. One day, my husband struggled to find the right words to communicate with a family member. His final text message was concise and to the point. Then, I realized that he unknowingly found his words using SAAVE. He responded, "There's too much *drama* surrounding yo *momma*." (Nope, he didn't learn SAAVE from me. He was already fluent before we married, thanks to his colleagues at AGH and his love for fish and grits Fridays. And no, I do *not* eat grits, said *with attitude*.)

P.P.S. Sweet Potato Brown is now in high school and faces a new challenge. He's *tall* and can now *ball*. His *kicks* are appropriate, and the girls think he's gorgeous. However, let's say "hypothetically," an African American classmate starts calling him a "nigger" quite regularly. Don't be confused; this is not the unfortunate expression of "What's up, my nigga?" that we discussed earlier and that some people welcome. This student places an angry emphasis on the "*er*," as seen in the movies. Perhaps he can tell that Sweet Potato Brown carries the genotype of European ancestry and wants to ensure he feels his pain. Would the school have the will to address this hot potato, or would they condone this abuse (interpersonal oppression) as acceptable for some students to endure? I know, I gotcha! It's complicated.

(Stop droppin' "the N-word" for 15 minutes a day; I promise it will transform your life!)

4. Why Do People Riot?

Disclosure Reminder…,

I spent a considerable amount of time in my marriage feeling muzzled. I noticed that things in my hands would become projectile, propelled forward with force, and others would turn into projectiles. (giggles) Let's stand for the national anthem: "…and the rockets' red glare, the bombs bursting in air, gave proof through the night that our flag was still there." This was a marvelous observation, and I could understand why some people riot. Martin Luther King Jr. once said, "A riot is the language of the unheard." No worries…my husband listens to me today, especially when I'm cookin'. The kitchen can be a dangerous place.

However, he played a crucial role in helping me write a poem many years ago in response to a question about rioting that I heard on the news one day. I, too, was a rioter for different reasons. (Sometimes folks lose their patience with bullshit and erupt. *Right, King?*) But in the end, I noticed the root cause was the same. While likely holding my shoe in one hand, I heard, "Rioting is not the answer," or "Why do they riot?" These folks must have never been married.

Here it goes!

11/15/2015

> Racism has its requirements as to how it will be treated
> Racism will not comply or listen
> If one is not able to communicate submissively to appease
> And respect its ego,
> Forget about honest emotions and listening to the heart
> When one talks about Racism,
> One must carefully choose words or phrases,
> Like "some," or "a few," or "it would appear"
> In order not to violate its pride
> If one cannot find a tactful way to attack it,
> Racism will often turn the tables and end up calling you a racist
> Racism also requires that you consider how it's being treated
> By the people it oppresses
> If you are going to call it out,
> Get ready!

Because Racism will say you have hurt me, too,
And will only consider your situation
If you are willing to allow its *feelings*
To stand as equal
To your life of hardship
Racism realizes that you must play its game
If you want to be heard
One remains powerless in defeating Racism,
Until one can fully play
It would appear Racism is less ignorant than once believed
Racism promotes inequality
By educational disadvantages,
But damn!
It requires, at the same time,
The highest level of educational thought and awareness,
Before you can get its attention to speak against it

Racism.

No worries…I don't riot anymore, unless I must. I don't need anyone to hear me, either. Presence was all I required to rise above my reactive patterns. Today, people listen to me because my Presence speaks louder than words. Presence speaks!

Peace,
    —Sher! (The Common Snook)
        Pause. Inhale. Exhale. Reflect.

(Sit in stillness with your eyes closed for 15 minutes a day; I promise it will transform your life!)

5. "The American Negro"

Okay, we're *gonna* laugh today!

Disclosure Reminder...,

One time, just a few years ago, when I was visiting New Zealand, a woman asked me with a rising tone at the end of her question, "What is your background? You don't resemble the American Negro." And no, she wasn't no granny. She should have known better.

Oh my god, talk about a punch in the chest. For a second, I genuinely thought she had used "the N-word" because I had never heard anyone use the term "Negro" when speaking to me. I didn't know whether to feel flattered or disgusted, but she was truly curious about my heritage. This surprised me because White Americans often assume my background and never inquire about who I am.

I thought, *What on earth is "the American Negro"? A bird? A prairie dog? A Pontiac?* What the hell was she talkin' 'bout!? *And did she call me a Negro on the sly?* However, there was a slim possibility that she was well-versed and was simply quoting the author James Baldwin, who often referred to Black Americans as "the American Negro." Alternatively, perhaps she watched, as a child on television, alongside the world, as White racists hosed Negroes down the street with fire hoses.

Man, that question threw me. I needed to contact their prime minister so she could correct her people. (Hmm...White folks on an island. That's concerning.) To me, this was a clear sign that White folks from Down Under needed to get out of the radioactive sun and travel more, and "the American Negro" needed to do the same.

Cheers to travel,
—Sher! (The Common Snook)
Pause. Plan. Travel.

P.S. This sermon leads to a bigger conversation.

(Sit in stillness with your eyes closed for 15 minutes a day; I promise it will transform your life!)

6. The Psychological Disadvantages of Racial Identity and the Power of Language Evolution

You may notice "Black" will sometimes be within quotation marks and sometimes not. It just depends on my perspective and feelings at that moment.

December 19, 2018...,

Quite a few disbelieving souls have crossed the path of my dreams. They say things like, "I don't know if we'll ever overcome racism," or "It'll probably never happen, or at least not in our lifetime." That feels rather condescending coming from someone who enjoys the privileges you hope to see for everyone. Racism frustrates the stew out of me, and I can't understand how a civilized world still operates under its system. My thoughts are not based on naivety but instead on pure disgust with humanity. What's the point of sharing opinions of hopelessness? If we don't believe in the possibility of change or can't envision a better world, then why bother fighting a war we have no chance of winning? If we don't believe humanity can evolve to respect all human life, then indeed, it will not happen in our lifetime.

I meditate on the structures of society, searching for the crack in its wall. One day, it will crumble, just as the Berlin Wall did when most never believed it was possible. Racism is a unique beast in that it must be dismantled from every conceivable angle. Since racism impacts so many aspects of our daily lives, we must prioritize deprogramming the racist mindset, reconstructing our society and social institutions with love, and harnessing the progressive evolution of culture and language.

I often write about the concept of race, a phenomenon with which I do not personally identify. When discussing race, I usually feel my hands are tied because I can't talk about racism without, to some extent, connecting with its racist classification system that lacks scientific validity (pseudoscience). I must refer to my brothers and sisters as Black to highlight the injustices they face, such as those expressed in the Black Lives Matter movement. This situation resembles a "double bind," where you're damned either way by your choices. You can't address the foolishness of race without reinforcing it! Systemic racism has constrained and controlled me with its language, forcing me to identify with its damaging implications.

325

Line after line, as I stroked or typed the word "black," I felt my entire body cringe at a term that perpetuates the issue of racism and the American race problem. How can I hope to dismantle racism when it may seem to some that I'm stressing about something trivial? Can't I join those who chant "Black Lives Matter" and be okay with the perspective many support today? I thought, *These lives matter, but could you do me a favor and stop calling them Black?* This plays a significant role in the mental struggle of why these lives don't seem to matter to some people—they're "Black."

We make very little progress in dismantling racism when we continue to build upon its racist foundation, which includes an unjustly structured society, often described as systemic or institutional racism. However, we also possess a language that is racist. A house wouldn't be fit for habitation if there were an issue with the foundation, and certainly, you wouldn't attempt to add a second floor to such an unstable structure. A no-brainer, right? Well, it should be no different in the fight against racism. Sometimes, it is necessary to replace some of the joists and support beams in the foundation that are rotten or cracked.

With that in mind, I made it my goal to address and dismantle racism at its roots. This must begin with accurately defining (not redefining) the diverse cultures of the many "People of Color" referred to as "Black" globally or "politically correct" as "African American" in the U.S.

The Evolution of Language

It's incredible how thoughts or images can exist without words; however, language is a unique tool that allows us to express our feelings and thoughts. English, no longer the sole language or mental expression of fair-skinned Europeans, is one of the most widely spoken languages in the world, encompassing speakers from diverse cultures and various skin tones. Specifically, in the U.S., consider the many "Black" phrases that have become second nature to most Americans.

The meanings of words shift with every new speaker. What was spoken and understood a hundred years ago may sound as foreign as a *completely different* language today. The evolution of language is a living organism that must continually change to reflect the people who speak it.

"Black" and "Negro," rather simplistic terms, were assigned to dark-skinned people by the original speakers of Romance and other European languages, which unfortunately carried a negative connotation. No matter how hard the "Black" communities worked to redefine the term "black," one could never completely erase the meaning it carries in the back of one's mind. Without the concept of "White," the concept of "Black" would never have come into existence. People with brown skin would have continued to live with dignity. Instead, White society defined and labeled a segment of humanity from a contrasting viewpoint of themselves, which forever established an unfavorable position, regardless of how hard some worked to redefine it.

The term "African American," introduced by Rev. Jesse Jackson (I can spot a Cherokee anywhere), gained traction in mainstream media in the early 1990s. He remarked, "It puts us in our proper historical context," which depends on whose historical account one claims to be theirs. "African American" sparked controversy among some who never identified with the distant land of Africa. It was somehow deemed the politically correct term for all "People of Color" in America. I recall thinking in the 7th grade in 1990 when I first encountered this new label, *Since when was anyone in my family from Africa?*

It was a good start to distancing from the racist and unfavorable description of "black." However, at the same time, the term uprooted the heritage of all "People of Color," forcing them to dream of or identify with a foreign land called Africa. While it was thoughtful and progressive at the time, it is an inaccurate description of "People of Color" and, incidentally, supports the misconception that "Black" people are only from Africa. It also created a divide. For instance, what do you call a person from the continent of Africa who is a rightful U.S. citizen? Are they African Americans, too? Not if you asked an African or a Black American; both would say "No!" without hesitation. Consequently, the phrase was turned around; there are also American Africans.

"Black" people have been mocked and dishonored across the globe since the beginning of colonialism. To feel "superior" requires making someone else inferior, and just about every culture has stepped on the heads of Black and Brown people to boost their sense of self. This stems from name-calling or negative descriptions of "People of Color."

For instance, the Spaniards, who are multiracial, called the people of the Philippines "little black people." Then, you have the people of Thailand who referred to black Africans as "frizzy hair." (That's creative!) However, nothing has been more dishonoring than being labeled with a term for "slave," which is still used in many Arab countries to refer to a "Black" person (Unknown Source). Moreover, let's not forget a term that continues to afflict Black Americans. How is it that I can't find a term from a White or Asian culture that honors those referred to as "black"?

As we know, words can be powerful, especially when they have power over you. They can move us forward or hold us back. I learned the power of words while living as a multiracial person. I went to places many of my "Black" friends could never have imagined going, all because I was never raised to believe I was "Black." I don't mention this to be arrogant or to raise eyebrows, but rather because my "Black" friends would tell me this: "You walked up in there like you were White," which was both mind-boggling and challenging for me to understand. (That was in 2007, by the way.) I realized I had a freedom that was primarily tied to how I viewed myself. I wasn't "Black," although I have light brown skin with a lovely afro and would qualify as "Black" under the absurd one-drop rule. For the most part, I avoided the psychological programming associated with being Black or White, particularly focusing on the concept of *Black* for this discussion. I was human, as my Cherokee grandmother always reminded me. Not only did I experience the unfolding of Martin Luther King Jr.'s dream of equality, but I also rose above the concept of race altogether.

Your Assigned Identity

Years ago, in a Quaker discussion circle, I watched a brilliant woman, Dr. Joy DeGruy Leary, author of the book *Post Traumatic Slave Syndrome*, present the theory she had developed. This was a remarkable project that revealed the reality of a collective cognitive dissonance within White cultures, which contributed to their desensitization towards feeling empathy for "People of Color." Most importantly, she demonstrated how American "Black" behavior could be viewed as a form of post-traumatic stress, which she termed "Post-Traumatic Slave Syndrome," and introduced a pathway toward healing from multigenerational trauma.

However, during her lecture, possibly as an opening argument, Dr. DeGruy took a moment to address—or almost criticize—"People of Color" who do not define themselves in a manner she considered appropriate or consistent with how White society has constrained their expression. She stated, "You've met these Black people who are not Black. How many of you have met these kinds of people? They look Black to me." Her argument aimed to explain why she believed some Black women struggle with self-acceptance. Although I might not have been her intended audience, as I couldn't relate directly, I could empathize with the sentiment of her argument, having not been treated kindly by many Black girls, which reflected the self-hatred she discusses.

For example, in junior high, around age fourteen, I recall telling my friends that I wasn't "red," again a label assigned to light-skinned people. "I'm beige," I declared boldly in an effort to change my nickname. (giggles) I wanted to put an end to "red." I didn't appreciate the pet name or the sexual harassment that came with it. My friends also knew that I disliked the name. As I mentioned in my sermon, "I'm Takin' Sexy Back," many darker-skinned women and girls also resent the name, or at least the attention and idolization that accompany it.

My friends began to taunt me, spitefully calling me "red." When I resisted, they shifted to calling me "beige" instead, but the taunting wouldn't stop. It felt like they were stoning me to death because they, too, hated "red," which also meant they sometimes hated me, "Red." I was caught in the middle of a war that wasn't mine—*Spike Lee*.

The taunting was so painful inside; I remember just sitting in the car, looking out the window, waiting for the torture to end while the three other girls in the backseat *took me down*. I could feel myself breaking inside. They wanted me to respond so they could crush me further. Instead, I sat silently as they laughed so loudly that I wouldn't be heard even if I had resisted. (Laughter used as a weapon is common in many African American communities.)

They found pleasure in viciously tearing me down and removing me from my throne of "white or light skin seen as better." My friends had collectively turned on me. Unfortunately, I possessed something they all despised, and I unknowingly allowed them to reveal this animosity, which was linked to their self-loathing and my favoritism. And these were my good friends, the *nice* Black girls.

Even though I understood Dr. DeGruy's point, she was viewing these individuals solely through the lens of her identity as a Black woman. She overlooked the fact that "People of Color," just like White people, have the right to express who they are. She joked that many claim to have Native American ancestry, which is entirely accurate if you study diversified American history. (I'm sure you can see she caught my attention.) However, in support of her argument, she suggested that these individuals were attempting to escape their Black identity. But honestly, one cannot escape having brown skin. Then, a question should arise regarding what they might be trying to escape.

"I am more than Black" likely represents the struggle. Perhaps connecting with their other roots liberates them somewhat from the stereotype of Black people being lazy, a notion also mentioned by Dr. DeGruy in her lecture. Multiracial Americans, such as Puerto Ricans, often evade this degrading label and are somewhat free from this aspect of the American race game. *(Whassup, Rosie Perez!)* However, suggesting one can only be Black because "they look Black" regardless of their background supports the White ideology that having "Black blood" erases culture and heritage. It implies that no matter who these individuals derived from, they are only Black as defined by "White Supremacy," as it only takes "one-drop." (Patel said, "You know, the people of the Caribbean are Indians from India…and African as well, of course." He added, "Look at their food, curry chicken and rotis! They're Indians! You can't erase our heritage!")

Those who demand respect and proper identification contribute to the conversation about a world that has historically left little room for personal expression and has often overlooked the individuality of "People of Color." The multiracial experience offers a unique perspective, boldly stating, "This is who I am." It challenges both ends of the racial spectrum by asserting, "It's not acceptable for you to define my identity." Indeed, just as transgender communities advocate for the use of specific pronouns, individuals who are "People of Color," biracial, multiracial, or cross-cultural deserve to be accurately recognized and respected, free from the pressure to choose sides or endure racist labels about their identities. Those who support restricting the expression of "Black" individuals should reflect on the origins of the belief that one can only be defined as Black.

Don't get me wrong; I understand that the term "Black" has been reclaimed and redefined with pride within many Black communities—the very Black communities that welcomed me into their inner circles. For instance, they taught me that wearing a scarf at night made for better hair management the following morning. Growing up in the 1980s and 1990s, I learned that their parents, who were public school educators, were graduates of Historically Black Colleges and Universities (HBCUs). They encouraged their children to follow in their footsteps. Even when I knew little about these highly reputable institutions (no, we didn't have cable to watch The Cosby Show when I was a kid), they brought me along and showed me how classy their culture was. I sometimes wished I had their stories of community, hair that could hold a fantastic style, and pride that could outshine the forces of racism. No matter how much I hoped for this to be my culture, it was never fully mine and is not a reality for all "People of Color."

Many vibrant cultures within Black communities have been able to counteract the degrading labels associated with being Black. Yet, the programming and negativity continue to trap millions, as they are still deeply embedded in our language, and deprogramming takes time and awareness.

Making a Wrong Right

Healing and restoration stem from correcting a wrong and returning something to its original condition. (The establishment of the notion of "black" is arguably one of the greatest conspiracies ever perpetrated against humanity!) I want to introduce you to "Pan Alpha." This respectful and restorative name appropriately honors and identifies individuals with brown and dark brown skin pigments who reflect many visible characteristics of the original human gene before its evolution, which produced our world's diverse skin colors and ethnicities. "Pan" speaks of a people who inhabited every continent that can support life but have been mischaracterized by a Eurocentric mindset. This mindset is misleading as it implies that "People of Color" originated solely from Africa, despite all of humankind tracing its origins to Africa. When the world labels these individuals as Africans or "black," which is not a nation, it erases the history and settlements established by our ancestors long before the arrival of those referred to as European or "White." Lastly, "Alpha" signifies the beginning of creation and the dominant gene of humanity, honoring its existence and survival. All it takes is "one-drop," and it continues to endure.

When we restore dignity to all "People of Color," we honor our shared humanity, rising together consciously and getting closer to understanding who we are collectively. Many individuals have been confined to the White man's definition of "black." However, Pan Alpha establishes a path to equality by providing significance and status—two qualities that many "People of Color" struggle to attain simply due to their dark skin. This concept can be embraced by a broad group of people and welcomed with pride. We can have Pan Alpha *Americans* and Pan Alpha *Africans*, allowing us to move beyond the label of "black" in humanity.

Nonetheless, Pan Alpha does not resolve all the issues surrounding race and its toxic byproduct, racism. However, it liberates us from the game of redefining words, or if I may add a bit of humor, it frees us from having to make chitterlings appetizing. It provides mental strength and significance, which can single-handedly transform lives.

I hope Pan Alpha will be welcomed in the evolution of language, just as Jesse Jackson's phrase "African American" was accepted. However, with change, there is always resistance. For one, some opposing "Black" forces may struggle with the fact that I identify as multiracial when required and not as "Black," which doesn't sit well with many "People of Color." Unfortunately, some won't be able to see that my demand to be correctly identified is my right. It is also a resistance to racism and "White Supremacy" and a continuation of the fight for freedom. (Or is *Black* merely a dumping ground to preserve *White?*) Anything less would force me to agree with the racist notion that "blackness" negates culture and erases ancestry, which is absurd and further reinforces the idea that "Black blood" represents impurity. If I must identify with the system, I am multiracial. My Nigerian heritage does not negate my Cherokee and German roots.

No Escaping

For years, many of my friends told me I wasn't Black or not Black enough because being Black in America is also about culture and understanding what it means to suffer due to being Black. "If I can exclude you, I feel better about myself," reflects the mentality. Additionally, how others perceive us can influence how we see ourselves. White people forcing "Black" upon me as my identity instead of asking about my ancestry and Black people insisting I wasn't Black likely liberated me from the foolishness of race. *(Thanks, y'all!)*

However, when you identify as anything other than Black, it doesn't go over too well with ~~many~~ Black Americans, and I have not found that to be a generalization. Forget about attempting to run for president as a biracial candidate or racial "minority"; you'd better choose a side and tweak your dialect if you want to win the Black vote. *(Right, Obama? Harris, did I hear you say, "Amen!"?)*

Raven-Symoné Christina Pearman-Maday made a similar "mistake" when she denied being African American. In 2014, she was interviewed by Oprah Winfrey, who appeared to be biased during their conversation. Pearman-Maday defended her position, stating that she had "the blood of many nations running in her veins" and that she was "American from Louisiana [and]…tired of being labeled"—Dammit! Her argument wasn't well received by Black communities, especially given Winfrey's influence, who remarked, "You're going to get a lot of flak for saying that you're not African American." (Who let the dogs out!?) Yet, I believe Pearman-Maday was observing her identity and may have consciously been rising above thought, which opens the door to freedom and liberation.

I bet she was kicking herself for giving in to at least being "Black" to satisfy Oprah, especially since she described herself as a "colorless" or perhaps a "raceless" person. But I think Pearman-Maday had more for us, yet it didn't appear Oprah was ready for what she had. Unfortunately, most of her audience also still strongly identified with labels as their identity, so they couldn't grasp or welcome her perspective and desire to detach from those labels. But that, too, is for another sermon: "Who Am I Without These Mental Labels?" (Uh-oh, no Oprah's Book Club for me. *Okay, Oprah, I'll say I'm Black if that helps.* [giggles] *Right, Obama? Harris, did I hear you say, "Amen!"?)*

Multiracial individuals are often questioned about their identity. At the same time, the essence of who we are lies in the inquiry itself or in why the question is posed in the first place: "What do you consider yourself?" However, why ask when there is only one acceptable answer? Multiracial individuals often need to clarify their position before they can accurately define themselves. One must prioritize the feelings of the individual asking the question above their own self-expression to avoid any misunderstanding. (Hmm...this sure sounds familiar.) They may assert, "Choosing to identify as multiracial isn't about denying heritage," which seems to temporarily soften the offense taken, but is not intended. This offense arises from the assumed belief that one thinks they're better than a "Black" person or is attempting to separate themselves. However, it's simply a difference in perspective.

Still, others believed I was trying to escape being "Black." They would spitefully declare in a demeaning way, "You're Black, too. Wait until you get pulled over!" "Black" was thus utilized as a weapon to humiliate and dehumanize, just as it has historically served to oppress an entire nation of people. These folks were unwilling to release me and seemed to curse me with blackness (internalized and interpersonal oppression), which raises the question of why.

Another example of how this interpersonal oppression affects others is the way some Black women respond to White mothers with biracial children. The White mother may not want to convey the typical Black experience to her children. Black women will address her with authority, as if she is oblivious and as if her children belong not to her but rather to the greater concept of the "Black race." "You need to teach them because, at the end of the day, they are still Black." (Or do they mean trapped?) How is this White mother supposed to confront this self-righteousness?

Nevertheless, this audacity can prompt an awakening in these White women. "THESE ARE MY CHILDREN—dammit!" (Oh my! I can hear the White women shoutin' and cheerin' into this book. My ol' homegirl from Tioga just did a cartwheel!)

Meanwhile, her biracial children will never be accepted as Black unless it appears that they are trying to escape. Many are unwilling to allow these children to be or to accept their mother's perspective, seeming to curse them with Blackness. It's almost as if they say, "At the end of the day, you must put the shackles back on" (internalized and interpersonal oppression), which again raises the question of why.

Many seem to resist the biracial or multiracial identity and insist that these individuals be labeled as "Black" because they themselves find no means of escape. When confronted about the threat of being pulled over, many argue, "I was just letting you know," rather than reflecting on their words and acknowledging their pain, as if all "People of Color" aren't aware of the struggles we face with law enforcement in America. The issue, expressed in a passive-aggressive manner toward biracial and multiracial individuals, is that "Black" is associated with considerable negativity and was never a name that "People of Color" (POC) chose for themselves. (Hmm...POC, another ugly description.) Some become angry when you refuse to accept the label they have accepted for themselves. "If I must eat this crap, you must eat it, too," is the mindset. These frustrated individuals fail to realize that mental freedom is a choice, and some don't know whether to embrace "Black"...or to stomp it.

Facing Our Feelings

We must first confront our feelings around the word "black" without the "thought-stopping" belief that we need to accept this label as our identity any more than we must embrace the terms "Colored" or "Negro." This mindset frees us from clinging to or defending something we have mistakenly considered an extension of ourselves. It's akin to a child who defends an abusive parent because that's all they know. If White people had not named you first, choosing to identify as "Black" would be unimaginable. You would have selected something honorable and respectful, not the opposite of white. ("Black" is like being named "Duque" in Spanish [pronounced like "dOO-keh"] and trying to convince Americans that it means "Duke" instead of "dookie." *Whassup, Meghan!*) The term has never truly represented the people it overshadows. Yet, it has likely created pocket-cultures that mirror the underlying etymology of how the word is framed and utilized in English—because words hold great power, forever putting "Black" people at a disadvantage. (It's hard to recover from "Duque," so to speak. *No pun intended, Babe!*)

In our minds, the understanding of words and images, along with our memories, shapes how we experience the world around us. Unfortunately, how others perceive us can also influence how we see ourselves. (We must understand how programming works or risk being programmed.)

Pan Alpha is such a powerful title, and if embraced, I can, unfortunately, see the resurgence of more derogatory terms, to which I reply, "Bring it on!" To hear backlash would confirm the appropriateness of the word. Nobody was shaken by "African American." Interestingly, I learned that very few "People of Color" use this term to describe themselves. They typically use the term in mixed company, which seems to make some White people feel more politically correct. Because they, too, sense there is something not right about the word "black" as it rolls off their tongues. (Even my Indian friends expressed feeling uncomfortable calling a person "Black.") Most of the professionals I interviewed admitted they had returned to using "Black" at home because it was what they grew up hearing. A few expressed dissatisfaction with the term "black," but "What else is there?" one individual asked. *(Whassup, Sweet-N-Salty!)*

Nothing Changes If Nothing Changes

"You never change things by fighting the existing reality. To change something, build a new model that makes the existing model obsolete" (R. Buckminster Fuller). Suppose we must still subject ourselves to the absurdity of the demographic checkbox. Pan Alpha should not be grouped with the Black or African American category. If individuals still wish to identify as Black or African American, that's acceptable, but we must honor Pan Alpha and the effort to eradicate racism from our language. Let Pan Alpha Americans be distinct and see how many people will proudly check that box.

All it takes is for a few to recognize the power of words and truth. The term "African American" slowly crept into society, becoming a household name. Pan Alpha signifies the progressive mindset that better represents the class of Americans and "People of Color" worldwide who are free or desire freedom from the oppression that still holds many captive.

When I see young people locking arms and chanting, "Black Lives Matter," I think Pan Alphas with immense pride. When I see Neil *de*Grasse Tyson, I think *brilliant* Pan Alpha. (He could be my father's twin!) When I see young "Black" boys struggling as early as elementary school, I see something greater: Pan Alphas who need to know they are a significant creation, and the description of Pan Alpha serves that purpose. The term "Pan Alpha" stands in stark contrast to the historical "White" narrative of "black" that has prevailed thus far. I hope you will join me in respecting humanity by appropriately identifying and defining "The People" across the globe who have been called "black."

Seeing things plainly,
—Sher! (The Common Snook)
Pause. Inhale. Exhale. Reflect.

P.S. Young people, this is my gift to you. Please take it and run with it! You're Pan Alpha, too!

P.P.S. Speaking of my peculiar psychological programming! One time in college, it had just started to rain. I was slowly driving down the mountain between the Oranges and Livingston, New Jersey, and somehow, my car became airborne. With a tacky concrete "Jersey wall" to my left and a rough, rocky mountain to my right, there was no safe place for my car to land. But somehow, a patch of grass appeared out of nowhere, and my trusty 1982 Volvo landed on all fours…like a house cat, as it went off the side of the mountain. (That sure sounds dramatic.)

My friend, riding with me, started to freak out while I processed what had just happened. He said, "Get back on the road!" *I had just hydroplaned and needed to gather myself,* I thought. (Safety first!) He shouted, "YOU DON'T UNDERSTAND THESE COPS. GET BACK ON THE ROAD!!!" I could tell he knew something I didn't. Despite being unable to drive due to being in complete shock with tears in my eyes, I agreed to get back on the road. (Hmm…Black folks can't even take a break after hydroplaning. White people, that doesn't seem fair. But nobody gets shot in a Volvo, right?)

(Stop *acting* Black for 15 minutes a day; I promise it will transform your life!)

Section VIII: Motherhood

In case you decided to skip the introduction and browse around, here's the **Disclosure Reminder**: Before diving in, I will say this: I'm simple. I love to laugh. Please don't confuse my humor with sarcasm; I always mean what I say. I test the limits. My words are plain. I often use "own" redundantly. I don't claim to know all the answers; my only intention is to be a vessel. Also, to connect with different experiences, I interchangeably use the terms "Consciousness," "Presence," "God," "Universe," "Source," "Divine," "Energy," "Christ/Krst," and "Light." Above all, reading my humor with a Southern accent is best. Enjoy!

Twenty eleven was one of the best years of my life, which felt more like a "Lovely Day." And then...everything went back to typical hell and disappointment. (giggles) Gainesville kicked me out again! It said, "Youse had yo baby; now get goin'!"

1. I Hide My Son in the Basement

Peacefully touring the Sydney Observatory in Australia with my son in early 2020.

Disclosure Reminder…,

I have always been passionate about sharing simple teachings that help people improve their lives. However, the principle of that "ruleth" scripture from the Bible kept me homebound for many years. "One that *ruleth* well [her] own house, having [her] *ch'rn* in subjection with all gravity; For if a [woman] know not how to rule [her] own house, how shall [she] take care of the church of God" (1 Timothy 3:4-5, King James Version of the Bible)? (Yes, I worked to make that scripture more gender-appropriate…out with the *he* and in with the *she*!)

One of my young fellows used to have me workin' overtime to earn the right to say, "I have risen above reactivity." He was my teacher just as much as I was his. He taught me that some people need a little extra love and have no interest in the Christian authoritarian parenting style, being *rulethed*, particularly due to trauma impacting their gene expression and life energy. My boy was so intense (mildly speaking) that I couldn't tell any struggling parent to follow me. As a matter of fact, if they had known what was going on behind our doors, they probably would have run from me.

I also found it interesting that many prominent spiritual teachers, such as Eckhart Tolle, Oprah Winfrey, Tenzin Gyatso, and Jorge Mario Bergoglio, who teach variations of mindfulness and how to overcome suffering, have either never *had* children or a classroom full of students with behavioral challenges. (giggles) I greatly respect many spiritual teachers, but I raise my eyebrow when they discuss child-rearing without having lived with a child who can yell all day. All…day…for like ten years. (I hear you, but you can't *whoop* everyone's ass. Corporal punishment, abuse, is outdated.)

338

Many argue that suffering is all in the head, which is true most of the time. (Two points for Buddhism, even though Buddhism isn't about winning.) However, a small percentage of us have been tortured like Job in the Bible (two points for Judaism for highlighting this reality), and no spiritual teaching can eliminate this kind of pain. If someone is stabbing you in the hand, it goes beyond mind-made suffering. (Stop with the mind games, acting like Buddhist beliefs should be applied to every situation. Hmm…that must be a privilege.) I don't care how much you remain present or joyfully in pain; your suffering…I mean, torture may persist and not budge except by "God's hand," policy changes, constant prayer (maybe), exorcism, or acupuncture. "The Game of Life" wants to see what you can handle without becoming homicidal or suicidal. (Hmm… some of y'all are feelin' me now.)

I used to have friends (without *ch'rn*/children) who would grunt when they felt my children needed discipline. The grunt seemed to suggest, "Are you going to let him speak to you like that?" Sometimes, I thought I had to respond to prove I was in charge of my household. But instead of losing my temper and beating the crap out of my kids to please my friends and assert my authority, I pulled my *sistas* aside. ("You ain't *gotta* go home, but….") I asked them to stop manipulating me and judging what came out of my son's mouth because beating children (violence!), as many religions teach, is not the solution. I told them there are some kids you can't beat unless you want to provoke a good slap upside the head. I'm sure they were rolling their eyes because we came from a church that used to preach, "Spare the rod, spoil the child."

Thank God I experienced an awakening regarding corporal punishment the same year my first child was born. This way, I didn't risk having my children walk away from me in adulthood, as often happens with *ch'rn* who are beaten in the name of sweet Jesus.

I read an article that changed my youthful perspective, which, "thought it knew something," then. It suggested that most behavioral problems parents encounter stem from improper supervision of their children and that *ch'rn* who were spanked were not more well-behaved than those who were not spanked. Oddly enough, the opposite was often true, meaning children who were spanked exhibited more behavioral issues. The article's author simply recommended improved supervision and meeting our children's basic needs before they had to ask for something. Basically, I got off my ass and off the computer. I started feeding my son before he was starving and had a tantrum, and I didn't try to run a real estate business with him in the room and not expect him to dump the flowerpot into my basket of clean laundry. I witnessed a miracle! Behavioral issues in early childhood and the need to react in frustration disappeared. I couldn't believe it was that easy.

However, they do grow older. Many would say my son was strong-willed, which was an understatement. He took me on the ride of my life, so I intentionally kept our lives small to meet his needs. I could empathize with parents who suffered without a break and faced judgment. (Tighten the neck, keep shopping, and ignore those staring. You know, children are meant to embarrass and humble you, and to help you detach because they are their own person and not you.)

These boys and girls do not need to be broken but embraced, because who will tackle the alligator that broke into the kitchen? There may come a time when you will need someone who isn't swayed by fear or intimidation to protect you physically. These folks were our warriors in the past, and they continue to exist today.

I am blessed to have two sons, one of whom is a monk and the other a Marine. For instance, we had a potentially catastrophic issue within our walls (the details aren't necessary), and, of course, my husband wasn't home. My "monk son" searched for prehistoric tools to open the wall without creating a mess. However, since time was of the essence, my "Marine son," who was twelve and almost six-foot tall, punched and tore a hole in the wall with his bare hands in less than a minute while my "monk son" was still digging for tools. (Uuhhahaha!) Sometimes, you need a little *menace* to take care of *business* (make it rhyme!). (If this were the Stone Age, he would have been the ladies' man.) You balance these energies by enrolling "the monk" in football and "the Marine" in violin.

Regardless, everyone tends to blame the parents, particularly mothers, when these strong-willed children enter the scene. Heaven forbid you don't seek the socially accepted counseling services that don't always work...if at all. And if that little booger does something wrong, they're going to blame you. Start your paper trail now!

I used to cringe when people praised me, claiming my one son was such a wonderful person, "because I raised him right." I would think, *well, wait until you meet my other son,* because you will undoubtedly blame me for his imperfections. As a result, I never accepted any compliments. We say all kinds of crap, thinking we know something, but some of us come into this world with more will and sometimes more baggage than others, and it has nothing to do with upbringing.

Charismatic Christians refer to it as a generational curse, Hindus see it as karma, Catholics and Muslims identify it as a demon, and Chinese Classical Five-Element Acupuncture describes it as an energy block. I call it a "Marine"! Whatever the heck it is, our job is to love and guide our children, hoping they choose the best life path. Fingers crossed!

Ultimately, the greatest gift we can give our kids is to raise ourselves first. Starting with stillness can be a game-changer for you and your children. I promise! Also, that's what 1 Timothy 3:4 in the Bible is talkin' 'bout. You must take care of your household (yourself) before you do anything else. Once you know you're spiritually sound, your suffering may diminish, or you may realize your challenges are beyond your control. This is where you can give your judgmental friends and relatives the middle finger.

Again, I teach from experience and am humbled to say I have witnessed and experienced much. I'm grateful for the parent my boys have allowed me to be, and I'm pleased with the young men they have become.

Bear hugs to parents who need a break,

—Sher! (The Common Snook)
Pause. Inhale. Exhale. Reflect.

P.S. If Classical Five-Element Acupuncture can remove energy blocks, a.k.a. "demons," that affect behavior, I'm sure you can imagine the many other conditions it can treat or blockages it can eliminate. Only those who are open to considering this possibility will know. (Hmm...is it still a *placebo effect* when you can see the demon leave the body and exit the window?)

P.P.S. A good African American citizen who was assisting me with my ballot at the polls instructed me to "Hit the [touch] screen like you're beating a baby," and my jaw dropped. I replied, "No, I do not beat babies." They responded, "Oh, you're one of those; you're part of the problem."

P.P.P.S. Speaking of menace! Did I ever tell y'all about the young lady I gave a ride home who was stranded in Gainesville over twenty years ago? We had a great time chatting for forty-five minutes, deep into the country, and check this! She said her stepdaddy was the child star Dennis the Menace. (Maybe she was fibbing.)

Anyways, Dennis...I mean, Mr. North, if what she said is true, you owe me gas money. (I know where you live!) However, since you served our state as a correctional officer, confined those fellas to Lake Butler, and probably warmed many hearts with that charming smile, I'll let you off the hook this time. 🐟

2. Mother's Day is a—BITCH!

Disclosure Reminder…,
Let me see if I can work this doohickey into a poem:

Mother's Day spotlights
All the love and recognition you get (big chuckles)
How *wonderful* it is to have children
Or whether your husband is home
Or you are raising these *ch'rn* alone
It's *special*! (sip)
Mother's Day, I paid no mind
Until my youngest was socialized
In the public schools
It is something folks…
I mean, MEN and children
Wouldn't remember (hiccup)
It is the teacher's responsibility
To push this ~~shit~~ propaganda
To send you tacky…I mean, crafty, handmade gifts
You would never get otherwise
And could live without
That's a lot of pressure
For one person to carry,
You know (hiccup)
Now, sometimes
I don't even tell 'em
It's Mother's Day!
To spare me (lighting and hitting a joint)
Nobody would remember otherwise
Without the teacher or…*yo* preacher
And umm…
What if you are called a *bitch*
The day before
Mother's Day
How would you feel????????????????????? (forehead on keyboard)
Sad, MAD, or glad? (enjoying chocolate)
If you don't celebrate

You're not phased
And might even say
Thank you, sweetheart
And move on
Which is the strength of motherhood (gulp)
But if you do celebrate
This horrid holiday
Because you enjoy pain (more chocolate)
The mind might take *bitch*
  To heart,
Cuz tomorrow is your *special* day
"How dare you!"

(bottle in hand, with a stagger)
You may say
Feeling entitled for a day
But listen here!
Christmas ornaments
Whether thoughtful or awful
Evangelistic or "ego-culturalistic"
Inconsiderate and deliberate
I do miss. (hiccup)

(Turn the bottle…I mean, the poem horizontal and put it up to your ear like a seashell to hear the mother's moan.)

Mother's Day is the day when your children graduate from high school. Honestly, I'm considering organizing a flash mob for moms right in the middle of the graduation ceremony. It's time for this outdated ceremony to change and honor the true graduates. Shoot, they should call our names, have us walk across the stage to receive our Mother's Day diplomas, and make our offspring cheer and celebrate, as is the public school tradition.

Well, umm…I did get this beautiful ceramic temple for Mother's Day, a school project. (giggles) By Li'l Snook van Gogh.

343

If you're from Gainesville, Florida, and have a child graduating from high school, we're *gonna* have an "Electric Slide" and "Cha-Cha Slide" after-party right there in the O'Connell Center parking lot, starting this year and every year thereafter. Gainesville is going to change the world by setting a new tradition! We're going to move Mother's Day from the beginning of May to the end of May—dammit! And those who don't have *ch'rn* graduating will finally have a day to look forward to.

I thank my babies for choosing me as their mother.

Chokehold Mother Hugs,
   —Sher! (The Common Snook)
Pause. Inhale. Exhale. Reflect.

P.S. It should be called Children's Day, as it is celebrated in many countries, including India. (Hmm…is Mother's Day another one of those European euphemisms?) Why didn't someone tell me after all this time?

P.P.S. How about this? "I hope your kids are just like you." We must put an end to that powerful curse. It's time to bless these babies and stop beating and cursing them. Look out for my future sermon: Father's Day is a—

BEACH! Coming soon! You're *gonna* have to look really hard to find it.

P.P.P.S. I have a secret! My children were not raised celebrating Christian holidays; instead, we appreciated the seasons. During the *Winter Solstice,* we exchanged one or two gifts at sunset, marking the start of a new day and season. (This is an excellent alternative to credit card debt and consumerism.) But thanks to my friendians…oops again, I mean, my Indian friends, I found liberation. They were like, "Shetty, stop being shitty; you know we Indians like to party. Why don't we celebrate your God, too? Let's get this *chapati* started right!" *(Harris, did I hear you say, "Amen!"?)* I said, "Okay, you bring the beer, biryani, and dhokla, and I will set up a Pagan Christmas tree."

(Sit in stillness with your eyes closed for 15 minutes a day; I promise it will transform your life!)

344

3. Why Should We Provide Lunch to Hungry Kids During the Summer?

He puts that sh*t on everything! No, my baby is not part Chinese, as my Chinese friends like to say. Those are Cherokee, Native American eyes (some say Algonquin), like Snoop Dogg's eyes—beeyotch! Now you know.

Disclosure Reminder...,

My husband, "the diplomat," serves on various nonprofit boards, so I prefer not to use his name. He must remain professional and watch what he says, and he is fortunate to have me as his wife. It's challenging for him to take me out to community events. Man, he gets nervous when the wrong, uncultured person corners me.

As I mentioned in a few sermons back, a curious White woman once asked about my heritage and told me that I did not resemble "the American Negro." I have been called and have experienced all sorts of nonsense in the name of peace and love. Yet, I smile, even though it's hard to bite my tongue because I know better: throwing pearls among *swine* isn't worth my *time*.

Once, I was talking to another White woman who was begging to be in my book...I mean, who frustrated me with her views on our country's national lunch program, which was starting to provide free lunches to hungry children during the summer months. Perhaps she believed it was better for them to starve than to use tax money to fund this initiative. In her defense, she argued that their mothers should be taking care of them and looked at me for agreement.

Biting my tongue at this dinner party, on the verge of tears, I said, "My mother was a nurse (because you know she thought these lazy mommas didn't work), and our refrigerator was always full." I learned how to make a mean sandwich with bologna (or baloney) on stiff whole wheat bread, complete with all the fixings, when she was at work. Now, almost in tears, I continued, "I'm thankful for the women in my neighborhood who used to feed me a hot lunch in the summer when my mom was at work." In my mind, I remember saying *thank you to Suzanne Kragiel and Kathy Leander*, who treated me like one of their own children; I have never forgotten their generosity. (Strangely, I can recall exactly what we had for lunch forty years ago.) Motherhood is a team effort, looking out for others, and expecting nothing in return.

There was somethin' *special* about having a White momma and a Jewish momma as my very own stay-at-home mommas. I felt doubly blessed. Mom's smile made lunch taste so much better than my bologna sandwich with all the fixings, of course. (Hmm…another reason I don't eat pork today.)

Hugs to caring moms,
   —Sher! (The Common Snook)
            Pause. Inhale. Exhale. Reflect.

P.S. I still remember when I was six, and my Jewish momma came over to the house after I had been discharged from Alachua General Hospital (AGH) with my broken arm, having fallen off the fire hydrant in my front yard. She gave me a coloring book and a bracelet with beautiful purple stones as she knelt next to me, which made me feel so *special*. Her Presence and kindness were remarkable.

Of course, having such wonderful stay-at-home mommas meant I was equally blessed with loving fathers. Thank you, Lucian Kragiel and Steve Leander. Witnessing how well they cared for their homes inspired my passion for home improvement. *(Lucian, I will send my son to bring you a copy of this book. Perhaps you could offer him some career guidance since "it takes a village to raise a child," you know. He's leaning toward a career in architecture and urban design.)* And if it hadn't been for Steve from *Joisy* loading us up in the back of his pickup truck, I would have never been to all those "Redneck" vacation hotspots, a.k.a. the Florida springs.

4. "You People Don't Eat this Kind of Cheese?"

Disclosure Reminder…,

Let's talk lunch again! This sermon and message could be short and straightforward, but I must represent N.W. Gainesville first. Then we will enjoy the cheese and my hidden message at the end. Don't get too distracted by this "prescription drug commercial" that has yet to find a remedy for this story.

In my formative years, I grew up in (played in) the notorious Environmental Protection Agency (EPA) Superfund site here in Gainesville, a toxic property once owned by Koppers Inc., a.k.a. the Stephen Foster Neighborhood. This was my home for nine years. The scent of pine and coal tar used to coat and treat the utility poles still brings me fond memories of the magical playground we discovered in the woods. But nothing could surpass the smell of Hogtown Creek flowing downstream from Koppers. (Technically, it was Springstead Creek, but we called it Hogtown.) Anyone else enjoy the smell of gasoline? It's a great hit of dopamine! Look it up!

When my parents divorced in the early 1980s, the judge ordered my father to buy my mother a house, so I suppose he thought the Superfund site on N.W. 3rd Street was the perfect place for his *ch'rn* to grow up. He was right; it was lovely! Better than his rural location, where cows once roamed free, on S.W. 91st. (Yep, they had free-range cows out there back in the day.)

And umm…I only mentioned his street because it marks a significant moment in Black History in Gainesville. "People of Color" did not live west of the newly built Oaks Mall in 1980, let alone in West Gainesville, except for a few pocket-neighborhoods: the Fifth Avenue and Pleasant Street Community, Porters Quarters, behind where the old Terwilliger Elementary used to be, and near Buchholz High. Okay, maybe there were five of us, like the beautiful woman and her family who used to own the rural post office on Tower Road, next to where the vacuum store is now. She knew *my daddy,* especially since he had ripped out his mailbox. (Now, don't destroy your mailbox; it's federal property. [giggles])

Anyhow, back to the Superfund site! We spent our summers picking blackberries in the woods that bordered our neighborhood and Koppers. We used to climb the ten to fifteen-foot mounds of telephone poles, often overgrown with vegetation, to reach the best berries. We especially enjoyed climbing to the top of Pine Mulch Mountain, which rose over twenty feet high, and then rolling

347

down to the bottom. It was a blast! We even used the fragrant mulch to carpet our forts and the leftover tree stumps as stools and tables.

We always stayed close to the edge of the woods, but we were really curious to see how the belt conveyor system worked, which transported the logs and violently stripped them of their bark. It was interesting to finally see this up close one weekend when the plant was closed. (Shhh!) We even *successfully reached* the railroad tracks in the woods, which used to cross N.W. 23rd Avenue and still cross N.W. 39th Avenue. (That was like finding the lost city of gold. Amazing!)

But, of course, every magical place must have a villain. We had to keep an eye out for the vicious, kid-hating men who drove the massive log trucks, cranes, and tractors in that area. We imagined their sole intent was to capture us. The thrill of the day was running and diving into the woods as fast as possible or hiding behind Pine Mulch Mountain. My brother, our Jewish friends, and I were fearless. (Hmm…I wonder if the high concentration of Jews was due to the Stephen Foster Neighborhood being known as a welcoming community where today you can find "Trump supporters," "insurrectionists," "preppers" "Rednecks," "gays," "Blackx," "Whites," "Jews," "freaks," "sex offenders," and "hippies" living side by side—one world, one people! *Whassup, Chas!*)

I'm sure that if we kids had a reunion today, half of us would test positive for toxins, autoimmune diseases, neurological disorders, cancer, infertility, food allergies, and, of course, autism. (Yes, I did say test positive. You know what I'm talkin' 'bout.) I really hope the twitch-like tremor in my leg and finger doesn't worsen. Either way, life has been full of adventures!

Okay, one more story before lunch! One afternoon, I walked home after a long school day *in* the Superfund site. I got my daily whiff of my favorite corner of Hogtown Creek, which I called Gasoline Corner. When I arrived home, I was struck by the beauty of early fall, where longleaf pine needles stood upright on the lawn. It was the perfect spot to relax in the sun, with the smells of fresh coal and pine in the air. It was a sure sign that Halloween was approaching.

Somehow, little me, who always took a daily nap, mistakenly fell asleep in the front yard. Poor Mrs. Pittman, who was nearly a hundred years old then and my best friend, discovered my lifeless body sprawled out in the grass. She thought for sure I was dead, but it was likely just the toxins seeping through the soil that had put me into a temporary coma. She called my name frantically while shaking my body vigorously. "*Sherry Baby*, wake up!" Thankfully, I awoke to her sweet smile, full of joy as if I had risen from the dead. Little Yappy

Dog was happy, too. The naps in the Superfund site were like no other! Okay, I'm done reminiscing.

*

In my last sermon, I shared how my White momma and Jewish momma cared for me as if I were their own. We were indeed a village, unaware of the toxins seeping into our soil and homes.

However, my third White stay-at-home momma, who was from New England, asked me one day if I wanted to stay for lunch, and of course, I did! I always looked forward to my White momma's home cooking. Casseroles were excellent in the 80s!

But she caught me off guard one day when she said, "You people don't eat this kind of cheese?" I remember looking at her with my five-year-old side-eye and saying, "Yes, I would still like to stay for lunch, but can we eat inside? The smell from Koppers is giving me a headache today." By now, you are aware that my siblings and I had just returned from living in Hawaii with our father. I should have told her, "No, I prefer fresh macadamia nuts from my backyard and organic kuawa." (I'm sure she thought we were just poor little half-Black kids, the ones who were safe to play with their children. She must not have known I was going to marry me a cheese-eatin' White man from New England one day and teach my fellow Southerners where this mysterious place was located.)

Still, she was right; I didn't know many people who looked like me who ate cheese, perhaps because dairy can give "People of Color" the shits. But that wasn't my problem back then. She was always right; she was right about everything. I had never tasted cheap-ass white bread fried in butter with a slice of cheese in the middle. That day, the cheese was *white American*. Seriously! She thought that cheese was *special*. In fact, it was the best thing I had ever tasted in my young life, and it may very well still hold the record!

I remember my friends eating their sandwiches cut into triangles, leaving the golden crust. I couldn't imagine why anyone would waste the best part of Golden Momma's golden delight, which I later learned was called a grilled cheese sandwich, after I told my mom what she said to me. **(Careful, mommas; five-year-olds *got* more awareness than most educated adults. They are watching you closely, so be mindful of what you teach them! They may write a book one day and thank you for your kindness.)**

I loved my White mommas even when some of them used to *try me* when I was only a baby, but my Jewish mommas never *tried me* with that nonsense. I had six of them, too. They tended to be relatively quiet about their Jewish heritage—except when Jewish grandma (Bubbeh!) would come to visit from

Miami or New York, of course. (Bubbeh did not play when it came to education and didn't want to hear anything about her grandchildren attending, say, a Waldorf School.) They also didn't pull out the Tanakh, the Hebrew Bible, and make me recite scriptures or memorize the Torah. I wonder what it was that made them a little different from the average White momma.

Cheers to grilled cheese sandwiches in the Superfund site,
    —Cher! (The Common Snook)
    Pause. Inhale. Exhale. Reflect.

P.S. Did I ever tell y'all I once fell into that toxic creek while searching for black fossilized shark teeth? I remember being terrified because we were warned that the creek was polluted. Amazingly, we never saw snakes or alligators in our area, which was common in most parts of Gainesville. (Hmm...I wonder why.)

P.P.S. It would be wonderful if the current owner of the Koppers site in Gainesville could complete the cleanup and donate the 49-acre land to *Betwixt,* transforming it into a nurturing school for boys. This act would serve as a heartfelt apology to the Gainesville community. Then, my old neighbors, particularly Zach Osbrach—a former builder who constructed the beautiful Green Leaf neighborhood—might appreciate this. (The community retains much of its beauty and some nurturing elements, not to mention the trees that were spared. *Zach, did you also build Cedar Ridge?* [giggles]) In addition to his work, he founded the Einstein Charter School, which serves students with dyslexia. He could provide valuable insights on establishing a school and guiding these boys in construction skills.

Additionally, the team at Atlantic Design Homes, who should consider offering my son an internship, could create a certified green school and temple that feels homey. Of course, it would need to be raised above the ground, providing adequate ventilation for our Super-*fun* School. Then, perhaps the social worker could visit to help heal the hearts of the wounded, recalling her words from my childhood when she comforted me, saying, "Sherry, now you must forgive her." (Nope!)

P.P.P.S. Speaking of Sherry baby! Did I ever tell y'all I met a woman who claimed to be the original *Sherry* from the 1962 "Sherry" song by Frankie Valli and The Four Seasons? Supposedly, she was "Frankie's sweetheart." And she was from *Joisy*, of course! (Yeah, right.) I met her right here in Gainesville, but I won't tell you where since I was probably still jumping for Jesus then. You know, I was in an organization similar to the mafia. ♟

5. Time

I need a smaller life
So I can be a "good" wife
Smaller like a mouse
Living in a tiny house
To ride and glide
To dance and prance
To find time to schedule a pap smear maintenance

An appointment…I never thought I would miss,
How nice it would be to lie on a table
(Insert your name here)
I know I sound unstable
"Scoot to the end, my dear"
"Not your whole body, just your derriere"

To focus on my health
And the inner self
To extract as many virtues
Hidden within the stony brook
You got it!
The youngest Snook

Perhaps I will treat myself to a crown
Or even better
A new gown
This sounds all too good to be true
Could happiness be as simple
as having time times two?

A few months before writing this poem, while cutting our three acres on my zero-turn mower (a meditative experience), a knowing from within came over me while I was bouncing and jerking back and forth with the rhythm of the mower. I was told, "You can either take care of this farm and house, or you can take care of yourself and your boys" (since my husband was always missing out due to work). That inner voice continued, "But if you don't get off this mower, you will die out here!" I thought for sure the warning was metaphorical.

Anyways, I told my husband I was selling the mower with the house and buying a townhome. I planned to turn my life into a vacation because no one would give me the time off I needed. Being the hero of my family was killing me.

One year later, while "flipping" another house, I discovered I had a brain aneurysm, which I realized had been with me for a few years due to my unusual headaches. I'm so thankful I didn't die out there on that mower and sacrifice my life to that old-ass house in hot-ass Georgia. (See! If you pay attention, you have time to choose a different path in life, even when death's door is just around the corner. And I loved that mower!)

Long Overdue Hugs,
— Sher! (The Common Snook)
Pause. Inhale. Exhale. Reflect.

P.S. I know it's impossible to scoot without bringing your whole body. I bet some of y'all didn't even catch that.

P.P.S. Ms. Juliette asked a family member of mine if he had ever been in a wheelchair. The question might seem odd coming from a woman who could *clearly see* your life. However, she often needed clarity to help align with our concepts of past, present, and future. Nevertheless, he probably didn't understand the significance of her question or that this event had already occurred.

About ten years later, he lost his leg due to diabetes and passed away shortly after. (I know, spooky. But we still have time to choose a different path. [He had ten years.] Yes, there are many options. Choose wisely!)

P.P.P.S. Speaking of time! When I turned forty-five, the chapter of motherhood was coming to a close. It was time for my young men to demonstrate their self-care skills before leaving the nest. Then, about two years later, my estrogen levels must have had a strange spike, and something came over me. I got this wild idea to make my young men a cup of hot cocoa, and they looked at me as if it were laced. My oldest asked, "What, is horse tranquilizer in there?" They were thrilled to catch a reassuring glimpse of the woman they knew as Mom.

(Sit in stillness with your eyes closed for 15 minutes a day; I promise it will transform your life!)

Section IX: Social Constructs: Individual and Collective Veils

In case you decided to skip the introduction and browse around, here's the **Disclosure Reminder**: Before diving in, I will say this: I'm simple. I love to laugh. Please don't confuse my humor with sarcasm; I always mean what I say. I test the limits. My words are plain. I often use "own" redundantly. I don't claim to know all the answers; my only intention is to be a vessel. Also, to connect with different experiences, I interchangeably use the terms "Consciousness," "Presence," "God," "Universe," "Source," "Divine," "Energy," "Christ/Krst," and "Light." Above all, reading my humor with a Southern accent is best. Enjoy!

The collective voice of society speaking outside the Florida Capitol after the Parkland School shooting in 2018. (TCS)

1. The Parables of Controlling Personalities: Codependency, Narcissism, and Others

Disclosure Reminder...,

Dear Friends and Family of those who suffer from codependency, narcissism, and related conditions:

Jesus often spoke in parables because he understood that the human mind often struggles to receive information directly, which can be challenging, especially when aiming to help individuals. Today, I've chosen to address not those suffering from these conditions but rather their friends and family. Sneaky? That's why I'm calling it a parable even though the stories are all true.

You might think that revealing my intentions would undermine the purpose of my letter. But honestly, it doesn't. That's how simple the mind is. You can address a letter to an entirely different audience while still intending to communicate with those who might avoid it. This creative technique, introduced by Jesus, provides just enough mental distance to suggest to these individuals that you aren't technically addressing them. It also lessens the need to listen defensively, hopefully allowing them to lower some barriers.

Interestingly, the mind isn't as clever as we once believed. It enjoys fooling itself and falls for the game of *Psych* every time. What nonsense! It says, "As long as you play by my rules and let me fool myself while still listening, I will." Great! I'm always up for a good challenge.

I imagine those who find this sermon uncomfortable will need to read it twice. The first time, the mind anticipates an attack on the ego, which means one isn't fully listening. You must reread it to truly absorb what I have to say.

Childhood can be a gruesome experience for some. Unfortunately, those who were abused or neglected as ch'rn/children or experienced trauma passed down through their DNA often create defense mechanisms to survive situations they can't change. Sadly, for many, the scars and behaviors from childhood follow them into adulthood. Many don't know whether it's safe to leave their superpowers behind. For those who have been guilt-tripped and manipulated, these behaviors manifest as a part of their personality. Their scars run deep.

These scarred individuals were left to create their own defense mechanisms to survive childhood. They use technicalities almost every millisecond of the day to deceive themselves into believing they are in control, "superior," entitled, and justified. These techniques, initially used as mind tricks to protect themselves,

354

are now also employed to excuse and permit themselves. They might say, "Well, I got there first. I'm taller. I'm pretty smart. It was in my yard. They're just *stupid*. You should have spoken up. You had every opportunity. Well, I told you. The letter isn't addressed to me. Well, I'm not controlling, so. Everyone is a little controlling, so. We all experience mental illness from time to time. What is life without a little narcissism? Everyone is a little narcissistic at times, so. Isn't life a competition?" You get the point.

Interestingly, their mind games stem partly from a mental block that convinces them they do not have the right to make their own decisions. Consequently, they devise clever ways to exercise their choices without completely violating their inner programming. I'm curious about the origins of this programming and who the programmer might be.

For instance, some people use religion to feel "superior," while others leverage it to justify their own decisions. Religion can also be used to control and condemn others or to escape from certain situations. Phrases like "She wasn't raised that way; she has no self-respect" enable judgment in the name of religion. Alternatively, people might say, "I feel God is 'calling' me to do this," which gives them a sense of free will they may not possess for some reason.

I strive to help anyone trapped by their mind who desires freedom. I'm fond of many of these individuals…well…most of the time, and unfortunately, I can see their gifts and talents beyond the mind games they play. But honestly, I wouldn't say I like that I can still see gold in some of the most challenging people. Isn't it just easier to condemn them as hopeless?

What they often fail to see, convincing themselves that others don't notice, is that they are abusive toward those they encounter almost every microsecond of the day. This may sound absurd, but they aren't entirely oblivious to their behavior, even though their minds quickly override their actions with a substitute "truth." They constantly elevate themselves by "one-upping and slamming" people to avoid the pain of feeling worthless. We can label this behavior as "random acts of manipulation." If you know one of these individuals, you'll likely be the one who bears the brunt of their attacks—snarky slams sandwiched with love-bombing—leaving you feeling insane or running for your life.

Here's a funny example a community member shared with me for this sermon. I said, "I would like to help further promote a local event." She responded resistantly, saying the event was not about helping but about sharing. (*Hmm*…I thought.) This was her way of maintaining control and avoiding the need to ask for help. She redefined the whole damn event in a game of resistance she was playing…with herself. Of course, I didn't offer help; instead, I chose to share. (giggles)

Another silly example was when I volunteered to help a local family with their home. While cleaning the yard, I noticed people digging holes and planting small ornamental plants and flowers directly into the lawn, rather than in the flowerbed. (Go figure!) I told the all-White team, "It's going to be a beast to weed and mow around those plants," and suggested removing the grass and expanding the flowerbed. They responded, "It's fine." Then, I was sternly reminded that the house was the priority, not the landscaping, which minimized and dismissed my insight. (Well, okay then!) It's hard to offer feedback to *"right" folks*. Even so, the one White man present that day pulled me aside and said I was correct in my thinking (Gee, thanks). (More in a minute. Sometimes tough broads devalue feminine women [hmm…or "Women of Color"] to elevate themselves, not realizing their frustration is with men…while acting like them.)

Codependency

Let's focus on codependency for a moment. First, it's important to acknowledge that some individuals give much of themselves to the world without expecting anything in return. This is called Love. Such individuals are sometimes targeted by controlling personalities. They may be mischaracterized as codependent because their kind intentions are misunderstood. Many therapists assign textbook definitions to certain behaviors without fully understanding how Love can function. (I sure hope I've saved a few of you; still, others may try to take this as an out.)

That said, codependency thrives on an unhealthy reliance on external validation. One of the easiest ways to spot a person with codependency is their tendency to offer unsolicited alternative opinions or excuses about someone or a situation they fear might cause discomfort for either you or themselves. Instead of accepting things as they are, they might say, "He talks to everyone like that," or "She was probably just…." They constantly put a positive or alternative spin on everything to skew your perception of reality, subtle gaslighting, while minimizing and disqualifying your experience. *(Right, Melissa?)* Many inaccurately judge situations due to their clouded vision. They hinder growth and successful resolutions by resisting anything that doesn't sound positive to their paranoid ears. They are like psychological nurses or firefighters, suturing up wounds without allowing them to bleed or dousing a fire before it even smokes. (Let it burn—dammit!)

Their strange behavior is often due to experiencing abuse in the past, usually during childhood. They constantly battle conflicting feelings of shame and inadequacy. "If I can keep Mommy or Daddy happy, they won't take their anger out on me." Or "If I can convince Mommy that Daddy wasn't being rude, maybe she won't start a fight with him, which ends with him beating me." Unfortunately, they feel safe only when everyone is happy, even if that means preventing anyone from expressing upset or discomfort.

Codependency becomes part of their personality. Coddling, disguised as helping, defines them because they never confront the fact that it serves as a means to protect themselves and fulfill a need. The mind says, "I will help this situation to my advantage." For this reason, many individuals pursue careers in helping professions, such as nursing. It's a validation paradise; they feel needed, which translates to love for them. However, being needed is not Love, as true Love arises only from within or through a being who also knows Love.

It's challenging to confront a codependent because they have everyone drinking from their cup and eating from their hands, worshiping their false, self-serving kindness. In this situation, those who are sane appear crazy, while the truly insane appear sane. *(Right, Melissa?) The Twilight Zone* episode "Nightmare at 20,000 Feet" vividly illustrates the experience of trying to warn someone about a controlling personality. The main character in the episode exclaims something like, "There's a *gremlin* on the wing!" which tried to rip off a panel of the airplane's wing while in flight, but nobody believed him.

You want to be stoned? Say something negative about these "angels" to their victims. These folks will protect the identity of the codependent because they, too, have fallen for their self-serving game. The codependent has succeeded, especially when you have become their puppet, and now you make it your goal to protect them and their identity. Some of these folks are also codependents, and their "friendship chain" can be endless. (You will see many of these puppets, Oompa Loompas, fighting for civil rights just because…it makes them feel good. Great, the more, the merrier!)

And if you ever ask them to cut it out and simply allow your feelings to be, watch out! Here's where they may become vindictive, resembling a narcissist, as they deceive themselves, you, and others; they will claim they were just being kind and helpful while portraying you as ungrateful, difficult, and undeserving. This behavior is known as blame-shifting, where sweet quickly turns to sour.

If you allow them to brush your hair, dress you, and take care of you, so to speak, they will behave because they feel secure when they are needed, all while using undermining language to keep you subservient and dependent on them.

"You've had a long day. How about you sit down? I'll make you something to eat because you must feel overwhelmed." Their offer to make you something to eat sounds nice, but you're not sure if you feel overwhelmed, even though you're starting to believe you do. "There, there," they say as they take your temperature and check you in permanently into their psych ward.

Here are some tools (defense mechanisms) that these personalities use to avoid processing their emotions:

- **Gaslighting** – making you feel as if you are crazy while attempting to alter your perception of reality. "I have no idea what you mean."
- **Blame-shifting** – "You're the one being abusive by writing this sermon," or "I'm sorry you didn't take that well."
- **Silencing** – one will not respond or acknowledge anything that might elevate another person, provoke their jealousy, or cause them to lose control. Additionally, they employ control, fear, and intimidation to keep their victims silent.
- **Redefining** – "That isn't being aggressive."
- **Reframing** – they rephrase what you said to make your opinion sound absurd. Here's one example I've heard more than once: They reframe my teachings on stillness and awareness (the state of no mental activity) as a void-like state of emptiness, likening it to a human blob. (giggles)
- **Rationalizing** – creating excuses.
- **Justification** – making themselves right.
- **Preemptive defense** – they might say, "I'm not perfect," or accuse you of labeling them as toxic before you even reach that point.
- **Withholding acknowledgment** – forcing you to prove or explain yourself repeatedly.
- **Shame** – "A real friend would…."
- **Putting words in your mouth** – "He's not as *stupid* as you think he is."
- My apologies: I must stop here, or I'll keep rolling, lol. (We must understand how programming works or risk being programmed.)

Certainly, some individuals possess the spiritual maturity to distinguish the defensive behaviors of controlling personalities from their true selves. Nevertheless, encountering toxicity can still pose life-threatening risks. Have you ever considered why you might develop joint pain after extended exposure to some of these individuals?

Many people drop terms like "codependency" and "narcissism" without fully understanding the behaviors associated with these conditions. These complex and multilayered issues make it incredibly challenging to comprehend and dismantle to address the true self, to the extent that many therapists feel uncertain about what they are addressing and can't be confident about which version of the self they are engaging with. (It's hard to keep up with Houdini, you know.) The behaviors are so perplexing that many professionals resort to coaxing the victims of these abusers to run for their lives, as they do not know how else to assist them. (Is it feasible? Can Black folks who suffer from racism flee collective narcissistic abuse?)

If you've heard "run," you might be thinking, "That's the prescription for the narcissist, while codependents are a different category; they are just people who excessively give, right?" Shoot, I wish that were true. However, when you experience both codependency and narcissism, it's hard to tell the twins apart. I've never encountered a codependent who lacks narcissistic traits or outright narcissism, and the same goes for the opposite. Furthermore, the psychological abuse they inflict to fulfill their needs is the same, so who cares how we label it?

Their self-protective behaviors are endless, as we already described in detail. Unfortunately, these scarred individuals may deceive themselves and the many people they encounter. However, if you're fortunate enough to witness their abuse consciously, take note: never respond to or identify their behaviors, as this leads to increased defensiveness and intellectual word salads that will leave your head spinning. It's best to simply observe them.

Many who struggle with narcissism find it challenging to recognize that their interactions with others can be cruel, abusive, and self-serving. Additionally, I advise against listing or sharing the details of the abuse you experienced with them. Some individuals take pleasure in having power over you, while others may exploit what you disclose (like my book) to further diminish you and elevate themselves. Remember, be quiet.

I must note that these individuals struggle with being labeled as abusive or narcissistic, often becoming defensive and shutting down completely. It is important to emphasize that codependency and narcissism are not identities; these terms merely describe a set of behaviors. We need to recognize that the pain, shame, and feelings of inadequacy make them challenging to engage with.

Therefore, you must comply with their demands to avoid hearing anything negative said about themselves if you wish to reach them, which, unfortunately, adds another layer of abuse for you through silencing. This situation often leads many to refrain from expressing how they have been mistreated or acknowledging that they have suffered narcissistic abuse.

These individuals are like wounded animals. First, you must earn their trust and help them lower their defenses before assisting them. However, many people are so hurt and scarred from their abuse that they can't provide the support they require.

I find it safest to say, "I don't like how I feel around you, and it's not my job to outline your inappropriate behaviors." This holds them accountable instead of making you responsible for how you feel. Most will only come close to apologizing by saying, "I'm sorry you feel that way." They never genuinely acknowledge how they have harmed you, instead shifting blame to your feelings. Furthermore, be warned! Some are highly deceptive and have learned to mimic empathy.

Learning Takes Time

Regrettably, it will take the average person many times, if not years, to realize that explaining their feelings to these "heart-hardened" individuals is futile when "they and their" feelings must be protected at all costs. In other words, they lack the appropriate empathy to prioritize your feelings over their own. (For your information, I refer to it as "appropriate empathy" to make empathy seem vague so my readers won't feel alarmed or caught off guard by the accusation of a "lack of empathy" they might have already faced. They struggle to accept this reality and will fight against you to alter your perception, as it significantly impacts their ego. While some possess empathy, their disconnection from emotions—a defense mechanism—leaves them unable to express it.)

For our relationship to continue, I tell them there must be authenticity moving forward. If they want my support, they can't call me pet names like "beautiful," "*hun*," "honey," or "sweetie," nor treat me as this spiritual guru or genie whom they hope won't call them out. Using pet names or constantly honoring and flattering someone can be a type of mind control and manipulation, which they will then deny doing. (Oh my, I got a little too close to providing an example that could give them just the right amount of fuel and an opportunity to attack. Never give them something to hang onto—like a letter.)

Additionally, I tell them they can't give me gifts because they are always laced with intentions or expectations. However, if they are persistent, I explain that I accept gifts without mental attachments since, for them, every gesture, step, or action is aimed at obtaining or influencing something. They aren't ready for freedom if they can't accept the terms. "You're terrible," they'll say. No, you can't give them an inch.

What has my experience been with these individuals?

As I have mentioned on numerous occasions, I was so graciously born into a toxic family, a petri dish for controlling personalities. I also survived a cult in my twenties right here in Gainesville, Florida, as if I didn't have enough of my family's dysfunction. I seem to be a magnet, as the "bugs" are attracted to the light. (That'll preach!) This awakening has led me to study controlling behaviors and groups for the past twenty years. I understand how these mind-patterns work. It's my hobby! A reputable university should award me an honorary doctorate, right? (Well, I suppose Fairleigh Dickinson University would be sufficient.)

As mentioned, cults are communities and churches led by "a charismatic leader who exercises undue influence and manipulation to control their followers" (*Elicit* sermon, "Guard Your Heart—from Whom?"). These leaders, often narcissistic personalities, are broken individuals who never overcame their childhood trauma. Moreover, there are many *cults of one* where an individual is either controlled by a narcissistic personality in a one-on-one dynamic, or those who endure this abuse often become *cults of one* themselves, as they are programmed and managed by their minds to protect their fragile inner selves. It may be easier to see each as a microcosm of larger systems of control, with the mind's self-defense mechanism, the *cult of one*, being one of the most difficult to overcome because, in a sense, it is ourselves.

The Endless Drama

Let me try to create a visual representation of how these microcosms of abuse and control (mental prisons) function in our lives. Several years ago, I ordered a set of Russian nesting dolls, as depicted in the first sermon, "Waking Up," where you open one doll to discover another inside and then another. This was meant to provide my children with a visual lesson about the endless mental prisons we must conquer. Just when you think, "That's it; I'm free," there's always one more waiting to be revealed.

We labeled the smallest one "the self." Although it is the smallest among all the others, its tormented mind, with its gripping control, is the hardest to break. Lying at the heart of each subsequent layer, or microcosm, as you will see below, the tormented self wields and manipulates its environment to satisfy the fragile ego.

The following is a list of divisive (or abusive) social constructs—essentially, the *stuff we humans* create in our minds and often agree upon—many of which are experienced through corresponding institutions. Each one involves exerting control over others, stepping on someone else's head to elevate oneself— sometimes, even multiple heads at once. As a result, whether looked at individually or collectively, these social constructs act as veils in our lives, dividing us and superficially separating groups of people. *(Please note that some of the terms and isms below have been modified or invented to suit this book.)* I also refer to this as my Tex-Mex breakdown because, again, it tastes the same and the outcome is the same, whether it's a taco, a bowl, or a burrito. In the end, it all produces the same shit:

- **Nationalism!** "I am this piece of land! This piece of cloth, this flag, is me, and these are my teammates…I mean, my people. And I will die for this land and these fabulous school colors." (Is this rugby?) This belief is anchored in a firm conviction that is seen as part of one's identity. Here, we encounter exclusivity, "superiority," dominance, and violence.
- **Religionism!** This is the only path to God, dictating how you should live your life, often expressed through religious dominance and violence.
- **Racial identity(ism)!** This defines who you are, and everything associated with this classification must be defended, representing a type of psychological abuse and control.
- **Racism!** Historically, it has been White over Black or any other "minority" group. Non-Whites are seen as inferior and are expected to submit to White power and control. This is White dominance and violence.
- **Sexism!** This has traditionally involved men oppressing women. Women face discrimination and exploitation, are regarded as inferior, are treated like property, and are expected to submit to men. This exemplifies dominance and violence perpetrated by men.
- **"Feminism!"** An often misunderstood, demonized, and hijacked term has also become a counterattack against sexism born out of frustration, which, unfortunately, often demeans men (the good ones), stripping

them of their dignity, talents, and gifts; it represents a form of dominance and violence carried out by women. (Meanwhile, "feminists" are shouting into this book and rippin' up the pages.)

- **Western medicine(ism)!** This notion is considered "superior" to all other forms of medicine and employs science as if it were definitive, dismissing the alternatives. Here, we observe dominance and aggression from the proponents of Western medicine. (This belief is as strong as Christianity in the collective view that it is "superior" to all other forms of medicine, and one cannot speak negatively about this approach without facing ostracism akin to that of a sinner.)
- **Cultism and controlling groups!** This involves one person or team manipulating and controlling a group for their benefit, typically financial, expressed through spiritual and psychological abuse and violence.
- **Familialism! (which can't be pronounced)** Individuals exert control over family members through manipulation, humiliation, fear, intimidation, and more. "Do what I say and meet my needs." This illustrates psychological abuse and domestic violence.
- **Selfism!** The mind (the ego) overshadows the true self. "I will not feel pain or face rejection." This insanity manifests through mental identifications and acts of self-inflicted violence.

Those who seek freedom exclaim, "I can't breathe; you're suffocating me!"

You may notice that some communities (the collective assholes) or individuals suffer from almost all of the above issues while others face just one or two. Interestingly, those the world judges for not aligning with the norm are often the closest to mental freedom—salvation! They merely need to overcome themselves.

Here's a quick riddle: What do you get when racism and narcissism merge in an individual who has also suffered from sexism and feelings of worthlessness? You guessed it: *"Karenism!"* As I mentioned earlier, the complexities of these controlling personalities are so challenging to understand and explain, even though we can see the insanity. Thankfully, groups that have experienced this multilayered abuse often create simple language to identify the behavior instead of breaking down the controlling games these individuals play, from gaslighting to blame-shifting. "Karen" summarizes the behavior well without losing too much sleep or yielding to their endless defense mechanisms. It also helps them avoid giving "Karen" something to cling to, which could be used to minimize or disqualify their experience. "Karen" seems to stop them in their tracks. *(Right, Melissa?)*

Each system of control stems from deep mental programming that shapes our beliefs, influences our behaviors and perspectives toward others, and affects how we perceive ourselves. When these beliefs are deeply ingrained, they become a part of our identity. When challenged, the mind reacts defensively, as if it were undergoing a physical attack. Consequently, we end up safeguarding *thoughts* we mistakenly turned into an identity. The closer the association to the self, the stronger the reaction. Moreover, we remain unaware that much of our programming triggers defensiveness. In essence, we defend our mental prisons without question.

Sometimes, it's easier to reach these people when they can see how others may also be unaware of their behaviors or trapped behind a similar mental prison or veil. (We all like company, right?) As mentioned earlier, *Plato's Allegory of the Cave* is an excellent work that helps people understand how their perception, sometimes distorted by their perspective, which becomes their reality, isn't necessarily accurate, yet changing it can be difficult.

Personally, surviving an abusive church opened my eyes to how someone (pastor, preacher, politician, parent, partner, etc.—as long as it starts with a "p") can program the human mind and what the mind will hide from us while defending itself without the individual knowing. There's also a level of being in a cult; although you may be a victim in a sense, you could rightly be defined as a narcissist for the duration of your stay and self-replacement. (Yep, I'm guilty, lol. Now, don't confuse that with a Christian narcissist.) This is because one replaces one's identity with the group's collective identity, which forms a false self. This is precisely what occurs in clinical narcissism. A false self rules them. Thankfully, a humble acceptance of the truth opens the door to liberation.

Labeling Can Be Painful

As you can see, I often refer to those who suffer from narcissism and codependency as "scarred individuals" because nobody likes labels, especially those who already feel worthless and ashamed inside. Even so, I still welcome the terminology because victims of this kind of abuse need language to express their experiences. It's challenging to show respect for the victim-perpetrator when so many are suffering because of their toxicity. But I do what I can.

Furthermore, if they are aware of their behavior, these individuals often desire freedom. However, most will spend their lives blaming others and never looking within. Many egos will insist that you leave it to itself. This would be akin to a demon pretending to be the person asking you to leave it alone, lol. "Don't tell me there's a sinkhole under the house; my ego wants to discover it…itself." Many people in cults behave similarly. Being right is more important than freedom and truth. Sadly, they will remain bound by their ego (their mind).

There's "Hope"

For those who possess a degree of self-awareness (which they will likely turn into a prize and intellectualize), there is hope, even when many professionals privately express doubt. It's just that most therapists aren't aware enough to recognize their own mind games. This isn't to devalue therapists but to recognize that overcoming the mind is challenging for us all.

Frankly, if a therapist isn't qualified to be a cult exit counselor or isn't exceptionally aware, they likely can't assist those trapped by their minds. This illustrates the complexity and layered nature of the mind. Nonetheless, the most crucial step is recognizing the need for help, which doesn't come easily until individuals have experienced many failed relationships. "Hi, my name is Barry, and I'm an alcoholic" is a great place to start, so to speak. If they're still in the "I'm not an alcoholic" phase, they aren't interested in personal growth yet, and I'm not interested in being abused.

Here is a simple test to assess a therapist's competency in addressing these conditions. Suppose a therapist cannot recognize that racism parallels the frameworks of narcissism and behaves similarly or employs the same tactics when addressing the behavior. In that case, they do not fully understand the condition and its thought patterns. They, too, are likely intellectualizing an idea at their client's expense and can only provide cognitive behavioral therapy to alleviate symptoms.

Therapist, are you aware that racism can be rightly described as a form of collective narcissism and codependency? Racism necessitates stepping on another's head to elevate oneself, and these racist individuals will gaslight their victims while justifying their actions. "Well, what was he doing looking around the home construction site?" or "I promise, they weren't being racist," attempting to "alter one's reality" when one knows damn well what they experienced. Before I mistakenly veer off topic, I must ask: who are their collective codependent counterparts that give these individuals the attention— positive or negative—they lavish to satisfy their fragile sense of self?

*

Don't Be Fooled by Intellectualization

Living locked behind the mind and its layers of veils won't prevent them from intellectualizing the concept of the veils. They will argue, "Isn't that the human struggle to overcome the many veils of life?" which has nothing to do with comprehending how veils operate and is, *in every way,* exhausting. For example, describing ice cream and tasting ice cream are two distinct experiences. This constant intellectualization makes them feel "superior" and in control. They are like puppies; they'll chew on anything you put in their path, rip out the inner guts, flip the item around, turn it inside out, and then use it to elevate themselves or beautifully tear you down. (giggles)

These individuals prefer to call the shots. Yet, freedom only comes through humility and letting go of the need for control. If we left each to their ego, as the mind craves, many would spend their entire lives imprisoned by their thoughts. For those who seek my assistance, I tell them, "You don't get to call the shots." This isn't about control; it's about surrendering to vulnerability. Freedom boot camp is about relinquishing control.

Through this process, some will agree to give trust a chance because they genuinely want help, but careful, because they are *slick* and *skilled.* They will try to manipulate you into accommodating their feelings, which they are largely disconnected from, as they live to avoid feeling anything at all. (I'm laughing like the nutty professor!) Whatever you do, don't give in!

They Want It Both Ways

They behave like children yet expect to be treated as mature adults. They also behave insanely yet expect you to engage with them like they are well, as if this time…or this time, they can be trusted. While posturing with authority like a politician, they will say, "Please hear me out. I'm not manipulating anyone…this time." (giggles) Whatever!

When they're ready to let go and be honest that they can't be trusted with a bottle of booze, so to speak, there will be no time…for a loooong time, a very loooong time, before they can be trusted again. Sipping is almost irresistible for them because their behaviors and actions are programmed and reactive. Observing the mind's reactive patterns and breaking them down takes time, much like building muscles or losing weight.

So, I tell them that I don't want to hear about their feelings and that they can't have it both ways. I will interact accordingly with the self they present. If they need their feelings stemming from the false self to be considered, they have come to screw with the wrong person. This may sound insensitive. If it does, you don't understand the behavior. Sympathize and make room for a hungry mosquito and see what happens. This is why it's easy for men to keep women in abusive relationships. Women often have a bad habit of considering feelings and puppy eyes. Don't fall for it.

If you mistakenly call out their behavior, they will seem clueless. Still, it's helpful to recognize that it doesn't matter whether their cluelessness is genuine or not because the goal remains the same. They need you to give in and express your feelings. Everything and every action can and will be used to their advantage to gain the upper hand. They will become the victim, critic, perpetrator, Houdini, savior, and intellectual as needed. For them, it's all about winning, which serves merely as a bandage for their psychological pain.

For example, one might say, "You've hurt my feelings, and I've had it with you and your nonsense. You're the narcissist!" or something like, "A real friend would [blah blah blah]." They don't have any real friends, so don't fall for that. As you can see, they become accusatory. I call this the shame-game blame-shifting combo. It's sad to say, but because most of us have a heart, we will give in and consider them; however, if you do, they've got you. You'll give an inch; they'll take a mile, light a joint, and burn you with it. It was just the hit their empty soul so craved.

They Respond to Awareness

Now that we have outlined their behaviors and some of the necessary boundaries, you might think that helping these individuals is hopeless. You're right, but what I offer isn't hope. The secret is that they respond well to awareness. They'll start to see what you see. Additionally, their behavior increases human Consciousness because you can't survive or avoid getting burned if you react to the multitude of offensive things they say. You can't respond! They're like ninjas and will take you down every time. (As you can tell, I have been slammed a few times. [giggles] I learn quickly, though.)

Ultimately, when you believe you've captured their attention, they might resort to criticizing your communication style or its length if necessary, or they may impose rules. There's always something more with these individuals. "You didn't have the decency to tell me this to my face?" Ignore them! Alternatively, they might say, "You don't have the credentials to speak on this topic." They will criticize, minimize, deflate, and disqualify anything to avoid facing pain or taking responsibility.

Moreover, let me take a moment to corner the brilliant and grandiose individuals who will surprise you by taking the high road instead of positioning themselves as victims to maintain their inflated sense of self. They'll say, "Sher, this was excellent!" Understand that if they get it, it means they don't have any issues. They are on the same level as you, and this is for everyone else, not them. "I couldn't have said it better myself," they will say. Play it safe and never accept compliments from these folks for their own good.

Remember, it's the little doses of medication they need every millisecond of their lives. Anything short of being honest with them is merely buying a ticket to play their games, where they're the cat, and you're the mouse. (You know, cats like to play with their food before they kill it, right?)

Keep It Simple

Today, I only offer these folks my awareness, but I'm open to helping them learn to practice stillness. That's all. *There is liberation for them just as there is liberation for you.* They are just as troubled as the average person, yet they carry an additional veil beneath all the others, which is significantly thicker and heavier. Again, this is because someone was screwing with their mind as a child, or trauma affected their DNA. (Probably both.)

But there is good news: As Jesus said, "Clear out the merchants from the temple, and you will meet God there." Conquering the mind is essential. As you can see, the prescription for good mental health and well-being hasn't changed.

Sitting in stillness and learning to clear the mind have lasting effects if one can move beyond merely discussing meditation and pretending to be an expert in what they cannot perceive. In their attempts to impress you with their intellect and spiritual jargon, they fail to recognize that codependency and narcissism represent a resistance to Consciousness, period.

However, I've experienced spurts of Consciousness, wisdom, and beauty from many of these individuals because "that of *God,*" the *Source,* the *Light,* the *Universe,* exists in each of us. (Wow, I used five words to express the *Divine* without using *Christ/Krst,* which now makes six.)

Some might say *with attitude,* "You make me sound like a monster." Well, every day, we have the opportunity to shape the life we wish to lead; let's create it consciously.

Don't Even *Try Me* Hugs,
  —Sher! (The Common Snook)
  Pause. Inhale. Exhale. Reflect.

P.S. When you help free one of these folks, their suffering is transmuted into gold. Priceless! (Hmm...here's a thought! I have encountered women from many cultures and find that those most controlled by their culture are often the most manipulative, meaning they are left with "no choice" but to constantly scheme to get their way. This behavior becomes a part of their personality. Can you imagine which culture might have some of the most honest and straightforward women? If I told you, you'd just assume I was being biased. That is so racist!)

P.P.S. This sermon nearly drained my soul, and the demons dared to lock my shoulder. That means it must be good!

P.P.P.S. My sensitivity check flagged the term "firemen" as non-inclusive in this sermon, but isn't the term "nurse" just as problematic? Sure, right...it's not gender-specific. Nurses should be referred to as "primary care providers" since they do all the work, and then family doctors should be called "primary doctors," right?

P.P.P.P.S. (There are only four quadruple **P.S.'s** in the book. Here's the fourth one!) If you tried to explain narcissism or narcissistic abuse to an Indian woman, many would be like, "Do you mean mother-in-law?" Or if you pointed out manipulation, mind tricks, or defense mechanisms, she might respond with a perplexed look, "Do you mean effective communication?" Or worse, try explaining codependency and the need for approval; it won't resonate with most Indians because codependency is taught and socially acceptable.

Very few Indians are raised to make their own decisions, and some don't know where to start, akin to my behavior when I left the cult. Many remain their parents' children for life, which is the opposite of *mukti* (liberation or freedom).

Here, you see, we have different words yet identical behaviors with varying levels of social acceptance. (The Indian women I know here in the U.S. who are free from their mothers-in-law's control *be* looking at them like Dobermans. "Don't you *try me*, woman! I will bite you!" as they dismantle the outdated social construct of being owned by their in-laws.)

(Stop *acting* crazy for 15 minutes a day; I promise it will transform your life!)

2. Black Folks! Stop Paying so Much Attention to Nonsense and the Past

Disclosure Reminder…,

Because I wasn't raised to mentally separate people by race, I didn't give White people any extra attention. As a result, I often missed the racist comments that they made. Racism wasn't something I expected to encounter. But thanks to my *sistas*, they would catch these comments for me like Johnny Bench, one of the greatest Major League Baseball catchers of all time.

Once upon a time (get ready for a pronoun rollercoaster ride), gender-neutral Goldilocks, whom I have the privilege of calling family, was irritated by my reservedness or quietness, a trait many people complained about. (giggles) They wanted to know what the heck I was thinking. Quietness can be unsettling for folks, especially for Goldilocks, who was accustomed to receiving *special* attention. (Yep, I *be* watching you.)

Anyhow, *they was pissed* that *they* couldn't read my mind and wanted to show *them's* disapproval of me. *They* said to a grown-ass woman something to the effect of "In our culture and family, we say please and thank you…" (Ouch!) As if my country-ass had said, "Gimme-a-sammich." (White people are *special*.)

Them's remark *was* definitely off-putting. First, *they tried me*, and second, I couldn't figure out what "culture" Goldilocks was talkin' 'bout. I'm also American and from the same region as *they was*, even though *I'm country*. Still, I wasn't cool enough to understand *them's* remarks…too chill to notice. More in a later sermon. (And I'm sorry about those pronouns. It was killing me just to try to write it. *They* should know "their" would be a lot easier than sayin' "them's." [giggles])

Apparently, *they was* talking to whom *them's* mind thought I was. But leave it to *Mochalocks*; unfortunately, my *sistas* have no problem interpreting or translating that kind of bullshit for me. They said to me, *"No they didn't!"* (That's SAAVE; no commas. Hmm…had I missed an opportunity to be hot?)

Interestingly, my lack of understanding described here demonstrates that subtle forms of racism are only as effective as their capacity to be understood. Fortunately, my mother didn't focus much on White folks, nor did she teach us about African American cultures or the issue of racism. Unfortunately, the two often seem intertwined. (It's interesting how those Cherokees seem to view themselves as humans, as though they own America. Even so, as a young child, I recall visiting the Martin Luther King Jr. Center for Nonviolent Social Change in

Atlanta with my mother's relatives. They cherished King like family because he freed Native Americans as well, so naturally, I embraced him as my own.)

(I certainly hope I use the following phrase correctly.) This whole situation is like a Catch-22—a no-win scenario. We must be aware of racism and how it functions in our society. After all, it can be deadly. However, this awareness ensures the intended impact of racism. You know, there's a shield against the pettiness of racism when you're unaware of it or don't speak their language. It's like that automatic response: "I know you are, but what am I?"

How can we protect our children while also avoiding the reinforcement of the racial stratification present in this country? For instance, when schools began teaching about enslavers and segregation during Black History Month, I used to tell my children, "That's White people's history," to prevent creating an identity around something that needed to be taught but could potentially make them feel like second-class citizens.

Avoiding Perpetuation

I'm also careful not to splatter the vomit of oppression or to spew it onto others. For instance, one of my Indian friends (you know, the folks from India who were named, invaded, and terrorized by the British) was headed to Horseshoe Beach in Dixie County. I remember sayin' under my breath, "What the hell!? You're going where?" But then I just smiled and said, "Have fun!" I refrained from sharing my gloomy story about when my husband and I stopped at Fanning Springs on our way to Horseshoe Beach in 2004.

We were newly married at the time and still holding hands. As we walked through Fanning Springs, a little White girl with a slow, deep Southern drawl said to her parents, "Mom-Dad (as if they were one creature), look at this." All I could think at that moment was, "From the mouths of babes speaks the heart," merging two scriptures from the Bible for this little rascal.

My husband became increasingly unsettled as we drove deeper into Dixie County's sea of Confederate flags. (*Hakuna matata*...it's just a cheap form of home security.) We headed over to the "Redneck" vacation hotspot, Horseshoe Beach. Who doesn't like to hook worms (not hookworms, lol) on a hook for vacation?

I loved the area, especially Old Town, Florida, where, ironically, many of my clients lived when I was a mental health caseworker. (Hmm...there must be something in the water.) It was a *special* place; it felt like I had stepped back in time, and I always felt welcome because all of "them" had a grandchild, niece, or nephew who resembled me. Even so, to ease my Yankee husband's growing stress with "his people" and my Rosewood massacre horror stories, I told him, "Don't get cranky, Yankee; you can put me in the trunk if necessary."

Well, did you know that Indian people are here to surprise White folks because they pop up everywhere that the rest of us Brown and Black folks won't travel? Read the following sentence in a deep, scary voice (preferably in Southern African American Vernacular English) as if you're speaking to an Indian person who doesn't know Florida History. "*Youse* didn't hear *'bout* what *happen* in Rosewood?" Black folks do not like Levy or Dixie County. (Okay, *most* don't like them.)

The Power of Uzi

However, our horror stories do not move Indian people in the slightest. They respond unshaken with a bouncy, joyful Indian/British accent, "Hey, Black people, 'we' were enslaved, too! But did you know the British starved our ancestors to death when they took all the food out of India to feed their soldiers in their wars? Despite this, we still have the largest population in the world—one point four billion, as a matter of fact!" (Hmm...that's alarming!)

Nearly fifteen million Indians lost their lives at the hands of the British within about fifty years—more than during the Holocaust, yet not even close to the number of Native Americans slaughtered in the name of colonialism and Christianity. Furthermore, that number could be as high as a hundred million, depending on the source or the date range from the late 1880s to the 1920s. Either way, it's a tragedy. We need to teach a diversified world history because nobody talks about how the British nearly destroyed India. (Hmm...maybe that's why they bounced back so quickly; they instead tapped into their inner strength. I hear some Indian folks shouting into this book, "Rename India so it vibrates!" [giggles])

Whose history is it!?

Anyways, all those horrible, barbaric, demonic stories of enslavers—I'm serious, that's White People's history. That's why many White folks don't want *White history* taught in Florida schools; instead, *defensiveness* will be the history that is taught.

For instance, the iconic bridge in Birmingham, Alabama, which the bicyclist I met showed me a picture of him crossing, was named after a Ku Klux Klan (KKK) leader. Many people believe the bridge should be renamed, which may be an emotional reaction to childish taunting, as seen in many gestures to exhibit "White Supremacy." White people need to rename the bridge and other such landmarks when they are ready and able to reflect Love. That's when it should happen! However, if they fail to create a world that respects all people, these monuments stand as reminders of the mental and spiritual state of a significant portion of White America.

We must make room for their awakening with a deep-seated desire to reflect an America that isn't rooted in hate, sends subtle messages of resentment, or postures against its own people. Naming the Montgomery to Selma Bridge after a KKK leader is embarrassing and dishonors America globally. Certainly, White America has leaders that all can embrace, yet when we don't see them honored, it makes me question the legacy of my White ancestry. Is there anything more to it than a legacy of violence and oppression? How is it that I struggle to think of White leaders who have a legacy of peace and love? John Woolman, a Quaker, comes the closest, and most Americans have no idea who he was. Ralph Waldo Emerson and R. Buckminster Fuller, both Unitarians, are also admirable. Nonetheless, Jimmy Carter, the 39th President of the United States, remains arguably the most memorable.

However, I had to research to learn more names, and many were worth noting. I was reminded of the heroic story of Viola Liuzzo, a White housewife and mother of five, who heeded Martin Luther King Jr.'s call to cross the Montgomery Bridge into Selma. Upon returning to the airport after a successful demonstration, she was shot and killed by members of the KKK at the age of thirty-nine. She gave her life for freedom and showed that racism and "White Supremacy" impact us all, similar to the death of John F. Kennedy, the 35th president of the United States. (Injustice threatens all, which these lives will forever represent.)

I believe the Civil Rights Movement pioneers would be honored if White America were to name the bridge after Mrs. Liuzzo…when ready, of course. As White America moves to make these changes, we will know that their capacity to know Love has grown. Until then, many of these monuments should remain, and we should acknowledge the ongoing spiritual struggles of many White individuals, as the outer is always a reflection of the inner.

White history (my history and, probably genetically, your history, too) keeps becoming uglier. What we defend is like a big big red arrow drawing attention to what we want to conceal. (That'll preach!) It's likely more effective that way. Children used to always find their Bible-thumping parents' *Penthouse* magazines, right?

Unfortunately, many descendants of various European ethnic groups (yep, they're ethnic, too) are mistakenly identified with the concept of *White,* which they believe defines their identity. Nobody is an idea. Nobody! How could something so irrational occur in humanity? (We must understand how programming works or risk being programmed.)

Oddly enough, this all sounds like a video game or some virtual reality simulation. We have made little progress with this kind of mental programming because some individuals dwell in a virtual world, clinging to things that don't exist. Doesn't that sound absurd? Unfortunately, many "People of Color" unknowingly participate in this video game instead of opting out by saying, "I'm not playing this game with y'all anymore."

Freedom!

Black folks, it's time to stop paying so much attention to nonsense and the past. Our South Asian friends are here to teach us something. Please pay attention!

When we feed into every petty thing our racist cousins do to elevate themselves, it keeps the family feud going. Perhaps we can confront them with our Consciousness instead of our reactivity and help them dissolve their mental patterns. (Say what!? Is that what Gandhi did?) With Consciousness, there is no "*No she didn't*" or "*Oh hell no!*" and earrings stay on. (Again, SAAVE; no commas.)

Squashing Oppression Hugs,
—Sher! (The Common Snook)
Pause. Inhale. Exhale. Reflect.

P.S. Look out for my sermon, "You Can Escape *White* if You Want To," especially if you're Jewish.

P.P.S. No worries, *cancel culture;* I hear you. What Mahatma Gandhi said about Black people does not qualify as racism because actual racism involves having power and control over a group. He had no control over Black people, but he certainly expressed prejudiced views, just like you.

Indians suffered from racism and were treated similarly to "Black" people. The truth is that Gandhi was demoralized and degraded by the British and their brainwashing. Unfortunately, he chose to trample on the dignity of Africans to elevate his already fragile sense of self instead of loving all people equally, as King did. Perhaps Gandhi didn't realize where the "sonic pop" and the "black" people of India came from. (Almost every culture of people has used and abused Pan Alphas to elevate themselves.)

Unfortunately, self-loathing is common among those who have experienced racism (narcissistic abuse). Understanding this allows you to recognize their suffering with compassion, even if some resort to the same techniques used against them. This phenomenon is known as the cycle of abuse. Gandhi was not racist but instead a victim of racism—more on that another time.

P.P.P.S. *(Hey Patel, Black folks want me to interject for a moment here.)* The Black experience in America is a bit more complicated than the horrific Indian experience under the British. (No worries…this is not a competition.) Both groups faced enslavement, but African Americans also lost their homeland, language, culture, and had their belief system replaced. (Shiiiit!) A portion of humanity was psychologically obliterated! *(Black people, can I keep talkin'?)*

Today, Black individuals are physically free, yet many remain prisoners of the mind. Some never escape the cult, so to speak. ("Whoomp! There It Is." Did you hear the bell…I mean, the bass? Every time the bass drops, a Black angel awakens and earns its wings. *Whassup, Jared!)* Thankfully, the British were unable to penetrate Hinduism. Hindus cannot be ruled…except by their spouses, their mommas, their gurus, their swamis, their yogis, and umm…their MILs. (giggles) Nonetheless, many Black people who have escaped religion have unknowingly adopted a type of mental Hinduism; sadly, even with this freedom, some still believe they are the White person's concept of "the N-word." This reflects the extent of the (narcissistic abuse) experienced. If you listen closely, you can still hear the White man or woman speaking through some of them. (Wow, that's spooky!)

"The enslaver no longer needs to teach his dogma because many Black people willingly pass down the teachings to their children, generation after generation" (*Elicit* sermon, "Black People: The Overlooked Similarities Between Racism and Religion and the Path to Liberation"). Or consider this quote from the cult sermon: "The great thing about mind manipulation or undue influence, as it's termed today, is that once you're wired, you don't require regular tune-ups because your friends and family typically share the same beliefs and speak the same language. You will pass these teachings down to your children ['Whassup, nigga!'], keeping the tradition alive. This mental programming ensures that oppression becomes cyclical and continues to thrive for generations" (*Elicit* sermon, "Guard Your Heart—from Whom?"). It takes time to deprogram and achieve mental freedom, and the process doesn't begin until you can recognize the programming or veil. This is why it's so challenging to escape a cult.

Any Black person who tries to take the high road and claim that the troubling behavior or situation of many Black folks today isn't a result of ancestral

enslavement and oppression by White folks has been misled! It's clear many were never taught American history and have no understanding of how undue influence works. It would be like saying White folks' privilege today isn't a result of the ancestral enslavement and oppression of Black Americans. (Oh my god! Could somebody get me a picture of Yin and Yang?) Don't be deceived by the <u>illusion of time</u>. This is where the past, present, and future seem to coexist. *(Patel, do you see how messy it is? Thank the gods for Shiva!)*

(Sit in stillness with your eyes closed for 15 minutes a day; I promise it will transform your life!)

3. "Nobody Is Racist"

Disclosure Reminder…,

Some years ago, I watched a story on the news about a Black family demanding an apology from a White woman who bumped into them at a Chipotle in the Midwest. What state of mind demands an apology from someone who chooses not to give one? Would this apology have erased or corrected the situation? Would it have determined in the mind who was right? Say, "Uncle" — dammit! Perhaps this is why insurance companies advise against apologizing after a fender bender.

Anyhow, the Black family could not force an apology out of the White woman to perhaps temporarily relieve their anguish, so of course, they called her "ignorant" and "racist." (Ouch!) The White husband was appalled and asked, "Who the fuck do you think you guys are?" (He sounded like he was from *Joisy* with that question. I do admire his calm. He was a teddy bear. Probably a Pisces because he had on a purple shirt.) *Anywho,* this accusation seemed to be a way of momentarily dethroning the White ruler of society. It also could have served as a pressure release to ease some of their deep-seated pain of still living in a White-dominated America. But, of course, the White family had something for them, too. You guessed it! A gun!

The gun would come after the gaslighting, of course, which, unfortunately, was used to defend all White people. As she said, "You cannot just walk around calling White people racist." She then went so far as to deny and minimize the experiences that every "Person of Color" has faced in this country at some point. She spoke in a knowing, condescending tone, saying, "This is not that kind of world. White people are not racist. No one's Racist." (Ouch!) Was she inciting a riot? As mentioned, Martin Luther King Jr. once stated, "A riot is the language of the unheard." Did she need to throw every "Person of Color's" experiences under the bus to relieve herself from the pain of name-calling?

It was a cowardly sucker punch to those who suffer from racism, but it was a slam dunk if you intended to stand your ground, walk away right, and avoid hurtful accusations. Not only did she not defend or deny being racist, but she instead declared, "No one is racist," to those who needed to be seen and heard.

As I observed the unawareness on both sides, "You gonna shoot me?" the mother asked, sounding surprised. I could see the emergence of an ego war. This was the age-old conflict between the mental concepts of *Black* and *White.* However, without taking sides on who was "wrong or right," I would like to focus our attention on the statement, "No one is racist." Please don't confuse my highlighting of the White woman's statement with a suggestion that she was wrong. I'm simply emphasizing the statement because it was *profound* and enlightening!

Many Whites will look for an escape when accused of racism to protect the identity they wish to believe about themselves. Being called "a racist" seems to really hurt White people's feelings.

After witnessing the foolishness, I looked at my husband and said, "She's right; 'No one is racist.'" He looked at me, perplexed, because he didn't know where I was going with this. After all, I had often expressed that I'd never met a White person who didn't deal with racism of the mind to some degree. (Hold on…maybe two—but they were Jewish, which I don't technically see as White. Okay…and a few others, but it's sure hard to count.) This isn't to say that more don't exist, but at least not in my very diverse world, which includes some of the most kindhearted White people that I consider dear friends and family. Meanwhile, my husband continued to take a bite of his dinner while keeping his eyes on me, peering over his reading glasses, suspicious that he was about to be cornered. (Perhaps you can see that genuine kindness comes from a place far beyond the mind.)

Let's take an intermission! Enjoy "The Sound of Silence" by Simon & Garfunkel for a moment of introspection. I'll be back shortly.

Unfortunately, most people are products of social conditioning, where free will is merely a construct that their minds convince them they have. If the essence of who we are is neither—the mind, the body, nor any of the mental labels—we adopt, then "No one is racist." To clarify, I explained to my husband that the mind is racist, and if we are not our minds, then "No one is racist."

Look at me! This was the first time I had successfully separated White people from the mental disease of racism, as I call it, that many Americans suffer from and spread from generation to generation. So that you know, I'm not referring to the racism that is redefined today to encompass every act of human ignorance. I'm speaking about the racism that asserts "superiority," looks down upon, dominates, controls, discriminates, and affects the peaceful existence of a group of people: the French over the Haitians, White Americans over Black Americans, the Germans over the Jews, the British over the Indians, and the British and other Whites over nearly every ethnicity, to name a few. Understood?

Yes, all people can be prejudiced and unkind to one another. This situation exists within the framework of racism, but it is not racism itself. If White people

378

were aware that they are not their minds, perhaps some would be more willing to examine the racism…in…their minds, which is reflected in the society that their minds work so hard to hide and deny.

Unfortunately, many White people do not know how to escape this monster in their heads because it is a part of White American culture(s) and a systemic issue. However, there is a path to avoid being ruled by this programming, eventually leading to deprogramming. All that is required is to become aware of racism in the mind, accept its existence, and not fear how it makes you feel about yourself. You cannot fault yourself for what you were not responsible for creating.

The belief about those feelings does not define who you are, either. Once you realize you are not your thoughts, you can begin to witness racism in your life fade away, avoiding denial or allowing your mind to lie to itself. Once again, this breakdown requires awareness and acceptance. As I've pointed out before, salvation at every level requires humility.

Still, very few people take the route I described above because the mind fears being associated with negativity. Those who endure this type of pain will do whatever it takes to avoid disapproval from the same mind that holds racist beliefs. The mind perceives avoiding these mental labels as essential to prevent feeling inferior. We can't have our little feelings getting hurt, right?

Regrettably, any mental trick to avoid confronting racism is a disservice to humanity and cultivates an environment for it to continue growing and thriving. In simpler terms, what you resist, persists. Unfortunately, these individuals remain prisoners of their minds.

I hope you can grasp the insanity of the mind in this example. It dares to masquerade as you, and when you attempt to confront it, it will shame the false version of yourself back into submission, escaping through denial. "You're racist. You're a disgrace, and you know it. Stop!!! No, I'm not racist," the mind retorts. It's a never-ending cycle. What a terrible psychological game of torment to play with oneself when freedom is an option.

Setting You Free Hugs,
—Sher! (The Common Snook)
Pause. Inhale. Exhale. Reflect.

P.S. What's the worst that could happen if we began to view those hurting as ourselves? I hurt because you hurt, and I'm sorry for the suffering this world has inflicted upon you. (Hmm…but it needs to be sincere. [giggles])

379

P.P.S. Speaking of countin' White folks on one hand! I met a regular ol' White man who works at the Home Depot off Tower Road in Gainesville. We got to talkin' 'bout refrigerators, Yeti coolers, camping…and Love. He shared some of that Love with me and let me know we were on the same team— beeyotch! Times are changing for sure!

(Stop playing mind games for 15 minutes a day; I promise it will transform your life!)

Why this picture? Well, it's Florida, of course! No other reason. I've always liked this photo because you can tell I'm standing relatively close to this big-mouthed creature who will eat you for dinner regardless of your race. Albert is not racist. (TCM)

4. You Can Escape *White* If You Want To; It's Not a Privilege

Disclosure Reminder…,

Speaking of privilege! I had an epiphany while driving past a store packed with SUVs and big-ass pickup trucks as if it were an Easter service. There's one group in America that has superstores to support their leisurely, privileged lifestyles. Excuse me, these folks are called sportsmen. Meanwhile, "Karen" is *pissed,* taking her wrath out on innocent people because she's home cookin' while he's out playing…again.

These stores are impressive and eye-opening, revealing who has the most leisure time in America. It doesn't matter if you are the bougie type of White guy who drives a Tesla or the blue-collar guy who prefers a Chevy; there's a big big, big-ass toy store for each. The locations are usually less than a mile apart for convenience. These sportsmen bring home $400 Yeti coolers from R.E.I. and can buy a boat from the other store. (Pardon me, R.E.I. is a co-op superstore. Progressive White folks love co-ops!)

Remember, my husband is a White guy. I still don't understand his love for camping, a need to sleep outdoors when there are folks whose lives are only a step up from camping. This must be the adult alternative to White boys living vicariously through gangster rap. *(Whassup, Jammin'son!)* Apparently, privilege can be tough, as some need to rough it to feel real. (That's deep. *Can you relate to this, Harry? Ask Meghan what she thinks.*) Hey, whatever floats your boat, right?

However, buying a $400 cooler to sleep outside is not a privilege. You can get a really fantastic hotel room with dinner included for that price. Don't get me wrong; I love camping, especially the kind where my husband takes our boys out for the weekend and leaves me at home. Our half-White boys, with their *half-*half-White privilege, little sportsmen that they are, love them some camping, too. One of them would be shootin' *stuff* if I let him.

Considering that I don't identify with "race," I told my husband one day, "You don't have to be White if you don't want to," and he looked at me strangely. (Rachel Dolezal knows what I'm talkin' 'bout. She tried to escape being White, but y'all wouldn't let her.) It's difficult to escape the cult, so to speak.

The notion of *White,* or even *Black,* is one of many mind-made identities that exist solely in our heads. *White* is an ideology; it's not real outside of the game of life in which we all participate. I also realized something powerful when I made that statement.

Interestingly, suggesting that "White people don't have to be White if they don't want to be" offers them a fleeting glimpse of their privileged lives. It was like a flash of light, allowing them to finally recognize that sweet White privilege. Who would want to relinquish White privilege? And when you consider the idea of giving it up, you start to see just how valuable it truly is and perhaps finally acknowledge the advantages you possess. Hmm…what is your hesitation, White allies? "I kind of like knowing I'm large and in charge and don't have to think twice about where I fit in society," an honest fellow once told me. I know; it's incredible. I can see. (You were supposed to read "I can see" with a Carol Burnett Southern accent and a side-eye.)

However, when it comes to the soul and entering the Kingdom of God, White is not a privilege, as many people are led to believe. Simply put, without so much "Christianese," we can also refer to this "*special* place" as connecting with "the Source." As the scripture states, "It's damn hard for a rich 'man' to enter the Kingdom of God," which could very well imply a *White man* (sorry, Babe) because *rich* is relative. Pardon the sexist language. White women, this is for you, too. *(Whassup, Jill and Becky!)* Please don't get worked up. I'm not talkin' 'bout your Heaven. If that's your perspective, we're on two different pages. Just so you know, you can still go to Hell or Heaven if you choose. It's all good! (This section completes a comment I made in the earlier Jewish sermon. Remember?)

The power that White people possess is an asset in this physical world. I don't express this to be offensive but to acknowledge the challenges White people face spiritually simply by identifying with the concept of *White. (Careful Jews!)* There is so much to give up. Jesus said, "Come and follow me," but you must lay down all those privileges first. Is it too good?

Oddly enough, I have noticed my husband's own awakening as he gets closer to embracing the idea. He recognizes that White is not who he is, but sometimes he can't resist returning for a taste because the cake is just too good to resist. And I'm guilty, too; sometimes, I use some of his *White* when I need to demand a refund or obtain some of those privileges he doesn't deserve. *White* still yields favorable outcomes, you know. I tell him, "You go in there and make demands with your corporate White tone." (By the way, that's the tone of entitlement.)

Did I ever tell y'all that with White privilege, you can push a big big tub full of cheap crap past the security checkpoint when exiting Walmart? Cheap crap could be falling all out of the cart! They told my good-looking husband, "Have a nice day!" (We hippies don't like plastic bags.)

On another day, my good-looking husband was driving under the influence of jet lag when he mistakenly ran a red light in Lady Lake, Florida, on his way home from the Orlando Airport just after midnight. (Thank goodness all the older White folks were in bed.) The officer pulled him over and asked for his license and registration, but he couldn't find any paperwork. While I was listening on the phone, my husband interrupted the young officer (with the tone of entitlement) and said, "I'm tired. I just got off an international flight. I've been looking for a charging station for this damn electric Mercedes the rental car company gave me, which was only half-charged. It's about to die! I've been driving in circles!" They began to chuckle like old friends, two good ol' boys.

Meanwhile, I'm on the phone, *pissed*! I'm in the background yelling, "Arrest his ass! He stole the Mercedes! Slam him to the ground!" He didn't even get a ticket for running the light and driving under the influence without registration. They should've taken the keys from his White-ass. But thankfully, the mosquitoes at the charging station woke his ass up.

However, unlike my earlier experience driving through Palatka that same month on my way back from the beach, a kind young White officer stopped me because I forgot to turn on my headlights at dusk. *(Yep, you remember me. I'm hard to forget. Ensure your buddies read this.)* While speaking with the young man, I told my son not to move because I spotted two poorly trained White officers creeping up behind us on his right. (That's how innocent people get shot!) He was completely unaware that two cops were standing just behind him. All he had to do was make one move, and they could have claimed they feared for their lives! (Those young men need better training and awakening!!!) I'm not sure why they were so aggressive, though. How many officers does it take to screw in a lightbulb? Sometimes, my son looks White at night, but maybe they thought he was Mexican or Latino that day since many assume he speaks Spanish. Anyhow, I wish my husband were there to interrupt them.

However, I do not take *White* to 504 (education accommodations) meetings for my son because it can be tough to tone it down in time. This attitude can really complicate things. White women don't realize they can't stand it, either. It isn't just the male ego they are frustrated with. This *thang*, like "Karen" (maybe we should call it "Egochad"), has a unique ego. You ain't getting accommodations easily when you have a White, white-collared daddy. Nobody has empathy for you. Hmm…I wonder why. (Add a little Carol Burnett personality to that last sentence as well, with a rising pitch at the end.)

I'm sorry, but *White* is not a privilege. (wink) Let's end this with one of my favorite country songs from 2020: "Better Together" by Luke Combs, which I dedicate to humanity. Even though he's talkin' 'bout a woman, I like the heart of the song, Yin and Yang, perfect harmony. Only a Pisces from Huntersville, North Carolina, could produce such a beautiful song. (You should hear my husband singing this song to me in the background.)

Hugs to my peeps who are diligently working to awaken and break free from the chains of *White*, bringing humanity closer together,
　　—Sher! (The Common Snook)

Pause. Inhale. Exhale. Reflect.

P.S. Surprisingly, my "Redneck" last name, which some of y'all may not know about, is also the name of an award-winning game fish in Florida. *The common snook* is a sought-after catch and one of the best! They are most recognized for their explosive strikes. (I warned you!) However, these sportsmen believe that anglers of all skill levels can handle *the common snook.* (They're right!) You also won't find a *common snook* in your local grocery store because this delicate meat or manna is too delicious to be packaged and resold as they do in the prominent big box religions. (I bet "Rednecks" are jealous of my last name.) Anyhow, they should stock a copy of my book in *Bass Pro Shops* so those sportsmen can read it while fishin', a.k.a. meditatin'.

P.P.S. Update! You should have seen my butt desperately digging through my sportsman's doomsday survival gear during Hurricane Helene…and of course, he wasn't home. (Probably fishin'.) Hmm…that $400 Yeti cooler sure came in handy when we lost power. "That man" even had a stove with propane tanks. Wow!

P.P.P.S. I suppose I need to give these "White" folks seeking freedom from the ideology a new liberating label. How about "F.A.I.R.," which stands for *fair, accepting, inclusive,* and *responsible*? Feel free to try it out! "I'm not White; I'm Fair!" (giggles)

(Stop *acting* White or right for 15 minutes a day; I promise it will transform your life!)

5. Cut from the Same Cloth: The Protective Veils of Black and White Americans

Let's activate our listening skills. This sermon requires hearing beyond what you perceive to be yourself.

Disclosure Reminder...,

The great author James Baldwin once said, "Negroes know far more about [W]hite Americans; it can almost be said, in fact, that they know about [W]hite Americans what parents—or, anyway, mothers—know about their children...." (*The New Yorker*, A Letter from a Region in My Mind). At the same time, many who relate to this perspective or understanding of Whites never harness the ability or tool to understand themselves better or inquire about what prevents White Americans from achieving this awareness. Certainly, it cannot be as simple as stubbornness.

Protective veils often exist among individuals or cultures that have been aggressors or have suffered abuse. This phenomenon can also be seen in unhealthy parent-child relationships. It's a way we shield ourselves from the pain of shame or endure situations we cannot physically change. In a sense, we deceive ourselves to avoid confronting painful truths.

Suppose a significant portion of White America wears a protective veil, which the rest of us claim to detect, that safeguards their sense of self. Is it possible that a comparable number of Black Americans have developed a similar protective veil to endure some of the most inhumane treatment? Once again, this resembles an unhealthy parent-child relationship between the abuser and the abused.

What's interesting about collective veils, a belief system embedded in a culture, is that they are passed down through generations, preserving the artificial notion of self along with the collective artificial idea of race and culture. Additionally, we can observe this collective veil in those who resist teaching inclusive and diversified American history. Counter beliefs or new perspectives (veils!) are formed to avoid confronting painful truths. These veils are so thick and well-constructed that the mind doesn't have to face the reality it seeks to avoid.

The simple fact that there are things we notice in others that they can't see should make us more open to hearing about the veils we cannot spot in ourselves. However, I've tested this theory in many situations, and common

385

sense is often not applied here. The mind does a fantastic job of protecting us from the decay, so to speak, that we fear would tarnish our identity if examined more closely.

If this idea is realized and I have your attention, again, is it possible that there are Black Americans trapped behind a veil they can't see through, similar to the veil that many can see in White Americans? If so, how do we learn to identify something if our minds protect us from seeing it?

Well, I'm glad you asked, and the answer is quite simple. Paying attention to defensiveness is essential since the truth often lies just behind what the mind passionately defends. Observing defensiveness reveals a veil that likely protects and projects an artificial version of yourself.

For example, forget about tackling this individually or helping a friend overcome strongholds, as opposition to the self will likely trigger an ugly defense mechanism. "You don't know me; I don't wear a veil. I know who I am. I'm not hiding from anything. A real friend wouldn't be so judgmental." Yep, you've spotted the veil or the false self talking back to you. "No, you didn't. This veil shit is bullshit," they will argue. (As you can see, I have experience talking with egos, but I've learned my lesson.)

Addressing this collectively and suggestively allows the mind to find an escape. It may say, "This doesn't apply to me. This is about them and not me." Again, this is why Jesus spoke in parables; egos dislike direct confrontation.

Subtleness also enables individuals to manage their feelings privately without needing to fully humble themselves, helping them avoid discomfort. Introspection and vulnerability take time and grow stronger with practice.

In simple terms, we can always see the speck in someone else's eye, but we often can't or are unwilling to see the plank in our own (referencing Matthew 7:3-5 from the Bible). Suppose we allow ourselves to trust and reflect, using our knowledge and insight to appreciate the lives of others. In that case, this can become a valuable tool for freeing ourselves from similar mental prisons. You got this! This book can help!

Setting You Free Hugs,
　—Sher! (The Common Snook)
Pause. Inhale. Exhale. Reflect.

P.S. You've heard the saying, "We are only as strong as our weakest link." America becomes its strongest and best when Pan Alpha Americans and White Americans are free. 異

6. Chi (Qi) or Is It Cancer?

Disclosure Reminder...,

As you have heard me share, Western medicine has by far the best emergency care services in the world...as they say. In a near-death situation, you are in some of the best hands. I can attest to this. I believe in giving honor where honor is due. However, Western medicine is a baby compared to some health treatments found in Eastern and African cultures, which feature therapies that date back over 5,000 years.

Good health and well-being should never be about who is right, Western versus "alternative" medicine. But for many, that's exactly how this debate registers in their minds. It's a competition to them: "us against them." (What foolishness!) And those who dislike this simplification of the games humanity plays, when we should all work together to improve the lives of those sick, they...I mean, the die-hard followers of Western medicine use its methods as the standard to assess validity. This is similar to how Christians use Christianity as the only source to measure truth. "Well, the Bible says...," they explain.

Regarding medicine, critics often say, "This has no scientific basis or hasn't been proven or supported by science." Western medicine is so dominant; yet again, it is still a child and behaves similarly to a child, demanding that others bow down to its authority to be seen as "superior." When promoting "alternative" health treatments, one must always include a disclaimer stating, "My treatment, which may help you, is not supported by 'the establishment' of Western medicine."

There are many aspects of this existence that we don't understand, and trying to fit everything into a single, limited system is futile. No worries...we are familiar with all the rebuttals framed as protecting people. For instance, Eastern medicine views new conditions like gender dysphoria differently—not as a condition at all or something that requires hormone therapy and surgical removal of genitalia. Instead, Eastern medicine focuses on removing energy blocks, just as they do with many of the other medical conditions that Western medicine neatly categorizes and attempts to treat or "correct."

These alternative medicines uphold the importance of nurturing the human soul. However, Western medicine has, so to speak, lost its soul. Almost every condition that humankind struggles with—outside of accidents or environmental toxins—has an emotional component. (Heck, I'm probably creating an energy block just from the emotions needed to address this insanity.)

*

Not too long ago, I visited my doctor for a routine exam. You know, the one where they say, "Scoot to the end of the table," and you're never quite there...that one. During the exam, my doctor seemed concerned as she removed her gloves, sat me up, and gave me *the hug of death.* You know "the hug." The one that says, "I have horrible news." I was thinking, *What the hell!?* I did not come there expecting to receive "the hug." She explained that she felt a strong pulse in my uterus. She looked me in the eye like my days were numbered and said she had never felt anything like that before in all her years of practicing medicine. (She must not have heard about me, though I did feel honored.) She wanted me to go for an ultrasound immediately since she was concerned that something was feeding blood to the area...in short, C A N C E R or another "pulsating aneurysm"!

Interestingly, just minutes before she had me hurry to the end of the table, I mentioned that I had recently started seeing an acupuncturist. I explained that after my first visit, he had miraculously treated me for over fifteen food sensitivities, along with subsequent headaches and physical pains that I had suffered from for more than fifteen years. Yes, after...one...treatment. I was *pissed*! It wasn't supposed to be that easy, especially since I was on the "No-Food Diet" and could only eat vegetables and protein. At the end of this appointment, my acupuncturist asked me how long I had been experiencing food sensitivities. I replied, "Since my oldest was born." He nodded and said, "Pregnancy, that'll do it."

I continued to explain to my doctor that I had initially sought out the acupuncturist because the pains I had in specific spots on the right side of my body for many years suddenly connected, becoming one and unified in a straight line. (So let me tell you the whole story.) I felt a shocking wave starting from my lower right molar, traveling down my neck, through my chest, centered through my nipple, down my hip, moving through my leg, and then finishing with the electric shock sensation through my toes. It was amazing!

The feeling was so intense that it caused my body to jerk as I lay in bed. Yet, I was fascinated because it formed a straight line that I could almost visualize...or see. Perhaps I was inside looking at it, as I remember the line being a weak grayish-blue color and not as vibrant as I knew it should be. (That's 4D quantum physics, lol.) I woke my husband and said, "Babe, I have an electric shock running from my head to my toes." I added, "It's like a meridian line of energy running through the body." I was also confident that if I had one on the right, I also had one on the left. (This shock wave or surge of energy led my husband to study acupuncture officially. The Divine knows how to capture our attention. "I'm going to electrocute your wife, alright?")

In the following weeks, this shocking sensation persisted, causing significant discomfort in my lower molar and prompting a visit to my dentist to ensure everything was okay. He took X-rays but found no issues.

I continued to research this experience, and each time I googled meridians in the body, I was led to acupuncture, but I couldn't find anything to validate my experience. As I continued to share my mystical story, I was referred to an acupuncturist in town.

I didn't want just any acupuncturist. Before they became my practitioner, this person had to validate my experience to earn my trust. (By the way, their spiritual state is paramount, while not perfect, but also not too flaky.) I explained my story to the soft-spoken gentleman who seemed to absorb me through the phone (again, 4D quantum physics, lol), and he responded that he'd never heard of anyone feeling their meridians or Chi (also known as Spirit, Prana, or life energy), but he didn't deny the possibility. (That, too, was an honor.) He said, "If I hear you correctly, what you are describing sounds like the stomach meridian, and I would guess that you have a lot of food sensitivities." (He was showin' off.)

Wow, he really caught my attention! Comfort foods like bread and butter, chocolate, peanut butter, coffee, alcohol :), dairy, and nuts were not a part of my life. It was so bad that I would be in trouble if I ever mistakenly ate anything sweet that was more than a gluten-free waffle with berries! Without seeing me, he said, "That's an easy fix," which I didn't take too seriously. After all, I had never tried acupuncture before, and I had those sensitivities for years.

So, back to the table exam and *the hug of death* from my primary care doctor. I asked if she thought the strong pulse had anything to do with my recent acupuncture appointment, which focused on reading pulses and tuning the body's energy. She said she didn't know, but it wouldn't hurt to run it by him. I was surprised and glad she was open to "alternative" medicine, or at least so I thought.

I contacted my acupuncturist, whom I like to refer to as Sensei, and told him everything verbatim. Honestly, I could have sworn I heard him giggle. He said, "You have a strong Chi, and it will serve you well." (I really liked how that sounded, lol.) He also mentioned that, unfortunately, traditional doctors are quick to suspect cancer. Still, he noted that my doctor's sensitivity was increasing because she could now detect a pulse in the human body that had always been present. She could feel the life energy known as Chi.

I relayed the message to my doctor, but by then, they weren't interested in hearing what I had to say or considering my acupuncturist's perspective, and they proceeded to order the ultrasound. I understood their position; this industry must follow specific protocols. At the same time, I was confident that my acupuncturist knew what he was talkin' 'bout and would not lead me astray. I contemplated canceling the ultrasound that my insurance *did not* cover. Still, I didn't want to risk being dismissed from their practice, as doctors often fear liability and have little tolerance for noncompliance. (Believe me, I have been excused before, lol.) So, I decided to pay for the ultrasound...*for her*...as a gift.

When asked, "What brings you here today?" during my ultrasound appointment, I shared both stories: my doctor's experience and my acupuncturist's explanation with the ultrasound technician and radiologist. I could tell they, too, were uninterested in hearing the story about my acupuncturist's Chi explanation. However, with a hint of arrogance, the two confirmed there was nothing in my uterus to be concerned about and seemed to giggle at the notion that my doctor said she felt a pulse—like she was being silly. (This giggling was getting out of hand.) My primary care doctor had to adhere to her science and protocol, and she didn't subscribe to what my acupuncturist suggested and confirmed that she felt. Yet her colleagues, in a way, mocked her for saying she felt a pulse. And I was caught in the middle with a $250 bill. (Hmm...I know just the price I'm *gonna* charge her for a copy of my book.)

At my next appointment, my acupuncturist explained that Chi, our life energy, resides in the lower abdomen. He even showed me a diagram of the unique hiding place of the *Cu Chi* on a poster on his wall. (giggles)

Regardless, I felt compelled to share this story after a friend urged me to see a doctor about some discomfort I was experiencing. I appreciated the concern; however, this individual is also a local physician, which makes them somewhat biased. I clarified that I don't rush to the doctor for every minor issue. I'm the type you would have to drag to the emergency room after a month of unbearable pain to discover something like a brain aneurysm, and I'll live to tell it—dammit!

My friend, the doctor, recognized my defiance and decided to challenge me. (*They* was about to take me down!) "You can't go inside and see what's going on," *they* said as if a Western doctor was the only one who could diagnose me.

They didn't realize I had never given up my right to analyze myself and explore within, without the need for an MRI. When they said I couldn't go inside to see what was happening, I almost asked *with attitude,* "Are you sure about that? Can you feel your Chi?" I wasn't worried about my discomfort because I knew my Chi was communicating with me as it always had. (I'm sorry, some of y'all will still require science to catch up with reality before you're willing to believe and learn to listen to your body that speaks.)

But let's not leave without the whole drama! There's more! This is for the locals and those with hospital bills and debt collectors as friends.

You know, after *the hug of death*, I reluctantly took my ass to the emergency room (E.R.) that same day because of my history of dismissing symptoms, "pulsating aneurysms." Well, UF Health Shands Hospital here in Gainesville had me sitting for six hours that day, but they were slick; they drew blood from all "fifty" of us in the waiting room to "expedite the service." This made me suspicious that this was their unethical way of charging folks without admitting them to the E.R. ("This would be like a mechanic charging you for pulling into their lot.")

Anyhow, after six hours without service, late into the night, I asked if I could go home. The staff agreed, and I was told I could get my bloodwork online the following day and return if needed. Do you know Shands sent me a $2,000 E.R. bill, even though I was never admitted to the E.R.? I never left the waiting room. I paid for my bloodwork, but not the *B.S.* E.R. charge.

Shands is going to make me sue them! They know most people would set up a payment plan because it would cost them more to sue, and they fear it would impact their credit. (But I don't give a SHIT, SHANDS!!!) They exploit the middle class because they know we like to buy shit on credit that we don't need.

Additionally, when I requested that my medical records and bill be reviewed to dispute the charges before they sent me to collections, they informed me that I had to pay them $50 first. (giggles) What does it say when you flip the U and F in *Shands UF?*

I should have written an article for the newspaper about the unpleasant nurse that day who told a beautiful African American college student who fell to the floor while vomiting, "Get up! You're not the only one who is sick in here!" (Still, she was right.) She didn't notice me watching her behind my mask, foggy glasses, and big ol' blanket. I bet she thought I was asleep. That's when I decided it was time for me to go home. I didn't want Grumpy Nurse, "Karen," taking care of me, especially since I had a demon nurse some years ago. Oh no, not again!

Hmm…I wonder if there's anyone I could call to handle this mess? Let me try this powerhouse, MD, MS, FCCM, FASN, Senior Associate Dean for Research Affairs at the University of Florida College of Medicine; Professor of Medicine, Surgery, Anesthesiology and Physiology, and Functional Genomics; and Director of the Intelligent Clinical Care Center. (Damn! That was a long-ass title…enough to make a man jealous…or stay home with the kids.) I bet folks listen to her. *See, SHANDS, I know how to play this game, too. You ripped off the wrong local.* Even so, bill collectors are here to build our character. No worries, I haven't F-bombed anyone…yet.

Anywho, I hold *the dramatic hug of death* responsible for this mess, and the fact that the medical industry, once again, has lost its soul. The industry exploits people for money and fails to teach physicians that there is a connection between the body, mind, and spirit, and that each individual has a unique energy pattern. When this pattern is out of balance, symptoms manifest physically, also known as illness. *(Whassup, Doc! I don't fault you; you're one of the best.)*

Many don't realize that Western medicine can become like a religion when its believers refuse to listen to anything that doesn't align with their understanding or "proven methods." This is where I say that science-minded people can become as stubborn and narrow-minded as religious folks. I never understand why some folks don't take a few seconds to hear the compelling testimonies of their friends. Instead, most would rather walk away "right" when *we humans* know so little about this existence. Let us not conclude life before it's over. We still have a great deal to learn.

Three-Thousand-Year-Old Chi Hugs,
    —Sher! (The Common Snook)
        Pause. Inhale. Exhale. Reflect.

P.S. For the record, since I live in the West and Westerners tend to sue and silence folks, I will comply and bow down to the allopathic gods and "Big Pharma" and say, "The FDA has not approved the content of this sermon."

P.P.S. Update! Shands UF (*Unbelievably Funny*) canceled my pseudo debt after dragging me through it for over a year. Someone must have made a phone call on my behalf. Hmm…they *gonna* fix my credit so I can buy cheap shit I can't afford? And what about my pain and suffering!? 🏃

7. "Pseudoscience"

Yes, that's Jesus in the background. My real estate agent gave me that picture as a gift.

Disclosure Reminder...,

"Pseudoscience" is a demonizing term that conveys contempt or disapproval, rendering someone else's contribution to the world inferior to the dominant view. However, it can be simply defined as a collection of beliefs assumed to be based on the scientific method. Still, the phrase carries a negative connotation and is often used from a position of "superiority" to undermine another form of knowledge. Strangely, those who speak English and are devalued by this approach continue to participate in this injustice—hopefully without being aware of it. English is complicated in that way.

Let's examine several perspectives: name-calling, terms, and phrases that stem from dominant views designed to counter-protest, crush, and/or reinforce a sense of inferiority in others, while elevating one's self-proclaimed "superiority." (I've always gotten a good chuckle out of Westerners who call some folks immigrants but refer to themselves as "expats." Wow!)

Some examples are:
- Racism and "White Supremacy" created and assigned terms like "Black," "Negro," "N-word," "K-word," "wetback," "White trash," "Jim Crow," "illegal," and "anti-Whiteness."
- Nationalism, paired with industrialism and its perceived "superiority" within the Western mindset, gave rise to the concept of the "Third World" and phrases like "developing nations." They also attack

opposing political, social, and economic perspectives with names like "socialists," "communists," "conspiracy theorists," "leftists," and "extremists."

- Religionism, particularly Christianity, has assigned names like "anti-Christ," "sinner," "lost," "heathen," "wicked," and "infidel."
- Western medicine(ism), under the umbrella of modern science, employs disparaging terms, such as "pseudoscience," "quacks," "anti-vaxxers," and "alternative medicine." *(Right, Robert Kennedy Jr.?)*
- Transgenderism has led to the creation of terms and phrases such as "transphobia," "hater," "cisgender," "women who ovulate," and "violence." (They understand how the demonizing game works.)

Now, let's examine the concepts of science and pseudoscience!

Science is a form of knowledge that extends beyond what is obtained through the scientific method. Labeling something as "pseudoscience" implies it lacks validity and suggests that modern science is the sole arbitrator of truth. This term is often used to dismiss other forms of knowledge and human experiences. Instead, it may be more appropriate to explore the various forms of knowledge and the methods through which they are acquired rather than resorting to a strong, demonizing term that completely shuts down a viewpoint. Pseudoscience has become synonymous with false knowledge, yet knowledge exists in many diverse forms.

Many alternate forms of understanding are far older than modern science, yet few people are interested in researching whether these methods could compete with or surpass contemporary science. (We can't have that, right?) Instead, we often focus on what generates revenue, and these ideas are frequently supported by falsified research *(Right, Robert?)* designed to create the illusion of scientific validity. This mainstream ideology has gained a following greater than that of Christianity and Islam combined. It has become the benchmark of all truth. In a way, I'm grateful the world has found this common ground, but at what cost? Like any religion, some extremists interpret everything literally and overlook the essence of the original teachings. *(Right, Robert?)*

These followers begin to accept the dogma as if it were "the only way," forgetting that science is a state of mind, not a fixed set of beliefs. They forget that "It's not a belief but a commitment to life, a dedication to seeking and being open to innovative ideas and new understandings" (*Elicit* sermon, "Mysticism as a Spiritual Path").

From the mentality of "us against them," it's challenging for Westerners to acknowledge that ancient Chinese knowledge might make the West seem like infants or even preemies. However, much of this ancient wisdom was destroyed during the Mao era. Most Chinese now embrace and support modern perspectives. Communism, like any other flawed economic system, breeds desperation. Unfortunately, many Chinese now prioritize money (math and science) over less recognized forms of knowledge.

Here's a fun fact! Only foolish minds—believe in science alone. *(Don't get offended, Bhutabhavyabhavatprabha.)* Oddly enough, many science followers accept history without question, which is often falsified and one-sided. Should we trust scientists who also believe in history? Or should we label them pseudo-scientists? They may argue, "Well, that's what happened!" Then I will respond, "Can you prove it?" It seems we are willing to accommodate only certain sources of knowledge.

You have heard me reference acupuncture throughout this book and the gentleman who treated me for more than fifteen food sensitivities after just one visit. Let me tell you a bit about his story: He was initially a pharmacist and researcher at the University of Florida's Shands Hospital for over three decades. (Uh-oh, here's an unexpected bunny trail! Sorry about that.)

Acknowledging he was a pharmacist for Shands UF sadly captures your attention. This is similar to stating that White researchers support the reality that the Americas had people of dark skin pigmentation before the African slave trade. However, if a Black person made this assertion without referencing the White arbiter of truth, it might not be as credible to some. The early American census reports that there were Black folks in the Americas before the slave trade. They counted them!

As a famous explorer once said, these people are just as numerous across the globe and depicted artwork of natives, featuring them with afro puffs at the back of their heads. Who else has afro puffs other than Pan Alphas? Many thriving cultures of various skin tones and hair textures existed here long before White folks arrived, just like on every other continent. Yet, heaven forbid we teach real American history. (This sound bite was brought to you by The Common Snook. Sorry, White folks, I don't remember all my references. However, this researcher often referred to White people as "albinos" or "an albino race." Unfortunately, I have forgotten his name. But Black folks have no problem considering the possibility. It's interesting how that works.)

Alright, back to the Shands UF pharmacist! He noticed research showing that acupuncture was as effective as, if not more so, than some drugs modern science prescribes for specific conditions. (Uh-oh, here comes the FDA!) This should capture the attention of any well-educated person. He began to question why we would prescribe potentially dangerous drugs when there are safer and more effective treatments available. (Somebody must not have told him about "Big Pharma." Shoot, I could have answered that question for him.)

His curiosity led him to study acupuncture and become a Classical Five-Element Acupuncturist while continuing to work at Shands Hospital. He prescribed drugs during the day and practiced acupuncture on the side. Beautiful! (I'm surprised they didn't feed his butt to the gators. I don't know how he got away with that.) If that isn't hypocrisy, I don't know what is. (I'm being funny, y'all! [giggles] No worries…I'm sure he "believed" in those drugs.) He was quite the Maverick with that kind of out-of-the-box thinking. Normal folks tend to be more conforming and arrogant. (Here, *normal* is not a compliment. Got it?) "That's pseudoscience or the placebo effect," they'll say, like a bonehead, which makes them feel "superior."

Anyhow, he became so obsessed with his research that he began decoding 3,000-year-old scientific evidence for boneheads, aligning with their religion and with the shallow mindsets that couldn't accept simple science like, "I was once lost, but now I'm found," or "I couldn't eat peanuts, but now I can." "Can you prove it?" they would ask. Or "Did you write it down?" because if you didn't document it, it didn't happen, right?

When you observe these types of results emerging from science predating the modern scientific method, common sense should prompt you to ask, "What is the source of this knowledge?" because it's clear that there is something greater than the scientific method. Asking this question doesn't make you anti-modern science; it simply indicates that you possess common sense and haven't subscribed to a pseudo-belief that denies the existence of something greater than human intellect. Some refer to it as God, for lack of a better word, but using common sense does not imply that you believe in deities or that the concept of a greater intelligence or higher power refers to a little man in your heart. (giggles)

Could there be knowledge that comes from beyond traditional intellect? The concept of connecting with our higher self suggests that there is. I wouldn't write this book if that weren't the case. Even though modern science hasn't caught up with explaining all aspects of our existence, it's foolish to dismiss something the human eye can validate. Acupuncture anesthesia speaks for itself, as doctors operate while the patient is awake and fully conscious. (Yikes!) I don't completely understand the science; however, seeing is enough to spark my curiosity. Even so, I wouldn't be so arrogant as to call it "pseudoscience" simply because it doesn't follow a methodology I am accustomed to. Again, pseudoscience tends to suggest falsity.

With that said, guess who was invited to speak to groups of doctors? You guessed it: the hypocrite, Mr. Pseudoscience, and his assistant, Placebo! Because some of those boneheads were starting to listen and use common sense, or they had witnessed, "She was once sick, and now she's healed." It'll get *ya* every time! That's why Jesus had folks on their knees—physicians, too. (Nope, I have no proof whether Jesus ever walked this earth, but the stories of Christ/Krst are still profound.)

In a sense, modern science and Western medicine have lost their souls, neglecting to acknowledge that there is a dimension to life beyond the physical. Classical Five-Element Acupuncture, which differs from traditional acupuncture in the U.S. (not *special,* of course and *careful* when they put a name in front of the science), aims to treat not only the symptoms but also the root cause, which almost always includes a mind-body component (except for those of us suffering from exposure to environmental toxins from playing in the Gainesville Superfund site as kids).

But heaven forbid anyone who supports these alternative methods or ancient treatments gets sick. Assholes will come out of the woodwork, saying, "How is that acupuncture working for you now?" What is wrong with humanity? Why the childish games? (These folks must have always been last in line in kindergarten—the same folks who don't allow others to merge in traffic.)

Knowledge is not about deeming one group or method superior or inferior; it is about understanding the nuances of each. Supporting Eastern medicine isn't about dismissing Western medicine. (Hmm…this line sure sounds familiar. "Identifying as multi-racial has nothing to do with denying heritage." We must move away from black-and-white thinking.)

I can't talk about ignorance forever. My only hope is that humanity will embrace knowledge and not reject it simply because it doesn't make sense to us or doesn't come from the "right culture." Not all knowledge derives from the scientific method, nor is the world subject to its validation. Scientific inquiry, research, and testing are necessary to avoid irrational conclusions. However, we must remain open to seeking all forms of knowledge and asking questions to prevent drawing faulty conclusions. This system of checks and balances works together nicely.

Just Plain Ol' Disappointed Hugs,
   —Sher! (The Common Snook)
Pause. Inhale. Exhale. Reflect.

P.S. Speaking of pseudoscience and irrational conclusions! After my brain surgery, I was on blood thinners for about six months to reduce the risk of clotting around the surgical site. This led to a menstrual cycle that wouldn't stop. I was bleeding to death. *(Thank you, donors, even the one with the demon, for the two bags of blood! [Yummy!] My husband has been donating blood ever since he joked with the nurse, "Fill'er up!")*

To hopefully resolve the issue, I was then referred to a gynecologist who scheduled me for uterine ablation surgery. Essentially, they were going to sterilize me (as warned, as a potential side effect) when my original issue was a brain aneurysm that had likely healed (and no longer needed the blood thinner). However, my insurance company would not cover another angiogram for six months to confirm whether my aneurysm had collapsed and healed, to stop the meds. Six months is the average recovery time for a seventy-year-old who no longer menstruates. Therefore, the risk of sterilization was the next best solution for me—not based on science but instead on insurance coverage protocol.

Hmm...I thought for sure that the head and the vagina were two different organs, but some people confuse the two or shave the wrong head during surgery. (Hush! I know the head isn't an organ. You know what I'm talkin' 'bout. And umm...y'all ever heard of yarrow tea? Shhh! It couldn't have been any worse than the coagulant the E.R. doctor mistakenly prescribed to me.)

P.P.S. Unfortunately, many of these alternative medicines attract a following similar to the spiritual parasites found in cults. As soon as humanity makes somethin' *special* or exclusive, its effectiveness is diluted, as often occurs in religion. Careful now!

P.P.P.S. Speaking of science! The British used education to position themselves as "superior" to the Indians. However, they had no idea that Indians would take "their science" of cataloging and labeling *stuff,* which was already ingrained in Indian cultures, to a level the British could never conceive. You know, they discovered 330 million gods, and the British only found one.

Go to India! There are "mad scientists" everywhere! I spoke to one gentleman for an hour about bugs and another about what the antelopes were eating in Delhi's Biodiversity Park as he crumbled fresh antelope droppings in his hands—"shit-ology." The work they have done to restore *our* ecosystem is remarkable! (*Shout out* to Biodiversity Park scientist!) 🏺

8. Phobia Baloney or *Holy Macaroni?*

Before you proceed, please read this sermon with an open heart, even though it has the dumbest title—ever! Try not to cram this new perspective into a box, as it may not align with anything you have probably heard— except in your own thoughts, which you may have denied. Sometimes, we don't listen to ourselves because what we feel or see contradicts what our minds prefer to believe.

Disclosure Reminder...,

I have read and heard from multiple sources that transphobia stems from colonialism and "White Supremacy," particularly because of the culture's strict adherence to the gender binary and its roles. (Hmm...I do understand their frustration.) Oh my, I thought, *White people are in trouble.*

I always strive to listen to every argument with my undivided, unbiased attention. While "White Supremacy" and systemic racism (a society that favors White people) are significant issues, those creating these arguments, likely a trans individual or an "ally," seem to blame White culture and norms for any opposition to their agenda. Of course, having someone to blame for our challenges allows us to avoid self-reflection, right?

It is nearly a fact that most major world problems can be traced back to a White man. Still, we can only arrive at this conclusion by investigating each situation individually. Failing to do so would mean blaming someone simply because they are an easy target, which is why a person is presumed innocent until proven guilty.

The White man is not the scapegoat for all of humanity's problems. (Oh my, never in a million years would I have imagined saying something like that. This must not be me. I must be channeling intelligence from a source beyond my mind. I'm in disagreement with my own words.) If anything, the White man's oppression of the world can be viewed as a gift designed to enhance human Consciousness. Instead of blaming them, let us use our suffering to awaken and rise to what truly matters above the childish games of supremacy: Okey-dokey, artichokey, enough of that spiritual *mumbo-jumbo*. Please don't close the book. I'm sorry. Let's get to the issue at hand, and I'll try to keep it simple.

How is "White Supremacy" the designer of transphobia regarding strict adherence to binarism and its roles when men globally cling to this and have restricted women? How far back are y'all going? If we keep going back, we might end up blaming humanity or religion for this mess (uh-oh, Judaism!), but y'all aren't ready for that. Indeed, colonialism has impacted many cultures. For example, there is a direct correlation between the development of the Taliban ideology that currently occupies Afghanistan and White people invading India, where it originated. White people seem to bring out the extremes in a lot of people. I get it.

"Sexism," within binarism, a relatively new term yet not a new phenomenon, isn't solely a product of White culture, even if its inception can be traced back to White people at some point in history. (I don't have time to figure that out, and what difference would it make today?) Men of almost every ethnicity can be united in that they have collectively taken advantage of women or have been seen as "superior" or more valuable in some form. Women have been expected to serve men on many levels. "I'm hungry," they say as they look to us for food.

Itching Ears and Recruiting the Wounded

However, when I observe this accusatory behavior mixed up in a "tossed word salad," I always trace the finger to identify the pointer. These individuals believe the rest of us aren't listening. They think those who suffer from racism and other forms of abuse will thoughtlessly join their movement simply because the language sounds familiar. Sadly, many do so without a second thought. I see it all the time. (We must understand how programming works or....)

The messages being conveyed sounded beautiful and were pleasant to hear. However, I didn't resonate with the sentiment of these messages; many expressed a language I didn't fully comprehend. I wondered if it was my age or if I simply wasn't their target audience, as I don't cling to racial and sexual identities.

They appealed to itching ears with an emotional message centered around collective pain, locking arms with those who resonated with terms and phrases like "transphobia," "full," "authentic self," "black and brown bodies," and "holding space," among others. There was a collective embrace of struggle and an understanding that these marginalized groups should unite. *What kind of emotional spirituality was this,* I wondered? **Today, sticking together and uniting should include all of us in *holy macaroni*...I mean, regardless of our differences. No longer limited by the shallowness of religion, race, sex, or gender, or finding unity in pain, but instead united by Love.** (Hallelujah! Holy macaroni, that was beautiful!) This is the human evolution I envision.

Unfortunately, uniting around pain seems to be more appealing to some. They cling to their mental-social identities and collectively sink deeper into their suffering. Most people are unaware of the alternative actions available to them. It feels reassuring to realize you're not alone. But does finding comfort with others who share similar pain genuinely enhance our lives? As the saying goes, "*Misery loves company,*" right?

Many prefer to have their emotions stroked without working to improve their situation or move beyond their pain. Togetherness is mistaken for progress. They fail to see that they are merely intellectualizing their pain and treating the symptoms rather than addressing the root causes. These wounded souls don't realize that what brings them down is the mental baggage connected to the labels or veils they believe define them. Again, instead of finding liberation, they find each other, uniting to join the beast I will introduce later.

These messages exemplify how language can be deceiving. Familiar "right language" or buzzwords can mislead us into nodding in approval when the underlying motive doesn't solve anything or contradicts our core beliefs—leaving many to join something because it seems right or is familiar. For instance, I use many Christian references to connect with my readers, which may lead some to assume I align with the Christian faith, even though I clearly state that I have no religion and *Betwixt* is religion-free. We can easily be fooled or moved into joining anything when we listen with itching ears.

The Diversity of Humanity

There exists a beautiful community of nonbinary, non-gender-conforming, and liberated individuals. For instance, Brittney Griner, the renowned Women's National Basketball Association (WNBA) star, does not fit neatly into our society's sexist and often White definition of beauty and femininity, with some individuals identifying or being pressured to identify themselves with a label. (Name it—Dammit!) I want to clarify that this sermon is not directed at them. (Hmm…have you ever noticed that when executive orders or bills are signed to protect women's sports, there is always a room full of gender-conforming White girls with yellow hair positioned for the photo opportunity? Oh my, I can now hear a few of those girls shouting into this book, "Blondes!" Oops, I stand corrected.)

Unfortunately, many unhealthy individuals exploit their struggles and the fight of others for civil rights to satisfy their need for power. In fact, I have a family member who does just that. She hijacks anyone's struggle or hardship as if it were her own, doing anything to put herself in the spotlight. This behavior is associated with histrionic personality disorder, which often coincides with narcissistic personality disorder. Sometimes, she needs reminders when her behavior escalates: "Your neighbor's house burned down, not yours, so cut it out." Please note for future reference, as I've mentioned before, "I use the term 'narcissism' to encompass all *Cluster B disorders* and mind-dominant behaviors, which I also describe as complete absenteeism from the body. This approach simplifies things since very few people understand *Cluster B disorders* and the clinical idea behind narcissism as someone who lives behind protective mental veils. The average person experiences this to varying degrees, which is more pronounced in those labeled as disordered" (*Elicit* sermon, "The Fruit of the Same Tree").

A similar behavior emerges when addressing racism and dealing with racial disadvantages. You will often see White people become the front-runners of the cause, which is described as the "White savior complex" or "White saviorism." For many, a good example of this is portrayed in the 2009 movie *The Blind Side,* featuring Sandra Bullock, where a White woman becomes the savior of a Black child. (Beautiful!) However, this "savior complex" is just a form of narcissism and codependency, a craving for power and attention, which many disguise as "helping others." (giggles) They will shout things like, "You're being antisemitic!" These individuals exploit those who suffer to garner attention and boost their self-esteem. Unfortunately, the transgender rights movement is overrun by many narcissistic personalities who don't mind attempting to change their sex/gender to make others bow down and conform. That's the bottom line. (Yes, we should help each other, but the goal shouldn't be to elevate our egos.)

The Mental Reality of the Notion of "Sexuality"

Power games are challenging to identify and confront because *we humans* tend to lie, deny, discredit, and minimize. Our minds do an incredible job of *avoiding owning lying* by simply choosing to believe what they prefer. Poof, the lie disappears. The mind might assert, "This is who I am; I'm a woman inside," when none of us is male or female internally (spiritually speaking) beyond our DNA makeup and/or the sex we were born with. (That'll preach.) All other factors are hormonal or merely behaviors we have adopted.

For instance, some people don't realize that women walk funny in high heels, not because of how they feel inside, but because they have hips. Men designed these back-breaking shoes initially to boost their egos and later realized they were perfect for sexualizing women. (What a shame!) Even so, others will mimic the sway, not understanding that it's due to how our bodies are built. We sway to gracefully balance fat deposits in feminine places. Nobody in their right mind would imitate the redistribution of cellulite and the need for more physical activity. (I sway more these days, sitting here writing this book for y'all.)

Surprisingly, after hearing arguments like, "I know I'm in the wrong body," some of you are motivated to stop and practice stillness unknowingly. You quiet yourself and look within to see if what they are saying makes sense. You try to feel this notion of being male or female in your body beyond what your mind tells you. When you do this, it further confirms the need to dismantle gender boundaries. Beyond what the mind tells us about being one sex or another, we find that we are the same inside—again, neither male nor female. How about that?

The problem these folks don't realize while they argue is that they aren't assessing "sexuality" or gender beyond the mind. The concept of "sexuality" that many accept exists only in their mental understanding, whether one identifies as "gay" or "straight." (Yep, it's all in your head.) It doesn't exist beyond the mind. I understand that not everyone can grasp this today. Give it time.

The Implications of Unchecked Toxicity

Transgenderism, *not transphobia,* stems from unchecked toxic masculinity and sexism prevalent in nearly every nation. These individuals are simply using the same means of controlling women and "minorities" to now exert control over those who have traditionally ruled the world and the family unit. We can thank social media for this rapid evolution. (Change is nice.) However, this is merely a long-awaited shift in power because we did not address sexism and racism appropriately. We allowed it to fester for too long. (Strangely, my racist sensitivity check fights to make White lowercase and flags transgenderism as outdated, but the use of "the N-word" is excellent, *completely acceptable*—no recommendation or counsel needed.)

As a result, transgenderism is the product being created and is becoming the new collective mindset. It's like voting for a new social construct to shape our beliefs, like voting for a new president every four years. However, abusive social constructs can persist for centuries as they do not operate like a political democracy and are reinforced by our mental programming, which can take years to dismantle, if at all, as seen in racism. When ideologies become collective, they stay with us and spread as quickly and extensively as a virus.

Those who are human (non-binary, transgender, non-gender conforming, etc.), for lack of better words, are likely not offended by my counterargument because they, too, feel overrun. The individuals who would argue with me are merely the personalities we hope to identify. Unfortunately, some individuals who don't fit neatly into the often sexist definitions of what constitutes a man or a woman…have been misled in the same way that "minorities" are buying into this new direction. "Hmm…smells and sounds like anti-racism to me, so I think I'll join them." This illustrates the consequences of denying the existence of sexism and racism while neglecting to teach diversified perspectives of history or sociology classes in our schools. (We must understand how programming works or risk being programmed.) If we don't, social media will educate them instead. Our youth need a strong understanding of how social norms and concepts are developed and how they impact our lives. Lessons on the frameworks of racism would be invaluable, enabling more individuals to quickly identify social constructs rooted in manipulation and control, as the methods to attract and sway followers have remained unchanged.

We also have a generation of Whites buying in, as well. They are tired of White dominance and the pain associated with the blatant disregard for human lives, which are treated as inferior and unworthy, and they are eager for something new. They aspire to live in a world that embodies inclusiveness and care for their fellow human beings, concluding the creation of mental blocks that deny their privilege over others. As I shared in my sermon, "The Fruit of the Same Tree," many progressive Whites are deliberately raising their children, mainly their boys, without regard for their masculinity or sex. They believe this approach is preferable to raising a racist and privileged White man like their father or relatives. As they seek liberation from the chains, they wish for the world to know, "I am more than White." (I avoided using the phrase *gender identity* since gender can be confusing and is also a social construct.)

Many Whites also recognize that "White Supremacy" harms or excludes them, as we observe the shrinking middle class. Others foolishly cling to the privilege that *White* used to afford previous generations. Still, who desires the notion of "superiority" as a prize while living paycheck to paycheck like the rest of America? Or who wishes to be part of a culture that labels some fellow humans as "White trash"? (I believe that is unique to the *White* ideology.) Many can now see that "White Supremacy" is a club or "religion" for only a select few and that it needs struggling Whites to keep buying into the falsehood of their "superiority" and, again, accepting mental tokens. This self-serving ideology has pushed many White folks out of the club who don't measure up to the standard, and many are jumping ship on *White,* which only supports a small percentage of America.

Religion, a primary transmitter of the *White* ideology, is attempting to retain its remaining supporters. However, many Whites are waking up and losing their patience with their religion rather than joining a rebranding of the Christian church. We have all seen the signs for these new churches starting at the local high school. "Church like you've never seen before," led by a pastor in ripped jeans and an untucked shirt. They are rejecting him and his trophy wife, too. They are finished with the manipulation of spirituality because the same self-serving system that glorifies one individual also often results in the wealth of one at the expense of others. And what do they gain? The warm, fuzzy feeling of "superiority," mental tokens in the form of "right religion," again, all while living paycheck to paycheck like the rest of America.

Surprisingly, many have begun to connect with the notion of God or Christ/Krst on their own. As they get closer to examining themselves and pursuing the Source beyond religion, they actively evaluate what to keep and what to discard, once more embodying the idea of "getting in where they fit in." Others are drawn to intriguing religious movements, such as the Hare Krishnas or various Eastern religions, which offer a richness and sense of freedom that their previous racial ideology could not provide. Again, many desire the world to know, "I am more than White." (These "White saviors" are finally saving themselves and will *not* sit idle as previous generations did. *Watch out!*)

Nevertheless, those who unthinkingly follow the transgender movement have their belief system replaced without realizing it, similar to what occurs in those who adopt racism or other controlling mind patterns. This is also how individuals end up in religious cults or join "Church like you've never seen before," as they struggle to separate or recognize that familiar language may be misleading. Gold plating something doesn't make it gold. One must be careful and think independently; don't drink the Kool-Aid just because *grape* is your favorite flavor.

Black people, you've seen this before! You were supposed to have learned. And if you think I'm aligning with an ideology that labels others as "sinners," I'm not. (expressed with frustration) I'm referring to those who understand the author James Baldwin's words about how the "Negro" knows better. I wouldn't be surprised to one day see water fountains and restrooms labeled "haters only" and for it to become illegal not to use specific pronouns. This would be similar to how a Black person couldn't address a White person by their first name and had to use the title Mr. or Mrs. (Calm down, "conspiracy theorist." If you don't recognize the conspiracy already alive and well in racism, you're likely just being dramatic. This kind of scheming is as White as apple pie.)

Let's replace the term "boy," which Whites used to refer to African American men, with "hater." The officer will say, "What did you say, hater? Did you look at *them* with disrespectful eyes?" "No, *officer*," instead of "No, *sir*" or "No, *ma'am,*" the second-class citizen will respond cautiously. You get the point. (Scary!)

Thought Patterns and Defense Mechanisms of Controlling Constructs

The mind patterns of individuals seeking power and control have remained consistent, much like a controlled group in an experiment. Again, they don't change; you can read them like a book if you pay attention. Let's take a moment to explore how transgenderism reflects the same thought patterns and defense mechanisms as racism and narcissism:

- **Gaslighting** – making you feel as if you are crazy while attempting to alter your perception of reality. Saying, "I am a woman," when you see a man. Or "There's no such thing as a biological man or woman."
- **Blame-shifting** – calling a person transphobic, making them the problem for disagreeing with their position.
- **Silencing** – one will not respond or acknowledge anything that makes sense or causes them to lose control. It also employs control, fear, and intimidation to keep its victims and any opposing voices quiet. Speak out, and you will be *canceled.*
- **Redefining** – calling women "cis-gendered" or "women who ovulate" instead of simply "women."
- **Reframing** – they will rephrase what you said to make your opinion sound absurd, framing and redefining disagreement as hatred or violence.
- **Rationalizing** – creating excuses.
- **Justification** – making themselves right.
- **Preemptive defense** – they might say, "I'm not perfect," or accuse you of labeling them as toxic before you even reach that point.
- **Withholding acknowledgment** – forcing you to prove or explain yourself repeatedly. They give word salads and circular answers to simple questions instead of acknowledging what you are saying or being willing to define what a woman is.
- **Shame** – they created the term "transphobia" to override disagreement. "You're a hater or violent," simply because you disagree with them, especially when teaching transgenderism to children.
- Putting words in your mouth.
- Defining the rest of society through their terminology and compelling everyone to adopt it. (Christianity and racism both engage in this practice.)

- Needing external validation to affirm themselves – "You go, girl!"
- Employing legal means to force people to support their agenda.
- The list goes on…

Let's take an intermission! Enjoy "Under Pressure" by Queen and David Bowie for a moment of introspection. I'll be back in just a moment.

The Mess

Now, you have men redefining what a woman is and continuing to rule over us as usual. We have conservative representatives from the far right on social media, predominantly White, appalled by what's occurring in our nation, which makes them appear sane for once. However, most won't stop to recognize that they are merely receiving a dose of their own medicine. Some of them present strong arguments to challenge the transgender movement yet are severely blinded by racism and the ideology of "White Supremacy." As they use words like "narcissism" to describe transgenderism, they fail to see that racism, too, is a form of narcissism.

My favorite far-right social media influencers include the bearded guy who thinks he knows everything and is probably thirty-nine but wishes he were forty, along with the ripped, redheaded guy with the ponytail you'd see at a rodeo-political event. The ripped dude and I would be working out on the same team if he would just *wake up*. It's so sad because we could totally be friends, laughing and rolling together. Still, I'm dumbfounded by what some people can keenly see in others yet completely miss in themselves.

When it comes to "White Supremacy" and racism, anything outside of acceptance forces individuals to either deny its existence or their involvement to avoid the pain of personal conviction or to embrace it with pride to avoid the pain of personal conviction. (It's goofy! That's also a beautiful sentence. No commas needed.) Yet, both paths ultimately serve the same goal. These defense mechanisms trap the individual in their mind or ideology. Humorously enough, my cult leader used to say, "If righteousness and purity make us a cult, then call us a cult!" Like fools, we would all respond, "Amen!" He reinforced a false sense of "superiority" (mental tokens), which ensured we would avoid confronting the truth about our ideology and church. You can see that "White Supremacy" plays the same games with its followers.

We need some of these smart White folks to stop defending their ingrained ideology and start collaborating with the rest of America like patriots to clean up the mess left behind by *our* ancestors. However, doing so would require humility and a willingness to take responsibility for something we didn't directly create. Like children, many respond, "I didn't do it."

Even so, is our species not to blame for the terrible affliction on humanity? It is our duty to clean up the mess they left behind. We are responsible, regardless of how we view it. Will you tell the animals searching for a place to call home, "I didn't cut down the forest or pollute the oceans"? Do they see you as separate from your species? No, they see you as part of a collective.

Once, I saw a turtle sitting before an alligator basking in the sun. As I approached, it decided to run for its life. I felt so offended. I thought, *How dare it view me as a greater threat than the alligator!* "I didn't do it," I said. Still, that wasn't how the turtle saw it, especially since it could see I was benefiting from my privileges by walking on cleared land that had once created a buffer between us. It held me equally responsible for my species' impact on the environment.

My youngest, passionate about forestry, has taken on the responsibility of helping restore what his species has destroyed. He could say, "This is the White man's doing," as he sits back, never questioning where the wood for his chair came from. Still, I ask, is the White man not a part of you or the rest of humanity, for that matter? To go a little deeper, your grandfather, who cut down the forest, lives in you. If you think I'm mistaken, check your DNA. You'll find he's still there.

But for those who are still *shaking their heads*, how about this? What if you inherited a piece of property that was trashed and owed back taxes, yet it was worth a few million? I bet *your ass* would take responsibility for your ancestor's mess then.

Taking responsibility today signifies maturity, as I shared with some local Quakers while writing this book. I mentioned, "Heck, all Americans with ancestry tracing back before Ellis Island have a genetic tie to this painful history. We're all responsible for this mess!" They didn't realize I was also speaking from my perspective as a White German, which they couldn't see beyond my skin color, even after I explained my ancestry. "I'm responsible for this mess, too," I continued. Strangely, they didn't seem to agree with my viewpoint and began *shaking their heads* like children (giggles) because acknowledging the truth is too painful for many. "I didn't do it!" they say. Moreover, those who benefit from the well-crafted American caste system are also responsible. Taking responsibility, once again, is a marker of maturity. It's honorable, and it's also a choice.

Most of us are cousins, of course! It was a messy affair led by White men suffering from toxic masculinity, you know. Folks were popping out with red afros and freckles. Let's reunite the family, but we must clean up the mess this time and pay what is owed.

The Mess Continued

Then we have people like Kelly Robinson, the president of the Human Rights Campaign, who, in 2023, was a witness in the U.S. Senate, sounding like *me* when I used to defend a local church that the community called a cult. Her responses seemed programmed. Was she drinking the *grape* Kool-Aid?

How is it that Robinson, a "Woman of Color," could not answer a simple question: "Is there a difference between men and women?" (That is how people are guaranteed not to vote.) Instead, she created a word salad to define what a woman is (while the Black woman represents the community of women closest to complete liberation from male dominance. Of course, this did not happen without the influence of racism and "White Supremacy" in the form of mass incarceration of Black men by the millions. However, liberation is still liberation, even with some assistance. Nevertheless, last I checked, he *is* "Irreplaceable"—*Beyoncé*.) Unfortunately, Robinson wasn't the only high-profile Black woman who faced difficulties answering similar questions that year. *("Order in the court! [bang, bang, bang] No more out of you, The Common Snook!")*

Some Say Transphobia Is the New Racism

Before we dig in deeper, let me reiterate that not every offensive human act amounts to racism. Some folks are just assholes and can't help it. (giggles) Nonetheless, personal ignorance does not correlate with possessing a collective power over another group. Racism is precisely that; it dominates over a group of people, affecting their right to exist peacefully.

Yet, many trans individuals, predominantly White (men), are now arguing that they are victims of "White Supremacy" and suggest they also suffer from a form of "racism" due to the mistreatment and discrimination they face in astonishing numbers. Still, we face several overlapping issues here. White trans individuals (men) are overshadowing their "minority" counterparts (the equalizers). These front-runners need to acknowledge that Black LGBTQ people endure racism *and* discrimination. There's a difference. This does not grant the entire movement, more specifically those who are White (men), permission to claim they are victims of "White Supremacy." (Oh my, I can hear a few White trans folks (men) shouting into this book.)

Additionally, opposing their demands and the desire to reshape and reprogram society and its responses is not in any way similar to racism. Conversely, defeating women in women's sports and invading our locker rooms is absurd and represents a form of dominance and control over us, like that of racism. It infringes upon our privacy and human rights to exist peacefully.

But heaven forbid someone to discuss safety concerns. The transgender movement will respond with statistics showing that although transwomen may be violating women psychologically, they are not physically endangering them. It is disheartening that women must defend their space by resorting to the fear of sexual assault as a weapon when it would be easier and more respectful to simply listen to them. Having a man or trans individual in the locker room feels intrusive. Private spaces for women, along with gender-neutral bathrooms and locker rooms, offer an easy solution, even if the "Dude (Looks Like A Lady)." But the goal is to be with the women, right? Because it's affirming, right?

Many "People of Color" don't know how to respond to the transgender movement because the Civil Rights Movement, for which many continue to fight, has been overshadowed by the transgender agenda. Unfortunately, those who lack a religious framework to provide a black-and-white perspective often feel lost and uncertain about their position. I urge you not to compromise your values. Rosa Parks (I spy a Cherokee in Alabama!) would be disappointed to see this, and Martin Luther King Jr. wouldn't be surprised that Black people did nothing to stop it.

The Graceful Swing from One Extreme to Another

Today, humanity embraces everything under the sun regarding sex, gender, pronouns, and the concept of the *sexual buffet*. (If you hear this term again, I coined it.) This "creativity" likely reflects a natural reaction to being under the control of religion, sexism, racism, and "White Supremacy" for so long. This resembles how Maslow's hierarchy of needs illustrates human necessities and behaviors. Here, we have a pendulum instead of a pyramid, demonstrating how we escape and respond to control. For example, if substances like alcohol were prohibited, we would all likely drink excessively to express our rebellion or freedom. "You can't control me, bitch!"

Have you ever noticed that there is a side to some African American cultures that acts as a perpetual middle finger to White norms and dominance? It's often expressed through the vibration of a car radio, a.k.a. bass. That represents the other side of the pendulum: liberation from control. (Here's one of my favorite songs to feel the bass, "Starboy" by violinist Josh Vietti. Someone needs to play that in a Box Chevy.)

Control, unfortunately, produces its complete opposite—being out of control. We swing from the pendulum hanging from *a bra* from one side to the other, until we eventually find balance in the middle. So, let us swing from insanity to insanity. It just makes sense so that we may find balance. When I left the control of religion, I was ready to experience everything, but thank goodness I didn't swing for too long. (Hey, get your mind out of the gutter. I did not "swing" for those with a different understanding of the word. [wink])

When we eventually swing back to the middle, hopefully, sooner than in the loooong era, again, of religion, sexism, racism, and "White Supremacy," the small transgender communities will have the right to exist peacefully. However, the rest will hopefully have received the mental health treatment or awakening needed for narcissism, and women, along with Black and Brown people, will not have allowed their suffering or their ancestors' legacy to be exploited to further an agenda that resembles the discrimination and oppression they fought tirelessly to overcome.

Understanding history is essential because history tends to repeat itself, although not in the way you might think. Come on, people. It's just that White people never believed their tricks would be used against them, and Black people never imagined they would participate, especially since Black Americans have not collectively retaliated against White people for their inhumane treatment. (Some might burn down a Target store or collectively reject some folks, but that's it.) We must awaken and rise in human Consciousness, people. This is just one of the many tricks the mind has made to rise to the top and rule the rest.

The LGBTQ Communities

The gay communities are also trying to figure out how the heck the transgender movement has gained prominence over theirs and become a central focus for youth to consider as an option. Moreover, lesbians are *pissed* with the bullshit men are pulling after all their hard work advocating for women's rights and standing for equality! (*Whassup to my homegirl,* who's been holding it down for women in commercial aviation. Whitney Houston would be proud of you. "How [do] I Know?" because "I'm Every Woman.")

The problem is that we disregarded human lives, ignored narcissism in our gay communities, and never imagined it would rise to the point of ruling over entire nations, much like racism and "White Supremacy" have done. (Whatever, religious folks! Those saying "Amen!" were the first to look the other way.) Yes,

411

there is narcissism within the gay communities, and when left unchecked, it can grow into a monster—monsterism! Again, what is narcissism? It's a condition of those who have been emotionally wounded and adopt a false self as a protection from feeling powerless in this world. (Hmm…sounds like our society might be responsible for this mess.)

Divided and Being Conquered

The transgender movement is like harvest time: what we sow, we shall reap. Society struggles to find unity today because White America has left this country divided. As you know, what is divided can be conquered. Instead of dismantling systemic racism and ensuring that everyone has access to the same opportunities, many White people continue to live comfortably in a divided world, with many of our Jewish brothers and sisters joining them, as well. Careful now!

Our nation is an ideal target for invaders due to our lack of unity. We have intelligent individuals who share the perspective of the late Muhammad Ali, who declined to serve in the Army because Black Americans were treated as second-class citizens. He didn't support our nation because it never supported him. He said, "Why should they ask me to put on a uniform and go 10,000 miles from home and drop bombs and bullets on brown people in Vietnam after so-called Negro people in Louisville are treated like dogs and denied simple human rights?" (*The New York Times*, 1967).

The collective White voice has shamed individuals like Ali, claiming that one is un-American if they resist racism by opposing the country's political agenda or if they oppose war to speak out against racism. (Hmm…public shaming/cancel culture is nothing new.) This collective will disregard your life of hardship and use the indoctrination of nationalism as the ultimate disqualifier that overrides your suffering. "This is where we must come together as Americans! But not there, where we treat you like dogs, and if you embarrass us by pointing out our cruel treatment of you or try to resist the abuse, we will force your submission and shame/cancel you if you don't comply." (Kaepernick, does this sound familiar?) This is also the power of racism, not to be mistaken for someone being a smartass who claims Mexicans love to chill. (They sure know how to enjoy life more than most. I saw some roofers taking a "siesta" the other day. When was the last time you took a nap under a shady tree?)

Oh man, we should have dismantled racism a loooong time ago because many Black Americans and other "minority" groups (the equalizers) are now embracing a new narrative that unifies their struggles with a beast no different from what we've known all along, whether discussing historical racism or the contemporary transgender movement. Perhaps its objective is to consume itself and finally create equality for all. That would be splendid if that were the case. However, this is why communism never works. Although the original intention of creating equality seemed like Utopia or Heaven, humans have a terrible habit of craving power and disguising their intentions to deceive the gullible. (Hmm…hopefully, the racist will move to Mars.)

The transgender movement may very well swallow racism and "White Supremacy." But then, what are we left with, as it also seeks to engulf women? (They're acting like men—pun intended!) Or will they engage in a Biblical-like battle where the Canaanites and the Moabites annihilated each other before Judah even got out of bed? (Sorry if I have the wrong "ites," but you get my point.) Unfortunately, we'll have to wait and see since the movement simply replaces one controlling social construct with another by hypnotizing and manipulating people's minds in a new direction. Even so, this leader is neither Martin Luther King Jr. nor Mahatma Gandhi, who graciously appealed to the belief systems of White people by embracing the lost essence of their religion. This movement is led by White people frustrated with themselves yet still armed with the same weapons used to control others. (That certainly doesn't sound like a plan for success.)

As amateur social scientists, let's observe these humans clawing their way to the top while repeatedly "…stepping on someone else's head to elevate [themselves]—sometimes, even multiple heads at once" (*Elicit* sermon, "The Parables of Controlling Personalities"). You know, it's the same nonsense; the game has never changed!

On the other hand, if I were White and understood how racism operates to control and devastate the lives of "minorities," I would run for my life or wake up and become a part of the solution. Power is shifting, even if our country builds the Great Wall of China across our southern border or Texas becomes its own country. Every party must come to an end.

Be warned! This new creation, ideology, or collective mindset is less divided by race, religion, or sex. It will have no tolerance for those who still are. No worries…there's still time to wake up before you, too, become a second-class citizen. They might have me saying, "Yes, they/them, she/her," which would violate my freedom of speech. But I can play along, too. This isn't new; it's like bringing bell-bottom jeans back. Aside from that, they will think I'm cool because religion, race, sex, and gender hold no authority in my life.

I hate to credit foolishness, but those who call "the woke movement" an ideology are correct. You must understand that an ideology is a set of beliefs held by a group that isn't necessarily true—like self-proclaimed "superiority," the idea that racism doesn't exist, the belief that Jesus is "the only way," the notion that men are the head of the household (men need to stop perpetuating this lie), or the assertion that you can change your sex. However, this critique of the ideology of "wokeness" sounds even more absurd coming from people governed by a similar ideology that we could reasonably label as "slept." Why can't we ever see the speck in our own eye? (I know, don't tell me; my "slept" joke was a flop.)

Moreover, we need new leaders and political parties—at least three or four—because one side votes against fundamental human rights, while the other has been overtaken by a similar controlling ideology positioned to replace the former. (Hmm…I know what y'all are thinking, but remember, *Betwixt* is a non-political spiritual organization. But nothing is stopping you from starting a *Betwixt Party*. [wink]) Unfortunately, we struggle to persuade more people to abandon the ideologies of the far right and left to find common ground and common sense in the middle. (Kumbaya.)

From Plato's works, it can be inferred that Socrates, another Greek philosopher, did not favor democracy because it allowed people to elect fools (dictators!) instead of prioritizing the common good of society. (Essentially, *boneheads* will elect *boneheads*.) For example, some privileged individuals vote based on religious principles, while others continue to fight for fundamental human rights. Additionally, many voters choose candidates based solely on their personal interests rather than what is best for everyone's well-being. *(Hush, Patel; I didn't ask for your opinion.)* Sure, the idea of less government sounds appealing, but no one wants to acknowledge the greater governing powers that rule our government.

Socrates believed this system of government would never be successful and would eventually lead to tyranny unless philosophers became leaders or vice versa. Education is essential for good leadership, you know.

I can respect his thinking and have observed its validity. However, philosophers aren't the answer. We don't need people who can intellectualize societal issues; instead, we need intelligent leaders who understand the power of Consciousness and can provoke human Consciousness to improve societal problems. The late Martin Luther King Jr. exemplifies that kind of leadership.

Is this *thang* global?

Some may believe the transgender movement is global. However, only a few countries regard the same issues as essential or are influenced by our leading concerns, even though we would like to impose them on others. Many world leaders are grappling with food scarcities and housing insecurities and don't have time to be cornered by the idea of "conform or be canceled." Asking where they stand on issues that are not central to everyone or their nation, in general, is like a Christian inquiring of a non-religious person or a follower of another faith how they feel about the resurrection of Jesus. This limited viewpoint resembles a child who can't understand that their desire for ice cream isn't the most pressing issue in the world or even recognized by others. Yet, they will insist on making it central as they address you from their narrow-minded perspective, which they present as "right" or "superior."

Sometimes, the only option is to stare back since responding to them first requires teaching them to recognize their ignorance. Unfortunately, when people conform or weigh in, it becomes easier to disguise the transgender agenda in our country. These limited perspectives often characterize those who, regrettably, become our leaders. Washington is full of them! But not Kenya! (giggles)

Moreover, the U.S. is the world leader in this movement. Seven other Western countries have banned gender-affirming medical interventions for minors, but our government has not. It won't yield to common sense because a more potent force is gaining traction with significant support. We have those who suffer from sexism *and* racism backing the cause. (Note this! Most doctors won't even perform a vasectomy on a man younger than thirty-five with no fewer than two kids. They will **not** cut his balls off.)

Don't be mistaken; this suffering from sexism and toxic masculinity affects men, too. Men feel lonely in a world that compels them to deny their femininity and fear intimacy and vulnerability. They aspire for more than always relying on women for support…so much so that some would prefer to be women rather than endure lonely lives. I don't blame *them*. Life is tough for many men.

How Controlling Social Constructs and Institutions Impact "Sexuality"

I can't leave without briefly mentioning how much religion has influenced this movement. Religious communities often act as the primary microcosm that supports other abusive social constructs, restraining and confining us instead of encouraging us to unfold and experience liberation and limitlessness.

For one, religion has significantly contributed to the oppression of women. Today, feminists continue to accommodate religion because it's tied to their faith. Unfortunately, they are waging a war against men instead of dismantling the social constructs created by men to justify the enslavement and oppression of women. These women can't confront religion directly because many would be left divided, so they never uproot the oppressor at its source.

A friend of mine noticed a male-to-female transgender individual who works in the community and sometimes gets frustrated with people who misgender him. His hair was cut short, and he was growing a mustache. She said, "Wow, you look different." He replied, "Yes, I'm transitioning back." When my friend, a great reporter, asked why, he responded, "Well, it's a long story, but I was raised in a cult here in Gainesville." He mentioned that the church ruined his life, and he now wanted to be his "authentic self" again, the man he was born to be. I looked at my friend and said, "Duh-uh!" I had "crossed roads" with that crazy, controlling church as well, and I had many friends who went there.

Observing the Mental Health Crisis and the Power of Transition

The men I have encountered who transitioned were all interestingly very narcissistic, completely dominated by their minds; nobody was home, resulting in total absenteeism from their bodies, much like the average heterosexual, for that matter. *(Whassup, Dakota!) Where did they go, and why did they leave?*

These individuals utilized their transition period within the religious setting to gain attention and compel everyone to submit to their agenda. (By the way, this was not your traditional spiritual community. If that isn't a game of power and control, I don't know what is.) I always remained silent to secure the best seat. We had older people misgendering all over, and it felt as if someone had granted the transitioning individuals the right to attack everyone. Who would body slam a precious eighty-year-old woman carrying a "Black Lives Matter" sign for calling them "son"? It was the power they had always craved when their parents and society were stifling them. The reverse abuse was disturbing to witness. (Many women who fought for equality found it challenging to accept a White man who benefited from both race and gender, suggesting he was now one of them. These women were not havin' it, and I just observed. [giggles])

Final Thoughts

Presence and inner stillness can heal all wounds, including toxic masculinity, false femininity, and racism, which are the root causes of today's issues. Honestly, there's not much difference between a stereotypical woman with fake boobs and booty and a man who tries to mimic that style. *Child please*; they look the same. Some of these young men said, "If you all can do it, I can do it too." For instance, when my oldest son was a baby, he had the ugliest laugh, sounding like Ernie from Sesame Street, until I realized he was mocking me. More power to the man-made and made-for-man women. (That was so hard for me to say.)

As I concluded in an earlier sermon, "The Fruit of the Same Tree":

> If anything, humanity has only taken baby steps toward understanding life, our purpose, and the paths we choose to take. We could do ourselves a favor by agreeing that it's okay not to draw conclusions. "CORRELATION DOESN'T EQUAL CAUSATION," these frustrated folks continue to shout into this book as if we have everything figured out. (eye-roll) We've been ruled by religion and other controlling constructs for ages. Indeed, we don't suddenly have it figured out, especially those of us from my generation or the fruit we produced.
>
> Furthermore, humanity remains largely unaware (asleep), living behind veils and false personas designed to shield ourselves from pain and reality. This is a trick the mind plays to protect us from suffering. I've observed that our world, which primarily participates in this self-preservation practice, produces the same fruit as if we were victims of the same condition. Observe, and let's continue to grow together.

When it comes to who's up to bat next, perhaps transgenderism signals the gradual emergence of an egalitarian society (where everyone is equal). Some might say, "Hey, anything but the current mess that has left many people behind and one group privileged." Honestly, I feel the same way. (wink) But we can learn from both history and the present, as the beast of sexism and racism still lingers; oppression is not the solution. Just wait for a natural disaster to strike; suddenly, we'll all appreciate big big men who can move big big *stuff* like trees or White men with chainsaws. *(Whassup, Snooks!)* Don't crush them too hard. The good ones, most men, are like man's best friend—pun intended! (Woof!) They love to please and are always eager to help. (Oh my, here comes a bunny trail!)

Holy macaroni, this sermon was finished! How did Kenya manage to get two *shout-outs* in one sermon? Speaking of our need for men! I can't leave without recognizing the masculinity and leadership shown by the Kenyan president, William Ruto, who agreed to send police to Haiti without posturing or threats of law and order—*hakuna matata*, just peace. We need men like the Kenyan president, willing to create environments where peace and femininity can thrive. He humanized the people of Haiti in the Western world when he stated, "The women and children in Haiti deserve peace the same way the women and children of Kenya do." He was like, "*Hakuna matata*, Haitians," and essentially said, "Sak pasé!" which means "Whassup!" in Creole. (Guess who's going to Kenya next year, the land of *holy macaroni*, where you can find Christians, Muslims, and Hindus embracing and loving each other. *[Whassup, Nairobi!]*)

Young ladies, how many of you will sign up to police Haiti? I didn't think so. We want and deserve equality and *equity*, but that doesn't mean we don't play different roles at times, right? We should be equally respected for our differences and what we bring to the table. I bow to the Divinity in Mr. Ruto because "Ain't no God coming down to do this work for us."

Questions from Dakota

Dakota: Sherguru, I have a question to ask before closing this sermon.

Sherguru: Of course, Dakota!

Dakota: Perhaps the mental illness you have experienced with some trans individuals stems from a world that denies who we are. I'm sure you can relate to this, having grown up multiracial, yet the world primarily treats you as if you are only Black. "This is who you are," they say.

Sherguru: I can follow you're thinking.

Dakota: I'm not a man, but most say, "I see a man." I'm sure you can understand what it feels like when the world wrongly identifies you and attempts to own your identity, Sher—guru.

Sherguru: Well, Da—kota, my goal was to make you to think. This is why it's time to rise above mental labels, because some people are not who *you think* they are. Unfortunately, many who identify as LGBTQ continue to partake in and play the roles of the gender binary (and many play them *hard*), diving deep into their mind identifications, never uprooting the antichrist or finding their freedom "to be." What if "gay or trans people" awakened and rose above labels instead of playing roles or assuming that sex reassignment surgery is the answer to their problems? Sadly, many "gay people" reinforce toxic masculinity and false femininity by adopting labels to "distinguish" themselves. "Okay, I'll agree to be your opposite or something less respected than who I am…so you can make yourself 'superior' and step on my head—

418

forever. I'll show you 'gay'—dammit!" You know, "Black people" participate in a similar game with "White people." (giggles) Please know you are beautiful just the way you are. Unfortunately, some never escape the cult, so to speak, and live not realizing there's a better way to be yourself, while a few, strangely, enjoy the pain and negative attention. Cheer up! Here's a song written by *our Father in Heaven* who loves us all: "It's Such A Good Feeling."

*

I'm back on track now! Additionally, what the world calls autism will inevitably drive this transition of power toward equality without the oppression of others. Individuals on the spectrum tend to be slow to adopt or conform to conventional social norms. I always say that "autism is humanity's way of self-correcting itself," likely resulting from trauma caused by living under the current toxic systems that influence our DNA and development before and after birth.

I know I have made no friends or allies—Black, White, Christian, Jewish, Gay, Straight, or Trans, except maybe Kenyans—with this sermon because it is for those who desire something more than mere allegiance to superficial categories and the current trajectory of the world. All I have to offer is freedom and a door beyond our mental concepts. (Holy macaroni! Do I see a few lesbians and a White man with stars and bars on his hat that appears to be floating on his head, saying, "I hear you"?)

In Peace and Love and Humble Hugs,
—Sher! (The Common Snook)
Pause. Inhale. Exhale. Reflect.

P.S. Hmm…have you noticed how one controlling ideology gives rise to another, much like how unprocessed hate or frustration breeds hate?

P.P.S. Did I ever tell y'all about the night my friends and I were preaching Jesus in my early twenties to the wild college students in downtown Gainesville? We hoped to invite those "sinners" to our Easter service.

While standing next to a nightclub on University Avenue, which I thought was closed, I saw an open door leading to a stairwell above the club. I was minding my own Christian business when a White drag queen started sashaying down the stairs, wearing a fancy robe. When I caught the queen's eye, he flashed me, revealing a red, white, and blue bikini with stars and stripes…with his bulge tucked, of course. I was shocked by his patriotism!

He came down the stairs with his microphone and asked me what I was doing. We chatted briefly, and I told him I was inviting folks to church. He said in a deep, muffled voice, "Do you want to come inside and invite the gays?" I replied, "Yes!" I could sense a part of him knew I wasn't a threat. He said, "You can come in, but your friends must stay outside," while eyeing them *with attitude* (like a Black woman) as if Christians disgusted him. (Yet, he saw something in me that he believed would benefit his audience.)

I wasn't sure how I felt about leaving my friends, but he seemed like a friendly person. I chose to trust him as he trusted me.

He opened the door, which was also his direct entrance to the stage, and closed it tightly behind me. It was like "Heaven" in Gainesville for these folks. The room was pitch black and filled with "gays," whom I could barely see because the spotlights had blinded me. He passed me the mic, and, full of excitement and zeal for the Lord, I invited the crowd to our Easter Service that year, held at the University of Florida Stephen C. O'Connell Center—beeyotch! It was an absolute blast!

When I finished and handed the mic back to him, he asked the crowd to "give it up for" me, and they *roared*, especially the lesbians. It was AWESOME! He even joked as I left, saying again in a deep, muffled voice, "I bet she was terrified." (He was lovely, and I'd like to meet him again one day, perhaps for a show, though I hope he kept his bulge because the show wouldn't be the same without it. [giggles])

As I rejoined my Christian posse outside, totally high on *Krst*, they thought I was the coolest for inviting "the gays" to church. Then, a young lady I had met earlier that evening, who was partying in the streets, asked if I could help her with a ride home because she was stranded. Of course…I said, "Yes." "Oh, What a Night!" Frankie Valli and The Four Seasons were right.

(Hey Dakota, stop "acting" gay for 15 minutes a day; I promise it will transform your life!)

9. Valuable Lessons from the Chinese

Disclosure Reminder...,

We have briefly touched on elements of Chinese life and culture, but I want to discuss a segment of Chinese history that may offer valuable lessons for us and will connect nicely with the two most recent sermons. I would guess that most people are either unfamiliar with or have a limited understanding of "Maoism," as the U.S. doesn't teach comprehensive world history, let alone American history. Nevertheless, as a sociology major, I studied Marxism, so I understand the basics of communism, which lies at the core of Maoism. Karl Marx was the intellectual behind what others used to birth communism. His theories and visions of a classless and communal society, which became known as "Marxism," are not reflected in modern-day communism. (*Shout out* to Instructor Waller, my childhood friend and sociology professor from SFCC. *Aww...I will never forget your sweet dog, Harry, the Irish Wolfhound.*)

I don't intend to give a thorough lesson on communism or demonize anyone's motives, since most social or economic movements begin with good intentions. However, they gradually erode, much like what we see in religion. And we know what happens when we make folks *special*, right? By now, you also recognize how people react to being controlled. In that sense, "communism" might have seemed like a logical, polarized option for the Chinese after being ruled by a dynasty for over 2,000 years.

When people possess very little power or wealth, the notion of equality and shared resources, as envisioned through communism, becomes appealing. It can be viewed as a beautiful gesture that the collective mindset seeks to share. That's why people join communes and co-housing communities...or run a Chinese "Walmart" Distribution Center right next to my house. (giggles) Sharing is caring, right?

Interestingly, this sharing embodies the essence of Jesus' teachings. However, acknowledging this likely leads people on the far right and left to construct additional barriers to defend their beliefs and the right to accumulate wealth. Perhaps the Chinese recognized the significance of Christ/Krst after all, understanding that phony treasures hold no real value, and that sharing is the heart of Christ/Krst. (My apologies to all the Chinese of Gainesville who used to frequent the distribution center in my neighborhood. I had to shut it down; there was too much traffic for my cat, Zen.)

Furthermore, I'm sure this economic system might also attract people in India who are still oppressed by the caste system. Possessing nothing but humility makes one more naturally willing to share and embrace the idea of shared resources, even though communism has yet to materialize in that way.

Either way, the People's Republic of China is a relatively young government, less than a hundred years old. Please pause and consider what America was doing at that same age and how many years it took to value all human life with equal rights. The Chinese will continue to evolve…hopefully faster than 350 years, and once again, they may demonstrate to the world what is possible. (What if a woman were to lead the People's Republic of China? I can think of around 50,000 young women who would be excellent additions to the Chinese leadership team. Migration changes you.)

Americans, please don't get weirded out because I'm not criticizing the Chinese or using derogatory terms like "dirty yellows," which I believe is a racial slur. (Uh-oh, bunny trail!) I became aware of this term in New Zealand a few years ago. Racial slurs and contempt towards the Chinese were pretty common and broadly accepted. (Yes, this was the same year someone referred to me as a Negro. Do you see a pattern?) The propaganda and dehumanization of the Chinese were so prevalent that I nearly left New Zealand with racist beliefs, questioning if they knew something about the Chinese that I didn't. (Patel remarked, "Hush, Sherguru; imagine having China as a neighbor." However, his tone was different, and he didn't dehumanize them.)

Unfortunately, simply sharing my experience and using terms I encountered, like "dirty yellows," upsets some people, as it reflects how blame-shifting operates to protect one's perceived self-image. These aren't my words; however, some will likely direct their frustration toward me for highlighting racism because everyone knows it's the "minorities'" unspoken responsibility to conceal it. As I have previously explained, "minorities" in Western countries often prioritize the feelings and discomfort of White people above their own. (Not today, sucka!)

Regrettably, the prevailing sentiment I perceived was contempt for the Chinese, which felt more offensive than being called a Negro. This led me to ponder what collective impression a foreigner might have when visiting our country. Who have we made into an enemy? Is it the Chinese, as well?

Anyways, I know it's uncommon to hear one of us speak about the Chinese without demonizing them. It isn't necessary. It's just that it's hard to digest from a Western perspective that the Chinese became a world power overnight. That isn't very comforting to the Western world. (It can almost be said the Chinese "don't die; they multiply." *RIP, Robin Harris*.) However, what the Chinese accomplished as an industrialized nation is remarkable! What they achieved, likely at the cost of human well-being, would have taken most nations decades to realize. (Hmm…that sounds like American history. Again, frightening!)

Warning! Some of you reading this are being hit by your American programming, your internal response to my neutrality. You might be thinking something like, "Bad, bad, bad," which is actually "good, good, good" because you may have uncovered another veil. We don't need to dislike people to disagree with their government. The Chinese are not communists but instead people just like you and me. (Only those rising in Consciousness will understand the last sentence.)

Anyhow, back to valuable lessons! I wonder what provoked the Chinese to say, "Enough is enough!" and respond aggressively to stabilize their nation. Hmm…outdated thinking, imperialism, and Japan come to mind. People who have been violated can be very defensive and reactive until they find the space to heal. (Have you ever had someone violate you to the point that it felt like they were putting their hand up your ass? Mothers-in-law sometimes do this and have you building your defense. Wow…what a beautiful metaphor!)

What's interesting about the Mao era, led by the Chinese leader Mao Zedong, is that so much knowledge was destroyed. Young Chinese, hungry for something new, swung hard from the pendulum and campaigned to eliminate "old ideas, old culture, old customs, and old habits" (the Four Olds). Though a dynasty no longer ruled them, similar to how the Southern states here in the U.S. were no longer Confederate states, the old ways still lingered. Reading about what transpired in China may be shocking for some who cling to knowledge, traditions, and relics of the past instead of pursuing human liberation. Still, nothing is ever lost when knowledge originates beyond human intelligence. This knowledge can't be destroyed as it didn't come from a book. Burn it, and it will surface again! (Y'all ever heard of the Tao Te Ching? The Tao, the indescribable, continues to emerge.)

Oh, *wao*! I hope we've learned from *Mao* because these young people will burn it down, which isn't always a literal fire but rather a metaphorical eternal flame. This is the reaction to old ways that need to change. Out with the "Four Olds," religion, sexism, racism, and "White Supremacy"! Change before they burn it down! Again, a riot is the language of the unheard (even though some use rioting as an act of terror). Please, let us listen. Can't we learn something from the Chinese, or are we above that? This may also be of interest to their neighbors! India, can you learn from your neighbors (your cousins!), the

Chinese, or are you above that? Many young Indians are tired of old traditions, too. Change! If not, young people will burn it down! "Grow or die!" they say.

Reflection here! Even if young people burn everything to the ground in a "Disco Inferno," Divine knowledge is never lost since it originates from a source beyond the mind and is not limited to the East or West, any racial group, or the scientific method—beeyotch! True wisdom is necessary to understand that. Pseudo-wisdom relies solely on books and the human ego. The prize is a Ph.D., which will soon be replaced by an intelligence greater than human intellect. (Isn't that interesting?)

Much of the ancient wisdom of acupuncture is thought to have been lost during the Mao era. However, I have witnessed that Divine wisdom is never destroyed. You heard me describe feeling my Chi and telling my husband that I believe there are meridian lines of energy running through the body, even though I never knew anything about the science of acupuncture.

I hope you enjoyed this lesson today, and may we learn from the Chinese.

Grow or Die Hugs,
—Sher! (The Common Snook)
Pause. Inhale. Exhale. Reflect.

P.S. Thank goodness for my peeps in Australia, especially my "bogans" from Adelaide, who helped redeem my concerning perspective of the Land Down Under. They kindly offered me a Vegemite sandwich and a jar of Vegemite to take home.

P.P.S. Hey, Chinese, speaking of valuable lessons! Did you know that you don't have to scheme in America for things to go your way? (Well…most of the time.) I have a feeling Americans are more helpful and willing than what you may have been accustomed to back home. (Well…most of us.) Be present…and transparent. That's enough. (wink)

P.P.P.S. Speaking of learning lessons from folks! Hmm…there are quite a few Jews mentioned in this book—over thirty, to be exact. What might that tell us? Yes, "Birds of a feather flock together," for sure. "It is true!" Jews are my people. Here's another one! Mm-hmm, "Many birds are not normal people." (*Right, Philly?* Can they say that?) That's a compliment! Again, *normal* is not a compliment. Got it? "It's time for the liberated Jews to *rise up* and stop chillin'," sure, that could be the message, too. Thank you for your feedback.

(Love the Chinese for 15 minutes a day; I promise it will transform your life!)

424

Section X: Less is More and Human Evolution

In case you decided to skip the introduction and browse around, here's the **Disclosure Reminder**: Before diving in, I will say this: I'm simple. I love to laugh. Please don't confuse my humor with sarcasm; I always mean what I say. I test the limits. My words are plain. I often use "own" redundantly. I don't claim to know all the answers; my only intention is to be a vessel. Also, to connect with different experiences, I interchangeably use the terms "Consciousness," "Presence," "God," "Universe," "Source," "Divine," "Energy," "Christ/Krst," and "Light." Above all, reading my humor with a Southern accent is best. Enjoy!

(TCS)

1. Rising Above Attachment to Culture

Disclosure Reminder...,

Okay, let's examine how culture shapes identity and, unfortunately, contributes to divisions among groups of people. Culture is a wonderful way to share our traditions and customs. Still, it resembles religion in that we must be careful about what we say regarding it to prevent folks from quarreling over trivial matters. People can easily be offended when discussing something that has become part of their identity. "This is how we do it" is important *stuff* to many people.

In simple terms, culture is simply a pattern of behaviors that differentiates us from one another or unites certain social groups. That's it! Unfortunately, as beautiful as diversity is, culture is often weaponized to diminish one group in comparison to another. Many people take great pride in idolizing how something is done. Culture is frequently used to excuse inflexibility and justify insanity, and it can even become a mini-god if one is not careful.

How Mystics Lose Friends and End Up on the Cross
(And Jesus said, "Amen!")

The oppression of women and other forms of unjust treatment can be justified in the name of culture. "We're Indian, so." Is not okay. (Yes, unacceptable! It's like saying "boys will be boys" to excuse their inappropriate behavior.) In my Indian circles, the cultural oppression of women that I have observed, which benefits men, is a veil thicker than religion and racism combined, and is often worn by both women and men.

The brokenness of the spirit I have witnessed in many Indian women is profound—brilliant women surrounded by an eerie silence and a collective pain that speaks through their eyes. In one friend, I could see the image of her mother being slapped reflected in her face every time she thought about challenging her husband. Yet the fear seemed to ignite an even greater determination to rise, as I could also see a raging river that could not be contained for much longer. (Uh-oh, no more biryani and dhokla for me! *To my homegirls, you know I love you with all my heart. This book would not be complete without the stories of the women who have impacted my life over the past twenty years. Some of y'all won't even read my book, so I'm not too concerned. Still, I told y'all I was writing a book. When we come together for chai, y'all be talkin' so much about those husbands [baby-husbands for some] and mothers-in-law; nobody ever asks about Shetty's book.* Again, "Shetty" is the Hindi pronunciation of my name.) I

426

have lived closely with Indians in five different communities to gain this insight. But my homegirl from Charlotte, with the Ph.D. in Soul Food, told me from the start, in front of her husband, *with attitude* in a declaring tone, "India is changing!" as if to say this change was starting with her household. (She's too spicy and feisty not to rise.) Even so, I was hesitant about speaking on this issue. Still, when I met Wing Commander Such and Such (she may not want to be connected to me by name) in India, who was the first woman to join the Indian Air Force in 1993 after six loooong years of fighting and petitioning the courts for change and her right to serve, and who is a well-known women's rights advocate, I heard the Divine say, "Speak—dammit!" (Oh my, is it a coincidence Billy Idol's "Rebel Yell" is playing in the background? Isn't that the feminist anthem!? Wow! I'll be back in a *sec*. I've *gotta* break it down.)

Unfortunately, manipulation and control are widespread globally, fostering codependent behavior and leading many individuals to accept prolonged abuse as a normal way of life. Many defend this programmed oppression with phrases like, "We're Indian, so," which further perpetuates their situation by shutting the door on their own liberation. (It's difficult to escape the cult, so to speak.) They long for freedom but simultaneously fight for the mental token of "the good wife." The programming is so ingrained that men don't have to worry about their wives stepping out of line because the women often enforce the rules (bad karma and interpersonal oppression) among themselves.

One woman remarked, "I can't believe she asked her husband to serve us." (Say what!? Liberated men are sexy! And my homegirls off Tower Road in Gainesville said, "Amen!") The programmed shaming was intense. These are the same women who often express frustration because their husbands don't lift a finger in the kitchen or handle any domestic work. How can he when his mother has handicapped him? Additionally, they serve their husbands while yearning for liberation yet expect their daughters-in-law to treat their sons like kings, never breaking the karmic cycle. "We're Indian, so."

As I have said before, "The great thing about mind manipulation or undue influence, as it's termed today, is that once you're wired, you don't require regular tune-ups because your friends and family ["Yo momma!"] typically share the same beliefs and speak the same language." (*Elicit* sermon, "Guard Your Heart—from Whom?").

Cultural doesn't mean it's acceptable, similar to how male and female circumcision, or what some call genital mutilation, is cultural for many around the world. (Yes, this includes male circumcision. I'm not suggesting they are the same, but both still leave scars on the human spirit. Male circumcision must be rather terrifying for a baby to endure.)

Also, the liberation of women means *all of us*. Anything less than *all* is a threat to our liberation globally. *(Right, King?)*

Indian men, if my husband can make dhokla from scratch—not "McDhokla" from a box but fermented overnight—so can you. If Mexican and Guatemalan men can make butter chicken in your local Indian restaurants, you can also make it in your kitchen. (To my Indian *bros who be* "throwing down" cookin' and can make a mean cup of chai, I'm not talkin' 'bout you. *Whassup, Abhi!*)

As one of the few large-scale cultures of men I am aware of outside some African communities—which have not lost their brotherly intimacy or connection to their femininity—I also recognize your desire for women's liberation. I could see it in your eyes when you often invited me to make my plate before the loooong line of men. You appeared uneasy as I observed your culture. Many Indian men, particularly those with mothers who may have worked outside the home or strayed from tradition, also seek this liberation. Namaste!

*Hey, Whatchamacallit…I mean, Patel, why **youse** so quiet? It was easier when we were pointing fingers at the Black folks robbing your stores, right? Baby-momma culture, as you mentioned, is just as detrimental as baby-husband culture. Black American women need men at home, and Indian women need liberation from the men in their homes, down the street, and around the corner. You know, there's a high chance that an uneducated Indian woman has the cure for prostate cancer in her kitchen, yet she's at home cooking and hand-feeding her baby-husband when she is truly a gift to the world. I know many of these women. Patel, don't be offended; you know I'm funny.*

Goofiness, Inflexibility, and Inclusivity

Humans take pride in some of the silliest things, such as how one holds a little pitchfork to shove food into their mouths. However, how you hold a fork does not define who you are. How you pass a joint may showcase class, but it also does not reflect your identity. Your habits do not determine who you are.

Growing up multiracial and multicultural, I sometimes wished I had a strong cultural tie to one group of people because, with culture, comes exclusivity and a sense of belonging. I first encountered this idea at age three. (As noted, I have an impeccable early childhood memory.)

428

When I attended the Santa Fe Community College Little School program in the red portables (I'm seeing red, but I could be mistaken), I was on the playground when the Chinese kids pulled me into their circle. They invited me to play with them…but they made it very clear that I should not play with the White kids, whom they kept at a distance. (giggles) They understood a little more about racism in America than I did. (Unfortunately, not much has changed for the Chinese since the 1980s.) That day, I was Chinese. I remember how it made me feel. I knew nothing about race or culture then, but I sure liked Chinese people. Culture can be like a country club if you allow it. (Uh-oh, here comes another story within the story! As church folks say, this bunny trail is attributed to the spirit leading. This one gets really local.)

Between 1980 and 1981, my preschool director at the college, whose name I oddly remember, must have been an awakened being because he worked diligently to unite our diverse group and teach our young parents not to pass down ignorance.

He always ensured they came in to do "crafts," a.k.a. "family therapy," disguised as gluing some kidney beans onto a popsicle stick picture frame with their children to experience the Presence in the holy presence of children. He emphasized the importance of showing love through undivided attention. Oh my, I cherished the times my mom joined our class for "family therapy."

Santa Fe Little School was likely the most diverse classroom in Alachua County that year, and Mr. Director was aware of it. I bet he never imagined that two-and-a-half to three-year-old me would be observing his passion. I even enjoyed seeing him around campus since he was active beyond his classroom, especially at the Harambee Club. I'm sure he also noticed the racial segregation perpetuated by his little students and me hanging out with my Chinese crew.

When I returned from Hawaii after being abducted by my father, I felt devastated. Little School told me I couldn't return to my safe little world because I was five by then. Instead, I attended nursing school (giggles) with my mother and then Preschool in the Historical African American Pleasant Street Community until kindergarten began.

Thankfully, five-year-old Yi…who would share the same pet name as me…and eventually earn a Ph.D.…was there to welcome me. (More on this poem in a later sermon.) And Emma, of course, with her cute, thick glasses and eyepatch, the only White girl in the school, always *had my back*. The little boys used to violate us girls, from sexually inappropriate remarks to swinging open the bathroom door while we undressed. **(Young children are watching you**

429

closely, so be mindful of what you teach them!) Still, Emma wasn't havin' it and devised a plan for us to look out for each other. Her vision may not have been the best, but her cognition was sharp. (She's probably a kick-butt social worker or women's rights activist today. *Whassup, Emma! I bow to you.*)

Anyhow, I remember leaving the red portables that day, listening to the sound of the wooden deck beneath my sad little feet. Little School was over for me. (If your children participated in the Santa Fe Little School Program, now located next to the Santa Fe Zoo, you can thank Mr. Director, a.k.a. Shelton Davis, Ed.D. That's his legacy.)

Freedom from Culture

As I have grown, I've come to accept that, not being raised culturally Black or White, and most closely with my Cherokee family—whose way of life was bulldozed and reflected much of the fragmentation seen in African American cultures, from food to housing and religion—I realized that my hippie parents gave me a gift. They were pioneers of their generation and chose not to limit my identity to a specific culture or set of beliefs. As Pearman-Maday argued, we were American. They followed their own path. My dad left for Asia in search of women and wives, which is what successful Western men do, right? (They value their submissive programming.) And my mom was a free spirit. What I once perceived as a deficiency, or what I was told I lacked, turned out to be a blessing in disguise. I didn't have a cultural identity to defend, which allowed me to embrace every walk of life.

Yet, I will admit that lacking a cultural identity allowed others who wielded culture as a weapon to sometimes dominate me. It's one of the many lessons to be learned from interracial marriage. Some individuals may be fixated on the idea, "This is how we do it," and intentionally resist change. (Boring!) Even so, when you realize someone has a strong need to do something a particular way, sometimes it's easier to let them be, much like a parent might make room for a child.

Individuals raised outside the dominant cultures are often regarded as "invisible" (I'm testing progressive jargon) and may have faced teasing. Some label us as "chameleons" or "Jews" in a derogatory sense and claim that we struggle with identity issues, but do we? If freedom is wrong, I don't want to be right.

For instance, when Europeans used religion to control Africans, they also recognized that erasing or replacing their culture was equally powerful. They must have thought, "The way we do it is better." (Hmm…missionary?) But

430

could this terrible affliction of the human spirit have served as another pathway to awakening for those who suffered or witnessed this hardship? Let's explore!

*

African American Cultures

African American cultures, unlike any other cultures in the world, are not exactly cultures of free will but, unfortunately, are the result of the collective resistance of White people, encompassing language, dialect, living situations, religion, and food. White America directly laid the foundation for American Black cultures yet could not suppress the expression of the Divine culture, which is Love.

Let's take a moment to appreciate Black cool! This unique quality, envied by the world, involves learning to thrive with very little, even when space for existence is denied. It represents a way of turning the cheek without missing a beat or letting the world impact your existence. Without the collective emergence of cool, many Black individuals would have struggled to find a means of self-expression.

Cool is wearing white sneakers while struggling to pay the bills. It means putting twenty-two-inch rims on a Box Chevy before getting the paint job. (And why is the back seat missing?) Cool is effortlessly doing a backflip without ever *stepping foot* in a gymnasium. Super cool is being able to respond with a phrase like "bleach-blonde, bad-built, butch-body" (Representative Jasmine Crockett of Texas). Cool represents how you survive discrimination and oppression without letting it destroy your soul. It has to do with overcoming a force and still thriving. That's why so few White people have mastered cool; it is a reaction to a cruel life situation. Even so, many attempt to mimic this coolness.

Cool requires a level of inner acceptance, yet it is most often expressed outwardly through the ego. However, it can be even more powerful when the ego is absent, as seen in Black and Brown women and men who have used their circumstances to awaken and bypass the outward cool entirely in exchange for the inner Krst. This can also be described as the ancient West African Cool, a transformative state of inner peace and love. When Martin Luther King took up his cross and gave his life for freedom (your salvation), some finally realized he was *Krst, the Cool Krst,* the awakened one. ("Did you hear the bass? Every time the bass drops...." [giggles])

Cool is what you must become when the world works against you...or worse, when someone talks about your eyelashes. Cool is a skill. For instance, Barack Obama, the 44th president of the United States, because of his background in many ways...wasn't cool. He became cool when he had to delicately navigate racism during his presidency. White people unknowingly extracted the kind of cool they envied, unfortunately, making Obama the coolest American president ever. (Sorry, Clinton, but good try.) "When they go low, we go high," said Michelle Obama, former first lady, proving my point: your life situation makes you cool.

As cool as cool may be, it remains a coping mechanism or survival tool. You will know the world has evolved and become more inclusive when Black people are no longer noticeably cool but just chill, like someone who grew up in Hawaii eating roadside kuawa.

Oddly enough, I met a Jewish guy who embodied both Black cool and West African Cool. (giggles) I could have sworn I was talking to a Black man. Strangely, many Latinos and Filipinos exhibit a similar cultural demeanor of coolness. (Hmm...I wonder why it seems to come so naturally for many of them.) Unfortunately, many Hawaiians have become cool, too.

Anyhow, did White America do some of us a favor while laying the foundation of Black cultures? Could they have inadvertently uncovered a treasure? While many cling to the notion of culture that fosters a sense of pride and belonging, could the absence of a solid culture, one not born from human resistance, or one that clings to individualism or collectivism, be the doorway to a culture that unites all people? It can be painful to imagine yet liberating to experience.

The culture reflected in human Consciousness is Love, which binds *us all* together, much like the power of jazz or the supernatural energy of *Soul Train*. (giggles) This culture values individual autonomy *and* group harmony, creating a socially conscious environment. Interestingly, this same Love has the power to free African Americans, or any marginalized community, from oppression if the gift is accepted. (*Shout out* to all the White and Jewish men who fantasized about moving their Chi on *Soul Train*, "You Should Be Dancing," and "Don't Stop 'Til You Get Enough." Pardon me for being distracting, but *Soul Train* could rightfully be described as the "Chi Train." *Whassup, Lee Bumblebee!*)

So, "What is human Consciousness," you say? Well, I'm glad you asked again. In its simplest form, it is the essence of who we are beyond all the mind-made identities, from race to culture and everything else you believe defines you. Some may never access this dimension (Love) within themselves due to the mental labels, possessions, and comforts they have accumulated in this physical world, which keep them from looking inward. Again, as the Bible describes, "It's harder for a rich 'man' to enter the Kingdom of God." You don't need more riches—whether culture or religion.

When people begin to recognize that they are more than just a cultural identity or that they possess no exclusive culture—while the rest of the world clings to this concept with pride—it becomes one of the greatest gifts that helps one rise above the limitations of this world. (I love long-ass sentences.) White America may have unknowingly given Black Americans the greatest treasure and a key to true freedom. However, only some have accepted this gift, as most desire what everyone else has, never realizing that the mirage is a phony treasure.

Mental freedom from culture or identity (one less merchant in the temple or one less thing to keep you bound) brings you closer to understanding who you truly are. We are among the few who possess this gift. Unfortunately, many forge an identity from the scraps left over from a deprived life. (And my White friends reading this sermon who seek to rise above exclusivity are saying, "I get it!")

I'm here to let you know that you don't need scraps, *fella*, to piece yourself together like *Cinderella* when you are a microcosm of the Universe. You didn't know? (*Hakuna matata*…you can keep your culture. But don't let it limit you. And umm…using a masculine noun alongside a feminine noun, such as *fella and Cinderella*, was my way of making that statement gender-neutral.)

Setting You Free Hugs,
—Sher! (The Common Snook)
Pause. Inhale. Exhale. Reflect. ♟

P.S. "'We are only as strong as our weakest link.' America becomes its strongest and best when Pan Alpha Americans and White Americans are free" (*Elicit*, "Cut from the Same Cloth"). We can grant ourselves this freedom, which will simultaneously liberate this country. America needs both Pan Alpha Americans and White Americans to elevate their Consciousness. We can change the world by first changing ourselves.

P.P.S. Did y'all know that the concept of race helps many to ignore the suffering of others because they aren't "your people," in a sense.

P.P.P.S. Back in the day, my mom was among the few educated mothers in the neighborhood. My White mommas would pull me aside to ask about nursing school and how she accomplished it. Naturally, I could answer their questions because I was there, too. (Hmm…Santa Fe owes me a nursing degree, lol) One even returned to school and became a nurse after her conversation with little me.

2. Rising Above Attachment to Family

Hold on to your seats, *momma's boys*. This is *gonna* be rough for some of you.

Disclosure Reminder...,

The family unit has evolved, yet many still cling to the belief that blood is thicker than water, paralleling one's often erroneous, ingrained beliefs. This way of thinking leaves no room for adoption and creates a barrier between this quirky little unit—a tyranny for some—that could genuinely be a part of the family of humanity, creating social harmony. Unfortunately, *we humans* tend to prefer subtraction and division over the prosperity of addition and multiplication. National division, cultural division, racial division, and family division—all of us need something to hold on to in order to enhance our sense of belonging, so we lean towards exclusivity instead of inclusivity.

There was a time when the family unit was crucial for survival. A family that *killed* together *chilled* together. It was that simple. We can refer to this as the pack mentality. There is a time and a season for everything. However, human evolution has surpassed the need to rely on these outdated, abusive packs, making the historical function of the family obsolete. But we know that change takes time, often hundreds or thousands of years. (Women, we are getting closer to the end of our enslavement!)

434

Let's examine a perspective on the caste system in India presented by spiritual teacher Jaggi Vasudev. There's no doubt that the practice is frowned upon today. Still, he suggests that some people don't appreciate its significance and that India was likely the first country to create a social welfare service that parallels what we have today in the U.S. (I'm not sure if the chicken came before the egg in this case. See references.)

Skill sets were divided into groups called castes, which functioned like a large family or nation. Marrying someone within your caste often meant being trained in the same skill set. Vasudev explained that this ensured knowledge was transferred from one generation to the next before the advent of higher education and possibly even before writing was employed to share information.

Each caste was responsible for providing food and assistance to those in need within their community. Haitians have a similar social service, although it is not organized under a caste system but through a collective social responsibility to care for the poor. *(Whassup, Haiti!)*

This alternative perspective on the caste system is delightful. It helps India save face, keeping young and vibrant Indian folks from flipping out and dismantling that nonsense right here—right now. We saw what happened in China during the Mao era, so perhaps preventing young folks from reacting (throwing the baby out with the bathwater) will help preserve the good of ancient India. Still, that's just one way of viewing a system that was ultimately a means to control and suppress people, creating a hierarchy where some are deemed inferior to others—*forever*, for example, with Aryans over the dark-complexioned population who are closely related to the Adivasi tribes and the First Peoples of Australia. (As you can see, I don't want to make lemonade out of the caste system that casts a shadow over India to this day.)

Humanity has been engaged in an endless power game to control the masses. Regardless of how humble or "Hebrew meek" (look it up!) we attempt to present our intentions, most cannot resist the urge to come out on top. They will leverage their position and status to enhance their self-image.

If you have ever heard of the surname Patel in the U.S., these business families from a lower Gujarat caste and other regions of India arrived in America decades before the Indian IT migration. They owned gas stations, convenience stores, liquor stores, learning centers, and restaurants. They built a respectable reputation in the U.S. and escaped the caste system that kept many at the bottom of the social hierarchy in India—*forever.* I wonder if they ever imagined that members of the more affluent caste of well-educated South Indians would, forty to fifty years later, arrive on American shores (well, the tarmac), bringing with them the mindset of the outdated caste system. (Now, don't confuse the Patels with the guys who wear the turbans. Those are Sikhs from Punjab in northern India. They established a new religion to escape the caste system. Brilliant! Noo, White folks, they aren't Muslims. They own pizzerias and Shell gas stations in New Jersey. And some of them can rap, too! [giggles])

Anyhow, would these new immigrants honor the Patels for giving India a presence in the U.S., or would some act as if they were "superior" to their fellow man? I'm sure you guessed it: the Patels were not given the respect they deserved. See, I bet you didn't even know this was happening in America. The oppression of the caste system manifests similarly to our sometimes "invisible" systemic racism. This is why adding "caste" as a legally protected category in California is so important to include alongside the current protected classes: race, color, religion, sex, national origin, age, disability, and genetic information, but it has yet to pass. For the Patels and many other families, the caste was back! (That's what happens when you don't *completely kill* the monster in the movie.)

Come on, light-skinned North Indian and South Indian Americans; we should at least thank the Patels for opening Kumon franchises to ensure your little one completes elementary school math by the second grade. (Please don't forget, I lived happily in an all-Indian neighborhood in Charlotte, North Carolina, a.k.a. Little India, so I can speak on this. And Indian people are not like Americans, who get offended by every little thing. At least, that hasn't been my experience...yet. [*And why is this here?* This must have been the spirit leading.])

Now, let's examine the tyranny we call the family unit, "ruled by its weakest member" (Irish playwright George Bernard Shaw). This concept is outdated in every possible way. Before any of you "blood is thicker than water" folks, like my husband's former backwoods *Yankalachian* mentality, get your feathers ruffled, this observation is meant for those seeking psychological freedom. This isn't to say we don't need each other. Family is lovely and has its place in our lives, but not to the extent that we create exclusive mini-kingdoms and tolerate their nonsense simply because they hold royal titles.

Those who grew up in strong families (or even unconventional ones) are led to believe that the family bond is the most significant in the world. This overlooks the reality that at least *half of us* have had a completely different experience and cannot relate to this idea presented as fact.

I'm one of those people for whom the early biological family unit fulfilled its role. I grew up without remaining a part of the clan, nor did I confine myself to the traditional family concept. I realized that the world is filled with wonderful people, and I have the right to choose who I consider family. It's a beautiful idea. It would be fantastic if more people could experience this freedom or Love.

Unfortunately, the phrase "blood is thicker than water" resonates with many, serving as an ugly way to make people feel unwelcome and reinforce a pack mentality. In earlier times, this mindset helped ensure the survival of the family unit, although in a very barbaric manner. Today, it keeps many adults under the control and authority of their parents. (I won't go into detail, but some of you in this situation know what I'm talkin' 'bout. And if you don't—hint, hint—you may still be defending ["Yo momma!"].)

We also need *woman* to embrace this idea of family and her "unconditional love." If her love were as perfect as *man* likes to imagine and require her to be, this world would be a different place. For one, we wouldn't be so divided because unconditional love knows no boundaries.

Many people, especially men and male spiritual teachers, believe in the concept of the unconditional "loving mother," often likened to the love of God. The comparison presents some difficulty because those are some big big boots for women to fill. (Hmm...maybe God is a woman after all. *Whassup, Lakshmi!*)

Women must find Love in themselves, no different than men. If few people know Love, do women (parents) love their children unconditionally? Women are incredible, but that doesn't mean they know God.

Momma's boys, I wouldn't be writing a book like this if unconditional love were a natural part of motherhood today. Sadly, she clings to this mental token— a myth—as if it were a badge of honor, because it creates a sense of *specialness* and ensures she behaves and stays in line. If she doesn't perform as men define her unconditional love to be, she will be shamed or canceled by both women and men alike, made to feel less than a woman. What a terrible mind game. It's difficult to escape the cult, so to speak. (Listen closely, sweet girl; Love should not be confused with your attachment or unwavering willingness to feed it, wash it, and raise it. Don't let your ego or the male perspective mislead you, *Mami*. "What's Love Got to Do with It?")

But again, we need women to embrace this idea of family because men have a terrible habit of going out for a hunt (chasing tail) and never returning. Sure, you can believe a dinosaur ate him if you like. But be thankful that few women are brave enough to step outside the programming. Someone must care for those kids. And if she chooses herself, again, we'll shame or cancel her when men do it every day. It works! ("What do we want? Freedom! When do we want it? Now!")

437

However, times are changing, and women are rethinking the role they are expected to play. For one, *woman* no longer needs *man* for protection. She can buy a gun if necessary. (But I still need my wonderful man. He knows I could be dangerous with a gun.) Nowadays, folks prefer thoughtful companionship that connects to their emotions (mental muscles) over physical strength.

The family unit should also evolve to be more sophisticated. When we recognize that we don't own anyone, we become less inclined to control or enslave another human being. We ought to raise our children to be independent and pursue interconnectedness rather than codependence, which involves manipulation by fostering dependency.

With freedom at every level, we can love at will and embrace all whom we choose to call family. And when these wonderful people leave us, whether due to the rhythm of life or by departing from this world, we release them freely without attachments. I understand it's difficult, but nothing is worth controlling or holding onto, as it only hinders our own freedom and spiritual growth.

Hugs without attachments,

—Sher! (The Common Snook)

Pause. Inhale. Exhale. Reflect.

P.S. Speaking of family! Did I ever tell y'all my baby sister was the 1989 Oaks Mall Cutest Baby winner? See, I haven't completely forgotten the folks I grew up with. She's still a cutie with all that…*aptitude. (Whassup, Kristin!)*

P.P.S. The world needs more women leaders because diverse perspectives are essential. I heard a woman ask a well-known spiritual teacher why most gurus are men. He responded, sounding progressive and inclusive, "What difference does it make what's in a person's pants?" Unfortunately, the progressive generation drank the Kool-Aid and cheered. They overlooked the fact that it was a valid question from a community where women are still undervalued. This was not the time to dodge the question and dismiss *woman* by throwing progressive beliefs in her face.

Why do men fear our leadership? Because our viewpoint could jeopardize their comfort and VIP status.

(Sit in stillness with your eyes closed for 15 minutes a day; I promise it will transform your life!)

3. Rising Above the Limitations of the Inner Beast, and the Restoration of Her Kingdom

Here, we have a complicated title for a complicated sermon.

Disclosure Reminder...,

Let's shift our focus and examine how some decisions we make without thinking contradict "best practices" for advancing humanity. These self-serving and often contradictory choices stem from our animal instinct to survive, rise, and evolve, which is often outdated. It resembles the mentality of those who believe "blood is thicker than water." I call this behavior the inner beast!

Some argue that we aren't animals, but I can't think of anything more barbaric than the oppressive social constructs we have already discussed. *We humans* are a mess.

Anyhow, I will let this sermon emerge organically and see what happens. This one will be a treat! I will allow y'all to watch how my mind translates what Consciousness sees without words. It will use analogies, allegories, and any tool to bring the information to the surface and paint a lovely picture. Please note that mystics aren't always precise the first time because we translate the unspoken into language, where there is always room for error as we search for the right words. I describe this as reading braille, but after a few attempts, I nail it...and nail that *thang* to the cross! And then say, it is finished!

My observation process often begins with noticing patterns or intriguing behaviors. I don't always verbalize my experiences or examine my observations further unless necessary. Still, I usually have a strong sense of knowing whether something is related, shares the same energy, or requires further investigation. When I'm ready to translate my observations into words, I turn on my mental computer. The mind is always eager to join the fun and starts making connections and noting additional patterns while I write. Sometimes, my mind gets ahead of itself, and I must feed the information back to the Source to determine if it's a keeper, a process I accomplish by being still. You know, there is an intelligence within that is greater than human intellect, right? With that understanding, you should always check with the Source to ensure that using your wisdom is wise.

*

Ruling Over the Beast

Speaking of using the mind as a tool and not being ruled by the inner beast! You may be wondering why there are so many songs in this book. Well, this is my surprise and gift to you! You'll never find another book like it! This phenomenon of songs popping into my head while writing is a blast. (Did you know I actually stopped and danced to most of those songs?) It may seem distracting to have music *spawning* at any moment of the day. Still, it's the Divine's way of ensuring I get the necessary nutrients to keep writing by moving my Chi, since I sometimes can write all day without food or water. (You know, "*woman* does not live by bread alone." "It is true!") However, if I told folks I'm a walking jukebox, they'd think I was crazy. (Wouldn't the world be a better place if we all had an inner orchestra or theme music and took a break now and then to move the Chi?)

That said, the mind is a fantastic tool when partnered with Consciousness. So today, I'm going to input a thought into the mental search engine: that Black women secretly support interracial marriage even though they cringe at its sight. (*Hakuna matata*...my mind knows this doesn't mean all.) Let's see what happens and who or what else gets drawn in as I use my observation skills (Consciousness) and pattern thinking to look around for similar behaviors. Warning: When writing my sermons, I often spew from multiple directions, which usually results in multiple sermons; however, there will only be one sermon today. I don't usually allow folks to see this, but you're in for a treat. And unfortunately, not everyone will have the capacity to follow my shifting currents. I get it! Still, this is unfiltered neurodiversity. Uh-oh, I can feel my tummy rumbling now. Hopefully, you can handle the mess. Here it goes!

Observations of the Inner Beast

Black mommas often ask me in a knowing and judgmental tone, "Are you okay with your son dating a White girl?" My response always catches them off guard because they wrongly assume I'm "whitewashed." After all, you know my husband is White...and handsome, too!

Sadly, many Black women are secretly hoping for their sons to marry White women while simultaneously casting judgment on those who seem to support interracial marriage. They often get frustrated when other men, besides their sons, follow this trend. (That's twisted!) Surprisingly, in my experience, most of these women pose this question with eager anticipation to fulfill this hidden desire. This behavior isn't necessarily self-hatred, as some might assume, but rather rooted in an instinctual urge to evolve and overcome racial injustice. They understand that life for their grandchildren (their legacy) will be a little sweeter with lighter skin, even though this contradicts their longing for equality and respect. It's about "survival of the fittest" and "mate selection."

However, we can't see that Black women promote this behavior in a manner similar to White women, ensuring the survival of racism (oops, there it goes!) because man is presumed to be the head of the woman or household. (There goes another punch from the Divine! It will spew from this point forward.) Nevertheless, there are many absent Black fathers, and women carry on without missing a beat. Either the media is doing a remarkable job influencing these boys, or Momma is guilty of partnering with the media. But everyone knows *woman* is the head and leader of humanity...I mean, the household, whether they admit it or not. Women teach and perpetuate damaging social constructs like racism. (Ouch! Of course, men, too. [eye-roll]) Still, the mother is the child's primary teacher during the formative years. Children are influenced by her perspective and are glued to her opinion. It's like a cord once connected the two. (You know, in Judaism, you're only Jewish if ["Yo momma!"] is Jewish because women keep these traditions alive. Not these men.)

Back to the...White Woman's Inner Beast

Besides being racially profiled by a few scared *momma's boys* during a traffic stop, the majority of the racism I have experienced has come from White women, which deserves our attention. History shows that from the resistance of the Civil War to some of the most atrocious acts of brutality against Black people in America, a White woman has often been the instigator. Men who are conditioned to believe that women are more peaceful or that the male ego is more dominant, unfortunately, view women through a stereotypical lens. What they don't realize or prefer not to admit is that *woman* often utilizes *man* to do her dirty work. *(Right, Hillary?)*

If I backed my words with academic research, you might be more open to considering this. However, I'm here to teach you to observe. You are the research and researcher! If you can be honest with yourself and move beyond your programming, life isn't all that difficult to see. You can perceive this whether you are the perpetrator or the victim. It works both ways. If we understood the male relationship with *woman*, we would see that *man* often expresses *woman's* emotions, demands, and wrath. Supreme Court Justice Clarence Thomas and his wife are a good example of this projection—or perhaps "puppetry" is a better word. (Pardon me, I must get off the floor from laughing.)

Men love to please and offer solutions so they can get back to chilling. "Here, *woman*, you happy now?"

For example, my husband's nonprofit exists today because I strongly encouraged him to go virtual and work from home in 2015. After all, sitting in Atlanta traffic was foolish. Many were resistant to the idea when he pitched it, but he had a more influential voice whispering in his ear at night. (Again, like Clarence Thomas and his wife.) And I won! (I bet she wins, too. Hmm…maybe married men shouldn't be allowed to serve on the Supreme Court.) *Anyways*, five years later, his nonprofit survived the pandemic because it had already transitioned to a virtual model, thanks to this woman. ("Behind every great *man*, there's a great [and assertive] *woman* [in charge].")

Now to the…Male Beast

Let's shift our focus to the male beast, Papa Bear, for a moment. *(Okay, you gonna use fairy tales now to reach the people?)* Momma Bear will say to reduce the male species' intimidation by her power cord while the cubs climb on his back like a toy, "Listen to your father," because…they don't. As he becomes frustrated and unable to escape them, she will ask sternly, "Do you hear your father speaking?" Again, because…they don't. They're now bouncing on his head. It's almost as if no cord ever connected the two to transmit this information. (Children love the heart of a father when he is awake.)

Papa Bear's job is to build and protect the camp. He's a "homemaker," a worker bee! He also ensures there's plenty of time for play and opportunities to sneak in as many snacks and honeycombs as possible. The cubs love his "Live Free or Die" attitude because Momma Bear tends to be uptight and doesn't appreciate sticky hands. As the head of the household and humanity, she *bears* the weight of the world on her shoulders. She's even responsible for protecting Papa Bear's enormous ego. It's a significant responsibility.

Hmm…while writing this, it sure the heck looks like women might be more dominant in masculine energy than their male counterparts, who like to chill and play. (Huh!) And some of them have the balls to "hang upside down" and paint pictures on the ceiling. That would be an interesting twist to the balance of Yin and Yang, discovering that men might be more dominant in feminine energy despite all that testosterone. You know, but with both balanced in the middle, one deviating slightly to the left or right. But due to our brainwashing, we can't fathom this. I should delete it instead of throwing my pearls before swine.

442

(*Whassup to my "TV-dad,"* who helped me crawl on the ceiling like Spiderman as a child!)

Zoom in and look at these men! *Man* can play in a messy house. *Man* will choose pleasure and snacks over structure any day, which is why many of them mess around (running *game*) without regard for the structure *woman* has established at home. Men are pleasure-seeking and will play before business any chance they get. Big big, big-ass toy stores like Bass Pro Shops and R.E.I. understand this truth. Hunting is all fun and *games*—no pun intended! Just ask a house cat or the common snook. (Ugh...*some* men. [eye-roll])

Over to the...Partnership Between the Beasts

However, women direct and teach in nearly every area of life. Women manage the schools, the most significant institution established to pass down knowledge. We oversee the home like CEOs. We lead the way while men assist in achieving the family goals. (Yep, "help meet!")

Man felt jealous of the power tool that *woman* had and made himself the head of *woman* when it's clearly not true, but rather the other way around. *Man gamed* the system and was *game* to take her down. We can't even flip 1 Corinthians 11:3 from the Bible because men would have a fit if they had to hear, ~~"Woman is the head of man."~~ Still, I won't say it because it's not exactly true. The two are equal partners, even though she is the head of the household, which is a microcosm of the world. As mentioned in my sermon, "Is It ADHD or Your Parenting?" I explained that both women and men possess feminine and masculine energy, and it appears men are a bit more dominant in feminine energy than women. *(Stop being ignorant. Ain't nobody talkin' 'bout twisting. Remember, boneheads, that masculine and feminine energy have nothing to do with "sexuality.")* Again, most can't fathom this because of the mental concept defining femininity created by men for us to play, which blurs their vision.

Like Tarzan, *man* is the lord of the jungle (his playground), and if he understood this and the significance of protecting this ecosystem, he would stop destroying it and making it ugly. He would return to building homes and towns that reflect Consciousness, as the great architect Christopher Alexander expressed in his book, *A Timeless Way of Building.* (My favorite Quaker gifted two of his books to my son because he recognized his passion for creating a beautiful world at such a young age. Wow! Both my sons are enthusiastic about preserving the jungle and enhancing its beauty.)

Well, perhaps my wiring isn't so strange after all. I create structure in our home while my husband and boys seize every opportunity to play. Isn't that interesting? Perhaps this is why men have man caves; women run and dominate the whole damn house. (See, men need safe spaces, too!)

Shift to the…Brainwashing and the Power of Words

The brainwashing around "sexuality" and the role women are expected to play is similar to how White America programmed many of my ancestors, Pan Alpha and Cherokee, to accept "Black" as their identity. Many years ago, I met a multiracial Cherokee woman in New Hampshire. I call her Adsila, who seemed disgruntled and lost, as if nobody had noticed she existed. I said, "You're Cherokee, right?" She replied, "I don't really know my ancestry and always assumed I was just mixed." I said, "You're certainly multiracial, but you're Cherokee. You look like my family; I can see it in your eyes." This beautiful woman, bearing the weight of the world on her shoulders, came alive and began to blossom. Words are powerful because how others see us can influence how we see ourselves (ladies!), as the guilty men turn the other way. (Oh my, channeling, translating, and writing is just as good as sex!)

Finally, to the…Restoration of Her Kingdom

If *woman* was restored to her role, we all know lesbians would have a bunch of children. She would be pro-life even if she had to apply progesterone cream because they are big big mommas with a lot of love to give, especially the butch ones! She would probably also be polyandrous (having more than one husband). We'd all call her the queen bee! Women 6'5" and taller would be at the top of the mate selections. Men would throw themselves at her feet instead of being intimidated by her. The real men would say, "That's a whole *lotta* woman," and beg to sow their seed. When she spoke, her twelve children would enthusiastically respond, "Yes, Big Big Momma!"

When the restoration occurs, she will take responsibility for her actions instead of behaving like an animal. She can't correct what she can't see because her role isn't adequately acknowledged, even though we blame her for everything. In a sense, she gets to call the shots without accepting responsibility when she doesn't behave nicely and lays down her uzi to tap her inner beast instead. Still, if her vision were clear and she understood the power of her influence, she could change the world tomorrow by starting at home. (Gandhi realized this, as well.) Remember, when you aim small, you hit big!

*

Please Don't Allow the Beast to Psych Your Mind with Wisdom

Back to the Black woman's inner beast, where I left off: I respond to their assumptions about my preferences for my sons by saying, "No, I'm not okay with them dating your average White young lady. It concerns me greatly because racism in America is still ingrained in a significant percentage of White Americans." Some never escape the cult, so to speak. (By the way, these are the kinds of realities that people like to silence. Again, I'm not talking about "haters." These are your average, everyday good people.) Anyhow, I don't want my sons to be subjected to the same unpleasant experiences as I encountered.

Nevertheless, enduring White dominance is more challenging for a "Woman of Color" than for a "Man of Color" because, once again, *woman* is "the head of the household," of course, and she doesn't have time for nonsense. I explain that I ask my sons if they want to deal with the ongoing challenges of the ingrained mental concepts within many White cultures and White dominance on a daily basis, as I kiss my husband on the cheek to reaffirm my love for him and his people. (Could this be *wise wisdom*? Relax, there's more to come.)

Most people struggle to accept my honest feedback because they are conditioned to deny the truth and instead rely on hope. My feedback causes cognitive dissonance arising from conflicting beliefs. People often ask, "Doesn't Love conquer all things?" because that's what they are expected to believe. However, they haven't fully experienced it. But yes, Love does conquer all! And it requires time, patience, perseverance, and Presence. But would I do it again if I knew better? (Hmm...women like me don't have as many options chasing her down. [giggles]) I'll get back to you on that as my husband postures with confidence.

The existence of abusive social constructs demonstrates that very few people, regardless of race, understand Love. As previously mentioned, if women genuinely practiced unconditional Love, as *momma's boys* would like to believe, racism would not persist today. (And they wouldn't be crazy today.) Additionally, unconditional Love would unite women, enabling them to overcome sexism more easily. It's that straightforward.

Either way, I'm prepared if the Divine sends me a beautiful White daughter-in-law who is ready to rise above societal programming...her momma's animal-like wisdom to protect the concept of race, which can't survive without racism. (Y'all know the notion of *White* cannot survive without racism, right? It's like the pair is inseparable.) *White* must be isolated or protected to ensure its survival because all it takes is one-drop...and it's gone. White also needed to be idolized and seen as *special* as a survival tactic because the natural human instinct to white skin triggers a cause for concern and can be startling. This response is similar to the reaction of seeing a snake, as children often react to those with albinism or my husband's vitiligo in this way. I used to tell the children in Little India as they approached my husband with caution, almost as if they had seen leprosy in a past life, "It's okay; you can touch his hand. He has vitiligo." We can see today that white or pale skin is not always related to a disease and won't kill the rest of us, right? (Hmm…how come I can't hear your response? Why the silence?) Anyhow, once racism is eliminated in America, the face of Americans will naturally resemble that of the diversity found in Puerto Rico or Cuba—like my sons. Love is beautiful!

Looking out for your family's interests can be seen as wise. However, this "wisdom" often violates humanity, is self-defeating, and limits us when this existence is so much more profound than self-preservation. What we believe to be the path to a good life or the illusion of safety—good, bad, or better—is a veil we must overcome. We must rise above the inner beast of wisdom, a collection of our knowledge and experience, to make just decisions, because our wisdom could be flawed or outdated. (I'm knowledgeable of this because I took Sociology of Knowledge eons ago in college. [wink])

Just because life has given you experience, which becomes your knowledge, using your wisdom doesn't necessarily make you wise, especially when intertwined with a need for survival. Making just decisions is a matter of opinion influenced by our belief system. Wisdom sometimes suggests killing your enemies or invading a neighboring country before they invade you. Humanity must move beyond wisdom and stop acting like animals. As mentioned before, thank God Black people have never collectively exercised extreme measures of "wisdom" when dealing with racism. Hopefully, we can begin to make decisions consciously, rather than relying solely on human "wisdom."

Babe, could you join me for a moment? Do you think folks were able to follow this sermon? Could they keep up with my shifting currents? Were there too many layers for the human mind to process at once? Please share your thoughts with me.

Babe: Well, watching your mind translate this information from the unspoken, as you say, has been a real treat.

Sher: Thank you, Babe. You make me feel *special.*

Babe: This sermon is loaded.

Sher: And that's why I said it was like spewing from both ends. It just came out of me violently without asking first, "Excuse me, I'm *gonna* plant myself right here and force you to delete some of those goofy sermons like "Mother's Day is a—BITCH," because you need to make room for me.

(Silence)

Sher: Babe, give me some feedback. I didn't even want to write this sermon and avoided peering deeper into my observation for a while, as I often do. We're right in the middle of editing! The book was supposed to be finished!

Babe: Well, this is a multi-layered sermon that you describe as the behaviors of the inner beast. You speak about masculine and feminine energy, as well as the behaviors that manifest as a result. You also discuss this skewed perspective on who is the head of the household, suggesting that women are the ones who make the decisions. To top it off, you discuss who holds the strongest influence when speaking to children within a family. You propose that because women are "secretly" in charge of their homes—not the men—and that their children really only listen to them, perhaps racism is most strongly perpetuated by White women. This perspective emerged, of course, only after you introduced a not-so-hypothetical viewpoint that Black women have regarding interracial relationships, which is...complicated. Yet, you suggest that many Black women encourage their sons to seek out White women as partners. Trying to hold and balance all these ideas is a lot to digest.

Sher: Well, that was a good summary. You got it! Don't worry about elaborating on *woman* being the head of the household and primary teacher of the children. There's no need to dwell on that since everyone can see this. Still, your insight into the challenges of interracial marriage could be helpful and further explain why I have concerns about our young men marrying your average White young lady. I'm sure folks were struggling with that remark.

(Long silence)

Babe: The answer most expect to hear is that it doesn't matter.

Sher: I don't give that answer.

Babe: I know you don't. You *never* take the easy out! Saying, "It's complicated," is probably the safest response.

(laughter)

Sher: And that's why you're a diplomat.

Babe: It's almost as if you should ask, what answer do you want me to give? There's an answer that says I want to stand on the side of love, so love who you want to love. Then there's an answer that acknowledges that racism is still alive and well, and I need to be honest with my children.

Sher: The latter nobody wants to hear. Babe, you know people like to believe that interracial marriage represents progress in the world. Remember when we used to walk into a new church and how quickly they would try to keep us? The image of our interracial marriage was good for business and created a false hope that "God" was changing hearts. Nobody wants to hear the ugly truth. As I've mentioned before, I've only encountered a couple or a few White folks who were free from the mental disease of racism. Unfortunately, my experience remains true to this day.

(laughter)

Babe: From what you're saying, it seems that many Pan Alphas deny their own reality and choose to fantasize about interracial marriage being something to desire. Look at our own marriage. For homogeneous marriages where race, culture, and religion align perfectly, the criteria for determining whether a relationship is a good fit can be pretty small. Do they have any underlying mental health issues? How financially stable are they? What is their family like? Do our family values align? For interracial marriages, without even discussing religion or culture, that checklist is far longer than anyone might initially think. Where will we settle and raise our kids? Where will they find acceptance? How racist are our family and extended families, and how might that manifest at family gatherings?

Sher: Babe, did you say *our* family? (laughter) Oh, I forgot they're my family, too.

Babe: How do we raise our children to avoid the racial pitfalls of being Black, Brown, or White? Where do we eat lunch? The last question sounds *stupid*, but remember when we drove just outside Athens, Georgia, with our kids and pulled over to that strip-mall Chinese restaurant for lunch? The restaurant, filled with White country folk and their families, all but stopped eating to glare at our multiracial family waiting for a table. It became so uncomfortable that we slowly backed out the door, and the Asian hostess quietly told us how sorry she was for our experience, as she had also witnessed what was happening. (Wow! Chinese people are apologizing for White folks' behavior. That proves we are more connected than you might imagine. You know, a White man marrying a "Woman of Color" is still a rare sighting; it's usually the other way around.) It was only one of several moments like this throughout our marriage that nobody warned us about when we committed to each other. The bottom line is it can be decades of hell for whoever takes that on in America." (laughter)

Sher: Wow, Babe-GPT, that was great feedback! But you forgot one thing. You didn't say anything about the hidden biases you had to overcome. Why *youse* being quiet? Are you intellectualizing again to avoid personal conviction? Now, White folks are praising your clarity, and you've stolen the stage...again. Hmm...I'm having "déjà vu. Do you remember the article you wrote, published in the local paper, that helped to clear your conscience for taking me into that funeral with all those big-ass Confederate flags without considering how I might have felt? And why didn't anyone from your family comment on the article? You were published! That was big big news! Yet they were silent, which spoke volumes about what they prioritized. You talked about the struggles we faced in New Hampshire, but no compassion was expressed. Nothing! Not a word from anyone. Still, your article made you a hero at the Quaker Meeting. They loved your introspection and self-reflection. They do enjoy talkin' 'bout White man's problems without ever correcting them, of course. Because if they can talk about them, it means they aren't impacted by them, right?

Babe: Which is worse, silence…or heroism!? (laughter)

Sher: Don't *be raising* your voice at me! Babe, you know you're my hero. Are you okay with me sharing this conversation? *(I'm sorry, Bette Midler, but I can't go down that road today.)*

Babe: You have my full support. We're just different people today. I know you questioned whether you'd do it again. But I wouldn't trade you for anything in the world because *you are the force that helps me soar.*

Sher: Oh Babe, stop. You're "Killing Me Softly…" (laughter)

As for humanity, we must rise above our animal instincts, the beast within. Our capacity to access Consciousness is the only thing that distinguishes us from all other…beasts. That's as close as I will get to a warm, fuzzy conclusion. Instead, reflect on this! (Cheer up! Here's a song, "Bird or Beast" by Terrence Ho and pianist Ed Legare, that connects us all. I love his voice, and we have the same birthday! This is my favorite song in the entire book! Only a Pisces from Gainesville, Florida, could produce such a beautiful song. *Whassup, Terrence!*)

I hope you enjoyed the show.

Bear Hugs,
　—Sher! (The Common Snook)
Pause. Inhale. Exhale. Reflect.

P.S. Who *ya* think raised all the lazy men who expect to be served? (*Give it up for* my mother-in-law, who managed to raise a helpful, hardworking man who's territorial, adventurous, playful, and snacky.)

P.P.S. *Sherguru, I've been meaning to ask, "What the heck is 'Yankalachia?'"* Well, the Appalachian Trail ends in New England, right? These Yankees share a culture similar to that of folks from Appalachia, even though it's a politically blue region. (giggles) Let's pronounce it together, (yanka-LAY-shuh), which should rhyme with Appalachia (appa-LAY-shuh).

P.P.P.S. It is finished! How cool; it's December 21, 2024! How 'bout a final lesson on **Consciousness for *Common and Country Folks*?** As we celebrate the

Solstice and my final sermon (but not the last sermon in the book), I recall explaining to my boys when they were little that the ancestors believed the sun died on the shortest day of the year, the first day of winter. Solstice means "sun stop."

We would head out for a winter walk and notice the long shadows following us. I explained that in the past, the dark days frightened many people who didn't understand the planet's natural rhythms. To overcome this fear and gloom, cultures worldwide decorated their homes with natural items to remind them of warmer days. Some would adorn their spaces with evergreen trimmings, cut down entire trees, and drag them into the house. Others filled their homes with lamps and lights to illuminate the darkness, as seen in the theme of Diwali. These celebrations were believed to encourage the gods to return the sun's warmth to the earth, with light conquering darkness, or good over evil. I explained to my sons that all the winter holidays around the world, such as Diwali, Christmas, Hanukkah, and Kwanzaa, shared similar themes. We called them the winter solstice holidays, with Diwali always leading the way.

Well, the celebrations and decorations seemed to work! Like clockwork, within a few days after the start of winter, it becomes noticeable to the naked eye that the sun starts to climb a little higher above the horizon, which suggests the gods are listening. The sun will continue to rise higher in the sky. The days will grow longer, with the sun eventually returning fully to the Northern Hemisphere, marking the arrival of spring.

Once again, the ancestors celebrated the return of warmer days, as the sun had been reborn and restored our planet's life, fertility, and vegetation (salvation). And the Pagans said, "Amen!" Yet, despite this common sense, Thomas Paine called these folks sun worshippers. In his book, *The Age of Reason,* he stated that "The Christian religion is a parody of the worship of the Sun, in which they put a name whom they call Christ, in the place of the Sun, and pay him the same adoration which was originally paid to the Sun." *And what's wrong with that, Thomas?* (No, I don't have a copy of that old-ass book or a page number for you. Ugh! What a waste of time when we have Google! However, I highly recommend *The Shortest Day: Celebrating the Winter Solstice* by Wendy Pfeffer. She has a book for each season. I hope your children enjoy her books as much as mine did. Happy Solstice and Happy Holidays to all!)

(Stop *acting* beastly for 15 minutes a day; I promise it will transform your life!)

4. Rising in Sophistication

Disclosure Reminder…,

In a global society, success hinges on finding common ground. Westerners cling to many outdated mental concepts while we face significant foreign influences that introduce even more obsolete ideas. Unfortunately, America hasn't yet adopted a more enlightened approach to human evolution, despite the presence of many great minds.

Let's explore the Abrahamic Ten Commandments, which embody values shared by most major world religions. We'll revise a few and add many more. However, one commandment will endure the test of time. See if you can spot Waldo! (My husband suggested I use "you" instead of "thou," but I believe "thou" effectively conveys my point.) Here we go:

- There are many paths to the Divine. (You are one of them!)
- Thou shalt know you are not your mind or body and miss God altogether by worshiping goofy mental idols like race and religion.
- Thou shalt not F-bomb thy neighbor.
- Thou shalt chill because life is short, and the only things that really matter are good food and friends.
- Thou shalt not abandon their elderly parents, so parents won't be tempted to hinder or handicap their children and tether them with chains.
- Thou shalt not kill (which includes war).
- Thou shalt know there are bigger things than sex and find something better to do.
- Thou shalt not steal, rob the Patels or sell cheap plastic shit to humanity and call it "capitalism." (And Patel said, "Amen!")
- Thou shalt not lie, use manipulation, or worse, think that people don't notice their behavior.
- Thou shalt not group people by skin color…and know that pinkish and yellowish "white" skin is just a type of albinism. (Hmm…is that why they call me "red" or "high-yellow"?)
- Thou shalt not enslave *woman*.
- Thou shalt not cover *woman* with a tent.
- Thou shalt be allowed to cry and experience emotions.
- Thou shalt let their son become a man and not raise a man-boy, *baby-husband*, or momma's boy.

- Thou shalt know the notion of "superiority" is child's play and is a sign of fear and feelings of inferiority.
- Thou shalt know that taking responsibility is a duty to humanity.
- Thou shalt listen or fear a riot.
- Thou shalt not put daughter-in-law and controlling mother-in-law under the same roof. (This practice benefits *baby-husbands* and is the Devil!)
- Thou shalt not follow a British/Western diet: cream, cake, and cookies. (Still, Taupo, New Zealand, has the best fish and chips!)
- Thou shalt be entitled to a simple home, food, water, healthcare, and education.
- Thou shalt not mandate recycling and composting before fundamental human rights or the end of White privilege.
- Thou shalt not rob the next generation of wisdom by moving to Lady Lake, Florida. (Thank you, Biden, for your service.)
- Thou shalt not equate hearing Arabic with terrorism, except if you failed college algebra.
- Thou shalt know that equality and *equity* make *woman* and *man* a fantastic team.
- Thou shalt cheer loudly when men move big big *stuff*.
- Thou shalt not "grab pussy" without permission.
- Thou shalt know that rap and country music are cousins.
- Thou shalt know math and that anti-abortion laws will not save the dwindling White majority. (White women will book a flight to NH.)
- Thou shalt not have unnecessary sex in the "country of Florida."
- Thou shalt know HIV should be over, and humanity can eradicate the disease.
- Thou shalt know conservatism is a resistance to human evolution, holding on to the past where Love doesn't live.
- Thou shalt know that progressiveness doesn't mean drinking every flavor of Kool-Aid.

Shared Hugs,
—Sher! (The Common Snook)
Pause. Inhale. Exhale. Reflect.

(Sit in stillness with your eyes closed for 15 minutes a day; I promise it will transform your life!)

Section XI: Your Pot of Gold

In case you decided to skip the introduction and browse around, here's the **Disclosure Reminder**: Before diving in, I will say this: I'm simple. I love to laugh. Please don't confuse my humor with sarcasm; I always mean what I say. I test the limits. My words are plain. I often use "own" redundantly. I don't claim to know all the answers; my only intention is to be a vessel. Also, to connect with different experiences, I interchangeably use the terms "Consciousness," "Presence," "God," "Universe," "Source," "Divine," "Energy," "Christ/Krst," and "Light." Above all, reading my humor with a Southern accent is best. Enjoy!

...or dhokla! (TCS)

1. Lord Vishnu and Followin' My Dream

Disclosure Reminder...,

"On today's episode of 🏠*House Whores*" as we like to say. Before returning to Gainesville, Florida, the nomads, who had "screwed around" with many many homes, lived between North Carolina, Georgia, and Florida for "business" (giggles) but got stuck in North Carolina due to an approaching virus. (That's what happens!) Our neighborhood, with approximately 400 residents, was surprisingly around 99% Indian and other South Asians, from Nepal to Sri Lanka. I didn't have to go to India because India came to me. I've never experienced anything like it in my life. The stories I could tell will one day become a children's book.

One evening, while chatting with some neighbors—since everybody and their grandma came outside during the golden hour (a sight to behold)—a little boy walking around the neighborhood pond greeted me with an engaging, high-pitched voice. He was surely a unique fellow, with the most angelic eyes and a mischievous smile that could light up a room. I'm not sure what I said to him, but he must have taken a liking to me because he showed up at our house the next day. Little did I know this was about to become a daily occurrence.

At the end of spring, my husband and boys set out for their annual camping trip to the mountains, leaving me home for the weekend. (My favorite kind of camping.) I was excited to have some time to myself. I didn't answer the door that day and drew the blinds. However, my new friend Vishnu came almost every hour looking for us. But as the sun set, I felt it was safe to go out and check the mail, and lo and behold, Vishnu appeared out of nowhere, thrilled to see me. "Sherry, there you are! I've been looking for you all day!" I glanced around briefly to see if anyone else could see him because his sudden appearance felt spooky. He certainly captured my attention because his timing seemed off to me. He was never down by the pond after dark, and it felt like he knew I was coming outside.

From then on, his visits became quite regular, especially since the school bus stop was in front of our house. Unfortunately, whenever he rang the bell, the adult in me would rather be busy when our boys were out.

Still, this was the pandemic. I thought, *Didn't I crave the company of a friend?* Ultimately, I realized it wouldn't hurt to give this sweet boy some of my time instead of dodging him, which took more time in the long run because he didn't give up easily, or perhaps it would be more accurate to say he never would. Sometimes, he would knock on my back door and call for me just in case I didn't hear him. (Oh my, how I miss that little boy.)

To my surprise, he didn't require much of my time. We had daily talks on the porch, which lasted no more than 15 minutes. At one point, he asked if I knew Spanish. I told him I had studied it for four years, but that was all. He replied, "Great, you can teach me!" I responded, "Vishnu, I don't speak Spanish."

He even went as far as to tell his mother to cancel his Spanish lessons because I could teach him. But this little boy was right and somehow had me teaching him a language I couldn't speak. We would have simple conversations in Spanish while sitting on the porch. He proved the theory that the student is the one who extracts knowledge from the teacher. Or, as I once heard spiritual teacher Richard Rohr say, "Be ready to be taught, and the teacher will arrive."

On other days, I would read him a story, or he would ask for water or a snack. He never took it by the hand but opened his mouth like a baby bird for me to feed him. This is common in Indian cultures and is often seen as an act of love or, at the very least, a clean hand. I felt honored that he viewed me as a friend or family member. I had been made an auntie, which neighbors from the same community or village in India are called.

As I experienced and observed his strangeness, I wondered whether I had befriended a Divine being. I could never hide from him because he would always find me. If I started to feel frustrated, he would stop by and ask if I wanted to go for a bike ride. My husband would respond by looking at me and saying, "Yes, Lord Vishnu, she needs to get out of the house."

Vishnu was also surprisingly Cupid (or Kama). He helped me see marriage as a journey of growing up and growing together (rising in Consciousness), having patience with my husband, and not letting his traumatic childhood affect our marriage. I began to realize that this incredible man had shaped me into the woman I am today, just as I had impacted his life, because we only receive what we need, right? I am awake today because of my husband, my best friend. Vishnu honored him as if he were a Telugu South Indian man—beeyotch! *("Vishnu, that's a little too far; he can get off his ass and make his own damn tea.")*

One day, he came over with granola bars in his pockets for our whole family, handing one to each of us. It was so heartwarming. My youngest, who was constantly ripping and running and never had time for Vishnu, paused momentarily and asked, "Is Vishnu Conscious?" I replied, "You see it, too." (It was also reassuring to know my children were listening and understood my teachings.)

As summer approached, my husband and I discussed making some changes in our lives. I expressed my love for our neighborhood, Little India, but I yearned to live in the countryside, with a bit more room to breathe and garden, as I used to. Additionally, I shared my childhood dream of having a swimming pool. Still, I envisioned that if I installed the pool in Little India, Vishnu and the entire neighborhood would be peeking through the fence since we were such a close-knit community.

With that, my husband and I considered selling our house and moving further into the countryside. The next day, Vishnu came over, as he did every day, for our afternoon chat, and I always gave him my full attention. Surprisingly, this time, he had some very specific questions about my life's desires. He smiled and said in his squeaky, high-pitched voice, "Sherry, can I ask you a question?" He always asked permission before posing more profound questions, perhaps to ensure I was engaged. "Have you ever thought about putting a swimming pool in your backyard?" he inquired. I glanced at him twice, and he patiently awaited my response. I could hear the Divine speaking to me. I sensed that I was being directed or guided, as Vishnu often captured my attention in this way. If you are conscious, you will find that the Universe is always speaking, whether through a flower or a Divine being.

That evening, I decided we should list the house because I was confident that the Divine, speaking through Vishnu, was telling me it was time to pursue my "dreams." But I didn't know where this dream would lead us.

For those of you who think I'm foolish, check this! About a week later, I listed our house and sold it myself in under twenty-four hours, and it sold for substantially more than its value. Let me repeat: substantially more than its value. I pocketed an unexpected $100,000 in cash in less than twenty-four hours because a little Telugu South Indian boy confirmed it was the right time to sell our house! (Again, I paid a healthy 1% buyer agent fee using Beycome.com. [giggles])

My experience with this young fellow was so remarkable that I even shared the story with his mother and older brother. I couldn't let the idea of strangeness hold me back from speaking. I told them we had nicknamed him Lord Vishnu. The teen looked to his mother and smiled; they could tell I didn't know Vishnu was the name of an Indian deity. His mother turned to me and said, "He was named after Lord Vishnu."

As I searched for our new home, I couldn't find a good fit. If I had predicted this from the start, we likely would have waited to list our house. I didn't know what to do or where we might find a suitable property in the country. Even so,

457

our time was running out to search for a home, so I called a family meeting and asked if they had any idea where we should settle in the meantime. Suddenly, my oldest said he had always wanted to live in Gainesville. I couldn't understand where this deep love for Gainesville came from since I only had horrific memories of fleeing a local church and being shunned by the congregation. Gainesville was a thing of the past, holding no appeal for me. (Hmm…it still doesn't.)

Well, I let an eight-year-old convince me to sell our house, so why not let my fourteen-year-old choose where we would move next? Honestly, we had no other choice since school was about to start. We selected a rental house off Zillow and signed a lease sight unseen. I had peace, knowing at least that this was my hometown.

Just like when I returned to Gainesville when I was five…once again to my surprise…the now forty-five-year-old Yi…who would share the same pet name as me…was finishing her Ph.D. She was there again to welcome me…yet had no memory of ever meeting me. I sent her proof: a photo of us together…at our preschool graduation…and she recognized it. "That's me!" She seemed to wonder…how that could be. (This poem, which was initially started in the *Elicit* sermon, "Rising Above Attachment to Culture," is now complete.)

The Baughman Center at the University of Florida.

As we settled back in Gainesville, followin' my dream has truly been Divine to me. I didn't return to *The Swamp* (Gainesville's nickname) because Gainesville was on my list. Instead, we popped through a wormhole, in a sense, followin' my dream. The feeling is hard to describe. I felt like a fugitive who had been caught. Something told me, "Time's up; you're going back to the *pen*." One moment, I was sitting on my porch with my young friend, and the next, I was back in my hometown twenty years later, with adolescents who would soon be starting their own lives, followin' my dream wherever it may lead. It just didn't seem possible to me. (And yes, to my friends who love 1980s rock with roots in Gainesville while eating pizza at Millhopper Leonardo's, you guessed it! "Runnin' Down A Dream.")

If you pay attention and listen, the Universe is always speaking.

Nudge, Nudge, Pay Attention Hugs,
—Sher! (The Common Snook)
Pause. Inhale. Exhale. Reflect.

P.S. This story isn't far-fetched for most Indian folks. (And Patel said, "Totally!") Some would have built a shrine in his front yard and begun worshiping him. "Lord Vishnu, come outside; we love you!"

P.P.S. Did I ever tell y'all that after a few days of moving back to Gainesville, I discovered all my neighbors were named "Sherry"? There were three of us in a row, just like in the movie *Heathers*. It was strange, but I had expected it because I was seeking confirmation on whether to buy the house we were renting. When my husband realized I was considering making a purchase, he said, "It's not for sale." I replied, "Sure it is!" Again, the Universe is always speaking. We were under contract a week later to buy the house with no damn pool! (Hmm…I wonder what it might be like to have a neighbor like me, listening, digesting, and regurgitating every word you said and didn't say while taking notes on intriguing patterns. I used to remind Sherry Chandler, who was all cute and *stuff,* "You know Heather Chandler was killed in the movie, right? Careful, cutie!")

(*Give it up for* Patel as he exits and reads the last line in Hindi! "Shanti se 15 minutes aankh band karke baithne se aap ki jindgi badal jayegi kasam se!")

2. Your Spouse or Partner is Golden

What I will share today applies to any committed long-term relationship, but I will speak from the perspective of a woman observing a man. Let's begin this service with the song "Solid" because it hasn't always been that way.

Disclosure Reminder...,

If you spiritually awaken first or are more aware than your spouse, watch out! Your marriage is about to get complicated because you can now see the mental games your spouse plays. They will either awaken, or you must learn to overlook their behavior and continue loving them unconditionally. And stop praying for the train to hit them; it doesn't work. (No worries...this challenging season can significantly enhance your Consciousness, and if you don't believe y'all play games, *ain't nobody awake anyways*. Back to "Pseudo-Chapter One"—off you go!)

Even so, don't let your ego get ahead of you because you wouldn't be the person you are today (close to awakening or awakened) without your spouse's bullshit. Be patient with them, and they will awaken in their own time...with a bit of help, of course. Some flowers are slow...slow as shit to bloom because you haven't quite learned to be patient yet.

"Awakening to mental veils is a process that unfolds beautifully, much like a flower. First, a bud emerges, slowly expanding in all directions. [They'll] notice things [they] hadn't seen before, which were always right in front of them, hidden by [their] mental veils. [They] may find that everything physical remains unchanged; only [their] perspective has grown. Once this unfolding process begins, it never stops, and the expansion becomes exponential." (*Elicit,* "Pseudo-Chapter One").

Be mindful to challenge him gently. (Nonsense!) I used to poke "that man" with a pitchfork and run if needed. ("Yo momma!") I was determined to wake his ass up if it killed me. This is the gift that only a life partner can give you, and give it to you good, which is probably the *complete opposite* of what you have been led to believe.

I'm tired of religious folks defining how feminine love should behave to satisfy the male ego. The way men instruct women on how to communicate with them or not communicate with them is counterproductive and restricts their spiritual growth. Silencing women only holds men back; I say this lovingly before I begin this rap.

460

*

Push Him 'Til He Pop

Confrontin' rebel
Quintessential
So bent (bent)
Caution (shun)
Understand (man)
Just jam (damn)

Yup, yup, he asking for it. I'm *gonna* give it to 'em
He knows it, it's real good *Forum*
I need to, see him tone it down
I'm hollerin', tossing words abound

Please stop. Get it? Get it?
The way he takes it, makes me want to hawk and spit it

Shawty, you know I'm New Age
We *gotta* get this thing movin' so we can turn a new page
He got me singing, "Hey *bro!*"
I'm tired of your 'tude with me
How 'bout you stop *trying me*
"Hey *bro!*" I'm tired of your 'tude with me
You need to stop resisting me

He asking for it, *yup, yup,* he asking for it
He asking for it, I'm going to serve it to 'em
He asking for it, *yup, yup,* he asking for it
He knows it, it's real good *Forum*

I said, your fits, your size, we have to compromise
I said, your wits, your size, are over-dramatized
I said, your fits, your size, we have to compromise
I said, your wits, your size, have got me desensitized (eye-roll)

(Ayo! Thank you for your inspiration, 50 Cent, Justin Timberlake, and Timbaland. I wrote this song first on the couch and then at my desk in the kitchen. I bow to the Divinity in you! Hmm...fifty cents is not a lot of money.)

Have you ever noticed how men often tell women who we are, what we want, and how we should behave? Most of us learn about relationships from religion, while others turn to social media. In African American communities, women frequently hear that they are *too this* or *too much of that* and should behave like *this* in order to get *that*...if they wish to be enslaved. (Interestingly, most of these women have no interest in enslavement. Hmm...I wonder why.)

The man who seeks a quiet, or in other words, silent woman, lacks the desire to grow. This indicates just how big big his ego truly is and the extent of the work he requires. (I hate to break it to you, but man is not the prize of life. *Right, Moni?*) That said, this is not to feed the "I don't need a man" attitude. Most of us will awaken through a committed relationship.

However, a real man who seeks growth desires a woman with an equal voice. He doesn't fear her wisdom. (I apologize for invoking the "real man" reference, but there's a big big difference between men who understand and respect the role of women and those who wish to control or dictate this role.) What your mind craves is often not what you truly need. If he wants a quiet woman, let 'em go...after her. Again, securing a man is not the prize of life, but finding a good man can be like finding gold. (We should all be gold diggers, lmao! Y'all, that means "laughing my ass off," *right, son?*)

For many, awakening comes when they realize the gift of a woman and how she can single-handedly transform their lives. Every man needs a woman who has his back. She is his greatest asset (quality, not property) because of her ability to see from multiple perspectives and the enormous weight she can bear. We have eyes like eagles because we must keep children alive. This is one reason why learning to see comes more naturally and quickly for women. Most of us possess a panoramic view of life, while men often maintain a narrower focus, which shouldn't be viewed as a negative trait. "With this system and screen, we'll get better surround sound and the highest resolution," he says. "Okay...if you say so." They work together harmoniously, like Yin and Yang.

The panoramic view ensures everything works together nicely, while the narrow view gets the job done—dammit! "You mean to tell me you already bought the damn car? I thought we were still running the numbers." This is how men make life fun. (Still, men worldwide, even in India, in their patriarchal society, know that *woman* is the head of the household. Yet we are okay with them believing otherwise, much like how we unconditionally accept and care for our children. "Isn't that sweet?" we say. Have you noticed that *ch'rn* come to the matriarch for everything and not "the life of the party"? "Mom, Dad said he's ordering pizza. Dad, Mom said, 'No, you're not; your cholesterol is high.'")

For those who feel constrained by the Christian definition of a *weak-ass-woman*, you must do your research and stop accepting what men want you to believe. I see women striving to be *weak-ass-meek* (putting duct tape over their mouths) when they know very well (damn well) that the distorted Christian definition of meekness does not represent who they are...or who they want to become. (Easily imposed on? That sounds like the language of rape culture.) Yes, controlling men desire submissive women, but can they handle the meek woman from the Hebrew translation? I didn't think so.

In your studies, you may discover you're "Hebrew meek"—beeyotch! That's one reason why Jewish women are a little different from your average White woman. They are "Hebrew meek!" Y'all remember Jesus? He was also "Hebrew meek." Black woman, be careful now; you're a threat to *weak-ass-meek*, and *weak-ass-men* will have to shut you down (and keep you down) because you aren't easily imposed on—even though many have been violated. I'm not even going to define "Hebrew meek," so you'll do your homework and stop mindlessly following *weak-ass-men*. When you find yourself saying, *"Oh hell naw,"* it's time to look up *anaw (or anav)*.

It is also unnecessary for me to define how a woman should behave, as you can see the character of a woman by observing yourself or the women you know. Women, like men, reflect the Divine when they are grounded. This understanding and affirmation arose from within when I recognized the Divine was working through me. However, I did not resemble, behave, posture, or speak like any spiritual teacher I knew who *acted spiritually*. (I couldn't do it if I tried.) Who I am is assertive. I do not need to be first or seen. I'm not concerned with what others think of me. I carry a heavy load. I am full of compassion. I'm willing to endure and sacrifice. I'm eager to speak out when needed. I am "Hebrew meek," if I must use such a term—a powerful tool used by the Divine, employed to carve out jewels. (Pardon my English, I *embody* "Hebrew meekness.")

Speaking of observing women! We are bold, especially because we challenge men twice our size. If men paused to consider, it's *actually* quite attractive. Our boldness is sexy! However, if he's the crazy type who wants to squeeze your neck, be careful what you say to him. Nonetheless, most men who aren't too broken or weak enjoy a good smack upside the head from our feminine boldness.

That's why they play football, and they especially like it when women tackle them. But their ego won't admit that. Love is to know how much he can handle. Remember, men are softies.

Hey guys! You want to feel and look weak? Use the word "emasculate" to dismiss a woman who isn't afraid to confront you. That's another one of those egotistical words where you are both the victim and the victor. Use it among yourselves because men surely devalue each other, but don't ever apply it to describe a woman's behavior unless she's ("Yo momma!"). But please know, if you must use that self-lubricated word to silence and disqualify a woman, you might have mom issues. This self-lubricated word sounds like a mix of ejaculate and castrate. How can they coexist?

One thing that's good about most White men is that they are less likely to choke you like the rest of them. (It's a joke.) Sometimes, I think I'd prefer somethin' physical, so at least I can see he's crazy underneath those good looks. Anyhow, they don't choke because they're already on top of the throne and prefer not to use physical force to break you. The White man's tricks and control games are more sophisticated and have been passed down through the generations.

While you're home with the babies, not working, losing your job skills, and becoming more dependent on his ass every day, he'll apply for a job in a rural part of America without asking you…to isolate you further from the rest of the world. What you can seclude, you can conquer! (Hmm…he must have learned the isolation technique from the cult, but I ended up loving it! Whatever! You move me to a Superfund site; I'll play in it! Move me to the White Northeast; I'll make best friends and assimilate better than a Jew. Shoot, I can also dance to The Lumineers, "Ho…Hey.")

Still, New Hampshire can be a beautiful place to accomplish such a task because no one will hear her cries or know she has been kidnapped—again. (Mm-hmm, you heard me right.) You don't take a "Woman of Color" to the backwoods of New Hampshire…I mean, *Yankalachia*, unless you have plans…that are bound to backfire, of course, because you picked the right woman. (Women always stash cash, especially if your man has you staying home with the *ch'rn*. Silent women have no cash stashed. Oops! Ladies, did I just disclose I have a secret? Fellas, the louder she is, the more cash she has stashed. It's just that simple. Because *we women* will be quiet and compliant to ensure our children are well cared for. The children will ask, "Mom, what did you say under your breath?")

464

If you're an Indian woman, ignore everything I just said about running your mouth, but do stash cash. Still, the Indian women I know, they *be* back-talkin' and shakin' their heads even when the consequences can be severe. They say shit that I would never say to my husband if he were Indian. "Over your mama's dead body, I will." And some are bold enough to go back to school and earn a doctorate—beeyotch! "You can call me doctor," she'll say. And she knows how to handle him. "Yo momma's rajma masala is bland, and her mooli parathas are stiff and dense." And when he gets nasty and wants to be stingy with the cash and do all the grocery shopping so she can't stash cash, she'll get him back, saying under her breath, "You can believe that's a chili if you want to," as she slips his ass a habanero. "Namaste," she says. Mexican women *be doin'* the same.

With my unwavering empathy and love for my husband, he also learned to see, even while his ego, the Terminator, was consistently protecting his little inner self and his perceived self-image. Men are complicated like that because they're wired to be defensive and safeguard their territory. (Woof, woof!) Of course, some of them take it a bit too far, especially those who have been exposed to other defensive or toxic men. ("What did you say, woman?")

"This man" was a mess and directionless, just like me. I joked when I first met him, "Damn! Your story is worse than that of the poor little Black child who was fatherless and raised their younger siblings, not knowing how to be a friend to them, only a parent, leaving them bitter because their siblings had a childhood, a father, and were well cared for. Also, imagine being the oddball in a household where everyone else had yellow hair and blue eyes. (That yellow hair and blue eye idolization and favoritism shit can be brutal for White kids who look like the mailman's kid or look like they are Italian, Greek, "Moor," North African, Middle Eastern, Jewish, Spanish, or Cuban—like they have "one-drop." Uh-oh, some of y'all are upset because I just passed out "the cooties," lol. *Whassup, DeSantis!*) My husband (let's keep this long-ass paragraph goin') didn't realize he was handsome growing up among all those White folks until he met me. He must have been sheltered, living up there in the backwoods. But at least he gets to partake in White privilege along with Italians and Jews today, even though he looks like he has at least "one-drop" of that Pan Alpha DNA; talkin' 'bout his grandfather is Cuban nonsense. (For the record, having a Cuban relative by marriage doesn't make you Cuban. You see, many White people are looking for a door to escape the pain of race, too, all while some frustrated Cubans are now shouting into this book, "We're White, too!" Forgive me, "White" Cubans. I know it's tough, but folks who carry the genotype of the motherland can spot a cousin's phenotype when others seem to miss it. Shhh! *Whassup, Pedrito!*)

Anywho, my husband's greatest superpower and gift that helped him accept veils was that he learned early in life that there are things you can't see, having escaped and dissected the inner workings of a cult. (He served two years longer than I did because he beat me there.) He learned to observe his reaction and defense patterns while I observed him consciously, sometimes with very few words exchanged. He could often anticipate his next move or reaction, while I waited for his next move or reaction. It was sexy, like dancing the tango. (Can you hear "Tango Cumparsita" in the background?) His gun was always loaded, so to speak, and he wore full-body armor, always anticipating a threat or surprise attack, so I mirrored the same anticipation.

Because of his inner world, he lived in a different world from my psychedelic-like experience. (giggles) Still, he knew I loved him and never intentionally provoked him. At the same time, I would never hide the truth from him, even if it might provoke him. Will he still shoot her? Of course! It's difficult not to pull the trigger when the gun is always loaded. Unfortunately, many of these broken White men go into law enforcement or are trained concealed carriers. *(Right, Babe?)* They are so damaged and powerless that no physical weapon can restore their dignity. At the same time, they encounter a reflection of themselves—this covert aggression—in African American communities, like the resistant young man we met at the beginning of this book who asked me, "Is *dis yo* house?"

I often responded to my *hubby* with, "You have an interesting inner world." This was meant to direct him inward so he could see that everything he experienced came from within and was often perceived by the dude with the gun. I would say, "Look how peaceful it is outside," as we watched a squirrel nibbling on a nut. (Hmm…some crazy bonehead must have told or shown my husband as a boy that this world was not a safe place and may have even dragged him by his hair. [Ouch!] They have the other kind of "rednecks" in the northeast that don't deserve to have the "r" capitalized. I'm sure some of those White folks didn't want me to marry this good-looking man like he was a prize, yet someone broke his spirit and rendered him powerless, causing him to always be on guard with his guns loaded—damn! They sent me a broke-ass man; he was both broken…and broke. When someone asked, "How black is she?" I should have asked, "How broke is he?" Let me cut it out. Now they finally know why he likes me: I'm funny. Here's our theme song, "The Way I Are," by Timbaland, Keri Hilson, and D.O.E.)

As I mentioned, nothing we experience ever occurs outside of ourselves. When we grasp this, we understand how crucial it is to nurture our spiritual selves and clear away the cobwebs. By cultivating inner peace, we create peace in the outside world, leading to global harmony—much more than anything the United Nations could achieve. We have the power to choose our responses, and we don't have to be governed by our minds, even when they say, "Take…her…ass…out. Make that woman submit." (Today, I pay *special* attention to individuals, particularly White men, who take non-traditional paths. They likely have a story to share and might be on the verge of awakening.)

If we have a *jacked-up* inner world, we will have a *jacked-up* outer world. My man lived in combat mode. Many men disguise this fear as masculinity while hiding behind real guns. Recognizing his own reactive behavior ultimately wore his ass out. He was tired of himself and his ego, and his mind eventually surrendered instead of directing his guns at me. He was awake and starting to surface like a budding flower. His expression of love shifted from inconsiderate masculine gifts like tech gadgets or the compass he gave me to help me find my way out of the backwoods in New Hampshire (wink) to more thoughtful gifts (Love) like the candle he brought home from Trader Joe's and a soft loaf of bread with butter, which I'll gladly take over a laptop or the latest cellphone any day. I'll be damned; this man was noticing me!

Only a strong man can handle a strong woman. *Weak brothas,* please step aside. I would remind my husband, saying, "You picked me and said I was solid and not ruled by my emotions," unlike the women he was accustomed to. (He's always had a way with words.) He never sought an easier, more compliant companion that he could control, which says a lot about men who do. Still, he did try to control me, especially when he was still under the influence…of Christianity. Thankfully, his intoxication didn't last long. (You know, it's easier to control *woman* when she believes it's her role to submit to *man* and when she follows a book written by *man* to validate her role.) However, he was just letting me know he was ready to get the party started…right? *(Thanks for the word, hummingbird.)*

I'm so thankful I never gave up on him or he on me (Thank you, Vishnu!), even though it was rough for a while with his militant-ass constantly barking orders. I'm impressed! This *brotha* cleaned up well, and he's handsome, too…with a little less hair today. (That's what happens when you bark too much.)

Thankfully, I could always see the jewel he was beneath all that trash baggage he used to carry. I humbly say **I wouldn't be the woman I am today** without my husband's brilliance and fantastic sense of humor. He's the missing piece of my puzzle. (giggles) I know it may sound cliché, but I'm completely serious. He reflected everything I needed and always caught the roaches like a gentleman. I am *forever* grateful to him. (By the way, men who raised *ch'rn* as children can build a house and cook, too—five ingredients or less—one box of Thrifty Maid holy mac 'n' cheese and a can of tuna—beeyotch!)

Hubby Hugs,
　　—Sher! (The Common Snook)
Pause. Inhale. Exhale. Reflect.

P.S. We have some of the biggest cockroaches in Gainesville. Nope, we don't use pesticides. Snooks always catch and release.

P.P.S. Did I ever tell y'all New Hampshire has some of the best-looking people in the country? And they all look alike with that stagnant gene pool. They *all* cousins!

P.P.P.S. Here's an interesting fact! Men raised under or impacted by toxic masculinity and false femininity who have been called ugly names or made to feel less of a man because they didn't play or follow football...or "grab pussy" without permission may find that they prefer a woman who doesn't adhere to traditional roles and appreciates them for being a loving man who also refuses to play those roles. (Damn...that was a long-ass sentence!) For some men (pay attention, Asian men), this might mean attracting a neurodiverse woman or even a Pan Alpha American woman. (I bet that offended some egos. [giggles]) But y'all can't handle what else I have because you're not ready for solid food. Some of y'all are choking on this meat. I'm sorry, but I don't serve milk. Grab some water. It's okay.

(Sit in stillness with your eyes closed for 15 minutes a day; I promise it will transform your life!)

3. The Path You Avoid Might Be Gold

Disclosure Reminder...,

Resistance is a path that doesn't flow smoothly, or worse, not at all...like a dry creek, and there are fewer *new discoveries*, if anything, along the way. (Boring!) Anyhow, we have countless paths to choose from each day. Most never stray far from their usual routes, which is why we sometimes feel like we're walking in circles. We must overcome our fears, be adventurous, and explore new paths.

Unfortunately, our strict adherence to religion, rituals, or habits can keep us trapped in a cycle of karma or behaving like a dog chasing its own tail. (This should not be confused with the Western idea of karma, described as "what goes around, comes around." Do your homework!) Still, when you realize that you can create the life you desire, you begin to enjoy all the endless possibilities instead of simply accepting what has long been the norm. You instead declare, "No, I want this path today," and pursue it. (This idea may not seem true for everyone; however, King and Gandhi proved the possibility.)

One day, purposely on Valentine's Day, I met over thirty of my neighbors because I wanted to host a tea party and invite all the attendees in person, if possible. To my surprise, almost everyone asked me into their homes for a chat. Neighbors, some of whom I had never met, offered me water, tea, a cheese dosa, and even an ice cream cone with homemade strawberry ice cream. It remains one of the most enjoyable days of my life because I chose a different path. You might miss your daily treasure if you avoid people for whatever reason. I like to believe there's gold along those paths, so I pursue them head-on.

Another path might be the communication you are avoiding. If something is difficult to say, instead of avoiding it, find the words to express yourself rather than letting situations dictate your life. When you do, you sometimes alter the path of people who are stuck. However, when you avoid these paths, your responsibility, you can rest assured that the situation will persist because, as I always say, "Ain't no God coming down to do this work for us."

Take care, teddy bear,
    —Sher! (The Common Snook)
                        Pause. Inhale. Exhale. Reflect.

4. The Missing Demographic

Disclosure Reminder...,

As mentioned in the last sermon, I hosted a delightful ladies' afternoon tea. It was a BYOTC (Bring Your Own *Tea-Cup*) party, and I invited all my neighbors. You were asked to attend if we had met at least once.

The turnout was remarkable! Nearly thirty-five women filled our home, representing twelve different countries: Canada, Brazil, China, Saudi Arabia, India, England, France, Haiti, Jamaica, the Philippines, Puerto Rico (because, you know, Americans don't realize Puerto Rico is part of the U.S. since we don't teach inclusive American history), and the U.S., of course. Technically, we would have had thirteen countries if we had included those of us from the "country of Florida." (I love *me some* Florida; I'm the number one patriot!)

I was reminded of this gathering because it was this party that inspired me to step into character and present my invitation using a Southern accent, along with elements of Southern African American Vernacular English (SAAVE). (Sometimes, I wonder if I'm channeling my inner Ms. Juliette, who spoke with a Southern accent and utilized SAAVE as needed.) I believe the audio version I made for those whom English is a second language is still available on social media. As you can see, I never stopped writing and channeling.

My beloved neighbor, who speaks limited English and has read the Tao Te Ching, even thanked me and said she enjoyed the invitation. It was the greatest compliment ever. (See, we all speak the same language.)

I wish I could show you our pictures because they were so elegant. Ladies were required to wear their Sunday best: floral dresses or skirts, hanfus, lehengas, and bling. White gloves and big ol' Southern-style hats were strongly encouraged. One rebellious millennial arrived in pants, but she was lovely, reminding us not to get too carried away and to remember how far we ladies have come because liberated women do not dress for men.

On top of that, you were required to bring a homemade dish on fine china since tacky aluminum pans were strictly forbidden. Can you imagine we had over thirty-five dishes? Also, *absolutely no ch'rn* were allowed, although the youngest lady who snuck in through the door under her big ol' hat was just ten or eleven, and the eldest, at ninety-five, will soon be seen on a Smucker's jelly jar, having attended a house party. That's why she's lived so long. And umm...the icing on the cake was that we had six male servants. Pardon me...I mean, a seasoned team of gentlemen waiters. Still, it was just a step up and a bit more diversified than a Paula Deen dream wedding.

470

Hold on. We also had a comedy show that had the ladies rolling with laughter until I introduced one of the waiters named "Gabriel." This was the highlight of teatime. In a high-pitched Southern accent, I remarked, "Gabriel is a good name, as I always hear folks say." Then I turned to our diverse crowd and said, "He came to the Muslims! The Christians! And the Jews! Mm-hmm, yes he did!" Despite that, there was no agreement. Oh man, you could've heard a fly croak up in there. But it's true; they must not have studied Abrahamic religions, although my Hindu *sistas* probably didn't get the joke either way.

My closing line on the invitation was that you could sit back and *belly up*, and the gentlemen would come and fill your *cup*. Men in bowties make handsome waiters, you know. (Ladies, they wore shirts. Cut it out!) It was indeed an honor to have them care for us that afternoon. I even brought my son out of the basement so he could join in being a blessing. But we did not give him a teapot. These *mens* even *manned* the kitchen and didn't break anything. It was the most excellent, action-packed two-hour house party...*ever!* I can only imagine it was the talk of the town.

Now, to the missing demographic!

I faced a significant challenge in reaching one *collective group*. These ladies had no idea, and neither did I, that I had sent out enough invitations to analyze the statistics, including the response rates of specific groups and their veils. I didn't like what I was witnessing. I was about to uncover how well America was doing in becoming one nation under God. Of course, many couldn't attend, but none of "the Karens" showed up—not one. (Please don't confuse this with name-calling. This is simply a diagnostic term from the African American Vernacular translation of the DSM-5.) Sure, I regretted inviting *them* when I knew better, but it was good to observe the sample results. This was telling as to who was still keeping their distance from the rest of us, especially when I had the *nations* in the house!

Unfortunately, I don't think it was a coincidence because the odds were too high. (Disproportionately high!) There was indeed a correlation! You should have seen my spreadsheet. And I'm sure my Chinese neighbor down the street, the statistician, could have quickly confirmed my findings, saying in broken English, "Calculations suggest 'Karen' neighbors *no* want to party with strange *Black girl* with all those Indian and Chinese friends." (Yep, I had Indian and Chinese [cousins!] in the same house. *Hakuna matata*...I won't make any Pakistani and Indian cousin jokes.)

However, these "*special*" women must not have heard that I don't identify with race. (See, we need to educate these "Karens" about Pan Alpha and the power of [one-DROP!] DJ Magic Mike style, of course. That was for my *bro*!)

All I can imagine is that my vernacular must have given them a fright, said with an English accent. Thank you, Alachua County Public Schools, for your historical busing program in the 1980s. Without you, I would never have become bilingual and would have endured all those years being called a White girl with no ass (well?), but thank God for Bridget...oops, I mean, *Brigit* for being my bridge. And, of course, Black folks in Gainesville still wouldn't know what a waffle or bagel was if it hadn't been for busing and my momma, of course, said with an uncoordinated head swivel and snap.

Or maybe it was because the invitation initially said BYODTC (Bring Your Own Damn *Tea-Cup*). Oh my god! I just had an epiphany; they must have thought I meant BYOB (Bring Your Own Bottle). Come on! Everybody knows I don't drink. I'd be a handful if I did.

I genuinely believe most of *them* wanted to come, but their minds were struggling with racism. (We must understand how programming works or risk being programmed.) I wish I could have told them, "No one is racist," and "You Can't Always Rely on the Past," because you are not your mind, and it shouldn't be running your life. Unfortunately, it all boils down to "Perception is Reality," even if we make it up and it isn't true. That sure sounds like insanity to me.

That said, we still have more work to do. These ladies avoided my party when it was golden!!! And my sheets *smell* like *Downy*, too!!! This should never have happened in G'ville! This ain't Levy or Dixie County...or the Panhandle! For some of *them*, this would have been the first time they had experienced a house party and enjoyed the company of so many wonderful people without needing to call the police...I mean, "the po-po." Despite that, I will give them a second chance at my book signing event and personally sign this page for them.

Please share this book of sermons with as many "Karens" as possible because she, too, is golden. K.A.R.E.N....K: Know you are loved. A: Accept yourself. R: Realize we are one. E: Extend a hand. N: Never lose hope. (Kumbaya, please don't pick on me, y'all.)

Peace Out and Namaste Hugs,
   —Sher! (The Common Snook)
        Pause. Inhale. Exhale. Reflect.

5. Keep It Simple

As I contradict the title, we will take a winding road this last time. This sermon will be like the Russian nesting dolls we discussed: You know, when you open one, you find yet another veil you must overcome. Except this doll is loaded with stories. Who knows, there might be six to twelve stories in one. (You'll see "story portal" in place of separating each story. You know, I'm running out of space.)

Disclosure Reminder...,

No worries...I'll host another tea party one day. Many of the big-time gurus will join if they can: Ms. Juliette Watts McCoy, Alice Walker, Pema Chodron, Mother Mary, Marianne Williamson, Oprah Winfrey, my *hubby*, Jesus, The Ripped Redheaded Dude with the ponytail, Jaggi Vasudev, Richard Rohr, Eckhart Tolle, Deepak Chopra, and Tenzin Gyatso (Stop it, "haters"; he probably cringes at the thought of children today.) Careful, *judgmental cancel culture,* before you inadvertently cancel yourself.

Also, I don't care if you think some of them have inflated egos (which is possible) or if mini-parasitic cults are *circling around* them. You know, spiritual parasites, right? By now, I'm confident you can spot these *special* folks. Yet, they're all invited!

Some leaders may require fancy purple chairs, as seen in some African American churches where the First Lady is seated. Their entourages could be so big that you might forget this event was about my tea party. (Hmm...I might need to reconsider that.)

I will also invite their "groupies" who are not interested in learning to raise human Consciousness because they're still stuck behind the veil of "I am someone *special* by association." These are the folks who often test me *(try me)* and help to build my character. You know, these little egos can be quite testy.

Do you sense a final story brewing? Remember, there will be many stories in one, but in the end, it will serve to remind you to keep this shit simple because complicated shit can be costly.

As mentioned in an earlier sermon, I contacted two spiritual organizations at different times over the years for different reasons. (Of course, it was different times for different reasons. Duh-uh!) I was providing thoughtful feedback because both organizations had significant operational malfunctions that affected my experience with their workshops. (You know, I've done this before.) Yet, no matter where I went or whom I called, I always encountered the same ego. How was that even possible?

As I mentioned, my gift is to see things plainly or for what they are. That's all. I notice things like missing book chapters or even an entire book printed inside out...if that's possible. Unfortunately, I can also spot loopholes (*gremlins*!) that could cost you millions, which most people won't point out. I can also tell when your company is ripping people off without you knowing. (wink) These *screw-ya-schemes* and company operational failures, I also call "loopholes" or "*screw-ya* loopholes." (Add it to your dictionary!)

(Story portal!) Once, I discovered that a local hotel and conference center had a shutter-like bathroom stall door installed backwards for over twelve years. I love it when folks ignore me as if I couldn't have discovered such a thing. (It's tough being me. I can't even confess to having *free power*.) But I wouldn't give up because I was getting a free night's stay and would be doing the backstroke in their pool for this discovery and for ignoring me, of course.

In this case, the shutter was angled open so that everyone passing by could see your business while you felt safe inside with the shutters closed. (Sometimes, what you can't see won't hurt you.) I couldn't believe my eyes; it took me a few seconds to process what I was witnessing. I recall saying out loud, "What the hell!?" This malfunction in the shutters went unnoticed due to the soft lighting and rustic, Banana Republic-like vibe. (Y'all remember the old Banana Republic stores?) This stall was at the end of the restroom, so it hadn't seen much traffic or visitors standing outside the door for the past twelve years. Plus, the door was traditionally ajar, allowing people to walk in without realizing the shutters had been wide open...for like twelve years. (That's a whole *lotta* ass.)

I know this stall well because I visited it often during my caseworker days when I was on the road. Hotels are the finest rest stops, by the way. And you better believe it: once I got someone to listen, they gave me a free room—hush money! (Locals listen for the clues and then take pictures with my book in front of the door.)

(Story portal!) I can also identify potential dangers and do my best to prevent them from happening. (Listen—dammit!) A few years ago, I nearly hit a little boy while driving. Actually, he would have hit *me* on his bike if I hadn't seen his little self coming out from under the bushes. He was a cutie riding that tiny bike and navigating this big big world. He couldn't have been more than five or six years old. Still, I suspected that I would encounter him again the next day at the same time, since he was biking home from school.

The following day, I approached the intersection of the four-lane highway more slowly than usual and told my son that I had a feeling the little boy we had seen the day before was about to emerge from those bushes. Just as I predicted, he popped out and came barreling through the crosswalk without a helmet. I told my son that someone might hit him if they didn't trim back the bushes. (This story still makes me tear up because children are so innocent and brave.)

As he safely crossed the intersection, I called the nearby school and asked to speak with the person in charge of school safety. The staff member who answered the phone responded *with attitude,* asking, "And what is your student's name?" I explained that I didn't have a student there and just wanted to speak with the person who handles safety issues. Again, *with attitude,* I was asked, "What is your concern?" (Apparently, this school only expected trouble from parents.) I said, "Please don't be alarmed." However, I mentioned that it was too complicated to explain twice, and it would be better to speak directly with that person, if that was okay. I was then transferred to the assistant principal, who answered the phone just like the secretary, "What's the problem?" They must have said, "Some woman on the line has 'beef' with you." Their attitude was contagious. Whatever happened to the sweet school secretary from the 1980s?

I explained that a huge, bushy-like tree was growing over the sidewalk and that I had nearly collided with one of their students. But you know, I had to add a bit of drama because folks won't listen without you fulfilling their emotional need for chaos. Folks can't even report a murder these days. So, I explained that I had encountered this student *twice*—dos veces!—and feared for his *life.* (Sometimes, almost rhyming captures their attention.) Then, this individual responded, "Well, that's the city's property." I replied, "Regardless of whose property it is [dammit!], the bush needs to be cut" because someone would nail this little boy one day. The assistant principal said, "Okay," like I was twisting their arm, "I'll see if the janitor will trim the bush," which meant the bush would never be cut. How could they do it when they never tried to pinpoint the tree's specific location? I also notified the local municipal authorities about this danger; the bush was never cut. Little man was fearless; faith, time, and space were looking out for him. That's how children survive.

(Story portal!) Speaking of *ch'rn!* We had a loud, overly jolly, friendly neighbor when we moved into our townhome (after I got off the mower for good, of course). The kids on the block adored him! However, he gave me the creeps. I told my son sternly, "I'm not responsible for the other kids, but you— are to stay away from him." This boy had the nerve to challenge me, saying,

"He's a nice guy…you always do that." I'm sure he could see the flames in my eyes as I glared back at him.

One night, I caught Mr. Jolly speaking to my son while taking out the trash in the dark. That's when I knew he was crazy because adults should know better than that.

Then, I noticed he had a business website on his truck. I looked it up, found out the name of our jolly neighbor, and googled him, of course. I couldn't believe it! The man popped up on the sex offender registry and was not living at his registered home address. His mugshot was enormous! I just left it on the computer so my son and husband, who were testing my patience, could see it. (That time, I got the head swivel and snap synchronized—beeyotch!)

(Story portal!) Let me share one last story to prove how strange I am! When my sons were younger, we watched the sci-fi kids' show *The Unlisted*. Have your children ever watched this show, which features the adorable Indian Australian twin brothers as the main characters?

On my birthday in early 2020, while strolling through a random park in Australia, I recognized a tree in the way you might remember an old friend, even though I had never been there before. "Hello there, you look familiar. Have we met before?" (giggles) I told my boys, "Hey, that's the tree from the show!!!" I didn't even recall the name of the series, but of course, they didn't believe me. My youngest said knowingly, "How is that possible when we're 10,000 miles away from home!?" (It's tough being me.) "Wasn't the show filmed in Australia?" I asked. "But how is that the tree, Mom?" he questioned. Again, I had to google—and prove it to them. From that moment on, I was the coolest mom ever. (Look it up! We even struck the same pose as the cast from the show.)

Observatory Park in Sydney, Australia, offers views of Sydney Harbor and is also the filming location of the Netflix series "The Unlisted."

Those four stories were meant to validate my eagle-like perception. Okay, now that I have qualified myself, here's the last story…I think.

I'm the type to walk through your scam door and accidentally catch you red-handed. Church leaders and gurus who are working the system hate to see me coming. I've come to accept that I'm like "Mayhem" to some of these folks. You know, the wild dude from the Allstate Insurance commercials. "Touchdown, yeah!" I discovered yet another.

There was a workshop series in which I convinced my poor family to join me for. It was a looong process, and I'm both thankful and surprised that they remained committed, which is unusual for them. However, the final class was live and required us to have our cameras on. I couldn't understand why they needed to see the inside of our house, so I informed them that there would be four of us, although I suspected it was to ensure no one else was in the room.

I explained that my entire family had attended the classes and asked if they could join me for the final session. They said no; all attendees must have separate accounts. Then, I asked if they could create one for each of them. They said that I would have to go online to do that. I asked, "Do you mean go back and pay $300 times three for them to retake the classes they have already completed?" They would never give me a straight answer. They would simply repeat, "Every attendee needs an account," because they knew it was *stupid* to require my family to retake classes they had already completed just to collect money. (I remember thinking, *If this is not a cult, please deviate from the script and talk to me like I'm a human.*) Additionally, you could only receive credit and progress to the next level by completing each class. There was no way my young men would sit through that class again, especially since it was a repeat of the book, teachings on Consciousness that I had already taught them.

Here's how the business model appears to me. "First, we'll sell the book; then we'll sell the book as a class; then as a workshop; and then as a fucking retreat! (Oh my, that sounds vulgar—no pun intended!) WHO CARES IF IT'S THE SAME SHIT REPACKAGED OVER AND OVER! We're going to make millions!" (Hmm…I should make a note of that, and the author forgot to mention creating online videos and podcasts.)

Amid all the back and forth, they refused to speak the truth: every attendee must pay because I found a *screw-ya-double-dippin'* loophole that exposed their goal of making as much money as possible—in your house. These are the resistant kinds of conversations that make you want to F-bomb. (It was a creative business model, similar to my father's business.)

Needless to say, I could *clearly see* their greed. Nonetheless, I gave them the middle finger and took it as a Divine reminder that the path to the Source within is simple and available to all for free.

Strangely, I began receiving various phone calls from "groupies" worldwide, urging me to complete the last class. (They had been giving out my number.) The first caller asked in a leading tone, "So, how did you like the classes?" The expected answer was to praise the guru's awesomeness to validate that they hadn't been deceived and that their volunteer work was essential. I replied, "I can't say I learned anything new since it was a repeat of the book." However, to spare this individual's feelings and keep them bound, I am ashamed to say I responded, "My boys found it interesting." Still, I'm not convinced that was enough. (Hmm…I wonder why it was so crucial for me to finish the last class. Were they *gonna* put me in a trance?)

I really enjoyed talking to them as I observed their approach and took notes, of course. Their persistence and enthusiasm made me feel like they were trying to recruit me, because once you reach a certain level—similar to network marketing or a pyramid scheme—your progress motivates you to stay engaged and invest more money. In this case, the goal was to attain the levels of spirituality they tried to sell you. "If I complete three levels, I can require folks to attach "saint," "mother," or "guru" to my name." ("Sherguru," does sound nice! Still, my goal is "Ghigau," which means "beloved or war woman" in Cherokee, similar to the meaning of "Sherry." It's given to a woman who impacts her community.) Anyhow, I wasn't coming back, no matter how *special* they made the cult initiation ceremony out to be. (We must understand how programming works or risk being programmed.)

You've been warned! Don't mess with Sher, who often mistakenly exposes deceitful or self-serving intentions. I'm clumsy that way.

Additionally, I'm the type who will inform your spiritual institution that spamming my email caused me to miss a few of the classes I paid for because the junk mail was a significant distraction. Good Lord, I couldn't figure out what was essential and what wasn't. Naturally, the ego that responded to my inquiry assumed I must have been the problem.

The "groupie" asked, "Did you follow the directions? We send notifications a few days before class." Once again, I explained that I had missed class because the overwhelming amount of junk mail had caused me to miss class notifications.

With that said, I requested credit toward another class. Anything! Because this *spiritual stuff* is all the same *shit*, just repackaged. They could have offered me any *class*, even the one where you stick a tube up your *ass*. It didn't matter to me. She said kindly that I received ample notifications. *(Oh no she didn't!)* But that was true. I'll give her that.

Giving me credit toward another class would have meant acknowledging that their spiritual guru's organization's practice of email spamming was counterproductive and tacky. But it's hard to believe that when you see them or the organization as "superior." (Not giving credits or refunds because you said so; again, sounds like my father's business model. You can make a lot of crooked money that way.)

I also mentioned that I was considering removing my name from their email list to address the issue of the junk mail, but I wasn't sure if I would still receive class notifications if I did. It felt like a Catch-22. They should have acknowledged whether this would happen, but they didn't seem to realize that this was a question.

After I got *absolutely nowhere* with them, I decided to remove my name from the junk mail list so I wouldn't miss any more classes for which I had received ample notification. I also did this because I started to think that perhaps I was the one complicating the process. (That's how blame-shifting works.) And certainly, I wasn't the only one seeing a potential *screw-ya-operational-failure* loophole regarding what might happen if I stopped the junk mail, right?

And guess what the fuck happened!? I fell headfirst into the "loophole" and have yet to receive another notification. By the time I realized this, the live classes were already over. It's okay to laugh; my husband is always laughing at me.

They were testing my character to see if I was the type to drop F-bombs. (And I am.) Still, I kept my cool because I was observing their behavior and their business model. I refrained from F-bombing even after they denied my request for partial credit toward another class.

The sweet ego stated, "Our policy states that no refunds will be issued once the class has started." (See, the ego never listened because I didn't ask for a refund; I specifically requested *integrity*.) And this was no $100 workshop. They gave me a run for my money. Priceless! (Oops! I have a side story within a story about how I learned to stop dropping F-bombs when people are screwing me over. It's a horror story! Want to hear it? Great!)

Once, the YMCA in New Hampshire (as if there's only one in the state) overcharged my credit card by $400, and the woman I needed to contact to resolve the issue was never available and wasn't returning my calls. I left a message nearly every other day for about three weeks. I have no idea why I never F-bombed; the situation indeed had it coming. Eventually, I reached her and resolved the issue. She was a lovely person with excellent customer service and apologized for not getting back to me.

A few weeks later, after the snow had melted, I was in the parking lot of my apartment complex when I noticed a paycheck stub on the ground next to my neighbor's car. We were friendly, but I didn't know her name. The stub was from the YMCA, and I saw the same name as the woman I had been trying to reach the month before.

Oh fuck! Was she my neighbor across the hall, who could have easily reported my yelling to the Department of Children and Families? My heart seemed to skip a beat as I peeked over my shoulder, feeling as though I was being watched. Our loudness and shit that piled up in the hallway surely warranted an F-bomb from the neighbors from time to time. But she was so kind to us. (She must have been practicing stillness.) I'm really thankful folks in New Hampshire don't judge you as quickly or meddle in your business as they do in the South. Still, they will drop a *wicked* F-bomb if necessary.

My visual memory could now recall a "Y" on the black shirt she often wore. For some reason, I passed the ultimate test and never lost my patience, even while I was contemplating it. Knowing what I could do that year, I had never felt so terrified as when I picked up her stub. I felt like I had been "caught," and thankfully, I have been on my best behavior since then. I treat everyone as my neighbor. (That would make a good addition to Leviticus 19:18 from the Bible— the command to "Love your neighbor as yourself.")

Oops, we just slipped into another story portal! As I revisit this miracle from a different perspective, I recall that this was the month I began the thirty-day vegetable juice cleanse, accompanied by a daily stillness session of at least 15 minutes. Coincidentally, I also shaved my head for the first time. Do you remember "Go Queer, but We Need Some of Y'all to Come Back," where I gave my husband and New Hampshire the middle finger—essentially the ultimate F-bomb? It was a powerful month that has proven to be a time of peace and increased sensitivity. I was living in harmony with Being. Still, please don't fuck around and shave your head, ladies or gents, without a plan to maintain balance.

Now, back to the spiritual organization that lacked integrity!

Sometimes, folks miss gold on a path that requires listening and compassion. They were right, and I was wrong. Plus, they had a policy to prove it! I wonder how many students they lost due to spamming. This illustrates why connecting with others can be so challenging: the mind needs to be *right*. And one is especially right when working for a guru or "a man of God" who is also right.

No money, merely a token, was lost on their end. I certainly thought they were in the business of teaching spirituality, but money appeared to be a priority. (Oh my god! I just had another epiphany! I forgot my "bank in America" would have taken care of that for me. "Hello, this is The Common Snook. I missed my workshop because the guru was spamming my email. So, I didn't receive the product I paid for." *Give it up for* my "bank in America" for redeeming their customer service!) Still, I couldn't have written my sermon, "Spiritual Assholes, *Specialness,* and You," without these experiences.

If you pay attention, you'll notice that the Universe always imparts wisdom. This class indeed taught me valuable lessons, and the costliest ones seem to teach me the most.

Now, cut it out. I didn't specify which two gurus or whether I mentioned them earlier, so don't be nosy. They can search for my name on their end to determine if the story pertains to them. Still, what a waste of time and valuable feedback when "Ain't no God coming down to do this work for us."

Today, your organization could be on fire; unfortunately, I must turn my head while it burns. I don't offer help or share my opinion with anyone. However, I still look out for *ch'rn* entrusted to the care of boneheads. Other than that, I just tell stories for those who can hear. "One time, I was walkin' down the street...."

These experiences served as a Divine reminder that you don't need any five-step program or *special* meditation retreat to connect with the Creator within, even though many provide helpful perspectives. They work not because of the guru but because there ain't nothing new under the sun. Most have just lost their way, and these folks sell it back to us, as seen in any religion.

We are also guilty of attending these retreats. We enjoy retreats and workshops that help us feel spiritual, where we can pose impressive, "sexy questions" about things we already know the answers to. The answer is always the same: be present and occupy your body, or go within, which requires being present and occupying your body. Or, as I teach, stillness, which is the act of occupying your body. I know...deep.

However, the late, beloved Dr. Hancock Talmor of Gainesville once said that people could heal themselves both emotionally and physically; yet most were unwilling to do the work. He remarked, "I need to make a living, so I offered them treatments," as he handed me his book, *Unconditional Healing,* as a gift. It was the most phenomenal book I had read at that time, and, of course, it resonated with what I already knew deep down inside, whether my intellectual self was fully aware of it or not.

Keep it simple, and you will find your treasure. George Fox, the founder of Quakerism, said "that of God in every man" can be accessed. Learn "to be" and connect with the Creator within, and the Source will impart wisdom and love to you. This should never be confused with human intelligence, religious doctrine, or unnecessary workshops with *special* gurus.

Keep an eye out for your invitation. I'll do my best to invite everyone to tea (including the original church ladies from the 2004 BYOTC), but please don't RSVP—*maybe*. I can't stand it when folks RSVP—*maybe*—as if something better than my tea party might come along. I hope you have enjoyed the liberation!

I bow to the Divinity in you,

—Sher! (The Common Snook)

Pause. Inhale. Exhale. Reflect.

P.S. Well, I'll be damned; I just spoke the biggest Southern-style tea party into existence—beeyotch! BYODTC!

P.P.S. Even though the British attempted to conquer the world for selfish reasons and eradicate all "People of Color" with their cream, cake, and cookies, they unknowingly gave the world one of the most precious gifts: the gift of a universal language. I would never have been able to speak to so many different cultures within this book without the gift of English and its evolution, of course.

P.P.P.S. These big-time gurus *be* making you feel bad when you fall short because they don't share their secrets. Well, I have one last secret that might bring you some comfort. Sometimes, I *cut up* because I still have *ch'rn* (a Marine) at home, and I have *neva' eva'* lost my connection to the Divine, said with a head swivel, wobble, "sonic pop," and snap. The awakened me *be* watching myself taking care of business.

I will put a pile of wet, dirty dishes *in* your bed if I must or drop you off a mile from home. But how you place the dishes *in* the bed makes all the difference. Wear a smile and pull the blanket over them. (giggles) And if I don't have time to rebalance my Chi after *cuttin' up* and before seeing my acupuncturist, Sensei will sometimes ask while taking my pulse, "Did someone rip out your flowers this week?" It's all good as long as you get back on the path.

(Sit in stillness with your eyes closed for 15 minutes a day; I promise it will transform your life!)

Epilogue

Many people believe a particular path or belief system is the answer to their problems or will save them or their children from this world. Please don't indoctrinate your children with more *isms*! The greatest thing we can do to improve our lives is to free our minds by changing ourselves.

Teach your children how programming works so they don't risk being programmed! In the book *Program or Be Programmed,* the author explains that the language of programming is the language of the future, and that humanity will either learn to program computers or be programmed and used by them. This idea has always resonated with me. However, as you know by now, I focus on the most sophisticated operating system: the human mind. We must understand how it functions and how it can self-program.

Additionally, we must learn to recognize the common language of those who wish to program our minds. "Hey, son, have you ever felt alone, as if nobody understands you? Do you feel like your parents have forgotten you?" Careful, they got you! For most of us, the answer will always be yes. But only you possess the answer to establish inner wholeness.

This understanding of yourself, connected to the Divine, is the essence of freedom. It reflects our individual and collective liberation from everything that divides and governs humanity. It signifies breaking free from our own illusions! (Yep, those veils!) Life and mental transformation are ongoing processes. When we actively engage with our bodies and resist letting our minds control our lives, we gain new perspectives and free ourselves. I invite you to join the ***Betwixt*** movement, which represents a commitment to life, nurtures your spiritual growth, and builds community between our differences—one world, one people!

As I mentioned in the introduction, "This is a long-ass book" because it would take some of you "a long-ass time to wake up." But it seems you made it to the end. "You Make My Dreams Come True." I hope you enjoyed pointing fingers and having that finger returned to you. Congratulations! Let's celebrate with a song to move your feet and stir your Chi. You deserve it!

If I were there with you or you were here with me, I would play "Lovely Day" by Bill Withers and look you in the eye just long enough to make you smile. However, I also enjoy celebrating and dancing to old-school hip-hop, so "Rapper's Delight" by the Sugarhill Gang wins today! (Don't act like you don't know…just feel the beat.)

Warm Hugs,

—Sher! (The Common Snook)
Pause. Inhale. Exhale. Reflect.

P.S. Did I ever tell y'all you can say just about anything; it could be totally off-topic? Still, if you say it with a Southern accent, you get a pass. For instance, I struggle with menthol addiction. No, not cigarettes—just straight-up menthol. Whenever the doctors ask if I abuse any substances, I always report menthol, and they *be* ignoring me. They never ask how much menthol I consume or how long this addiction has been with me.

I chewed about "five kilos" of gum while writing this book. I'm *feening* just thinking about taking a hit. For those of you who smoke menthol cigarettes and can't beat the addiction, it's because it's not just the nicotine ruling the body. It's that menthol! Still, Consciousness can overcome addiction, too. Be present and stop thinking about taking a hit. (*Shout out* to all the spiritual *junkies*! You are not your mind or your body. [wink])

(Hey, sit in stillness with your eyes closed for 15 minutes a day. I promise [the Divine] will transform your life. I bow to the Divinity in you!)

Nods and Credits

To the apple of my eye, you bold man who declared, "I choose her to be my wife." *I'm so grateful for your endless love, support, and fantastic sense of humor. You willingly became a main character in this book and a model student. You're my spiritual teacher, editor, interpreter, spokesperson, and best friend— my sweetheart.* (When I asked my husband if he preferred "beeyotch or dammit" at the end of my sentences where I mention being able to "build a house and cook, too," he replied, "I don't know, Honey; they both sound so wonderful.")

I send much love to my sister, Dr. Raman, from my building, South Concord Meadows, who gave me the big big book on mysticism.

To my homegirls from India: *I am deeply thankful to you. You have had a profound impact on my life, more than I ever could have imagined, and your contribution has greatly enhanced the enjoyment of this book. You welcomed me into your culture and treated me like family. Nandita, thank you for feeding and checking on my children while I was in India, allowing me to take a much-needed break from this book. Words cannot express my gratitude.* Some, like my son, even wondered whether India was part of my past life, as the culture and language, specifically Marathi, felt familiar and seemed to follow me as I followed them. *Thank you, Vd. Aruna, for the <u>curry tree</u>!*

Thank you, Kapil, for your passion and vision of a better world and for being bold enough to befriend me. (Millennials are bold! How many Indian men do you know who have a homegirl and *be* challenging her?)

To my BFFs in New Hampshire, *you made me feel like a teenager again: Lee, thank you for choosing me as your friend that day in the basement of the Unitarian Church and for being my first friend in a new world. Jessica, you're incredible! Thank you for being a reliable friend. I love you both.*

I credit Debbie, also known as Grandma Debbie, from the same building, South Concord Meadows on the South Side, for helping me get this far. *Oh boy*, I struggled to build the confidence to share my work! I've always been told that I am too direct in my communication or don't spend enough time on small talk. Feeling inadequate, I often kept my thoughts to myself. As a visual artist and art teacher, I couldn't understand why writing felt so unforgiving. I was born with a piece of graphite in my hand and always believed that art was for everyone. I worked hard to convince my students that they, too, had a place in the studio.

Still, the writing scene was different. It revolved around the concepts of "right" or "wrong," or "good" or "bad." It didn't welcome all of us…not even a spot on the fridge. This changed when a new friend moved in down the hall. *Debbie, you liberated me from my frustration and the criticism that once crippled me. When I asked for advice on softening my voice, you had every opportunity to steer me in another direction. Instead, you encouraged me to embrace my voice. You also showed me that I could address sensitive topics while still keeping friends (White friends). My words can be hard to swallow; nonetheless, you never shut me down and encouraged me to keep expressing my thoughts. I wouldn't be sharing my experiences without you and your continual reminder to keep writing.* This must be one of the greatest gifts anyone has ever given me.

Many thanks to everyone who took the time to read my manuscript and provide feedback, recognizing that tending to human emotions, political correctness, or defining an audience beyond all of humanity was not a priority. A *special* thanks also goes to my Jewish neighbor. *Philip, you're a lifesaver. Thanks for all your insightful ideas and especially for spelling "skrrt" after checking with Jay-Z, of course.*

Thank you, Quakerism; Gainesville, Florida; New Hampshire (New England); Kirstin and Australia for "No worries," and Snoop Dogg for "Beeyotch!"

Thank you to all my "sister-wives," as affectionately I call those who partied with me in my twenties, jumping for Jesus. *I love you with all my heart. We share a connection that only those who have experienced a cult or the Marines can understand.* Although we have all gone our separate ways, in my eyes, you will always be my "sister-wives." (wink) I hope we cross paths again—perhaps for tea! *(Whassup, Kim Chi!)*

Finally, I thank everyone I met along the way, especially Ms. Juliette Watts McCoy, the greatest reflection of the Divine I have experienced, who allowed me to sit in her Presence. Of course, thank you to my parents for being my door to this world and instilling in me a love of music and a unique perspective. *Also, big big thanks to you for giving me stories. Unlike our friendship, your stories will last a lifetime. I could not have written this book without you.* (wink)

Reference

Books

Eckhart, Meister. (2009). *The Complete Mystical Works of Meister Eckhart.* Translated and edited by Maurice O'C Walshe. Revised with a Foreword by Barn McGinn New York, NY: The Crossroad Publishing Company.

Hassan, Steven. (2000). *Releasing the Bonds: Empowering People to Think for Themselves.* Danbury, CT: Aitan Publishing Company.

Holt, John. (1981). *Teach Your Own.* Random House Publishing Group.

King James Bible. (2017). King James Bible Online. Https://www.kingjamesbibleonline.org/ (Original work published 1769)

King, Martin Luther Jr. (1998). *The Autobiography of Martin Luther King Jr.* Edited by Clayborne Carson. New York, NY: Grand Central Publishing.

Rushkoff, Douglas. (2003). *Nothing Sacred. The Truth About Judaism:* New York, NY: Crown Publishers.

Rushkoff, Douglas. (2010). *Program Or Be Programmed: Ten Commands for a Digital Age. USA: OR Books.*

Talmor, Hanoch, M.D. (1999-2006). *Unconditional Healing: Personal and planetary healing for the new Millennium.* Gainesville, FL: Hanoch Talmor, M.D.

Williams, Lawrence. (2010). *The Heart of Learning.* Oak Meadow Curriculum. Brattleboro, VT: Oak Meadow School.

Movies, Shows and Videos

Chechik, Jeremiah S. (1989). *National Lampoon's Christmas Vacation.* USA.

Donner, Richard. (1963). "Nightmare at 20,000 Feet." *The Twilight Zone.* USA.

Gerwig, Greta. (2023). *Barbie.* United States: Warner Bros. Pictures.

Key, Keegan-Michael and Peele Jordan. (2015). Turbulence. *Key and Peele.* Retrieved from https://www.youtube.com/watch?v=kH6QJzmLYtw

Lehmann, Michael. (1989). *Heathers.* United States: New World Pictures.

Wayans, Keenen Ivory. (1988). I'm Gonna Git You Sucka. (Metro-Goldwyn Mayer Studios Inc. and Ivory Way Productions.) USA.

Online Sources

Baldwin, James. (November 9, 1962). Letter from a Region in My Mind. *The New Yorker.* Retrieved from https://www.newyorker.com/magazine/1962/11/17/letter-from-a-region-in-my-mind

Fuller, R Buckminster. (n.d.). Quote retrieved from Good Reads, https://www.goodreads.com/quotes/133403-we-should-do-away-with-the-absolutely-specious-notion-that

Mack, Kristin and Palfrey, John. Capitalizing Black and White: Grammatical Justice and Equity. Retrieved from https://www.macfound.org/press/perspectives/capitalizing-black-and-white-grammatical-justice-and-equity

Thomas, Zoey. (March 26, 2024). Protest of Chinese student recruitment ban draws crowd outside Board of Governors meeting at UF. *The Independent Florida Alligator.* Gainesville, FL. Retrieved from https://www.alligator.org/article/2024/03/faculty-protest

Vasudev, Jaggi. (n.d.). Why does Sadhguru wear a turban? Retrieved from https://www.sadhguruwisdom.org/wisdom/the-benefits-and-dangers-of-shaving-your-head/why-does-sadhguru-wear-a-turban/ The Truth About The Caste System & How We Can End It Retrieved from https://isha.sadhguru.org/en/wisdom/article/how-to-end-caste-system-india

Wikipedia. List of murdered hip-hop musicians. Retrieved from https://en.wikipedia.org/wiki/List_of_murdered_hip_hop_musicians

Index

The Table of Contents and the Song Index must do for now. However, I promise to compile an index one day and post it online, especially for my Quakers who want to see how many times they appear in this book.

Song Index

(Hmm…that's quite a list, honoring those who help to move the Qi. I can't believe I let y'all listen to my jukebox. I should make a Spotify playlist.)

Jackson, Michael. (1979). "Don't Stop 'Til You Get Enough." *Spotify.*, 432
Jackson, Michael. (1982). "Thriller." *Spotify.*, 223
Jett, Joan. (1981). "I Love Rock 'N Roll." *Spotify.*, 283
John, Elton. (1983). "I'm Still Standing." *Spotify.*, 95
JUVENILE, Lil Wayne, Mannie Fresh. (1999). "Back That Thang Up." *Spotify.*, 124, 276
K-Ci & JoJo, (1997). "All My Life." *Spotify.*, 97
Lennon, John. (1969). "Give Peace A Chance." *Spotify.*, 270, 283
Lumineers. (2012). "Ho Hey." *Spotify.*, 464
M.S. Subbulakshmi. (1970). "Bhaja Govindam." *Spotify.*, 299
Mellencamp, John. (1982). "Jack & Diane." *Spotify.*, 143
Men At Work. (1981). "Down Under." *Spotify.*, 223
Michael, George. (1984). "Careless Whisper." *Spotify.*, 86
Mr.C. (1998). "Cha Cha Slide." Spotify., 344
Oates, John and Hall, Daryl. (1982). "You Make My Dreams (Come True)." *Spotify.*, 483
Peaches & Herb. (1978). "Reunited." *Spotify.*, 242
Petty, Tom. (1989). "Runnin Down A Dream." *Spotify.*, 458
Petty, Tom. (1989). "Love Is A Long Road." *Spotify.*, 143
Pink. (2012). "Blow Me (One Last Kiss)." *Spotify.*, 96
Pitbull, Dilijit Dosanjh and Neeraj Shridhar. (2024). "Bhool Bhulaiyaa-3!." *Spotify.*, 270
Planet Patrol. (1983). "Play at Your Own Risk." *Spotify.*, 283
Prince. (1985). "Raspberry Beret." *Spotify.*, 150
Railroad, Grand Funk. (1974). "Some Kind Of Wonderful." *Spotify.*, 259
Rihanna. (2012). "Diamonds." *Spotify.*, 125
Rodgers, Nile & Chic. (1979). "Good Times." *Spotify.*, 117
Rogers, Fred. (1968). "Won't You Be My Neighbor." *Spotify.*, 163
Rogers, Fred. (1969). "It's Such A Good Feeling." *Spotify.*, 419
Rolling Stones. (1981). "Start Me Up." *Spotify.*, 242
Shaboozey. (2024). "A Bar Song Tipsy." *Spotify.*, 129
Simon & Garfunkel. (1964). "The Sound of Silence." *Spotify.*, 378
Simon, Paul. (1972). "Me and Julio Down by the Schoolyard." *Spotify.*, 51
Sledge, Sister. (1979). "We Are Family." *Spotify.*, 264
Sugarhill Gang. (1981). "Rapper's Delight." *Spotify.*, 483
Survivor. (1982)."Eye of the Tiger." *Spotify.*, 283
Swift, Taylor. (2014). "Shake It Off." *Spotify.*, 64
Tag Team. (1993). "Whoomp! (There It Is). *Spotify.*, 215
Tech Panda and Kazan. (2022). "Dillagi." *Spotify.*, 282
Tech Panda and Kenzani. (2023). "Kulli." *Spotify.*, 282
The Notorious B.I.G. (1997). "Hypnotize." *Spotify.*, 283
The Rolling Stones. (1978). "Miss You." *Spotify.*, 283
The Trammps. (1976). "Disco Inferno." *Spotify.*, 424
Timbaland, Keri Hilson and D.O.E. (2007). "The Way I Are." *Spotify.*, 466
Toto. (1982). "Africa." *Spotify.*, 223
Tsvetaeva, Kate. (2012). "Tango Cumparsita." *Spotify.*, 466
Vietti, Josh. (2018). (Original song by The Weekend.) "Starboy." *Spotify.*, 410
will.i.am and Britney Spears. (2012). "Scream & Shout." *Spotify.*, 98
Wilson, Charlie. (2017). "I'm Blessed." *Spotify.*, 283
Withers, Bill. (1977). "Lovely Day." *Spotify.*, 283, 483